The Prescriber's Complete Handbook: Comprising The Principles Of The Art Of Prescribing

Armand Trousseau

THE PRESCRIBER'S
COMPLETE HANDBOOK,

COMPRISING THE

PRINCIPLES OF THE ART OF PRESCRIBING.

A MATERIA MEDICA CONTAINING ALL THE
PRINCIPAL MEDICINES EMPLOYED,

CLASSIFIED ACCORDING TO THEIR NATURAL FAMILIES, WITH THEIR
PROPERTIES, PREPARATIONS AND USES, AND

A CONCISE SKETCH OF TOXICOLOGY.

BY M. TROUSSEAU,

PROFESSOR OF THE FACULTY OF MEDICINE, PARIS, AND

M. REVEIL.

EDITED, WITH NOTES,

BY J. BIRKBECK NEVINS, M.D.

LONDON:
HIPPOLYTE BAILLIERE, 219, REGENT STREET,
AND 290, BROADWAY, NEW YORK, U.S.
PARIS: J. B. BAILLIERE, RUE HAUTEFEUILLE.
MADRID: BAILLY BAILLIERE, CALLE DEL PRINCIPE.

1852.

LONDON:
Printed by Schulze and Co., 13, Poland Street.

DEDICATION

TO

FLEETWOOD CHURCHILL, ESQ., M.D.

HONORARY M.D. OF TRINITY COLLEGE, DUBLIN, AND HONORARY FELLOW OF
THE KING AND QUEEN'S COLLEGE OF PHYSICIANS, DUBLIN.

————————

My dear Churchill,

When I had first the good fortune to become acquainted with
you, you were earnestly engaged in laying a solid foundation for
the celebrity you now so deservedly enjoy; and in dedicating the
following Work to you, I not only gratify my personal feelings of
regard, and my ambition to have my name, even in such a way,
associated with yours, but I am trying to repay part of the debt
which I have always felt that I owed you, for your example of
unflagging industry, even more than for your repeated exhorta-
tions so to work during those first years of expectancy, anxiety,
and often of disappointment, which await nearly every medical
man, as to enjoy the satisfaction of feeling that I had at any rate
done my best to deserve success, whether success should attend
my labours or not.

For the measure of prosperity which I have attained, I am
conscious how much I am indebted to your example and advice;
and that you may long live to enjoy your own reputation, with
daily increase, is the sincere desire of

Your attached friend,

J. BIRKBECK NEVINS.

LIVERPOOL, JUNE, 1852.

AUTHORS' PREFACE.

In publishing this little Book, we make no pretence to having done anything original. We have simply endeavoured to be useful to students and to practitioners at the commencement of their career, and have tried to say all that appeared to us essential in as few words as possible, and we hope with success.

We shall, however, briefly point out those portions of our Work in which we have slightly departed from the beaten track.

Except the part devoted to a short sketch of toxicology, everything has been done with a design; viz., that of making our Readers acquainted with medicines, their preparations and their properties.

In order to avoid confusing the mind of the student, we have classified all the medicines taken from the vegetable and the animal kingdoms, not according to their medicinal properties, but according to their natural characters; so that we can see at a glance what are the medicines contained in such or such a family of the vegetable kingdom; by which means we can seize upon affinities that would otherwise escape us. But in the tables in which vegetable substances are arranged according to the order of their natural families, we have taken care to mention the part of the plant which is employed, its principal preparations, the different modes in which it is administered, and lastly, the class in which it is placed in our treatise on therapeutics.

In the "*Art of Prescribing*," we have endeavoured to be as elementary as possible, insisting, however, with great care upon the valuable details scattered through the best treatises on pharmacy, and so ably illustrated in the very valuable works of Messrs. Soubeiran, Mialhe and Bouchardat.

We have thought it desirable to give a Short Sketch of Pharmacy, which is intended especially for those medical men who, residing in country places, are obliged to prepare their own medicines.

The "*Magistral Formulary*" which we have given differs from all that have been published hitherto. All the medicines have been arranged in the order adopted in our Treatise on Therapeutics. We have not attempted to copy the thousand and one prescriptions with which all collections of formulæ swarm; but we have inserted those which we most frequently employ, and the efficacy of which we have proved by our own experience.

We have taken great care to point out with precision the doses suitable for different ages, and to lay down minutely the methods of administering them; so that each series of formulæ may take up one class of medicines.

For the sake of students, as well as of practitioners who do not reside in large towns, a Sketch of Toxicology was necessary: we have made it very short, but nevertheless so complete, that every medical man may, by a little attention, arrive at positive results in a medico-legal examination. We have laid special stress upon the treatment of Poisoning.

Such is the Book which we now publish; not, truly, with any ambition for glory, but simply to satisfy a desire which has been often expressed to us by the students who attend our lectures.

TRANSLATOR'S PREFACE.

To the foregoing unassuming Preface, the Translator has little to add; for if the authors of a work claim little credit to themselves, to how much less is he entitled who simply renders the result of their labours into another tongue. With few exceptions, his duty has been confined to the simple office of translating; though he has occasionally added an explanatory or illustrative note, which is always indicated by the mark §., the portion for which he is responsible being enclosed within a parenthesis.

Upon one portion of his Work it is necessary to make a few remarks; viz., the way in which he has reduced the French doses ordered in the original into English ones. In the tables at the commencement he has given the exact reduction, so that the Reader has the means of finding the English quantities which correspond with the original ones, to the most minute degree of exactness; and he has, throughout the Work, retained the French weights, as well as given their English equivalents, that his Readers may be able to judge how far he has departed from exactness—which he acknowledges to having done in most instances, though within narrow limits of error. For example, the gramme is the standard of weight used throughout by the Authors; and it equals 15·438 grains, or 15½ grains nearly; 4 grammes will therefore equal 61·75, or 61¾ grains; and 100 grammes will equal ℥iii, ʒi, gr. xliii. Now English medical men are in the habit of ordering solid substances by drachms and ounces, and mixtures, of one, three, eight, or twenty, &c., fluid ounces; and if the quantities prescribed come to a drachm more or a drachm less than a three ounce mixture, the druggist will unquestionably comply with the prescriber's intention in filling a three-ounce phial. Upon this principle, then, the Translator has omitted fractional parts, and has rendered 1 gramme by gr. xv, 4 grammes by ʒi, and 100 grammes by ʒiii. But he has in some cases taken a greater liberty even than this. In the tables at the commencement of the work the doses are given as follows: 4 to 10 grammes, 5 to 15 grammes, 20 to 50 grammes, &c.; and he has rendered these by ʒi to ʒiiss, ʒi to ʒss, and ʒv to ʒiss. Now it is evident that both 4 and 5 grammes cannot be correctly represented by ʒi; but where the margin is left so wide in the original as from 5 to 15, the error is not of the smallest consequence in translating 5 grammes as ʒi, instead of ʒi gr. xix. So, also, in the "*Magistral Formulary,*" he has always adopted the English weight which corresponds most nearly in round numbers with the French quantity prescribed; because although this is never quite exact, the error amounts to nothing when compared with the discretion allowed in the dose—from 1 to 4, 1 to 10, or even 1 to 16 pills in the day being the discretion allowed by the Authors. In the case of mixtures, also, which are to be administered by spoonsful and glassfuls, the difference of dose, arising from variation in the size of these measures, and the degree to which they are filled, will altogether outweigh the difference between ʒiss (the quantity employed by the Translator to represent 50 grammes), and ʒiss gr. lii, which is the true equivalent. He trusts, therefore, that no practical inconvenience will arise from this slight departure from exactness.

LIVERPOOL, JUNE, 1852.

CONTENTS.

	Page
Authors' preface	v
Translator's preface	vii
Table of weights, ancient and modern	1
Pharmaceutical nomenclature	5
Classification of simple medicines in their natural families	9

ACOTYLEDONS.

Algues, Algæ, Sea-weeds—*Coralline blanche*, white coral; *mousse de Corse, coralline de Corse*, Corsican moss; *carrageen (mousse perlée ou d'Irlande)*, pearl, or Irish moss 10

Champignons, Fungi, Mushrooms—*Agaric blanc*, larch agaric; *agaric amadouvier*, amadou, or German tinder; *ergot de seigle, seigle ergoté*, ergot of rye . . . . . . —

Lichens—*lichen d'Islande*, Iceland moss; *orseille*, archil; *parelle d'Auvergne*, craw-fish-eye lichen . . . . . —

Fougères, Filices, Ferns—*Fougère mâle*, male fern; *capillaire du Canada*, Canada maiden hair; *capillaire de Montpellier*, Venus's maiden hair . —

Lycopodiacées, Lycopodiaceæ, Club-Mosses—*Lycopode (soufre végétal)* . 12

MONOCOTYLEDONS.

Aroïdées, Aroideæ, (Arum Tribe)—*Arum (gouet, ou pied de veau)*, arum; *acore vraie*, acorus, or sweet flag 12

Cyperacées, Cyperaceæ, Sedges—*Souchet long et rond*, long and round galingale; *Carex ou laiche des sables (salsepareille d'Allemagne)*, German sarsaparilla, sea sedge . . . . —

Graminées, Gramineæ, Grasses—*Chiendent*, dog's tooth; *canne de Provence (grand roseau)*, great reed-grass; *canne à sucre*, sugar-cane; *avoine*, oats; *orge*, spring barley; *riz*, rice . . . —

Colchiacées, Melanthaceæ (Colchicum Tribe)—*Colchique d'automne*, meadow saffron (Colchicum); *ellébore blanc*, white hellebore; *cévadille (poudre des capucins)*, sabadilla . . . 14

Palmiers, Palmaceæ, (Palm Tribe)—*Dattes*, dates; *sagou*, sago; *sang-dragon (en roseau)*, dragon's blood, (in reeds) . . —

Liliacées, Liliaceæ, (Lily Tribe)—*Scille*, squill; *aloés*, aloes . . 16

Page

Asparaginées, Asparagineæ—*Asperge*, asparagus ; *salsepareille*, sarsaparilla   16

Iridées, Irideæ—*Iris de Florence*, fleur de lis ; *safran*, saffron   —

Amomées, Zingiberaceæ—Arrow-root ; *cardamome*, cardamoms ; *galanga*, galangale   —

Orchidées, Orchidaceæ—*Vanille*, vanilla ; *salep*, salop   18

DICOTYLEDONS.

Conifères, Coniferæ—*Genévrier*, juniper ; *huile de Cade* ; *sabine*, savine ; *térébinthine de Bordeaux, Strasbourg, ou Venise*, turpentine, &c.; *poix de Bourgogne*, Burgundy pitch   —

Pipéritées, Piperaceæ—*Poivre noir et blanc*, black and white pepper; *poivre à queue (cubèbe)*, tailed pepper (cubebs)   —

Cupulifères, Cupuliferæ—*Chêne rouvre*, the oak; *noix de galle*, nut-galls   —

Juglandées, Juglandaceæ, (Walnut Family)—*Noyer*, the walnut .   20

Salicinées, Salicaceæ, (Willow Tribe)—*Saule*, willow ; *peuplier*, poplar   —

Ulmacées et Morées, Ulmaceæ and Urticaceæ, (Elm and Nettle, or Mulberry Tribe)—*Orme pyramidal ou champêtre*, the elm ; *contrayerva*, contrajerva; *figuier*, figs; *pariétaire*, pellitory of the wall; *murier*, mulberry   —

Cannablées, Cannabinaceæ, Hempworts—*Chanvre indien*, Indian hemp; *houblon*, hops   —

Euphorbiacées, Euphorbiaceæ, (Spurge Tribe)—*Euphorbe*, euphorbium; *mercuriale*, dog's mercury; *caoutchouc*, caoutchouc; *tapioka*, tapioca; *ricin (palma Christi)*, castor oil; *petit pignon d'Inde (croton)*, croton-oil; *cascarille*, cascarille, *cascarilla* ; *buis, box-tree*   —

Aristolochiées, Aristolochiaceæ, Birthworts—*Serpentaire de Virginie*, serpentary ; *azarum cabaret*, asarabacca   22

Daphnées or Thymélées, Thymelaceæ, (Daphne Tribe)—*Garou*, mezereum   —

Laurinées, Lauraceæ, Laurels—*Laurier commun ou d'Apollon*, sweet bay; *sassafras*, sassafras; *cannelle de Ceylan*, cinnamon; *camphre*, camphor   —

Myristiées, Myristaceæ, (Nutmeg Tribe)—*Muscade*, nutmegs   24

Polygonées, Polygonaceæ, (Buck-wheat Tribe)—*Bistorte*, bistort; *patience ou pareille*, patience, sharp leaved dock; *rapontic*, French rhubarb; *rhubarbe*, rhubarb; *sarrasin*, sarasin   —

Chénopodées, Chenopodiaceæ, (Goosefoot Tribe)—*bette ou poirée*, white beet; *betterave*, beetroot   —

Labiées, Labiatæ, (Pea Tribe)—*Lavande*, lavander ; *menthe*, mint ; *marjoline*, marjorum ; *thym*, thyme; *mélisse*, balm ; *hyssope*, hyssop; *sauge*, sage   —

Scrophularinées, Scrophularineæ, (Figwort Tribe)—*Véronique*, speedwell ; *gratiole*, hedge hyssop; *digitale pourprée*, purple foxglove; *bouillon (molène)*, mullein   26

Solanées, Solanaceæ, (Nightshade Tribe) — *Tabac*, tobacco ; *stramonium (Pomme épineuse)*, thorn apple ; *jusquiame*, henbane ; *belladonne*, deadly nightshade ; *douce amère*, bitter sweet or woody nightshade ; *morelle*, common nightshade ; *pomme de terre*, potato ; *alkekenge coqueret*, winter cherry   —

Page

Boraginées, Boraginaceæ, (Borage Tribe)—*Bourrache*, borage; *consoude*, comfrey; *cynoglosse*, hound's tongue; *orcanette*, alkanet . . 28

Convolvulacées, Convolvulaceæ, (Convolvulus Tribe)—*Turbith*, turbith; *jalap*, jalap; *scammonée d'Alep*, scammony . . . —

Gentianées, Gentianaceæ, (Gentian Tribe)—*Gentiane jaune*, gentian (yellow); *petite centaurée*, lesser centaury . . . . —

Logoniacées-Strychnées, Logoniaceæ, (The Logania Tribe)—*Noix d'Igasur* (*Fève de St. Ignace*), Saint Ignatius' bean; *noix vomique*, nux vomica; *fausse Angusture*, false Angustura bark . . . —

Apocynées, Apocynaceæ, (The Periwinkle Tribe)—*Laurier rose*, oleander; *pervenche*, periwinkle 30

Jasminées, Jasminaceæ, Jasmine-worts—*Manne*, manna; *olivier*, olives . —

Styracinées, Styraceæ, (Storax Tribe)—*Benjoin*, benoin . . —

Synanthérées ou Composées, Synantheraceæ or Compositæ, (Dandelion and Daisy Tribe)—*Laitue cultivée*, cultivated lettuce; *chicorée*, chicory; *arnica*, arnica; *bardane*, burdock; *pied de chat*, mountain everlasting, or cat's foot; *grande absinthe* (*Aluine*), common wormwood; *armoise*, common mugwort; *semen-contra d'Alep*, semen contra, semen cinæ; *camomille*, chamomile; *pyrèthre*, pellitory; *aunée officinale*, elecampane 32

Valérianées, Valerianaceæ, (Valerian Tribe)—*Valéraine sauvage*, common wild valerian . . . . . . —

Rubiacées, Rubiaceæ, (Cinchona Tribe)—*Garance*, madder; *ipécacuanha annelé*, ipecacuanha; *cainça*; *quinquina gris officinal*, grey cinchona bark; *quinquina rouge*, red cinchona bark; *quinquina jaune*, yellow bark 34

Caprifoliacées, Caprifoliaceæ, (The Honey-suckle Tribe)—*Sureau*, elder —

Ombillifères, Umbelliferæ—*Ache*, celery; *cigue officinale*, hemlock; *cigue vireuse* (*cicutaire aquatique*), water hemlock; *petite cigue* (*éthuse*, *faux persil*, *ache des chiens*), fool's parsley; *persil*, parsley; *anis vert*, aniseed; *phellandrie aquatique*, fine-leaved water dropwort; *assa-fœtida*, assafœtida; *gomme ammoniaque*, ammoniacum . . . —

Grossulariées, Grossulariaceæ, (Currant Tribe)—*Groseille*, currants . 38

Myrtacées et Granatées, Myrtaceæ, (Myrtle Tribe)—*Girofle ou gérofle*, cloves; *grenadier*, pomegranate . . . . —

Cucurbitacées, Cucurbitaceæ, (Gourd Tribe)—*Bryone*, bryony; *coloquinte*, colocynth; *concombre cultivé*, common cucumber; *elaterium*, (*concombre sauvage*), elaterium, wild or squirting cucumber . . . —

Rosacées, Rosaceæ, (Rose and Strawberry Tribe)—*Coing*, quince; *pêcher*, peach; *rose rouge ou de Provins*, red, or Province rose; *benoite*, herb. avens; *cusso*, *kousso*, *cousso*, kousso; *amandes*, almonds; *laurier cerise*, *ou laurier amande*, cherry-laurel 40

Légumineuses, Leguminosæ, (Pea Tribe)—*Réglisse*, liquorice; *mélilot*, melilot; *séné*, senna; *casse*, cassia; *cachou*, catechu; *gomme arabique*, gum arabic or acacia; *gomme adragante*, tragacanth; *copahu*, copaiba or copaiva; *baume de Tolu*, balsam of Tolu; *indigo*, indigo; *fenu grec*, fenugreek 42

                                                                    Page
Térébinthacées, Terebinthaceæ, (Tribe yielding Turpentine)—*Myrrh*,
    myrrh; *encens ou oliban*, olibanum   42
Rhamnées, Rhamnaceæ, (Buckthorn Tribe)—*Jujubes*, jujube; *nerprun*,
    buckthorn .   .   .   .   —
Rutacées, Rutaceæ, (Rue Tribe)—*Gayac*, guiacum; *rue*, rue; *angusture
    vraie*, cusparia; *bois amer de Surinam*, quassia   .   .   44
Ampélidées, Ampelideæ, (Grape Tribe)—*Vigne*, vine   .   .   —
Guttifères, Guttiferæ, (Trees or Shrubs yielding a resinous juice)—*Gomme
    gutte*, gamboge; *cannelle blanche*, canella   .   .   .   —
Aurantiacées, Aurantiaceæ, (Orange Tribe)—*Citron*, citron; *oranger*,
    orange   .   .   .   .   —
Ternstræmaniées or Camelliées, Ternströmiaceæ, (Tea Tribe)—*Thé noir et
    vert*, black and green tea   .   .   .   .   .   —
Tiliacées, Tiliaceæ, Lindenblooms—*Tilleul*, linden tree   .   .   —
Malvacées, Malvaceæ, (Mallow Tribe)—*Guimauve*, marsh-mallow; *mauve*,
    mallow; *coton*, cotton; *cacao*, cocoa   .   .   .   46
Linées, Linaceæ, (Flax Tribe)—*Lin*, linseed   .   .   .   —
Caryophyliées, Caryophyllaceæ, (Clove Pink Tribe)—*Œillet rouge*, clove
    pink; *saponaire*, soapwort   .   .   .   .   .   —
Polygalées, Polygalaceæ, (Milk-wort Tribe)—*Polygala de Virginie*, Senega;
    ratania, rhatany root   .   .   .   .   .   —
Violariées, Violaceæ, (Violet Tribe)—*Violette*, violet   .   .   —
Crucifères, Cruciferæ, (Stock, or Wallflower Tribe)—*Cresson de Fontaine*,
    water-cress; *raifort sauvage*, horseradish; *erysimum ou vélar (tortelle,
    Herbe aux chantres)*, common hedge mustard; *moutarde noire*, black
    mustard   .   .   .   .   —
Fumariacées, Fumariaceæ, (Fumitory Tribe)—*Fumeterre*, fumitory   .   —
Papaveracées, Papaveraceæ, (Poppy Tribe)—*Chélidoine*, celandine; *coque-
    licot*, red poppy; *pavot blanc*, white poppy; *opium*, opium; *morphine*,
    narcotine, *codéine*, and their salts   .   .   .   50
Nymphéacées, Nympheaceæ, (Water-lily Tribe)—*Nymphæa or nénuphar*,
    water-lily   .   .   .   .   —
Ménispermacées, Menispermaceæ, (Cocculus Tribe)—*Colombo*, colomba;
    coque du Levant, cocculus indicus   .   .   .   .   —
Renonculacées, Ranunculaceæ, (Butter-cup Tribe)—*Ellébore noir*, black
    hellebore; *staphisaigre*, stave-sacre; *aconit napel*, monk's-hood; *pi-
    voine*, peony   .   .   .   .   .   .   —

PRODUCTS OF THE ANIMAL KINGDOM.

Mammifères, Mammalia, Animals which suckle their young—*Civette*, civet
    cat; *castor*, beaver; *ivoire*, ivory; *porc*, hog; *ânesse*, ass; *chevrotain
    porte-musc*, musk deer; *cerf*, stag; *chèvre, bouc*, goat, male and female;
    mouton, brébis, sheep, ditto; *bœuf, vache*, ox and cow; *cachalot*, sperm
    whale; *marsouin*, the dolphin   52
Oiseaux, Aves, Birds—*Poule*, the common hen   .   .   .   —

Page

Reptiles, Reptilia, Reptiles—*Tortue*, the tortoise; *vipère*, the viper; *grenouille*, the frog . . . . . . ,. 54
Poissons, Pisces, Fishes—*Morue*, the cod fish; *esturgeon*, the sturgeon . —
Mollusques, Mollusca, Soft-bodied Animals (without internal skeletons)—*Sèche*, cuttle-fish; *limaçons*, *escarottes*, snails (edible); *huître*, the oyster; *moules*, muscles . . . . . . —
Annélides, Annelides, Worms—*Sangsues*, leeches . . . —
Crustacés, Crustacea, Crabs, Shrimps, &c.—*Ecrévisse*, the crab; *cloportes*, the wood-louse . . . . —
Insectes, Insecta, Insects—*Poux, de tête, de corps, du pubis*, lice, of the head, the body and the pubis; *puce*, fleas; *cantharides*, Spanish, or blistering fly; *cochenille du Nopal*, cochineal; *noix de galle*, nut-galls; *abeille*, the bee 56
Polypiers, Polypi, Polypes—*Coralline blanche*, white coral; *corail rouge*, red coral; *éponge*, sponge . . . . . — .

MEDICINES SUPPLIED BY THE MINERAL KINGDOM AND CHEMISTRY.

Oxygène, oxygen; *chlore*, chlorine; *iode*, iodine; *soufre*, sulphur; *phosphore*, phosphorus . . . . —
Arsenic, arsenic; *eau*, water; *eaux minérales*, mineral waters . 60
Acides chlorhydrique, sulfhydrique, azotique, hydrochloric, hydrosulphuric, nitric acids . . . . —
——— *sulfureux, sulfurique*, sulphurous, sulphuric . . 62
Alcool sulfurique (eau de Rabel), sulphuric alcohol . . . —
Acides phosphorique, carbonique, borique, cyanhydrique, phosphoric, carbouic, boracic, hydrocyanic acids . . . . —
Potasse, potash; *caustic de Vienne*, caustic of Vienna . . —
Iodure, sulfure et cyanure de potassium, iodide, sulphuret and cyanide of potassium; *sulfate et nitrate de potasse*, sulphate and nitrate of potash; *nitrate fondu*, fused nitre; *acétate et bitartrate de potasse*, acetate and bitartrate of potash; *tartrate borico-potassique*, borico-tartrate of potash —
Hypochlorite de potasse, hypoclorite of potash; *soude et sels de soude*, soda and its salts; *chlorure de sodium, de baryum*, chloride of sodium, of barium; *phosphate de chaux*, phosphate of lime; *ammoniaque*, ammonia; *acétate et chlorhydrate d'ammoniaque*, acetate and hydrochlorate of ammonia; *magnésie blanche*, white magnesia; *sulfate de magnésie*, sulphate of magnesia 64
Sulfate d'alumine et de potasse, sulphate of alumina and potash; *fer limaille et fer réduit par l'hydrogène*, iron filings and iron reduced by hydrogen; *péroxide de fer anhydre et hydraté*, anhydrous and hydrated peroxide of iron; *safran de Mars, aperient*, saffron of Mars, aperient; *Ethiops martial*, Ethiop's martial; *iodure de fer*, iodide of iron; *eau ferrée*, rusty water; *sulfate de fer*, sulphate of iron; *bleu de Prusse*, Prussian blue; *tartrate de potasse et de fer*, potassio-tartrate of iron; *lactate de fer*, lactate of iron; *boules de Nancy*, bolus of Nancy; *oxyde blanc de zinc*, white oxide of zinc; *sulfate de zinc*, sulphate of zinc . . . 66

Page

Protoxide de plomb, protoxide of lead; *carbonate de plomb*, carbonate of
lead; *acétates neutre et tribasique de plomb*, acetate and tribasic acetate
of lead; *étain*, tin; *sous-nitrate de bismuth*, subnitrate of bismuth; *sulfate de cuivre*, sulphate of copper; *tartrate de potasse et de cuivre*, tartrate of potash and of copper; *mercure*, mercury . . 68

Eaux phagédéniques noire et jaune, black and yellow wash . —

Bioxyde de mercure, binoxide of mercury; *bisulfure de mercure*, bisulphuret of mercury 70

Chlorures, iodures et cyanure de mercury, chlorides, iodides and cyanide of
mercury; *sulfates et nitrates de mercure*, sulfates and nitrates of mercury . . . . —

Pommade citrine, citrine ointment; *nitrate d'argent crystallisé et fondu*,
crystallized and fused nitrate of silver; *chlorure d'argent*, chloride of
silver; *chlorure d'or*, chloride of gold; *chlorure d'or et de sodium*, chloride
of gold and of sodium; *oxyde blanc d'antimoine*, white oxide of antimony; *antimoine diaphorétique*, diaphoretic antimony; *sulfures et oxy-
sulphures d'antimoine*, sulphurets and oxysulphurets of antimony; *beurre
d'antimoine*, butter of antimony; *émétique*, tartar emetic; *acide ar-
sénieux*, arsenious acid; *liqueurs de Fowler et de Pearson*, Fowler's and
Pearson's solutions; *sulfures d'arsenic*, sulphurets of arsenic; *savons médi-
cinal et animal*, medicated and animal soap . . . 72

Alcool, alcohol; *éthers*, ethers; *liqueur d'Hoffmann*, Hoffmann's anodyne
liquor; *sirop d'éther*, syrup of ether; *aldehyde*, aldehyde; *chloroforme*,
chloroform; *acides acétique, citrique, lactique, oxalique, tartrique*, acetic,
lactic, oxalic and tartaric acid 74

THE ART OF PRESCRIBING 77
Table of incompatible substances 118

SHORT SKETCH OF PHARMACY 125

MAGISTRAL PRESCRIPTIONS 206
Table indicating the value of different quantities . . . 217
Tonics; reconstituent or analeptic medicines . . . 218
Astringents furnished by the mineral kingdom . . . 227
———— furnished by the vegetable kingdom . . . 230
Alteratives 236
Irritants 256
———— from the vegetable kingdom . . . 267
———— from the animal kingdom . . . 268
Emollient or antiphlogistic medicines . . . 270
Emetics from the vegetable kingdom . . . 275
———— from the mineral kingdom . . . 276
Purgatives and laxatives 278
Laxatives furnished by the mineral kingdom . . 280
Saline purgatives 283
Drastic purgatives 285
Excitants of the muscular system, or excitatives . . 287

	Page
Narcotics (stupefiants) .	289
Anæsthetic medicines	304
Anti-spasmodic medicines	305
Neuro-sthenic tonics	311
Excitants or stimulants	318
Sudorifics	322
Diuretics	324
Emmenagogues .	326
Balsamic stimulants	327
Sulphurous stimulants	331
Sedatives—contra-stimulants	335
Antiseptic absorbents	339
Anthelmintics	340
HELMINTHOLOGY .	345
OUTLINES OF TOXICOLOGY	346
Irritant poisons	356
Narcotic poisons	434
Narcotico-acrid poisons	448
Septic or putrefactive poisons	470
Appendix (Act of Parliament for regulating the Sale of Arsenic) .	478

TABLES OF WEIGHTS,

ANCIENT AND MODERN.

The (French) physician and the pharmaceutist ought to comply with the demands of the law which has established the decimal system.

A cube of distilled water, measuring a centimetre,* at its greatest density (*i. e.* 4⁰ of the centigrade, or 39·2⁰ of the Fahrenheit thermometer), weighs 1 gramme, or 15·438 grains Eng.,† which is the unit or standard of the new weights. The word *gramme* is the Greek name for the weight which the Romans called a *scruple*.

The divisions of the gramme are:

The *decigramme,*	0·10,	the tenth part of a gramme; or 1·544 of a grain, or 1½ grain, nearly.
The *centigramme,*	0·01,	the hundredth part of a gramme; or 0·154 of a grain, or 1/6 of a grain, nearly.
The *milligramme,*	0·001,	the thousandth part of a gramme; or the tenth part of a decigramme; or 0·015 of a grain, or 1/66 of a grain, nearly.

The multiples of a gramme are called:

The *decagramme,*	or	10 grammes,	or	154·4 grains,	ʒiiss, nearly.
The *hectogramme,*	or	100 ,,	or	1544 ,,	℥iii—ʒii, ,,
The *kilogramme,*	or	1,000 ,,	or	15540 ,,	℥xxxii—ʒi, ,,
The *myriagramme,*	or	10,000 ,,	or	154400 ,,	℔xxvii, ,,

---

* 0·39371 of an inch.

† The necessity for adding *Eng.* arises from the circumstance that the French grain does not correspond with the English grain, to which latter the French weight employed in this work are reduced in this translation.

B

Physicians ought, in their prescriptions, to write the weights at full length; but certain short signs are still used, which should be explained.

The law of July, 1837, has made the employment of the decimal system compulsory, in all calculations after 1840.

The ancient French standard of weight is the pound weight of "marc," which equals 16 ounces, or 500 grammes (*i. e.*, 16 oz. and 39 grs. troy). By the *exact* division of these weights, we arrive at fractions which are seldom taken into account (see the table below). In the sequel of this work we have adopted the following divisions:

The kilogramme	= 2 pounds Fr.	or	℔ii ℨviii ʒi Ɔi Eng.	that is	℔ii ℨviii, nearly.
1/2 „	= 1 „	„	℔i ℨiv Ɔii	„	℔i ℨiv, „
1/4 „	= 1/2 „	„	ℨviii Ɔi	„	ℨviii, „
The ounce	= 1/16 „	„	ʒi gr. iiss	„	ʒi, „
1/2 „	= 1/32 „	„	ʒss gr. i 1/4	„	ʒss, „
The gros (drachm)	= 1/128 „	„	ʒi gr. 1/4	„	ʒi, „
1/2 „	= 1/256 „	„	ʒss gr. 1/8	„	ʒss, „
The grain	= 1/10000 „	„	gr. ·77	„	gr. 3/4 „

1000 grammes are written	1 kilogramme.		
500 „	„	1 pound, or ℔.	
250 „	„	1/2 „ „ ℔β.	
30 „	„	1 ounce, or ℨi.	
15 „	„	1/2 „ „ ℨβ.	
4 „	„	1 gros (or drachm), or ʒi.	
2 „	„	1/2 „ or ʒ β.	
1/20 „	„	1 grain, or gr. i.	

Thus ℔ signifies pound, ℨ means ounce, ʒ indicates drachm; and their halves are expressed by β*. We should add, that a scruple is represented by Ɛ or Ɔ, and equals 24 grains.†

After the signs, the numbers are expressed by Roman figures, which are known throughout the world. So that

	ʒi,	ʒii,	ʒii,	ʒiv,	ʒv,	ʒvi,	ʒvii,	ʒviii,	ʒix,	ʒx, &c.
signifies	1	2	3	4	5	6	7	8	9	10 ounces, &c.

In the same way for drachms, pounds and scruples;

and ℨβ and ℨiβ signify 1/2 an ounce, and 1 ounce and 1/2.

Grammes are indicated by a comma being placed on the right of the figure, whilst decigrammes, on the contrary, are placed on the right of the comma; on the right of the decigrammes are

---

* Thus the French symbol β corresponds with the English symbol ss, or ſſ, in meaning half.

† The French scruple does not quite equal the English scruple, for although it consists of 24 French grains, these are only equal to 18·5 English grains.

placed the centigrammes; and lastly, at the right of these, are placed the milligrammes. So that we write:

$$1, \quad = 1 \text{ gramme.}$$
$$0,1 \quad = 1 \text{ decigramme.}$$
$$0,01 \quad = 1 \text{ centigramme.}$$
$$0,001 = 1 \text{ milligramme.}$$

And if there are at the same time grammes, decigrammes, centigrammes and milligrammes, each of them keeps its place, thus:

1,525 = 1 gramme, 5 decigrammes, 2 centigrammes, and 5 milligrammes, or 1 gramme and 525 milligrammes, and so on.

We have just given the reduction of ancient into modern weights, which is most generally employed; and having said that this reduction is not exact, we now think it necessary to give a table made with more exactness, though still not with mathematical precision:

POUNDS.	GRMS.	GRS. Eng.	OZS.	GRMS.	GRS. Eng.	GROS. DRS.	GRMS.	GRS. Eng.
1	500	7719	1	31·25	482·44	1	3·9	60·21
2	1000	15438	2	62·50	964·88	2	7·80	120·42
3	1500	23157	3	93·75	1447·32	3	11·71	180·62
4	2000	30876	4	125·00	1929·76	4	15·62	240·83
5	2500	38595	5	156·25	2412·20	5	19·53	301·04
6	3000	46314	6	187·50	2894·64	6	23·43	361·25
7	3500	54033	7	218·75	3377·08	7	27·34	421·46
8	4000	61752	8	250·00	3859·52	8	31·25	481·66
9	4500	69471	9	281·25	4341·96	9	35·15	541·87
10	5000	77190	10	312·50	4824·40	10	39·00	602·08

GRS. French.	GRMS.	GRS. Eng.	OBSERVATIONS.
1	0·054	·77	
2	0·110	1·54	Round numbers most commonly used :*
3	0·162	2·31	
4	0·217	3·09	1 ounce = 30 grammes or 463·2 grains English.
5	0·271	3·86	1 drachm = 4 „ 61·8 „ „
6	0·325	4·63	1 grain = 0·05 „ ·77 „ „
7	0·379	5·40	½ ounce = 15 „ 231·6 „ „
8	0·434	6·18	½ drachm = 2 „ 30·9 „ „
9	0·488	6·95	½ grain = 0·025 „ ·39 „ „
·10	0·542	7·72	

* From this table it is evident that the French ounce and drachm employed in prescriptions, nearly correspond with the English ounce and drachm, whilst the French grain is only about ⅔ of the English grain.

We strongly recommend practitioners to adopt one of these divisions: the one which we employ appears to us the most convenient. They ought especially to avoid giving the ounce different values—as, for example, 30 grammes, 31,25 grammes or 32 grammes, or reckoning the gramme at 18,43 grains, and 60 centigrammes at 10 grains—a practice likely to create great confusion in the mind. To a stranger, the confusion will be still greater. Thus the scruple sometimes equals 20 grains, and sometimes 24 grains.

The medicinal pound is always divided into 12 ounces:

The ounce.   .   .   .   8 gros or drachms.
The drachm   .   .   .   3 scruples.

For other countries, the following table gives the principal reductions :*

COUNTRY.	POUND.	OUNCE.	DRACHM.	SCRUPLE OF 24 GRAINS.	SCRUPLE OF 20 GRAINS.	GRAINS.
	grs. E.	grs. E.	grs. E.	grs. E.	grs. E.	grs. E.
Spain . . .	5324	444	55·4	18·3	,,	·769
Tuscany . .	5242	900	54·5	18·2	,,	·757
Rome . .	5237	437	54·4	18·2	,,	·756
England . .	5760	480	60	,,	20·	1·000
Austria . .	6497	541	67·7	,,	22·5	1·126
Germany and Russia.	5526	460	57·7	,,	19·1	·959
Prussia . .	7221	451	56·4	,,	18·7	1·064
Holland and Belgium.	5697	475	59·3	,,	19·7	·987
Sweden . .	5501	458	57·3	,,	19·1	·953
Piedmont . .	4746	396	49·4	,,	16·4	·817

(Soubeiran, *Traité de Pharmacie.*)

FRENCH MEASURES OF CAPACITY.†

Eng. Apothecaries Measure.

	Cub. In. Eng.	Gallons.	Pints.	Ounces.	Drs.	M.
Millilitre .	·0610	...	...	...	...	16·3
Centilitre .	·6103	...	...	...	2	43
Decilitre . .	6·1028	...	...	3	3	2
Litre . .	61·028	...	1	15	1	43
Decalitre .	610·28	...	1	12	1	16
Hectolitre .	6102·8	2	0	1	4	48
Kilolitre . .	61028·	22	0	12	6	24
Myrialitre .	610280·	220	7	13	4	48
		2200				

* This table is computed in grammes in the original, but is here reduced to English grains.

† In the French, Codex fluids are seldom ordered by measure, but generally by weight.

PHARMACEUTICAL NOMENCLATURE.

The chemical nomenclature established by Messrs. Guyton de Morveau, Fourcroy, Lavoisier, &c., has rendered such services to science, that all chemists have adopted it without restriction even to the present day. Some have, however, of late years, given too great an extension to the principles laid down by the great chemists we have just named, from which have arisen names so uncouth or difficult to be remembered, that, although seeking to establish the rules of a nomenclature applicable to organic chemistry, no one has yet arrived at any precise results.

The art of pharmacy anciently embraced names given by chance and without any signification; but Messrs. Henry, Guibourt, Béral and Chéreau have latterly sought to establish rules of pharmaceutical nomenclature, which, without being adopted in an absolute manner in the present day, are still so much used, that we are obliged to give a table of the ancient and modern names. In doing this we shall follow the order indicated by M. Soubeiran, which we have adopted in the definition of each pharmaceutical preparation to be described in the course of this work.*

Ancient Names.		Modern Names.		English Names.
CODEX.	HENRY and GUIBOURT.	BÉRAL.	CHÉREAU.	
Poudres.	Poudres.	Poudres.	Pulvérolés.	Powders.
Pulpes.	Pulpes.	Pulpes.	Pulpolites.	Pulps, e. g. Tamarinds.
Sucs.	Sucs.	Sucs.	Opolés (officinaux). Opolides (magistr.)	Juices ; some of them correspond with "Inspissated juices."
Fécules.	Fécules.	Fécules.	Amydolés.	Feculæ, e. g. Starch, Sago, &c.
Huiles.	Huiles.	Huiles.	Oléol.	Oils.

* All the following preparations are described in full in the "Short Sketch of Pharmacy" in this work.

Ancient Names.		Modern Names.		English Names.
CODEX.	HENRY and GUIBOURT.	BÉRAL.	CHÉREAU.	
Solution par les huiles.	Huiles médicinales (Elœolés).	Elœolés.	Elœolés.	Solutions in oil, e. g. Lin. Camph.
Eaux distillées.	Hydrolats.	Hydolats.	Hydrolats.	Distilled waters.
Huiles volatiles (huiles essentielles).	Huiles volatiles (essences).	Oléolés.	Oléolats.	Volatile or distilled oils.
Solution par les huiles volatiles.	„	Myrolés.	„	Solution in volatile oils, e. g. Lin. Crotonis.
Acolats, (esprits).	Alcoolats.	Alcoolats.	Alcoolats.	Spirits.
Solutions par l'eau.	Hydrolés.	Hydrolés.* Hydrolatures	Hydrolés.	Watery solutions.
Tisanes.	Hydrolés.	Tisanes.	Hydrolés.	Diet drinks, e. g. Gruel, linseed tea.
Apozèmes.	Hydrolés.	Apozèmes,	Hydrolites.	Decoctions.
Potions.	Hydrolés.	Potions.	Hydrolites.	Draughts, mixtures.
Mucilages.	Hydrolés.	Mucilages.	Mucolites.	Mucilages.
Teintures alcooliques.	Alcoolés.	Alcoolés. Alcoolatures.	Alcoolés.	Alcoholic tinctures.
Teintures éthérées.	Ethérolés.	Ethérolés. Ethérolatures.	Ethérolés.	Ethereal tinctures.
Vins médicinaux.	Œnolés.	Œnolés. Œnolatures.	Œnolés.	Medicated wines, e. g. Vin. Ipecac.
Bières médicinales.	Brutolés.	Brytolés.	Brutolés.	Medicated Beer.
Vinaigres médicinaux.	Oxéolés.	Acétolés. Acétolatures.	Acétolés.	Medicated vinegars, e. g. Acet. Colch.
Médicaments avec le sucre.	Saccharolés.	Saccharolés.	Saccharolés.	General name not applied to any specific preparation.
Sirops.	Sirops.	Sirops.	Saccharolés liquides.	Syrups.

* The termination in é is employed by M. Béral for solutions which do not furnish an extract by evaporation, and that in ature for those which do. In general, we are in the habit of giving the termination é to preparations made with dried substances, and the termination ature to those which have fresh plants for their base. This rule applies to substances in water, alcohol, ether, &c.

Ancient Names.		Modern Names.		English Names.
CODEX.	HENRY and GUIBOURT.	BÉRAL.	CHÉREAU.	
Mellites, Miels.	{ Mellites. Oxymellites.	{ Hydromellés. Acétomellés.	{ Hydromellés. Acétomellés.	{ Honeys and oxymels.
Oléosaccharum.	{ Elæ saccharum. Saccharrures.	} Saccharolés.	{ Oléosaccharolés.	Oleosaccharum ; volatile oils dropped upon a lump of sugar, &c.
Gelées.	Gelées.	Gelées.	{ Sacchorolés mous.	} Jellies.
Pâtes.	Pâtes.	Pâtes.	{ Saccharolés ductiles.	Pastes; no corresponding Eng. prep.
Conserves.	Electuaires.	Conserves.	{ Saccharolés mous.	} Confections.
Tablettes.	Tablettes.	Tablettes.	{ Saccharolés solides.	} Lozenges.
Pastilles.	Pastilles.	Pastilles.	Pastilles.	Pastilles.
Electuaires.	Electuaires.	Electuaires.	{ Saccharolés mous.	Electuaries.
Extraits.	Extraits.	Extraits.	Apostolés.	Extracts.
Espèces.	Espèces.	Espèces.	Spéciolés.	"Species," e. g. Species for Aromatic Confection, for Conf. Pip. Nign., &c.
Poudres comp.	Poudres comp.	{ Poudres comp.	} Pulvérolés.	{ Compound powders.
Pilules et Bols.	Pilules et Bols.	{ Pilules et Bols.	{ Saccharolés solides.	} Pills and boluses.
Capsules.	,,	,,	,,	{ Capsules, e. g. of Copaiba, &c.
Granules.	,,	,,	,,	Granules ; no corresponding British preparation.
Cérats.	Elæocérolés.	Liparoïdés.	Oléocérolés.	Cerates.
Pommades.	Liparolés.	Liparolés. Excipient simp. Liparoïdés. Excipient comp.	} Stéarolés.	{ Pomatum, e. g. Cold Cream.
Onguents.	Rétinolés.	Rétinoïdés.	{ Oléocérolés résineux.	} Ointments.

| Ancient Names. | | Modern Names. | | English Names. |
CODEX.	HENRY and GUIBOURT.	BÉRAL.	CHÉREAU.	
Emplâtres ou Onguents solides.	Rétinolés.	Rétinoïdés.	Stéarolés solides.	Ointment plasters ; (no such class in English Pharmacy).
Emplâtres vrais	Stéaratés.	Stéaratés.	Stéaratés.	Plasters.
Cataplasmes.	Cataplasmes.	Cataplasmes.	„	Poultices.
Fomentations.	Hydrolés.	Hydrolotifs.	Hydrolés.	Fomentations.
Lotions.	Hydrolés.	Hydrolotifs.	Hydrolés.	Lotions.
Liniments.	Elæolés (oily), Alcoolés (alcoholic), Ethérolés (ethereal), etc.	Elæolés. Alcoolées. Alcoolatures, etc.	„ „ „	Liniments, oily, e. g. Lin. Ammon.; Alcoholic, Lin. Saponis ; Ethereal ; no English preparation.
Collyres.	Hydrolés. Liparolés. Poudres. Alcoolats, etc.	Hydrolotifs. Poudres. Alcoolats. Alcoolés, etc.	„ „ „ „	Collyria, eye-waters. Powders do not generally come under this head in English, but when burnt alum or calomel is blown into the eye, it would in French come under the head of Collyrium.
Bains.	Hydrolés.	Hydrolotifs.	Hydrolés.	Baths.

CLASSIFICATION

OF

SIMPLE MEDICINES

IN THEIR

NATURAL FAMILIES.

FRENCH AND ENGLISH COMMON NAMES.	LATIN NAMES.	PART EMPLOYED.	FORMS OF ADMINISTRATION.
			ACOTY
			Algues, Algæ,
CORALLINE BLANCHE, white coral.	Corallina officinalis.	The whole plant.	Infusion and jelly.
MOUSSE DE CORSE. CORALLINE DF CORSE, Corsican moss.	Fucus helminthocorton.	Ditto.	Ditto.
CARRAGÉEN (Mousse perlée ou d'Irlande), pearl, or Irish moss.	Fucus crispus.	Ditto.	Decoction and jelly.
			Champignons,
AGARIC BLANC, Larch agaric.	Boletus laricis.	The whole plant.	Powder.
AGARIC AMADOUVIER, amadou, or German tinder.	Boletus ignarius.	Ditto.	,,
ERGOT DE SEIGLE. SEIGLE ERGOTÉ, ergot of rye.	Sphacelia segetum. (LÉVEILLÉ.)	The whole fungus.	Powder.
			Lichens,
LICHEN D'ISLANDE, Iceland moss.	Lichen Islandicus.	The whole plant.	Decoction and jelly.
ORSEILLE, Archil.	Roccella tinctoria.	Ditto.	Employed to prepare Archil—a dyeing material.
PARELLE D'AUVERGNE, craw-fish eye lichen.	Variolaria Orcina.	Ditto.	Employed to prepare litmus.
			Fougères,
FOUGÈRE MALE, male fern.	Nephrodium felix. (MAS.)	The root.	Powder and decoction.

DOSES FOR ADULTS.	DOSES FOR CHILDREN.	THERAPEU-TICAL CLASSI-FICATION.	OBSERVATIONS.
LEDONS.			
Seaweeds.			
20 to 30 grms. ʒv to ʒi.	10 to 20 grms. ʒiiss to ʒv.	} Anthelmintic.	{ Considered in the present day as a polype.
Ditto.	Ditto.	Ditto.	{ Principally administered as an infusion in milk.
Ad libitum.	Ad libitum.	{ Emollient.	
Fungi, Mushrooms.			
{ 0,05 to 0,25. { 3/4 gr. to 4 grs.	{ 0,01 to 0,05. { 1/6 gr. to 3/4 gr. { seldom used.	} Drastic.	
„	„	{ Hemostatic ; checks bleed-ing.	The amadou employed in sur-gery ought to be free from nitre.
{ 0,50 to 4 grms. { 7 grs. to ʒi.	0,25 to 0,30. 4 grs. to 8 grs.	Exciting agent. Hemostatic.	{ It contains ergotin, which is employed in solution to check hæmorrhages, in doses from 8 grs. to 15 grs. in 4 ounces of water, or in pills.
Lichens.			
Ad libitum.	Ad libitum.	{ Emollient and bitter tonic.	The lichen is deprived of its bitter principle by washing it with boiling water, or with alkaline carbonates. Its substitutes are *Pulmo-naire de chêne*, or Lungs of the oak, and *Lichen pixidé*.
Filices, Ferns.			
{ 10 to 20 grms. { ʒiiss to ʒv.	5 to 10 grms. ʒi to ʒiiss.	{ Anthelmintic. { Expels tape-worms.	The ethereal extract is em-ployed in the dose of 1 to 4 grammes (gr. xv. to ʒi). The fresh leaves answer for making mattrasses upon which children may sleep.

FRENCH AND ENGLISH COMMON NAMES.	LATIN NAMES.	PART EMPLOYED.	FORMS OF ADMINISTRATION.
			Fougères,
CAPILLAIRE DU CANADA, *Canada maiden hair.*	*Adianthum pedatum.*	The whole plant.	Infusion and syrup.
—— DE MONTPELLIER, *Venus's maiden hair.*	*— capillus Veneris.*	Ditto	Ditto.
			Lycopodiacees,
LYCOPODE (Soufre végétal), *lycopodium (vegetable sulphur).*	*Lycopodium clavatum.*	The powder enclosed in the capsules.	Used externally.
			MONOCO
			Aroïdees, Aroïdeæ
ARUM (Gouet, ou Pied de veau), *arum.*	*Arum vulgare.*	The root.	Powder.
ACORE VRAIE, *acorus,* or *sweet flag.*	*Acorus verus,* or *calamus.*	Ditto.	Ditto.
			Cyperacees,
SOUCHET LONG et ROND, *long and round galingale.*	*Cyperus longus* and *rotundus.*	Ditto.	"
CAREX ou LAICHE DES SABLES (Salsepareille d'Allemagne). *German sarsaparilla; sea sedge.*	*Carex arenaria.*	Ditto.	"
			Graminees,
CHIENDENT, *dog's tooth.*	*Triticum repens.*	The root or rhyzome.	Tisane, decoction.
CANNE DE PROVENCE (Grand roseau), *great reed-grass.*	*Arundo donax.*	The root.	Ditto.
CANNE A SUCRE, *sugarcane.*	*Saccharum officinarum.*	The sugar.	Bases for syrups, pâtes, &c.
AVOINE, *oats.*	*Avena sativa.*	The fruit.	Tisanes, decoctions.

DOSES FOR ADULTS.	DOSES FOR CHILDREN.	THERAPEU-TICAL CLASSI-FICATION.	OBSERVATIONS.
Filices, Ferns.			
15 to 30 grms. 3ss to 3i.	15 to 30 grms. 3ss to 3i.	(*Béchiques*). Expectorant.	Substitutes : Black maiden hair, *Asplenium adian-thum nigrum*, and Hart's tongue, *Scolopendrium officinale*.
Ditto.	Ditto.	Ditto.	
Lycopodiaceæ, Club-Mosses.			
Every dose.	Every dose.		Employed for rolling pills, and drying up the excoriations which occur in the thighs of infants.
TYLEDONS.			
(Arum Tribe.)			
0,50 to 1 grm. gr. viii to gr. xv.	0,10 to 0,25. gr. iss to gr. iv.	Drastic.	Little used.
1 to 4 grms. gr. xv to 3i.	0,50 to 2 grms. gr. viii to 3ss.	Excitant ; general stimulant.	Ditto.
Cyperaceæ, Sedges.			
„	„		Employed formerly, but not at present.
„	„		Employed to adulterate sar-saparilla. It is easily distinguished by its clean and easy fracture.
Gramineæ, Grasses.			
30 to 50 grms. 3i to 3ii.	30 to 50 grms. 3i to 3ii.	Emollient. Diu-retic.	Succedaneum : Great creeping dogs'-tooth grass *Cynodon dactylon*.
Ditto.	Ditto.	Emollient. Re-pels milk from the breasts.	
Every dose.	Every dose.	Sweetening. Gently laxative.	The beetroot, maize, maple-tree, &c., yield the same sugar. Uncrystallizable, and called *mélasse* (molasses).
30 to 50 grms. 3i to 3ii.	30 to 50 grms. 3i to 3ii.	Emollient.	Furnishes gruel. The chaff is employed to make mat-trasses for children and for women in child-bed.

FRENCH AND ENGLISH COMMON NAMES.	LATIN NAMES.	PART EMPLOYED.	FORMS OF ADMINISTRATION.
			Graminees,
ORGE, *spring barley.*	*Hordeum vulgare.*	The fruit.	Tisanes, decoctions.
RIZ, *rice.*	*Oryza sativa.*	Ditto.	Ditto.
			Colchicacées, Melanthaceæ
COLCHIQUE D'AUTOMNE, *meadow saffron* (*Colchicum*).	*Colchicum autumnale.*	Bulbs and seeds.	Tincture of the bulbs.
ELLÉBORE BLANC, *white hellebore.*	*Veratrum album.*	The root.	Powder and tincture.
CÉVADILLE (Poudre des capucins), *sabadilla.*	*Veratrum sabadilla.*	The fruit.	Powder.
			Palmiers, Palmaceæ,
DATTES, *dates.*	*Phœnix dactylifera.*	The fruit.	Tisane and decoction.
SAGOU, *sago.*	*Sagus Rumphii.*	Fecula extracted from the trunk.	Puddings and soups.
SANG-DRAGON (en roseau), *dragons' blood,* (*in reeds*).	*Calamus draco.*	Extract.	Extract in powder or pills.

DOSES FOR ADULTS.	DOSES FOR CHILDREN.	THERAPEU-TICAL CLASSI-FICATION.	OBSERVATIONS.

Gramineæ, Grasses.

30 to 50 grms. ʒi to ʒii. Ditto.	30 to 50 grms. ʒi to ʒii. Ditto.	Emollient. Ditto.	We make a distinction be-tween *pearl* barley and *hulled* barley. From all these fruits, and from wheat, (*Triticum sativum*), we obtain starch (*amidon*). The starch of the gramineæ, under the influence of dias-tase or of the diluted mi-neral acids, is converted into sugar of starch (*glu-cose*). (See note upon Dias-tase, article Feculæ. See Index).

(Colchicum Tribe.)

1 to 4 grms. gr. xv to ʒi (of the tincture).	2 to 6 drops.	Diuretic. Dras-tic. Anti-gout.	The seeds are less active. As a drastic, give double the dose.
By drops.	By drops.	Drastic.	Succedaneum : Black helle-bore, *Helleborus niger*, (Ranunculaceæ).
,,	Employed ex-ternally to kill lice.	Ditto.	These three substances con-tain Veratrin, which is pow-erfully drastic, and is em-ployed externally in neu-ralgia, in doses from 0·01 to 0·06, 1/6 of a gr. to 3/4 gr.

(Palm Tribe.)

30 to 50 grms. ʒi to ʒii.	30 to 50 grms. ʒi to ʒii.	Expectorant.	The four pectoral fruits are : Dates, Jujubes, *Zisiphus vulgaris*, (Rhamneæ), Figs, *Ficus carica*, (Urtiaceæ), and Raisins, *Vitis vinifera*, (Vitaceæ).
Every dose.	Every dose.	Emollient. Ana-leptic, (resto-rative after illness).	
0,50 to 1 grm. gr. viii to gr. xv.	0,10 to 0,30. gr. iss to gr. v.	Astringent.	Enters into the composition of the escharotic powder of Rousselot. Dragon's blood in mass is supplied by *Dra-cæna draco*, (Asparagineæ), and that in small sticks by *Pterocarpus draco*, (Legu-minosæ).

FRENCH AND ENGLISH COMMON NAMES.	LATIN NAMES.	PART EMPLOYED.	FORMS OF ADMINISTRATION.
			Liliacees, Liliaceæ
			THIS FAMILY FURNISHES, THE LILY, THE
SCILLE, *squill.*	*Scilla maritima,*	The bulb.	Powder, tincture, and extract.
ALOËS, *aloes.*	*Aloë, soccotrina, spicata, linguæformis.*	The evaporated juice.	Powder and tincture.
			Asparaginees,
ASPERGE, *asparagus.*	*Asparagus officinalis.*	The root and turio (leafy stem).	Tisane and syrup.
SALSEPAREILLE, *sarsaparilla.*	*Smilax sarsaparilla, medica, officinalis, etc.*	The root.	Tisane, syrup, and extract.
			Iridées,
IRIS DE FLORENCE, *fleur de lis.*	*Iris florentina.*	The rhyzome.	Powder. Used as peas for keeping issues open.
SAFRAN, *saffron.*	*Crocus sativus.*	The stigmas.	Powder, tisane, infusion, and syrup.
			Amomees,
ARROW-ROOT (a name adopted in French from the English.)	*Maranta - arundinacea.*	The fecula (of the root).	Puddings and soups.
CARDAMOME, *cardamoms.*	*Amomum Cardamomum.*	The fruit.	Alcoholic tincture.
GALANGA, *galangale.*	*Alpinia galanga.*	The root.	Powder.

DOSES FOR ADULTS.	DOSES FOR CHILDREN.	THERAPEU- TICAL CLASSI- FICATION.	OBSERVATIONS.

(Lily Tribe.)

GARLIC, THE ONION, THE ESCHALOT, &c.

DOSES FOR ADULTS.	DOSES FOR CHILDREN.	THERAPEU- TICAL CLASSI- FICATION.	OBSERVATIONS.
0,05 to 0,50. 3/4 gr. to gr. viii.	0,01 to 0,5 1/6 gr. to grs. viii.	Diuretic.	Promotes suppuration, when externally applied.
0,20 to 0,60 gr. iii to gr. ix.	0,02 to 0,10. 1/3 gr. to gr. iss.	Drastic.	Three principal kinds: Soc- cotrine, caballine and he- patic.
Asparagineæ.			
15 to 30 grms. ʒss to ʒi.	8 to 15 grms. ʒii to ʒss.	Diuretic.	The root is one of the five aperient roots; the others being: Petit Hous, Rus- cus aculeatus, Butcher's broom, (Asparagineæ), and the roots of Parsnip, (Per- sil, F.), Wild celery, (Ache, F.), and Fennel, (Fenouil, F.), (Umbelliferæ).
15 to 30 grms. ʒss to ʒi.	8 to 15 grms. ʒii to ʒss.	Sudorific, puri- fying to the blood.	Succedaneum: The roots of Smilax squina, (Aspara- gineæ).
Irideæ.			
Not used inter- nally.	Not used inter- nally.	Irritant.	Issue peas may also be made of cultivated peas, of me- zereon, of unripe oranges, and of caoutchouc.
0,50 to 1,0 grm. gr. viii to gr. xv.	Not used for infants.	Emmenagogue.	Enters into the laudanum of Sydenham, and the caustic sulfo-safranique of Velpeau. (See Acid, Sulphuric).
Zingiberaceæ.			
Every dose.	Every dose.	Analeptic. (See Sago, p. 14).	
Not used inter- nally.	Not used inter- nally.	Excitants.	Greater, lesser, and round, or clustered cardamoms are known familiarly.
0,25 to 1,0 grm. gr. iv to gr. xv.	Not used.	Ditto, and spice.	Succedanea: Ginger, Amo- mum zingiber; Zedoary, Kempferia longa; (Manig- uette, F.), Grains of Pa- radise, Amomum grana paradisi, (Zingiberaceæ).

C

FRENCH AND ENGLISH COMMON NAMES.	LATIN NAMES.	PART EMPLOYED.	FORMS OF ADMINISTRA- TION.
			Orchidées,
VANILLE, *vanilla.*	*Vanilla aromatica.*	The fruit.	Tincture and powder.
SALEP, *salop.*	*Orchis mascula* or *Morio.*	The bulbs.	Puddings and soups.
			DICOTY
			Conifères,
GENÉVRIER, *juniper.*	*Juniperus communis.*	The fruit.	Infusion, fumi- gation.
HUILE DE CADE, (no English representa- tive).	*Juniperus oxicedrus.*	Empyreuma- tic oil.	External use.
SABINE, *savine.*	*Juniperus sabina.*	The twigs.	Infus., powder, and ess. oil.
TÉRÉBENTHINE DE BORDEAUX, STRAS- BOURG, or VENISE, *turpentine, &c.*	*Pinus maritima* and *sylvestris. Abies ex- celsa.*	Resinous juice.	Pills, vol. oil.
POIX DE BOURGOGNE, *Burgundy pitch.*	*Abies excelsa.*	Solid resinous juice.	Plaster.
			Pipéritées,
POIVRE NOIR et BLANC, *black and white pepper.*	*Piper nigrum.*	The grains.	Powder and Pi- perin.
POIVRE A QUEUE (Cu- bèbe), *tailed pepper* (cubebs.)	*Piper cubeba.*	The grains.	Powder, oleore- sinous extract.
			Cupulifères,
CHÊNE ROUVRE, *the oak.*	*Quercus robur.*	The bark and acorns.	Powder and de- coction.
NOIX DE GALLE, *nut- galls.*	*Quercus infectoria.*	Tannin.	Pills and solu- tion.

DOSES FOR ADULTS.	DOSES FOR CHILDREN.	THERAPEU- TICAL CLASSI- FICATION.	OBSERVATIONS.

Orchidaceæ.

| 0,50 to 2 grms. gr. viii to 3ss. | 0,25 to 1 grm. gr. iv to gr. xv. | Excitants, aro- matic. | It is reduced to powder by the aid of sugar. The crystals which cover it are benzoic acid. |
| Every dose. | Every dose. | Nourishing food | |

LEDONS.

Coniferæ.

30 grms. 3i.	15 to 20 grms. 3ss to 3v.	} Excitant.	Acts upon mucous membranes, especially upon that of the bladder. Succedaneum: *Bourgeons de sapin,* F., tops of the Silver Fir, *Abies pectinata.*
„	„	„	In affections of the skin. (§. and Veterinary surgery).
0,10 to 0,25. gr. iss to gr. iv.	} Not used.	Emmenagogue.	The powder is used for dressing indurated chancres.
0,50 to 1 grm. gr. viii to gr. xv.	In the form of syrup from 30 to 40 grms. 3i to 3x.	} Excitant.	Tar is obtained by their combustion.
Unlimited.	Unlimited.	{ Excitant. Rubefacient.	Succedaneum: Black pitch.

Piperaceæ.

| 0,10 to 0,25. gr. iss to gr. iv. | } Not used. | Exciting spice. | |
| 15 to 30 grms. 3ss to 3i. | } Not used. | Excitant. | Employed against discharges, (§. In the original, the above very general expression is employed; for Cubebs act beneficially upon other discharges from mucous membranes, as well as simple gonorrhœa. The dose appears enormous). |

Cupuliferæ.

| 20 to 30 grms. 3v to 3i. | 10 to 20 grms. 3iiss to 3v. | } Astringent. | Tannin. See Nutgalls, below. |
| 0·50 to 1 grm. gr. viii to gr. xv. | 0,10 to 0,40. gr. iss to gr. vi. | } Ditto. | Antidote to poisoning by the organic alkalis and by tartar emetic. |

c 2

FRENCH AND ENGLISH COMMON NAMES.	LATIN NAMES.	PART EMPLOYED.	FORMS OF ADMINISTRATION.
Juglandées, Juglandaceæ			
NOYER, *the walnut.*	*Juglans regia.*	Fruit and leaves.	Decoction and extract.
Salicinées, Salicaceæ			
SAULE, *willow.*	*Salix alba.*	Bark. Salicine.	Decoction.
PEUPLIER, *poplar.*	*Populus nigra.*	The tops; small twigs.	Enters into poplar ointment.
Ulmacees et Morees, Ulmaceæ and Urticaceæ			
ORME PYRAMIDAL or CHAMPETRE, *the elm.*	*Ulmus campestris.*	The bark.	Decoction.
CONTRAYERVA, *contrajerva.*	*Dorstenia contrayerva.*	The root.	Ditto.
FIGUIER, *figs.*	*Ficus carica.*	The fruit.	Ditto.
PARIÉTAIRE, *pellitory of the wall.*	*Parietaria officinalis.*	The whole plant.	Infusion.
MURIER, *mulberry.*	*Morus nigra.*	The fruit.	Syrup.
Cannabiées, Cannabinaceæ,			
CHANVRE INDIEN, *Indian hemp.*	*Cannabis indica.*	The leaves.	Infusion.
HOUBLON, *hops.*	*Humulus lupulus.*	The fruit (cones).	Ditto.
Euphorbiacees, Euphorbiaceæ			
EUPHORBE, *euphorbium.*	*Euphorbia antiquorum.*	Gum-resin.	Powder. Pills.
MERCURIALE, *dog's mercury.*	*Mercurialis annua* and *perennis.*	The whole plant.	Honey.
CAOUTCHOUC, *caoutchouc.*	*Iatropha, Elastica, etc.*	Thickened juice.	,,
TAPIOKA, *tapioca.*	*Iatropha Manihot.*	Fecula of the root.	Puddings and soups.

DOSES FOR ADULTS.	DOSES FOR CHILDREN.	THERAPEUTICAL CLASSIFICATION.	OBSERVATIONS.
(Walnut Family).			
20 to 30 grms. 3v to 3i.	10 to 20 grms. 3iiss to 3v.	Antiscrophulous.	
(Willow Tribe).			
10 to 20 grms. 3iiss to 3v.	Not used.	Febrifuge.	Salicine is employed in doses of 3/4 gr. to gr. xv.
External use.	„	As an ointment for promoting suppuration.	The charcoal is employed by Dr. Belloc in certain affections of the stomach.
(Elm and Nettle or Mulberry Tribe).			
15 to 30 grms. 3ss to 3i.	Not used.	Antisyphilitic.	
10 to 20 grms. 3iiss to 3v.	Ditto.	Against the bite of a serpent.	
15 to 30 grms. 3ss to 3i.	10 to 20 grms. 3iiss to 3v.	Expectorant.	
15 to 30 grms. 3ss to 3i.	10 to 20 grms. 3iiss to 3v.	Diuretic.	
20 to 30 grms. 3v to 3i.	10 to 20 grms. 3iiss to 3v.	Cooling and refreshing.	The syrup is used in gargles.
Hempworts.			
5 to 10 grms. 3i to 3iiss.	Not used.	Stupefying.	The extract bears the name of hashish or hachich, (Churrus). It is employed as a stupefiant in doses of gr. iss to gr. iii.
10 to 20 grms. 3iiss to 3v.	5 to 10 grms. 3i to 3iiss.	Bitter.	Enters into beer.
(Spurge Tribe).			
0,05 to 0,20. 3/4 gr. to gr. iii.	0,01 to 0,02. 1/6 to 1/3 gr.	Drastic.	Succedaneum : Euphorbia, (fruit), Euphorbia lathyris.
External use. 30 to 60 grms. 3i to 3ii.	10 to 20 grms. 3iiss to 3v.	Laxative.	The honey is only employed in glysters.
„	„	„	Employed to make sounds, pessaries, and other surgical instruments. Replaced in making these instruments by linseed-oil, boiled until thick.
Every dose.	Every dose.	Emollient. Analeptic. (See Sago, p. 14).	

FRENCH AND ENGLISH COMMON NAMES.	LATIN NAMES.	PART EMPLOYED.	FORMS OF ADMINISTRA- TION.
Euphorbiacées, Euphorbiaceæ			
RICIN (Palma Christi), castor-oil.	Ricinus communis.	Fruit and oil.	Draughts and glysters.
PETIT PIGNON D'INDE (Croton), croton-oil.	Croton tiglium.	Ditto.	Pills and draughts.
CASCARILLE, cascarilla.	Croton cascarilla.	The bark.	Powder and fumigations.
BUIS, box-tree.	Buxus sempervirens.	Ditto.	Decoction.
Aristolochiees,			
SERPENTAIRE DE VIRGINIE, serpentary.	Aristolochia serpentaria.	The root.	Powder. Infusion.
AZARUM CABARET, asarabacca.	Azarum europeum.	The leaves and root.	Infusion.
Daphnees or Thymelees,			
GAROU, mexereum.	Daphne gnidium.	The bark.	Pomatum. Caustic to the skin.
Laurinees,			
LAURIER COMMUN or D'APOLLON, sweet bay.	Laurus nobilis.	The leaves and fruit.	Pomatum.
SASSAFRAS, sassafras.	Laurus sassafras.	The wood.	Maceration. Tissue.
CANNELLE DE CEYLAN, cinnamon.	Laurus cinnamomum.	Bark, essence.	Powder, wine and tincture.
CAMPHRE, camphor.	Laurus camphora.	Concrete essential oil.	Pills and powder.

DOSES FOR ADULTS.	DOSES FOR CHILDREN.	THERAPEU- TICAL CLASSI- FICATION.	OBSERVATIONS.
(Spurge Tribe).			
15 to 30 grms. ₃ss to ₃i.	5 to 10 grms. ₃i to ₃iiss.	} Laxative.	
1 to 4 drops.	{ 1/2 drop to 1 drop. ●	} Drastic.	{ The oil is employed externally as a blistering derivative.
1 to 4 grms. gr. xv to ₃i	} Not used.	Aromatic.	
{ 8 to 15 grms. ₃ii to ₃ss.	} Ditto.	Bitter.	
Aristolochiaceæ, Birthworts.			
5 to 10 grms. ₃i to ₃iiss.	2 to 6 grms. ₃ss to ₃iss.	Excitant.	
{ 0,5 to 1,50. gr. viii. to ₃i.	{ 0,10 to 0,20. Seldom used. gr. iss. to gr. iii.	} Emetic.	
Thymelaceæ (Daphne Tribe).			
„	„	Blistering.	{ The bark is employed as a blistering substance; the pomatum to promote sup- puration from issues.
Lauraceæ, Laurels.			
External use.	External use.	Ext. excitant.	
5 to 10 grms. ₃i to ₃iiss.	2 to 6 grms. ₃ss to ₃iss.	} Sudorific.	{ Four sudorific woods: Sassa- fras, Guiacum, Sarsaparilla and China-root, (Squine, *Smilax æquina,* See Sar- sap. p. 17).
0,50 to 1,50. gr. viii to ₃i.	0,10 to 0,30. gr. iss to gr. v.	Excitant. Sto- machic.	{ Succedanea: *Laurus cassia,* (*Cassia*), *Laurus malaba- trum*), &c.
0,20 to 0,50. gr. iii to gr. viii.	0,05 to 0,10. 3/4 gr. to gr. iss.	Anti - spasmo- dic.	{ Excitant in a larger dose. Sprinkled upon blisters, to prevent the action of the cantharides upon the mu- cous membrane of the bladder.

FRENCH AND ENGLISH COMMON NAMES.	LATIN NAMES.	PART EMPLOYED.	FORMS OF ADMINISTRATION.
		Myristicées, Myristaceæ	
MUSCADE, *nutmegs.*	*Myristica moschata.*	Fruit and fixed oil.	Powder. Pills.
		Polygonées, Polygonaceæ	
BISTORTE, *bistort.*	*Polygonum bistorta.*	The roots.	Decoction.
PATIENCE or PARELLE, *Patience, sharp leaved dock.*	*Rumex acutus* or *patientia.*	Ditto.	Ditto.
RAPONTIC, *French rhubarb.*	*Rheum rhaponticum.*	Ditto.	Powder and maceration.
RHUBARBE, *rhubarb.*	*Rheum palmatum.*	Ditto.	Powder.
SARRASIN, *sarasin.*	*Polygonum fagopirum.*	The fruit.	Fecula.
		Chenopodées, Chenopodiaceæ	
BETTE or POIRÉE, *white beet.*	*Beta cicla.*	The leaves.	To dress blisters.
BETTERAVE, *beetroot.*	*Beta vulgaris.*	The root.	Employed to yield sugar.
		Labiées, Labiatæ	
LAVANDE, *lavender.*	*Lavandula spica* or *vera.*	The whole plant.	Infusion and fumigation.
MENTHE, *mint.*	*Mentha piperita* or *crispa, viridis, etc.*	Ditto.	Injection. Distilled water.
MARJOLAINE, *marjorum.*	*Origanum marjorana.*	Ditto.	Ditto.
THYM, *thyme.*	*Thymus vulgaris.*	Ditto.	Ditto.
MÉLISSE, *balm.*	*Melissa officinalis.*	Ditto.	Ditto.
HYSSOPE, *hyssop.*	*Hysopus officinalis.*	Ditto.	Ditto.

DOSES FOR ADULTS.	DOSES FOR CHILDREN.	THERAPEU-TICAL CLASSI-FICATION.	OBSERVATIONS.
(Nutmeg Tribe).			
0,20 to 0,40. gr. iii to gr. vi.	5 to 10 grms. ʒi to ʒiiss.	Excitant. Spice.	The arillus of the musk is employed under the name of *Mace*. (§. There is evidently an error, perhaps typographical, in the doses here mentioned. Even if they are transposed, two drachms is a very large dose for an adult. It is probable that the dose for children in this case ought to be substituted for that in the next article: Bistort.)
(Buck-Wheat Tribe.)			
10 to 20 grms. ʒiiss to ʒv.	0,05 to 0,10. 3/4 gr. to gr. iss.	Sudorific.	
15 to 30 grms. ʒss to ʒi.	5 to 15 grms. ʒi to ʒss.	Tonic purgative.	Succedaneum: Sorrel, *Rumex acetosa.*
2 to 4 grms. ʒss to ʒi.	1 to 2 grms. gr. xv. to ʒss.	Ditto.	
0,50 to 1 grm. gr. viii to gr. xv.	0,05 to 0,50. 3/4 gr. to gr. viii.	Emollient food.	Tonic, in doses of gr. iii to gr. viii; purgative, from gr. viii to gr. xv.
Every dose.	Every dose.		
(Goosefoot Tribe).			
,,	,,	Food.	Succedaneum: Spinage, *Spinacia oleracea.*
,,	,,	Sweetening.	
(Pea Tribe).			
10 to 20 grm. ʒiiss to ʒv.	5 to 10 grms. ʒi to ʒiiss.	Excitant.	
10 to 30 grms. ʒiiss to ʒi.	Ditto.	Ditto.	Succedanea: Different species of mint.
Ditto.	Ditto.	Ditto.	Succedanea: *O. vulgare* and *O. dictamus.*
Ditto.	Ditto.	Ditto.	Succedaneum: *Thymus serpyllum.*
Ditto.	Ditto.	Excitant, and antispasmodic.	
Ditto.	Ditto.	Excitant.	Succedanea: Rosemary, *Rosmarinus officinalis,* Ground ivy, *Glechoma hederacea,* Germander, *Teucrium chamedrys.*

FRENCH AND ENGLISH COMMON NAMES.	LATIN NAMES.	PART EMPLOYED.	FORMS OF ADMINISTRA-TION.
Labiees, Labiatæ			
SAUGE, *sage*.	*Salvia officinalis.*	The whole plant.	Injection. Distilled water.
Scrophularinees, Scrophularineæ			
VÉRONIQUE, *speedwell*.	*Veronica officinalis.*	Ditto.	Infusion.
GRATIOLE, *hedge hyssop*.	*Gratiola officinalis.*	Ditto.	Ditto.
DIGITALE POURPRÉE, *purple foxglove*.	*Digitalis purpurea.*	The leaves.	Powder. Infusion.
BOUILLON BLANC (Molène), *mullein*.	*Verbascum thapsus.*	Ditto.	Infusion.
Solanées, Solanaceæ			
TABAC, *tobacco*.	*Nicotiana tabacum* and *rustica.*	Ditto.	Infusion. Fumigation.
STRAMONIUM (Pomme épineuse), *thorn apple*.	*Datura stramonium.*	Leaves and seeds.	Infusion and smoking.
JUSQUIAME, *henbane*.	*Hyosciamus niger.*	Ditto.	Ditto.
BELLADONE, *deadly nightshade*.	*Atropa belladona.*	Leaves.	Powder.
Ditto.	*Ditto.*	Alcoholic extract.	Ditto.
Ditto.	*Ditto.*	The root.	Injections.
DOUCE AMÈRE, *bitter sweet, or woody nightshade*.	*Solanum dulcamara.*	The stalks.	Tisane.
MORELLE, *common nightshade*.	*Solanum nigrum.*	The whole plant.	Decoction.
POMME DE TERRE, *potato*.	*Solanum tuberosum.*	The rhizomes.	Fecula.

DOSES FOR ADULTS.	DOSES FOR CHILDREN.	THERAPEU-TICAL CLASSI-FICATION.	OBSERVATIONS.
(Pea Tribe).			
10 to 30 grms. ʒiiss to ʒi.	5 to 10 grms. ʒi to ʒiiss.	} Excitant.	
(Figwort Tribe).			
15 to 30 grms. ʒss to ʒi.	8 to 15 grms. ʒii to ʒss.	} Ditto.	
Ditto.	Little used.	Purgative.	
0,10 to 0,50. gr. iss to gr. viii.	0,02 to 0,05. 1/3 gr. to 3/4 gr.	Contra-stimu-lant.	Contains *digitaline*, employed in doses of 0,001 to 0,006, (1/60 gr. to 1/10 gr.), the dose being gradually increased. (⅓. The dose of digitalis scarcely ever exceeds gr. ii to gr. iii with English practioners).
15 to 30 grms. ʒss to ʒi.	Little used.	Sudorific. Expectorant.	
(Nightshade Tribe).			
0,25 to 1 grm. gr. iv to gr. xv.	Not used.	Stupefiant.	Contains *nicotine*. An active poison, used in doses of 0,001 to 0,01, (gr. 1/60 to 1/6).
1 to 4 grms. gr. xv to ʒi.	Ditto.	Ditto.	Contains *daturine*.
Ditto.	Ditto.	Ditto.	Contains *kyosciamine*.
0,05 to 0,20. gr. 3/4 to gr. iii.	0,01 to 0,05. gr.1/6 to gr.3/4.	Ditto.	In doses of 0,01 to 0,05, (gr. 1/6 to gr. 3/4) against hooping-cough.
0,01 to 0,05. gr. 1/6 to gr.3/4.	0,001 to 0,0005. gr. 1/60 to gr. 1/120.	Ditto.	Four kinds of extract: 1st. alcoholic ; 2nd. extract with the starch ; 3rd. extract without starch; 4th. extract by infusion. Arranged in the order of their activity.
0,06 to 0,20. gr. 3/4 to gr. iii.	0,01 to 0,05. gr.1/6 to gr.3/4.	Ditto.	Tincture from 10 drops to 15.
15 to 30 grms. ʒss to ʒi.	5 to 10 grms. ʒi to ʒiiss.	Sudorific and purifying to the blood.	
10 to 20 grms. ʒiiss to ʒv.	Not used.	Stupefiant.	This dose is intended to apply to injections.
Every dose.	Every dose.	Emollient food.	Varieties of food obtained from the *Solanaceæ*: Tomata, *Solanum lycopersicum*, and Mad-apple, *Aubergine, Solanum melongana*.

FRENCH AND ENGLISH COMMON NAMES.	LATIN NAMES.	PART EMPLOYED	FORMS OF ADMINISTRATION.
			Solanees, Solanaceæ
ALKEKENGE COQUERET, winter cherry.	Physalis Alkekengi.	The fruit.	Decoction and syrup.
			Boraginees, Boragineæ
BOURRACHE, borage.	Borago officinalis.	Leaves and flowers.	Infusion.
CONSOUDE, comfrey.	Symphytum officinale.	The root.	Decoction.
CYNOGLOSSE, hound's-tongue.	Cynoglossum officinale.	Bark of the root.	Powder.
ORCANETTE, alkanet.	Anchusa tinctoria.	The root.	Colouring matter.
			Convolvulacees, Convolvulaceæ
TURBITH, turbith.	Convolvulus turpethum.	Ditto.	Powder.
JALAP, jalap.	Convolvulus jalapa and oryzabensis.	Ditto.	Powder and tincture.
SCAMMONEE D'ALEP, scammony.	Convolvulus scammonea.	The dried juice.	Powder.
			Gentianees, Gentianaceæ
GENTIANE JAUNE, gentian (yellow).	Gentiana lutea.	The root.	Powder and decoction.
PETITE CENTAUREE, lesser centaury.	Erythræa centaurium.	The whole plant.	Infusion.
			Logoniacees-Strychnees, Logoniaceæ—Sometimes
NOIX D'IGASUR (Fève de Saint Ignace), Saint Ignatius' bean.	Ignatia amara.	The seeds.	Powder.
NOIX VOMIQUE, nux vomica.	Strychnos-nux-vomica.	Ditto.	Powder, extract, and tincture.

DOSES FOR ADULTS.	DOSES FOR CHILDREN.	THERAPEU- TICAL CLASSI- FICATION.	OBSERVATIONS.

(Nightshade Tribe).

| 5 to 10 grms. ʒi to ʒiiss. } | Little used. | Diuretic. | The *growing* calyx is em- ployed as a febrifuge, (Gen- dron). |

(Borage Tribe).

| 15 to 30 grms. ʒss to ʒi. 15 to 30 grms. ʒss to ʒi. | 10 to 20 grms. ʒiiss to ʒv. Ditto. | Sudorific. Diu- retic. Astringent. | |
| 0,50 to 1 grm. gr. viii to gr. xv. } | Little used. | Calming sub- stance. | Basis of pills of hound's- tongue with opium and henbane seeds, |

(Convolvulus Tribe).

0,25 to 1 grm. gr. iv to gr. xv. }	Not used.	Drastic.	
0,50 to 1 grm. gr. viii to gr. xv.	0,20 to 0,40. gr. iii to gr. vi. }	Ditto.	The resin of jalap is employed in doses from 0,25 to 0,50, (gr. iv to gr. viii).
0,25 to 2 grms. gr. iv to ʒss. }	Ditto.	Ditto.	Succedanea: Smyrna scam- mony, *Periploca scammo- nea;* Montpellier scam- mony, *Cynanchum Mons- peliacum,* (Asclepiadeæ).

(Gentian Tribe).

| 4 to 10 grms. ʒi to ʒiiss. Ditto. | 2 to 5 grms. ʒss to ʒiss. Ditto. | Bitter tonic. Ditto, and febri- fuge. | |

included amongst the Apocynaceæ—**(The Logania Tribe).**

| Little used. | Little used. | Excitants of the central and conducting nerves. | Contains much *strychnia,* and little *brucia.* |
| 0,05 to 0,50. 3/4gr. to gr. viii. | 0,01 to 0,05. 1/6 gr. to 3/4gr. } | Ditto. | Contains much *brucia,* and less *strychnia.* Strych- nine and its salts are em- ployed in doses from 0,001 to 0,005 (1/60 gr. to 1/12 gr.) |

FRENCH AND ENGLISH COMMON NAMES.	LATIN NAMES.	PART EMPLOYED.	FORMS OF ADMINISTRATION.
Logoniacées-Strychnées, Logoniaceæ—Sometimes			
FAUSSE ANGUSTURE, false angustura bark.	*Strychnos-nux-vomica.*	The bark.	Powder.
Apocynées, Apocynaceæ			
LAURIERROSE, *oleander.*	*Nerium oleander.*	Ornamental plant.	Not used.
PERVENCHE, *periwikle.*	*Vinca major* and *minor.*	The whole plant.	Infusion.
Jasminées, Jasminaceæ,			
THE TWO PLANTS HERE NAMED ARE GENERALLY CONSIDERED			
MANNE, *manna.*	*Fraxinus ornus* and *rotundifolia.*	Concrete juice.	Dissolved in milk. Glysters.
OLIVIER, *olives.*	*Olea Europæa.*	Oil extracted from the fruit.	Medicated oils.
Styracinées, Styraceæ			
BENJOIN, *benzoin.*	*Styrax benzoin.*	Resinous juice. Balsam.	Tincture and fumigations.
Synantherées ou Composées, Synantheraceæ			
LAITUE CULTIVÉE, *cultivated lettuce.*	*Lactuca sativa.*	The leaves.	Distilled water.

DOSES FOR ADULTS.	DOSES FOR CHILDREN.	THERAPEU- TICAL CLASSI- FICATION.	OBSERVATIONS.

included amongst the Apocynaceæ—(**The Logania Tribe**).

| 0,05 to 0,50. 3/4 gr. to gr. viii. | 0,01 to 0,05. 1/6 gr. to 3/4 gr. | Excitants of the central and conducting nerves. | Contains more *brucia* than *strychnia*. It differs from pure Angustura bark *Cusparia febrifuga*, (Rutaceæ), by having its edges cut perpendicularly, and by becoming *red* on the addition of a drop of nitric acid. The strychnia and brucia are in the state of *igasurates*. |

(**The Periwinkle Tribe**).

| Not used. | Not used. | Acro-narcotic poison. | |
| 10 to 20 grms. 3iiss to 3v. | Ditto. | Repels milk from the breasts. | |

Jasmine-worts.

AS BELONGING TO THE OLEACEÆ BY ENGLISH BOTANISTS.

| 20 to 40 grms. 3v to 3x. | 10 to 20 grms. 3iiss to 3v. | Laxative. | We distinguish manna in tears, or *geracy*, and manna in sorts, or *capacy*. |
| Every dose. | Every dose. | Ditto, internally. | |

(**Storax Tribe**).

| 4 to 8 grms. 3i to 3ii. | 2 to 4 grms. 3ss to 3i. | Expectorant. | The tincture, mixed with water, constitutes "Virgin's milk." Substitutes : *styrax* and *storax*. (Same natural family). |

or Compositæ (**Dandelion and Daisy Tribe**).

| 30 to 100 grms. 3i to 3iii. | 20 to 50 grms. 3ss to 3iss. | Soothing. | Lettuce juice, evaporated to dryness, constitutes *thrydace*. *Lactucarium* is the thickened juice obtained by incision. They are employed in doses from 0,25 to 1 grm. (gr. iv to gr. xv). The wild lettuce *Lactuca virosa*, employed as an extract, is much more powerful. |

FRENCH AND ENGLISH COMMON NAMES.	LATIN NAMES.	PART EMPLOYED.	FORMS OF ADMINISTRATION.
	Synanthérées ou Composées, Synantheraceæ		
CHICORÉE, *chicory.*	*Cichorium intybus.*	The leaves and root.	Purified juice. Tisane.
ARNICA, *arnica.*	*Arnica montana.*	Flowers and root.	Tisane. Infusion.
BARDANE, *burdock.*	*Arctium lappa.*	The root.	Tisane. Decoction.
PIED DE CHAT, *mountain everlasting, or cat's foot.*	*Gnaphalium dioïcum.*	The flowers.	Tisane. Infusion.
GRANDE ABSINTHE, (Aluine), *common wormwood.*	*Artemisia absinthium.*	The whole plant.	Tisane. Infusion. Tincture.
ARMOISE, *common mugwort.*	*Artemisia vulgaris.*	Ditto.	Tisane. Infusion.
SEMEN-CONTRA D'ALEP, *Semen contra, semen cinæ.*	*Artemisia contra.*	The fruits and their envelope.	Tisane. Infusion. Powder.
CAMOMILLE, *chamomile.*	*Anthemis nobilis.*	The flowers (heads).	Tisane. Infusion.
PYRÈTHRE, *pellitory.*	*Anthemis pyrethrum.*	The root.	Tincture.
AUNÉE OFFICINALE, *elecampane.*	*Inula helenium.*	Ditto.	The pulp externally applied. Tisane.
	Valérianées, Valerianaceæ		
VALÉRAINE SAUVAGE, *common wild valerian.*	*Valeriana officinalis.*	Ditto.	Powder, extract, tisane, and infusion.

DOSES FOR ADULTS.	DOSES FOR CHILDREN.	THERAPEU-TICAL CLASSI-FICATION.	OBSERVATIONS.

or Compositæ (Dandelion and Daisy Tribe).

DOSES FOR ADULTS.	DOSES FOR CHILDREN.	THERAPEU-TICAL CLASSI-FICATION.	OBSERVATIONS.
30 to 50 grms. ʒi to ʒiss.	15 to 30 grms. ʒss to ʒi.	Bitter tonic.	The roasted root constitutes coffee of chicory. Succedaneum: *Pissenlit*, (Fr.) Dandelion, *vulgo*, Piss-a-bed, *Taraxacum dens leonis.*
4 to 10 grms. ʒi to ʒiiss.	1 to 5 grms. gr. xv to ʒiss.	Excitant of the nervous system.	
20 to 40 grms. ʒv to ʒx.	10 to 20 grms. ʒiiss to ʒv.	Purifying sudorific.	Succedanea: Greater centaury, *Centaurea centorium*; Blessed thistle, *Centaurea benedicta*, or *Cnicus benedictus.*
15 to 30 grms. ʒss to ʒi.	Ditto.	Expectorant.	Succedaneum: Coltsfoot, *Tussilago farfara.*
10 to 20 grms. ʒiiss to ʒv.	2 to 8 grms. ʒss to ʒii.	Bitter vermifuge.	Succedanea: *Artemisia pontica* and *maritima*; Common tansy, *Tanacetum vulgare*; Estragon, *Artemisia dracunculus*; Wild chamomile, *Matricaria parthenium*; Cresson de Para, *Spilantus oleracea.*
10 to 30 grms. ʒiiss to ʒi.	Little used.	Emmenagogue.	
4 to 8 grms. ʒi to ʒii.	0,50 to 2 grms. gr. viii to ʒss.	Vermifuge.	Substitute: Semen-contra of Barbary, *Artemisia Judaica.*
4 to 15 grms. ʒi to ʒss.	2 to 8 grms. ʒss to ʒii.	Stimulant tonic.	A small dose assists emetics. Substitutes: Maronte, *Artemisia cotula*; and Yarrow, *Achillea millefolia.*
External use.	Little used.	Relieves toothache.	
15 to 30 grms. ʒss to ʒi.	8 to 15 grms. ʒii to ʒss.	Expectorant.	In poultices, to hasten the formation of pus in abscesses.

(Valerian Tribe).

DOSES FOR ADULTS.	DOSES FOR CHILDREN.	THERAPEU-TICAL CLASSI-FICATION.	OBSERVATIONS.
4 to 10 grms. ʒi to ʒiiss.	1 to 4 grms. gr. xv to ʒi.	Anti-spasmodic.	Succedaneum: Great valerian, *Valeriana Phu.*

D

FRENCH AND ENGLISH COMMON NAMES.	LATIN NAMES.	PART EMPLOYED.	FORMS OF ADMINISTRATION.
			Rubiacees, Rubiaceæ
GARANCE, *madder.*	*Rubia tinctorium.*	The root.	Colouring matter.
IPECACUANHA ANNELÉ, *Ipecachuana.*	*Cephælis ipecacuanha.*	Ditto.	Powder, extract, syrup, &c.
CAINÇA.	*Chiococca angwifuga.*	Ditto.	Tisane. Decoction.
CAFÉ, *coffee.*	*Coffea arabica.*	Roasted seeds.	Infusion.
QUINQUINA GRIS OFFICINAL, *grey cinchona bark.*	*Cinchona condaminea.*	The bark.	Powder, tincture, syrup, and wine.
— ROUGE, *red cinchona bark.*	*— cordifolia.*	Ditto.	Tisane, decoction, and maceration.
— JAUNE, *yellow cinchona bark.*	*— lancifolia.*	Ditto.	Extracts, soft and hard.
			Caprifoliacees, Caprifoliaceæ
SUREAU, *elder.*	*Sambucus nigra.*	Fruit. Flowers, and bark of the root.	Flowers in infusion.
			Ombellifères,
ACHE, *celery.*	*Apium graveolens.*	The root.	Infusion.

DOSES FOR ADULTS.	DOSES FOR CHILDREN.	THERAPEU- TICAL CLASSI- FICATION.	OBSERVATIONS.
(Cinchona Tribe).			
"	"	"	
1 to 2 grms. gr. xv to ʒss.	0,25 to 0,50. gr. iv to gr. viii.	Emetic, and ex- pectorant in small doses.	Substitutes: Ipeca ondulé, *Richardsonia brasiliensis;* Ipeca stria, *Psicotria eme- tica;* Ipeca blanc, *Viola emetica.*
10 to 15 grms. ʒiiss to ʒss.	4 to 8 grms. ʒi to ʒii.	Diuretic.	(†. Violent emetic and drastic. Used by the natives of Brazil as a certain remedy for serpent bites. Lind. Veg. King. p. 763).
40 to 100 grms. ʒx to ʒiii.	30 to 60 grms. ʒi to ʒii.	General stimu- lant.	Antidote to poisoning by nar- cotics. Coffee conceals the bitterness of all bitter sub- stances.
8 to 30 grms. ʒii to ʒi.	1 to 8 grms. gr. xv to ʒii.	Bitter tonic.	Grey cinchona contains little quinine and much cincho- nine; red, almost as much of one as of the other; and yellow, more quinine than cinchonine. These alkaloids exist in the state of quinates in the cinchona bark. Qui-
Ditto.	Ditto.	Antiseptic.	nine and its salts, and, amongst others, the neutral sulphate, are employed as
Ditto.	Ditto.	Febrifuge.	antiperiodics, in doses from 0,50 to 1,50, (gr. viii to gr. xxiv).
(The Honey-suckle Tribe).			
20 to 40 grms. ʒv to ʒx.	10 to 20 grms. ʒiiss to ʒv.	Sudorific.	*Elder rob* is the extract of the juice of the laxative fruit. The inner bark is employed as a purgative and diuretic, in doses of from 2 to 6 grms. (ʒss to ʒiss).
Umbelliferæ.			
15 to 30 grms. ʒss to ʒi.	8 to 15 grms. ʒii to ʒss.	Excitant; gene- ral stimulant. Diuretic. Aperient.	Succedanea: Archangel, *An- gelica archangelica;* Pars- ley root, *Apium petrose- linum;* Fennel root, *Fœ- niculum dulce;* Root of broad-leaved hog's fennel, *Imperatoria ostrutium.*

FRENCH AND ENGLISH COMMON NAMES.	LATIN NAMES.	PART EMPLOYED.	FORMS OF ADMINISTRATION.
			Ombellifères,
CIGUE OFFICINALE, *hemlock.*	*Conium maculatum cicuta major.*	The entire plant.	Powder and extract.
—— VIREUSE, (Cicutaire aquatique), *water hemlock.*	*Cicutaria aquatica.*	Ditto.	Ditto.
PETITE CIGUE, (Éthuse, Faux persil, Ache des chiens), *fool's parsley.*	*Æthusia cynapium.*	Ditto.	Ditto.
PERSIL, *parsley.*	*Apium petroselinum.*	Ditto. The root.	Juice. Tisane.
ANIS VERT, *aniseed.*	*Pimpinella anisum.*	The fruit.	Powder, tincture, infusion.
PHELLANDRIE AQUATIQUE, *fine-leaved water dropwort.*	*Phellandrium aquaticum.*	Ditto.	Powder of the fruit.
ASSA-FŒTIDA, *assafœtida.*	*Ferula-assafœtida.*	Inspissated juice. Gum. Resin.	Powder, tincture.
GOMME AMMONIAQUE, *ammoniacum.*	*Dorema ammoniacum.*	Ditto.	Ditto.

DOSES FOR ADULTS.	DOSES FOR CHILDREN.	THERAPEU-TICAL CLASSI-FICATION.	OBSERVATIONS.

Umbelliferæ.

DOSES FOR ADULTS.	DOSES FOR CHILDREN.	THERAPEU-TICAL CLASSI-FICATION.	OBSERVATIONS.
0,05 to 1 grm. gradually increased. 3/4 grs. to gr. xv.	0.01 to 0,20. 1/6 gr. to gr. iii.	Stupefiant. Resolvent of tumours, when applied in poultices.	There are four kinds of extract of conium, as is also the case with belladonna, p. 26. It contains cicutine (conine, conicine, conine), which is employed in doses of 0,001 to 0,02, (1/60 gr. to 1/3 gr.)
Ditto.	Ditto.	Ditto.	
Ditto.	Ditto.	Ditto.	Confounded with parsley. It differs in its strong odour, its leaves of a dark green, its reddish stem, and its white flowers; those of parsley are yellow. Fools' parsley has no involucre, (½. and is distinguished from all other Umbelliferæ by having three drooping bracteæ, all hanging down from the same side of the umbel.)
10 to 20 grms. ʒiiss to ʒv.	4 to 10 grms. ʒi to ʒiiss.	Diuretic. The juice is used to cure emissions of semen. (Lallemand).	
15 to 30 grms. ʒss to ʒi.	8 to 15 grms. ʒii to ʒss.	Carminative. Excitant.	The carminative species are fruits of Anise, Fennel, Caraway, Carum carui; and Coriander, Coriandrium sativum. Substitutes: Cumin, Cuminum cyminum; Dill, Anethum graveolens; and Starry Anise, or Badiane, Illicium anisatum, (Magnoliaceæ).
0,50 to 3 grms. gr. viii to gr. l.	0,25 to 0,50. gr. iv to gr. viii.	Diuretic. Narcotic.	Employed to assist expectoration in phthysis.
0,25 to 2 grms. gr. iv to ʒss.	0,10 to 0,40. gr. iss to gr. vi.	Anti-spasmodic.	Succedanea, Sagapenum, Ferula persica; Galbanum, Bubose galbanum; Opoponax, Opoponax chyronium.
0,50 to 3 grms. gr. viii to gr. l.	0,20 to 0,60. gr. iii to gr. ix.	Ditto. Expectorant.	

FRENCH AND ENGLISH COMMON NAMES.	LATIN NAMES.	PART EMPLOYED.	FORMS OF ADMINISTRA- TION.
Grossariées, Grossulariaceæ			
GROSEILLE, *currants.*	*Ribes rubrum.*	The fruit.	Syrup, jelly.
Myrtacées et Granatées,			
GIROFLE ou GÉROFLE, *cloves.*	*Caryophyllus aroma- ticus.*	The unex- panded flowers.	Essence, pow- der and tinc- ture.
GRENADIER, *pomegra- nate.*	*Punica granatum.*	The fresh bark of the root.	Decoction and tisane.
Cucurbitacées, Cucurbitaceæ			
BRYONE, *bryony.*	*Bryona alba* and *di- oica.*	The root.	Powder.
COLOQUINTE, *colocynth*	*Cucumis colocynthis.*	The fruit.	Powder and tincture.
CONCOMBRE CULTIVÉ, *common cucumber.*	„ *sativus.*	Ditto.	Pomatum.
ELATERIUM, (Con- combre sauvage), *ela- terium, wild* or *squirt- ing cucumber.*	*Momordica elate- rium.*	Ditto.	Extract.
Rosacées, Rosaceæ (Rose			
COING, *quince.*	*Cydonia vulgaris.*	The fruit and seeds.	Syrup and jelly.
PÊCHER, *peach.*	*Amygdalus persica.*	The flowers.	Ditto and infu- sion.

DOSES FOR ADULTS.	DOSES FOR CHILDREN.	THERAPEUTICAL CLASSIFICATIONS.	OBSERVATIONS.

(Currant Tribe).

| | | | Succedanea: Black currant, *Ribes nigrum ?* (*rubrum* in the orig.); Gooseberry, *Ribes uva crispa*; Strawberry, *Fragaria vesca,* (Rosaceæ); Bramble, *Rubus idæus,* (Rosaceæ), and Mulberry, *Morus nigra,* (Urticaceæ). |
| 30 to 60 grms. ʒi to ʒii. | 20 to 40 grms. ʒv to ʒx. | Cooling. Refreshing. | |

Myrtaceæ (Myrtle Tribe).

| 2 to 8 grms. ʒss to ʒii. | 0,50 to 2 grms. gr. viii to ʒss. | Aromatic. Excitant. | Succedanea: Allspice, *Myrtus pimenta*; Clove-cinnamon, *Myrtus caryophyllata.* |
| 15 to 40 grms. ʒss to ʒx. | 10 to 20 grms. ʒiiss to ʒv. | Anthelmintic. Expels tapeworms. | |

(Gourd Tribe).

0,25 to 1 grm. gr. iv to gr. xv. 0,10 to 0,40. gr. iss to gr. vi.	0,05 to 0,25. 3/4 gr. to gr. iv. 0,01 to 0,05. 1/6gr.to gr.3/4.	Drastic. / Ditto.	
Every dose.	Every dose.	Emollient.	The four cold seeds are the Cucumber, the Melon, *Cucumis melo*; the Gourd, *Cucurbita lagenaria,* and the Water-melon, *Cucumis citrullus.*
0,10 to 0,30. gr. iss to gr. ivss.	0,02 to 0,05. 1/3 gr. to 3/4gr.	Drastic.	(§. These doses are very large, compared with those generally prescribed in this country).

and Strawberry Tribe).

			Substitutes: The Apple, *Malus communis*; the Pear, *Pyrus vulgaris*; the Peach fruit, *Amygdalus persica*; Cherries, *Cerasus caproniana.*
30 to 60 grms. ʒi to ʒii.	20 to 40 grms. ʒv to ʒx.	Emollient; checks diarrhœa.	
15 to 30 grms. ʒss to ʒi.	8 to 15 grms. ʒii to ʒss.	Laxative.	

FRENCH AND ENGLISH COMMON NAMES.	LATIN NAMES.	PART EMPLOYED.	FORMS OF ADMINISTRATION.
			Rosacees, Rosaceæ (Rose
ROSE ROUGE ou DE PROVINS, red, or Provence rose.	Rosa gallica.	The flowers.	Conserve, honey, injection and infusion.
BENOITE, herb. avens.	Geum urbanum.	The root.	Powder, tisane, and decoction.
CUSSO, KOUSSO, COUSSO, kousso.	Brayera anthelmintica.	The flowers.	Powder and infusion.
AMANDES, almonds.	Amygdalus communis.	The seeds.	Emulsion and tincture.
LAURIER CERISE ou LAURIER AMANDE, cherry-laurel.	Cerasus-lauro-cerasus.	The leaves.	Distilled water
			Legumineuses, Leguminosæ
RÉGLISSE, liquorice.	Glycyrrhiza glabra.	The root.	Tisane, maceration.
MÉLILOT, melilot.	Melilotus officinalis.	The whole plant.	Ditto, infusion.
SÉNÉ, senna.	Cassia senna (Linneus).	The leaflets, fruit, pods, (improperly called follicles).	Ditto, glyster, infusion.
CASSE, cassia.	Cassia fistula.	The fruit.	Pulp, confection and tisane.

DOSES FOR ADULTS.	DOSES FOR CHILDREN.	THERAPEUTICAL CLASSIFICATION.	OBSERVATIONS.
and Strawberry Tribe).			
25 to 50 grms. ʒvi to ʒiss.	10 to 20 grms. ʒiiss to ʒv.	Astringent.	The Hundred-leaved Rose, *Rosa centifolia*, is employed for preparing rose-water. Agrimony, *Agrimonia eupatoria*, and the Bramble, *Rubus fructicosus*, are also astringent.
15 to 30 grms. ʒss to ʒi.	8 to 15 grms. ʒii to ʒss.	Ditto.	Substitutes: Strawberry-root and Tormentilla, *Tormentilla erecta*.
10 to 20 grms. ʒiiss to ʒv.	5 to 10 grms. ʒi to ʒiiss.	} Destroys tapeworms.	
15 to 30 grms. ʒss to ʒi.	8 to 20 grms. ʒii to ʒv.	} Emollient.	The bitter variety contains amygdalin and synaptase, which reacting upon one another, in contact with warm water, form hydrocyanic acid and essence of bitter almond. The latter is employed as a sedative in doses of 1 to 4 drops.
{ 4 to 30 grms. { ʒi to ʒi.	1 to 4 grms. gr. xv to ʒi.	} Soothing.	Substitutes: Distilled water of bitter almonds. All the trees amongst the *Rosaceæ* furnish indigenous gum.
(Pea Tribe).			
30 to 60 grms. ʒi to ʒii.	20 to 40 grms. ʒv to ʒx.	} Emollient.	
{ 20 to 30 grms. { ʒv to ʒi.	10 to 20 grms. ʒiiss to ʒv.	} Excitant.	Succedaneum: Tonka bean, *Koumarouma* or *Dipteris odorata*.
15 to 30 grms. ʒss to ʒi.	2 to 8 grms. ʒss to ʒii.	Cathartic. Purgative.	Alexandrian senna is a mixture of several species of Cassia. It is adulterated with Redoul, *Coriaria myrtifolia*, (Coriareæ). (⅓ which is poisonous, and has sometimes caused death, Lind. Veg. King. p. 476), and Argel, *Cynanhum arguel*, (apocynaceæ).
8 to 15 grms. ʒii to ʒss.	4 to 10 grms. ʒi to ʒiiss.	} Laxative.	Succedaneum: Tamarind, *Tamarindus indica*. The pulp is adulterated with prunes.

FRENCH AND ENGLISH COMMON NAMES.	LATIN NAMES.	PART EMPLOYED.	FORMS OF ADMINISTRATION.
		Légumineuses, Leguminosæ	
CACHOU, *catechu.*	*Acacia catechu.*	The extract.	Powder, extract and syrup.
GOMME ARABIQUE, *gum arabic or acacia.*	*Acacia vera.*	Proximate principle.	Powder, syrup, &c.
GOMME ADRAGANTE, *tragacanth.*	*Astragalus verus* and *creticus.*	Ditto.	Powder, mucilages.
COPAHU, *copaiba or copaiva.*	*Copaifera officinalis.*	A turpentine, Oleo-resin, (improperly called a balsam).	Emulsions, pills, glysters.
BAUME DE TOLU, *balsam of Tolu.*	*Myroxylon Toluiferum.*	Resinous juice.	Syrup, lozenges
INDIGO, *indigo.*	*Indigofera tinctoria.*	Dyeing material.	Opiate powder.
FENU GREC, *fenugreek.*	*Trigonella fænumgræcum.*	The seeds.	Poultices.
		Térébinthacées, Terebinthaceæ	
MYRRHE, *myrrh.*	*Balsomodendron myrrha.*	Resin.	Powder.
ENCENS or OLIBAN, *olibanum.*	*Boswelia serrata.*	Ditto.	Ditto.
		Rhamnées, Rhamnaceæ	
JUJUBES, *jujube.*	*Zisiphus vulgaris.*	The fruit.	Tisane, decoction.
NERPRUN, *buckthorn.*	*Rhamnus catharticus.*	Ditto.	Syrup, rob, (*i. e.* a vegetable juice, boiled with sugar or honey).

DOSES FOR ADULTS.	DOSES FOR CHILDREN.	THERAPEU-TICAL CLASSI-FICATION.	OBSERVATIONS.
(Pea Tribe).			
2 to 6 grms. ʒss to ʒiss.	0,50 to 2 grms. gr. viii to ʒss.	} Astringent.	{ Succedaneum: Kino, *Nauclea gambis*, (Rubiaceæ), &c.
15 to 30 grms. ʒss to ʒi.	8 to 15 grms. ʒii to ʒss.	} Emollient.	Substitute: Gum Senegal.
1 to 2 grms. gr. xv to ʒss.	1 to 2 grms. gr. xv to ʒss.	} Ditto.	
15 to 30 grms. ʒss to ʒi.	2 to 4 grms. ʒss to ʒi.	{ Excitant of mucous mem-branes.	
{ Of the syrup, 30 to 50 grms. { ʒi to ʒii.	10 to 30 grms. ʒiiss to ʒi.	} Expectorant.	{ Substitute: Balsam of Peru, *Myrospermum peruife-rum*.
{ 10 to 30 grms. { ʒiiss to ʒi.	5 to 15 grms. ʒi to ʒss.	} Anti-spasmodic	
Every dose.	Every dose.	{ Emollient. Re-solvent.	{ The "Resolvent Farina" con-tains, in addition to Fe-nugreek, Beans, *Faba vulgaris*; Bitter vetch, *Orobus vernus*, and Lu-pins, *Lupinus albus*, of each equal parts. Lentils, Haricots. Peas, &c., &c., the flour of which possesses similar properties.
(Tribe yielding Turpentine).			
			{ Employed in fumigations. Succedanea: Bdelium, *Edeulotia africana*; Ele-mi, *Icica icicariba* (Tere-binthaceæ).
{ 0,50 to 2 grms. { gr. viii to ʒss.	0,25 to 1 grm. gr. iv to gr. xv.	} Excitant.	
{ 0,50 to 2 grms. { gr. viii to ʒss.	0,25 to 1 grm. gr. iv to gr. xv.	} Ditto.	
(Buckthorn Tribe).			
20 to 80 grms. ʒv to ʒi.	10 to 20 grms. ʒiiss to ʒv.	} Expectorant.	
20 to 40 grms. ʒv to ʒx.	10 to 20 grms. ʒiiss to ʒv.	Purgative. Ca-thartic.	{ Employed in preparing blad-der-green, used in paint-ing.

FRENCH AND ENGLISH COMMON NAMES.	LATIN NAMES.	PART EMPLOYED.	FORMS OF ADMINISTRATION.
Rutacées, Rutaceæ			
GAYAC, *guiacum.*	*Guajacum officinale.*	Wood and resin.	Tisane, extract.
RUE, *rue.*	*Ruta graveolens.*	The whole plant.	Powder.
ANGUSTURE VRAIE, *cusparia.*	*Galipea cusparia.*	The bark.	Ditto.
BOIS AMER DE SURINAM, *quassia.*	*Quassia amara.*	Wood.	Tisane, maceration.
Ampélidées, Ampelideæ			
VIGNE, *vine.*	*Vitis vinifera.*	Fermented juice of the fruit.	Tisane, injection.
Guttiferes, Guttiferæ (Trees or			
GOMME GUTTE, *gamboge.*	*Cambrojia gutta.*	Dried juice.	Powder, pills.
CANNELLE BLANCHE, *canella.*	*Canella alba.*	The bark.	Powder, tisane.
Aurantiacées, Aurantiaceæ			
CITRON, *citron.*	*Citrus medica.*	The fruit.	Lemonade.
ORANGER, *orange.*	*Citrus aurantium.*	The flowers and leaves.	Tisane, distilled water.
Ternstræmaniées or Camelliées,			
THÉ NOIR et VERT, *black* and *green tea.*	*Thea Bohea* and *viridis.*	The prepared leaves.	Tisane, infusion.
Tiliacées, Tiliaceæ,			
TILLEUL, *linden tree.*	*Tillia Europæa.*	The flowers.	Tisane, infusion, distilled water.

DOSES FOR ADULTS.	DOSES FOR CHILDREN.	THERAPEU-TICAL CLASSI-FICATION.	OBSERVATIONS.
(Rue Tribe).			
20 to 30 grms. ζv to ζi.	5 to 10 grms. ζi to ζiiss.	} Sudorific.	
0,50 to 1 grm. gr. viii to gr. xv.	little used.	Emmenagogue.	
			Differs from false Angustura, *Strychnos nux vomica,* (Apocynaceæ), in being cut with a bevilled edge, and not being reddened by nitric acid. See p. 30.
0,50 to 2 grms. gr. viii to ζss.	0,25 to 1 grm. gr. iv to gr. xv.	} Bitter tonic.	
4 to 10 grms. ζi to ζiiss.	2 to 5 grms. ζss to ζi.	{ Tonic. Strengthening to the nerves.	Succedaneum: Simarouba, *Quassia simarouba,* (Ru-taceæ).
(Grape Tribe).			
100 to 200 grms. ζiii to ζvi.	50 to 100 grms. ζiss to ζiii.	Tonic. Exci-tant.	{ Four kinds of wine: Red, white, generous or liqueur, and sparkling.
Shrubs yielding a resinous juice).			
0,50 to 1 grm. gr. viii to gr. xv.	0,10 to 0,25. gr. iss to gr. iii.	} Drastic.	
8 to 20 grm. ζii to ζv.	4 to 10 grms. ζi to ζiiss.	} Excitant.	Succedaneum: Winter's bark, *Drimys Winterii,* (Mag-noliaceæ).
(Orange Tribe).			
10 to 20 grms. ζiiss to ζv.	4 to 15 grms. ζi to ζss.	} Cooling.	{ Substitutes: Orange, *Citrus aurantium;* Lemon, *Ci-trus limonum,* &c.
20 to 40 grms. ζv to ζx.	10 to 20 grms. ζiiss to ζv.	} Anti-spasmodic.	{ Variety: Bitter orange. Bitter tonic. The bark.
Ternströmiaceæ (Tea Tribe).			
15 to 30 grms. ζss to ζi.	8 to 15 grms. ζii to ζss.	} Excitant.	
Lindenblooms.			
30 to 50 grms. ζi to ζii.	10 to 30 grms. ζiiss to ζi.	} Anti-spasmodic.	{ (§. If the bracts are used along with the flowers, an astringent effect instead of an anti-spasmodic one is produced. Lindley, Veg. King. p. 372.)

FRENCH AND ENGLISH COMMON NAMES.	LATIN NAMES.	PART EMPLOYED.	FORMS OF ADMINISTRATION.
			Malvacées, Malvaceæ
GUIMAUVE, *marsh-mallow.*	*Althæa officinalis.*	The root and flowers.	Tisane, syrup, &c.
MAUVE, *mallow.*	*Malva sylvestris.*	The flowers and leaves.	Tisane, lotions.
COTON, *cotton.*	*Gossypium herbaceum.*	The down covering the seeds.	Tampons, (plugs).
CACAO, *cocoa.*	*Theobroma cacao.*	The seeds.	Chocolate, butter.
			Linées, Linaceæ
LIN, *linseed.*	*Linum usitatissimum.*	The seeds.	Poultices, tisane.
			Caryophyllées, Caryophyllaceæ
ŒILLET ROUGE, *clove pink.*	*Dianthus caryophyllus.*	The flowers.	Tisane, syrup.
SAPONAIRE, *soapwort.*	*Saponaria officinalis.*	The root and entire plant.	Ditto.
			Polygalées, Polygalaceæ
POLYGALA DE VIRGINIE *senega.*	*Polygala senega.*	The root.	Powder and tisane.
RATANIA, *rhatany root.*	*Krameria triandra.*	Ditto.	Decoction and extract.
			Violariées, Violaceæ
VIOLETTE, *violet.*	*Viola odorata.*	The flowers.	Infusion and syrup.
			Crucifères, Cruciferæ (Stock
CRESSON DE FONTAINE, *water-cress.*	*Sisymbrium nasturtium.*	The leaves.	The juice and syrup.
RAIFORT SAUVAGE, *horseradish.*	*Cochlearia armoriaca.*	The root.	Wine and tincture.

DOSES FOR ADULTS.	DOSES FOR CHILDREN.	THERAPEU-TICAL CLASSI-FICATION.	OBSERVATIONS.
(Mallow Tribe).			
20 to 40 grms. 3v to 3x.	10 to 30 grms. 3iiss to 3i.	Emollient. Ex-pectorant.	
20 to 40 grms. 3v to 3x.	10 to 30 grms. 3iiss to 3i.	Ditto.	
External use.	External use.	External ab-sorbent.	
Every dose.	Every dose.	Emollient and nourishing.	
(Flax Tribe).			
Every dose.	Every dose.	Emollient.	
(Clove Pink Tribe).			
10 to 30 grms. 3iiss to 3i.	10 to 20 grms. 3iiss to 3v.	Excitant.	
15 to 40 grms. 3ss to 3x.	10 to 20 grms. 3iiss to 3v.	Sudorific.	
(Milk-wort Tribe).			
0,50 to 2 grms. gr. viii. to 3ss.	0,10 to 0,50. gr. iss to gr. viii.	Excitant.	Emetic in doses from gr. viii to gr. xv. (§. This dose rarely excites vomiting in this country).
of the extr. 0,50 to 4 grms. gr. viii to 3i.	0,50 to 1 grm. gr. viii to gr. xv.	Astringent. Hé-mostatique, (cheeks bleed-ing).	The extract, made into a soft paste (*bouillie*), is used to relieve fissures round the anus (Trousseau).
(Violet Tribe).			
10 to 20 grms. 3iiss to 3v.	5 to 10 grms. 3i to 3iiss.	Sudorific. Ex-pectorant.	Emetic in larger doses, espe-cially the root. Substi-tutes: Heart's-ease, *Viola tricolor*; Wild pansy, *Viola arvensis.* (§. Both described as the same plant by Hooker and Arnott).
er Wallflower Tribe).			
10 to 30 grms. 3iiss to 3i.	5 to 10 grms. 3i to 3iiss.	Anti-scorbutic.	Succedaneum: Scurvy-grass leaves, *Cochlearia offici-nalis.*
10 to 20 grms. 3iiss to 3v.	5 to 10 grms. 3i to 3iiss.	Ditto.	

FRENCH AND ENGLISH COMMON NAMES.	LATIN NAMES.	PART EMPLOYED.	FORMS OF ADMINISTRATION.
Cruciferes, Cruciferæ (Stock			
ERYSIMUM ou VÉLAR, (Tortelle, Herbe aux chantres), *common hedge mustard.*	*Erysimum officinale.*	The entire plant.	Tisane and syrup.
MOUTARDE NOIRE, *black mustard.*	*Sinapis nigra.*	Seeds and flour.	Poultices, pediluvia, (footbaths).
Fumariacées, Fumariaceæ			
FUMETERRE, *fumitory.*	*Fumaria officinalis.*	The entire plant.	Tisane and syrup.
Papaveracées, Papaveraceæ			
CHÉLIDOINE, *celandine.*	*Chelidonium majus.*	The entire plant.	Little used.
COQUELICOT, *red poppy.*	*Papaver rheas.*	The flowers.	Tisane, infusion, syrup.
PAVOT BLANC, *white poppy.*	*Papaver somniferum album.*	The fruit, (capsules).	Decoction, extract.
OPIUM, *opium.*	Ditto.	Dried juice.	Extract and compound wines.

DOSES FOR ADULTS.	DOSES FOR CHILDREN.	THERAPEU-TICAL CLASSI-FICATION.	OBSERVATIONS.
or Wallflower Tribe).			
10 to 30 grms. ʒiiss to ʒi.	5 to 15 grms. ʒi to ʒss.	} Anti-scorbutic.	White Mustard, *Sinapis alba*; the whole seeds are taken internally, in doses of 20 to 40 grms. (ʒv to ʒx.) The active principle of black mustard is the essence, which does not exist before-hand, but is formed, on contact with water, by the reaction of *myrosine* upon *myronic acid.* White mustard contains only *myrosine.* Boiling water, alcohol and acids, are opposed to the formation of the essence; hence these bodies ought never to enter into the composition of mustard poultices.
{ Dose variable. For foot-baths, 100 to 200 grms. ʒiii to ʒvi. For entire baths, 1000 grms. ℔iiss.	Pediluvia. 50 to 100 grms ʒiss to ʒiii. Entire baths, 500 grms. ʒxv.	Anti-scorbutic. Externally. Rubefacient.	
(Fumitory Tribe).			
15 to 30 grms. ʒss to ʒi.	10 to 20 grms. ʒiiss to ʒv.	{ Bitter tonic. Purifier of the blood.	
(Poppy Tribe).			
Little used.	Little used.	Narcotic.	} The yellow juice is used to destroy warts.
15 to 30 grms. ʒss to ʒi.	10 to 20 grms. ʒiiss to ʒv.	Soothing. Sudorific. Su-	The seeds furnish white, or poppy-oil, which is emollient and laxative; the syrup called "Diacodium" is made from the extract of poppy. Dose, 20 to 40 grms. (ʒv to ʒx.)
{ Of the fruit, 15 to 30 grms. ʒss to ʒi.	} Ditto.	Narcotic.	
0,05 to 1 grm. gr. 3/4 to gr. 15.	{ 0,001 to 0,01. 1/60 gr. to 1/6 gr.	} Ditto.	The laudanum of Sydenham is used in the dose of 0,50 to 4 grms. (gr. viii to ʒi) The laudanum of Rousseau, in the dose of 0,25 to 2 grms. (gr. iv. to ʒss) There are five species of opium: 1st. Constantinople; 2nd. Egyptian; 3rd. Indian; 4th. French or English; 5th. (the one most used). Smyrna.

E

FRENCH AND ENGLISH COMMON NAMES.	LATIN NAMES.	PART EMPLOYED.	FORMS OF ADMINISTRA- TION.
Papaveracées, Papaveraceæ			
MORPHINE, NARCO- TINE, CODEINE, and their salts.	Papaver somniferum album.	Proximate principles.	Powder and syrup.
Nympheacées, Nympheaceæ			
NYMPHÆA or NÉNU- PHAR, water-lily.	Nymphæa alba and lutea.	Flowers and roots.	Tisane.
Menispermacées, Menispermaceæ			
COLOMBO, columba.	Cocculus palmatus.	The root.	Powder, tisane.
COQUE DU LEVANT, coc- culus indicus.	Anamirta cocculus.	The fruit.	Not used.
Renonculacées, Ranunculaceæ			
ELLÉBORE NOIR, black hellebore.	Elleborus niger and viridis.	The root.	Powder and wine.
STAPHISAIGRE, stave- sacre.	Delphinium staphi- sagria.	The seeds.	Powder.
ACONIT NAPEL, monk's- hood.	Aconitum napellus.	The entire plant, the leaves.	Extract and tincture.
PIVOINE, peony.	Pæonia officinalis.	Flowers and roots.	Tisane, little used.

DOSES FOR ADULTS.	DOSES FOR CHILDREN.	THERAPEU-TICAL CLASSI-FICATION.	OBSERVATIONS.
(Poppy Tribe).			
0,01 to 0,05. 1/6 gr. to 3/4 gr.	0,001 to 0,01. 1/60 gr. to 1/6 gr. }	Narcotic.	
(Water-lily Tribe).			
20 to 40 grms. ʒv to ʒx.	10 to 20 grms. ʒiiss to ʒv.	Emollient. Vulgarly anti-aphrodisiac. (Allays venereal excitement).	
(Cocculus Tribe).			
5 to 10 grms. ʒi to ʒiiss.	2 to 5 grms. ʒss to ʒiss.	Bitter tonic.	
		Stupifying.	Employed to poison fishes.
(Butter-cup Tribe).			
0,05 to 0,20. gr. 3/4 to gr. iii.	0,01 to 0,05. gr. 1/6 to gr. 3/4. }	Drastic. Sternutatory.	
External use.	External use.	Destroys lice.	
0,06 to 0,25. gr. 3/4 to gr. iiiss. }	0,01 to 0,05. gr. 1/6 to gr. 3/4. }	Stupifying.	
Every dose.	Every dose.	Antihysterical.	

FRENCH AND ENGLISH COMMON NAMES.	LATIN NAMES.	PART USED.	FORMS OF ADMINISTRATION.
MAMMIFÈRES, MAMMALIA, Animals			
CIVETTE, *civet cat.*	*Viverra civetta.*	Peculiar secretion.	Pills. Perfumery.
CASTOR, *beaver.*	*Castor fiber.*	Castoreum, a secretion.	Pills. Tincture.
IVOIRE, *ivory.*	*Elephas africanus* and *Indicus.*	Weapons of defence, canine teeth.	Sundry surgical
PORC, *hog.*	*Sus scropha.*	Axonge, lard.	Pomatums and ointment.
ANESSE, *ass.*	*Equus asinus.*	Milk.	Food.
CHEVROTAIN PORTE-MUSC, *musk deer.*	*Moschus moschiferus.*	Secretion or concretion.	Powder. Tincture.
CERF, *stag.*	*Cervus elaphus.*	Horn, horns.	Jelly. Calcined horn.
CHÈVRE, BOUC, *goat, male and female.*	*Capra ilex.*	Milk; formerly the blood.	Milk. Food.
MOUTON, BREBIS, *sheep, ditto.*	*Ovis aries.*	Milk, bones, gelatine, animal charcoal.	Food.
BŒUF, VACHE, *ox and cow.*	*Bos taurus.*	Milk, bones, gelatine, animal charcoal, bile, butter.	Ditto.
CACHALOT, *sperm whale.*	*Physeter macrocephalus.*	Spermaceti and ambergris.	Pomatums. Tincture of ambergris.
MARSOUIN, *the dolphin.*	*Phocæna communis*	The fat.	Phocenic acid.
OISEAUX,			
POULE, *the common hen.*	*Phasianus gallus.*	The egg and the shell.	Albumen and oil.

DOSES FOR ADULTS.	DOSES FOR CHILDREN.	THERAPEU-TICAL CLASSI-FICATION.	OBSERVATIONS
which suckle their young.			
0,20 to 2 grms. gr. iii to ℥ss.	0,05 to 0,50. gr. 3/4 to gr. viii.	Antispasmodic.	Digitigrade carnivorous.
Ditto.	Ditto.	Ditto.	Rodent.
instruments, speculums, toys. &c.		Absorbent when calcined.	Pachydermatous. Animal with a trunk.
Every dose.	Every dose.	Emollient.	Ditto, without a trunk.
Ditto.	Ditto.	Ditto.	Ditto. Solid-hoofed. Ass's milk, more nearly than any other, approaches the human milk in constitution.
0,15 to 2 grms. gr. ii to ℥ss.	0,05 to 0,25. gr. 3/4 to gr. iv.	Antispasmodic.	Ruminants without horns. Musk is furnished by the male.
Calcined, 0,50 to 4 grms. gr. viii to ℥i.	0,25 to 2 grms. gr. iv to ℥s.	Emollient. Absorbent.	Ruminants with large and deciduous horns. Rasped hartshorn is employed for making jellies. When calcined (phosphate of lime), it enters into the decoction of Sydenham.
Every dose.	Every dose.	Emollient.	Ruminants with short and persistent horns.
Ditto.	Ditto.	Ditto.	Ditto.
Ditto.	Ditto.	Ditto.	Ditto. Extract of bile is antispasmodic in doses of 0,25 to 1 grm (gr. iv to gr. xv).
Of ambergris 0,25 to 2 grms. gr. iv to ℥ss.	0,25 to 2 grms. gr. iv to ℥ss.	Emollient. Ambergris is antispasmodic.	Cetacea.
Little used.	Little used.	Antispasmodic.	Phocenic acid is the same as valerianic acid. Cetacea.
AVES, BIRDS.			
Every dose.	Every dose.	Emollient.	Calcined egg shells are absorbent. (¼. They consist of carbonate of lime-chalk.) Gallinæ.

FRENCH AND ENGLISH COMMON NAMES.	LATIN NAMES.	PART USED.	FORMS OF ADMINISTRATION.
REPTILES, REPTILIA,			
TORTUE, *the tortoise.*	*Testudo Europæa, etc.*	The flesh and the eggs.	Soups.
VIPÈRE, *the viper.*	*Vipera* or *Coluber berus.*	The flesh.	Powder and soups.
GRENOUILLE, *the frog.*	*Rana esculenta.*	Ditto.	Soups.
POISSONS,			
MORUE, *the cod fish.*	*Gadus morrhua.*	Oil from the liver.	Oil from the cod-fish and skate.
ESTURGEON, *the sturgeon.*	*Accipenser huso.*	Swimming bladder, isinglass, pure, gelatine.	Jellies and soups.
MOLLUSQUES, MOLLUSCA, Soft-bodied			
SÈCHE, *cuttle-fish.*	*Sepia officinalis.*	Bone of the cuttle-fish, *Os sepiæ.*	Powder.
LIMAÇONS, ESCARGOTS, *snails (edible).*	*Helix pomatia.*	The flesh.	Soups.
HUÎTRE, *the oyster.*	*Ostrea edulis.*	Ditto, and calcined shells.	Shells. Powder.
MOULES, *muscles.*	*Mytilus edulis.*	The flesh.	Food.
ANNÉLIDES,			
SANGSUES, *leeches.*	*Sanguisaga officinalis* and *medicinalis.*	The whole animal.	For local blood-letting.
CRUSTACÉS, CRUSTACEA,			
ÉCREVISSE, *the crab.*	*Astacus fluviatilis.*	The eyes, that is to say, a calcareous concretion found in the stomach.	Soups made of flesh. The eyes in powder.
CLOPORTES, *the wood-louse.*	*Oniscus asellus.*	The whole animal.	Powder.

DOSES FOR ADULTS.	DOSES FOR CHILDREN.	THERAPEU- TICAL CLASSI- FICATION.	OBSERVATIONS.
REPTILES.			
Every dose.	Every dose.	Food. Emol- lient.	Chelonian reptiles.
Not used.	Not used.	„	Ophidian reptiles.
Every dose.	Every dose.	Emollient.	Batrachian reptiles.
PISCES, FISHES.			
20 to 40 grms. ʒv to ʒx.	10 to 30 grms. ʒiiss to ʒi.	Anti-scrophu- lous.	Cartilaginous fishes.
Every dose.	Every dose.	Emollient.	Sturgeons. Cartilaginous fishes.
Animals (without internal skeletons).			
0,50 to 4 grms. gr. viii to ʒi.	0,25 to 2 grms. gr. iv to ʒss.	Absorbent.	Cephalopodous molluscs (♦. having the feet surround- ing the head). The sepia used in painting is ex- creted by this animal.
Every dose.	Every dose.	Food. Emol- lient.	Gasteropodous molluscs (♦. crawling by means of a flattened contractile disk under the belly).
0,50 to 4 grms. gr. viii to ʒi.	0,25 to 2 grms. gr. iv to ʒss.	Absorbent.	Acephalous molluscs (♦. with- out heads).
Every dose.	Every dose.	Food.	Acephalous molluscs, poison- ous under certain unknown circumstances.
ANNELIDES, WORMS.			
„	„	Debilitating.	Hirudines.
CRABS, SHRIMPS, &c.			
0,50 to 4 grms. gr. viii to ʒi.	0,25 to 1 grm. gr. iv. to gr. xv.	Absorbent.	Ten-legged crustaceans. The lobster, *Astacus mariti- mus.* The stomachic con- cretion (the eyes) is phos- phate of lime.
Not used.	Not used.	Not used.	Isopodous crustaceans (♦. hav- ing the feet of equal length).

FRENCH AND ENGLISH COMMON NAMES.	LATIN NAMES.	PART USED.	FORMS OF ADMINISTRATION.
			INSECTES,
Poux, de tête, de corps, du pubis, *lice, of the head, the body and the pubis.*	*Pediculus humanus, capitis, pubis (morpion).*	,,	,,
Puce, *fleas.*	*Pulex irritans.*	,,	,,
Cantharides, *Spanish, or blistering-fly.*	*Cantharis vesicatoria.*	The whole animal.	Powder. Tincture.
Cochenille du Nopal, *cochineal.*	*Coccus cacti.*	Ditto.	Dyeing matter.
Noix de galle, *nut-galls.*	*Cynips gallæ tinctoriæ.*	Excrescence formed upon the *Quercus infectorius.*	Decoction. Tannin.
Abeille, *the bee.*	*Apis mellifica.*	Honey, wax.	Honeys. Cerates. Pomatums. Ointments.
			POLYPIERS,
Coralline blanche, *white coral.*	*Corallina nodosa.*	The whole animal.	Jelly. Syrup.
Corail rouge, *red coral.*	*Isis nobilis.*	The whole tubes.	Powder.
Éponge, *sponge.*	*Spongia officinalis.*	The whole animal.	Calcined, and also prepared with wax and string.

DOSES FOR ADULTS.	DOSES FOR CHILDREN.	THERAPEUTICAL CLASSIFICATION.	OBSERVATIONS.
INSECTA, INSECTS.			
„	„	„	Parasites.
„	„	„	Suckers.
Internally. 0,02 to 0,10. 1/3 gr. to gr. iss.	0,01 to 0,05. gr. 1/6 to gr. 3/4.	Vesicant.	Coleoptera heteromera. Trachelides.
„	„	„	Hemiptera. Hemoptera. Gallinsectes. Kermes animal. *Coccus illicis.*
Tannin. 0,50 to 5 grms. gr. viii to 3i.	0,25 to 1 grm. gr. iv to gr. xv.	Astringent.	Hymenoptera pupivora (♀. or Cynipidæ).
20 to 40 grms. 3v to 3x.	15 to 30 grms. 3ss to 3i.	Emollient. Laxative.	Hymenoptera.
POLYPI, POLYPES.			
15 to 30 grms. 3ss to 3i.	10 to 20 grms. 3iiss to 3v.	Anthelmintic.	Polypes in cells.
External use.	External use.	Dentifrice.	Polypes.
Calcined. 0,50 to 2 grms. gr. viii to 3ss.	0,25 to 1 grm. gr. iv to gr. xv.	Used, after being calcined, to cure goitre.	Polypes. When prepared with wax and a string, it is employed to dilate fistulous sinuses.

CLASSIFICATION OF MEDICINES

SUPPLIED BY THE

MINERAL KINGDOM AND CHEMISTRY.

COMMON FRENCH AND ENGLISH NAMES.	FORMS OF ADMINISTRATION.	DOSES FOR ADULTS.
OXYGÈNE, *oxygen.*	Inspiration.	,,
CHLORE, *chlorine.*	Fumigations.	
IODE, *iodine.*	Tincture, &c.	0,06 to 0,30. gr. 3/4 to gr. v.
SOUFRE (Fleur de), *sulphur (flowers of).*	Pomatum. Lozenges.	0,50 to 4 grms. gr. viii to ʒi.
SOUFRE (Précipité, Magistère de soufre), *precipitated sulphur, (magistry of sulphur).*	Ditto.	Ditto.
PHOSPHORE, *phosphorus.*	Powder. Pomatum.	0,01 to 0,05. gr. 1/6 to gr. 3/4.
ARSENIC, *arsenic.*	Powder. Fumigations.	0,001 to 0,05. gr. 1/60 to gr. 3/4.
EAU, (Protoxyde d'hydrogène), *water, (protoxide of hydrogen).*	Baths. Douches. Basis of tisanes and hydrolats.	Every dose.
EAU, Glace artificielle, *water,* artificial ice made from sulphate of soda. 8 parts; 50° F. to 2° F.		
EAUX MINÉRALES SALINES PURGATIVES, *purgative saline mineral waters.*	Copious draughts.	1 to 2 bouteilles. 1 to 2 bottlesful.
EAUX SALINES MURIATIQUES, *saline waters containing muriates.*	Ditto.	Ditto.
EAUX SULFUREUSES, *sulphurous waters*	Copious draughts. Baths. Douches, &c.	1 to 2 verres. 1 to 2 glasses.
EAUX ALKALINES, *alkaline waters.*	Ditto.	Ditto.
EAUX FERRUGINEUSES, *ferruginous (or chalybeate) waters.*	Ditto.	Ditto.
EAUX ACIDULES GAZEUSES, *gaseous (or sparkling) acidulous waters.*	Draughts.	Ditto.
ACIDE CHLORHYDRIQUE, Cl H, *(hydrochloric acid,* H Cl, *(muriatic acid).*	Lemonades. Collutoires. See p. 82.	For internal use. 1 to 4 grms. gr. xv to ʒi.
ACIDE SULFHYDRIQUE, SH, *hydrosulphuric acid,* (HS), *sulphuretted hydrogen, H. and sulphur.*	Lotions. Baths.	,,
ACIDE AZOTIQUE, NITRIQUE, AzO⁵ HO, *nitric (azotic) acid* NO⁵ HO.	Lemonades.	1 to 4 grms. gr. xv to ʒi.

DOSES FOR CHILDREN.	THERAPEUTICAL CLASSIFICATION AND OBSERVATIONS.
„	Air contains O21, N 79, CO^2 ·0004. Disinfectant. Antidote to prussic acid.
0,01 to 0,05. gr. 1/6 to gr. 3/4.	Alterative, anti-scrophulous; substitute, bromine (Brôme).
0,25 to 1 gr. gr. iv. to gr. xv.	Sudorific. External use. Anti-psoric. Flowers of sulphur should be washed, to remove the sulphurous and sulphuric acids, which they always contain.
Ditto.	
0,01 to 0,02. gr. 1/6 to gr. 1/3.	Excitant. Used in exostosis.
0,001 to 0,02. gr. 1/60 to gr. 1/3.	Alterative. In affections of the skin and larynx.
Every dose.	Excitant. Sedative, tonic, &c., according to its temperature.
hydrochloric acid, 5 parts; temperature reduced from +10° to —17° C., i. e. from	
1/4 to 1/2 bouteille. 1/4 to 1/2 a bottleful.	Seidlitz, Epsom, &c. Alterative. Resolvent. Purgative.
Ditto.	Balaruc, Bourbonne, Hamburg, Wiesbaden, &c. Laxative and resolvent.
1/2 to 1 verre. 1/2 to 1 glass.	Bonn, Cauterets, Barèges, Enghein (¼. Harrogate), &c. Sudorific. Expectorant. Anti-herpectic.
Ditto.	Vichy, Vals, Ems, Carlsbad, M.-Dore, &c. Alterative. Resolvent.
Ditto.	Spa, Passy, Bussang, Bagnères of Bigorre, &c. Tonic. Restorative to the constitution.
Ditto.	Seltz, St. Galmier, Contrexeville, &c. General excitants of the digestive organs.
1 to 2 grms. in 1 litre d'eau. gr. xv to ʒss in 1 3/4 pints of water.	Stimulant. Used in affections of the liver, and in rubefacient foot-baths, to the amount of 125 grms. (ʒiv.)
„	Sudorific. Anti-psoric. The gas is a poison which causes putrefaction (septic).
1 to 2 grms. in 1 litre d'eau. gr. xv to ʒss in 1 3/4 pints of water.	Stimulant. Caustic when concentrated.

COMMON FRENCH AND ENGLISH NAMES.	FORMS OF ADMINISTRATION.	DOSES FOR ADULTS.
ACIDE SULFUREUX, SO^2, *sulphurous acid*, SO^3.	Fumigations.	„
ACIDE SULFURIQUE, SO^3, HO, *sulphuric acid*, SO^3, *oil of vitriol*, (huile de vitriol).	Lemonades.	1 to 4 grms. gr. xv. to ʒi.
ALCOOL SULFURIQUE, (Eau de Rabel), *sulphuric alcohol*.	Ditto.	2 to 10 grms. ʒss to ʒiiss.
ACIDE PHOSPHORIQUE, $PhO^5 3HO$, *phosphoric acid*, P^2O^5, 3HO or PO^5, 3HO.	Lemonades. Lotions.	1 to 2 grms. gr. xv to ʒss.
ACIDE CARBONIQUE, CO^2, *carbonic acid*.	Seidlitz water.	Every dose.
ACIDE BORIQUE, BO^3 (Sel sédatif de Homberg), *boracic acid* (*sedative salt of Homberg*).	Mixtures. Lemonades.	1 to 6 grms. gr. xv to ʒiss.
ACIDE CYANHYDRIQUE, C^2Az,H, (Prussique, médicinal), *hydrocyanic* (*prussic*) *acid*, HCy or NC^2, H.	Mixtures.	1 to 15 gouttes. 1 to 15 drops.
POTASSE, KO, HO, (Potasse à la chaux; pierre à cautère), *potash* (*caustic*) *hydrated*.	Mixtures. Collyriums, &c.	0,01 to 0,10. gr. 1/6 to gr. iss.
CAUSTIQUE DE VIENNE. The *caustic of Vienna* contains quick lime and caustic parts.		
IODURE DE POTASSIUM, (Hydriodate de potasse), *iodide of potassium* (*hydriodate of potash*).	Mixtures. Pomatum.	0,50 to 4 grms. gr. viii to ʒi.
SULFURE DE POTASSIUM, (Foie de soufre), *sulphuret of potassium*, (*liver of sulphur*).	Baths. Pomatum.	15 to 60 grms. ʒss to ʒii.
CYANURE DE POTASSIUM, (Prussiate de potasse), *cyanide of potassium*, (*prussiate of potash*).	Mixtures. Lotions.	0,01 to 0,10. gr. 1/6 to gr. iss.
SULFATE DE POTASSE, (Sel de Duobus), *sulphate of potash*, (*sal de Duobus*).	Copious draught.	4 to 15 grms. ʒi to ʒss.
NITRATE DE POTASSE, (Sel de nitre), *nitrate of potash* (*saltpetre*).	Tisanes.	2 to 8 grms. ʒss to ʒii.
NITRATE FONDU, (Cristal minéral; sel de prunelle), *fused nitre*, (*sal prunella, mineral crystal*).	Ditto.	Ditto.
ACETATE DE POTASSE, (Terre foliée de tartre), *acetate of potash*, (*terra foliata tartari*).	Tisanes. Mixtures.	2 to 10 grms. ʒss to ʒiiss.
BITARTRATE DE POTASSE, Crême de tartre), *bitartrate of potash*, (*cream of tartar*).	Tisanes.	4 to 10 grms. ʒi to ʒiiss.
TARTRATE BORICO-POTASSIQUE, (Crême de tartre soluble), *tartrate of potash*, (*soluble tartar*).	Ditto.	10 to 30 grms. ʒiiss to ʒi.

DOSES FOR CHILDREN.	THERAPEUTICAL CLASSIFICATION AND OBSERVATIONS.
,,	Anti-psoric. Used as a vapour-bath.
1 to 2 grms. gr. xv to ʒss.	Astringent. Caustic when applied externally. The " Caustic sulfo-safranique" of Velpeau.
1 to 5 grms. gr. xv to ʒi.	Astringent. Used in hæmorrhages. Contains alcohol, 3 parts; sulphuric acid, 1 part.
0,50 to 5 grms. gr. viii to ʒi.	} Used in exostoses.
Every dose.	Excitant to the digestive organs.
0,50 to 2 grms. gr. viii to ʒss.	} Astringent.
1 to 5 drops.	Sedative. The medicinal acid contains by weight 1 part of hydrocyanic acid, to 8·5 parts of water; (§. i. e. nearly 19 per cent., which is six times the strength of the dilute hydrocyanic acid of the Ph. L. The French dose appears very large when this is taken into account.)
0,01 to 0,05. gr. 1/6 to gr. 3/4.	} Alterative. Caustic when externally applied.
potash of each equal	} Caustic of Filhos. Potassa, 50 parts; quick-lime, 60 parts.
0,05 to 0,25. gr. 3/4 to gr. iv.	Alterative. Resolvent. Used in tertiary syphilis. Substitute, bromide of potassium.
2 to 10 grms. ʒss to ʒiiss.	} Anti-herpetic. Sudorific.
0, 01 to 0,05. gr. 1/6 to gr. 3/4.	Sedative. Fomentations in headache, 8 to 12 grms. (ʒii to ʒiii), to ʒviii of water.
1 to 4 grms. gr. xv to ʒi.	} Purgative. Checks the secretion of milk.
Ditto.	Diuretic. Sedative in doses from 30 to 60 grms. (ʒi to ʒii) (§. which should be given in a large quantity of fluid).
Ditto.	Ditto.
1 to 5 grms. gr. xv to ʒi.	} Ditto.
Ditto.	Laxative. Little used.
2 to 10 grms. ʒss to ʒiiss.	} Ditto.

COMMON FRENCH AND ENGLISH NAMES.	FORMS OF ADMINISTRATION.	DOSES FOR ADULTS.
HYPOCHLORITE DE POTASSE, (Eau de javelle; chlorure de potasse) *hypochlorite of potash, (chloride of potash)*.	Lotions. Mixtures. Fumigations.	0,50 to 2 grms. gr. viii to ʒss.
SOUDE ET SELS DE SOUDE, comme les sels de potasse, *soda and its salts, like those of potash.*		
CARBONATE DE SOUDE, (Sel de soude), *carbonate of soda, (salt of soda).*	Alkaline baths.	100 to 200 grms. ʒiii to ʒvi.
BICARBONATE DE SOUDE, *bicarbonate of soda.*	Lozenges. Vichy water.	0,50 to 2 grms. gr. viii to ʒss.
SULFATE DE SOUDE, (Sel de Glauber), *sulphate of soda, (Glauber's salt).*	Copious draughts.	15 to 45 grms. ʒss to ʒiss.
BORATE DE SOUDE, (Borax,) *biborate of soda, (borax).*	Gargles. Collutoires.	0,50 to 8 grms. gr. viii to ʒii.
TARTRATE DE POTASSE ET DE SOUDE, (Sel de Seignette, de la Rochelle,) *tartrate of potash and soda, (Seignette, Rochelle salt).*	Copious draughts.	10 to 20 grms. ʒiiss to ʒv.
CHLORURE DE SODIUM, (Sel marin; chlorhydrate de soude), *chloride of sodium, (sea salt, muriate of soda).*	Baths. Lotions.	200 to 500 grms. ʒvi to ℔iss.
CHLORURE DE BARYUM, (Chlorhydrate de baryte,) *chloride of barium, (hydrochlorate, muriate of barytes).*	Copious draughts.	0,50 to 2 grms. gr. viii to ʒss.
PHOSPHATE DE CHAUX, (Os calcinés, corne de cerf calciné; yeux d'écrivisses), *phosphate of lime, (burnt bones, calcined hartshorn, crabs' eyes.*	Powder.	0,25 to 1 grm. gr. iv to gr. xv.
AMMONIAQUE, AzH³, (Alkali volatil), *ammonia,* NH³, *(volatile alkali).*	Mixtures. Frictions. Pommade de Gondret.	For internal use. 4 to 20 gouttes. 4 to 20 drops.
ACÉTATE D'AMMONIAQUE, (Esprit de Mindererus), *acetate of ammonia, (spirit of Mindererus).*	Mixtures.	2 to 10 grms. ʒss to ʒiiss.
CHLORHYDRATE D'AMMONIAQUE, (Sel ammoniac), *hydrochlorate of ammonia, (sal-ammoniac).*	Mixtures. Lotions.	0,05 to 0,50. gr. 3/4 to gr. viii.
MAGNÉSIE BLANCHE et CARBONATE, *magnesia, white (usta) and carbonate of.*	Powder.	0,50 to 4 grms. gr. viii to ʒi.
SULFATE DE MAGNÉSIE, (Sel d'Epsom, de Sedlitz), *sulphate of magnesia, (Epsom and Seidlitz salts).*	Copious draughts.	15 to 45 grms. ʒss to ʒiss.

DOSES FOR CHILDREN.	THERAPEUTICAL CLASSIFICATION AND OBSERVATIONS.
0,25 to 1 grm. gr. iv to gr. xv.	Disinfectant. Antiseptic. Succedanea · The hypochlorites of soda and lime (chlorinated soda and lime.)
50 to 100 grms. ʒiss to ʒiii.	In baths. Alterative. Resolvent.
0,25 to 1 grm. gr. iv to gr. xv.	For a bath. Alterative. Resolvent. Succedanea: Carbonate and bicarbonate of potash.
5 to 15 grms. ʒi to ʒss.	Purgative. Substitute: Phosphate of soda.
0,50 to 4 grms. gr. viii to ʒi.	Astringent. Used in thrush.
5 to 10 grms, ʒi to ʒiiss.	Purgative.
100 to 200 grms. ʒiii to ʒvi.	For baths. Resolvent.
0,25 to 0,50 in 1 litre. gr. iv to gr. viii in 1 3/4 pints of water.	Anti-scrophulous. Resolvent. Substitute: Chloride of calcium.
0,25 to 0.50. gr. iv. to gr. viii.	Absorbent.
2 to 10 gouttes. 2 to 10 drops.	Alterative. Against intoxication. Externally applied. Rubefacient, vesicant and caustic, according to its degree of concentration.
1 to 5 grms. gr. xv to ʒi.	Alterative. Diuretic.
0,02 to 0,20. gr. 1/3 to gr. iii.	Resolvent. Alterative.
0,25 to 2 grms. gr. iv to ʒss.	Absorbent. Antidote to poisoning by arsenious acid.
5 to 15 grms. ʒi to ʒss.	Purgative.

F

COMMON FRENCH AND ENGLISH NAMES.	FORMS OF ADMINISTRATION.	DOSES FOR ADULTS.
SULFATE D'ALUMINE et DE POTASSE, (Alun), *sulphate of alumina and potash, (alum)*.	Pills. Mixtures. Injections.	Internal use. 0,10 to 0,35. gr. iss to gr. v. External use. 0,50 to 4 grms. gr. viii to ʒi.
FER, (Limaille de fer porphyrisée; fer réduit par l'hydrogène), *iron, (iron filings, iron reduced by hydrogen)*.	Powder. Pills.	0,50 to 2 grms. gr. viii to ʒss.
PEROXYDE DE FER ANHYDRE DE COLCOTHAR, *anhydrous peroxide of iron, ferri sesquioxidum, Colcothar*.	Ointment of Canet, (♃. or *Emplastrum roborans*).	Every dose.
PEROXYDE DE FER HYDRATÉ ou HYDRATE DE PEROXYDE DE FER, *hydrated peroxide of iron, (ferrugo)*.	Antidote to poisoning, by arsenious acid.	Ditto.
SOUS-CARBONATE DE FER, (Safran de Mars, apéritif), *sub-carbonate of iron, ferri sesquioxidum, saffron of Mars, aperient)*.	Powder. Pills.	0.20 to 2 grms. gr. iii to ʒss.
ETHIOPS MARTIAL, Fe²O³, FeO, (Oxyde-noir de fer), *Ethiop's martial, (black oxide of iron)*.	Ditto.	Ditto.
IODURE DE FER, *iodide of iron*.	Pills and Mixtures.	0,05 to 0,50. gr. 3/4 to gr. viii.
ROUILLE, (Eau ferré, eau-et fer oxydé), *rusty water, (water and oxidized iron)*.	Copious draughts.	Every dose.
SULFATE DE PROTOXYDE DE FER, (Vitriol vert; couperose verte), *sulphate of (protoxide of) iron, (green vitriol, green copperas, or simply copperas)*.	Syrup. Lotions. Baths.	0,25 to 0,50. gr. iv to gr. viii.
CYANURE DOUBLE DE FER, (Bleu de Prusse), *double cyanide of iron, (percyanide of iron, Prussian blue)*.	Powder. Little used.	0,25 to 1 grm. gr. iv to gr. xv.
TARTRATE DE POTASSE et DE FER, *potassio-tartrate of iron*.	Pills. Mixtures.	0,50 to 4 grms. gr. viii to ʒi.
LACTATE DE FER, *lactate of iron*.	Ditto.	0,25 to 1 grm. gr. iv to gr. xv.
BOULES DE NANCY, (Tartrate de potasse et de fer avec des plantes aromatiques), *bolus of Nancy, (potassio-tartrate of iron with aromatics)*.	Solution.	External use. Every dose.
OXYDE BLANC DE ZINC, (Fleurs de zinc), *white oxide of zinc, (flowers of zinc)*.	Pills. Powder.	0,05 to 0,25 gr. 3/4 to gr. iv.
SULFATE DE ZINC, (Vitriol blanc), *sulphate of zinc, (white vitriol)*.	Injections. Collyria.	0,10 to 1 grm. gr. iss to gr. xv.

DOSES FOR CHILDREN.	THERAPEUTICAL CLASSIFICATION AND OBSERVATIONS.
Internal use. 0,05 to 0,25. gr. 3/4 to gr. iv. External use. 0,25 to 2 grms. gr. iv to ʒss.	Astringent. Burnt alum is employed as a caustic.
0,10 to 0,50. gr. iss to gr. viii.	Tonic. Restorative after illness.
Every dose.	Drying. Absorbent.
Ditto.	Astringent.
0,10 to 0,50. gr. iss to gr. viii.	Tonic. Reconstituant (see iron, above).
Ditto.	Ditto.
0,05 to 0,25. gr. 3/4 to gr. iv.	Anti-scrophulous. Reconstituant. The syrup is given in doses of 30 to 100 grms. (ʒi to ʒiii).
Every dose.	Tonic. Reconstituant. (♃. Although not in general professional use, this medicine, under the name of "Smithy water," because obtained from the tank in which blacksmiths slake their red-hot iron, is frequently and beneficially employed by the poor as a restorative after illness, or as a tonic in gradual debility, in many parts of Yorkshire, and possibly elsewhere.
0,10 to 0,20. gr. iss to gr. iii.	Astringent. The pills of Blaud contain sulphate of iron and carbonate of potash, of each, gr. iii. One to six to be taken daily. The pills of Vallet contain protocarbonate of iron and honey.
0,10 to 0,50. gr. iss to gr. viii.	
0,10 to 1 grm. gr. iss to gr. xv.	Tonic. Reconstituent.
0,10 to 0,50. gr. iss to gr. viii.	Tonic. Succedaneum: Citrate of iron.
External use. Every dose.	Applied to bruises.
0,01 to 0,05. gr. 1/6 to gr. 3/4.	Anti-spasmodic. Emetic in a large dose.
0,05 to 0,30. gr. 3/4 to gr. ivss.	Astringent.

COMMON FRENCH AND ENGLISH NAMES.	FORMS OF ADMINISTRATION.	DOSES FOR ADULTS.
PROTOXYDE DE PLOMB, (Litharge, massicot), *protoxide of lead, (litharge, massicot).*	Basis of plasters.	External use.
CARBONATE DE PLOMB, (Céruse), *carbonate of lead, (whitelead, cerussa).*	Powder. Ointment of Rhazés.	0,15 to 0,25. gr. 3/4 to gr. iv.
ACÉTATE NEUTRE DE PLOMB, (Sucre et sel de Saturne), *acetate of lead (neutral), (sugar of lead, salt of Saturn.)*	Pills.	0,01 to 0,20. gr. 1/6 to gr. iii.
ACÉTATE TRIBASIQUE DE PLOMB, (Extrait de Saturne), *tribasic acetate (diacetate) of lead, (Goulard's extract of lead).*	Mixed with water.	External use. Every dose.
ÉTAIN, *tin.*	Powder. Filings.	0,50 to 2 grms. gr. viii to ʒss.
SOUS-NITRATE DE BISMUTH, (Blanc de fard), *subnitrate (trinitrate) of bismuth, (white cosmetic).*	Powder. Pills.	0,50 to 5 grms. gr. viii to ʒi.
SULFATE DE CUIVRE, (Vitriol bleu; couperose bleue), *sulphate of copper, (blue vitriol, blue copperas).*	Collyria. Injections.	0,10 to 0,50. gr. iss to gr. viii.
SULFATE DE CUIVRE AMMONIACAL, (Eau céleste, *(ammonio-sulphate of copper).*	Ditto.	Ditto.
ACÉTATE NEUTRE DE CUIVRE, (Verdet; cristaux de Vénus), *neutral acetate of copper, (verdigris, crystals of Venus).*	Ointment.	External use.
ACÉTATE DE CUIVRE TRIBASIQUE, (Vert-de-gris), *tribasic (di-) acetate of copper, (verdigris).*		
TARTRATE DE POTASSE et DE CUIVRE, *tartrate of potash and of copper ;* is when boiled with the sugar of diabetes.		
MERCURE, (Argent vif), *mercury, (quicksilver). Pharmaceutical preparations which contain it in the metallic state.*	Eau mercurielle, *Mercurial water.* Mercure saccharin, *Saccharine mercury.* Mercure gommeux, *Gummy mercury.* Pilules bleues. *Blue pills.* Pilules de Belloste. Pilules de Sédillot.	Internal use. 0,10 to 0,50. gr. iss to gr. viii.
	Simple and double mercurial ointment. Plaster of Vigo. (See Index.)	External use. Every dose.
EAU PHAGÉDÉNIQUE NOIRE, *black wash.*	Lotions.	Ditto.
EAU PHAGÉDÉNIQUE JAUNE, *yellow wash.*	Lotions and Dressings.	Ditto.

DOSES FOR CHILDREN.	THERAPEUTICAL CLASSIFICATION AND OBSERVATIONS.
External use.	Astringent. Simple plaster is a stearate, margarate and oleate of lead.
0,01 to 0,06. gr. 1/6 to gr. 3/4.	Astringent. Desiccative.
Ditto.	Astringent.
External use. Every dose.	Astringent. Mixed with common water, it constitutes "White water," "Vegeto-mineral water," and "Goulard's lotion."
0.25 to 1 grm. gr. iv. to gr. xv.	Anthelmintic.
0,10 to 2 grms. gr. iss to 3ss.	Used in diarrhœa and gastralgia.
0,05 to 0,20. gr. 3/4 to gr. iii.	Astringent. Caustic in a large dose. (§ Generally emetic in the larger dose here prescribed for adults.)
Ditto.	Ditto.
External use.	Caustic. Egyptian ointment contains honey and protoxide of copper. Verdigris is obtained from vinegar and metallic copper.

employed to recognize sugar in the urine; the blue test forms a brick-red precipitate

0,05 to 0,20. gr. 3/4 to gr. iii.	
	Alterative, resolvent, and anti-syphilitic.
External use. Every dose.	
Every dose.	Anti-syphilitic. Prepared from calomel and lime-water.
Ditto.	Anti-syphilitic. Prepared from corrosive sublimate and lime-water.

COMMON FRENCH AND ENGLISH NAMES.	FORMS OF ADMINISTRATION.	DOSES FOR ADULTS.
BIOXYDE DE MERCURE, (Précipité rouge), *binoxide of mercury, (red precipitate).*	Pills. Pomatum.	External use. 1 to 4 grms. to 30 grms. of axonge or cerate. gr. xv to ʒi, with ʒi of lard.
BISULFURE DE MERCURE, (Vermillon; Cinabre), *bisulphuret of mercury.*	Fumigations.	4 to 10 grms. ʒi to ʒiiss.
PROTOCHLORURE DE MERCURE A LA VAPEUR, (Calomel à la vapeur), *protochloride of mercury prepared in a state of vapour, calomel in vapour.*	Lozenges. Powder.	0,25 to 2 grms. gr. iiiss to ʒss.
PROTOCHLORURE PAR SUBLIMATION, *protochloride obtained by sublimation.*	„	Not used.
PROTOCHLORURE PAR PRÉCIPITATION, (Précipité blanc), *ammonio-chloride of mercury, (white precipitate).*	Powder. Pomatum.	External use. 1 to 10 grms., with 30 grms. of axonge. gr. xv to ʒiiss., with ʒi of lard.
BICHLORURE DE MERCURE, (Sublimé corrosif), *bichloride of mercury, (corrosive sublimate).*	Solution. Pills.	0,01 to 0,10. gr. 1/6 to gr. iss.
PROTO-IODURE DE MERCURE, *proto-iodide of mercury.*	Pills. Pomatum.	0,01 to 0,20. gr. 1/6 to gr. iii.
BI-IODURE DE MERCURE, *biniodide of mercury.*	Ditto.	0,01 to 0,10. gr. 1/6 to gr. iss.
IODURE DE MERCURE ET DE POTASSIUM, (Iohydrargirate de potassium), *iodide of mercury and potassium, (iodohydrargyrate of potassium).*	Ditto.	Ditto.
CYANURE DE MERCURE, (Prussiate de mercure), *cyanide (prussiate) of mercury.*	Ditto.	0,01 to 0,05. gr. 1/6 to gr. 3/4.
SULFATES DE MERCURE, *sulphates of mercury.*	Little used.	0,01 to 0,10. gr. 1/6 to gr. iss.
NITRATES DE MERCURE, *nitrates of mercury.*	Ditto.	Ditto.

DOSES FOR CHILDREN.	THERAPEUTICAL CLASSIFICATION AND OBSERVATIONS.
Same as for adults.	Anti-syphilitic. Slightly caustic.
1 to 4 grms. gr. xv to ʒi.	For a vapour-bath, in syphilis.
0,06 to 1 grm. gr. 3/4 to gr. xv.	Alterative. According to Law's method, 3/4 of a grain of calomel, and gr. xv of sugar, are made into 12 or 24 powders ; one to be taken every half-hour, until salivation is produced. (§ He states that 3 grains will produce salivation. The first of these preparations is made by subliming calomel, and causing the vapour to meet steam proceeding from another vessel. The mixed steam and calomel vapour are conducted into cold water when they are condensed, and the calomel is obtained in a state of exceeding fineness. Fr. Codex.)
Used alone.	
Same as for adults.	
0,01 to 0,02. gr. 1/6 to gr. 1/3.	Alterative. Anti-syphilitic. The solution of Van Swieten contains the thousandth part of its weight of corrosive sublimate. ʒi of the solution contains gr. ss. (§ The dose prescribed for adults (gr. iss) is much greater than English patients either require or will bear.)
0,01 to 0,05. gr. 1/6 to gr. 3/4.	A greenish-yellow colour. It is used in secondary syphilis.
Ditto.	A beautiful red colour. Used in secondary syphilis.
Ditto.	Yellow, citron-coloured. Crystallized. Secondary syphilis.
0,001 to 0,005. gr. 1/60 to gr. 1/12.	Secondary syphilis.
0,005 to 0,05. gr. 1/12 to gr. 3/4.	Sub-sulphate, or turbith mineral. Secondary syphilis.
Ditto.	Sub-nitrate. Turbith nitrate. Acid nitrate is caustic. Secondary syphilis.

COMMON FRENCH AND ENGLISH NAMES.	FORMS OF ADMINISTRATION.	DOSES FOR ADULTS.
POMMADE CITRINE, *citrine ointment*, (*Ung. hydr. nitr.*)	Frictions.	10 to 40 grms. ʒiiss to ʒx.
NITRATE D'ARGENT CRISTALLISÉ, *crystallized nitrate of silver.*	Collyria. Injections. Pills.	Internal use. 0,01 to 0,05. gr. 1/6 to gr. 3/4.
NITRATE D'ARGENT FONDU, (Pierre infernale), *fused nitrate of silver,* (*lunar caustic*).	Ditto.	Ditto.
CHLORURE D'ARGENT, *chloride of silver.*	Pills.	0,05 to 0,25. gr. 3/4 to gr. iv.
CHLORURE D'OR et CHLORURE D'OR et DE SODIUM, *chloride of gold and chloride of gold and sodium.*	Frictions over the gums. To be mixed with some inert powder.	0,01 to 0,05. gr. 1/6 to gr. 3/4.
OXYDE BLANC D'ANTIMOINE, (Fleurs argentines d'antimoine), *white oxide of antimony,* (*argentine flowers of antimony*).	Powder. Mixtures.	1 to 4 grms. gr. xv to ʒi.
ANTIMOINE DIAPHORÉTIQUE, (Bi-antimoniate de potasse), *diaphoretic antimony,* (*biantimoniate of potassa.*)	Ditto.	Ditto.
SULFURE D'ANTIMOINE HYDRATÉ, (Kermès; Oxysulfure d'antimoine), *hydrated sulphuret of antimony,* (*Kermes' mineral*).	Ditto.	0,05 to 2 grms. gr. 3/4 to ʒss.
OXYSULFURE D'ANTIMOINE, *oxysulphuret of antimony;* (Crocus metallorum) antimony; soufre doré d'antimoine, *golden sulphuret of antimony;* persulfure		
PROTOCHLORURE D'ANTIMOINE, (Beurre d'antimoine), *protochloride* (*butter*) *of antimony.*	External use.	External use.
TARTRATE DE POTASSE et D'ANTIMOINE, (Emétique; tartre stibié) *potassio-tartrate of antimony,* (*tartar emetic*).	Mixture. Ointment.	0,05 to 0,15. gr. 3/4 to gr. ii.
ACIDE ARSÉNIEUX, (Oxyde blanc d'arsenic), *arsenious acid,* (*white oxide of arsenic*).	Mixture. Pills.	0,01 to 0,05. gr. 1/6 to gr. 3/4.
LIQUEUR DE FOWLER, (Arsénite de potasse), *liquor potassæ arsenitis,* (*Fowler's solution*).	Mixture.	2 to 20 drops,
LIQUEUR DE PEARSON, *Pearson's solution.*	Ditto.	2 to 15 drops,
SULFURE JAUNE D'ARSENIC, (Orpiment, Ar S³; sulfure rouge, Réalgar Ar S²), *yellow sulphuret* (*orpiment*) *of arsenic,* Ar S³, *red sulphuret, Realgar,* Ar S².	"	"
SAVON MÉDICINAL et ANIMAL, *medicated and animal soap.*	Pills and Baths.	Every dose.

DOSES FOR CHILDREN.	THERAPEUTICAL CLASSIFICATION AND OBSERVATIONS.
6 to 20 grms. ʒi to ʒv.	Prepared from olive-oil, lard, and the acid nitrate of mercury Anti-psoric.
0,01 to 0,05. gr. 1/6 to gr. 3/4.	Checks (ʒ chronic) diarrhœa. Astringent. Used in epilepsy.
Ditto.	Caustic, when externally applied.
0,02 to 0,10. gr. 1/3 to gr. iss.	Used in epilepsy. Substitutes, the bromide and oxide of silver.
0,01 to 0,02. gr. 1/6 to gr. 1/3.	Anti-syphilitic. Caustic when dissolved in eau régale (ʒ Aqua regia, nitro-hydrochloric acid), and applied externally.
0,05 to 2 grms. gr. 3/4 to ʒss.	Expectorant. Contra-stimulant.
Ditto.	Expectorant. Sudorific.
0,05 to 0,40. gr. 3/4 to gr. vi.	Expectorant. All the preparations of antimony are emetic in large doses.

crocus ; oxysulfure silicaté, *silicated oxysulphuret* ; verre d'antimoine, *glass of* hydraté, *hydrated persulphuret*.

External use.	Caustic.
0.001 to 0,005. gr. 1/60 to gr. 1/12.	Emetic. Contra-stimulant. Counter-irritant, when externally applied. 0,50 to 1 grm. (gr. viii to gr. xv.)
0,01 to 0,05. gr. 1/6 to gr. 3/4.	Alterative. Febrifuge (ʒ only in intermittents). Caustic externally.
1 to 5 drops.	Alterative. Contains one hundredth part of arsenious acid, and a fiftieth part of arsenite of potash.
1 to 10 drops.	Alterative. Used in affections of the skin. Contains 1 part of arseniate of soda, and 30 parts of water.
,,	Destroys the hair (depilatory).
Every dose.	Alterative. Resolvent. Stearate, oleate and margarate of soda.

COMMON FRENCH AND ENGLISH NAMES.	FORMS OF ADMINISTRATION.	DOSES FOR ADULTS.
ALCOOL, $C^4 H^6 O^2$, *alcohol*.	Basis of alcoolés and of alcoolats. See p. 6.	"
ÉTHER SULFURIQUE, $C^4 H^5 O$, (Ether hydrique), 1st class),* *sulphuric ether, ether, (hydric ether, 1st class.)*	Mixture. Inhalation.	10 to 40 drops.
ÉTHER CHLORHYDRIQUE, $C^4 H^5 Cl$, *hydrochloric ether, 2nd class.*	Ditto.	Ditto.
ÉTHER IODHYDRIQUE, $C^4 H^5 I$, 2nd class, *hydriodic ether, 2nd class.*	Ditto.	Ditto.
ÉTHER NITREUX, $C^4 H^5 O + AzO^5$, (*nitric ether of pharmaceutists, 3rd class), nitrous ether, (hyponitrous ether).*	Mixtures.	Ditto.
ÉTHER ACÉTIQUE, $C^4 H^5 O + C^4 H^3 O^3$, 3rd class, *acetic ether.*	Ditto.	Ditto.
LIQUEUR D'HOFFMAN, *Hoffman's anodyne liquor.*	Ditto.	20 to 60 drops.
SIROP D'ÉTHER, *syrup of ether.*	Ditto.	20 to 100 grms. $\mathfrak{z}v$ to $\mathfrak{z}iii$.
ALDEHYDE, $C^4 H^2 O^2$, *aldehyde.*	Inhalations.	"
CHLOROFORME, $C^2 HCl^3$, (*perchloride of formyle), chloroform.*	Inhalations. Mixtures.	4 to 15 drops.
ACIDE ACÉTIQUE, $C^4 H^3 O^3 + HO$, *acetic acid (diluted with water, vinegar, radical vinegar).*	Lotions.	Internal use. To be made agreeably acid.
ACIDE LACTIQUE, $C^6 H^5 O^5 + HO$, *lactic acid.*	Mixtures.	0,10 to 0,50. gr. iss to gr. viii.
ACIDE OXALIQUE, $C^2 O^3 + HO$, *oxalic acid.*	Little used.	"
ACIDE TARTRIQUE, $C^8 H^4 O^{10} + 2 HO$ *tartaric acid.*	Syrup.	Of the syrup. 30 to 100 grms. $\mathfrak{z}i$ to $\mathfrak{z}iii$.

(‡. * The three classes of ethers here referred to are, 1st. simple ether, $C^4 H^5 O$, is replaced by some other element, *e. g.* chlorine Thus sulphuric ether, 1st class, is combined with some acid, *e. g.* hyponitrous or acetic, which forms as it were a

DOSES FOR CHILDREN.	THERAPEUTICAL CLASSIFICATION AND OBSERVATIONS.
,,	Excitant. General stimulant. See " Art of Prescribing," Art. Wines.
5 to 20 drops.	Anti-spasmodic. Anesthetic.
Ditto.	Anti-spasmodic.
Ditto.	Anti-spasmodic. Used in strumous affections.
Ditto.	Anti-spasmodic.
Ditto.	Ditto.
10 to 40 drops.	Contains: Ether, 1 part; alcohol, 1 part.
10 to 30 grms. ʒiiss to ʒi.	Contains: Ether, 1 part; simple syrup, 16 parts.
,,	Anti-spasmodic. Anesthetic.
2 to 8 drops.	Ditto.
Same as for adults.	Refrigerant. Alterative. Caustic, when applied externally, in a concentrated form.
0,05 to 0,20. gr. 3/4 to gr. iii.	Used in exostosis.
,,	Irritant poison. Alterative in very small doses, 0,01 to 0,05 (gr. 1/6 to gr. 3/4.
20 to 40 grms. ʒv to ʒx.	Alterative. Substitutes: malic and citric acid. Lemonades, syrups of acid juices.

which is taken as the type of the ethers generally; 2nd. ethers in which the oxygen $C^4 H^5 + O$; hydrocloric ether, 2nd class, $C^4 H^5 + Cl$. In the 3rd class, ether, $C^4 H^5 O$, salt, of which the ether is the base; e. g. acetic ether, $C^4 H^5 O$ + acetic acid, $C^4 H^3 O^3$).

ART OF PRESCRIBING.

THE purpose of the "Art of Prescribing" is to give rules for administering medicines so that they may be at once agreeable and convenient, for making their effects more certain, for apportioning their dose, and frequently for combining them together.

The chief means for accomplishing these objects are: Varying the pharmaceutical forms; the mode of application; the doses; the intervals between the administration of the medicines, and the other substances with which they are combined.

All these contrivances are founded upon scientific data, supplied by therapeutics properly so called, by pharmacy, by medical natural history, by physics and chemistry.

In order to prescribe well, it is necessary to pay attention to a great number of circumstances relating to the articles of the *materia medica*, as well as to the patients themselves.

We shall now pass all these subjects in review, taking care to attribute to each that share of influence which belongs to it; and in so doing, we shall treat of the habitual use, of the tolerance, and of the accumulation of medicines in the system: important questions, which we do not find conveniently developed elsewhere.

Special sections will be devoted to what we have called the "means" of the art of prescribing; and we shall give several examples of pharmaceutical formulæ, from which we shall only have afterwards to extract what is of most general application, in order to lay down the rules which ought to preside over the construction of a prescription.

This order appears to us at the same time the most useful and the most logical.

CONSIDERATIONS RELATING TO MEDICINES.

QUALITIES OF MEDICINES.

It is important to administer only medicines of good quality, and the physician will only have a perfect guarantee on this subject by taking care to prescribe the best commercial kinds, and such as have been but recently submitted to pharmaceutical preparation of the most advantageous character.

. 1. **Commercial varieties.**—The varieties of vegetable drugs depend upon differences in the botanical species which supply them; or, when the plants are the same, upon their different conditions of age, soil, and climate, &c., and still more upon the nature of the processes, often fraudulent, to which they are subjected. It is not always the quality which is absolutely the best that we ought to seek for in medicines; for we may often prefer an inferior kind, but one which is less easily adulterated and is more abundant in commerce.

In many cases it may even be necessary, especially in the country, to be content with medicines of similar or analogous properties, that is to say with *succedanea*, or the best substitutes we can find.

Therapeutical agents placed in the same class may, in general, supply the place of one another, if account is taken of the difference of dose; (§ *e. g.* Jalap and scammony are both placed in the therapeutical class of cathartics, and may if necessary be substituted for one another, bearing in mind that the first must be given in larger doses than the second.)

To find the substitutes for any particular medicine, it will be necessary to consult the article which is specially devoted to it.

2. **Age of the preparations.**—Extracts and other officinal preparations lose their properties in the course of time, which is a circumstance that ought never to be forgotten, especially in the case of very active medicines. A single instance will suffice to show the importance of this caution.

In the Necker Hospital (Paris), we had submitted a young girl, affected with chorea, to the employment of the alcoholic extract of nux vomica for twenty days. From a grain and a half (0,1—10 centigrammes), the dose had been gradually increased to fifteen grains and a half (1 gramme), without the patient perceiving any particular effect. Surprised at this inertness of the medicine, we made inquiry how long it had been prepared, and the extract was found to be very old. We caused another to be made, and took the precaution of prescribing, not fifteen grains, as of the old, but only nine grains (0,6); nevertheless the symptoms of poisoning were such, that according to all appearances, twice that quantity would inevitably have caused death.

Amongst the substances which ought especially to be pointed out as undergoing a constant change, we may mention the cyanide of potassium, which, when pure, is a very violent narcotic poison, in the dose of three grains (0,2—20 centigrammes); but in the course of time, and depending also upon the process employed in its preparation, it may contain carbonate, formiate, and cyanate of potash—bodies which are nearly inert. Cyanide of potassium, therefore, on account of the changes just mentioned, ought to be excluded from internal administration as a medicine. The distilled water of bitter almonds, and that of the cherry laurel (*Prunus laurocerasus*), also change rapidly, and their active principle (essential oil) is converted into benzoic acid.

Similar accidents may happen, under similar circumstances, with other energetic substances. The difference of energy observed between two totally distinct preparations, the one old, and the other new, is found, though in a less degree, between a portion of a medicinal mass, and the mass itself from which it has long been separated, provided that the medicines change in direct proportion to their division. We therefore advise practitioners—1st, not to send to their patients a supply of medicine more than sufficient for a few days; 2nd, to reduce the dose each time they renew the supply, so that the fresh dose may equal the last but one; and 3rd, to desire the druggist not to use preparations which are too old.

3. **Pharmaceutical preparations.**—Under this title we comprehend the forms which are given to medicines in the druggists' shop, and even in the chemists' laboratory. The following are a

few general precepts relative to their selection. We ought to give the preference to those preparations in which the doses of the active principles admit of being most exactly estimated; and we therefore prescribe syrup of opium rather than syrup of poppy; and strychnine, or, better still, the sulphate of strychnine, rather than St. Ignatius's bean, &c. Moreover, we are sometimes so happy as to have at our disposal inferior preparations, but disguised by some odd name, which conceals their real nature. In the face of a sick person who has absolutely refused to take opiates, the syrup of karabé* has relieved more than one physician from his difficulty.

Some substances exist in greater purity in one state of combination than in others: thus antimony is only perfectly free from arsenic in tartar emetic, and in kermes mineral, which are therefore the two combinations that ought to be employed.

As a general rule, we may say that medicinal substances are so much more easily received into the system, as they are more analogous to the chemical principles distributed through our organism.

It is on this principle that insoluble substances surpass others when the question is to determine dynamic effects. It appears that their solution by means of the fluid secretions is a commencement of assimilation.

We ought furthermore to choose, amongst insoluble substances of the same kind, the one which is most easily attacked by our humours; that is to say, that which is most hydrated. Amongst those of different kinds we should choose one whose affinities are the least satisfied, or the combinations of which are the least stable.

We ought to follow the opposite rule with regard to soluble medicines, when we search for their general action. In this point of view the saline form is the most convenient. All these rules are however subject to many exceptions, and mutually modify one another. They will even be often sacrificed to dislikes on the part of the patient, or to other considerations into the enumeration of which we cannot now enter.

---

* Syrup of extract of opium. Fr. Codex.

CHANGES (MUTATIONS) OF MEDICINES.

There are very few agents of the *materia medica*, which preserve in the midst of the economy the form under which they have been administered, and the whole of the changes which they undergo between the moment of their application and that of their removal are described under the title of "mutations."

In medicines we ought to distinguish an immediate or local, and a remote, or general or dynamic action. This latter supposes a preliminary absorption and conveyance into the circulating current, and it appears that it only belongs to bodies which are soluble without decomposition in the liquids of the body, or are susceptible of being dissolved in consequence of certain reactions.

Forms under which medicines are absorbed.—The substances whose absorption can take place directly are those which are already dissolved in water, or are soluble without undergoing any decomposition from the humours that lubricate the absorbing surfaces, which can render them insoluble.

We lay stress upon these words *dissolved* or *soluble*, because " soluble" in common language means solubility in water, and implies that the matters dissolved in any other vehicle can also be directly absorbed if they are miscible without change in our humours. Ethereal and alcoholic tinctures in general come under this head.

The substances which can immediately penetrate into the "second ways"* are, the mineral alkalies, and up to a certain point all the alkaloids; the vegetable, and some mineral acids; all the alkaline, and some other salts; and a great number of principles.

On the other hand, substances, which, not being dissolved, are at the same time insoluble in water, or even when dissolved are precipitated by the reaction of the humours, can only be absorbed after undergoing transformation.

(§ * The expression, " second ways," is seldom used by English writers. The *primæ viæ*, or "first ways," are the mouth, stomach, and small intestines, through which most substances first enter the body. The "second ways" here spoken of are the lacteals, or absorbent vessels, through which substances are removed from the *primæ viæ* into the blood, and so carried into the system.)

Transformations are effected by four classes of agents :

1. The *acids*, which are chiefly found in the stomach (the lactic and chlorhydric).*

2. The *alkalies*, which are met with especially in the small intestines, but which belong equally to the serosity of blisters, to the lymph and to blood.

3. *Alkaline chlorides*, which are diffused everywhere.

4. *Certain neutral bodies containing nitrogen*, which produce peculiar changes in certain bodies. Such are the animal *diastase* found by M. Mialhe in the saliva; *pepsin* (Showan), and the *pancreatic* juice (Bernard); the action of which upon matters consisting of flesh is entirely independent of its alkalinity.

Bodies soluble in acids.—These are, all the metals, (except those of the last division,† which have scarcely any affinity for oxygen); and nearly all the metallic oxides. These last unite directly with the acid of the gastric juice, but the first decompose water, in order to be previously oxidized, from which arises the disengagement of pure hydrogen, and sometimes of sulphuretted hydrogen, producing offensive eructations. To the above must be added the vegetable alkalies, and some principles which are allied to them.

Bodies soluble in alkalies, are in general all those which by their affinities approach acids; and acids properly so called. We may mention amongst the metalloids sulphur, phosphorus and

---

(§ * Generally called, by English chemists, "hydrochloric or muriatic acid." Most acids are composed of hydrogen, combined with an element or some compound body termed a "radical." British chemists generally place the hydrogen first in the name, and the other body afterwards, because the hydrogen, giving the acid properties, and being constantly present, they think it of the most importance. French chemists, on the contrary, place the hydrogen last, because, being always present, its name may almost be taken for granted; whilst the other body, being the one which gives the characters by which one acid is distinguished from another, is put in the first place. Hence British chemists say, hydrochloric, hydrocyanic acids, &c., placing the hydrogen first, from its importance; the French chemists say, chlor-hydric and cyan-hydric acids, placing the chlorine and cyanogen first, because they distinguish these acids from one another, and from others, which also contain hydrogen.)

(§ † Metals are divided into:

1. Metals yielding alkalies   by oxidation,   . *e. g.* Potassium.
2.   ,,   ,,   alkaline earths ,,   ,,   .   . *e. g.* Calcium.
3.   ,,   ,,   pure earths   ,,   ,,   .   . *e. g.* Aluminium.
4.   ,,   which decompose water at a red heat,   . *e. g.* Iron.
5.   ,,   which do not   ,,   ,,   .   . *e. g.* Arsenic.
6.   ,,   which have so little affinity for oxygen, that their oxides are reduced to the metallic state } *e. g.* Mercury and Gold.) by heat . . . . .)

iodine. Amongst the metals those which only give doubtful bases, and especially their combinations with a large amount of oxygen (§. *e. g.*, Alumina, which is a feeble metallic base, and arsenious and arsenic acids, which contain large proportions of oxygen, are soluble in solution of potash). Certain oxides, such as the protoxide of antimony are soluble both in the acids of the stomach, and in the alkalies of the intestines. In this way may be explained the prolonged action of certain metallic oxides, which can combine both with acids and bases to form soluble compounds.

In the organic kingdom nearly all colouring matters are soluble in alkalies. In all these cases compounds analogous to "*salts*" are formed.

According to some authors this does not always happen, for fatty and resinous matters, in their opinion, are not converted into soaps (§ fatty salts), but are simply made into emulsions by alkalies.

Bodies soluble in alkaline chlorides.—The compounds soluble in these are not numerous, and they have the common character of belonging to the last class of metals (§. gold, platinum, &c., see p. 82), the chlorides of which possess the character of acids, when in relation with those of metals which furnish more powerful bases. They are all the oxides and salts of lead, mercury, silver, gold, and platinum.

But the quantity of these three kinds of solvent which is contained in the animal fluids is so small, that M. Mailhe[*] has adopted it as a general formula for associating matters insoluble by themselves, with a certain amount of their special solvent.

We believe that we shall often attain the same end by a different proceeding; for which we shall give certain rules:

RULES FOR THE ADMINISTRATION OF MEDICINES REQUIRING ACIDS, ALKALIES, OR CHLORIDES FOR THEIR ABSORPTION.

They ought to be given in small doses, and at short intervals, but we shall have occasion to return to this point.

Medicines requiring acids.—They ought to be combined with

---

[*] "Art de Formuler," Paris, 1845.

the smallest possible quantity of water, for fear of diluting the gastric juice, or of forcing the substance to pass through the pylorus too rapidly.

Alkaline drinks ought to be avoided. Should we then recommend acid drinks? It will perhaps be better rather to have recourse to some device for increasing the quantity of acids in the stomach. This device consists in provoking the secretion by the aid of some agreeable alimentary substances. In certain cases, however, the same end is attained by associating the medicine with sugar, honey, or fecula (§. starch, arrow-root, &c.), which are easily transformed into lactic acid. This is the secret of the advantages presented by chocolate and medicated biscuits.

Experience proves that medicines administered during a meal are borne even by stomachs which are easily excited to vomiting; a precaution which is too often neglected.

Medicines requiring alkalies.—To favour the absorption of medicines requiring alkalies for their solution we reasonably advise slightly alkaline drinks; but we ought to observe that in the administration of acid or alkaline liquids it is necessary to employ very small doses; for Mr. Bernard has proved that an excess of acid suspends or diminishes the gastric secretion, whilst a quantity of alkali larger than is necessary to saturate the acids of the stomach increases that secretion. Does this imply then, that we ought to administer an excess of alkali in order to increase the acid secretion? We think not; for this excess of alkali cannot fail to produce disturbances more injurious than useful.

For our part, we prefer moderately provoking the flow of bile into the small intestine by the aid of a small dose of some cholagogue purgative.* For example, we mix a little powdered ipecacuanha with the medicine, and give it under the form of a pill.

Medicines requiring alkaline chlorides.—As the medicines which require these are very active, and as a small dose suffices to produce the desired effect, it will be almost idle to try and assist them. We must be content with administering them in finely divided doses.

Forms under which the medicines pass through the current of the circulation.—We cannot admit, as absolutely proved,

(§ * Chole, bile, and Ago, I move. Medicines to excite the biliary system.)

the whole series of transformations through which chemists assert that medicines pass when they arrive in the blood. In our opinion they make too rigorous an application of the laws of Berthollet (§. *i. e.*, the general laws of *inorganic* chemical combinations and decompositions); and, moreover, the curious facts to which we have just called attention, make it sufficiently evident how careful we ought to be in our inductions, when we attempt to transfer the laws of mineral chemistry to the organic world. Sulphate of iron and carbonate of soda, when placed together, ought by double decomposition to produce sulphate of soda and insoluble carbonate of iron; but, lo! this effect does not take place if a small quantity of albumen is dissolved in the liquid. And does not the serum of the blood present this condition?

Quantities have also their influence upon the play of affinities, which they sometimes reverse. All those who have made many chemical experiments know how remarkably even very energetic reagents remain powerless to produce the effect theoretically foreseen, if they are employed in too small a quantity.

Now, in a given instant, there passes into the blood by way of absorption an infinitely small quantity of a medicine, and especially if this medicine is insoluble by itself. How then, after these considerations can we avoid hesitating to admit, as if absolutely certain, the precipitates which are supposed to be formed by the salts of iron in the presence of the albumen and the alkalies of the blood?

We have chosen this example because it is one of the most important; but these observations will apply to many others.

In conclusion, notwithstanding the works of eminent chemists, we are not yet sufficiently instructed as to the changes which medicines undergo when they have arrived in the vascular system. What appears to be most fully proved is that some of them are oxidized, as the materials of the blood; since we find them under this, as it were, burnt form, in the products of secretion, and especially in the urine. It is thus, as the experiments of Messrs. Wœhler, Millon, and Laveran, have proved, that the salts of potash and soda with an organic acid are generally converted into carbonates, in consequence of this oxidizing action.

MODE OF ACTION OF MEDICINES.

Writers on Therapeutics* have not dared to attempt to penetrate the secret of the intimate action of medicines; but chemists have made a bold attempt in this path, and have put forth notions against which we cannot be too much on our guard.

According to them, chemical form regulates everything; and if they have shown that every mercurial preparation passes into the state of bichloride, it becomes henceforth useless to employ anything else than corrosive sublimate. Thus, also, they take no account of intermediate states, and of many other circumstances worthy of attention; they only look to the ultimate reactions. They disregard the nervous system, and recognise nothing but coagulants and solvents, solutions and precipitates.

Sulphate of quinine (according to them) only acts by the alkalies of the blood precipitating its insoluble quinine, which then goes to obstruct the capillary vessels, and to impede and retard the course of the blood. Now, to fight the chemists with their own arms, has it not been shown already that quinine can be dissolved by alkalies? Has not this been proved by M. Calvert and others? Cannot the blood, which is essentially alkaline, effect this solution? Have they not also tried to explain the contra-stimulant action of tartar emetic by a like decomposition; that is to say, by the precipitation of the oxide of antimony by alkaline liquids, so that this medicine acts in a purely mechanical manner? But here also we may remind these chemists that they have themselves stated the solubility of oxide of antimony in alkaline liquids: and once more we may repeat that the blood is in this condition. It is necessary, therefore, to attribute the contra-stimulant action of the emetic to some other cause, and we content ourselves with repeating here, that the absorption of the emetic, and its subsequent passage into the urine, is not proved with certainty in every instance in which it is borne by the stomach.

Sound physiology revolts at such pretentions. For ourselves we formally reject them on the ground that they are exclusive and absolute. We are far from refusing to chemical form some

* The medicinal effects of medicines.

share of influence in the action of medicines; but we are still further from attributing the whole importance to it.

The grand phenomena, of which the blood is the seat, only depend indirectly upon the form and special nature of the chemical compounds which form part of it. It is not by virtue of the chloride of sodium that sea-salt prevents the coagulation of fibrine; for sulphate of soda, and what is still more, sugar do so also. The salts contained in the serum, taken as a whole, are very slightly coagulating, and yet they take away from water its property of dissolving the blood globules.

These examples suffice to show that it is in facts of a higher order than those which have been invoked by chemists, that we must look for the explanation of the proximate effects of medicines.

In our opinion the principal part belongs to modifications of the nervous system, and to changes which the blood undergoes in its organization and its physiology, or as it may be called in its vitality.

ELIMINATION OF MEDICINES.

Whenever medicinal substances have nothing corresponding to them in the animal organism, it appears that they cannot be assimilated, and that in consequence they ought to be thrown out of it; which does in fact happen with each of them, after a variable length of time, according to circumstances which it is difficult to appreciate.

It would be interesting to search out the laws which preside over this elimination; for the continuance of the action of a medicine is in proportion to the length of time which it remains in the system, and it is often useful to keep the body under the prolonged influence of a certain therapeutical effect.

We must not, however, forget, that notwithstanding the oft repeated axiom: *Sublatâ causâ tollitur effectus*, effects may remain even after the removal of the agent, just as they cannot be manifested immediately after its absorption. From which it follows, that clinical observation is much more useful under these circumstances than merely chemical experience: for the former gives us directly the results which interest us, whilst the latter only leads us by the more circuitous and uncertain road of induction, or of inference.

We have mentioned above that the salts of organic acids are transformed, and it is probable that all substances of this nature undergo similar modifications; but it is often difficult to determine their character. Thus we know how difficult it is to explain the changes experienced by asparagus juice and oil of turpentine, which communicate characteristic odours to the urine. Experiments have, however, been undertaken to determine the rapidity of absorption of certain substances, and the changes which some of them undergo; so that in the present state of science we are able to classify substances which are eliminated by the urine in the following manner:

1. **Substances which pass into the urine with little or no change.**—Carbonates; nitrate of potash or of soda; sulphocyanide of iron, and ferrocyanide of potassium (in 20 minutes), borate of soda; and the chlorides of barium and of calcium, &c.

Principal colouring matters.—Indigo and madder in 12 to 15 minutes; rhubarb in 20 minutes; gamboge in 25 minutes; black cherries in 45 minutes; elder berries in 75 minutes; volatile oil of turpentine produces the odour of violets, and the oils of valerian, saffron, garlic, castoreum, and asparagus, cause a peculiar offensive odour.

2. **Substances which pass into the urine in a state of combination.**—Sulphur, phosphorus, iodine (in 5 minutes); sulphuric, sulph-hydric* (HS.), iodhydric† (HI.), gallic and benzoic acids, &c.

8. **Substances which are decomposed.**—Alkaline salts of the vegetable acids (Wœlher, Millon, Lavaran, Stenberger) are converted into carbonates. The alkaline sulphurets pass into the state of sulphates; according to M. Gélis, the lactate of iron does not pass into the urine, whilst the sulphate of the same base does. *A-propos* of the salts of iron, M. Mialhe asserts, that those which are decomposable by the alkalies of the blood, do not pass into the urine; upon which he founds a theory upon the formation of blood globules, which requires confirmation from exact experiments.

(§ * Hydrosulphuric.)   (§ † Hydriodic. See note, p. 82.)

ACCUMULATION OF MEDICINES.

Under this head are confounded two totally distinct phenomena, one of which may be turned to use in the administration of
medicines, whilst the other is always an accident which we ought
carefully to avoid.

ACCUMULATION OF ACTION.

The first phenomenon is always physiological, and may be
stated as follows. That, in continuing the use of a medicinal
substance, it happens that whilst successive doses remain equal,
their effects gradually increase.

This depends upon the interval of time which elapses between
two consecutive doses. If the intervals are so short that the
effect of the first dose still continues when the second is administered, the two effects are added together. Suppose that the first
effect (equal to 10) may be still represented by half its former
value, the result will be an effect half as powerful again as the
first; that is to say, equal to 15. At the moment of the third
dose, the effect of the first will still remain with (§ say) the fifth
part of its original intensity, that of the second will be reduced
to half, and the total effect will be represented by 17. Ad-
mitting that in the next interval the action of the first dose has
entirely passed away, the effect will never exceed 17, provided
that no change is made in the prescription.

We can easily comprehend all the possible combinations in
this way, and the law of these progressions would be mathe-
matically exact, if habit and other circumstances did not introduce some irregularities. The phenomena of accumulation are
so much more marked, as the action of medicines is prolonged,
and the doses are more numerous during its continuance.

Such is the general law. Its application to particular instances requires an exact knowledge of the duration and rate
of decrease of the action of each medicine; but here is a chasm
in medical science which remains to be filled up.

ACCUMULATION OF DOSES.

There is another kind of accumulation which is peculiar to medicines that must undergo transformation before being able to act; such as insoluble medicines, and those whose active principle can only be developed by the aid of some chemical influence.

So long as circumstances are not favourable to this solution, or to the formation of a new principle, repeated doses of medicine accumulate in the *primæ viæ** without producing any notable effect. Then, if these circumstances alter, the changes are effected, and the system is all at once overcharged with agents, very energetic, and perhaps even poisonous; from which arise accidents more or less severe, which have long since been pointed out, but without the explanation being furnished. We shall avoid them by giving insoluble medicines in very divided doses, and by assisting their solution by means which we have already pointed out.

CONSIDERATIONS RELATIVE TO PATIENTS.

It may be said that all persons are affected by medicines in a peculiar manner; or, in other words, that every patient has his peculiar medical constitution.

Amongst the peculiarities which thus distinguish different individuals, some are evidently united under general laws of the organization, whilst others appear at present to be exempt from them, and are considered as inherent in the individual himself. The first have been classified, and referred to the influence of sex, age, temperament, habits, profession, and diseases, &c. The others, that is to say, those which have not yet been linked with their causes by any rational connection, constitute what it is usual to describe under the name of *idiosyncracies*.

AGES, SEXES, TEMPERAMENTS.

Anatomical and physiological modifications, produced by the progress of age, exert no doubtful influence upon the action of medicines.

(§ * Note, p. 81.)

Common observation has taught us, that a dose which would pass unnoticed in an adult, powerfully disturbs the organization of an infant at the breast. This result might be anticipated. For do we not see, that a given quantity of a medicinal agent might not produce any effect at all, if it was spread out upon too great a surface, or diluted in too large a mass of blood in a man of ordinary stature, whilst it would have a very energetic action if it was concentrated upon a surface, or in a liquid mass twenty times less; which is the case in a new-born infant? In the same way we can understand the difference in the effects observed in little men compared with those of a lofty stature.

But the entirely peculiar susceptibility of infants finds its chief explanation in the predominance of their nervous system, the actions of which, brought into play by the most trifling causes, often exhibit themselves by convulsions. A condition precisely opposite, that is to say, a defect of nervous action, entails upon old people consequences practically analogous.

What we have said about infancy applies equally to the female sex, and even to a nervous temperament or a weak constitution, whether present in men or women.

It is to avoid useless repetitions that we have united in the same paragraph the most general considerations relative to all these important circumstances. As to facts of a more limited application, which also arise from different conditions of age, sex, &c., we designedly omit them, in order not to exceed the limits which we have proposed for ourselves.

PROFESSIONS, HABITS OF LIFE, DIET.

Habits and professions beget modifications of three kinds.

Some of these correspond with ages, sexes, and temperaments, upon which we shall not dwell any further, whilst others constitute abnormal states of organs or functions, more or less compatible with health, the nature of which derangements being known, the consequences are easily deduced from them.

There is a kind of habit which merely consists in introducing into the system, substances capable of reacting upon medicines which are mingled with them. For example, people who are great eaters of salt ought to absorb calomel with extreme facility. On the other hand, ought we not to attribute to the small amount of salt in the usual diet of children, the scanty proportion of alkaline chlorides which they present, and consequently the difficulty which we experience in salivating them?

We attach therefore to diet, the word being taken in its most extended sense, a certain number of facts which it is useful to know.

Furthermore, amongst persons who have long been subjected to scanty food, we observe the same diminution of alkaline chlorides as in children; and the proportion of other secretions is equally affected. This special fact and some others are included under the general law: "That the composition of our humours always bears a relation to that of the substances taken into the system as food or medicine."

Too abundant nourishment, and especially a recent meal of fatty matters hinders the absorption of medicines; and drinks taken in too large a quantity produce the same effect. On the other hand, a deficient supply of food or drink, bloodletting, or in a word, anything which diminishes the mass of the blood favours the absorbent power.

Fatty matters appear to oppose the absorption of every soluble medicinal substance, by coating the surface of the mucous membrane of the stomach; and they retard it also in the case of matters whose absorption into the *secundæ viæ** requires the aid of alkalies, by rendering the intestinal fluid neutral, or even, it is said, making it acid.

(§. NATIONAL DIFFERENCES. CLIMATE.

(The influence of these circumstances has not been touched upon by the French authors of this work; but they are of sufficient importance to deserve notice.

(Dr. Paris (Pharmacologia), on the authority of Dr. Harrison, has pointed out the effect of residence in Italy and regions bordering upon the Mediterranean on the constitution of English people who have gone to reside there. "Narcotics act with greater force, even in smaller doses in Naples than in England; a three-grain dose of extract of hyoscianus, which the patients had been in the habit of taking in England without any unpleasant consequences, produced temporary amaurosis in two patients. I have treated several cases of epilepsy with nitrate

---

* See note, p. 81.

of silver successfully in Italy, though I certainly had not the same success in England. Mercury also is more active in its effects than in our own country; and the doses of medicines prescribed by English physicians in their own country excite universal astonishment amongst the faculty in Italy."[*]

(Mr. Twining says, "In acute dysentery it has never been necessary to use active depletion by blood-letting among natives to such an extent as among Europeans; neither have we occasion to employ purgatives so freely. Smaller doses are in general sufficient, and we must be more reserved in the employment of calomel and blue pill. We seldom need more than half the dose of jalap or castor-oil that is prescribed for Europeans; and the blue pill also is to be reduced to half the quantity, for destructive atonic fluxes are apt to follow the employment of large quantities."[†]

("I am always averse to the administration of mercury to any great extent in the remittent fever of natives. It is not uncommon to see those who have used much of it in the course of fever, acquire morbid susceptibility to atmospheric vicissitudes for a year or two; and they are apt to become permanent valetudinarians, either from rheumatism or dysentery."[‡]

(Mr. Annesley[§] gives some interesting tables, containing amongst other subjects the amount of sickness amongst the native and European troops, of which the following summary is a fair representation. Though there are some discrepancies in particular districts, still it furnishes a good illustration of the effect of climate and constitution. Whilst the proportion of cases of fever and rheumatism was about two in Europeans to one amongst the natives, and the cases of cholera were nearly equal, those of hepatitis amongst Europeans were one hundred, whilst there was but one amongst the same number of natives; of dysentery there were forty-seven cases amongst Europeans to two amongst natives, and of diarrhœa eight to two.

(The proportion of sickness was two hundred and seventeen amongst Europeans to seventy amongst the natives, and the deaths were respectively in the several districts specified, 9, 4, 7,

* "Pharmacologia," edit. 9, p. 121.
† "Diseases of Bengal," 2nd edit., Vol. I., pp. 191, 192.
‡ "Diseases of Bengal," 2nd edit., Vol. II,, p. 346.
§ "Diseases of India."

6, 2, and 4 amongst Europeans, to 2, 2, 2, 3, 1, and 3 amongst the natives: making the per-centage of mortality twice and a half as great amongst Europeans as natives. At the same time, it is proper to mention that Mr. Annesley does not make any marked distinction in his directions for treating the two different classes of men.

("As far as I have observed, the Lascar sailors, when ill, generally commend themselves to Allah, and either recover, or die quickly. I generally found that the proper doses for them were about half what I should give to a European." (Mr. Paterson). The extensive experience of Mr. Busk on the 'Dreadnought' Hospital ship, to which sailors from all parts of the world are daily brought, is of value. In a letter on this subject, he says, "With reference to Swedes, Norwegians, Danes, Russians, Fins, and Germans, and, in fact, to all European nations, I am not aware that we ever make any difference in the doses of drugs. In the case of Blacks, or Lascars, and South Sea Islanders, I do not know that I have remarked any peculiarities. The Lascars, from their habits, require to be allowed tobacco and opium, and we are careful in taking blood from them; but as venesection is very rarely indeed practised in the 'Dreadnought,' I do not know that this amounts to much. The moral management of coloured people requires more tact and attention, than is, I think, often supposed necessary."

(Lastly, we may mention the difference of treatment required in town and country practice, even in our own land; as many a student finds, to his cost, when he attempts to transfer the principles and practice of the treatment of Londoners in London hospitals—gin drinkers, and porter drinkers, and people who sometimes have little either to eat or drink, to the more robust inhabitants of the country parts of the north of England; and we sometimes hear of the smile of incredulity with which a London examiner listens to a country student's account of the bleeding and calomel inflicted upon the colliers and farmers of Northumberland and Yorkshire, &c.)

HABITUATION, AND TOLERANCE OF MEDICINES.

We place these two subjects together, less for the purpose of establishing their resemblance, than with the design of exhibiting their difference.

According to us, *habituation* (§. "habitude") consists in the action of a medicine becoming progressively weaker; *tolerance*, on the contrary, is produced by the absence of reaction against an agent which is more or less poisonous.   We only *accustom* ourselves to a thing gradually; but sometimes *bear* it on the first trial.   The insensibility which habitual use begets increases indefinitely, whilst the (§. power of enduring) *tolerance* of a medicine often ceases all at once, and loathing succeeds to the oppression.

From this it follows that we may support, for many years enormous quantities of a poison to which we have become *habituated*, whilst we cannot continue, beyond a few days, without danger to life, the use of large doses of a poisonous substance, which has only been retained at first by virtue of its *tolerance*.

The phenomena of *tolerance* have not been studied beyond the instance of the preparations of antimony; and the word itself was created by the school of Rasori, who highly vaunted these preparations as contra-stimulants "especially when they were *tolerated*."   The benefits of this tolerance do not appear to us particularly mysterious; when the tartar emetic is not rejected by vomiting, it is absorbed in a larger proportion than usual; the efficacious dose is therefore greater than common, and this is the whole mystery.   However, this principle is not absolute, for it has been attempted to explain the contra-stimulant action of the emetic by an irritation which it produces upon the mucous membrane of the stomach, and its absorption has been denied.   It is also said that the salt does not pass into the urine; but this fact requires to be proved.

Habituation (*habitude*) is observed in a great number of cases. M. Bouchardat maintains that he can lay down the following rules from his experience: " 1. We *cannot* habituate ourselves to substances which act as a poison to *all* beings in the organic scale.   2. We *can* habituate ourselves to substances, which, although rightly considered as poisons to individuals to whom they are administered, nevertheless, spare some beings in the scale of organized nature."

Habituation seems then to be possible, provided the poison does not arrest the phenomena essential to life, but only strikes those animal functions, which are a luxury, so to speak, since they only belong to a privileged class of organized beings. This will lead us to admit two sorts of poisonous substances; some directly impeding the chemico-organic phenomena, and others acting through the intervention of the nervous system. The first kill even plants; the second are only fatal to animals; and their effects are so much the more violent, as they are exerted upon animals placed higher in the scale.

The law which we have just laid down has not been verified in a sufficiently great number of cases to be admitted as absolutely certain; and we are not at present in a position to say what are, and what are not the substances, to which we can become habituated.

Every one knows that we are easily habituated to opium—witness the Orientals. But without speaking of the opium-eaters, some persons have taken, under our own eyes, extraordinary quantities of this medicine. Thus, we have seen a sick person, under our care, in the Necker Hospital, take nearly 6½ drachms (25 grammes) of opium in a day, and examples of this kind are not excessively rare.

Certain poisons, such as worari, the origin of which is not perfectly known, are without action when introduced into the mouth, and even into the stomach, as M. le Docteur Bernard has recently proved, whilst they immediately kill animals wounded by arrows tipped with them. This kind of tolerance appears to depend upon the property possessed by healthy mucous membranes of not absorbing poisons, whilst they become mortal as soon as absorption takes place.

DISEASES.

The nature and intensity of diseases have an evident influence upon the action of medicines, but it is at present little studied.

The more intense a disease, the greater is the quantity of a medicinal substance which it can *saturate* (if we may adopt the word). Thus, after very vivid nervous excitement, a larger quantity of opium is necessary to produce calm and sleep.

With reference to the nature of diseases, we know that in febrile affections emetics act with facility; but the opposite is the case in nervous diseases. In certain forms of gastralgia every medicine capable of producing any local irriration becomes a violent emetic.

It is asserted that the gastric juice is very acid in chronic gastritis, hypochondria, diabetes, worms, and gouty affections. This is disputed, at any rate, in diabetes; but if the fact is true in some other cases, medicines which are soluble by the aid of acids, ought, under these circumstances, to produce a much more prompt and decided action.

In the case of jaundice from retention of bile, medicines soluble by the aid of alkalies will no longer be absorbed.

In general, a surface which secretes much, absorbs with difficulty. Thus, calomel will not produce salivation if a copious diarrhœa exists, even when it is not thrown out of the system.

IDIOSYNCRACIES.

As we have already seen, we comprehend under the name of *idiosyncracy* all the individual differences which we cannot bring under a general law. The term therefore serves as a veil to our ignorance. But in proportion as our knowledge advances, we either limit its use, or at least give it a more precise signification, and perhaps it does not mean more than a particular condition of the nervous system.

In reference to individual differences which sick persons present with regard to the action of medicines, we may range them under three classes.

1. Some experience the usual effects, but in a more intense degree than common. For example, in ourselves the smallest dose of opium produces nettle-rash.

2. Others only experience one of the effects proper to the medicine. Thus, some substances are always purgative to one person, always emetic to another.

3. There are some sick persons who experience effects unusual, and altogether extraordinary.

Idiosyncracy sometimes renders the employment of an innocent remedy, if not dangerous, at least annoying. Gaubius cites an example of a man who was quite as ill from the use of powdered crabs' eyes (§. phosphate of lime, see p. 64) as other persons are from the employment of arsenic. After the application of a blistering plaster a general erysipelas sometimes follows. Antimony sometimes causes salivation, which is not accompanied by

H

loosening of the teeth, or by fœtor of the breath. A druggist of Tours was the prey to a cruel dyspnæa whenever he prepared powdered ipecacuanha. M. Chevalier has known a lady who cannot take powdered rhubarb without immediately having an erysipelatous rash upon the skin, although she can take an infusion of the same substance without any inconvenience.

It is necessary to pay great attention to these idiosyncracies; to which, moreover, patients, warned by previous experience, take care to call the attention of the physician.

Having thus passed in review the principal circumstances which modify the effects of medicines, as well on the part of patients as on that of medicines themselves, and having pointed out the most general laws which preside over their effects, it remains for us to turn our attention to what we are accustomed to call the *" means of the art of prescribing."*

METHODS OF APPLYING MEDICINES.

We apply to every accessible part of the body the medicines whose action ought to be entirely local, that is to say, topical.* Those whose influence can only be exerted after absorption and conveyance into the circulating system, are generally applied to the skin and the digestive and pulmonary mucous membranes.

When we wish to produce absorption through the external skin two methods present themselves: 1. Through the skin remaining entire; 2. After we have removed the epidermis in order to increase its power of absorption.

Enepidermic Method,† (J. Pelletan).—Christiern made us acquainted with this method under the name of *Iatraleptic;‡* it is also the *Anatripsalogic§* method of Bréra; and the *Eispnoïc∥* (absorption by inhalation) of Cruikshank and Duval.

These methods vary according to the properties of the medicine.

---

* From τοπος, topos, a place.

† Εν, en, upon; επι, epi, upon; δερμα, derma, the skin; application to the outside of the epidermis, or cuticle.

‡ Ιατρος, iatros, a physician; αλειπω, aleipo, to anoint; a mode of curing by ointment.

§ Ανα, ana, up and down; τριβω, tribo, to rub.

∥ Εις, eis, into; πνεω, pneo, to breathe.

If it is soluble in water, we may dissolve it, and give it under the form of local or general baths, or soak cloths in it (fomentations, lotions), or make it enter into the composition of poultices, either by using these solutions instead of water, or by simply pouring them upon the surface of an ordinary poultice. The same thing may be done with alcoholic and oily liquids. In the latter case, the preparation takes the name of *liniment* if the oily body is cold, and of *embrocation* if it is hot.

Absorbtion is favoured by friction of the skin. Other greasy bodies, such as pomatums and ointments, are spread upon the skin without further trouble (*unctions*), or are accompanied by friction as above; and it is this which constitutes *frictions*, properly so called. The friction doubtless acts by wearing away the epidermis and exciting the skin, which is more or less reddened. Previously washing the part has the effect of cleansing the skin from the greasy coating which covers it, and which would hinder the absorption of substances that are dissolved in water.

Matters capable of making a paste with water constitute true *cataplasms*, or poultices.

The enepidermic method is often employed, but fresh practical investigations are necessary to give it as much reputation as it deserves. In order to do this, it will be indispensable to take into account the different conditions of the skin in health and in disease; for absorption may be influenced by its dryness or greasiness, by its activity or inertness. We know, in fact, that nitrate of silver does not colour parts which are the seat of erysipelas. Moreover, even very active substances applied to various parts of the body are not absorbed with equal rapidity, for there is little or almost no absorption by the skin covering cellular tissue, whilst it is rapid enough over parts where lymphatic vessels or veins are abundant, as the axilla and the internal part of the thighs. The laws described by M. Dutrochet, under the name of *endosmosis*, will certainly be of great importance in elucidating this question, so much more easy in the present day, as we are better acquainted with the intimate structure of the skin, with its affections and its mode of absorption.

We ought to add, that whenever the enepidermic method is employed, it is indispensable that the substances shall be completely dissolved; so that we advise practitioners to employ vehicles appropriate for effecting their solution. (See the Formulary).

Endermic* method.—When we wish to employ this method, we must begin by removing the epidermis by means of a blistering substance. The one which we should chose is the blistering ammoniacal solution (§. Liq. Ammon. Fort.) It is important for success to take all those precautions upon which we have long insisted in the employment of ammonia. (§. The precautions here alluded to have probably been clinical ones, for the subject is not again adverted to in this work. When ammonia is used for the purpose of raising a blister, it is applied by means of a *small* sponge fastened to the end of a piece of stick, and soaked in the strong solution of ammonia, but not applied to the skin until the superfluous liquid has ceased to run. It should then be rubbed briskly upon the part which we wish to vesicate for ten or fifteen minutes, which are generally required before vesication is produced. Sometimes an ointment (Gondret's pomatum, see Index) is used instead).

This method was invented by M. Lembert, and applied at first by him, along with M. Bailly. Orfila had previously employed it in his toxicological experiments. It has already rendered great service to the medical art, when the object is to produce rapid absorption of energetic substances, which ought to act upon organs near the place of application.

The endermic method is of peculiar value in producing rapid absorption of the organic alkalies, especially those which, like morphia, are soluble in the alkaline fluids of the system. M. Rougier, of Lyons, in the first instance, and afterwards M. Mayor, of Geneva, have proposed to denude the skin by means of a hammer with a round head, dipped in boiling water, and immediately applied to the part which we wish to blister. Strychnine, used by M. Rougier in this way, has yielded him the most favourable results. We should add that the application to the dermis of substances, which are insoluble either mediately or immediately, ought to be avoided.

Method by ingestion.—We comprehend under this title all those proceedings by which medicines are conveyed into the

* Εν, en, upon; δερμα, derma, the skin; the application of remedies to the true skin, the epidermis being removed.

digestive system. This is sometimes effected by the mouth, sometimes by the anus. The first plan ought to be used in nearly every circumstance, and the second only obtains the preference when there is an invincible repugnance on the part of the patient, or the medicines are susceptible of being digested, and thus converted into inert substances.

Ingestion by the stomach is the only possible plan when we wish to make medicines enter into the circulation, which are only soluble by the aid of acids or of alkalies. In this latter case we administer, as we have already said, (p. 84), abundant drinks, to oblige the medicine to pass into the pylorus as rapidly as possible; in addition to which, different artifices have been put in practice to mask the disagreeable flavour of the medicines, which are accordingly sweetened or mixed with aromatics, or enveloped in wafers or in gelatinous capsules.

Method by inspiration.—This method is founded upon absorption by the pulmonary mucous membrane. This end may be attained by charging the atmosphere with medicated vapours,* but it will nearly always be more convenient to make the patient smoke cigars from which the active principles, such as camphor and mercury, may be disengaged. It is important to tell him to fill the cavity of his mouth with smoke by a sucking action, and then to take breath into his lungs, that is to say, to breathe by his mouth.

We believe that it is possible to apply all volatile substances in this way, or at least such as are easily converted into a gaseous state.

Method by infusion into the veins.—We shall simply mention this plan; for although we advise the injection of active substances directly into the veins in desperate cases, it is a double edged weapon.

Method by introduction into the substance of organs.—The first suggestion of this plan belongs to M. Palaprat. It is accomplished by means of a platinum needle, which is plunged into the tissue by one end, whilst by the other it communicates with the pole of a galvanic battery, the acid of which is charged with a medicinal salt.

This method cannot be too limited in its application.

---

* See the article, "Fumigations," for a fuller account of this plan.

Method by inoculation. — This method is related to the iatrapeltic; and certainly, if we consider that vaccination preserves from small-pox, whilst viruses and animal poisons (*e. g.* from the viper and rattlesnake) can be swallowed with impunity, it is clear that this mode of absorption may be of great use in medicine.

All these modes of administering medicines should be present in the mind of the practitioner, because they may often replace one another. Certain substances are so repulsive, or the patients are so susceptible, that it is impossible to administer them in a liquid form by the mouth, and we must have recourse to other plans, such as pills, capsules, or glysters, or the endermic method.

DOSES.—INTERVALS OF ADMINISTRATION.

The considerations to which we have lately paid attention, suffice to show that the dose can only be fixed when we have taken account of the age, sex, habituation and idiosyncracy of the patient, and of the intensity and nature of the disease, &c.

As to age, the doses vary in the proportions which have been laid down in a general way by Gaubius. A whole dose is given to an adult, which is taken as unity, and the following table shows the proportions which ought to be observed:

Under 1 year	.	. 1/15 to 1/12 of the dose.
At 2 years	.	. 1/8
„ 3 „	.	. 1/6
„ 4 „	.	. 1/4
„ 7 „	.	. 1/3
„ 14 „	.	. 1/2
„ 20 „	.	. 2/3
From 20 to 60 years	. 1	the full dose.

Above sixty years of age, an inverse proportion is to be followed.

This last rule, given by Gaubius, cannot be taken without restriction; for it is very certain that a number of medicines may be administered to old people above sixty in the same doses as for adults, as is amply proved by the practice of the physicians to the Salpêtrière and the Bicêtre. Moreover, under certain circumstances, it is necessary to push doses with old people; when, for example, we wish to produce a blister, or to excite sweating or a flow of urine.

The other rules also are not without exceptions, for children bear larger doses of calomel than adults.

For women, we nearly always prescribe rather smaller doses than for men.

Different circumstances, especially climates, make the doses vary; thus the English and the inhabitants of the North bear stronger doses of medicine in their own climate than in a hot country; in Italy for example.

If the medicine is applied to the gastric surface, smaller doses are necessary than for the intestinal surface or the skin. Thus the doses for a glyster ought to be double or even treble of those administered by the mouth.

To counterbalance the effects of habituation we must increase the successive doses of a medicine, the use of which requires long continuance. It will be useful also to change the form of the medicine. Thus, when from habituation we have begun to give a patient large doses of extract of opium without producing the desired effect, we may obtain it by administering laudanum or the salts of morphia, even in doses which are relatively smaller.

We have now said sufficient to indicate the general laws by which we must proportion the doses to the effects which we wish to obtain, after taking attendant circumstances into account; but as to the absolute amount of the dose, ought we to continue giving such as have been generally prescribed up to the present time? Homœopathists only administer quantities infinitely small, which is absurd. Allopathists, on the contrary, often employ doses which are too large, and given at too long intervals, which involves inconveniences of more kinds than one.

1. It is often abused. Calomel is given in doses of two or three decigrammes (gr. iii to gr. ivss) once a-day to excite salivation: only a very small portion dissolves, the rest passes away with the fœces.

2. The medicine produces a different effect from that which we expect. Thus, to take the same example, calomel in a large dose is a purgative.

3. It does not produce the desired effect. Calomel again might furnish us with a proof of this fact: but it is rendered

perhaps more evident still by sulphate of quinine employed in acute articular rheumatism.

When we give this substance to the amount of two grammes (ℨss) daily, in two doses of one gramme each, the fever reappears in the intervals, and the rheumatism is unyielding. If, on the contrary, we give a more feeble dose on the whole, but divided into several portions, the sedative action continues, the pulse remains low, and the treatment is successful.

We can perfectly understand how this may happen, when we see that sulphate of quinine passes into the urine in half an hour after the medicine has been swallowed. The system is not slow in being relieved from it, and therefore to keep it saturated, it is necessary to renew the supply at short intervals.

4. A careless increase of the dose occasions accidents. Thus, sulphate of quinine, in an overdose, causes deafness. Insoluble medicines produce a kind of accumulation, which also possesses danger; and we might multiply facts in support of each of these propositions.

We ought generally to prescribe in divided doses, taking care to make the intervals between them short,

1. Medicines insoluble by themselves, which can only be absorbed by the aid of solution in the fluids of the *primæ viæ*.

2. Medicines, the dynamic action of which ought to be continuous and prolonged, in order to be efficacious.

3. Those which, before passing into the circulation, would revolt the digestive canal, if given in too large a dose.

4. Substances capable of becoming poisonous.

But if we condemn excessive doses, we are equally ready to blame insufficient ones.

Practitioners ought not to forget that the action of medicines is not simply proportioned to the amount, but that each remedy has a dose below which it either produces no effect, or one contrary to that which we are seeking from it; and it is precisely the efficacious quantity which it is necessary to introduce into the system, either at one dose or in several portions taken near together.

The hour of the day at which a medicine should be given also deserves attention.

Purgatives should be taken early in the morning or late at night; and the same remark applies to *alteratives*. *Diuretics* should be taken more frequently during the day than the night, when we desire their special action upon the kidneys; for the greater heat of the bed during the night converts them, for the most part at any rate, into sudorifics. *Soothing* medicines should be given at night to promote sleep, or some time before the pain appears, when it is periodic.

Pills ought generally to be taken during a meal, especially those which from the nature of their constituents may exert a dangerous action upon the stomach (pills of nitrate of silver, arsenic, &c.) It is, however true, that it is sometimes better to employ these substances in solution. The same may be said of substances which are only soluble in the acids of the stomach. As to those which can be absorbed directly, it is usual to prescribe them on an empty stomach in the morning.

The intervals between the doses must be regulated by the nature of the medicine and of the disease. The object which we have in view ought also to regulate us in the prescription. The effects of diffusible stimulants, as ammonia and ether, are very fugitive, and we are therefore obliged to repeat them at short intervals. If we wish to soothe pain and to procure sleep, we employ opium in large doses and at long intervals ; if, on the contrary, we desire to obtain its stimulant effects, we give it in small doses and at short intervals.

COMBINATIONS OF MEDICINES.

The different ends proposed in combining and mixing medicinal substances may be reduced to the following heads :*

1. TO AUGMENT THE ACTION OF A MEDICINE.

A. *By mixing different preparations of the same substance.*—Thus, when the stomach will not bear powdered cinchona bark,

(§. * In the original of this work no acknowledgment is made of the source whence the present chapter was derived, viz., Paris's " Pharmacologia." But though this omission may be pardonable in a French work, avowedly a compilation, and intended for French students, it would be inexcusable in the translator if he did not state that the pith of the following chapter is taken almost verbatim from Paris's " Pharmacologia"—all the rules having been literally copied from that admirable work to which, in many other places also, the authors have been indebted.)

we may employ the decoction; but as its action is mnch less than that of the powder, we add the tincture and extract, in order to increase it. The following law may be laid down: *When all the active principles of a medicine are not soluble in the same vehicle, and it is impossible to administer it in substance, we must have recourse to a mixture of its different preparations.* This rule is applied every day, when we strengthen an infusion or decoction by adding a certain quantity of tincture or extract of the same plant.

B. *By combining medicines of the same class; that is to say, substances which by themselves produce similar immediate effects, but with less energy than when they are combined.*

It is well known that there is no more certain emetic than a mixture of ipecacuanha and tartar emetic. Manna purges to a degree which may be represented as one, senna as two; but the two substances combined purge as four, or more.

Bitter tonics, astringents, cathartics, emetics, diuretics, antispasmodics and narcotics produce a much more powerful effect when combined than when taken separately. We ought not, however, to neglect the excellent rule given by M. Chapman: "Prescribe," said he, "*stimulating* remedies separately, and you will economise your resources in a great number of diseases of debility. By neglecting this caution, we often weaken the susceptibility of the patient to all substances of this class." M. Magendie also asserts that, by varying the different preparations of the same narcotic, we can sustain its action upon the system without increasing the dose, better than by using the same throughout. It is equally useful occasionally to suspend the administration of remedies in chronic diseases, and then to resume them, in order to avoid the influence of habituation, which renders the patient insensible to their effects.

C. *By adding to a medicine substances of a different nature, which do not exert any action upon itself, but render either the stomach, or some other organ, or the whole system, more sensible of its influence.*

There is no medical man who does not know how much more certain the influence of mercury is rendered by combining it with opium. Some have, indeed, almost said that opium can revive the effects of mercurial preparations, even after they have ceased for some time. The augmentation of the sudorific properties of antimony, when associated with opium, is a fact gained by our science.

The purgative action of jalap is remarkably assisted by ipecacuanha. Cullen has observed that senna leaves infused with some bitter plant exert a stronger purgative effect, even in smaller doses, than when employed alone. The aqueous infusion of rhubarb, also, to which columba root has been added, becomes more active. The bitter principle increases the activity of purgatives, even when it does not itself possess any laxative property, as the experiments of Dr. Paris upon elaterium appear to prove;* where he has stated that the bitter principle contained in elaterium considerably increases the purgative action of the substances with which it is associated.

Mercury is more easily absorbed when combined with some animal matter. We are in the constant habit of prescribing the milk of a cow or a goat which has been subjected to mercurial frictions, in order to enable a patient to bear this remedy, who could not take it under any other form; and the milk of a mother, placed under mercurial treatment, is given to an infant affected with syphilis. It appears that mercurials, and especially corrosive sublimate, are advantageously modified in their action —*dulcified*, as it is called—by the contact of animal substances, and espesially of those styled albuminoid, such as albumen, gluten, casein, &c. We must moreover add, that if Messrs. Péligot and Reveil have not been able hitherto to prove the presence of mercury in the milk of mothers under mercurial treatment, it is nevertheless probable, that in the present day, when the process of analysis is more exact, it will be possible to discover mercury in the milk, as it has already been found in the blood and in the urine.

Bleeding very often favours the action of purgatives, emetics, mercury, &c.

It may be generally stated, that purgatives notably facilitate the action of alteratives and diuretics.

A change of habits and of diet also acts in an advantageous manner, and considerably aids the action of medicines. It is not desirable, however, that this change should be too disagreeable to

---

* "Pharmacologia," ed. 9, p. 390,

the patient, or we may obtain an effect quite different from the one which we desire.

2. THE DIMINUTION, OR EVEN DESTRUCTION OF TOO IRRITANT AN ACTION OF A MEDICINE.

In the language of the schools it is said that a medicine is *corrected.*

A. *By a mixture which increases or diminishes its solubility.*

Senna frequently produces colic; to lessen the intensity of which it is sometimes associated with aromatics, such as anise and coriander, or ginger. By mixing gamboge with some insoluble substance we prevent the nausea which generally accompanies its administration. Drastics often produce colic, which is easily avoided by the addition of a small quantity of some alkali; for example, aloes combined with soap, or an alkaline salt, acts much less upon the rectum, and no longer causes tenesmus. The action of bichloride of mercury is increased by alkaline chlorides, and especially by the chlorhydrate of ammonia (Am. Mur.), whilst it is diminished by albumen, casein, gluten, and analogous substances.

B. *By combination with some substance which is capable of preserving the stomach, or the whole system, from its deleterious effects.*

It is to obtain this result that we administer corrosive sublimate with decoction of guiacum, with opium, gum, or some mucilaginous vehicle. Antimony and its preparations act as diuretics and diaphoretics, when they do not produce vomiting or purging. Opium appears to be the substance which most effectually preserves the stomach from the emetic effects of antimony; aromatic stimulants, mucilages, and emollient substances are also sometimes employed with advantage.

Furthermore, opium generally hinders the action of emetics, of which we see an example in Dover's powder, which contains sulphate of potash 125, nitrate of potash 125, powdered ipecacuanha 30, powdered liquorice 30, and extract of opium 30 parts, and which, even in the dose of 1 to 2 grammes (gr. xv to ʒss) is neither narcotic nor emetic. From which the following consequences result, especially in the treatment of poisoning, viz. : that opium should be given to combat the effects of emetic poisons, and that, in turn, they should be employed to destroy the action of narcotics; though it is true, that when emetics have been given in large doses, they act in the first instance by expelling the poison, and afterwards by counterbalancing its narcotic action.

3. TO OBTAIN AT THE SAME TIME THE EFFECTS OF TWO OR MORE MEDICINES.

A. *By employing substances which produce the same result in the end, but have not the same mode of action.*

Purgatives are often combined with the common design of purging; but one increases the peristaltic action of the bowels, another produces a more abundant exhalation from the intestinal mucous membrane, and a third acts upon neighbouring organs, so as to increase their secretions into the intestines.

Calomel is associated with squill and digitalis to obtain diuretic effects. The calomel and digitalis promote absorption, whilst the squill exerts its influence chiefly upon the kidneys, yet the common result of these two kinds of action is *diuresis.*

B. *By combining substances the action of which is entirely different, but intended to answer several indications.*

In painters' colic, purgatives are successfully combined with anti-spasmodics, and in spasmodic colic these two kinds of medicine are employed with equal success. Tonics also are combined with purgatives in dropsies and in amenorrhœa. Purgatives and alteratives united are powerful in obstinate constipation, and in syphilis, &c.; and examples may be multiplied *ad infinitum.*

4. BY THE MIXTURE OF SEVERAL SUBSTANCES TO FORM A NEW REMEDY, THE EFFECT OF WHICH COULD NOT BE OBTAINED FROM ANY OF THE COMPONENTS TAKEN SEPARATELY.

A. *By combining without chemical reaction, medicines endowed with powers essentially different from each other ; but, which by their union produce different effects upon the system, from those which they would occasion separately.*

It is difficult enough to explain the singular property of certain combinations. It is thus, that a mixture of ipecacuanha and opium produces a powerful diaphoretic; whilst we know that neither ipecacuanha nor opium taken alone possesses this influence. It is probable that several natural medicines owe their efficacy to such combinations.

It is in this way that electuaries, and all the preparations of the ancients which contained a multitude of medicines, acted.

B. *By chemically combining substances that give rise to new compounds which bring out the active principles of one of the components.*

Sulphuric acid united with potash forms a salt (sulphate of potash), which has only a gentle action upon the system, whilst both the components are remarkably caustic.

The anti-emetic draught of Rivière is prepared by mixing lemon-juice and bicarbonate of potash; the citric acid acts upon the carbonate, decomposition takes place at the moment of combination, carbonic acid is disengaged, and it is by this carbonic acid that the vomiting is checked.

Yeast or leaven poultice owes its antiseptic properties merely to the development of carbonic acid produced by the decomposition of the ingredients during fermentation.

It would be difficult, if not impossible, to show beforehand what will be the chemical composition resulting from the mixture of two neutral organic substances. It has required the grand labours of Messrs. Robiquet and Boutron, Liebig and Wœhler, to prove that two neutral substances as inoffensive as amygdalin (the bitter principle of bitter almonds), and synaptase, or emulsin (the albuminous constituent of the almond) can give rise to two poisons, as energetic as the essence of bitter almonds and cyanhydric (hydrocyanic), or prussic acid.

M. Bernard has proved, moreover, that these two substances can react upon one another even in the stomach, and give rise to the two poisons just named. This learned physiologist has even made use of this reaction, to prove that the division of the pneumogastric nerve, or the eighth pair, arrests the digestive process; for, the section of this nerve being made in a dog, if we administer to this animal first synaptase, and then amygdalin even a long time afterwards, these two substances meeting in the stomach the animal will die poisoned by cyanhydric acid and essence of bitter almonds. If, on the contrary, we make a dog in a natural state take synaptase, and amygdalin only an hour afterwards, the animal will not be inconvenienced, because of the digestion and assimilation of the synaptase; which is completed by the time the amygdalin is swallowed, so that these two substances do not meet either in the stomach or elsewhere in a state of purity.

The "Looch blanc" (white lohoc, or linctus—soft confection) of the *codex*, contains a small quantity of bitter almonds, and the reaction which we have just pointed out is shown by the production of hydrocyanic acid and essence of bitter almonds; but in so small a quantity that they are of no dangerous consequence. If, however, we add calomel to this linctus, that substance, which, administered alone is free from danger, is converted into two deadly poisons, the bichloride and bicyanide of mercury; and poisoning, followed by death, has occurred from such a mixture.

Certain medicines, when combined, lose some of their physiological properties without our being able to attribute the cause to any chemical change; and without its being certain that the curative action has been modified. We have already mentioned that coffee and tannin destroy the bitterness of sulphate of quinine, sulphate of magnesia, and the greater number of bitter substances. Washed animal charcoal acts in the same way in many instances; and the odour of musk disappears when it is mixed with milk of almonds; and M. Reveil asserts that camphor acts in the same way. Lastly, M. Planche has pointed out important changes which are produced in the consistence and smell of resins and gum-resins when combined with camphor, which destroys the offensive odour of assafœtida. We have still to learn whether the curative properties are not also modified by such mixtures; but upon this question experience must decide.

Cyanide of potassium is a very energetic poison; but if combined with protocyanide and sesquicyanide of iron, it forms two salts, ferrocyanide, or yellow cyanide, and ferrycyanide, or ferridcyanide, or red cyanide of potassium, both of which salts are without action upon the system, and may be given without inconvenience in doses of 50 to 60 grammes (ʒiss to ʒii), whilst the pure cyanide of potassium inevitably kills in doses of 0,30 to 0,50 (gr. ivss to gr. viii); and it is a curious thing, that not only are its curative and poisonous properties masked, or destroyed in the ferrocyanide and ferrycyanide of potassium, but its chemical ones also; for the iron itself cannot be indicated by the proper tests.

5. TO GIVE A MEDICINE A SUITABLE FORM.

We have already mentioned, that the physician ought as far as possible to adapt the form of his medicines to the taste or caprices of his patients, by concealing their odour and disagreeable flavour, though always without sacrificing their efficiency. It is also very important to choose a pharmaceutical form, which may prevent spontaneous chemical decomposition. We generally attain this end, by adding to the prescription aromatics, or essential oils. Sugar prevents ointments from becoming rancid, and a dry place and a moderate temperature will almost always be the most favourable for keeping them in.

As to the most efficacious form for particular medicines, we shall consider this in speaking of the different pharmaceutical forms, such as infusions, powders, draughts, mixtures, &c.

Chemical and pharmaceutical errors to be avoided in the composition of a prescription (" Magistral formula.")

The chemical and pharmaceutical errors which are liable to be committed arise from the following causes.

1. *Combining substances which cannot mix, or which do not produce compounds of a uniform consistence, or suitable to the required pharmaceutical form.*

This is what we call committing an error in the *mechanism* of the prescription. A fault of this kind is more injurious to the reputation of the physician, than to the health of the patient; but in certain cases the mistake may be disagreeable. A few examples will suffice to show the nature of these errors. We cannot order camphor and copaiba under the form of pills without employing some intermedium, such as hard boiled yolk of egg; for instead of obtaining a pill mass we should have a mixture of the consistence of syrup.

Calomel should not be prescribed in a watery vehicle, as it is insoluble in water, and its administration would therefore be difficult. We ought to add some medium such as mucilage, albumen, &c.

We must take care not to mix substances which will produce a mass too hard or difficult of digestion, as will be the case if we mix myrrh with iron, and add liquor potassæ instead of carbonate of soda. It is also desirable not to use large quantities of powdered gum or mucilage, especially in such pills, as are generally made in large quantities; for, at the end of a few days these pills become extremely hard, and pass through the bowels unaffected by them. (§ It is in accordance with this principle that most of the pill masses of the Ph. Lond. are made up with treacle or soft soap, instead of with gum or hard soap).

2. *Placing the medicines under such circumstances that their active principles cannot be developed.*

It is well known that the essential oil of bitter almonds, of mustard, and of horse-radish, are only produced in consequence of a true species of fermentation. It is necessary therefore to avoid heating preparations which contain these medicines as their bases, above 75° C. (167° F.), and not to add any substance, such as alcohol, strong acids, or camphor, which may hinder the fermentation. (§ On this principle, vinegar has been omitted from the mustard poultice in the last edition of the Ph. L.)

3. *Mixing substances which decompose each other, and whose action is thereby changed, or entirely destroyed.*

We might here give a table of incompatible substances; but we shall first show a few examples to make this kind of mistake easily understood; and we shall at the same time lay down some rules which may assist the physician in avoiding this error.

To a mercurial pill preparation, nitric acid must not be added; for it would form nitrate of mercury, which might kill the patient. The styptic action of acetate of lead is destroyed by combination with alum, or with the acidulated infusion of roses, or small doses of sulphate of magnesia if used at the same time. (§ It must, however, be borne in mind, that decompositions are sometimes intentionally produced, and at other times are disregarded, as immaterial, though not designed. Thus, sulphate of zinc and acetate of lead, both soluble separately, produce soluble acetate of zinc, and insoluble sulphate of lead, which is precipitated. But in this case the decomposition is intentional; for the acetate of zinc is the medicinal agent really wanted, and it is conveniently obtained from the above mixture. Again: acetate of lead and tincture of opium produce soluble acetate of morphia and insoluble meconate of lead; and yet they are frequently combined in glysters to check diarrhœa or to relieve tenesmus; for the quantity of acetate of lead (say Mxxx of the Liq. Plumbi

I

Diacet.) is far more than sufficient to remove all the meconic acid from the laudanum; and therefore there are still in the glyster soluble acetate of morphia (soothing), an excess of soluble acetate of lead (astringent), and the precipitate of insoluble meconate of lead, which is simply disregarded as being of no consequence, good or bad.) Lime water forms an insoluble compound with tannin, which we regard as inefficacious.

The rules which have been established are purely chemical, and are as follows:

1. Whenever two salts in a state of solution *can*, by the exchange of their acid and base, *form* a soluble and *an insoluble salt*, or two insoluble ones, *the decomposition always takes place;* unless, which is very rare, the soluble and insoluble salt form a double salt during their combination. (§ This is called the "Law of Berthollet.")

Thus, chloride of barium and sulphate of soda ought not to be prescribed together, for they will be decomposed and form sulphate of barytes, which is insoluble, and chloride of sodium, which is soluble. The same decomposition takes place if acetate of lead is mixed with a soluble sulphate; for an insoluble sulphate of lead is formed, and a soluble acetate, of soda for example, if we have taken sulphate of soda. Nitrate of silver ought not to be associated in a mixture with a soluble chloride, for we shall have chloride of silver, insoluble, and a soluble nitrate. (§. Chlorides are however sometimes purposely combined with nitrate of silver for the sake of the resulting chloride of silver, which is preferred in some cases to the nitrate for internal administration. See also p. 113).

2. If the two soluble salts which are mixed are not of such a nature as to form a soluble and an insoluble salt, the solution is not disturbed, and possibly there may be no decomposition. (§. It is, however, generally supposed that each acid combines with each base, and a decomposition therefore does take place; but if all the resulting salts are soluble, we have no proof that this change has actually occurred. *e. g.* If carbonate of soda and nitrate of potash are combined, the carbonic acid may be divided between the soda and potash, and form carbonate of soda and carbonate of potash, and the nitric acid also may form nitrate of soda and nitrate of potash; but although this probably does occur we have no proof of it).

3. If a soluble and an insoluble salt are placed in contact, and their elements are capable of forming two insoluble salts, the decomposition will take place; but we must add, that this reaction is extremely rare at ordinary temperatures.

4. In mixing any salt with an acid, we shall always have a decomposition if the acid added is either more fixed or more soluble than that of the salt. (§. *e. g.* If sulphuric acid is added as a refrigerant to liquor ammon. acetatis, the sulphuric acid being more fixed than the acetic acid, forms sulphate of ammonia, and the acetic acid becomes free in the solution. This species of decomposition is seldom of any consequence, except in the following case).

5. Salts, the acid of which is gaseous (*e. g.* carbonic acid) or possessed of a feeble affinity for the base, (*e. g.* lactic or gallic acid), are always decomposed by more fixed acids, or when the acid added can form an insoluble or even merely a less soluble compound with the base of the salt.

6. Oxides and acids mutually saturate each other; their effects are nullified, and they give rise to a new compound.

7. Alkaline oxides (§. *e. g.* potash, soda) precipitate other oxides and the vegetable alkalies from their saline solutions; but the oxide precipitated is often soluble in an excess of the alkaline oxide, (§. *e. g.* oxide of zinc precipitated by liquor potassæ from sulphate of zinc is re-dissolved by an excess of potash). The same alkaline oxides disengage from their combinations volatile bases, such as ammonia, nicotine, &c.

Potash and soda decompose all the salts of the last five classes, and most of those of the first. (See p. 82.)

8. Vegetable substances containing tannic or gallic acid precipitate gelatine, albumen, vegetable alkalies, and the oxides of most of the salts of the last five sections. We ought to avoid prescribing tartar emetic and a bitter or astringent decoction in the same mixture, for without this precaution the tartar emetic will be decomposed and lose its properties. We may, however, combine quinine with preparations of iron.

Soluble substances.—We may foresee the reactions, which are consequences of the law of Berthollet, (see p. 114,) by knowing that all the bicarbonates, acetates, and nitrates, and sulphates with the exception of those of barytes, tin, antimony, mercury and bismuth; that the carbonates of potash, soda and ammonia; the phosphates of the same bases; all alkaline sulphurets; the iodides of the three first divisions; all chlorides except the protochloride of mercury, (calomel), and the chlorides of lead and silver; and all the salts of potash, soda and ammonia, which have an excess of acid, are *soluble* in water, provided only that the acid itself is not insoluble, like silicic and antimonic acid; and even the silicates and antimoniates of potash and soda are soluble in an excess of alkali.

We must not, however, forget that a great number of salts, such as nitrate of bismuth, protochloride ("butter") of antimony, and the nitrates and sulphates of mercury are decomposed by water into soluble acid salts and insoluble basic salts. (§. *e. g.* In the preparation of medicinal nitrate of bismuth, the metal is dissolved in nitric acid, and the solution is then thrown into water, which converts it into two salts of bismuth, one containing a large excess of acid (an acid salt) which remains dissolved in the water; the other containing a large excess of bismuth, the base, (a *basic* salt), which is insoluble and is precipitated).

Lastly, we advise that acids should never be mixed with substances capable of being coagulated by them, such as albumen, casein, milk of almonds, &c.

Insoluble substances.—The sulphates of barytes, tin, lead, antimony, bismuth and mercury; all the carbonates except those mentioned above as being soluble; the phosphates, borates and sulphurets of the last five sections; and the iodides of the last three are *insoluble* in water.

We again advise that mercurial preparations, even calomel, should never be combined with hydrocyanic acid or bodies which are capable of forming it, such as locks or emulsions containing bitter almonds, or the distilled waters of the cherry laurel or bitter almond; for we have already mentioned (p. 111) that the protochloride of mercury, of little activity when administered alone, is transformed by hydrocyanic acid and the simple alkaline cyanides, into bichloride and bicyanide of mercury, both of which are violent poisons. It is therefore only with a full recollection of these circumstances that alkaline chlorides, and especially hydrochlorate of ammonia, should be mixed with insoluble metallic preparations, and especially with mercurial compounds, which, according to M. Mialhe, are converted in this case into corrosive sublimate, the action even of which salt is increased by alkaline chlorides, as it forms double salts with them, which are more easily absorbed.

As a last rule to be observed with respect to chemical reactions, it may be stated, that acid substances should never be placed in contact with vessels of copper, iron, lead or marble, but that glass or porcelain vessels only should be employed. And the same precaution will be useful in the case of tartar emetic, and corrosive sublimate.

The table of incompatible substances which we are about to give, is as complete as we could make it; but some omissions may have escaped us. They will, however, be somewhat remedied by remembering that, if a substance is endowed with well marked therapeutical or poisonous properties, independent of those which may exert a chemical effect upon the tissues, its mode of action will neither be changed nor destroyed by the combinations which it forms; provided always that the new compounds are not insoluble in water.

Before treating of incompatibility, we ought to mention that there are three varieties of it: *physical incompatibility*, of which we have treated in speaking of the pharmaceutical form of a medicine; *physiological incompatibility*, of which we have spoken in treating of idiosyncracies; and lastly, *chemical incompatibility*, which is now about to occupy us.

Though some authors say that there is not always a physiological or therapeutical, when there is a chemical, incompatibility—that, in short, the formation of a precipitate does not always prevent medicine from acting—still it does diminish or retard its action; but this is all the effect produced, if the precipitate is capable of being acted upon by the fluids of the system. Thus ferruginous preparations are combined with quinine every day, and tannin with the alkaloids: and corrosive sublimate—which, when alone, acts too powerfully upon the stomach—is combined with albumen, gluten, or milk, and is then more easily borne.

It is not necessary to give two incompatible medicines at the same time, in order to produce decomposition: it is sufficient if they are given within a very short interval of each other. Thus a sick person, who has been treated with lead externally, or even internally, will present a discolouration of the skin, if he takes a sulphur bath four or five days after the lead treatment has been discontinued. If a person is rubbed with iodide of potassium shortly after having applied Vigo's plaster (Empl. Hydr. c̄. Am.)* or the Neapolitan ointment (Ung. Hydrarg.), iodide of mercury and caustic potash will be formed, which will cause vesication. So also vomiting occurs if lemonade made with tartaric acid is taken five or six days after the administration of white oxide of antimony.

TABLE OF INCOMPATIBLE SUBSTANCES.

Absinthium.

With: the sulphates of iron and zinc, acetate of lead and tartar emetic.

Acetate of Ammonia.

With: concentrated acids, the fixed alkalies, nitrate of silver and corrosive sublimate.

Acetate of Morphia. See Acetate of ammonia.

With: iodine and the free salts of iron. (§. In a mixture of the ordinary degree of dilution, there is not one of these so-called incompatibles with which morph. acet. may not be combined.)

Acetate of Lead.

With: sulphuric and most other acids, alkalies, alum, borax, alkaline carbonates, lime, hydrosulphates or sulphureta, milk, most animal matters, magnesia, soap, most neutral salts, alkaline sulphates, tannin and substances containing it, opium, and preparations containing meconic, quinic and igasuric acids, &c. (§. In short, with nearly all substances, except distilled water and solid opium. See, however, note, p. 113.)

Acetate of Potash.

With: most acids, nearly all the acid fruits, and a great number of salts.

Acetate of Potash and of Iron.

With: strong acids, lime-water, hydrosulphates or sulphureta, bitter and astringent vegetable infusions, &c.

Acetic Acid. See Citric acid.

Acid, Arsenious, or White Oxide of Arsenic.

With: lime-water, decoction of quinine and infusions of astringent substances, with nitrate of silver and the soluble sulphureta. (§. It is the best plan to give arsenious acid in the form of liquor potassæ arsenitis, uncombined with any other substances.)

Acid, Citric.

With: mineral acids, alkalies, alkaline carbonates, emulsions, milk, the salts of lead and lime, &c. (§. Citric acid is often combined with alkaline carbonates, for the sake of the effervescence and the resulting neutral salt.)

Acid, Hydrochloric.

With: alkalies, alkaline carbonates, nitrate, and all the salts of silver, the salts of lead, and the proto-salts of mercury, &c.

Acid, Hydrocyanic, its Compounds, and their **Products containing Cyanogen.**

With: the mineral acids, chlorine, the oxides of antimony and of mercury, nitrate of silver, the salts of iron, most metallic salts, sulphureta, &c. (§. Hydrocyanic acid is often beneficially added to bitter infusions containing some dilute mineral acid; and it forms a valuable addition to the Mistura Ferri. Comp. in phthysis, though it changes the colour of the mixture, and is, chemically speaking, incompatible with it.)

(§ * This is really a much more compound plaster than the Empl. Hydr. c̄. Ammoniaco; but its essential constituents and principle of action are the same.)

Acid, Nitric.

With: salifiable bases, carbonates, &c.

Acid, Oxalic. See Acid, citric.

With: all the salts of lime, and those of the second division.

Acid, Sulphuric.

With: alkalies, carbonates, emulsions, hydrochlorates, milk, nitrates, sulphurets, and the salts of barytes, lime, *lead*, &c. (§. The last is the most probable mistake to be made, as both lead and dilute sulphuric acid are valuable remedies in internal hæmorrhages. They ought not to be given together, unless a considerable interval elapses between the dose of one and that of the other.)

Acid, Tartaric. See Acid, citric.

With: lime-water (§. and salts of potash).

Aconitum Napellus. See Solanaceæ (poisonous).

Alcohol, Alcooles and **Alcoolats** (See p. 6).

With: gummy and albuminous substances, such as milk, &c.

Alum.

With: acetate of lead, alkalies and their carbonates, ammonia, lime, emulsions, infusion of quinine, magnesia, nutgalls, the salts of mercury, and most metallic salts.

Ammonia.

With: acids, alum, and acid and metallic salts.

Angustura (Cusparia) Bark (tincture).

With: concentrated acids, infusion of galls and of cinchona, potash, corrosive sublimate, and the phosphates of iron and of copper. (§. Though incompatible with *concentrated* acids, which are never likely to be prescribed with cusparia, it is usefully combined with *dilute* nitric acid and laudanum in chronic dysentery, &c.

Arnica.

With: acetate of lead, the mineral acids, and the sulphates of iron and zinc, &c.

Arseniate (neutral) of Soda. See Arsenite of potash.

Arsenite of Potash.

With: lime-water, decoctions or infusions of cinchona, the soluble sulphurets, and the soluble salts of silver, copper, &c. See Acid. arsenious.

Bichloride and Biniodide of Mercury. See Deutochloride or Deutoiodide of mercury.

Borax, or **Sub-borate of Soda.**

With: acids, the chlorides of lime and magnesia, potash and the sulphates.

Butter of Antimony (Protechloride).

With: water, which converts it into hydrochloric acid and oxychloride of antimony, or powder of Algaroth. *See* Tartar emetic.

Calomel or **Protechloride of Mercury.**

With: acids, which convert it into poisonous corrosive sublimate; alkalies and lime-water, which decompose it; chloride of sodium or common salt, which makes it pass into a state of bichloride; copper, iron, lead; the sulphurets of antimony and of potassium; loochs containing milk of almonds, cherry-laurel water, bitter almonds, or any liquid containing hydrocyanic acid, all of which convert it into bichloride and bicyanide of mercury. See p. 111.

Calumba. See Colombo.

Camphor.

The resins of the gum-resins (*e. g.* ammoniacum, myrrh) form very soft masses with it, and musk loses its odour in contact with camphor.

Carbonate of Ammonia.

With: acids, the oxides of the two first classes of metals, and metallic and earthy salts, and corrosive sublimate.

Carbonate of Lead. See Acetate of lead.

Carbonate of Potash and of Soda.

With: acids, alum, hydrochlorate of ammonia, the chlorides of mercury, lime-water, tartar emetic, nitrate of silver, and the sulphates of copper, iron, magnesia, zinc, &c. (§. The bicarbonate of potash or soda is not incompatible with sulphate of magnesia, with which it forms a clear solution, whilst it possesses the property of almost concealing the taste of the salts).

Catechu. See Tannin.

Chamomile, Infusion of.

With: infusion of cinchona and of the vegetable astringents, with nitrate of silver, the salts of lead, solution of gelatine, corrosive sublimate and sulphate of iron.

Chlorine.

With: gelatine, nitrate of silver, (§. and colouring substances added to a mixture for the sake of colour).

Chloride of Barium.

With: alum, the carbonates, the alkaline and metallic nitrates, and the soluble phosphates and sulphates.

Chloride of Calcium.

With: boracic, phosphoric and sulphuric acids, and their salts, with alkalies and their carbonates.

Chloride of Gold.

With: alkalies and vegetable juices, gums, saccharine and extractive matters, and the proto- salts of iron and tin.

Chloride of Sodium or **Common Salt.**

With: sulphuric acid, the mineral acids, the salts of silver and calomel.

Colocynth.

With: acetate of lead, the fixed alkalies, nitrate of silver and sulphate of iron.

Colombo.

With: acetate of lead, lime-water, infusion of galls and of cinchona, and corrosive sublimate.

Conium. See Solanaceæ (poisonous).

Acids lessen the activity of conium. Preparations which have hemlock for their basis, are more active in proportion as they have been prepared at a lower temperature.

Cream of Tartar, or **Tartrate of Potash.**

With: strong acids, the salts of lime and lead, and antimonial preparations.

Cyanide of Potassium.

With: all acids, even feeble ones, and most metallic salts, especially those of mercury.

Deutochloride of Mercury (Bichloride — Corrosive Sublimate).

With: alkalies and their carbonates, copper, tartar emetic, iron, metallic mercury, lead, soap, vegetable substances containing tannin, and the soluble sulphates. Albuminous substances diminish its action. (§. There is scarcely anything with which it is desirable to combine corrosive sublimate, except muriate of ammonia and decoction of sarsaparilla.)

Deutoiodide of Mercury.

Its solution in alcohol is decomposed by undistilled water. The soluble iodides dissolve it, and render it more active.

Digitalis.

The salts of iron, lead and silver precipitate infusion of digitalis. Does a therapeutical incompatibility result from this? (§. It does not, if the experience of the effects of Tinct.

Ferri. Mur. and digitalis are to be our guide in giving the answer.) Digitalis is incompatible with acetate of lead, infusion of cinchona, and the iodide of potassium, with free iodine.

Ether, Hydrochloric.

Water separates it from its alcholic solution.

Fruits.

Containing acetic, citric, malic, oxalic acid—*e. g.* cherries, citrons, raspberries, pomegranates, gooseberries, mulberries, oranges, apples, crabs, sorrel, &c.—are incompatible with alkalies, the alkaline carbonates, emulsions, milk, and salts containing chlorine.

Gums.

With: alcohol, acids, subacetate of lead, (§. nitrate of silver, and most metallic salts.)

Hops.

With: the mineral acids, and the salts of silver, iron, mercury and lead.

Hydrochlorate of Ammonia.

With: nitric and sulphuric acid, oxides of the second class, and the salts of silver and of lead.

Iodine and the Iodides.

With: substances containing starch (amydon) or the vegetable alkalies. (§. Iodine combines with most metals on simple contact; it loses its corrosive, and consequently its counter-irritant properties when added to the fixed alkalies, and iodide of potassium decomposes nearly all the metallic salts, forming insoluble compounds with most of them. Both iodine and the iodides ought therefore to be prescribed with as few additions as possible.)

Ipecacuanha.

With: vegetable acids and astringent infusions. Opium modifies its action. See p. 109.

Kermes Mineral.

With: all the acids, and the soluble sulphurets and chlorides.

Kino.

With: the mineral acids, tartar emetic, gelatine, and the salts of silver, lead and iron,

Laudanum. The same as for opium, which see.

Lime.

With: acids, carbonates, and infusions of columba, rhubarb and cinchona.

Nitrate of Silver.

With: hydrochloric and hydrocyanic, tartaric, arsenic and arsenious acids, the soluble cyanides, the fixed alkalies, the soluble carbonates, the chlorides, iodides, and alkaline sulphurets, tannin, and substances containing it. In the last case the organic substances decompose it. (§. It is decomposed by so many substances when in solution, that in this form it should be prescribed by itself alone. When made into pills, bread crumbs should not be used, as the mass quickly becomes hard; but some soft extract (*e. g.* Ext. Gent.) should be employed; and acetate of morphia should be preferred to muriate, unless the physician is indifferent whether he is administering nitrate or chloride of silver.)

Nitrate of Potash.

With: sulphuric acid and alum, and the sulphates of iron and copper, magnesia and zinc. (§. It is often given along with sulphate of magnesia without any disadvantage.)

Oak Bark.

With: acetate of lead, alkaline carbonates, lime-water, gelatine, corrosive sublimate, and the sulphates of iron and zinc.

Opium.

With: alkalies,? ammonia, the carbonates of potash and soda,? nitrate of silver,? acetate of lead,? and corrosive sublimate (at any rate, unless it is in the form of pill), and the salts of copper,? iron,? mercury? and zinc. Infusion of galls, and tannin, &c., precipitate opium, but are not truly incompatible with it, because the compounds they form are very active. The bodies most incompatible with opium, and which most diminish its activity, are iodide of potassium with free iodine, and solutions giving off chlorine.

Acetate of lead forms, with tincture of opium, meconate of lead and acetates of morphia and codeia, so that its action is little changed; but on account of the decomposition which is shown by the precipitate of meconate of lead, this combination ought to be avoided.

(§. All the substances above mentioned are theoretically and chemically incompatible with solutions of opium, if both the solution and the incompatible addition are concentrated; but in the ordinary degree of dilution employed in dispensing medicines, laudanum is constantly added to solutions of the alkalies or their carbonates, without the smallest change of importance. All the substances to which the translator has added a note of interrogation are daily prescribed along with opium in the form of pills, or with laudanum in that of solution, with benefit, such as proves that there is no essential impropriety in the combination.)

Oxide of Zinc and Tutty (impure oxide).

With: acids, salts, and acid juices.

Phosphorus.

With: water, which precipitates it from its alcoholic and ethereal solutions.

Sub-nitrate of Bismuth (Nitrate, Tris-nitrate), Pearl-white, Cosmetic.

With: hydrosulphuric acid and the soluble sulphurets. After being applied to whiten the skin, sulphurous baths would blacken it.

Sub-phosphate (Phosphate) of Soda.

With: hydrochloric, nitric and sulphuric acids, lime, magnesia and chloride of barium.

Sulphate of Copper.

With: acetate of lead, alkalies, borax, alkaline carbonates, and infusions and tinctures containing tannin.

Sulphates of Iron.

With: acetate of lead, alkalies and their carbonates, borax, hydrochlorate of ammonia, nitre, metallic oxides of the first two classes, and most metallic salts; those substances which form an insoluble compound with sulphuric acid; soap, and the tartrate of potash and of soda; tannin, and substances containing it, such as galls, oak bark, canella, cinchona, catechu, &c. According to some authors, the precipitates of the salts of iron, with tannin and vegetable astringents, retain medicinal properties. (§. In the Mistura Ferri. Co. and the Pil. Ferri. Co., sulphate of iron is intentionally combined with alkaline carbonates. See note, p. 113.)

Sulphate of Magnesia.

With: acetate of lead, and muriate of ammonia, barytes and lime, nitrate of silver, metallic oxides of the second class, and the carbonates (§. but not the bi-carbonates of potash and soda. Vinum colchici and calcined magnesia prescribed together, in conjunction with sulphate of magnesia, form a bulky, insoluble mass.)

Sulphate of Morphia.

With: most metallic oxides.

Sulphate of Potash. See Sulphate of soda.

Sulphate of Soda.

With: the salts of barytes, lime and lead, &c.

Sulphate of Zinc.

With: alkalies, alkaline carbonates, milk, mucilage, the salts of lead, barytes and lime, sulphurets, and tannin and vegetable substances containing it. See p. 113.)

Super-arseniate of Potash. See Arsenite of potash.

Protochloride of Iron.

With: alkalies and their carbonates, astringent vegetable infusions, mucilage of gum arabic, and the salts of morphia.

Quassia-Amara,

With : acetate of lead and nitrate of silver.

Quassia-Simarouba.

With : acetate of lead, alkaline carbonates, infusions of catechu, galls and cinchona, and corrosive sublimate.

Rhatany. See Tannin.

Rhubarb.

With : strong acids, lime-water, tartar emetic, astringent infusions? (see p. 107), corrosive sublimate, and the sulphates of iron and zinc. A high temperature must be avoided.

Senna.

With : strong acids, alkaline carbonates,? lime-water and tartar emetic. A high temperature lessens its action.

Soap, Medicinal.

With: acids and all soluble salts, except those of potash, soda and ammonia, and with substances containing tannin.

Solanaceæ (poisonous).

Most substances precipitate the preparations of the poisonous solanaceæ; but the only mixtures which are truly incompatible are those which give off chlorine or iodine.

Tamarind.

With: alkaline carbonates, lime-water, tartar emetic and the salts of potash.

Tannin.

With: mineral acids, alkalies and their carbonates, albumen, emulsions, gelatine, the metallic salts of the last four classes, and especially those of antimony and iron. (See Sulphate of iron, above.)

Tartar, Emetic.

With: concentrated acids, gallic acid, the metallic oxides of the first two classes and their carbonates, soap, most bitter and astringent substances, rhubarb, cinchona, the soluble sulphates (§. except sulphate of magnesia, the action of which it promotes), tannin and all the plants containing it. Opium diminishes its emetic action, but increases its diaphoretic properties.

Tartrate of Potash.

With : all acids, even weak ones, which form an acid tartrate (cream of tartar), lime-water, chloride of barium and the salts of lead.

Tartrate of Potash and Iron.

With : strong acids, sulphuretted hydrogen, lime-water, astringent vegetable infusions and sulphurets.

Tartrate of Potash and Soda. See Tartrate of potash.

Tea.

With : lime-water, gelatine, the salts of iron and metallic salts.

Unguentum Citrinum, (Ung. Hydrarg. Nitr.)

which contains nitrate, stearate, margarate, oleate, and elaïdate of mercury, is decomposed by contact with organic substances, such as lard or cerate. The mercury is then restored to the metallic state, and the mixture becomes black, (§. The same blackening occurs if the ointment is rubbed with a steel or iron spatula.)

Unguentum Hydrargyri (Double Fr.) **Neapolitan Ointment.**

With: iodine and iodides, chlorine and chlorides.

Vegetables containing Tannin

are: agrimony, silver-weed (*Potentilla anserina*), hips, oak-bark, pomegranate, galls, blackberries, red roses, tormentilla (§. nearly all the plants belonging to the natural families of the *Cupuliferæ* (oak tribe), *Gentianaceæ* (gentian), *Rosaceæ* (roses, brambles, &c.), and *Salicaceæ* (willow tribe), &c.

The incompatible substances are those mentioned under the article, "Tannin," which see.

*3. Prescribing such a method for the preparation of the medi-
cines, as does not attain the end proposed, or is of such a nature as
to change and destroy the efficacy of the substances employed.*

There are some substances which lose all their active properties
when prepared in one way rather than in another. Thus, the
essential oil and the distilled water of the cherry-laurel or of
bitter almonds have a well marked poisonous action, but their
watery extracts, on the contrary, are innocent. When we prescribe an infusion of juniper berries, the remedy is nearly inert,
unless we take care to have them first pounded. But it is need-
less to multiply examples of this kind, and we shall content
ourselves with saying that some medicines are soluble in water,
either hot or cold, whilst others are only soluble in alcohol,
ether, or oil; and it is therefore important not to leave the
prescription indefinite as to their mode of preparation.

SHORT SKETCH OF PHARMACY.

Definition.—Pharmacy is the art of choosing, collecting, preserving and preparing medicines. That portion of the science of medicine which treats of medicinal agents is termed Pharmacology, and is divided into three heads: 1. Medical natural history, or *materia medica;* 2. Pharmacy properly so called; 3. Therapeutics, (§. or the *modus operandi*), the medical properties and the proper applications of medicines. The art of prescribing likewise forms a part of pharmacology.

The choice and recognition of a medicine depends upon its having been defined by its most marked chemical and physical properties, so as to be distinguished from all others.

Collection.—The most favourable time for the collection of medicines has been named by Van Helmont the *balsamic time.* It varies much, and has great influence over their properties. Age, soil and the effect of cultivation have generally a well marked influence, and with the exception of emollient and mucilaginous substances, those parts of vegetables ought to be chosen, the flavour and odour of which are most decided.

In most cases the pharmaceutist ought to employ the kinds prescribed by the Codex, (French Pharmacopæia), yet substitutions are daily made; but it is always? (§. generally) from the same natural family, and even from the same genus, that the substitute (succedaneum) is chosen. Thus several species of *Rumex* may replace the *Rumex patentia*, and we employ indifferently *Symphytum tuberosum* and *S. officinale*, (comfrey), *Helleborus niger* and *H. viridis*, whilst we could not substitute white hellebore (*Veratrum album*) without inconvenience.

Roots are collected in spring and autumn, *woods* in winter, *barks* at the same time as roots, taking care, however, to select individuals which are neither too young nor too old. *Leaves* are gathered when the plant is in full luxuriance; *flowers* when they are full blown, with the exception of the red or Provence rose; *fleshy fruits* a little before their perfect maturity; *dry fruits* when the pericarp and the seeds are fully developed, but always before they change colour. The negligence which is shown in gathering certain capsular fruits explains the uncertainty of their therapeutical effects, as we see in the case of poppy seeds and the fruit of senna, &c.

Seeds are collected when perfectly ripe, that is to say, at the time of the natural dehiscence, if the fruit is dehiscent, or of the maturity of the pericarp if the fruit is indehiscent.

Those parts of plants which are to be employed whilst fresh, should be gathered in the early morning; when, on the contrary, we wish to keep them, it is better to collect them soon after sunrise, when the dew which covers them has evaporated. If they are gathered when wet, they become black whilst drying.

Drying those parts of plants which are collected in this country (France), ought to be done in such a way as to preserve the colour and flavour as much as possible. This operation is effected, in the first instance, by the sun in drying-rooms (a chamber under the roof, in which air circulates freely), and at last by a stove. When the substances are very fleshy, as the roots of the water-lily, elecampane, &c., they are divided into thin slices; the flowering tops, as melilot and lesser centaury, are placed in little packets, not too close together, so that the air may circulate amongst them, and they are surrounded by paper.

By means of graduated compression and drying, effected with care, we may remove from plants all the water which they contain; and if they are afterwards soaked in water, they imbibe it and resume their former appeararance and qualities. It is by this means that M. Masson, head gardener to the Horticultural Society of Paris, has been able to preserve kitchen-garden plants, such as cabbages, spinach, lettuces, &c.

Medicinal substances ought to be kept in suitable places; volatile ones should be enclosed in bottles carefully stopped with ground stoppers; deliquescent salts in a dry place; and flowers with bright colours, powders, the salts of antimony and of silver, and hydrocyanic acid should be kept in the dark.

OF THE PARTICULAR FORMS TO BE GIVEN TO MEDICINES

AND OF THE GENERAL PRINCIPLES WHICH OUGHT TO REGULATE THEIR PREPARATION AND ADMINISTRATION.

Of pharmaceutical forms, some are dependent upon the chemical properties of the active principle: thus, one principle is soluble in alcohol, another in ether, and a third in oils, &c., from which we have *alcoolés* (alcoholic tinctures) and *éthérolés* (ethereal tinctures), &c.

These forms must not give way when they are really important, though they may sometimes be sacrificed to the repugnance of the patient, of which we have spoken in another chapter.

We shall now give examples of each form.

AFFUSIONS.

Affusion is not a form of medicine, but a mode of applying it. Some persons will perhaps be surprized to see it mentioned here; but as there are certain precautions which ought to be taken in prescribing affusions, we have thought that they were not foreign to our subject.

Affusion consists in pouring upon various parts of the body either hot or cold water, or water medicated by the addition of sundry substances. The composition of these medicated waters will be treated of hereafter, under the head of *Lotions*.

Affusions are generally made with cold water, that is to say, from 12° to 18° Centigrade, or 54° to 64° Fahr. Their duration varies from two to ten or fifteen minutes. Affusion only differs from *douche* in the latter being poured from a more elevated place, in smaller quantities, but with more considerable force. (§. Cold affusions, whether in the form of simple washing with cold water or in that of the shower-bath, plunge-bath, &c., are valuable tonics to the system generally, and frequently restore delicate persons to vigour better than any other means; but unless properly used, they are productive of harm rather than good. They ought to be used *whilst the body is still hot, the moment the patient rises from bed*. If this is attended to, and the body is well rubbed immediately afterwards, a glow of warmth follows the application of the cold, and an increased strength is the result; but if a child, for example, is taken out of bed, and allowed to *become cool* before the water is poured on, it frequently happens that there is not vigour to restore the circulation to the skin, and injury rather than benefit is the result).

As to the word *Embrocation*, which has never been well defined, we employ it as a synonym for *Lotion* or *Fomentation*. Other writers have wished to make it into a special medicinal form, asserting that it differs from a fomentation in the short length of time it remains upon the skin, in the proportion of medicines which it contains being much greater than for fomentations, and in the nature of these medicines, which is always oily or fatty. Lastly, it has been also said that an embrocation is not a form of medicine, but simply a mode of application, consisting in soaking pieces of flannel, &c., with a liquid, which is always oily and of the ordinary temperature, and placing them in contact with a circumscribed region of the body, for a longer or shorter space of time. According to the sense which we apply to the word embrocation, it will always be possible to prescribe a lotion or fomentation instead of it, after what we shall now say.

In *pharmacy*, a lotion or lavage consists in washing a substance with the intention of separating some foreign matters. It is thus that we wash gum to remove a bitter matter; calomel to dissolve corrosive sublimate; flowers of sulphur to remove sulphurous acid, &c. In these cases we employ the word lotion, because the liquid exerts a solvent power; whilst we restrict the term lavage to cases in which the washing has only a mechanical action, such as the washing to which we subject plants to remove adhering earth. We conceive, moreover, that for a lavage the vehicle employed should always be water, whilst for a lotion it will vary according to the substance to be dissolved.

In *medicine*, on the contrary, we give the name of lotions and fomentations to liquid medicines intended to warm, to moisten, or to wash the external parts of the body, when they are themselves affected with maladies, or cover more deeply seated parts which are diseased.

Fomentations, like lotions, are applied by means of flannel, linen, cotton, or sponges soaked in different liquids, such as decoctions and aqueous infusions; vinous, alcoholic or ethereal fluids, solutions of acids or other substances, and oils, &c.

There is no well established distinction between lotions and fomentations; but we may say that fomentations are applied for a longer or shorter time upon the affected part, whilst lotions are only employed to wash the part, without remaining applied; so that fomentations approach more nearly to embrocations.

The quantities of fomentations and lotions to be prescribed are not strictly defined, and from two or three hundred grammes (℥vi to ℥x) to as many kilogrammes (℔v to ℔viii) are sometimes prepared. We ought, in prescribing them, to mention the temperature to be employed, the proper vehicle, the place for their application, the method of keeping them hot, and how soon they are to be repeated. (§. In applying a fomentation of simple hot water, or of water medicated with poppy heads, &c., the benefit derived is very much dependant upon the mode of application: and more harm than good sometimes results from neglect of the following rule, viz.: *never to let the patient become chilled during their application.* This is effected by the simple precaution of always employing *two* flannels, and having these large enough. If one only is used, the skin becomes chilled during the time occupied in removing the flannel, soaking it in the water, wringing it out, and re-applying it; but if two are used, one of them is ready, and can be applied the moment the other is taken off, by which means the part is never exposed to the air, no matter how long the fomentation is continued. In some diseases, *e. g.* rheumatism, peritonitis, &c., the patient is scarcely conscious of a degree of heat which scalds the nurse's hands. In this case, the fomenting flannels should be put into a towel, by which means they may be wrung out without being handled by the nurse, and may be applied far hotter than can be done by any other method).

Soapy Fomentation,

Soft soap	30 grms. (℥i.)
Washings of (wood?) ashes. .	130 grms. (℥iv.)

To be applied hot, by means of a flannel, and to be renewed several times daily. Application: scrophulous tumours.

(§. The French text merely says "ashes," but wood ashes are no doubt intended, both from wood being the chief fuel in France, and from the nature of wood ashes; as they always contain carbonate of potash, which alkali is known to be of value in scrophula.)

K

Antineuralgic Fomentation.

Cyanide of potassium . . 1 grm. (gr. xv.)
To be dissolved in :
Distilled water . . . 100 grms. (℥iii.)

Folds of linen are to be soaked in this solution, and applied to the painful part (forehead, orig.), and care must be taken to renew them frequently.

Antiherpetic Mercurial Lotion.

	ADULTS.	CHILDREN.
Corrosive sublimate. . .	8 grms. (℥ii.)	4 grms. (℥i.)
Alcohol	q. s.	q. s.
When dissolved, add:		
Distilled water. . .	190 grms. ℥v and ℥vi.)	200 grms. (℥vi.)

From 1 to 4 table-spoonfuls to be mixed with 500 grms. (℥xvi) of very hot common water. It will be useful to employ a wooden, porcelain, or glass spoon.

Lotion of Vegeto-Mineral Water.

Spring water . . . . 250 grms. (℥viiss.)
Tribasic acetate of lead . . 4 grms. (℥i.)
Alcohol. . . . . 30 grms. (℥i.)

Mix.

DECANTATION.

Decantation helps to assist washings, and has for its object the separation of matters of different density, and it is necessary to use it, in order to accomplish their complete separation. In this operation we make use of wide-mouthed vessels, broader at the bottom than the top, and pierced with several holes just above the lower part. The syphon and pipette, &c., are also used.

FILTRATION.

Filtration is an operation which consists in separating liquids from substances which they hold in suspension. For this purpose they are made to pass over bodies, the pores of which will allow the passage of the fluid, but not of the suspended matters; and whatever may be its character or arrangement, an apparatus which accomplishes this is a filter. It is most frequently made of unsized (blotting) paper, linen, cotton or woollen cloth, carded cotton, sand, powdered glass for acids, charcoal, &c.

In making a filter, our choice is determined by the nature of the substances to be filtered. Paper is most commonly employed; but as it always contains some soluble salts, it ought first to be carefully washed with warm water, especially when it is intended for liquids to be afterwards analysed, or to serve as beverages; a precaution which is too often omitted in the filtration of whey. When we wish at the same time to render a liquid clear, and to remove its colour, or an offensive flavour or odour, we employ filters made of washed *animal* charcoal; but we must not forget, especially in toxicological researches, that the charcoal always retains a small quantity of the salts which were even perfectly dissolved in the liquid. Charcoal acts by virtue of its porous character, and it has been shown by M. Bussy, that its properties vary with its physical condition.

When we wish to filter very volatile liquids, such as ethereal ones, a closed apparatus is used, such as is recommended by Messrs. Riouffe and Donovan.

VAPORIZATION AND EVAPORATION.

To evaporate or vaporize a body, is to convert it into vapour; but in practice the following difference is established between the operations. We speak of *vaporization* when we merely consider the vapour and its effects; for example, fumigations, vapour baths, &c. In evaporation, on the contrary, we only consider the residuum; for example, the extracts left by evaporation.

The ease with which bodies are converted into vapour is increased:

1. By the temperature being raised. (§. This requires no comment).

2. By the pressure being diminished. (§. The air presses upon all bodies, and acts as a great hindrance to their being converted into vapour. When this pressure is removed, as by the air-pump, some bodies, like ether, boil violently and are rapidly converted into vapour at the common temperature of the air; and all liquids boil, *i. e.* are rapidly converted into vapour 140° F. lower when the pressure of the air is removed, *i. e.* in a vacuum, than when it is still present. Hence, if we wish to evaporate a liquid quickly, we may either accomplish it by increasing the heat, or by removing the pressure of the air by placing it under an air-pump; and this latter plan is adopted in the preparation of some vegetable extracts and of sugar, which are injured by the heat that would otherwise be necessary).

K 2

3. By increasing the surface exposed to the air, by stirring the liquid. (§. The larger the surface exposed to the air, the more rapidly is the vapour carried away, and room made for fresh steam; hence, liquids evaporate more quickly in broad shallow vessels than in deep narrow ones; and stirring the liquid so as to make its surface into little waves, increases the surface, and promotes evaporation).

4. By heating the substances in vessels which are good conductors of heat. (§. If the vessel is of metal, the heat is conducted to a larger surface of the liquid than if it is made of earthenware or glass, which being bad conductors, allow the heat only to be applied to the bottom of the liquid).

(§. 5. By constantly bringing a fresh current of air over the surface of the liquid. Air can only carry off a certain amount of vapour, and when it contains this quantity, which varies with the degree of heat, it is said to be *saturated*, and evaporation then ceases until that portion of air is removed, and a fresh supply, free from vapour, is brought over the liquid. In this way it is that wet bodies dry so much more quickly on a windy day than on a still one; for the wind carries away the air which has absorbed its share of moisture, and brings a constant fresh supply. The influence of a current of air is much more important in the case of spontaneous evaporation, or evaporation unaided by artificial heat, than when such heat is employed, in which case it is of comparatively little importance).

There are three kinds of evaporation: 1. *In vacuo.* See Section 2, above. 2. Spontaneous. See Sect. 5, above. 3. By the aid of heat.

FUMIGATION.

Fumigation is a mode of applying sundry medicines which have been converted into vapour. It is a sort of vapour bath, applied to an external or internal surface of the body. Medicinal fumigations are composed of steam alone, or of water charged with aromatic principles, with alcoholic solutions, acids, different gases such as chlorine and sulphurous and hydrosulphuric acid, resins and burnt animal substances, &c.

In prescribing a fumigation, we must fix upon the medicinal substances, and when necessary, explain the manner of directing the fumigation to the part affected, and fix the length of time it is to be continued, and the intervals between each administration. It will sometimes be necessary to order the fumigation to be received upon flannel or some other kind of cloth, and to recommend that the skin should be rubbed with it.

Aromatic Fumigation.

Thyme . . . . . . As much as is wished.

Put it upon a chafing-dish (§. the lid of a warming-pan), to volatilize its aromatic portion, which is to be received upon a cloth, and applied to the debilitated member.

Fumigations of tobacco are employed per anum in strangulated hernia, and other kinds are used internally in affections of the air-passages and of the mouth. *Medicated cigars* have been invented, made with belladonna, stramonium and digitalis, &c. and M. Trousseau has also caused cigars to be made of paper previously impregnated with a medicinal solution and dried. In this way corrosive sublimate, arseniate of soda, and other medicines, have been of real service. Substances are also frequently put into a pipe.

Soothing Fumigation.

Stramonium. . | Of each, equal parts, in sufficient quantity to fill a single
Sage. . . | pipe.

(§. In spasmodic asthma stramonium is smoked alone, to the extent of three or four pipes or more, at varying intervals.)

The medicinal substances are frequently thrown upon hot cinders, so as to produce smoke in the room, which is chiefly done in fumigations with benzoin, frankincense, juniper berries, savin tops, burnt sugar, coffee, &c. These fumigations are employed to mask offensive odours, and in this case there is no prescription to be written.

(§. Nitric, or rather, perhaps, nitrous acid, is sometimes used as a fumigation by simply pouring a small quantity of fuming nitric acid into a saucer upon the table near which the patient is sitting. In some cases of phthysis and of chronic bronchitis with excessive expectoration, the acid fumes thus diluted with air and received into the lungs, have produced great relief by checking the secretion and improving the condition of the mucous membrane generally. It is quite under the patient's control, and may be used two or three times a day, according to circumstances and the relief produced).

INHALATION.

Inhalation consists in the inspiration of gases or vapours, and therefore approaches fumigations ; but the first of these operations is always effected by the mouth, and rarely by the nose.   Since the discovery of the anæsthetic properties of chloroform, ether, &c., this method of applying medicines has assumed a new importance.   Thus, inhalations of hydriodic ether are employed in strumous affections.   Chlorine, mixed with air and steam, has long been advised in different cases, (§. chiefly phthysis), but in the present day is nearly abandoned.

PULVERIZATION AND POWDERS.

The form of powder is one of the most convenient for the administration of medicines, as it presents the active principle in all its integrity, and it assists other operations also, for it more easily mixes with solvents, and readily forms intimate combinations.

Pulverization has for its object the reduction of a body to very small particles, with which end in view we must take account of the texture of the substance to be powdered, so as to use a mortar, a rasp, or a file, as may be most convenient. Whatever the instrument used, the body to be powdered must be very dry, especially in the case of organic matters ; and as spontaneous drying might in certain cases be too slow, they must be divided into small portions and dried in a stove.

Some substances before being powdered must undergo preliminary operations.   Thus, egg-shells and oyster-shells are calcined, and the powder is afterwards washed with boiling water. So, also, the *os sepiæ* and crabs' eyes are washed in order to remove an animal matter, which by putrefying, would give an offensive odour to the powder.

At other times we are obliged to soak the substances in water, as is done with rice and sago ; and so also nux vomica and St. Ignatius's bean must be subjected to the action of steam. As to silicated stones, it is indispensable to make them red hot, and then plunge them into cold water, after which they become friable.

The methods of pulverization most frequently employed are the following :

Contusion consists in striking heavy blows upon a body in a mortar. If much powder escapes, or if it is dangerous or disagreeable when breathed, or if the substance is high priced, the mortar should be covered with a skin of leather, to which the pestle is attached. (§. The irritating powder which arises from aloes may be prevented by adding a few drops of olive oil previous to commencing the operation).

Trituration is employed to reduce substances to powder which soften with the heat produced by percussion, and is accomplished by giving the pestle a circular movement round the interior of the mortar. *Gum-resins* are powdered in this way, after being first slightly dried.

Grinding consists in breaking up hard bodies by means of instruments of various forms, such as mills with iron teeth, grindstones, cylinders, &c. (§. Nux vomica is directed by the Ph. Ed. to be ground in a coffee-mill for making the extract. Capsicum pods and cantharides are more conveniently powdered in this than in any other way, owing to the very irritating powder which arises from them when pulverized in a mortar).

Pulverization by rubbing. Carbonate of magnesia, white-lead and agaric are almost the only substances reduced to powder by this method, in which a horse-hair sieve is placed over a sheet of paper, and the substance is gently rubbed through.

Porphyrization takes its name from the table of porphyry or marble upon which bodies are rubbed to powder (sometimes dry, and at other times moistened with some liquid) by means of a slightly convex stone rubber. It is indispensable that the porphyrizing table should be harder than the substance to be powdered.

Materials soluble in water (*e. g.* tartar emetic) or altered by that liquid (*e. g.* iron) should be powdered dry.

Pharmaceutists cannot be too strongly urged to porphyrize with great care ointments containing insoluble bodies, especially such as are intended for application to the eyes, such as the pomatum of Lyons, of Desault, (§. which contains red precipitate, tutty, acetate of lead, burnt alum and corrosive sublimate. Codex) and of oxide of zinc, &c.

Dilution, called also *levigation*, is employed to separate powders of different densities, or such as are mixed with coarse bodies either lighter or heavier than the powder we wish to obtain. The mixture is to be stirred rapidly in a large quantity of water, when the foreign bodies either come to the surface if lighter, or fall first to the bottom if heavier than the powder required, which is then obtained by pouring off the water which still holds it suspended, and allowing it to subside. This proceeding is often employed in commerce and the arts, (§. and is the method adopted for obtaining *very* fine *(impalpable)* powders, and for making the creta preparata of the pharmacopœias).

Pulverization by the aid of an intermedium. A great number of bodies cannot be powdered by themselves: thus we are obliged to add alcohol to camphor (§. and to hard compound extract of colocynth), and sugar to vanilla and gold leaves, in order to powder them. Fusible metals are powdered by means of heat. (§. Thus zinc and tin may be powdered by melting them, and pouring them into a mortar, heated a little above their melting-point, and stirring them rapidly as they cool.) Phosphorus is powdered by means of lime-water and heat, and the mixture is stirred up till it cools.

It is to pulverization through an intermedium that we ought to refer pulverization by means of chemical reaction: such for example as preparing powdered gold by means of chloride of gold dissolved in water, to which oxalic acid, or protosulphate of iron, is added, when the following changes occur:

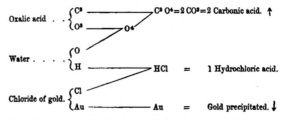

Proximate principles (*e. g.* starch, gum) ought to be powdered without anything being rejected, which is not the case with vegetable substances; for their first portions are sometimes rejected, as in grey cinchona (§. which, being partially covered with lichens, these will be the parts first broken off and powdered), and sometimes the last, as in red and yellow cinchonas, ipecacuanha and rhatany.

Powders are either *simple* or *compound*. The first is obtained by the pulverization of a single substance, the second, by a mixture of several powdered medicines. In preparing a compound powder, each of the component substances must be powdered separately, unless that is impossible; in which case we must resort to pulverization by the intermedium of one of the substances entering into the composition of the powder, and must make them as fine as possible.

Mineral substances are always porphyrized; but this is not always the case with vegetable ones. Sternutatory powders (snuffs) ought always to be coarseish. Substances to be made into emulsions are powdered by an intermedium. Whenever these substances easily undergo change it is best to add them to other powders only as they are required.

Substances which attract moisture ought not to form part of a compound powder; and although we have advised that powders should be made very fine, there are some bodies which must not be too finely divided; such as rhubarb and guiacum; but these are exceptions.

Powdered substances ought to be mixed with great care; and after being well triturated together, they should be returned into a sieve the bottom of which is not very tightly stretched, and passed through it several times; and as the heaviest substances sometimes fall to the bottom of the jar in which they are kept, the mixing should be renewed from time to time.

Powders are employed when a remedy is insoluble, or when it would irritate the stomach if given in an undivided form (for example, camphor); and powders may even be prescribed independently of the above conditions, if the physician thinks them the most suitable form.

Powders enter into both internal and external preparations, according to their nature, and the properties of their components.

Powders, either simple or compound, are given suspended in some vehicle, such as honey or an electuary, unleavened bread or soup, or they are made into the form of a pill. The dose for active substances (narcotics, and some vegetable alkalies, &c.) is from 1 to 10 centigrammes (gr. 1/6 to gr. iss) at first, gradually increased. Less active powers are given from the commencement, in doses of 10 centigrammes to 1 gramme or more (gr. iss to gr. xv or more).

When very active substances—such as strychnine, arsenious acid and chloride of gold—are to be administered under the form of powders, they are mixed with inert powders, such as gum, sugar or marsh-mallow.

DENTIFRICE POWDERS.

Powders, liquids, and some kinds of opiate intended to cleanse the teeth, are termed *dentifrices*. If they are in the form of powder or paste, they ought to be extremely fine and smooth; and the use of acid materials should be avoided as much as possible. It is better to employ neutral, or better still, alkaline substances.

Antiseptic Dentifrice Powder.

Red cinchona bark, very finely powdered . } Of each, ℥i.
Vegetable charcoal, „   „   „ .
Oil of mint, or of cloves . . . . 6 drops.

Porphyrise with care.

Ferruginous preparations quickly blacken the teeth. M. Mialhe attributes this colouration to a tannate of iron, and advises a powder containing tannin as a dentifrice, in order to form a soluble acid tannate of iron.

PULPES, PULPS.

Pulps are medicines of a soft consistence, either formed of the parenchyma of vegetables mixed with the juice which they contain, or obtained by a mixture of powders with a sufficient quantity of water. The substances which answer for the preparation of pulps may be either fresh or dried, whole or powdered; they are made either cold or hot, but most of them are prepared by heat (that is to say, by boiling, which gives them a better consistence); which should always be employed when it can be done without injury (that is, when the pulp does not contain any volatile ingredient). If it does, heat will alter its properties. Thus, the pulp of a raw onion would be rubefacient, but when cooked, it is emollient and maturative.

Boiling is indispensable in the preparation of pulps from dried substances; at least they must be made from the powder by the aid of boiling water. The boiling is effected in several ways: 1. By cooking the ingredients upon a coal fire. 2. By enclosing them in paste, and heating them in an oven. 3. By boiling them in water, or exposing them to steam.

Pulps easily undergo change; and those of cassia, tamarind, hips (§. and prunes) are the only ones now employed. They often contain copper, derived from the pans in which they have been boiled.

In prescribing them, the physician need only indicate the name and quantity thus:

> Pulp of raw onions .   .   .   . q. s. for a sinapism.
> To be applied to the calf of each leg.
> (§. Sinapism really means "mustard poultice," and is seldom used in any other sense in this country. By the French it is sometimes employed to indicate a rubefacient application generally.)

or

> Pulp of cooked onions .   .   . q. s. for a poultice.
> To be applied to the tumour.

or, again:

	ADULTS.	CHILDREN.
Pulp of cassia	5 grms. (ʒi 1/4.)	2 grms. (ʒss.)
> To be taken, at two doses, in wafer bread.

But to complete the prescription, and to follow the practice which we wish to establish both in internal and external applications, the physician ought to say whether he wishes the pulps to be prepared with or without heat, from the fresh or dried plant, and whether whole or powdered. There are only the pulps of cassia, tamarind and cynorrhodon (hips) which are prepared and kept cold in the present day; all others are prepared at the moment they are wanted. For internal use they are generally made into conserves. They may be given in doses of 2 to 3 grammes (ʒss to ʒ 3/4) in stewed prunes, in wafer bread, or suspended in some aqueous or vinous vehicle, as a mixture. Externally, they are employed to make poultices and glysters. The dose must be according to the purpose intended (§. e. g. for a poultice or other use).

SUCS, JUICES.

Juices are magistral medicines, either liquid, or soft and liquifiable by heat, obtained by pressing entire vegetable bodies, or
some portions of them. There are perhaps no preparations
which change so quickly; and therefore pharmaceutists never
keep vegetable juices except in some of the ways to be mentioned
immediately. The physician need only order them in amount
proportioned to his wants, without having to prescribe the mode
of their preparation. He should indicate the dose and the name
of the juices which he wishes for; and if it is necessary to combine those of several plants, or if he has to add any other substances, this must be specified.

Every body which is liquid or liquifiable by heat, and is contained in the organic tissues, may be considered as a juice; and
they are divided into five classes, according to their nature, viz.:
Aqueous, oily, resinous, and milky juices, and 5thly, essential
oils.

AQUEOUS JUICES.

Aqueous juices.—The nature of the vehicle characterizes them
as being without any fatty or resinous ingredient. They are
subdivided into three classes, which are well defined in their
composition, viz., *extractive, saccharine* and *acid* juices.

Extractive juices.—These contain *albumen, chlorophylle* and
extractive matter, and various salts. *Vegetable albumen* possesses
the same properties as that of the egg, and exists in plants in a
state of solution or suspension. It is coagulated by a temperature of 40° to 60° C. (104° to 140° F.) *Chlorophylle*
(*chloros*, green; *phyllos*, a leaf) is the green colouring matter of
leaves. The name of *chromule* (*chroma*, colour) has been given to
all colouring matters which are not white or green: but this
distinction is not made in the present day; whatever is not white
is called chlorophylle. This colouration is owing to the air
enclosed in the cellular tissue. Chlorophylle approaches resins
in its composition and properties; like them, it is softened by
heat, dissolved by alcohol and fatty bodies, and is slightly combustible. *Extractive matter* is not well defined: it varies in every
plant, but always possesses certain prominent features of resem-

blance in flavour, colour, &c. (§. being of a brownish colour, and at first soluble in water, but being rendered insoluble by long continued boiling or exposure to the air.)

Extractive juices require to be clarified; for which purpose they must be filtered cold. Clarification is a long process but may be expedited by using several filters. Another process, which is more rapid, is sometimes injuriously employed, viz., heating the juice to ebullition and filtering it whilst hot; but we must never forget that when the albumen is coagulated, and the chlorophylle and most of the extractive matter is removed along with it, the juice thus obtained is almost without flavour, and of merely a slight yellow colour; whilst if filtered cold, it possesses a brown colour, and a much more decided flavour. Extractive juices are always intended for internal use. They may be taken in the morning, or may be repeated several times a day. They are sometimes also employed in gargles, collyria, lotions, injections and glysters.

Saccharine juices.—Under the name of *sugar*, every substance is included which, under the influence of an active ferment (leaven or yeast), and of a suitable temperature (35° to 50° C., 95° to 122° F.), is converted into alcohol and carbonic acid (alcoholic fermentation). Under other circumstances, such as the ferment being too feeble, or the temperature too high, sugars undergo other kinds of fermentation, viz., the lactic, butyric and viscous fermentations; *i. e.* they are converted into lactic or butyric acid, or into a viscid, mucilaginous substance.

The different kinds of sugar are divided into four groups:

1. *Cane sugar,* furnished by the sugar-cane, the beet-root, maize, chestnut, the sugar-maple tree, and all fruits which contain sugar and no acid.

2. *Grape sugar,* furnished by saccharine and acid fruits, glucose or sugar of starch, and the sugar of diabetic urine.

3. *Sugar of milk,* which exists especially in the milk of the herbivora.

4. *Mushroom sugar,* found by M. Wiggers in ergot of rye.

(§. *Cane* sugar is too well known to require description. *Grape* sugar is not so sweet as cane sugar, and is granular rather than crystalline. It contains more of the elements of water than cane sugar, but it is less soluble in water and alcohol. Sugar of *milk* admits of being crystallized upon a thread like sugar candy: it is less sweet than cane sugar, and not so soluble in water. *Mush-room* sugar corresponds in essential properties with grape sugar, and like it, is capable of being converted into alcohol by fermentation. It consists of $C^{12} H^{13} O^{13}$, which is one atom less water than grape sugar ($C^{12} H^{14} O^{14}$). Gregory).

All these sugars are converted by acids and ferments into grape sugar; and molasses, or uncrystallizable sugars, are the products of change in different kinds of sugar. These things being premised, we will return to the saccharine juices.

Saccharine juices are characterized by the presence of cane sugar, and the absence of any considerable quantity of acid. They are obtained by dividing the substances containing them by various mechanical methods, and submitting the pulpy mass to strong pressure; afterwards clarifying the juice by cold filtration, and coagulating the albumen by means of heat. They contain *cane sugar, vegetable albumen, malic acid* and *malate of lime* in small quantities, *extractive* and *colouring matter, pectine* and *pectic acid.* Left to themselves, they undergo alcoholic, lactic or viscous fermentation, according to the temperature, and the nature of the juice itself.

Acid juices are characterized by the presence of a free vegetable acid in considerable abundance. They are *tartaric* acid in grapes, *citric* in oranges and citrons, *malic* in pears, apples, the elder and the mountain ash, and lastly, *malic and citric mixed* in gooseberries, strawberries, raspberries, cherries, &c., and *oxalic* acid in wood sorrel and rumex. They generally contain also sugar of the grape variety. Acid juices are prepared by breaking up the parenchyma, pressing out the juice and clarifying it, sometimes by simple filtration, sometimes by allowing fermentation just to commence. When exposed to a temperature of 25° to 30° C. (77° to 86° F.) they undergo alcoholic fermentation.

Preservation of juices.—M. Gay Lussac has shown that this fermentation cannot take place without access of air, and every method for their preservation is founded upon this important observation. The most ancient process consisted in pouring upon the surface of the juice, a thin layer of almond or olive oil, which does not easily become rancid. A method called "*mutisme*" has also been proposed, which consists in introducing a little sulphurous acid into the juice, which acts either by appropriating to itself the oxygen of the air, or according to M. Desfosses, by forming a combination with the ferment, which renders it incapable of exciting fermentation. This sulphurous acid may be obtained by burning a sulphur match in the jars intended to hold the juice, or by introducing a small quantity of sulphite of lime. But the plan most to be preferred is that of M. Appert, as modified by M. Gay, which consists in putting the juice into bottles surrounded with hay, which are then placed in a flat-bottomed pan full of cold water, which is to to be boiled and kept at this temperature for about half an hour. The bottles, whilst still hot, are to be closed and kept in a cellar, after the cork has been firmly fastened down by means of string or iron wire.

OILY JUICES.

Oily juices are empirically divided into *liquid* oils, which are *drying* or *not drying; soft* oils, *greases; solid* oils, *suets;* and *soft odorous* oils, or *butters.*

Fatty bodies may be considered as mixtures in variable proportions of the proximate principles, *stearine,* which is solid; *margarine,* which is soft; and *oleine,* which is fluid; so that the consistence of a fatty body depends upon the predominance of one or other of these principles. Under the influence of alkalies, stearine, margarine and oleine are converted into stearic, margaric and oleic acids, and into glycerine or the sweet principle of oils. According to another theory, glycerine is supposed to exist from the first, so that fats ought to be considered as stearates, margarates and oleates of glycerine; which latter, being a feeble base, is simply separated in the form of a hydrate by alkalies.

Fats ought to be divided chemically into four groups:

1. Fatty bodies upon which alkalies have no effect, viz.: *cholesterine, ambreine, ceraine, myricine, castorine.*

2. Those which are changed by alkalies into glycerine and a fatty acid, which are partly volatilized and partly decomposed by heat, viz: *stearine, margarine, oleine, ricinine* and *palmine.*

3. Those which are changed by alkalies into oleic and margaric acid, and into a greasy matter which cannot be converted into soap, viz.: *cetine* and *cerine.*

4. Those which are converted by alkalies into glycerine and

volatile fatty acids, and into oleic and margaric acids, viz.: *butyrine, hircine,* and *phocenine.*

Liquid fatty bodies are prepared by division and simple expression of the substance containing them, but the process is often assisted by the action of heat, which is indispensable when the fatty bodies are solid or soft.

Fatty substances ought to be kept from the contact of air. They form the basis of cerates, pomatums, ointments, plasters, and medicated oils; they are insoluble in water, but are soluble in ether; when not volatile, they are decomposed by heat into very variable products, the chief of which are inflammable gases.

Oils are employed internally in a state of purity in emulsions and looches, in doses of 8 to 30 grammes (ʒii to ʒi) or more, croton oil or oil of tiglium excepted, which is only given internally in doses of one to four drops, whilst externally it is used as a revulsive. Oils form the basis of liniments; are employed in glysters; and are applied superficially in poultices.

RESINOUS JUICES.

Resinous juices are obtained by natural exudation or by making incisions into various plants of the natural orders of *Coniferæ* and *Terebinthaceæ*, in which cases they are especially designated as *turpentines;* whilst they are denominated *balsams* when they contain benzoic or cinnamic acid. The absence of which acids essentially distinguishes resins from balsams.

Resins and resinous juices are insoluble in water; are fusible, rough to the touch, conduct electricity badly, and are soluble in alcohol, ether and fatty bodies.

Uverdorben distinguishes three classes of them:

1. *Resins which are strongly electro-negative,* which combine with alkalies, are soluble in ammonia, the solution frequently not depositing resin during a quarter of an hour's ebullition, and the alcoholic solution of which does not redden litmus. Such are colophane and one of the resins of copal.

2. *Resins moderately electro-negative,* which redden litmus when dissolved in alcohol. They are soluble in ammonia in the cold, but their ammoniacal solution when boiled deposits the resin. The resin of the pine (common resin), which when combined with soda forms *vegetable grease,* belongs to this class, as does the resin of copaiva.

3. *Resins feebly electro-negative*, the solution of which only reddens litmus when at the boiling-point. They are soluble in caustic alkalies, (liquor potassæ et sodæ), but not in ammonia, and they do not decompose carbonate of soda. Benzoin and the balsams of tolu and Peru belong to this class.

By contact with the air resinous juices lose their essential oil and solidify, and with magnesia they form solid compounds; a circumstance which is of importance in their administration.

MILKY JUICES.

Milky juices take their name from the milk-like character which they possess, and which is due to caoutchouc or resinous matters which they hold suspended. Lettuce juice is the only one amongst them which is used in medicine; when evaporated it goes by the name of *thridace* or *lactucarium*.

ESSENTIAL OILS.

Essential or volatile oils, or essences, are proximate principles which sometimes exist ready formed in the vegetables furnishing them, and at other times owe their formation to the reaction of certain principles upon each other, (*e. g.* essences of mustard and bitter almonds. See pp. 41 and 49).

They are always bodies rich in carbon and in hydrogen (§. many of them consisting of these two elements alone); they are insoluble in water, but are soluble in alcohol and ether; and they are divided, according to their consistence, into solids *stéaroptène*, (camphor), and liquids, *eléoptène*, (oil of lemons). Chemically, they are divided into three classes:

1. *Hydrocarbons, essences.* Nearly all of these are isomeric, like the oils of turpentine, copaiva, savine, lemon, &c., (§. which are all $C^{10} H^8$).

2. *Oxygenized essences,* which, according to M. Dumas, may all be considered as oxides of some hydrocarbon. Such are the oils of the *Labiatæ*, (§. *e. g.* oil of lavender, $C^{16} H^{14} + O^2$), of the *Umbelliferæ*, (§. *e. g.* oil of anise, $C^{20} H^{12} + O^2$), and of the *Lauraceæ*, (§. *e. g.* camphor, $C^{10} H^8 + O$, though this scarcely comes strictly under the head of *oil*).

3. *Azotized (nitrogenized)* or *sulphurous essences,* which are generally the result of reactions, which are only produced by the action of water and a suitable temperature upon the substance

L

from which they are obtained; such as the essence of mustard, of horse-radish, and of other *Cruciferæ*.

When exposed to the air, essential oils become converted into resin, and are solidified; some are converted into acids, like the essence of bitter almonds, which by absorbing oxygen, produces benzoic acid.

Some essences are obtained by pressure, in cases where a large quantity is accumulated in a single point, such as the essential oils of the *Aurantiaceæ*; and others by distillation with water, such as the oils of the *Labiatæ* and the *Lauraceæ*.

They are employed internally in mixtures and oleo-sacchara (see Index) in the dose of a few drops; externally, they are used as fumigations, and for glysters and liniments, and are poured upon the surface of poultices.

FECULÆ.—STARCHES.

These are officinal medicines, employed for both internal and external use. Internally, they are prescribed in the form of jellies (§. *blanc-manges*) and tisanes, and they are also administered in glysters. Externally, they are employed as poultices and for making soothing fomentations.

In chemistry, as well as in pharmacy, the words fecula (starch) and amidon (amylum) indicate one and the same thing; but in domestic economy, on the contrary, we designate, under the name of fecula, such ternary* substances as are rendered blue by iodine, and can be used as food, (§. *e. g.* starch, arrow-root, tapioca), whilst we apply the term amidon to the feculæ which are separated by putrefaction from the gluten of the cereals (*Gramineæ*), and which, tainted principally with lactic acid, are employed in the arts, and sometimes in medicine, but are never used for food.

The name of "farina" (or flour) is given to seeds and the fruit of the *Gramineæ* when reduced to powder. It is principally composed of amidon, (or starch), gluten and fatty? (§. saccharine) matters.

Iodine renders feculæ blue, as we have said, and the degree of colour is more intense in proportion as the starch grains are larger. The iodide of amidon heated to 60° or 80° C. (140° to

(§. * Containing these elements, *e. g.* starch, $C^{12} O^{10} H^{10}$.)

176° F.) loses its colour, but regains it on cooling; .(§. but a temperature below 100° F. is sufficient to prevent the formation of the blue colour in the first instance). It is only when *free* that iodine produces this colour, the iodides and hydriodic acid only colouring starch when the iodine is set at liberty (§. as by the addition of nitric or sulphuric acid, or chlorine). Under the influence of *diastase*, a neutral azotized principle which is formed during the germination of barley, and also when boiled for many hours with diluted mineral acids (sulphuric), starch is converted into *dextrine*, and *glucose* or starch-sugar. (§. One part of diastase is capable of converting 2000 parts of starch into sugar).

MEDICINES PREPARED BY SOLUTION.

Of **solution generally.**—By solution or dissolution is understood an operation which consists in making a body melt in a liquid. There is, however, a distinction between solution and dissolution. We call that a "solution" in which, by simply removing the liquid, we can recover the body dissolved, of the same character as it was before the operation; whilst we speak of a "dissolution" when a solid has undergone some chemical change, as for example, when we dissolve a metal in an acid; but in a simple solution no chemical action occurs, as when we make sugar or gum dissolve in water; but this distinction is seldom made.

A reduction of temperature always accompanies the solution of a solid body in a liquid, (§. or the conversion of a solid body into a liquid without solution; from which circumstance we are able to obtain cooling lotions and freezing mixtures; the first by mixing powdered salts, such as saltpetre and sal-ammoniac with cold water, and allowing solution to proceed slowly and gradually; and the latter by mixing together salt and snow or ice, which are both solid bodies, but rapidly form a liquid compound when mixed. The reduction of temperature when the solid bodies become liquid is so great that the thermometer falls to 0° F., or 32° below freezing). On the contrary, the temperature is raised whenever dissolution takes place, because it is accompanied by chemical action.

Bodies generally dissolve better with heat than in the cold,

L 2

—

and agitation also facilitates solution. A substance entirely soluble in a liquid is easily dissolved if placed upon a porous diaphragm upon the surface of the liquid. If substances are mixed which are of different degrees of solubility, we must vary the mode of proceeding according to the end proposed, which remark is also applicable when soluble substances are mixed with insoluble ones.

The nature of the vessel in which we operate is generally of no consequence; but if the liquid or the matter to be dissolved is capable of acting upon metals, we must employ vessels of glass or porcelain. If the materials are volatile, or are liable to be altered by heat, we must operate with close vessels in the first case, and in the cold in the last.

It now remains for us to point out succinctly the different modes of solution, to treat of the substances which can be dissolved, and to study the particular action of each solvent.

Maceration is an operation which consists in submitting one or more substances to the action of a liquid of the temperature of the surrounding air. It is preferred for volatile principles, or for such as are alterable by heat, and the product takes the name of maceration, or *macéré*. (§. There is no equivalent term in our language nearer than "cold infusion.") Medicated wines and tinctures are prepared by maceration. (§. These "*macérés*," or cold infusions, are more aromatic than when made by heat, as the aromatic principle, which is often volatile, is not dissipated. They also keep better than hot infusions, because they do not dissolve the starch, which generally soon decomposes when dissolved).

Infusion consists in pouring a boiling liquid upon the substances which we wish to dissolve. It is preferred for bodies of a delicate texture, and which easily yield their principles. If the tissue is hard, it must be divided in the first instance. The solution obtained goes by the name of *infusion*.

Digestion consists in keeping a liquid below the point of ebullition for a longer or shorter period, along with the body whose active principles we wish to remove. If the liquid is volatile, we operate in close vessels, such as stills, so as to recover the volatilized products by condensing them.

Decoction differs from the preceding operation, in the liquid being kept for some time at the boiling-point, so that the temperature varies with the nature of the liquid. It will be 100° C. (212° F.) for water; 78° C. (172° F.) for alcohol; 35° C. (95° F.) for ether. Here also we operate in a distilling apparatus in the case of volatile liquids.

Decoction is always employed when we wish to attack bodies which are difficult to penetrate, or when we wish to dissolve principles which are insoluble at a lower temperature, or such as are only formed by ebullition, such as gelatine; but it must always be avoided when the substance is easily altered, such as rhubarb, cassia, senna, liquorice, &c., and also when we operate upon bodies which contain volatile ingredients, unless we wish to separate the volatile, and merely to preserve the fixed principles. (§. The aromatic ingredient in vegetable bodies, which is commonly a volatile oil, is generally impaired, if not entirely dissipated by boiling, and therefore decoctions are much less aromatic and agreeable than infusions of the same substances).

In these operations we ought to remember that principles which are insoluble by themselves, are sometimes dissolved by the aid of others, so that guiacum (resin), which is insoluble, is extracted from the root by boiling in water.

Lixiviation consists in pouring a hot or cold liquid upon a powdered substance disposed in layers more or less thick, and more or less beaten down, according to the nature of the materials. Sometimes it is even necessary to macerate or infuse the powder previous to putting it into the vessel. The apparatus goes by the name of the *apparatus for displacement.*

(§. Lixiviation is generally confined to the solution of saline matters from insoluble substances with which they are mixed. Thus, the ashes of wood are "lixiviated," by which means the carbonate of potash contained in them is dissolved, and the charcoal and other insoluble ingredients are left behind.)

SOLUTIONS BY WATER (HYDROLÉS).

TISANES, DIET DRINKS.

A *tisane* is an aqueous solution, slightly charged with medicated principles, which is employed as an ordinary drink by sick persons.

Tisanes ought to be but slightly unpalateable to the taste, and they should be frequently changed, simply to avoid tiring the patient. When taken hot, they have a sudorific action. The quantity to be prescribed daily varies from a demi-litre (about 3/4 of a pint) to two or more litres (3 or 4 pints) ; but except in special cases we ought not to go beyond three litres, as a larger quantity is very weakening.

Tisanes may be sweetened with sugar, honey or syrup; they may be diluted with milk or whey, or, in certain circumstances, a small dose of wine, tincture, extract, or expressed vegetable juice, salts, acids, &c., may be added; but they should never be added until after the liquor has been strained.

Tisanes are taken hot or cold, by glassfuls or by cupfuls, during the course of the day, at intervals more or less distant, but always some time before or after a meal.

They are prepared by infusion, decoction, maceration and digestion. Infusion ought to be prescribed for aromatic plants, or plants containing extractive principles allied to starch, which we wish to separate; and the flowers and leaves of vegetables, the fruits of the umbelliferæ, sassafras root and canella bark should be treated by infusion. Decoction is employed for very dense substances, the principles of which are only dissolved by the aid of heat. Barks, woods, roots, the fruit of cereals (wheat, &c.), furnish tisanes by decoction. We must, however, observe, that all roots cannot be treated by decoction; for there are some which contain so much starch that, by long continued boiling, they would give a tisane so thick as to be disagreeable to the taste, without any additional efficacy. These substances ought to be pounded and treated in the cold, or by simple infusion.

The following table, drawn up by M. Robert, which has been taken from the manual of M. Soubeiran, may be useful for consultation in this respect.

Roots containing Starch, or Amylum.

Rest-harrow (ononis), aristolochia (serpentary), belladonna, herb-bennet (geum), calamus aromaticus, nasturcion, carrot, columba, cabbage, black hellebore, male fern, strawberry, galanga (a species of alpinia), ginger, marsh-mallow (althæa), the hop, ipecacuanha, iris (orris root) iris nostras, jalap, mallow, water-lily, the nettle, sorrel, dock, parsley, pæony, radish, liquorice, monks' rhubarb (rumex alpinus), rhubarb, sarsaparilla, sassafras, Virginia-snake root, China root, tulip, turbith (ipomœa turpethum), valerian and zedoary.

Roots which do not contain Starch, or Amylum.

Angelica, elecampane (inula helenium), borage, chicory, comfrey, mustard, onion, taraxacum and squill.

Maceration is also employed in cases where the principles are alterable by heat, as in the tops of wormwood and rhubarb root, which yield tisanes by simple maceration.

When substances contain a bitter principle which we wish to remove, they should be first treated with hot or cold water, or be slightly boiled. Iceland moss (lichen islandicus) is treated in this way, when we only wish to have its mollifying properties. It is important to strain the tisane before adding salts, acids or syrups. In these mixtures we must take into consideration the incompatible substances which have been pointed out. (See "Table of Incompatibles," p. 118.)

Tisanes are chiefly made from the materials at the time they are wanted; thus a tisane is prescribed with emollient materials, bitter materials, &c.

In prescribing a tisane, it is nearly always sufficient to prescribe the base (the materials), the excipient (the vehicle, *e. g.* water) and the proper pharmaceutical operation.

Sudorific Tisane.

	ADULTS.	CHILDREN.
Sudorific "species" (½. Guaiacum wood. sarsaparilla and smilax china, of each, equal parts), Codex	60 grms. (℥ii.)	40 grms. (℥x.)
Digest them for four hours in:		
Hot water	1000 grms. (℥xxxii.)	500 grms. (℥xvi.)
Strain, and add:		
Compound syrup of sarsaparilla :	60 grms. (℥ii.)	40 grms. (℥x.)

To be taken, in five doses, in the course of the day.

Alkaline Tisane.

	ADULTS.	CHILDREN.
Crystallized bicarbonate of potash .	2 grms. (ʒss.)	0,50 centigrms. (gr. viii.)
Tincture of cinnamon / vanilla of each .	1 grm. (Mxv.)	10 drops.
Simple syrup	60 grms. (℥ii.)	40 grms. (℥x.)
Water	1000 grms. (℥xxxii.)	500 grms. (℥xvi.)

Mix. To be taken daily by cupfuls at a time.

LEMONADES.

Drinks which have a mineral or vegetable acid for their base go by this name. They are therefore distinguished into mineral and vegetable lemonades. They ought to be sweetened like tisanes, and in the same proportions.

Sulphuric Lemonade.

Common water .	. .	1000 grms. (℥xxxii.)
Simple syrup .	. .	60 grms. (℥ii.)
Sulphuric acid .	. .	q. s.

To be agreeably acid (§. about ℥ss of acid. s. dilut:). To be taken as a common drink during the day.

We may proceed in the same way for other mineral lemonades. Vegetable lemonades are prepared with vegetable acids or acidulous fruits, When prepared from fruits, they are made by maceration or infusion; and when obtained by infusion (called *lemonade cuite*, cooked lemonade), they are better borne by the stomach, because they contain muco-saccharine matter.

Citric Lemonade.

	ADULTS.	CHILDREN.
Crystallized citric acid . . .	2 grms. (℥ss.)	0,75 centigrms. (gr. xii.)
Sugar	60 grms. (℥ii.)	40 grms. (℥x.)
Oleo-saccharum of citron. . .	1 grm. (Mxv.)	0,50 centigrms. (gr. viii.)
Water	1000 grms. (℥xxxii.)	500 grms. (℥xvi.)

Mix. To be taken by glassfuls in the day.

Acid fruits, and acetic, citric and tartaric acids may be replaced by their syrups in the dose of 60 grms. (℥ii) to a kilogrm. of water (℥xxxii).

APOZEMES, APOZEMS.

(§. A term formerly used by British writers as synonymous with decoctions.)

Apozems, like tisanes, are solutions in water of the proximate principles of vegetables, but they differ from them by containing a much larger proportion of the medicinal principles, and in never being employed as an ordinary drink for the patient. Apozems are magistral preparations, little used in the present

day, their disagreeable taste having not a little contributed to
their falling into neglect; and as the sick are often slow in
digesting, they frequently remain like a weight in the stomach,
which is not without inconvenience. These medicines answer
for special indications, being sudorific, purgative, &c.; and those
most frequently used are the "white decoction of Sydenham,"
"decoction of herbs," the anti-scorbutic apozem, the tisane of
Feltz, &c.,* Although apozems are magistral preparations, it is
sufficient to indicate the quantity to be employed, (custom having
consecrated their formulæ). They are prescribed cold or tepid,
in one dose, or in several, in the morning, fasting, or at different
hours of the day. They should only be prepared for a single day
at a time, for if long kept, they decompose.

For medicines which may be regarded as a kind of apozem,
the physician has generally no occasion to make a prescription.
It is sufficient to indicate the medicine which he desires, and the
pharmaceutist will prepare it very well from this indication.

BOUILLONS, BROTHS.

Bouillons are obtained by boiling the flesh of certain animals
in water. Care must be taken to let them grow cold, in order
to remove the fat. For the rest (all the world knowing how to
make broth), the physician has only to prescribe it, without saying how it is to be prepared.

It has lately become the fashion to give the name of "broth of
herbs" to a liquid in which herbs have been boiled, with the
addition of butter and salt, but it is more truly an apozem.
Broths are either alimentary or medicinal. Alimentary broths
are prepared from the flesh of full-grown mammiferous animals
(the ox, sheep, &c.); whilst medicinal ones are made with less
nourishing kinds of flesh, such as veal, chicken, &c.

Herbs may be added to broths, keeping in view the desired
object; they should be emollient, aromatic, &c.

(§. * The white decoction of Sydenham contains: Powdered hartshorn, 1; bread
crumbs, 3; gum arabic, 1; sugar, 4; orange-flower water, 2 parts; and common
water, q. s.—Codex.

(The anti-scorbutic apozem contains: Burdock, rumex patientia, horse-radish root,
cochlearia officinalis leaves, fresh water-cress, fresh buckbean leaves (menyanthes),
of each, 1 part; water, 125 parts.—Codex.

(The tisane of Feltz contains: sarsaparilla, 64; isinglass, 10; powdered sulphuret
of antimony, 80; water, 2000 parts.—Codex.)

MUCILAGES.

Mucilages are preparations which have for their base gum or some other analogous principle, held in solution or suspension in water. Mucilages are liquid, but they are generally of the consistence of white of egg. For the rest, their consistence is proportioned to their different purposes; and they are rendered more or less liquid by using a greater or less quantity of water.

Mucilages may present various colours. That of quince seeds is reddish; and the root of the marsh-mallow furnishes one of a light yellow colour. The substances employed to prepare them are gum-arabic, gum-dragon, mallow and marsh-mallow (malva and althæa) roots, grain (e. g. groats), linseed, flee-wort (plantago psythium), feculæ.

In a prescription, the physician indicates the quantity of the mucilage and the name of the plant or of the organ which furnishes it.

Mucilages are employed, diluted with water, under the form of tisanes, or by tea-spoonfuls, sweetened with sugar, syrup, &c.

Mucilages of gum are especially indicated as a medium for suspending substances which are not soluble in a vehicle, or for giving tenacity to pâtes and lozenges.

EMULSIONS.

An emulsion is a liquid magistral medicine, of a milky appearance, and of a white or yellowish-white colour, prepared either from oily seeds and water, or from oil suspended in water by means of mucilage, or the yolk of an egg, or sugar, or from resins and gum resins suspended in the same way.

Those emulsions are called false which are prepared by suspending oils, resins or gum-resins in water by means of mucilage or yolk of egg. True emulsions are only prepared from sweet almonds, pistachio-nuts, hemp seeds and the seeds of the melon, pumpkin, water-melon and cucumber. The last four seeds are called "the cold seeds."

Powders and salts may be mixed with emulsions, but we must be careful not to add acid or alcoholic liquids, as they coagulate them. The acids form an insoluble compound with the vegetable albumen, and the alcohol appropriates the water of the emulsion to itself, and the albumen is equally coagulated. Tisanes and emulsions are sometimes mixed in equal parts; for example, the tisanes of barley (barley-water), of dog's-tooth and of gum (mist. acaciæ).

Emulsions easily undergo change, and ought only to be prescribed for immediate use. The quantity to be employed in the twenty-four hours should not exceed 500 to 600 grammes (ʒxvi to ʒxx).

Simple Emulsion, or Milk of Almonds.

Almonds	30 grms. (ʒi.)
Sugar	30 grms. (ʒi.)
Cold water	500 grms. (ʒxvi.)
Orange-flower water . .	15 grms. (ʒss.)

Pound the almonds (having first blanched them) in a marble mortar with the sugar, add a little water, and make a uniform paste, to be diluted afterwards with the remainder of the water. Strain it through a linen or woollen cloth, and add the orange-flower water.

The emulsions are all made after the above fashion. Whether for emulsions or for linctuses, we advise that both sweet and bitter almonds should be prescribed by weight, and not by number, as is often done, for the size of the almonds is liable to vary.

Emulsion of Copaiva.

	ADULTS.	CHILDREN.
Common water	350 grms. (ʒxii.)	150 grms. (ʒv.)
Copaiva	60 grms. (ʒii.)	10 grms. (ʒiiss.)
Mucilage of gum arabic. . .	60 grms. (ʒii.)	10 grms. (ʒiiss.)
Simple syrup.	60 grms. (ʒii.)	20 grms. (ʒv.)

Make an emulsion, to be taken by a coffee-cupful at a time in the course of the day.

Purgative Emulsions, with Castor Oil.

	ADULTS.	CHILDREN.
Fresh castor oil	30 grms. (ʒi.)	10 grms. (ʒiiss.)
Rub the oil in a mortar with half the yolk of an egg, and add:		
Common water	200 grms. (ʒvi.)	100 grms. (ʒiii.)
Orange-flower water } of each	30 grms. (ʒi.)	30 grms. (ʒi.)
Simple syrup . . }		

SOLUTIONS BY ALCOHOL (ALCOOLÉS), TINCTURES.

The alcohol of wine (spirits of wine)* which is the only one employed in pharmacy, is the product of the decomposition of the sugar contained in the juice of the grape under the influence of a ferment, which is only formed by contact with the air. It is a colourless liquid, with a highly aromatic odour and a sharp and burning taste, and it may be condensed as a *bi*hydrate of bicarbonated hydrogen.

Bicarbonated hydrogen . $C^4 H^4 + 2$ water $2 HO = C^4 H^6 O^2$, or as a *mono*hydrate of ether . $C^4 H^5 O + 1$ water $HO = C^4 H^6 O^2$, its entire formula being as above, $C^4 H^6 O^2$.

Amongst simple bodies, alcohol dissolves phosphorus, sulphur, iodine and bromine; and amongst compound ones, resins, volatile oils, nearly all acids and the alcaloids, tannin, grape-sugar and fatty bodies at a high temperature. It does not dissolve gum, starch, vegetable nor cane-sugar when anhydrous, but if diluted with water it does dissolve it.

Anhydrous, or absolute alcohol, as it is called, is obtained by distilling commercial alcohol with bodies which have a great attraction for water, but which cannot act upon itself chemically, such as quick lime, dried carbonate of potash, &c. (§. This limitation as to the kind of substance for removing the water is important, as sulphuric acid is often employed for removing water from gases, and is so generally at hand that a young student might be tempted to employ it. If he did so, he would obtain ether instead of anhydrous alcohol).

Eau-de-vie (brandy) is obtained by the distillation of wine, and ranges from 47° to 65° per cent. (18·5 to 24.5 Cart.), and has a refreshing and agreeable flavour. It is frequently made from commercial alcohol and water, coloured with burnt-sugar, (caramel), and often has acrid matters added to give it a high flavour. The taste is the best means of detecting these adulterations.

(§. * Although commonly called "spirit of wine," the alcohol used by British pharmaceutists is never obtained from wine, but is distilled from malt. It does not differ in its chemical properties, but its flavour and odour are less aromatic.)

ALCOHOLIC TINCTURES, (ALCOOLÉS).

Tinctures are officinal preparations, obtained either by the solution, maceration or digestion of the principles of certain substances in alcohol, or by the simple mixture of alcohol with an acid or alkaline liquid. They are simple when they contain the active principles of a single substance, and compound when they contain those of several.

The *Codex* employs alcohol of three degrees of strength: 1. Of 88 per cent. (34° Cartier, sp. gr. 843), for resins and balsams, such as those of ambergris, tolu and amber, &c. 2. Alcohol at 80 per cent. (31° Cartier, sp. gr. 861) for substances containing resinous principles and essential oils, like aloes, anise, castoreum, musk, nux vomica, vanilla, saffron, &c. 3. Alcohol at 56 per cent. (21° Cartier, sp. gr. 920) for matters of an extractive nature, *e. g.* absinthium, cantharides, colchicum, opium, guiacum, ipecacuanha, cinchona, squill, valerian, &c.

With some few exceptions, the proportion of the substance to the alcohol should be as 1 to 4.

Alcoolatures are medicines so named by M. Béral, and only differ from tinctures (*alcoolés*) in being prepared from fresh substances. The principal alcoolatures are those of aconite, belladonna, digitalis and hyosciamus.

(§. *Percolation* is not adopted by the French Codex for making tinctures, nor has the London College prescibed it in their last Pharmacopœia. It consists in reducing the solid substance to a powder, more or less fine, according to circumstances, pressing it more or less firmly upon a broad-bottomed filter, and allowing the alcoholic liquid gradually to trickle through it, dissolving the active principle in its passage. According to the Ph. Ed., the tinctures which are not so well prepared by percolation as by simple maceration, are Tr. Aloes, Al. c Myrrha, Assaf., Benz. Co., Camph., Castorei., Ammon., Guiaci., Guiaci. Co., Kino., Opium, Op. Ammon., Op. Camph., Quassia Co., Tolu. All the others are more conveniently made by percolation).

MEDICATED WINES, (ŒNÉOLÉS).

A wine is called medicated when it holds in solution one or more medicinal principles. Fermentation, maceration and alcoholic tinctures may furnish medicated wines.

When employed pure, or added to a tincture, a tisane, or any other vehicle, they are given internally in the same doses as vinegars; but those containing opium or narcotic substances, (*e. g.* veratrum), are only taken by drops. Externally, they are employed in frictions, fomentations, lotions and glysters, &c., and the doses are then increased; but the wines of opium and of narcotic substances are always prescribed in very small quantities.

Three kinds of wine are used in their preparation :

1. *Red wines*, rich in tannin, and containing also tartaric, œnanthic* and acetic acids, bitartrate of potash, tartrate of lime, a yellow colouring matter, and a blue ditto, which is reddened by acids, and is held in solution by alcohol.

2. *White wines*, which contain either very little or no blue colouring matter, or tannin.

3. *Generous wines*, which approach white wines in composition, but are richer in sugar and alcohol. These last are employed in operating upon substances of a delicate nature or easily changed, such as saffron, opium, &c.

4. Sparkling (effervescing) wines, which are not employed medicinally.

MEDICATED VINEGARS, (ACÉTOLÉS).

Officinal, liquid medicines, formed of vinegar, and charged by maceration with different medicinal principles.

They are employed internally as well as externally. Internally, they are mixed with tisanes, mixtures, &c., in quantities varying from 4 to 15 grammes (ʒi to ʒss), and are given by tea-spoonsful when taken alone by the mouth. Externally, they are employed in frictions, fomentations, lotions and fumigations, &c., and the doses are not more precise.

Vinegar from wine ought alone to be employed. *Oxycrate* is made with vinegar ʒi, cold water ʒxxx. Medicated vinegars are simple or compound.

MEDICATED ALES (BRUTOLÉS).

These are magistral medicines resulting from the action of

(§. * Œnanthic acid, in the form of œnanthic ether, is the cause of the peculiar odour of wine, which adheres so obstinately, as to enable us to say whether a vessel has or has not contained it.—*Greg. Chem.*)

beer upon certain substances, such as cinchona, savin tops, the leaves of the lesser centaury, and anti-scorbutic plants, &c. They are little used in France. The physician has only occasion to order them, the druggist not requiring any particular formula for preparing them. They should only be ordered in the quantity immediately required, on account of the facility with which they change.

SOLUTIONS BY ETHER.

ETHEREAL TINCTURES (ÉTHÉROLÉS).

These are officinal liquid medicines produced by the solution of volatile oils, balsams, resins, wax, several fatty substances, various colouring principles of vegetables, several mineral salts, and some simple substances in an ether (see p. 74), but chiefly in sulphuric ether.

Ethereal tinctures are employed like alcoholic ones, but their action is not so powerful, and the doses must be larger (§ and the stimulating influence of the ether itself bears a greater proportion to the effect of the medicinal substance dissolved in it, than is the case in alcoholic tinctures; in which the effect of the alcohol is often so trifling compared with that of the substance contained in it, that it may generally be disregarded, which cannot be done in the case of ethereal tinctures). It is necessary to remember in prescribing ethereal tinctures, that though easily *mixed* with water, they are so slightly *soluble* that they sometimes separate when left at rest.

SOLUTION BY OILY BODIES.

MEDICATED OILS (ÉLÆOLÉS).

These are liquid officinal medicines, formed by the solution of various substances in olive oil. Some of them are employed internally as emulsive mixtures, but they are chiefly intended for external use.

Medicated oils are obtained by maceration or digestion, and are simple or compound (baume tranquille, still-balsam). Olive-oil, which ought alone to be employed in their preparation, is often adulterated by white or poppy-oil. This fraud is recognized by means of fuming nitric acid, or the acid nitrate of mercury, which quickly solidify pure olive-oil, whilst solidification is much slower in proportion as the poppy-oil is more abundant.

SOLUTION BY ESSENTIAL OILS (MYROLÉS).

Messrs. Henry and Guibourt have given the name of *myrolés* to volatile oils holding fatty, resinous, or other substances in solution. Two of these preparations are still employed, viz., *baumes de soufre anisé* and *térébenthiné,** which are solutions of sulphur in the essential oils of anise and turpentine. Amongst the compound ones are the *baume de vinceguère* or *de condom*.

OF DISTILLATION,

AND THE MEDICINES OBTAINED BY DISTILLATION.

Distillation is always performed in closed vessels, and is intended to separate volatile parts from those which are either less volatile, or not volatile at all. Bodies which are capable of being converted into vapour are the only ones which can be distilled.

Of the three kinds of distillation practised by the ancients one only remains to us (for extensive use) this is distillation per *ascensum*, or upwards, by means of an alambic, still, &c. As to distillation per *latus*, or laterally, by a retort, it is only employed in operating upon very small quantities, and distillation per *descensum*, or downwards, is entirely abandoned. (§ This last observation only applies to pharmaceutical operations, for distillation by descent is still practised in distilling zinc from its ores. Distillation *in vacuo* does not properly come under the head of distillation, as its object is the removal of the volatile parts which are lost by the operation, whilst the object of distillation, properly so called, is the separation and preservation of the volatile portions).

An alembic made of tinned copper, consists of the body, the water-bath, the head, and the worm enclosed in a tub of cold water. In distillation from a retort, the apparatus is composed

(§. * " Balsamum sulphuris anisatum and terebinthinatum."—Ph. Ed. 1722.)

of the retort, its tube or beak, and a tubulated globular receiver, to which a long tube is attached, in order to carry off noxious, or unnecessary, or uncondensible gases. The retort may be heated by a naked fire, a gas flame, a sand-bath, a water-bath, a salt-bath, or an oil-bath, according to the greater or less volatility of the liquid to be distilled. The condensation of gases by a Woulf's apparatus is only a species of distillation, which, however, we shall content ourselves with having simply named in this place.

DISTILLED WATERS (HYDROLATS).

These are liquid officinal medicines obtained by the distillation of water from one or several substances. Their basis, according to the researches of chemists, is formed of volatile principles of a very varied nature. Essential oils appear to be the active portion of these preparations.

Internally, distilled waters are employed as an excipient or vehicle for juleps, mixtures, and potions, and they are sometimes put into tisanes.

Externally they are employed in collutoires (See definition), collyria, fomentations, gargles, injections, glysters, and lotions. The doses depend upon the nature of the different preparations of which they form part.

Essential oil predominates in distilled waters, but they must not for all that be considered as simple solutions of an essence; for the attempts to obtain them by mere artificial mixture have not hitherto succeeded. Lastly, certain distilled waters contain special principles; e. g., that of valerian contains valerianic acid, and that of pepper is ammoniacal.

Distilled waters are prepared by the distillation of substances in contact with water, or sometimes with steam. The first mode is indispensable for the distilled waters of bitter almonds and of mustard, and is employed for that of lettuce and horse-radish. Experience has pronounced in favour of distillation by steam, for roses, orange flowers, linden, balm, hyssop, &c. Different apparatuses have been proposed for performing this distillation; but the one described by M. Soubeiran in his "Treatise on Pharmacy" ought to be preferred.

Fresh vegetables are generally employed for making distilled waters; but the dried plants are preferred for those of melilot,

M

marjoram (origanum), linden, &c., in all which cases a prelimi-
minary maceration is very useful.

Distilled waters are subject to changes, the nature of which is
not very well known; thus, orange-flower water often contains
acetic acid, from which we may see how imprudent it is to keep
it in copper vessels; for which bottles made of wrought iron
ought to be substituted. Orange-water, when well prepared by
the distillation of the flowers is reddened by sulphuric acid,
whilst what is made artificially by mixing distilled water and oil
of neroli (orange) is not reddened by that acid.

Distilled waters should be kept in a cool and dark place.

ALCOOLATS (ESPRITS) SPIRITS.

This name is given to officinal pharmaceutical preparations,
procured by the distillation of alcohol from one or more medicinal substances.

Spirits are employed internally in mixtures, or are added to
tisanes, in the dose of a few drops, once or oftener in the day.
They may be taken on sugar, or mixed with syrup. Those
which contain essential oils in large quantity, or resins, are
precipitated by water, and generally give it an opaque tint.

Externally they are employed in fomentations, frictions, fumigations, injections, and lotions. The doses are then less precise,
and may be from 30 to 60 grammes, or more (ʒi to ʒii).

ÉTHÉROLATS (ETHEREAL SPIRITS, ESPRITS ÉTHÉRÉS).

By the name of etherolats is designated the product of the
distillation of ether from one or more medicinal substances.
They consequently contain only the volatile principles of plants,
and are little used.

ACÉTOLATS (ESPRITS ACÉTIQUES, ACETIC SPIRITS).

Concentrated, or crystallizable, or glacial acetic acid, boils
at 120° C. (248° F.). When most concentrated it still contains
an equivalent of water, and is represented by the formula
$C^4H^3O^3 + HO$; but it is wine vinegar which is exclusively employed in the preparation of medicated vinegars and acetic
spirits; 100 parts of good vinegar ought to saturate 10 parts
of pure and dry carbonate of potash. Its saturating power may,

it is true, be increased by adding mineral acids, such as sulphuric, nitric, or hydrochloric acid, the presence of which is recognized by the means indicated in the article on poisoning by the acids (See Toxicology).

Acetic spirits are then the products of the distillation of vinegar from one or more medicinal substances, and they contain only volatile products; they are simple when they contain the principles of only a single substance, and compound when they contain several. This class of medicines is little used.

MEDICINES PREPARED BY EVAPORATION.

EXTRACTS.

An *extract* is the product obtained by evaporation from a maceration, an infusion, a decoction, or a clarified or unclarified juice. Extracts are made from vegetable or animal substances. Their composition is extremely complicated, and these medicines cannot be fully relied on when employed, owing to the different methods followed in their preparation.

They are divided according to the mode of their preparation into five classes:

1. Extracts prepared from vegetable juices, (§. formerly called inspissated juices).
2. Extracts, the vehicle for the extraction of which is water.
3. Extracts prepared by wine.
4. Extracts prepared by alcohol.
5. Extracts from animal matters.

The extracts from vegetable juices are preferable to all the others, if they are prepared in a vacuum; but it is very seldom that such are met with amongst pharmaceutists. After them we must have recourse to aqueous and alcoholic extracts, and we shall not dwell upon vinous extracts, for there are only two in use in the present day; viz., the extract of wine of opium, or *laudanum opiatum*, and the extract of black hellebore of Bacher.

The activity of alcoholic extracts is generally much greater than that of corresponding aqueous ones, and it is therefore necessary to guard against substituting one for the other. Alcoholic extracts are most frequently employed in pills, because if we make them enter into mixtures they render them turbid and disagreeable. Watery extracts are more readily

M 2

added to mixtures, owing to their more easy solubility. The doses of extracts generally cannot be laid down with precision, for they vary in every case. We may, however, say that they are the same as those of the corresponding powders.

Extracts of the juices of fruits are termed *robs*. Extracts prepared by means of ether and vinegar are little used; for we only employ the ethereal extract of male fern, and the acetous extract of opium. Lastly, the extract of ox-gall is the only one prepared from animal substances.

Extracts are of three degrees of consistence; soft, when they are of the consistence of honey (ext. of juniper); hard, or of pill consistence, when they can be rolled in the fingers without sticking (ext. of opium); and dry, when they are brittle (thridace, Lactucarium).

Extracts have also received different names, according to the principles which predominate in them. Thus, we speak of gummy, mucilaginous, resinous, and gum-resinous extracts.

In extracts prepared from the juice of plants, it is indispensable to distinguish those which contain fecula, from those which are depurated, or without fecula, for the first are more active because they contain all the principles of the plant, whilst the second have lost some of them by the separation of the chlorophylle and the albumen at a high temperature, a part of the extractive matters, and the volatile constituents.

It has been already mentioned, that extracts prepared from the juice of fruits are called *robs*, a term which it is scarcely worth while retaining, for it is easy to distinguish two extracts of the same plant, when one is prepared from the leaves, and the other from the fruit, as in the case of belladonna. We may add, that the robs of elder (Sambucus), and of buckthorn (Rhamnus) are the only ones employed.

We may add, that by a new process of evaporation *in vacuo*, M. Granval, Pharmaceutist to the Hospital at Rheims, prepares extracts of great purity, and of such activity, that if his process is adopted, the therapeutical action of the extracts so prepared is so much increased that all the doses must be considerably diminished.

Extracts are employed under the form of powder if they are dry; and of pills, draughts, mixtures, glysters, &c.

The doses are very variable. For the very active extracts

(nux vomica, aconite, belladonna, and opium), they vary from 0,01 to 0,20 centigrammes (gr. 1/6 to gr. iii). The other extracts, which are nearly inert, such as gentian, buckbean (Menyanthes), chicory, and sarsaparilla, may be employed in every dose.

MEDICINES HIGHLY CHARGED WITH SUGAR.

SACCHAROLÉS.

All medicines which contain a large quantity of sugar take the name of *saccharolés*. According to their consistence they are divided into:

1. Liquid—syrups, honeys, and oxymels.
2. Soft—conserves, jellies, pâtes.
3. Solid—Oleo-sacchara, saccharures, lozenges, and pastilles.

SYRUPS.

Liquid officinal medicines, of a viscid consistence, produced by the concentrated solution of sugar alone or sugar mixed with honey, in water, wine, or vinegar. Syrups are generally charged with the active principles of one or more medicinal substances. They are only employed internally, and are given by themselves, or mixed with a draught, an emulsion, a tisane, &c.

They are employed as an excipient or a medium in certain preparations, pills, &c. They are given by tea-spoonfuls or table-spoonfuls in doses from 4 to 15 grammes (ʒi to ʒss), and in mixtures from 30 to 60 grammes (ʒi to ʒii). Even when they contain the most poisonous agents they are always made in such a way that they may be safely given in doses of 30 grammes (ʒi).

A syrup when well prepared ought to be transparent, with some few exceptions; and when too deep in colour for us to judge of its clearness, it must be diluted with water, and the mixture should not present any muddiness if the syrup has been well prepared. The most certain method of obtaining a transparent syrup is to use the best sugar.

Simple syrup, or syrup of sugar, is the basis of a great number of compound syrups, and is prepared, first, by simple solution, and secondly, by boiling and clarifying by means of albumen, paper, and charcoal.

Many plans are adopted in preparing medicated syrups. 1. By simple solution. In this operation sugar of good quality must be used, and melted at a gentle heat in the proportion of 2 parts of sugar to 1 of the liquid; but for the juices of fruit the proportion of sugar is rather less. The following are prepared by simple solution.

1. Syrups with distilled waters: orange-flower, mint, rose, &c.

2. Syrups with acid juices: gooseberries, strawberries, cherries, blackberries, citrons, &c.

3. Syrups with the juices of plants: asparagus, peach-blossoms, water-cress, &c.

4. Syrups with aromatic or changeable infusions: violets, red poppy, tolu, digitalis, &c.

5. Syrups with vinous solutions: syrup of (cinchona) bark, syrup of saffron.

Syrups by simple solution and evaporation.

Syrups of buckthorn, nettle, and fumitory.

Syrups clarified by means of albumen.

Syrups of marsh-mallow, snails.

Syrups obtained by mixture with simple syrup and evaporation.

Syrups of gum, ipecacuanha, poppy (diacodium), extract of opium, tartaric and citric acids, and rhatany.

Syrups obtained by mixture with simple syrup without evaporation.

Syrup of acetate of morphia, sulphate of quinine, and the salts of the alkaloids.

Syrups prepared by a mixed method.

This method is employed for aromatic substances, which ought also to furnish fixed principles. In this case, the substance is first subjected to distillation, and a first syrup is made by simple solution with the distilled liquid, and a second with the decoction which remains in the body of the still, and the two are afterwards mixed. Or we may make a very concentrated syrup with the decoction, and then add the distilled liquid. The antiscorbutic syrups, and amongst the compound syrups that of erysimum, and amongst the simple ones, the syrups of peach-blossoms made from the dried flowers are obtained in this way.

Distilled waters, solutions, macerations, digestions, infusions, decoctions, vinous liquids, the juices of fruits or of plants, and emulsive liquids are all employed for making simple syrups. A method very much used in the present day, and which yields syrups of a uniform constitution, consists in preparing the syrups with the extracts dissolved in water, and adding simple syrup. As to the compound syrups they are made:

1. By distillation; *e. g.* syrup of erysimum, (anti-scorbutic).
2. By decoction; *e. g.* simple syrup of sarsaparilla.
3. By decoction and infusion; *e. g.* compound syrup of sarsaparilla, or the cook's syrup.
4. By infusion; *e. g.* syrup of the five aperient roots. (§. The *greater* aperient roots are smallage, fennel, asparagus, parsley, and butchers broom; the *smaller* are grass, madder, eryngo, capers and chammoc).
5. By infusion and maceration; *e. g.* syrup of rhubarb, or the compound syrup of chicory.
6. By digestion; *e. g.* syrup of calf's lights.

PRESERVATION OF SYRUPS.

A well prepared syrup ought to show 32° (§ sp. gr. 1·286) when boiling, and 33° or 34° (§ sp. gr. 1·298 to 1·309) when cold. If too much concentrated they crystallize, if too little they ferment. In this latter case pharmaceutists are in the habit of correcting them by boiling them over again.

Syrups ought to be kept in a cool place. M. Mialhe advises that they should be enclosed in bottles whilst hot, and that these should be turned with the neck downwards. Syrups of the juice of fruits are subject to a change which nothing can prevent, viz., the cane-sugar which is employed in their preparation is converted into grape-sugar, and the whole crystallizes into a mass. We may, however, to a certain extent prevent this change by closing them up whilst hot, and keeping them in a cellar.

MELLITES (HONEYS).

Honeys are syrups in which the sugar is replaced by honey.

The honey which is produced by bees (*apis mellifica, hyménoptères*) is a mixture in variable proportions of a crystallizable sugar analogous to that of the grape, and an uncrystallizable one, of a little vegetable acid, and of odorous and colouring principles very variable in nature and quantity, a little wax, and an azotized matter named *couvain*. It is often bleached by exposure to the air, and rendered white by mixing it with starch, which is recognized by the effect of iodine.

Honey is clarified by simply boiling it. If we wish to prepare compound honeys, we employ unsized paper, moistened with water, for this clarification; and indeed honey should always be purified, to accomplish which object we are advised to boil it with carbonate of lime or magnesia.

A simple "honey" is merely water and purified honey boiled to the consistence of a syrup, and frequently decolourised by animal charcoal.

A *hydromel* is a mixture of honey and water, or of syrup and honey, either with or without the addition of other medicinal principles, and is a species of tisane.

> Syrup of honey.   .   .   60 grms. (℥ii.)
> Cold water   .   .   .   1000 grms. (2 livres—℥xxxii.)
> Mix. To be drunk, by a glassful at a time, during the day. ·

The compound honeys in use are those of mercuriale (dog's mercury), and red roses (*miel rosat*), and that of (acetate of) copper, or the unguentum egyptiacum, which is only employed externally.

Oxymels differ from honeys in their water being replaced in their preparation by simple vinegar, forming simple oxymel, or by compound vinegars, forming oxymel of squill, &c.

SACCHAROLÉS MOUS (SOFT PREPARATIONS OF SUGAR).

CONSERVES (CONFECTIONS, ELECTUARIES).

These are officinal medicines, which ought to be comprised under the generic name of electuaires, from which they only differ in being formed of a single medicinal substance and the excipient (the vehicle). However the Codex of 1837 admits compound conserves also.

We must, however, add, that conserves always contain sugar as their basis; whilst electuaires seldom contain it.

Conserves may be prepared in five different ways :

1. With fresh plants; *e. g.* water-cresses.
2. With dried plants, by boiling; *e. g.* elecampane.
3. With the fresh plants by boiling; *e. g.* marmalades.
4. By boiling the plants with sugar; *e. g.* angelica.
5. With dried plants reduced to powder; *e. g.* roses.
(See Electuaries, p. 171).

GELÉES (JELLIES).

This name is given to preparations medicinal and alimentary, and officinal, or magistral, which are principally formed of sugar, and a gelatinous or mucilaginous matter. They may be divided into:

1. Animal jellies, which owe their consistence to gelatine; *e. g.* calves-foot jelly.

2. Vegetable jellies, which owe their consistence to cooked feculæ; *e. g. lichen islandicus;* or to gelatinous principles of a vegetable origin (pectine, pectic acid); *e. g.* quince, apple, currant and rashberry jellies, &c.

3. Vegeto-*animal* jellies, which are prepared by the decoction of certain vegetables, to which is added Corsican moss gelatine.

Animal jellies quickly putrify; feculent vegetable jellies can be preserved for a short time; and those of fruits are more easily kept.

Jellies possess the advantage of giving to the patient but little of a nutritive or medicinal principle, though under a large bulk, and they just serve to cheat his appetite. They are generally employed internally; but some among them are prescribed in glysters, as a means of nourishing the patients in certain cases. The doses employed vary from 15 to 100 grammes (ʒss to ʒiii).

PATES, (PASTES).

This name is given to officinal compound medicines of the softness of bakers' dough, but which do not stick to the fingers. They are formed of sugar and of gum, dissolved in water or in some medicinal substance. They are evaporated, so as to unite these principles by degrees, and give them the pliancy and the consistence of paste. They are employed internally in doses more or less variable. Pâtes, properly so called, are divided into *transparent*, or such as are made without agitation, like jujubes

of brown liquorice, and *opaque*, or such as are made with agitation, like the pâtes of marsh-mallow, lichen, &c. caustic and cos-
The name of pâtes is also given to different the preceding
metic preparations, which have no analogy with
medicines.

SACCHAROLÉS SOLIDES, (SOLID PREPARATIONS OF SUGAR)

ELÆO-SACCHARUM, OLEO-SACCHARUM.

This name is given to mixtures (or possibly to combinati
of sugar and essential oil, which ought then to be miscible
water. They are obtained by trituration, and the pr
one drop of essential oil to a drachm of sugar.
obtained by rubbing a piece of sugar upon the
fruits of the *Hesperideæ* (orange) tribe. This la
a more fragrant product than the first. (§
is sometimes given to a lump of sugar upon
drops of an essential oil have been placed).
internally in powders, electuaries, mixtures,

SACCHARURES.

A generic name, which designates offi
cines that are solid, and formed by the
medicinal principles, which are disso
getable juices.

TABLETTES AND PASTILLES, (MO

Officinal, solid, dry, brit
spherical form, prepared
or aromatics. Pastilles
each other, but the n
medicines which ar
contain sugar and
blettes) is given t
substances unit
still, of gum-t

ANOMALOUS COMPOUND MEDICINES.

ELECTUARIES, (CONFECTIONS, OPIATES).

The medicines designated by the name of electuaries are of the consistence of soft paste, and are generally composed of powders or extracts united by means of a syrup, of sugar, honey, or a conserve. Pulps, salts, gum-resins, essential oils and distilled waters, &c., may also serve for the composition of electuaries. These preparations still bear the name of *confections* or *opiates*, though the Codex only applies the name of opiates to electuaries which contain opium. Electuaries are officinal or magistral medicines, and are divided into *simple* and *compound*. They are simple when they are formed of a single medicinal body and of the excipient, and are called compound when they have been prepared with an excipient and several substances. (§. One of the French electuaries, Theriaca, certainly does contain *several* substances, for it is composed of seventy-two ingredients).

Electuaries possess the great advantage of rendering the administration of powders less offensive to the sick.

Astringent Electuary.

	ADULTS.	CHILDREN.
Extract of rhatany	2 grms. (ʒss.)	1 grm. (gr. xv.)
Conserve of red roses . . .	120 grms. (ʒiv.)	60 grms. (ʒii.)
Syrup of poppy (white) . . .	8 grms. (ʒii.)	4 grms. (ʒi.)
Catechu (powdered)	1 grm. (gr. xv.)	0,50 centigrms. (gr. viii.)

Mix. To be taken by a spoonful at a time.

Electuary, with Myrrh.

	ADULTS.	CHILDREN.
Powdered myrrh	4 grms. (ʒi.)	1 grm. (gr. xv.)
Honey	15 grms. (ʒss.)	10 grms. (ʒiiss.)

Tonic Electuary.

	ADULTS.	CHILDREN.
Powder of yellow cinchona . .	48 grms. (ʒiss.)	15 grms. (ʒss.)
„ „ wild valerian . .	8 grms. (ʒii.)	2 grms. (ʒss.)
„ „ juniper berries . .	8 grms. (ʒii.)	2 grms. (ʒss.)
Honey	q. s.	q. s.

Let an electuary be made.
Dose: Two boluses daily, of ʒss each, for adults, or gr. viii each for children.

PILLS.

Pills are medicines of the consistence of stiff paste which does not stick to the fingers, of a round form, and not exceeding 40 centigrammes (gr. vi) in weight. This kind of preparation is employed, especially when the substances are energetic in small volumes, and have a disagreeable odour or flavour. Their effect is sometimes not produced until long after they have been swallowed, their solution in the stomach being more or less slow.

All medicinal substances may enter into the composition of pills; their preparation is therefore extremely varied.

1. When the ingredients are solid, a soft or liquid excipient is prescribed.

2. If they are soft or liquid, their excipient will be some inert powder.

They are commonly rolled in some vegetable powder, or sugar, or magnesia, to prevent their adhering together, and to conceal their odour and flavour. They are sometimes even covered with gold or silver leaf, but we must avoid this plan whenever mercury, free iodine or sulphur enters into the composition of the pills. At other times, as in the case of boiled turpentine, they are preserved in water.

Oil, vinegar, oxymel of squill, syrups, bread-crumb, extracts, mucilages and inert powders are the excipients most frequently used.

Mucilages (§. and bread-crumb) have the inconvenience of making the pill-mass hard when it dries, and on this account they ought to be avoided as much as possible.

Volatile oils do not hold the pill-mass well together, unless they are rich in resinous ingredients. They should be very rarely used.

Alcohol, in the dose of a few drops, softens gums and gum-résins, (§. camphor and compound extract of colocynth) and gives them a convenient consistence.

Excipients which are easily drawn out should be chosen in preference to others; such are soap, honey and the syrups, which answer the purpose perfectly.

An excipient will be useless when the materials have naturally the required consistence; and extracts are generally in this condition.

Solid excipients which absorb superabundant liquids the most perfectly are always to be preferred.

Syrups, extracts, mucilages and honey are the most convenient excipients for uniting powders.

The inert powders of liquorice, marsh-mallow and starch are usefully employed for giving the requisite consistence to extracts and soft matters.

Soap unites fatty matters very well, (§. and is useful in purgative pills to aid their solubility).

There are some substances which soften when they are mixed together, *e. g.* camphor and copaiva; and we must therefore add an appropriate excipient, such as yolk of egg. The same thing is sometimes observed when we mix some extracts, and especially extract of ox-gall, with alkaline matters.

In making pills, it is frequently necessary merely to decide upon the basis, leaving the pharmaceutist to choose the excipient; but in certain cases, the excipient itself being active, it is necessary to fix the dose.

It is common to prepare a quantity of pill-mass, which is to be divided into a certain number of pills, which shall weigh from gr. 3/4 to gr. vi, of which the patient will take one or more, at different hours during the day, taking care to swallow a small quantity of some liquid each time, to assist their solution.

It is generally said, that pills should be taken on an empty stomach, and at a considerable distance from a meal; but for ourselves, we think that it is nearly always better to take them during a meal; first, because the stomach does not then find itself immediately under the influence of substances, which, if not always dangerous, seldom fail to act more or less disagreeably; secondly, because its absorbent action is more certain; and lastly, because they are then taken more easily.

Antineuralgic Pills.

ADULTS.

Extract of stramonium · } of each 50 centigrms. (gr. viii.)	
Watery extract of opium }	
Oxide of zinc . . . . 8 grms. (ʒii.)	
Excipient . . . . . q. s.	

For 40 pills.

From one to eight may be taken in the course of the twenty-four hours, and the dose should be pushed until the patient experiences hallucinations, or at any rate, considerable disorder of vision.

Pills for Chronic Catarrh of the Bronchi and Bladder.

	ADULTS.		CHILDREN.
Turpentine	15 grms.	(℈ss.)	10 grms. (ʒiiss.)
Balsam of Tolu . . .	2 grms.	(℈ss.)	1 grm. (gr. xv.)
Ammoniacum	4 grms.	(ʒi.)	2 grms. (℈ss)
Watery extract of opium. .	40 centigrms. (gr. vi. {		25 centigrms. (gr. iiiss.)
Excipient	q. s.		q. s.
For 78 pills.	To take 5 daily.		To take 1 to 4 daily

Antigastralgic Pills.

	ADULTS.	CHILDREN.
Nitrate (tris-nitrate) of bismuth . . . } of each . Chalk . . . }	4 grms. (ʒi.)	2 grms. (℈ss.)
Extract of opium . . . {	0,20 centigrms. (gr. iii.)	0,05 centigrms. (gr. 3/4.)
Conserve of roses . . .	q. s.	q. s.

For 48 pills. To take 4 or 5 daily.

(§. The dose of nitrate of bismuth is very small compared with that usually prescribed by British physicians, who seldom give less than gr. v to gr. x for a dose; whilst in this case it is not quite gr. iss.)

Tonic Pills of Sulphate of Quinine.

	ADULTS.	CHILDREN.
Sulphate of quinine. . . {	0,20 centigrms. (gr. iii.)	0,10 centigrms. (gr. iss.)
Extract of dandelion (taraxacum) .	q. s.	q. s.

For 8 pills, of which the patient may take 4 in the course of the day.

Copaiva Pills.

Balsam of copaiva } of each. . equal parts.
Calcined magnesia }

To be made into pills of 40 centigrms. (gr. vi) each, of which 2 to 4 must be taken daily.

We may add, that the form of pills is very inconvenient in the case of children, from the difficulty of making them swallow them. They ought therefore to be very small, and not to exceed 0,02 to 0,05 centigrammes (gr. 1/3 to gr. 3/4).

CAPSULES.

Medicines of a repulsive flavour are sometimes introduced into vesicles, formed of some substance which is soluble in the stomach. It is generally gelatine, sugar, or a mixture of sugar and gum, which forms the capsules. Pills are also frequently covered with one or two coats, by dipping them into a gummy or gelatinous solution, and afterwards drying them.

BOLS (BOLUSES).

A bolus is only a pill which exceeds 40 centigrammes (gr. vi) in weight; but it is necessary to add, that boluses are generally of a softer consistence than pills, and that the form of a sugar-plum is given to them to assist their being swallowed, and they are covered with gelatine, or some similar substance.

GRANULES.

Granules, introduced into practice by Messrs. Homolle and Quevenne, are formed of nothing but sugar and a medicinal substance. Their preservation is indefinite, and their solution is always easy. They are intended to supplant common pills, principally in the administration of very active medicines. They generally contain 1 milligramme (gr. 1/60) of the active ingredient.

POTIONS.

A *potion* is a liquid medicine, intended to be taken by the spoonful. There are several kinds of potions; but the distinctions are purely conventional, and it is difficult enough to give well marked distinguishing characters to each of the varieties admitted.

Custom has consecrated four kinds of potion; viz., the julep, the looch or loch, the mixture, and the potion properly so called.

JULEPS.

The word julep, comes from a Persian expression, which means "sweet drink." A julep is a drink generally composed of distilled waters, infusions, and syrups. Sometimes mucilages and acids are added; but never powders or oily substances, which could interfere with its transparency.

Juleps are often prepared of sedative, soothing, expectorant, or refrigerant substances. They contain from 125 to 250 grms. (f ℥iv to f ℥viii), and are given by table-spoonfuls, or in two or three doses. It is generally in the evening that they are taken.

Soothing Julep.

	ADULTS.	CHILDREN.
Syrup of extract of opium . . .	8 grms. (℥ii.)	2 to 4 grms. (℥ss to ℥i.)
Syrup of Tolu	30 grms. (℥i.)	20 grms. (℥v.)
Orange-flower water	25 grms. (℥vi.)	15 grms. (℥ss.)
Distilled lettuce water	125 grms. (℥iv.)	68 grms. (℥iiiss.)

To be made *secundum artem*, and taken, by a table-spoonful at a time, from hour to hour.

LOOCHS, LOCHS, LOKS (LINCTUSES).

The looch, or linctus, is a drink of greater consistence than that of the julep, and is similar to that of a syrup. The basis is almost always mucilage, and oils, or active medicinal substances, frequently enter into it.

Three kinds of looch are distinguished according to their colour, viz.: the white, the green and the yellow. The white looch takes its colour from the emulsion which forms part of it; the green owes its colour to saffron and syrup of violets, which mixing their yellow and blue colours form a green; and the yellow arises from the yolk of egg which it contains.

The formulæ of the different looches being consecrated by long custom, it is sufficient to prescribe them in the following way:

White Pectoral Looch or Linctus of the Codex.

(℞. Sweet almonds (blanched) . . . ℥ii and ℥ii.
Bitter almonds   „   . . . ℥ii.
White sugar. . . . . ℥ii.
Oil of almonds . . . . . ℥ii.
Gum tragacanth (powdered). . . ℥ii and gr. xiv.
Orange-flower water . . . . ℥ii.
Water . . . . . . ℔i, ℥iii and ℥v.)

or :

White Pectoral Demi-Looch of the Codex.

(℞. There is no preparation of this name in the *Codex*; but the Looch Huileux contains about half the above ingredients, and is probably the one meant.)

The green looch is not much used, and is prescribed like the white one. As to the yellow one, it is frequently employed for the same purposes as the yellow emulsion or mulled eggs. It is prescribed in the same way as the white looch.

The *Codex* indicates a fourth species of looch, called "looch without emulsion," which differs from the foregoing in being made without emulsion. Lastly, we ought to mention "marmalade looches," a name given by M. Opoix, pharmaceutist at Provence, to mucilaginous preparations analogous to looches, but in which the almond emulsion is replaced by butter of cocoa, and oil of sweet almonds. According to M. Opoix, these looches alter less quickly than common ones.

Looches are given to the extent of 125 grammes (ℨiv). When we wish to prescribe a compound looch, we state what substance the pharmaceutist is to add to the white looch. The nature of the medicine may sometimes require a particular mode of mixing, which the physician ought also to specify.

Kermetised Looch.

	ADULTS.	CHILDREN.
Kermes mineral	1 grm. (gr. xv.)	0,10 centigrms. (gr. iss.)
White looch	No. 1 (℥. 125 grms.—ℨiv.)	No. 1 (℥.125 grms. ℨiv.)

To be taken, by a table-spoonful at a time, from hour to hour. To be stirred before being taken.

Looch, with White Oxide of Antimony.

	ADULTS.	CHILDREN.
White oxide of antimony . . .	5 grms.(gr. lxxv.)	1 to 2 grms. (gr. xv to ʒss.)
Rub the oxide with a little syrup, and add :		
White looch	125 grms. (ℨiv.)	125 grms. (ℨiv.)

A table-spoonful to be taken from hour to hour. To be stirred before being taken.

Laxative Looch, for Children.

White looch of the *Codex*	No. 1 (℥. 125 grms.—ℨiv.)
Syrup of white roses, or of peach flowers . .	30 grms. (ℨi.)

Mix. One half to be taken at night, and the other half the next morning.

MIXTURES.

Mixtures are potions which, in a small volume, contain a considerable quantity of an active principle; from which definition we see that they do not differ essentially from potions properly

N

so called. M. Cottereau thinks that the name of mixture ought to be confined to very active liquid mixtures, administered in very small quantities, or by drops, in some suitable vehicle, or upon sugar. For certain medicines mixtures is synonymous with mingling.

Tonic Mixture.

(Example of a mixture approaching the sense of potion.)

	ADULTS.	CHILDREN.
Dry extract of cinchona	8 grms. (ʒii.)	1 grm. (gr. xv.)
Water	200 grms. (ʒvi.)	100 grms. (ʒiii.)
Syrup of Tolu	60 grms. (ʒii.)	30 grms. (ʒi.)

Mix. A table-spoonful to be taken every hour.

Obstetric Mixture. (Mixture in the sense of M. Cotereau.)

Freshly powdered ergot of rye . .	1 grm. and 50 centigrms. (gr. xxiii.)
Simple syrup	30 grms. (ʒi.)

Mix. Take a spoonful every ten minutes, taking care to shake it each time.

Mixture against Chilblains. (In the sense of mingling.)

Balsam of Peru. . . .	15 grms. (ʒss.)
Dissolve it in alcohol. . .	125 grms. (ʒiv.)

Add:

Hydrochloric acid . . .	4 grms. (ʒi.)
Tincture of benzoin . . .	15 grms. (ʒss.)

To be rubbed upon the affected part several times a day.
To be kept in a blue or black bottle, and labelled, "For external use."

POTIONS PROPERLY SO CALLED.

Under the name of potions properly so called are designated all those mixtures which are neither juleps nor looches.

Potions are composed of an aqueous vehicle, (distilled waters, infusions, decoctions, &c.), and of a syrup, honey, oxymel, or conserve, in which sundry medicinal principles are dissolved or suspended.

The proportions of the vehicle and of the sweetening substance are variable, but they may be stated at 1 or 2 parts of the sweetener to 3 or 4 parts of the vehicle. Like a julep, a potion is generally from four to eight ounces.

Before indicating the peculiarities belonging to the preparation of the different species of potion which we have described above, we may remark that in any mixture whatever, if we wish to add ethers, Hoffman's solution, (§. Sp. Æth. Sulph. Co. Ph. Lond.), or, in short, any volatile substance, we must take care to write them the last, in order that the pharmaceutist may only add them at the moment before corking the phial, by which means all loss will be avoided. Moreover, M. Soubeiran thinks it would be better to direct the mixture of the ether with the syrup, in accordance with the observation of M. Boulay, who has stated that there is a great affinity between sugar and ether. We may also repeat, that the insoluble or slightly soluble salts, (e. g. sulphate of quinine, and in general, all the salts of the vegetable alkalies), become soluble on the addition of a few drops of the acid which enters into their composition. Thus, in the febrifuge potion containing sulphate of quinine, we write the prescription thus :

Febrifuge Potion.

	ADULTS.	CHILDREN.
Sulphate of quinine	1 grm. (gr. xv.)	0,95 centigrms. (gr. iv.)
Alcoholized sulphuric acid (eau de Rabel, (see p. 62) . . . . . }	10 drops.	3 drops.
Simple distilled cinnamon water . .	80 grms. (ʒiiss.)	20 grms. (ʒv.)
Syrup of orange peel	25 grms. (ʒviss.)	20 grms. (ʒv.)

Mix. To be taken immediately, upon the occasion of the attack, in four doses, with an interval of half-an-hour between the doses.

Potions composed of soluble substances, the transparency of which is preserved.

It is sufficient in this case, in prescribing, to indicate the name and the dose of each substance. The mixture forms naturally.

Diuretic Mixture.

	ADULTS.	CHILDREN.
Oxymel of squill	15 grms. (ʒss.)	5 grms. (gr. lxxv.)
Distilled pellitory water . . .	125 grms. (ʒiv.)	100 grms. (ʒiii.)
Mint water	30 grms. (ʒi.)	15 grms. (ʒss.)
Nitric alcohol*	2 grms. (ʒss.)	0,50 centigrms. (gr. viii.)

Mix. To make a potion, which is to be kept in a well-stopped phial. To be taken, in the course of the day, by a table-spoonful at a time.

(§. * Acid. Nitr. 100; Spt. Rect. 300 parts. Mix. *Codex.*)

Anti-spasmodic Mixture.

	ADULTS.	CHILDREN.
Syrup of nymphæa (water-lily) . . .	30 grms. (ʒi.)	20 grms. (ʒv.)
Distilled water from linden flowers } of each „ „ „ orange flowers } of each	60 grms. (ʒii.)	40 grms. (ʒx.)
Sulphuric ether	4 grms. (ʒi.)	10 drops.

Mix, in a phial, carefully corked.
To be taken, by a spoonful at a time, from hour to hour.

Mixtures composed of insoluble substances, the transparency of which is impaired.

The substances which impair the transparency of a mixture, are: resins, gum-resins, fixed and volatile oils, camphor, certain alcoholic or ethereal tinctures, powders, extracts and electuaries. We shall examine in order, mixtures which contain these different substances.

Mixture, with Resin, or Gum-Resin.

In order to incorporate a resin or a gum-resin with a mixture, it is necessary, in the first place, to reduce it to a very fine powder, and then to mix the powder by trituration with the yolk of an egg (when we make use of the yolk of an egg in a mixture, it is always well to begin by adding a little water). This first operation being completed, we add the liquid which constitutes the bulk of the mixture. Instead of yolk of egg, we sometimes employ mucilage of gum, or some other inter-medium, but it is not so good a plan, for the division of the resins or gum-resins is less perfect.

Purgative Mixture.

	ADULTS.	CHILDREN.
Resin of jalap . . . . . {	40 centigrms. (gr. vi.)	0,20 centigrms, (gr. iii.)

Mix it with half the yolk of an egg, and add:

	ADULTS.	CHILDREN.
Milk of sweet almonds	200 grms. (ʒvi.)	60 grms. (ʒii.)
Syrup of marsh-mallow. . . .	30 grms. (ʒi.)	30 grms. (ʒi.)

To be taken at once.

Copaiba Mixture.

	ADULTS.
Oleo-resin of copaiva	20 grms. (ʒv.)
Yolk of one egg	
Triturate together the copaiva and the yolk of egg, and add:	
Syrup of mint	60 grms. (ʒii.)
Distilled linden water	125 grms. (ʒiv.)

Mix. To be taken in eight doses.

In mixtures containing gum-ammoniacum we often add oxymel of squill. It is necessary to direct that they shall be well rubbed together before adding the yolk of egg. When the dose of ammoniacum does not exceed 10 or 15 centigrammes (gr. iss or gr. iiss) we may omit the egg.

Mixture, with the Gum-Resin, Ammoniacum.

	ADULTS.	CHILDREN.
Gum-ammoniacum, in powder . .	4 grms. (ʒi.)	1 grm. (gr. xv.)
Oxymel of squill . . .	60 grms. (ʒii.)	20 grms. (ʒv.)
Rub the ammoniacum thoroughly with the squill, and add:		
Yolk of one egg		
Distilled water of penny-royal . .	200 grms. (ʒvi.)	100 grms. (ʒiii.).)
„ „ „ peppermint. . .	125 grms. (ʒiv.)	60 grms. (ʒii.)

To be taken, during the day, by a table-spoonful at a time.

Mixtures with fixed oils.

Fixed oils are divided by means of yolk of egg or mucilage. The latter should be preferred, because the oils are more perfectly divided, and the colour of the compound is not changed. When, however, the oil is naturally consistent, like castor-oil, the yolk of egg thickens the mixture less, and should be preferred.

Purgative Mixture, with Castor Oil.

	ADULTS.	CHILDREN.
Fresh castor oil	30 grms. (ʒi.)	10 grms. (ʒiiss.)
Yolk of half an egg		
Triturate them together, and add:		
Syrup of orange flowers . . .	40 grms. (ʒx.)	20 grms. (ʒv.)
Common water	60 grms. (ʒii.)	40 grms. (ʒx.)

Mix the whole. To be taken at once.

Purgative Mixture, with Croton Oil.

	ADULTS.	CHILDREN.
Croton oil	3 drops.	1/2 a drop to 1 drop.
Gum arabic	{ 20 centigrms. (gr. iii.)	10 centigrms. (gr. iss.)
Rub the oil with the gum, and add :		
Simple syrup	15 grms. (ʒss.)	15 grms. (ʒss.)
Infusion of chamomile . . .	100 grms. (ʒiii.)	40 grms. (ʒx.)

To be taken in one or two doses.

In order to be exact, we ought to add that oily mixtures, in which the greasy matters have been made into an emulsion, might take the name of emulsion, and in that case we should define the word emulsion as follows : a liquid medicine containing oil or resinous substances held in suspension by means of gummy or albuminous substances.

Mixtures with volatile oils.

When volatile oils enter into a mixture in small doses, we simply mix them with syrup, or triturate them with sugar, which make an oleo-saccharum miscible with water. If, on the contrary, the oil is employed in a considerable dose, the yolk of an egg is employed as an intermedium.

Vermifuge Mixture.

	ADULTS.	CHILDREN.
Volatile oil of turpentine . . .	90 grms. (ʒiii.)	2 grms. (ʒss.)
Yolk of one egg.		
Syrup of wormwood . . .	30 grms. (ʒi.)	30 grms. (ʒi.)
Mint water (distilled) . .	90 grms. (ʒiii.)	90 grms. (ʒiii.)

The mixture of the volatile oil is only to be added at last.
To be taken in four doses, from hour to hour—the phial to be shaken, before the mixture is taken. (§. There is probably some typographical error in the doses in the original; for the disproportion between 3 *ounces* for an adult, and ½ *drm.* for a child, is so great, that its intention was probably to make the dose for children 20 grms., instead of 2, which would make the whole dose ʒv—about the ordinary one in such a case.)

Mixture of camphor.

If we make camphor enter into a mixture, we must take care to direct that it shall be first pulverized by means of a few drops of alcohol, and then divided by the aid of mucilage of gum-arabic, or of yolk of egg. Sometimes treating the camphor with alcohol may be neglected, and the trituration may be confined to the mucilage or the yolk of egg.

If camphor is associated with a tincture it must be first triturated with it in order to be dissolved, and the solution must afterwards be mixed with syrup.

Camphor Mixture.

	ADULTS.	CHILDREN.
Camphor, in powder . . . {	60 centigrms. (gr. ix.)	0,20 centigrms. (gr. iii.)
Triturate the camphor with a quarter of the yolk of an egg, and add:		
Saccharine emulsion	200 grms. (ʒvi.)	100 grms. (ʒiii.)
Syrup of sulphate of morphia . . .	30 grms. (ʒi.)	{ 2 to 4 grms. (ʒss to ʒi.)
Simple syrup	15 grms. (ʒss.)	20 grms. (ʒv.)

Mix. To be taken, by a table-spoonful, every hour.

It has been proposed to divide camphor by means of magnesia, a process which M. Soubeiran considers defective, for if the magnesia is removed from the mixture, the dose of camphor cannot be appreciated, as the magnesia retains some of it. If, on the contrary, the magnesia is left in the mixture, it is more disagreeable to the patient than it need be.

Mixtures containing tinctures.

A good number of tinctures, and especially such as contain gum-resins or oily matters, such as tincture of assafœtida, castoreum, myrrh, scammony, gamboge, aloes, ammoniacum, &c., when mixed with water, lose the materials which they held in solution, and form clots. This inconvenience is remedied by taking care to triturate these tinctures with sugar or the syrup of the mixture, before adding them to the water. This precaution is unnecessary when the principles contained in the tincture are soluble in water, or when they are precipitated in a very fine state of division. Nevertheless, there is no disadvantage in always prescribing the trituration of tinctures with syrup, and by this means we may sometimes avoid giving the patient a disagreeable mixture.

Anti-hysteric Mixture.

	ADULTS.
Compound syrup of wormwood	30 grms. (ʒi.)
Tincture of assafœtida	1 grm. (Mxx.)

Mix them carefully in a mortar, and then add:

Distilled water of valerian . . } of each . .	60 grms. (ʒii.
" " " orange flowers }	
Sulphuric ether	8 grms. (ʒii.)

Put the whole into a well-corked bottle. To be taken, by a tea-spoonful, every hour.

Mixtures with powders.

Powders should be very finely divided before entering into a mixture. It is necessary to triturate them first in syrup or with a little sugar, in order to have them thoroughly divided and better suspended, and the remainder of the liquid may afterwards be added. Mucilage of gum-arabic may be employed for suspending powders, and it is chiefly used with mineral powders.

Emetic Mixture, containing Ipecacuanha.

	ADULTS.	CHILDREN.
Ipecacuanha, in powder	2 grms. (ʒss.)	1 grm. (gr. xv.)
Syrup of maiden-hair	30 grms. (ʒi.)	30 grms. (ʒi.)
Common water	150 grms. (ʒv.)	60 grms. (ʒii.)

Mix. This mixture is to be given in three doses, every quarter of an hour.

Kermetised Mixture.

	ADULTS.	CHILDREN.
Gum tragacanth, in powder . .	1 grm. (gr. xv.) {	0,50 centigrms. (gr. viii.)
Kermes mineral . . . . {	10 centigrms. (gr. iss.)	0,10 centigrms. (gr. iss.)
Triturate them with:		
Syrup of Tolu	30 grms. (ʒi.)	30 grms. (ʒi.)
And add:		
Infusion of hyssop . . .	125 grms. (ʒiv.)	125 grms. (ʒiv.)

To be taken, by a table-spoonful, every hour.

Mixtures with extracts, electuaries or conserves.

Extracts ought to be triturated in a mortar with the syrup and the vehicle, in order that they may be perfectly divided. This is a better plan than dissolving them by the aid of heat, which only yields them imperfectly divided.

Electuaries and conserves are diffused through the vehicle by simple trituration.

Anthelmintic Mixture.

	ADULTS.	CHILDREN.
Alcoholic extract of the bark of pomegranate . . . . . }	25 grms. (℥vi.)	4 grms. (℥i.)
Syrup of citron juice ⎫ Mint water . . ⎬ of each . . Linden water . . ⎭	60 grms. (℥ii.)	30 grms. (℥i.)

To be taken by a table-spoonful at a time.

FATTY OR RESINOUS MATTERS FOR EXTERNAL USE.

CERATES (ÉLÆOCÉROLÉS).

These are external officinal medicines formed of oil or wax, and sometimes of spermaceti. Their consistence is always soft; but it varies with the proportions of the substances employed. We very seldom, however, content ourselves with the simplicity above-mentioned in the composition of cerates, but add liquids, extracts, salts, powders, &c. They are used spread upon linen, or lint, and they are also employed to lessen the friction in using sounds. They are also used in liniments. There are no particular directions necessary in prescribing them; as it is sufficient to mention the dose, and the mode of employment.

The mode of preparation varies according to the nature of the substances which we wish to incorporate. Liquids, especially those of a watery nature, ought to be added in small quantities, and the mixture bleached by the interposition of air and water amongst its particles. As an example of the kind of preparation, we shall give the formula for preparing simple cerate, and the cerate of Galien.

Simple Cerate.

Take of oil of sweet almonds . . . . 3 parts.
    „   „ white wax . . . . . 1 part.

They must be melted by a gentle heat, and poured.into a marble mortar slightly warmed, and triturated with a wooden pestle, in order that they may be perfectly divided. By trituration with very finely divided powders or extracts, dissolved in water, we obtain compound cerates.

Cerate of Galien.

Take of White wax	.	.	.	.	.	1 part.
Oil of sweet almonds		.	.	.	.	4 parts.
Rose water	.	.	.	.	.	3 parts.

Operate as for the Simple Cerate (above), and add the rose water by small quantities, constantly stirring.

POMMADES, POMATUMS ("Graisses médicamenteuses" of the *Codex*).

(LIPAROLÉS).

Pomatums never contain resinous matters, but are composed always of fatty substances of a soft nature, and charged with aromatics and medicines. They are generally officinal preparations; but are sometimes specially prescribed, in which case it is necessary to know, that these medicines are prepared by simple mixture, by solution, and by combination.

Pomatums are prepared by simple mixture or incorporation, when they are composed of mineral, vegetable, or animal powders, of aqueous or alcoholic extracts, or of aqueous, vinous, or alcoholic liquids. When mixed with lard, to which a little wax is sometimes added, to give them a firmer consistence, they are the only pomatums for which the physician has to give special directions; all the others being officinal, it is sufficient to give the name.

Pomatum of Iodide of Lead.

Iodide of lead	.	.	.	.	5 grms. (gr. lxxv.)
Axonge (lard)	.	.	.	.	15 grms. (ʒss.)

Mix them, and rub the neck therewith morning and evening, and leave upon the part a piece of blotting paper impregnated with the pomatum.

Pomatums, like cerates, are intended for external use, and are spread upon lint or linen, or are used by means of friction. Care must be taken, that when used for frictions they are prepared by porphyrization (p. 135), especially if they are composed of mineral substances.

We advise, that whenever soluble substances are made into pomatum, their solution in some appropriate liquid should be directed.

Antimonial Pomatum.

Take of Tartar emetic, in powder .   .   **4** grms. (ʒi.)
     Water .   .   .   . q. s. about 8 grms. (ʒii.)
     Lard .   .   .   .   . . 30 grms. (ʒi.)

Mix them carefully.

Ioduretted Pomatum.

Take of Iodide of potassium .   .   .   **4** grms. (ʒi.)
     Water .   .   .   . q. s. about 4 grms. (ʒi.)
     Lard .   .   .   .   . . 30 grms. (ʒi.)

Mix them carefully.

Pomatum of Iodine and Iodide of Potassium.

Take of Iodide of potassium .   .   .   **4** grms. (ʒi.)
     Iodine .   .   .   .   .   . 1 grm. (gr. xv.)
     Water .   .   . q. s. about 8 grms. (ʒii.)
     Lard .   .   .   .   . . 30 grms. (ʒi.)

Mix them carefully.

We have already mentioned, that it is necessary to porphyrise soluble substances with great care.

Pomatums may be divided, according to their nature, into three classes :

1. *Pomata by simple mixture; e. g.* mercurial and iodine pomata, &c.

2. *Pomata by solution; e. g.* camphor, and phosphorus pomata, &c.

3. *Pomata by chemical combination; e. g.* oxygenised, and citrine pomata, &c.

OINTMENTS (RÉTINOLÉS MOUS).

An ointment is a pomatum composed of resinous matters, united with an oil or an animal fat, and not containing metallic substances. Their consistence is generally pasty, and they are only employed for external use. They differ from pomatums, which are softer, and do not contain resins, and from plasters, which are harder, adhesive to the skin, and do not melt with the heat of the body.

In common language, the words "balsam" and "ointment" are confounded; but the term "balsam," though applicable to certain ointments, does not embrace them all. *Ointment* ought to designate medicines suitable for anointing the body; and *balsam* should be restricted to resinous pomata, destined to be applied to injured parts, or such as are likely to be so: at least, such is the opinion of M. Soubeiran. Ointments are officinal medicines, and the physician has no occasion to prescribe the mode of making them; he need but direct the mode of applying them. It is sometimes necessary to sprinkle the surface of an ointment with some animal or vegetable substance (*e. g.* opium), which ought always to be very finely powdered, and it is also important to use only a very thin layer of ointment, as these preparations only act by the surface which is immediately in contact with the body.

Ointments are employed in frictions, or are spread upon linen, leather, or lint. They are sometimes employed as the excipient for other medicines, powders, liquids, &c.

OINTMENT-PLASTERS (RÉTINOLÉS-SOLIDES).

This preparation only differs from the last in containing more solid materials.

It is incorrect for ointment-plasters to be named plasters, as we often see done. The plasters of mucilage, conium, and belladonna, are comprised in this class of medicines.

PLASTERS PROPERLY SO CALLED (STÉARATÉS).

We have defined plasters in speaking of ointments. Plasters, properly so called, have as their basis the combination of oxide of lead (litharge), with oleic, margaric, and stearic acids. Some are prepared by the intervention of water, and others are made without this liquid, and are called brulés (burnt).

Plasters are applied externally, and are spread thinly upon linen or calico cloth, upon thin silk, or more frequently still upon white leather, to which a suitable form is to be given.

> Take of plaster of white-lead sufficient to be spread upon a piece of silk, the size of a crown piece, to be applied to the part affected, with neuralgia.

Simple plaster is then a stearate, margarate, or oleate of lead; it is the basis of compound plasters, like those of gum-diachylon (empl. Galbani), the plaster of Vigo (empl. Hydr. c Ammoniac); emplatre diapalme (simple plaster 32, Wax 2, Zinc. Sulph. 1), &c.

The only burnt plaster employed is the "onguent de la mère," which is also a true soap, and contains, moreover, acetate of lead, and burnt matters.

Soaps, properly so called, approach plasters (stearates) in their composition; that is to say, they are stearates, margarates, and oleates of potash (soft soaps), or of soda (hard soaps); and fat and olive-oil are employed in preparing both soaps and plasters.

Plasters may be prepared by double decomposition, for which purpose it is sufficient to dissolve white soap in water, and to mix a solution of neutral acetate of lead with it. Soluble acetate of soda is then formed, and insoluble stearate, margarate, and oleate of lead; but the simple plaster thus obtained is hard, and difficult to work up.

EXTERNAL MEDICINES,

MORE ESPECIALLY MAGISTRAL ONES.

SPARADRAPS (§. No corresponding English officinal preparation).

This name is given to tissues made of cotton or silk, or to papers prepared with some composition of the nature of a plaster, which is sometimes spread upon one surface only (sparadrap of gum-diachylon, or empl.' Galbani made into a spararadrap); sometimes upon both surfaces (toile de mai, or white wax 8, oil of almonds 4, Venise turpentine 1, *Codex;* blistering papers or tissues), (§. court plaster, and the blistering tissues now in use are the chief representatives of this class of medicines. They are considered preferable to ordinary blistering and other plasters, from their greater elegance and cleanliness).

ÉCUSSONS (SHIELDS, OR MEDICATED CUSHIONS.).

An écusson, or shield, is a magistral medicine intended for external use, and made of pieces of linen, taffeta, leather, or sparadrap of gum-diachylon (galbanum) covered with a layer of some medicine of variable nature. It may be Burgundy pitch, some extract, an electuary, an ointment, plaster, &c. If the shield does not stick conveniently to the skin, the physician should take care to make it do so by a margin of adhesive plaster.

The size of the shield is determined by the extent of the space which we wish to cover. There is no rule to be laid down in this respect, and we simply recommend not to give too great a thickness to the medicated surface, as we advised for plasters. The size of the shield should be exactly defined by the physician, who ought to give a model for it, or to indicate its diameter.

Thus he may prescribe a shield of Vigo's plaster, 10 centimetres (4 inches) in diameter, or 10 centimetres (4 inches) long, and 6 (2½ inches) broad.

Sometimes even a piece of a sparadrap, cut of the proper size, constitutes by itself a shield; but in other cases we put certain materials for plasters upon it.

VÉSICATOIRES (BLISTERING PLASTERS).

This name is given to plasters (écussons) which are used to raise a blister. For this purpose they are prepared with cantharides plaster, and then lightly covered with the powdered fly. In order to prevent the action of the cantharides upon the mucous membrane of the bladder, blistering plasters are sprinkled with a little powdered camphor, or better still, are moistened with camphorated ether, which leaves a thin layer of camphor. In all these cases the layer should not be too thick, for in that case the plaster would not take effect.

When the blistering substance is soft, we may prevent it from spreading beyond the desired limits, by surrounding the plaster with a band of gum-diachylon, which has the effect of preventing the blistering plaster from changing its place.

BOUGIES.

This name is given to instruments destined to be introduced into the urethra. They are made of some material for plasters, of india rubber, gutta-percha, or of thickened linseed-oil.

SOUNDS.

They differ from bougies only in being hollow. They are made of the same materials, or of silver.

PESSARIES.

These are intended to be introduced into the vagina. They are made of linen, silk, caoutchouc, gutta-percha, thickened linseed-oil, boiled leather, ivory, wood, &c.

SUPPOSITORIES.

' This name is given to officinal or magistral medicines of a firm consistence, a conical or oblong form, a variable thickness, not exceeding that of the little finger, and from 2¼ to 5 centimetres (1 to 2 inches) long. Their weight is never greater than 40 grammes (℥x).

Suppositories are intended to be introduced into the rectum, and to remain there for some time. They are most frequently prepared of cocoa, butter, honey thickened by heat, soap, suet, or wax. Resinous, saline, metallic (§. or opiate) powders, are sometimes added. Lastly, we may employ plasters or emollient roots made of a suitable shape, and smeared with fresh butter, or some oily body.

When suppositories are not intended to act as purgatives, they should only be introduced after the patient has been to the water-closet.

Purgative Suppository.

Powdered colocynth .	. . . .	2 grms. (℈ss.)
Common salt .	. . . .	4 grms. (℥i.)
Thickened honey	. . . .	30 grms. (℥i.)

To be made into a cone, and introduced into the rectum, and left there until it produces a stool.

Suppository, to recall a suppressed Hæmorrhoidal Discharge.

Cocoa butter .	. . . .	8 grms. (℥ii.)
Powdered aloes	. . .	20 centigrms. (gr. iii.)
Powdered tartrate of antimony	.	5 centigrms. (gr. 3/4.)

To be formed into a suppository. A similar one is to be introduced every day until a severe pain is felt round the margin of the anus.

(§. Suppositories made with a scruple or half a drachm of soap, and 4 or 5 grains of opium, are often of eminent service in relieving the tenesmus of acute or chronic dysentery. And when made of soap alone, they often answer better than purgatives with children, whose bowels do not act, simply because they are too idle to make the attempt to have a stool).

CATAPLASMS (POULTICES).

A cataplasm is an external medicine of the consistence of thick hasty pudding, and is intended to be applied to some part of the body. They are composed of pulps, powders, different kinds of flour, and various liquids. Oils, ointments, resins, gum-resins, salts, camphor, milk, decoctions of plants, wine, and vinegar, &c., are sometimes added.

Cataplasms are employed either raw or cooked. Those made of flour of mustard, which loses its active principle by heat, and those made of the pulps of plants prepared in the cold, ought always to be raw.

When made of flour of mustard they bear the especial name of *sinapisms*, and ought always to have nothing but water for their vehicle; which liquid should always be cold or tepid. We sometimes sharpen sinapisms with pepper, or cantharides, or their alcoholic tincture.

Cataplasms prepared by heat are much the most numerous. They are made of pulps, or different kinds of farina. Those made of pulps are valuable, from the water being separated with difficulty; and those made of farinas are better in proportion, as the particular kind used preserves for a length of time the water which it has absorbed. The flour of *phalaris canariensis* (the grass yielding canary-seed) appears to preserve its moisture better than any other, and ought to be more frequently used than it is; but perhaps the experiments of M. Duportal require repetition, though too little importance has been attached to this property, which he appears to have sufficiently proved. It is principally like local baths that emollient poultices appear to act; we have often proved in the hospital, that even before their application, linseed poultices have produced an effect upon litmus paper, comparable to that of the most powerful acids.

The preparation of a poultice is very simple; nevertheless, care is requisite that it should be of uniform consistence, and well held together, for clots or lumps increase the pain of the patient.

Many precautions must be taken when we wish to add certain medicines to a common poultice.

1. Whenever we wish to employ aromatic plants, it is best to

use them in the state of powder. We may cover the face of the poultice by means of some liquid proper for giving the powder a suitable consistence, and for moistening the cataplasm. We may also make a decoction highly charged with the plant, and pour it upon the poultice.

2. All substances (e. g. powdered conium, safron, camphor, acetate of lead, &c.), which might lose their medicinal virtue by the action of the heat necessary for making the poultice, ought to be added to it when it has partially cooled, or is quite cold. The surface of the poultice being the part really efficacious, by its immediate contact with the sick part, we must take care to cover it with the substances of which we have just spoken, instead of incorporating them with its mass, as is often done.

3. Wines, tinctures, and oils, are to be simply poured upon the poultice.

4. Salts, soaps, and extracts, require to be previously dissolved in a sufficient quantity of water, and then spread over the poultice.

5. Ointments, pomatums, and all greasy bodies being diffused at first in a little oil, should then be spread upon the face of the poultice, whilst it is still sufficiently hot to melt them.

We may remark, that when a poultice contains greasy substances it preserves its heat longer, sticks less to the skin, and causes less coldness when it is removed.

A bread crumb or linseed-meal poultice is made well enough by all the world, and it is therefore unnecessary to detail the mode of proceeding in prescribing it; but we ought to fix the quantity to be employed, to prescribe the substances which we wish to add, to indicate in what manner they are to be incorporated with it, and lastly, to specify to what part of the body it is to be applied. The prescription should also state, whether it is to be cold, tepid, or hot, and how long it is to remain upon the patient.

We think it is desirable, in prescribing a mustard poultice, to direct how it is to be prepared, for many persons still think that they should heat the mustard, or add vinegar to it.

Anodyne Poultice.

Emollient poultice .   .   .   .   . 160 grms. (℥v.)
Laudanum of Sydenham.   .   .   . 2 grms. (℥ss.)

The laudanum is to be poured upon the face of the poultice, before it is applied hot to the belly.

Antiarthritic Poultice.

Bread crumbs .   .   .   .   . 1 kilogrm. (℥xxxii.)
Water . }
Alcohol } of each, equal parts, q. s.

To give the bread crumbs the consistence of a poultice; heat it upon a gentle fire. The poultice being made, add to the surface:

Extract of opium.   .   .}
   „   „ stramonium } of each   . 5 grms. (gr. lxxv.)

Dissolve them in water, and make them of a fluid consistence.
Then sprinkle the surface with:

Camphor (in powder).   .   .   . 15 grms, (℥ss,)

Apply the poultice, when tepid, to the painful joint, and leave it on at least three days. Cover it over with oil-cloth and flannel, to keep in the moisture.

Suppurative Cataplasm.

Make an emollient poultice, of the weight of   . 500 grms .(℥xvi.)

Add:

Pulp of the bulbs of the lily, prepared by heat . 60 grms. (℥ii.)
Onguent de la mère .   .   .   .   . 30 grms. (℥i.)

Previously diluted with:

Oil .   .   .   . q. s.

Mix the whole carefully, and apply it hot, for twenty-four hours, to the affected part.

Vinegar Poultice.

Bread crumbs .   .   .   .   . 60 grms. (℥ii.
Solution of chloride of sodium .   .   . 15 grms. (℥ss.)
Vinegar .   .   .   . q. s.

Boil them together. To be applied, cold, to bruises, and renewed several times a day.

COLLYRIA.

This name is given to officinal or magistral preparations, especially intended for diseases of the eyes; they are either dry, soft, liquid, or in the taste of vapour.

Dry collyria are always composed of very finely-divided powders, which are blown into the eye through a tube or quill. Alum (burnt), borax, sugar, sulphate of zinc, oxide of

zinc, cuttle-fish bone (§. and calomel), reduced by porphyrization to a very fine powder, form the dry collyria most frequently
used.

Dry Collyrium.

Burnt alum		
Sulphate of zinc ⎬ of each. . . . 1 grm. (gr. xv.)		
Borax		
Powdered white sugar . . . . 2 grms. (ʒss.)		

Soft collyria are nearly always ointments, or more especially
pomatums. They are particularly employed in diseases of the
eye-lids. In making use of them, the eye and the edge of the
eye-lids are smeared with a piece about the size of a pin's head
every day, or every other day, according to need. These ointments and pomata are sometimes mixed with substances of
different natures, and we thus obtain more or less compound
collyria.

Soft Collyrium.

Oxide of zinc.	.	.	.	. 80 centigrms. (gr. xii.)
Calomel	.	.	.	. 60 centigrms. (gr. ix.)
Camphor	.	.	.	. 40 centigrms. (gr. vi.)
Fresh butter.	.	.	.	. 8 grms. (ʒii.)
Cocoa butter.	.	.	.	. 2 grms. (ʒss.)

Mix them thoroughly.

Liquid collyria are made either of distilled waters, or decoctions which are frequently heightened by saline substances or
alcoholic liquids, or of solutions of salts or extracts, and the
eyes are washed with them, by means of a camel's hair pencil, or
a small piece of linen rag, once or oftener in the day. Compresses soaked in the collyrium, may also be applied to the eye.
The quantity to be ordered varies from 100 to 300 grammes, or
more (ʒiii to ʒix).

Narcotic Collyrium.

Extract of the juice of stramonium	.			20 centigrms. (gr. iii.)
„ „ opium	.	.	.	. 10 centigrms. (gr. iss.)
Rose water	.	.	.	. 125 grms. (ʒiv.)

Dissolve them.

Collyrium of Nitrate of Silver.

Distilled water. . . . . . 30 grms. (ʒi.)
Crystallized nitrate of silver . . . 5 grms. (gr. lxxv.)

(§. This is probably a mistake for 5 decigrms. (gr. viii) ; for 8 or 10 grains to the ounce, is a very common strength ; but nearly a drachm and a half to the ounce is an unheard of strength in this country.)

Employed in thrush and the purulent ophthalmia of new-born infants, either as a collutoire (see p. 197), or as a collyrium.

Simple Collyrium.

Rose water . . . . 125 grms. (ʒiv.)

Collyria in vapour, are gases or vapours, to the action of which the eyes are exposed. Those most frequently used are liquid ammonia and the balsam of Fiovarenti,* a little of which is poured into the palm of the hand, and then rubbed over both hands, which are then held to the eyes so as to cover without touching them. (§. These are stimulating vapours, and are used in chronic conjunctivitis. As an anodyne in intolerance of light, and continued pain after sclerotitis, for example, a few drops of hydrocyanic acid are used in the state of vapour, being put into a glass of a proper shape made for the purpose, and volatilized by the heat of the hand. Sometimes acetic ether and other preparations, are used in the same way for the relief of incipient cataract).

GARGARISMS (GARGLES).

These are liquid magistral medicines, which generally have water for their vehicle, and are intended for affections of the mouth and throat. The physician ought not to neglect telling his patient that he must only wash his mouth and throat with the gargle, and not swallow it; for serious accidents might result if it were swallowed by mistake. It often happens, however, that the patients do swallow a certain quantity notwithstanding every precaution. We must therefore avoid making gargles of such substances as may cause severe accidents in small doses, though not perhaps amounting to poisoning.

We advise the same attention in cases in which, the patient

(§. * This balsam contains sixteen ingredients: resins, gum-resins and spices. They are macerated for several days in spirit, which is afterwards distilled from them; and the distilled spirit constitutes this notable preparation.)

being himself unable to gargle, we are forced to inject the gargle upon the parts affected; in which case a part of the liquid is almost certainly swallowed. (§. In the case of infants and children, who cannot gargle, we may attain our object by making the gargle sweet, soaking a bundle of rag in it, and placing this in the mouth. The child sucks the rag, and the gargle acts upon the throat in being swallowed).

The composition of gargles is very variable, for they are formed of solutions, infusions, or decoctions, to which salts are sometimes added, of extracts, tinctures, and acids, or other substances, which are often very energetic. These magistral preparations contain some sweetening ingredient.

Water, milk, wine, and vinegar, diluted with water, are most commonly used as the excipient.

The quantity of liquid is a glassful, or more; but it should not exceed a litre (1¾ pints). Gargles may be prescribed cold, tepid, or very hot, according to the case, and they are employed at intervals, more or less close.

Acidulated Gargle.

Common water	.	.	.	.	125 grms. (℥iv.)
Simple syrup	.	.	.	.	15 grms. (℥ss.)
Sulphuric acid.	.	.	.	.	15 drops.

Hydrochloric Gargle.

Infusion of cinchona	.	.	.	.	125 grms. (℥iv.)
Hydrochloric acid	.	.	.	.	15 drops.
Honey of roses	.	.	.	.	30 grms. (℥i.)

COLLUTOIRES (No representative in English).

Collutoires are magistral preparations, of a thick consistence resembling that of a concentrated syrup; but there are some instances of dry collutoires. These medicines are applied by means of a camel's-hair pencil, or of a morsel of sponge. They differ from gargles in their consistence, and in not being used for affections of the throat. Collutoires are sometimes prescribed with the intention of facilitating the sialogogic action of certain substances.

Boracic Collutoire.

Borax } of each . . . . . 16 grms. (℥ss.)
Honey }

Dry Collutoire of Borax.

Borax . . .} of each . . . . 10 grms. (℥v.)
Powdered sugar }

Collutoire, to relieve Tooth-ache.

Powdered pyrethrum } of each . . 15 grms. (℥ss.)
Opium . . . }

Macerate them for an hour in :

Vinegar . . . . 190 grms. (℥vi.)

Filter. To be applied by means of a camel's-hair pencil.

INJECTIONS.

Injections are liquid medicines, intended to be introduced by means of a syringe into certain canals, or different natural or unnatural cavities in the body ; and they may regarded as a kind of internal lotion. The basis is almost always a watery vehicle, a decoction, infusion, or solution ; to which certain substances have been added, suitable for increasing its energy. In prescribing an injection we must take care to fix its temperature, which will be either cold, or a little above the temperature of the body, according to the indications to be fulfilled. We must at the same time direct how long it is to be retained.

Irritant Injection.

Hot port wine . . . . . 500 grms. (℥xvi.)
Alcohol, at 36° (sp. gr. 835) . . . 20 grms. (℥v.)

Mix.

Soothing Injection.

Decoction of linseed . . . . 200 grms. (℥vi.)
Opium . . . . 20 centigrms. (gr. iii.)

Injection of Distilled Pine-Water.

Distilled pine-water . . . . 200 grms. (℥vi.)

Add :

Common water, at 30° C. (86° F.) . 1000 grms. (℥xxxii.)

LAVEMENTS (GLYSTERS).

A lavement, or glyster, is an injection specially intended for that portion of. the intestines, which is comprised between the rectum and the iliocecal valve (the colon).

Glysters, intended to act either locally upon the intestinal mucous membrane, or by sympathy or absorption upon the rest of the system, are very variable in their nature. Most medicinal preparations may be made to enter into them, and nutritive substances are carried into the intestines by means of glysters, and then exposed to absorption.

The quantity of liquid is from 125 grammes ($\overline{3}$iv) to 500 grammes ($\overline{3}$xvi) for adults; and less than this for children. The temperature should be from 24⁰ to 30⁰ C. (77⁰ to 86⁰ F.).

It is important, when we wish to administer a glyster containing an active substance, to precede it by one composed of simple water, in order to clear the intestines of fœcal matters, and to allow of the more direct action of the second.

Glysters may be prepared from insoluble substances; but we must not forget to employ some intermedium in this case, which will most frequently be yolk of egg.

Glyster, for Fissures of the Anus.

Extract of rhatany	5 grms. (gr. lxxv.)
Water	250 grms. (ℨviii.)

To be retained for half an hour or an hour. It should be preceded by a simple glyster, so as to produce a stool beforehand.

Anti-spasmodic Glyster.

Assafœtida	30 grms. (ℨi.)

Suspend it in:

The yolk of an egg . . . .

And add:

Decoction of marsh-mallow root . .	250 grms. (ℨviii.)

Starch Glyster.

Starch	15 grms. (ℨss.)
Common water	500 grms. (ℨxvi.)

Diffuse the starch minutely through half the water; boil the other half, and pour it upon the mixture of starch and water, and administer the glyster.

LINIMENTS.

By a liniment is understood an unctuous liquid, generally containing oil, which is employed to anoint the skin, by means of friction with the hand, flannel, or cotton, &c. Sometimes the cloth, soaked in the liniment, is left upon the skin like a fomentation.

Fixed oils and fats are the general bases of liniments, to which are added alkalies, salts, acids, soaps, metallic compounds, gum, resins, balsams, ointments. Tinctures, or oils by themselves, sometimes constitute a liniment. Lastly, in certain cases the white or yolk of egg, water or alcohol, is employed as the basis, in which case it is necessary to add honey or mucilage, in order to give the liquid a certain consistence.

We ought, in prescribing, to indicate the mode of mixing the substances composing the liniment, and the way to use it. The quantity to be prepared varies from 40 to 125 grammes (ζx to ζiv).

Volatile Liniment.

Olive oil	125 grms. (ζiv.)
Liquid ammonia	15 grms. (ζss.)

Mix them in a well corked bottle, and rub the liniment over the parts affected with rheumatism by means of a flannel.

Sedative Liniment, for Ulcerated Piles.

Extract of stramonium . . .	2 grms.	(ζss.)
Hydrochlorate of morphia . .	30 centigrms.	(gr. ivss.)
Yolk of one egg		

Beat the substances together, to make a liniment. Let fledgets of tow be soaked in it, and applied to the principal hæmorrhoidal tumours.

BATHS.

A bath is a medicine into which the whole of the body, or some particular part is plunged, and allowed to remain for a longer or shorter time. Baths are divided into two classes, general and local, according as the whole body or only a part is immersed in it. Partial baths again are subdivided into demi, or sitting-baths, hip-baths, foot-baths or pediluvia, hand-baths or maniluvia, and head-baths or capitiluvia, (shower-baths). They are also distinguished, according to their nature, into *liquid* baths, (soft water, sea-water, natural or other mineral waters, baths containing solutions, or medicated baths); into *soft* baths, (mineral sediments, refuse (*marc*) after pressing grapes or olives, horse or cow-dung); into *dry* baths (sand, ashes, bran, plaster of Paris, earth); into *gaseous* baths (chlorine, hot air, sulphur, &c.), and into baths of aqueous or medicated vapours (simple or medicated steam-baths).

As to their temperature, baths are either very cold, cool, temperate, or hot.

When the temperature is less than 12⁰ C. (53⁰ F.) it is very cold.

> „ „ from 12⁰ to 18⁰ C., (53⁰ to 64⁰ F.), cold.
> „ „ from 18⁰ to 25⁰ C., (64⁰ to 77⁰ F.), cool.

These different baths are prescribed as tonics.

When the temperature is from 25⁰ to 30⁰ C., (77⁰ to 86⁰ F.), it is temperate, and possesses properties essentially hygienic.

Lastly, from 30⁰ to 38⁰ C., (86⁰ to 97⁰ F.), it is hot, and is regarded as debilitating.

When considered in reference to their composition, baths are simple or compound. The first are made of pure water of a specified temperature; the second are prepared of water charged with principles which are more or less active, (mucilaginous, emollient, gelatinous baths, &c.), or of natural or artificial mineral waters. Baths of sea-water ought to be considered as medicated mineral baths.

Soft baths are furnished by hot sediments or dregs, such as the refuse of grapes and olives, at the moment of their removal from the tub, whilst still heated by the fermentation. Horse-dung is not employed in the present day; and we may say the same thing of solid baths. (§. In some country places, poultices made of cows' dung are still employed as a resolvent domestically, and I have known them successful in resolving the swelling after abscess of the breast, after the failure of other means.)

As to gaseous or vapour-baths, they have for some time past been in frequent use. The methods of applying them, which have been brought to singular perfection, have greatly facilitated their employment. Hot air, chlorine, steam by itself or charged with aromatic principles, sulphurous and hydrosulphuric acid, cinnabar, &c., are employed to compose them.

When we prescribe a bath, we must always take care to fix the temperature and the amount of any active principle if it is a medicated one. The part of the body for which the bath is ordered should be specified. The length of time it is used may extend from some minutes to several hours; and the quantity of water varies from two litres (about 3½ pints) to forty, or more, (about 9 gallons), according to the intention with which it is employed. The physician should indicate whether it is to be repeated, and at what intervals.

Aromatic Bath.

Aromatic species* . . . . . . 1000 grms. (℔iii.)

Boil for a quarter of an hour in:

Common water . . . . q. s.

Add to the decoction:

Essence of soap (§. soap dissolved in alcohol) . 125 grms. (ʒiv.)
Sal-ammoniac . . . . 60 grms. (ʒii.)

For a bath, made with twelve pailsful of water, which is to be used for an hour, and repeated three times a week.

Gelatinous Bath.

Gelatine . . . . 1000 grms. (℔iii.)

Dissolve it in:

Warm water . . . . 1500 grms. (℔ivss.)

And add it to the water of a common bath.

Mercurial Bath.

Bichloride of mercury . . . . . 15 grms. (ʒss.)

Dissolve it in:

Alcohol . . . . 125 grms. (ʒiv)

Pour it into a wooden bath, containing sufficient common water.

We may dissolve the sublimate in distilled water instead of the alcohol. The wooden bath is only ordered because the mercury attacks common baths; but this alteration is of little real importance. We have latterly been advised to add sal-ammoniac, with the intention of checking the decomposition of the sublimate, which takes place to a slight extent. For this purpose we may employ the following formula:

Corrosive sublimate } of each . . . 15 grms. (ʒss.)
Sal-ammoniac. }

Dissolve them in:

Water . . . . q. s.

Pour the solution into the water of a common bath.

(§. * Aromatic species: Dried leaves of sage, common and wild thyme, hyssop, mentha aquatica, marjoram and wormwood, of each, equal parts. Fr. *Codex*.)

Sulphurous Bath.

Dry sulphuret of potassium .	.	. 20 grms. (ʒv.)
Common water .	. . .	. 750 grms. (℔ii.)

Dissolve, and pour them into a bath.

DOUCHES.

This name is given to jets or threads, more or less considerable, of either pure or medicated water, falling from a certain height, or gushing out with more or less force, and directed in either case to different parts of the body by means of pipes. The difference between a douche and an affusion is, that in the latter the liquid comes from a source nearer the part to which it is directed.

Douches are ascending, descending, or lateral, and come either in a jet or a broad sheet, in a fine thread or as from the rose of a watering-pot. Pure and medicinal waters are the liquids most frequently used for douches, but we may employ all such solutions as are convenient for baths, taking care, however, to increase the dose of the medicinal substance, because the action of the douche, being only in passing, must be compensated by the greater energy of its ingredients.

In prescribing a douche, we ought to specify its kind, and the temperature, (see p. 201), its height or direction, and the length of time it is to be used, together with the region of the body to which it is to be applied, and whether it is necessary to repeat it.

Douche, containing Sulphuret of Sodium.

Sulphuret of sodium .	. . .	. 30 grms.	(ʒi.)
Chloride of calcium .	. . .	. 8 grms.	(ʒii.)

Dissolve them in a kilogrm. (ʒxxxii) of water, and add:

Water .	. . . . . .	. 40 kilogrms. (8 gallons.)

To be received, upon the swollen part, for a quarter of an hour, the fall being two metres (6½ feet), and in a slender jet.

TROCHISQUES.[*]

This name was formerly given to medicines composed of one or more dry substances, reduced to powder, and made into the form of a round lozenge by the aid of some intermedium which was not composed of sugar, such as mucilage, some vegetable juice, or bread-crumb, &c. The absence of sugar in trochisques was the only distinctive character which could be pointed out between them and lozenges. More recently, the form of these preparations has been changed, and has been made conical or pyramidal. In the present day trochisques are abandoned, with the exception of escharotic ones.

As these are officinal preparations, the physician has no occasion to direct how they shall be made. Moreover, there are only two, the basis of one of which is corrosive sublimate mixed with minium (red-lead), and of the other, corrosive sublimate alone. The trochisques have the forms of grains of oats, weigh about 15 centigrammes (gr. iiss), and are employed externally for opening venereal bubos and scrophulous tumours. They are also introduced into fistulas, &c.

Escharotic Trochisques.

Corrosive sublimate 2 parts ; starch .   .   .   16 parts.
Mucilage of gum tragacanth   .   .   .   q. s.

Mix. To be divided into troches of about gr. iiss each. Fr. *Codex.*

ESCHAROTICS.

Medicines intended to burn the skin, or to destroy fungou flesh, or to form a scar, are named *escharotics ;* when they are more feeble, they are termed *catheretics.*

In the present day, both are confounded under the general name of caustics, and are divided into :

1. *Actual caustics ;* those which have a free and sensible cause for their effect (viz. heat), and which can exercise their influence at a distance, such as moxa, red-hot iron, &c.

2. *Potential caustics ;* those whose influence remains latent, and which can only produce the effect of fire when in actual

(§. * The term, Trochisci, or Troches, is commonly used in this country to indicate lozenges. It is necessary to bear in mind, that it is not used in this sense in the Fr. *Codex.*)

contact with some animal matter, *e. g.* caustic potash, nitric acid, &c.

Escharotics are soft, solid, or liquid, and have different forms, according to the manner in which they are employed. Those most commonly used amongst simple medicines, are burnt alum; fused nitrate of silver (lapis infernalis), solid, or in a concentrated solution; proto-chloride of antimony (butter of antimony); chloride of zinc (butter of zinc); potash and lime (cauterizing stone).

Amongst compound caustics we may name the following: Vienna caustic, formed of equal parts of quick-lime and caustic potash; Filho's caustic, which contains rather more lime, and is obtained by fusion; the arsenical powder of Rousselot, or Brother Côme;* the sulfo-safranique paste of Rust and Velpeau,† and the paste of Cauquoin, made of chloride of zinc, &c.

Moxas.—Combustible matters which are applied to the skin, and made to burn it, are thus named. Every substance capable of burning may be used as a moxa, but it is necessary that the combustion should be gradual, and amadou and absinthium are chiefly employed. Percy's moxas are made of tow or cotton, moistened with saltpetre; and the stem of the sun-flower, the pith of the elder, and wafers soaked in saltpetre, &c., have also been employed.

(§. * Bisulphuret of mercury, and powdered dragon's blood, of each, 2 parts; arsenious acid, 1 part; carefully powdered and mixed, and made into a paste, when required for use, by means of salion or gum-water. Fr. *Codex.*)

(§. † See acid, sulphuric, p. 63.)

MAGISTRAL PRESCRIPTIONS.

The number of ingredients should scarcely ever exceed three or four.—GAUBIUS.

We are now in a position to lay down the rules, which ought to guide the practitioner when he is about to write a prescription; but before entering upon this subject it is necessary to give a few definitions.

Medicine.—Everything which is administered to a sick person, with the intention of curing him, is called by this name. A medicine is *simple,* when it consists of only a single substance, such as gum; but it is necessary to remark, that a simple medicine may be composed of several elementary principles. It is said to be *compound* when it is made by the combination of several medicinal substances. *Theriaca** (an electuary in the Fr. *Codex*) is a type of a compound medicine.

Medicines are again divided into *officinal*† and *magistral*‡.

Officinal medicines ought to be found ready-made in the shop of the pharmaceutist, and they are not very susceptible of change

---

(§. * It is to be hoped that, calling this medicine a "type" of anything to be imitated, is a typographical error; for it is composed of 1 drastic, 2 mild purgatives and 3 astringents; 3 turpentines and 2 emmenagogues; 1 nauseating and 9 bitter expectorants; 6 drumbeats and 9 antispasmodics; 1 opiate and 7 stimulants; 9 carminatives, 7 aromatics and 8 tonics; an ounce and a half of dried vipers; sherry wine; and one substance the properties of which I cannot find.)

(§. † From *Officina,* a shop; because ordered to be kept ready made.

(§. ‡ From *Magister,* a master; because ordered by a master of his profession. By English writers on *materia medica,* all those preparations are called "officinal" for which formulæ are given in the Pharmacopœias whether kept by the druggists, ready made or not.

from the effects of time; *e. g.* distilled waters, conserves, tinctures, wines, syrups, pastilles, powders, &c. *Magistral* medicines are only prepared in proportion as they are wanted, according to the directions of a physician. In this category we may mention tisanes, apozems, potions, emulsions, juleps, mixtures, liniments, poultices, &c. It is more especially to magistral medicines that what we are about to say in this treatise will apply.

Formule (prescription).—To make a prescription (formule), is to give directions in writing to the pharmaceutist, according to certain conventional rules, prescribing the kind of medicines to be used, their number and their dose, the pharmaceutical form which is to be given to them, and the manner in which they are to be administered.

Ordonnance (also a prescription).—The term "ordonnance" is confined to indicating in writing, the name of the medicine, its dose, and the manner in which it is to be used. In an ordonnance the physician may, however, give the patient directions as to the regimen which he is to follow, and may also recommend such and such hygienic precautions.

An ordonnance differs therefore from a formula, though the two words are often used as synonymous; (§. and by English writers no distinction is ever made between them; but the same word "prescription" is employed for both). The distinction between them is founded upon the classification of medicines into officinal and magistral. We *order* ("on ordonne") an officinal medicine; we *prescribe* ("on formule") a magistral one. (§. Thus :

℞ Pil. Rhei Co. gr. v. hora somni sumenda

is an "ordonnance," for it contains merely the name of an officinal medicine, the dose, and the manner of administering it ; but

℞ Rhei, gr. x.
　Aloes, gr. v.
　Ol. Menthæ piperitæ, gr. ii.
　Mist : Acaciæ q. s.

M. ut fiat massa, in pilulas iv dividenda, quarum capiat æger
duas, hora somni—

is a "formule," for it contains the names of the medicines to be
used, their dose, the pharmaceutical form to be given them, and
the mode of administration; but both these examples are called
simply "prescriptions" by English writers).

A prescription may be either simple or compound. It is
simple when it contains only one principal medicine, and compound when it unites several active substances. We advise
physicians to make their prescriptions as little compound as
possible, for the simplest are unquestionably the most frequently
successful in their results, and the most easily made; they are
free from serious errors, and from chemical reactions, more or
less important; and they seldom inspire disgust in the patient.
What physician does not know how difficult it is to appreciate
exactly the effects of even a single substance? How much then
is this difficulty increased, when he has to disentangle the effects
due to each of the bodies which form a compound medicine?

The constituent parts of a prescription.

A magistral prescription comprises three principal parts:
1. The *inscription*; or the names and doses of the substances to
be used; 2. the *subscription*; or what relates to the preparation
or preservation of the medicine; and 3. the *instructions*; or the
directions for its administration.

A prescription generally contains several medicinal substances,
and according to the office which each fills, they have received the
name of: 1. the *basis*; 2. the *excipient*; 3. the *adjuvant*; 4. the
corrective, or *corrigant*; and 5. the *intermedium*.*

Basis.—The basis, or principal medicine, constitutes the substance of the prescription; and we ought not only to know in
what dose to prescribe it according, to the nature of the substance, but also according to the form in which we wish to give
it, or the result we desire to obtain. It is thus that very
different doses are prescribed in an emetic draught, according as
we take emetina or ipecacuanha as the basis; and nux vomica

(§. * For much of the present chapter, the authors are indebted to Paris's "Pharmacologia.")

will not be given in the same doses if we prescribe the extract, as if we order the tincture. Sulphate of quinine will be prescribed in much smaller doses as a simple tonic, than when given as an active febrifuge; that is to say, the dose will vary according to the effects upon which the physician reckons.

The basis of a prescription may be *compound; e. g.* in prescribing a mixture of tartar emetic and ipecacuanha as an emetic, these substances are employed together as the active ingredients, and constitute the basis of the vomit. Lastly, the nature of the basis ought always to be so related to that of the excipient, that no decomposition or chemical reaction may change its properties, unless such a change takes place intentionally.

Excipient.—The excipient is the substance which gives the preparation its particular form and consistence. It is sometimes a solvent. Water is employed as the excipient in tisanes, apozems, emulsions, lemonades, &c. The distilled waters of plants (which are still water) answer the same purpose in potions, mixtures, &c. Light infusions, macerations and aqueous solutions are the excipients in juleps. Emulsions are also employed as excipients for looches; and, lastly, syrups, honeys, pulps, conserves, sugar and powders, &c., are every day prescribed as excipients for pills and boluses. The exact quantity of the excipient necessary for a magistral preparation is seldom prescribed, being generally left to the judgment of the pharmaceutist, though it is important to be exact in some cases. The excipient is generally a substance of little activity, but in some cases it is employed as the *adjuvant*, or even as the *corrigant*, in the prescription.

Adjuvant.—The adjuvant, as its name indicates, comes in aid of the basis, the action of which it augments, and in certain cases even calls into activity. We may, strictly speaking, consider the adjuvant as a new base, and the base then becomes a compound one. The adjuvant may sometimes be dispensed with, if the substance employed at the basis is sufficiently active.

Corrigant or corrective.—The corrigant is the substance employed: 1. to conceal the flavour or odour of the base, and it is then selected from the edulcorants (sugar, syrup, honey, &c.), or the aromatics (distilled waters, essences, tinctures, oils, &c.) Gold

P

and silver leaf, with which pills are sometimes covered, are employed for the same purpose. 2. To diminish over activity in the base, and sometimes to lessen its corrosive action; in which case, inert or mucilaginous powders are usefully employed, such as liquorice, marsh-mallow, starch and gum-arabic; or some syrup of such a character as shall not decompose the base. The taste of the patient will sometimes decide us in our choice of a corrigant, but the quantity must never be such as to destroy the effect of the medicine.

Intermedium.—It remains for us to say a few words upon the intermedium, which is only a variety of the excipient.

In employing an intermedium, we do so with the intention of uniting two substances which are not by themselves miscible with each other or with the excipient, and by its assistance we suspend them when they are made into a mixture. Yolk of egg and mucilage are the intermedia most generally used in a preparation which contains water, and at the same time resinous, oleo-resinous, or oily matters, or oil itself.

The nature of the intermedium is not an indifferent matter, and the quantity to be employed depends upon the dose of medicine to be suspended or mixed.

In order that a prescription may be well made, it is not necessary to unite all the five elements of which we have just spoken. The base and the excipient are the only two parts absolutely necessary, for there are many medicines which have no need of an adjuvant. The agreeable flavour and odour of some, and the mild and harmless nature of others render the intervention of a corrigant unnecessary. And, lastly, most substances are sufficiently miscible by themselves to do without an intermedium. We may also mention that a single substance may be capable of answering two or more purposes: thus, the adjuvant may act as a corrigant also, as when the addition of soap to aloes or to extract of jalap lessens their griping properties and at the same time promotes their action. In the same way neutral salts correct colic which follows the use of resinous purgatives, and accelerate their action.

Rules to be observed in drawing up a prescription.

Custom has fixed the rules for drawing up each of the three parts which constitute a magistral prescription, and no physician can transgress them without appearing ignorant in the eyes of the druggist who is charged with making it up.

The first two parts of a prescription, viz. : the *inscription* and the *subscription*, have reference to the druggist ; the third is the affair of the sick man, or of those who take care of him.

1. The prescription ought to be written either in common language or in Latin ; and when a substance has several names, those which are best known ought to be used ; or the scientific name should be written, and afterwards, in a parenthesis, the common one, *e. g.* bichloride of mercury (corrosive sublimate). But we are at liberty, when necessary, to conceal from the patient the name of a medicine which might be offensive to him, or which he had already refused to take, and which we fear he might again reject. Thus, we may prescribe cigars of Dioscorides instead of arseniacal cigars, or Neapolitan ointment instead of mercurial ointment, &c., and the Latin names may be used with the same intention. It is also well not to use the common language, when the name of the medicine may put people upon the scent of a disease, which the patient has an interest in concealing from them.

2. At the head of the prescription is to be indicated the pharmaceutical form which we wish to be given to the medicine, and when possible, its nature should be specified. Thus, *potion, decoction, pills,* &c., or better still, *tonic potion, diuretic pills, emollient tisane,* &c., are written as its title. The title is sometimes fixed at the same time with the mode of preparation, *e. g.* we say : "make the mixture according to art."

3. Custom has made it usual (℥. in France) to place a P, which means *prenez,* take, or, (℥. throughout the world) an R, or the sign ℞, which means *recipe,* take, before the substances which are to constitute the prescription. For ourselves, we regard these signs as completely useless, and only allude to them as a memorial of the past.

4. Each substance is to be written in a single line, that it may be easily distinguished from the others. If we wish to order several analogous medicines, for example, the roots, leaves, or flowers of different plants, we must take care to place their names immediately one under another, and we may, for the sake of shortness, write the word which is common to them all before the first medicine only.

(§. *E. g. Tinctura aromatica sulfurica.* Fr. *Codex.*)

℞ Root of Roseau aromatique (*Acorus calamus*).
    ,,   ,,   Galanga (*Galanga officinalis*).
    Flowers of Camomile (*Anthemis nobilis*).
    Leaves of Sage (*Salvia officinalis*).
      ,,   ,,   Wormwood (*Absinthium officinale*).
      ,,   ,,   Mint (*Mentha crispa*).
    Cloves, &c., &c.)

The order in which the ingredients in a prescription should be written is sometimes indifferent; but they are generally put down in the order of the pharmaceutical operations to which they are to be submitted.

As a general rule, the base should come first, then the adjuvant, next the excipient, or intermedium, and lastly, the corrigant.

If an excipient is used, the weight of which cannot be precisely fixed, as for instance, in pills, it should not be written until the last place, after all the substances the dose of which can be exactly fixed. And it is important to remember that volatile substances should always be added last, whatever may be the part they play in the prescription.

After each substance, the precise dose is fixed (§. in France) by means of decimal weights. The kind of unit employed (*e. g.* grammes, decigrammes, kilogrammes, &c.) should always be written in full, the authorized signs being employed in certain cases, which are left to the discretion of the physician. It is useless attempting to justify this last exception, for the serious mistakes, too often committed, sufficiently account for our fears. Whether we use abbreviations or not, the weight of the ingredients, and not their bulk, must be fixed, for the medicinal properties of bodies depend upon the quantity of matter, and not upon its volume. These directions must be attended to with special care when very active medicines are prescribed.*

When two or more substances follow each other immediately, and are employed in the same dose, they may be united by a brace, and the weight is then only written once; or they may be preceded (§. in English prescriptions, followed) by the ab-

(§. * In the Edinburgh *Pharm.*, the medicines were formerly ordered by weight, as is still done in the Paris *Codex*; but this plan has now been discarded in the case of liquids, which are so much more easily measured than weighed.)

breviation aa, or ana,* which signifies *of each.* When the proportion of a substance is indefinite, and is left to the discretion of the druggist, the abbreviation q. s. placed after the name, indicates that he must use *quantum sufficiat,* as much as may be sufficient. These two contractions, and the one to be immediately mentioned, are the only ones which can be retained without inconvenience.

5. The particular method of preparing medicines should sometimes be specified. It is frequently sufficient merely to order the mixture of the substances specified in the prescription, and to mention what is the desired form, which is then written simply thus: "Make a potion, mixture, pill, &c., according to art," or this abbreviation may be used, F. S. A. P., that is to say, *fiat secundum artem potio.* But as the therapeutical properties of certain substances depend upon the processes to which they are subjected, it is necessary in many cases, when such substances are used, to indicate the order and the manner of combining them ; a remark which we consider to be of the highest importance. Whenever a substance may be used in infusion or decoction, it is necessary also to fix which of these two forms shall be preferred.

Colombo is more bitter when made into an infusion than into a decoction; and Iceland moss becomes emollient and soothing after a slightly prolonged decoction, whilst it is bitter after simple infusion. Certain substances ought to be submitted to infusion and others to decoction, to obtain all their medicinal principles. Cinchona only yields the whole of its active ingredients to decoction, whilst this process is singularly injurious to serpentary. Certain mixtures can only be made under certain conditions; for example, when we make a compound decoction of sarsaparilla, the sassafras ought not to be added until the other ingredients are already boiled, (§. for its active principle is a volatile oil, which would be dissipated by boiling). Decoctions of Iceland moss and sarsaparilla are sometimes employed in phthysis; in which case the decoctions ought to be made separately, and aftewards mixed; for without this precaution the

(§. * Doctors are so often accused of writing dog-Latin, that it really seems unwise to make matters worse still by mixing up a little Greek as well. a.a is just as truly a contraction of *alterius alteriusque,* as it is of *ana*; and the one has the advantage of being in the same language as the prescriptions, whilst the only recommendation of the other is, that it shows the prescriber is not confined to one or two languages for the means of expressing his wishes.)

lichen (moss) would lose its properties from long continued boiling, whilst the sarsaparilla, on the contrary, requires it.

The physician then, who knows with what intention he writes his prescription, ought to indicate the mode of making it up; and he will often obtain the desired effect only in proportion, as his compound conforms to the rules which we have just laid down.

The mode of preparation is sometimes interwoven with the *inscription;* certain manipulations being indispensable before we are able to proceed with the succeeding substances.

6. The physician should not only give *vivâ voce* directions as to the manner of administering the medicine, but he should also write down in a language familiar to the patient, or those who have the care of him what is to be done with the medicine—whether it is for internal or external employment, and whether is is to be taken at once, or made into several doses, &c. If the medicine is to be taken internally, he must mark the dose to be taken each time; whether by spoonsful, cupsful, or drops. If the preparation is for external employment, he must specify the part of the body to which it is to be applied. The regimen (diet, clothing, &c.), and other precautions which the medicines may make necessary, should be also carefully laid down.

It is unnecessary to advise the physician to exercise the greatest caution in his choice of expressions, especially when treating syphilitic diseases or affections peculiar to females. What we have said elsewhere upon the selection of words with respect to the *inscription,* equally applies to the *instruction.*

We generally take care to put, in the first place, the directions which the druggist is to copy upon the label attached to the medicine. To conclude his prescription, the physician dates and signs it, and then puts the name of the person for whom it has been given. This precaution tends to avoid all mistakes on the part of the druggist or the nurse. If it should sometimes be desirable to conceal the name, the physician will not have anything to put after his signature.

MODEL OF A PRESCRIPTION.

Balsamic Potion.

		ADULTS.	CHILDREN.	
Inscription.	℞ Oleo-resin of copaiva .	30 grms. (℥i.)	10 grms. (ʒiiss.)	(Basis.)
	Yolk of egg . . .	No. 1.	No. 1.	(Intermedium.)
	Syrup of Tolu . . .	30 grms. (℥i.)	20 grms. (ʒv.)	(Adjuvant.)
	Distilled water. . .	60 grms. (℥ii.)	50 grms. (℥iss.)	(Excipient.)
	„ „ of hyssop	25 grms. (ʒvi.)	10 grms. (ʒiiss.)	(Corrigant.)

Subscription.

Make the copaiva into an emulsion, with the yolk of the egg, in a mortar: add the syrup by degrees, and then the distilled waters.

Or:

F. S. A. P. (Fiat secundum artem potio.)

Instruction.

Two table-spoonfuls of this potion to be taken at a time, taking care to shake the phial well each time. Half a glass of sugared water to be taken after each spoonful.

Diet.

Date.

Name of the patient. Signature.

In the case of medicines intended for external use, or of such as are altered by light, the physician should state that they must be put into black or blue vessels.

We cannot leave the subject of what is important in drawing up a magistral prescription, without advising the physician to *write legibly*, the most serious mistakes having arisen from bad writing; and we must not neglect to *read over the prescription*, however simple it may be, for it is the only means of being certain that it is correct.

Even when the prescription is finished, the practitioner ought still to shield himself by certain precautions.

In order that he may not give false impressions to the patient, or be considered ignorant, it is well that he should describe to him carefully both the weight and the volume, the form and other qualities of the medicine which he has prescribed. He must see, that the name which he has given to the medicine is not altered by the pharmaceutist; for changes of this kind, even when not really important, and when the prescription is dispensed with perfect accuracy, are still very objectionable, for the sick person may be afraid of some mistake in consequence of them.

The physician must take account of the length of his patient's purse, even when different remedies might produce the same results: for in the case of a poor man he will prefer sulphate of magnesia to seidlitz powders, and these to lemonade or citrate of magnesia; he will prefer valerian to musk, morphia to codeia, and cinchona to sulphate of quinine, &c. But though this substitution may be made by the physician, it can never be permitted to the druggist.

In no case ought the druggist to make any change in the prescription, unless the error is a palpable one, and he ought never to make observations upon it to the patient or messenger; and if he considers a change indispensable he ought to apprize the physician of it, and if possible, see him before making the alteration.

It is necessary for the physician to calculate what is the proportion of the bodies in each dose of the medicine, if the patient is to divide it into several doses. This is a precaution of the highest importance, for if part only of a mixture, for example, has been taken, but yet has produced certain effects, either expected, or otherwise, they must not be attributed to the entire quantity, or disagreeable consequences might ensue in another case from such a miscalculation.

(§. Students are strongly advised, when first beginning to write prescriptions, to indicate the quantities for each dose, rather than the entire quantity for the whole number of doses. By this means they will become much more familiar with the doses and effects of drugs, than if they prescribe in the ordinary way. They will find it far more instructive to order.

℞ Jalapæ, gr. vi.
Potassæ Bitart. gr. xviii.
Zingiberis, gr. iss.
M. ut fiat pulvis. Mitte vi tales; quorum capiat æger unum, 3tia q. q. hora, donec alvi liquidæ prodeant,

rather than

℞ Pulv. Jalap. comp. ʒiiss in Pulv. vi dividend; quorum, &c.)

If all these things are carefully attended to, it will never happen that the physician orders a mixture of some drops only to be taken by the spoonful, or a soft or solid medicine to be taken by glassfuls.

It is proper to remember, that a mixture contains generally from 100 to 150 grammes (℥iii to ℥v); that tisanes are prescribed by 1000 grammes (℥xxxii); apozems by 400 or 500 grammes (℥xii to ℥xvi); opiates and electuaries are prepared in quantities of 50 to 200 grammes (℥iss to ℥vi) at a time; the weight of pills should not exceed 40 centigrammes (gr. vi), above which they become boluses, which ought to weigh 1 gramme (gr. xv); and lastly, gargles are prescribed to the amount of 200 or 250 grammes (℥vi to ℥viii); glysters by the 500 grammes (℥xvi); demi-glysters 250 grammes (℥viii); and quarter-glysters (℥iv), &c.

We shall conclude these general observations by giving the value of different quantities, such as are adopted by the Fr. Codex.

A coffee-spoonful (nearly identical with our tea-spoonful)	equals	5 grms.	(ℨi 1/4.)
A common mouth- (table) spoonful, or 4 coffee-spoonfuls	„	20 grms.	(℥v)
A glassful, or 8 table-spoonfuls	„	160 grms.	(℥iiiss.)
A pinch of leaves or flowers	(at least)	5 grms.	(ℨi 1/4.)
A handful „ „ „	„	40 grms.	(℥x.)
20 drops of æther	equals	0,35 centigrms.	(gr. vss.)
20 drops of alcohol or tinctures	„	0,45 centigrms.	(gr. vii.)
20 drops of distilled water	„	0,70 centigrms.	(gr. xi.)
20 drops of Sydenham's laudanum	„	0,75 centigrms.	(gr. xiss.)
20 drops of Rousseau's laudanum	„	1,10 centigrms.	(gr. xviss.)
A cupful	about	200 grms.	(℥vi.)
A basinful, or 2 cupfuls.	„	400 grms.	(℥xii.)

All syrups may be employed in doses of 30 grammes (℥i), and some of them in unlimited doses; but never by drops. It is generally better to prescribe any medicine by weight rather than by drops, because these may be larger or smaller, according to the manner of pouring them out, the size of the bottle holding the liquid, (§. and the thickness of the lip of the bottle).

TONICS;

RECONSTITUANT OR ANALEPTIC MEDICINES.

FERRUGINOUS PREPARATIONS;

INSOLUBLE PREPARATIONS OF IRON.

Metallic iron is employed under three forms; 1. iron filings; 2. iron filings porphyrized; and 3. iron reduced by hydrogen.*

Ferruginous Pills.

Take of Iron filings with a metallic lustre. 15 grms. (ʒss.)
Soft extract of cinchona.   .   .   5 grms. (gr. lxxv.)
Some inert excipient   .   .   .   q. s.

Mix them carefully, and divide the mass into 100 pills, which are to be rolled in powdered gum.—From 1 to 10 to be taken daily, during meals.

Used. In simple chlorosis; anæmia, and convalescence from intermitting fevers.

(§. * This preparation, although metallic, when first made, has ceased to be so before being used; for the moment it is exposed to the air, the iron, which was in the form of an impalpable powder, takes fire spontaneously, and becomes oxidized. In this form, however, it is probably more active than in any other; for its state of oxidation is low, and it is in an extremely fine powder. Now experience has proved, that the lower the oxidation of the ferruginous compounds, and the more active their properties; and the more finely any substance is divided, the more easily is it acted upon by the fluids of the body, dissolved, and conveyed into the system.

(This substance is prepared by passing hydrogen gas over red-hot peroxide of iron, during which process the hydrogen and oxygen combine and form steam, leaving the iron behind in the metallic state.)

Others.

Take of Iron reduced by hydrogen,

or

Iron filings, porphyrized,

or

Sub carbonate of iron (ferri sesquioxid.)	. 15 grms.	(ʒss.)
Sub-nitrate of bismuth (nitrate of B.) .	. 20 grms.	(ʒv.)
Watery extract of opium . . .	. 0.20 centigrms.	(gr. iii.)
Syrup of gum.	. q. s.	

Mix, and divide into 125 pills. From 1 to 10 to be taken daily, during meals.

Used. In chlorosis, with pain in the stomach (gastralgia), or in the bowels (enteralgia), or a tendency to diarrhœa.

Others.

Take of Iron reduced by hydrogen .	4 grms.	(ʒi.)
Powdered cinnamon .	. 2 grms.	(ʒss.)
Aloes	. 0,50 centigrms.	(gr. viii.)
Syrup of gum . .	. q. s.	

Mix. For 30 pills. From 1 to 6 to be taken daily.

Used. In chlorosis; anæmia, with constipation and loss of power in the digestive canal.

Tonic Ferruginous Pills.

Take of Iron reduced by hydrogen.	. 10 grms. (ʒiiss.)	
Dry extract of cinchona } of each	5 grms. (gr. lxxv.)	
Powdered rhubarb. . }		
Syrup of gum	. q. s.	

Mix, and divide into 80 pills. To be taken like the last, and in similar cases.

Other Pills.

Take of Hydrated peroxide of iron in powder	15 grms.	(ʒss.)
Powder of belladonna root .	. 0,25 centigrms.	(gr. iv.)
Extract of chicory . . .	. 10 grms.	(ʒiiss.)

Mix, and divide into 100 pills. From 1 to 10 to be taken daily, during meals.

Used. In chlorosis, accompanied with gastralgia and constipation.

Antichlorotic Pills.

Take of Iron filings, porphyrized .	. 4 grms. (ʒi.)	
Extract of wormwood .	. q. s.	

Mix, and let 36 pills be made, S. A. 3 or 4 to be taken night and morning.

Antichlorotic pills. (Blaud.)

Blaud's pills are made of sulphate of protoxide of iron (green sulphate) and carbonate of potash; but their decomposition not being complete, the pills contain sulphate of potash and carbonate of iron, beside the two salts which enter originally into their composition. Besides this, they are very easily changed, and we therefore prefer the following formula :

Blaud's Pills (modified).

Take of Pure crystals of sulphate of protoxide of iron . . . . . } 10 grms. (ʒiiss.)

Powder this, and dry it in a stove at 40° C. (104° F.), and add :

     Dry carbonate of potash . . . . 10 grms. (ʒiiss.)
     White honey . . . . . 5 grms. (gr. lxxv.)

Mix, and divide into 50 pills. From 1 to 10 to be taken daily.

Pills of Vallet.

Take of Honey of iron of Vallet. . . 20 grms. (ʒv.)
     Powdered marsh-mallow . . q. s.

Mix, and divide into 100 pills. From 1 to 10 to be taken daily in chlorosis.

The honey which enters into this preparation prevents the peroxidation of the iron, so that these pills have a more permanent consitution than those of Blaud's, and ought to be preferred.

Ferruginous Powders.

	ADULTS.	CHILDREN.
Take of Iron reduced by hydrogen, or		
Powdered hydrated peroxide of iron.	8 grms. (ʒii.)	2 grms. (ʒss.)
Powdered sugar . . .	20 grms. (ʒv.)	4 grms. (ʒi.)

Mix them carefully, and divide the mixture into 20 equal packets. From 1 to 4 to be taken daily, in the first spoonful of soup, or in biscuit wafer.

Used in anæmia, and after hæmorrhages and intermittent fevers.

Tonic Powders.

Take of Sub-carbonate of iron (ferri. sesquiox. Ph. L.)
Powdered columba
Sub-nitrate of bismuth (nitrate of B. Ph. L.) } of each   10 grms. (ʒiiss.)

Mix them carefully, and divide the mixture into 20 equal packets. 1 to be taken night and morning, during a meal.

Used in the same cases as the preceding, and to check diarrhœa.

Stomachic Tonic Powders.

	ADULTS.	CHILDREN.
Take of Iron reduced by hydrogen	4 grms. (ʒi.)	2 grms. (ʒss.)
Powdered cinamon „ gentian } of each	2 grms. (ʒss.)	1 grm. (gr. xv.)
Calcined magnesia		

Mix them accurately, and divide the mixture into 20 packets. To be taken like the last, and in the same cases.

Used in pyrosis, and atony of the digestive canal.

Antineuralgic Tonic Powders.

Take of Carbonate of iron . . . 50 grms. (ʒiss.)
Powdered valerian root . . 10 grms. (ʒiiss.)

Mix, and divide into 50 packets. From 1 to 10 to be taken daily.

Used in obstinate neuralgia of the temporo-facial nerves, accompanied with chlorosis.

Restorative Tonic Powders.

	ADULTS.	CHILDREN.
Take of Iron reduced by hydrogen	10 grms. (ʒiiss.)	4 grms. (ʒi.)
Powdered grey cinchona	10 grms. (ʒiiss.)	5 grms. (gr. lxxv.)
or		
Dry extract of cinchona.	2 grms. (ʒss.)	1 grm. (gr. xv.)

Mix, and divide into 20 packets. From 1 to 4 to be taken daily.

Used in anæmia, and at the close of intermittent fevers.

Powders for Children.

Take of Sub-carbonate of iron. . . 2 grms. (ʒss.)
Powdered crabs'-eyes . . . 4 grms. (ʒi.)
Sub-nitrate of bismuth . . 6 grms. (ʒiss.)
Powdered sugar . . . . 6 grms. (ʒiss.)
Laudanum of Sydenham . . 10 drops.

Triturate the laudanum accurately with the sugar, add the other powders by small portions at a time, and divide the mixture into 20 packets. 2 to be taken daily.

Used for anæmiated children, weakened by diarrhæa after being weaned, and hæmorrhages or intermittent fevers, &c.

Ferruginous biscuits.

Iron reduced by hydrogen, and also hydrate of (oxide of) iron, are often beneficially given to children in the form of lozenges, chocolate, and biscuits, &c.

Dentifrice Powder

(To prevent the teeth from being blackened by preparations of iron),

Take of Powdered cinchona
Tannin   . . } of each . 10 grms. (ʒiiss.)
Vegetable charcoal

Porphyrize them with care, and add:

Essence of cloves . . . 5 drops.

A soft brush is to be moistened, and dipped into the powder; the teeth are to be rubbed with it, and the mouth washed with water, to which a few drops of water of Bottot have been added.

Syrup of Iron and Rhatany. (Ricord.)

Take of Syrup of Tolu . . . . 500 grms. (ʒxvi.)
Sub-carbonate of iron . . 10 grms. (ʒiiss.)

Mix them by agitation, and add:

Extract of rhatany . . . 10 grms. (ʒiiss.)
Dissolved in a sufficient quantity of warm water.

From 4 to 6 spoonfuls to be taken daily. To be shaken before each dose.

Used in blenorrhæa, and mucous oozings from debility.

Nail, or Rusty Water. (Eau de clous ou ferrée.)

Take of rusty nails . . . . . A handful.
Boiling water . . . . 1000 grms. (ʒxxxii.)

Pour off the water the next morning. To be taken by glassfuls in the course of the day (see p. 67.)

SOLUBLE PREPARATIONS OF IRON,

OR

FERRUGINOUS PREPARATIONS CAPABLE OF BEING ABSORBED IMMEDIATELY.

Ferruginous Solution. (Hôpital de l'Ourcine.)

Take of Tartrate of potash	. .	100 grms. (ʒiii.)
Distilled water	. .	500 grms. (ʒxvi.)

Dissolve and filter. A table-spoonful to be taken pure, or mixed with some tisane.

Used in chlorosis, anæmia, chloro-anæmia, and phagedenic syphilitic ulcers.

N.B. For ferruginous and gaseous compounds, see "Traité de Thérapeutique," Art. Fer.

Ferruginous Potion.

	ADULTS.	CHILDREN.
Take of Tartrate of potash and iron . .	8 grms. (ʒii.)	2 grms. (ʒss.)
Distilled water	100 grms. (ʒiii.)	100 grms. (ʒiii.)
„ „ of cinnamon . .	20 grms. (ʒv.)	10 grms. (ʒiiss.)
Syrup of Tolu	30 grms. (ʒi.)	30 grms. (ʒi.)

Mix them. From 1 to 4 table-spoonfuls to be taken daily in the same cases as the last.

Ferruginous Water of Boules.

	ADULTS.	CHILDREN.
Take of Boules de Nancy* . . .	2 grms. (ʒss.)	1 grm. (gr. xv.)
Water	1000 grms. (ʒxxxii.)	1000 grms. (ʒxxxii.)

Dissolve. Used externally in lotions for blows and bruises; and taken internally to the extent of from 2 to 4 glassfuls daily.

(§. * This is a complicated preparation, made by acting upon iron filings, by a decoction of aromatic species (see p. 202), subsequent evaporation, solution along with impure cream of tartar in a fresh decoction, evaporation, and again a repetition of the solutions and evaporations, &c.. until the mass is at length made into balls, which are the "Boules de Nancy," and consist of an impure tartrate of iron, mixed with a large quantity of vegetable extract. The whole process of manufacture occupies something more than two months.)

Ferruginous Syrup.

Take of Syrup of Tolu . . . . 500 grms. (℥xvi.)
Tartrate of potash and iron . 10 grms. (ʒiiss.)
Cold water . . . q. s.

Dissolve the salt in the water, and add the solution to the syrup. From 2 to 6 spoonfuls to be taken daily.
Used in chlorosis, anæmia, &c.

Syrup of Iodine and Iron (Iodo-ferré). (Mialhe.)

	ADULTS.	CHILDREN.
Take of Syrup of sugar . . . . 500 grms. (℥xvi.)	500 grms. (℥xvi.)
Tartrate of potash and iron		
Iodide of potassium . } of each 10 grms. (ʒiiss.)	4 grms. (ʒi.)
Cinnamon water . .		
Water . . . . q. s. about 8 grms. (ʒii.)	8 grms. (ʒii.)

Dissolve the salts in the filtered water, add the syrup, and shake them together. From 2 to 6 table-spoonsful to be taken daily.
Used in scrophulous affections, accompanied with chlorosis.

Syrup of Iodide of Iron.

	ADULTS.	CHILDREN.
Take of Iodine . } of each . . . 2 grms. (ʒss.)	1 grm. (gr. xv.)
Iron filings }		
Water . . . q. s. about 80 grms. (ʒiiss.)	80 grms. (ʒiiss.)
Boil them together for some minutes, filter, and add :		
Boiling syrup of gum, evaporated } 500 grms. (℥xvi.)	500 grms. (℥xvi.)
to 35°; *i. e.* to sp. gr. 1·32 . }		
Syrup of orange-flower water . 100 grms. (℥iii.)	100 grms. (℥iii.)

Mix them carefully, and keep them in a bottle of coloured glass, and excluded from the air. To be taken like the preceding, and in the same cases.

Injection of Iodine and Iron (Iodo-ferrée).

Take of Iodine . } of each . 1 grm. (gr. xv.)
Pure iron filings }

Boil them in :

Water . . . . . 200 grms. (℥vi.)

Filter them, after a few minutes' ebullition, and add :

Syrup of gum. . . . 30 grms. (℥i.)

Mix. Used as an injection; to be employed from 2 to 6 times a-day in gonorrhœa.

N.B. The syrup of gum is put into the solution to prevent the peroxidation of the iron. See pp. 218, 220.

Ferruginous Lotion.

Take of Sulphate of protoxide of iron (green sulphate) 10 grms. (ʒiiss.)
Tannin . . . . 2 grms. (ʒss.)
Water . . . . 60 grms. (ʒii.)

Carefully triturate the sulphate of iron, and add the tannin by little and little, and then the water. It will form tannate of iron, grayish at first, but blackening in the air in proportion as the iron becomes peroxidized.

Used for touching phagedenic syphilitic ulcers two or three times a-day.

Ferruginous Pills.

Take of Tartrate of potash and iron (tar-} 15 grms. (ʒss.)
trate ferrico-potassique) . .}
Soft extract of cinchona . . 10 grms. (ʒiiss.)
Excipient . . . . . q. s.

Mix and divide into 100 pills. From 1 to 15 to be taken daily.
Used in the treatment of phagedenic syphilitic ulcers, and in most cases in which the internal use of iron is indicated.

Others.

Take of tartrate ferrico-potassique (see above) . 15 grms. (ʒss.)
Soft extract of rhatany . . . . 5 grms. (gr. lxxv.)
Excipient . . . . . . q. s.

Mix, and divide into 100 pills. From 1 to 10 to be taken daily.
Used in chlorosis accompanied by menorrhagia; and in anæmia from hæmorrhage.

Tonic-Astringent Pills.

Take of Copaiva balsam .} of each . 10 grms. (ʒiiss.)
Extract of gentian }
Sulphate of iron } of each . 5 grms. (gr. lxxv.)
Kino . . }
Excipient . . . . q. s.

Mix, and divide the mass into pills of 1 decigramme (gr. iss). From 4 to 16 to be taken during the day, made into 3 or 4 doses.
Used in chronic mucous discharges and leucorrhœa.

Q

Pills of Lactate of Iron.

	ADULTS	CHILDREN.
Take of lactate of iron	4 grms. (ʒi.)	1 grm. (gr. xv.)
Powdered liquorice . . .	4 grms. (ʒi.)	1 grm. (gr. xv.)
Honey	q. s.	q. s.

Mix, and divide into 40 pills. From 1 to 6 to be taken daily.

Pills of Citrate of Iron.

The citrate of iron possesses the same properties as lactate of iron, and is given in the same cases and in the same doses.

Astringent Pomatum.

Take of Sulphate of protoxide of iron, powdered, and dried   20 grms. (ʒv.)
Lard . . . . 50 grms. (ʒiss.)

Mix them intimately by porphyrization.
Used for anointing parts affected with traumatic, or merely local erysipelas.

Astringent Solution. (Velpeau.)

Take of Sulphate of protoxide of iron.   60 grms. (ʒii.)
Water . . . . . 1000 grms. (ʒxxxii.)

Dissolve. Used in lotions and fomentations, in the same cases as the preceding pomatum.

Ferruginous Baths.

	ADULTS.	CHILDREN.
Take of Sulphate of protoxide of iron .	1000 grms. (ʒxxxii.)	100 grms. (ʒiii.)

Dissolve it in the water contained in a bath of well tinned copper, and not of zinc or wood.
Used for persons for whom preparations of iron are indicated, but whose stomach will not bear the iron.

N.B. These baths leave an indelible rusty stain upon the towels used for drying the skin.

ASTRINGENTS FURNISHED BY THE MINERAL KINGDOM.

LEAD.

Mixture.

Take of Carbonate of lead (cerussa) . 10 grms. (ʒiiss.)
Mucilage of gum-arabic . . q. s.

To make a soft paste to be spread upon the temple or the forehead in cases of facial neuralgia, and to be renewed several times a-day. If the pain is very severe, we may add to the above:

Extract of opium . . . 2 grms. (ʒss.)

. Diffused in:

Water . . . . . 8 grms. (ʒii.)

Astringent Pills.

Take of Neutral acetate of lead . 1 grm.   (gr. xv.)
Powder of white agaric . 0,50 centigrms. (gr. viii.)
Syrup of opium . . q. s.

Mix, and divide into 10 pills. From 1 to 4 to be taken daily to moderate the swéating in phthysis, and to check chronic colli-quative diarrhœa.

Astringent Lotion.

Take of Liquid sub-acetate of lead (extractum saturni)   30 grms. (ʒi.)
Spring, or river water . . . . 500 grms. (ʒxvi.)
Alcohol, at 36° (sp. gr. ·835) . . . . 25 grms. (ʒvi.)

Mix. Used for vaginal injections in cases of leucorrhœa, for lotions and fomentations in acute and chronic eczema, and in pruritus of the vulva.

Astringent Gargle.

Take of liquid sub-acetate of lead . . 30 grms. (ʒi.)
Water . . . . . 150 grms. (ʒv.)

For a collutoire, to be held in the mouth in excessive mercurial salivation.

N.B. This gargle has the serious objection of blackening the teeth.

Antidysenteric Glyster.

	ADULTS.	CHILDREN.
Take of Solution of acetate of lead . {	10 to 100 grms. (ʒiiss to ʒiii.)	2 to 10 grms. (ʒss to ʒiiss.)
Distilled water . . .	500 grms. (ʒxvi)	160 grms. (ʒv.)

For a glyster, to be given during the most acute part of a dysentery.

SULPHATE OF ALUMINA AND POTASH, (ALUM).

Astringent Potion.

Take of Alum	10 grms. (ʒiiss.)
Water	200 grms. (ʒvi.)
Syrup of Rhatany . . .	60 grms. (ʒii.)

Dissolve the alum in the water, and add the syrup. To be taken in 4 doses, with an interval of half an hour between them. *Used* in hæmoptysis, and uterine hæmorrhages.

Astringent Pills.

	ADULTS.	CHILDREN.
Take of Powdered alum	10 grms. (ʒiiss.)	4 grms. (ʒi.)
Powdered kino	10 grms. (ʒiiss.)	4 grms. (ʒi.)
Syrup of gum	q. s.	q. s.

Mix, and divide into 100 pills. From 2 to 10 to be taken daily. *Used* in chronic diarrhœa and chronic menorrhagia.

Astringent Glysters.

	ADULTS.	CHILDREN.
Take of Alum	10 grms. (ʒiiss.)	2 grms. (ʒss.)
Water.	500 grms. (ʒxvi.)	150 grms. (ʒv.)

Dissolve. *Used* as a glyster in diarrhœa.

Astringent Injections.

Take of Alum	8 grms. (ʒii.)
Decoction of walnut leaves .	1000 grms. (ʒxxxii.)

Dissolve. *Used* for vaginal injections in leucorrhœa.

Astringent Gargle.

	ADULTS.	CHILDREN.
Take of Alum	10 to 30 grms. (ʒiiss to ʒi.) {	2 to 6 grms. (ʒss to ʒiss.)
Water	500 grms. (ʒxvi.)	200 grms. (ʒvi.)
Syrup of mulberries .	100 grms. (ʒiii.)	60 grms. (ʒii.)

Dissolve the alum in the water, and add the syrup. To be used as a gargle several times a-day in chronic diseases of the throat, which have caused much alteration in the tone of the voice, or deafness. Used also in alterations of the voice without any appreciable lesions of the throat ; in œdema, with dropping of the uvula.

Collutoire.

Take of Powdered alum . . . . 4 grms. (ʒi.)
White honey . . . 20 grms. (ʒv.)

Reduce the alum to a very fine powder, and rub it upon a porphyrizing slab with a few drops of water.

Used as a collutoire, with which to smear several times daily the mouths of children affected with thrush, or with mercurial inflammation of the tongue, &c.

Mixture for Croup.

Take of Powdered alum. . . . 10 grms. (ʒiss.)
White honey . . . . 40 grms. (ʒx.)

Prepare it like the collutoire above. Half a spoonful of this mixture to be given to the child every hour, and powdered alum is at the same time to be blown down its throat every 4 hours. Used also in diptheritis, even when the change in the tone and strength of the voice proves that the larynx is affected.

Odontalgic Mastic. (Foullon, dentist.)

Take of Resin of mastic (*pistacia lentiscus*) . 2 grms. (ʒss.)
Powder it, and dissolve it in :
Ether. . . . . . 6 grms. (ʒiss.)
Add :
Powdered alum . . . . 4 grms. (ʒi.)
„ gum-arabic . . . q. s.

To make a soft paste, which is to be put into the hollow of carious teeth. The mastic hardens by the evaporation of the ether. It cures the pain in the teeth, and often checks the decay.

SULPHURIC ACID.

Astringent Tisane.

Take of Eau de Rabel (alcool sulfurique, p. 62) .	8 grms. (ʒii.)
or	
Sulphuric acid	2 grms. (ʒss.)
or, better still, sufficient to make it agreeably acid to the patient's palate.	
Decoction of barley	1000 grms. (ʒxxxii.)
Syrup of catechu	30 grms. (ʒi.)

To be drank by glassfuls in the course of the day.
Used in pulmonary, uterine and nasal hæmorrhages, &c.

ASTRINGENTS FURNISHED BY THE VEGETABLE KINGDOM.

TANNIN.

Pills.

	ADULTS.	CHILDREN.
Take of Tannin.	1 grm. (gr. xv.)	{ 0,15 centigrms. (gr. ii 1/3.)
Soft extract of rhatany. . .	2 grms. (ʒss.)	1 grm. (gr. xv.)
Excipient	q. s.	q. s.

Mix and divide into 20 pills.   From 1 to 10 to be taken daily.
Used in chronic diarrhœa, colliquative sweats and hæmorrhages.

Compound Powder of Tannin.

	ADULTS.	CHILDREN.
Take of Tannin	1 grm. (gr. xv.)	{ 0,15 centigrms. (gr. ii 1/3.)
Sugar.	10 grms. (ʒiiss.)	10 grms. (ʒiiss.)

Rub them accurately together, and divide into 20 equal packets.
From 1 to 10 to be taken daily in preserve or unfermented bread.
Used in the same cases as the last.

Glyster.

	ADULTS.	CHILDREN.
Take of Tannin . . .	{ 0,50 centigrms. (gr. viii.)	0,15 centigrms. (gr. ii 1/3.)
Water. . . .	250 grms. (ʒviii.)	150 grms. (ʒv.)
Laudanum of Sydenham . .	10 drops.	2 drops.

Dissolve the tannin in the water, and add the laudanum.
Used in the same cases as the powders above.

Injection.

| Take of Tannin | . | . | . | . | . | 1 grm. (gr. xv.) |
| Water | . | . | . | . | . | 100 grms. (ʒiii.) |

Dissolve. Used as an injection up the urethra in chronic
gleet; up the nose in epistaxis, or chronic catarrhal discharge,
(coryza); and the ears, in discharge from them.

Solution for Lotions.

| Take of Tannin | . | . | . | . | . | 10 grms. (ʒiiss.) |
| Water | . | . | . | . | . | 500 grms. (ʒxvi.) |

Dissolve. Used as a lotion for scrophulous ulcers.

Suppository of Tannin.

| Take of Tannin | . | . | . | . | . | 1 grm. (gr. xv.) |
| Cocoa butter | . | . | . | . | 4 grms. (ʒi.) |

Melt the cocoa butter by a gentle heat; reduce the tannin to
a fine powder; mix it with the cocoa butter, and stir them until
the fatty matter is nearly congealed; then put it into a paper
mould, and fix a small tape into the suppository, which is to be
used in cases of bleeding piles, and of mucous discharges from
the rectum. Also in cases of thread-worms and fissures of the
anus.

Solution for Uterine Hæmorrhages.

| Take of Tannin | . | . | . | . | . | 20 grms. (ʒv.) |
| Water | . | . | . | . | . | 10 grms. (ʒiiss.) |

Dissolve, and moisten plugs (tampons) of tow in the solution,
which are to be applied to the neck of the uterus; or larger plugs
may be used, if intended to be placed in the vagina.

Used in inflammation of the mucous membrane of the vagina,
and especially in the case of pregnant women.

GALLS, OAK-BARK, &c.

Astringent Glyster.

| Take of Powdered galls | . | . | . | 4 grms. (ʒi.) |
| Water | . | . | . | . | 500 grms. (ʒxvi.) |

Boil them down to 400 grms. (ʒxii), and strain.
Used in chronic diarrhœa, and excessive hæmorrhage from piles.

Astringent Tisane.

Take of Coarsely powdered oak-bark .   80 grms. (ʒiiss)
Water .   .   .   .   . 1100 grms. (ʒxxxvi.)

Boil them down to 1000 grammes (ʒxxxii), and strain.

Used as an astringent, and as an antidote in poisoning by antimonials and the vegetable alkaloids.

Astringent Injection.

Take of Powdered galls .   .   .   10 grms. (ʒiiss.)
,,   bistort   .   .   5 grms. (gr. lxxv.)
Walnut leaves .   .   .   15 grms. (ʒss.)
Water .   .   .   . 1000 grms. (ʒxxxii.)

Boil them down to 800 grammes (ʒxxvi), and strain.

Used in cases of "whites" and in pruritus of the vulva.

CATECHU, KINO, SANDRAGON, (DRAGON'S BLOOD).

Pills.

	ADULTS.	CHILDREN.
Take of Catechu or kino	2 grms. (ʒss.)	1 grm. (gr. xv.)
Syrup of gum	q. s.	q. s.

Mix, and divide into 10 pills.   From 1 to 10 to be taken daily.

Used in intestinal hæmorrhages and chronic diarrhœa.

Powders.

Take of Powdered extract of catechu .   .   . 1 grm. (gr. xv.)
,,   sugar .   .   .   . 2 grms. (ʒss.)

Mix and divide into 10 powders.   From 1 to 4 to be taken daily by children affected with chronic diarrhœa.

Astringent Tisane.

	ADULTS.	CHILDREN.
Take of Decoction of rice . . .	1000 grms. (ʒxxxii.)	500 grms. (ʒxvi.)
Powdered catechu or kino .	2 grms. (ʒss.)	1 grm. (gr. xv.)
Syrup of quince . . .	100 grms. (ʒiii.)	60 grms. (ʒii.)

Used in the same cases as the above powders.

Astringent Potion.

	ADULTS.	CHILDREN.
Take of Pure kino	2 grms. (ʒss.)	1 grm. (gr. xv.)
Water	100 grms. (ʒiii)	100 grms. (ʒiii.)
Mix by trituration, filter, and add :		
Syrup of quince . . .	30 grms. (ʒi.)	30 grm. (ʒi.)

Used in chronic diarrhœa, dysentery and hæmoptysis.

Astringent Collutoires.

Take of Powdered catechu or kino . . 10 grms. (ʒiiss.)
Honey of roses . . . . 10 grms. (ʒiiss.)

Mix.   Used in swelling and ulceration of the gums.

RHATANY.

Tisane.

	ADULTS.	CHILDREN.
Take of Powdered rhatany root . . 40 grms. (ʒx.)		10 grms. (ʒiiss.)
Water . . . . . 1000 grms. (ʒxxxii.)		500 grms. (ʒxvi.)
Boil, then strain, and add :		
Syrup of quince . . . 100 grms. (ʒiii.)		60 grms. (ʒii.)

Used in hæmorrhages, melena and chronic diarrhœa.

Astringent Pills.

	ADULTS.	CHILDREN.
Take of Dry extract of rhatany . . . 10 grms. (ʒiiss.)		4 grms. (ʒi.)
Excipient . . . . . q. s.		q s.

Mix, and divide into 50 pills.   From 1 to 15 to be taken daily.
Used in hæmorrhages, chronic diarrhœa and excessive bronchial, urethral, or uterine mucous flux.

Astringent Potion.

	ADULTS.	CHILDREN.
Take of Soft extract of rhatany . . . 2 grms. (ʒss.)		0,50 cent. (gr. viii.)
Water . . . . . 100 grms. (ʒiii.)		80 grms. (ʒiiss.)
Dissolve, filter, and add :		
Syrup of quince . . . . 40 grms. (ʒx.)		30 grms. (ʒi)

Mix.   To be taken in 4 doses in hæmoptysis.

Glyster.

	ADULTS.	CHILDREN.
Take of Soft extract of rhatany . . 5 grms. (gr. lxxv)		0,50 cent. (gr. viii.)
Tincture of rhatany . . 4 grms. (ʒi.)		1 grm. (gr. xv.)
Water . . . . . 250 grms. (ʒviii.)		125 grms. (ʒiv.)

Dissolve the extract in the water, filter if the solution is not clear, and add the tincture.
Used in bleeding piles, fissures in the anus, and chronic dysentery.

Gargle.

Take of Soft extract of rhatany   .   .   10 grms. (ʒiiss.)
     Mixture of rhatany   .   .   15 grms. (ʒss.)
     Water   .   .   .   .   250 grms. (ʒviii.)
     Syrup of mulberries   .   .   60 grms. (ʒii)

Dissolve the extract in the water, and add the syrup and tincture. To be held in the mouth, in order to bathe the tongue and gums in mercurial salivation, painful ulcers of the gums, and a spongy condition of the mouth.

Mixture.

Take of Dry extract of rhatany   .   .   10 grms. (ʒiiss.)
     Mucilage of quince seeds   .   .   q. s. to give the
        consistence of a soft electuary.

Powder the extract, and afterwards add the mucilage.

Used to relieve the pain of hospital gangrene, bleeding and painful ulcers, the surface of blysters which are covered with a pultaceous secretion, and which are tending to gangrene. Applied also to fissures of the anus, the nipples, or the lips, and to ulcerated chilblains.

Decoction for Injections.

Take of Powdered rhatany root   .   .   50 grm.   (ʒiss.)
     Water   .   .   .   .   1 kilogrm. (ʒxxxii.)

Boil them down to 800 grammes (ʒxxvi).

Used for vaginal injections, in leucorrhœa; up the rectum, in hæmorrhoids with great bleeding, and applied as a lotion or fomentation in cases of fissured anus.

MONESIA, PAULLINIA, CREOSOTE, AND SOOT.

Potion.

	ADULTS.	CHILDREN.
Take of Extract of monesia (*chrysophyllum glyciphyllum*). . . .	2 grms. (ʒss.)	0,25 to 0,50 cent. (gr. iv to gr. viii.)
Water	100 grms. (ʒiii.)	60 grms. (ʒii.)
Syrup of gum . . .	40 grms. (ʒx.)	30 grms. (ʒi.)

Dissolve the extract in the water; filter if necessary, and add the syrup. To be taken in 4 doses.

Used in chronic diarrhœa.

Powders.

Take of Powdered extract of Paullinia (*Paullinia sorbilis*) . 5 grms. (gr. lxxv.)

Divide it into 10 packets. From 1 to 5 of them to be taken at the beginning of a periodical headache, and one packet night and morning for several days about the expected period of its return, as a preventive measure.

Creosote for Tooth-ache.

Take of Pure creosote   .   .   5 grms. (gr. lxxv.)
Tincture of pyrethrum .   10 grms. (ʒiiss.)

Mix them, and soak a little cotton in the mixture, and put it into the hollow tooth.

Desiccative Pomatum.

Take of Creosote   .   .   .   2 to 8 grms. (ʒss to ʒii.)
Cerate   .   .   .   30 grms. (ʒi.)

Used for dressing indolent ulcers.

Pomatum for Psoriasis.

Take of Naphthaline   .   .   .   8 grms. (ʒii.)
Lard washed in rose-water .   30 grms. (ʒi.)

Mix. *Used* by means of friction in psoriasis and other cutaneous eruptions.

Anthelmintic Mixture for Children.

Take of Soot from wood (sifted)   .   .   8 grms. (ʒii.)
Roasted coffee (powdered) .   15 grms. (ʒss.)
Water   .   .   .   .   125 grms. (ʒiv.)

Boil them together, strain, and add :

Simple syrup   .   .   .   50 grms. (ʒiss.)

To be taken in a single dose in the morning, fasting, by children who are affected with round worms, (ascaris lombricoides).

Anthelmintic Glyster.

Take of Sifted wood-soot   .   .   25 grms. (ʒvi.)

Boil it in:

Water   .   .   .   .   200 grms. (ʒvi.)

Strain. For a glyster to be given in the evening for several days in succession, half an hour before the child goes to bed, to destroy thread worms, (oxyuris vermicularis).

OIL OF PAPER, (PYROTHONIDE).

Make cigars of white blotting-paper, and gently inhale the smoke into the larynx night and morning, for the cure of chronic superficial ulcerations of the larynx.

Antidartrous Lotion.

Take of Oil of paper   .   .   .   10 grms. (ʒiiss.)
       Water   .   .   .   1000 grms. (ʒxxxii.)

Mix.   For lotions.

Pomatum.

Take of Oil of paper .   .   .   4 grms. (ʒi.)
    Benzoinated lard .   .   30 grms. (℥i.)

Mix.   For smearing over parts covered with scurf.

ALTERATIVES.

METALLIC MERCURY.

Pills.

Take of Fluid mercury } of each .   . 3 grms. (gr. xlv.)
    White honey }

Rub them together until the mercury is extinguished, and add:

        Powdered rhubarb .   .   1 grm. (gr. xv.)
         ,,   liquorice .   .   q. s.

Mix, and divide into 40 pills. From 1 to 3 to be taken in the course of the day.

Used as a laxative, in the treatment of secondary syphilis, and as an antiphlogistic.

Pills.

Take of Double mercurial ointment (Ung. Hydrarg. } 6 grms. (ʒiss.)
    fort. Ph. L.) .   .   .   .   .   .
    White soap .   .   .   .   .   6 grms. (ʒiss.)
    Powdered liquorice .   .   .   q. s.

Mix, and divide into 60 pills. To be taken like the above. (§. It has been stated that the mercurial ointment salivates readily when taken in the above form after the common Pil. Hydrarg. had failed to produce that effect).

Resolvent Pomatum.

Take of Double mercurial ointment } of each   15 grms. (ʒss.)
      Poplar ointment.   .   . }

Mix.   To anoint swollen parts.

Pomatum.

Take of Double mercurial ointment   .   .   30 grms. (ʒi.)
      Alcoholic extract of belladonna   .   4 grms. (ʒi.)

Mix.   Used for frictions; and in peritonitis and amaurosis.

Softening Plaster.

Take of Plaster of Vigo*   . } of each   .   .   Equal parts.
   ,,   ,,   Conium }

Press the two plasters together, and with the mixture make shields, (écussons, p. 189), which are to be applied to enlarged ganglions and to bubos, and which are to surround the testicles in orchitis and inflammation of the epidydimis.

Ophthalmic Pomatum.

Take of Binoxide of mercury (red precipitate)   .   .   0,25 centigrms. (gr. iv.)
    Tutty (oxide of tin), or, better still, oxide of } 0,50 centigrms. (gr. viii.)
     zinc .   .   .   . }
    Fresh lard   .   .   .   . 10 grms.   (ʒiiss.)

Mix, and rub them most carefully upon the porphyrizing table, and make an ointment.

Used as an ointment to the edges of the eyelids in chronic inflammation of them; rubbed upon the skin when affected with scurf or eruptions, and especially with vesicular ones (rupia), and upon cauterized surfaces.

Powder for External Use.

Take of Binoxide of mercury   .   .   .   .   0,50 centigrms. (gr. viii.)
    White precipitate (protochloride of mer- } 1 grm.   (gr. xv.)
     cury by precipitation)   .   .   . }
    Powdered sugar   .   .   .   .   30 grms.   (ʒi.)

Mix and porphyrize them. Preserve them for use in a well-stopped wide-mouthed bottle, which is to be kept in the dark and in a dry place. To be taken disguised in tobacco, in the treatment of ozena; to improve the character of bleeding unhealthy ulcers, hospital gangrene and wounds covered with false membrane.

(ʒ. * This is nearly the same as the Empl. Ammoniaci c. Hydrarg. Ph. L.)

Compound Powder.

Take of Protochloride of mercury prepared }
  by sublimation . . . } 0,10 centigrms. (gr. iss.)
Sugar . . . . . . 3 grms. (gr. xlv.)

Mix, triturate them with care, and divide them into 20 equal
packets.

Used internally. One packet every one or two hours to produce a general mercurial affection of the system and swelling of
the gums, in acute peritonitis, pleurisy, pericarditis, acute synovial
rheumatism, iritis, acute syphilitic laryngitis, and dysentery.
Used also to produce a gentle purging and to destroy intestinal
worms, and in dyphtheritis of the pharynx and trachæa.

Externally it is taken concealed in tobacco at the commencement of acute coryza, two or three times a day, and in the same
way in chronic coryza and in ozena. It is applied to the surface
of unhealthy wounds, of hospital gangrene, and cutaneous dyph-
tharites.

It is also blown into the eye (§. through a quill) in chronic
ophthalmia and in opacity of the cornea.

Powder for Sprinkling.

Take of White precipitate . . . . 5 grms. (gr. lxxv.)
 Perfumed starch (common hair-powder) 100 grms. (ℨiii.)

Mix them carefully. To powder the head of children affected
with lice, or with pityriasis of the scalp.

Powder for Dressings.

Take of White precipitate }
 Powdered savine. } of each. . 2 grms. (ʒss.)

Mix them carefully. To soften indurated chancres, which are
to be washed several times a day with aromatic wine, and covered
each time with this powder. When the induration has disappeared, pure white precipitate or calomel is to be used.

Pills for External Use.

Take of White precipitate }
 Powdered gum . } of each. 0,50 centigrms. (gr. viii.)
Honey . . . q. s.

Mix, and make into 10 pills, which are to be rolled and kept in
powdered gum. Dissolve one of these pills in a spoon with one
or two drops of water, so as to make a kind of clear soup. Carry

this soup to the bottom of the throat with the forefinger in cases of chronic angina of the pharynx, or to the root of the tongue and the glottis in cases of hooping-cough. Introduce a drop of this preparation between the eyelids in cases of catarrhal scurvy or scrophulous ophthalmia. Apply it to fissures of the anus, the breasts or the lips.

Calomel Pills.

		ADULTS.	CHILDREN.
Take of Calomel prepared by sublimation . {		0,50 centigrms. (gr. viii.)	0,20 centigrms. (gr. iii.)
Extract of gentian . . . {		0,50 centigrms. (gr. viii.)	0,50 centigrms. (gr. viii.)
Gum-arabic		q. s.	q. s.

Mix, and divide into 20 pills. From 1 to 10 to be taken daily. *Used* as a laxative and in cases of worms, &c.

Dry Collyrium.

Take of Calomel . . .	0,20 centigrms. (gr. iii.)
White oxide of zinc .	0,50 centigrms. (gr. viii.)
Powdered sugar . .	2 grms. (3ss.)

Mix, and porphyrize them. The powder is to be blown into the eye, through a quill, in chronic ophthalmia, and in specks on the cornea.

Liniment.

Take of White precipitate . . . . . } of each {	0,50 centigrms.
Red " (binoxide of mercury) } of each {	(gr. viii.)
Oil of sweet almonds	4 grms. (3i.)
Lard	2 grms. (3ss.)

For a liniment to be applied by a camel's-hair pencil to the whole external auditory canal, in cases of otorrhœa (discharge from the ear); and to the edges of the eyelids in cases of chronic palpebral ophthalmia.

SOLUBLE MERCURIAL PREPARATIONS.

Amongst the soluble preparations of mercury, the bichloride, and occasionally, but very rarely, the cyanide have been employed internally : the others, such as the sulphates, nitrates, &c., are almost entirely abandoned. Even the acid nitrate of mercury, so often employed as a caustic, is generally replaced in the present day by the monohydrated nitric acid.*

We shall give chiefly the formulæ into which the bichloride of mercury (corrosive sublimate) enters. They may be divided into five classes:

1. Preparations in which corrosive sublimate possesses its own peculiar properties.

2. Those in which its action is augmented.

3. Those in which its action is modified by combination with extractive matters.

4. Those in which its effects are still more modified by albuminous substances.

5. And, lastly, those in which the corrosive sublimate is entirely decomposed.

1. *Medicines which contain corrosive sublimate without alteration.*

Van Swieten's Solution.

Take of Bichloride of mercury (corrosive sublimate)   1 grm. (gr. xv.)
Alcohol . . . . 96 grms. (℥iii.)

Dissolve the salt in the alcohol, and add:

Distilled water .   . . . . 904 grms. (℥xxix.)

This solution contains the thousandth part of its weight of corrosive sublimate, (§. and is, practically speaking, identical in strength with the Liq. Hydrarg. Bichlor. Co. Ph. L.)

Used in secondary syphilis, in doses of 1 to 2 spoonfuls in a glass of water. It ought to be administered by a wooden, and not a metallic spoon.

Solution for Lotions.

Take of Bichloride of mercury . . 0,25 cent (gr. iv.)
Eau de Cologne . . . 100 grms. (℥iii.)

Dissolve. A tea-spoonful of this solution to be put into a glass of water, and used as a lotion to kill lice on the head, the body, or the pubis. Used also to cure dartres, &c.

Solution for Injections and Lotions.

Take of Bichloride of mercury . . 10 grms. (℥iis.)
Alcohol . . . . 100 grms. (℥iii.)

* (§. According to Mr. Phillips there is no such liquid, the smallest quantity of water with which nitric acid can remain permanently combined being 1½ equivalents.)

Dissolve. From 1 to 4 tea-spoonfuls are to be mixed with 32 grammes of very warm water, and the mixture is used for injections and lotions in the same cases as the *eau phagédénique*, (yellow wash).

N.B. Sponges should never be used for applying these lotions, as they rapidly harden, and become useless. This phenomenon is due to the combination of the animal matter with the sublimate, (§. on which principle a solution of corrosive sublimate is used for hardening brains before they are dissected.)

Bath of Corrosive Sublimate.

	ADULTS.	CHILDREN.
Take of Bichloride of mercury .	15 to 30 grms. (ʒss to ʒi.)	2 to 4 grms. (ʒss to ʒi)
Alcohol . . .	100 grms. (ʒiii.)	50 grms. (ʒiss.)

Dissolve, and add to a bathful of water. (See Compound baths of corrosive sublimate, p. 242).

Antisyphilitic Gargle.

Take of Corrosive sublimate . . 0,05 cent. (gr. 3/4.)
Distilled water . . . 250 grms. (ʒviii.)

Dissolve. For a gargle for syphilitic ulcers.

Pomatum (Ointment) of Cyrillus (modified).

Take of Corrosive sublimate . . 1 grm. (gr. xv.)
Lard . . . . 20 grms. (ʒv.)

Mix upon a porphyrizing slab.

Used in dartres and venereal ulcers to the extent of 2 to 4 grms. (ʒss to ʒi).

Vermifuge Glyster.

	ADULTS.	CHILDREN.
Take of Bichloride of mercury .	0,10 cent. (gr. iss.)	0,02 cent. (gr. 1/3.)
Distilled water . .	200 grms. (ʒvi.)	100 grms. (ʒiii.)

Dissolve. To be administered as a glyster by means of a glass syringe, to destroy thread worms, (ascaris vermicularis).

2. *Medicines in which the action of the corrosive sublimate is augmented, or at least in which the remedy is less easily decomposed.*

Van Swieten's Solution Modified. (Mialhe.)

Take of Bichloride of mercury (corrosive sublimate) . 0,40 cent. (gr. vi.)
Hydrochlorate of ammonia ⎫ of each . . 1 grm. (gr. xv.)
Chloride of sodium . . ⎭
Distilled water . . . . 500 grms. (ʒxvi.)

R

Dissolve the salts in the water. From 1 to 2 table-spoonfuls to be taken night and morning in the same cases as the common solution of Van Swieten. (§. The composition of this solution corresponds more nearly than that of the common solution (p. 240) to the Liq. Hydr. Bichlor. Co. Ph. L., but it is not quite so strong, 13 parts of this French preparation being equal to 10 of the London one).

Compound Bath of Corrosive Sublimate.

	ADULTS.	CHILDREN.
Take of Bichloride of mercury	15 to 30 grms. (ʒss to ʒi.)	2 to 4 grms. (ʒss to ʒi.)
Hydrochlorate of ammonia (sal-ammoniac) . }	30 grms. (ʒi.)	5 grms. (ʒi 1/4.)

Triturate with care, and dissolve the salts in sufficient water (about 250 grammes, ʒviii), and add the solution to a common bath. Baths of sublimate ought to be taken in vessels made of wood, not of metal, especially copper. Zinc and tin also precipitate mercury from its solutions, but this inconvenience is less liable to happen with the compound than with the simple bath of corrosive sublimate.

Used to destroy lice on the body; in the treatment of chronic diseases of the skin; of constitutional syphilitic affections, either with or without any cutaneous affection, especially in women and children; and in chronic rheumatism and swelling of the joints.

Cosmetic Lotion.

Take of Bichloride of mercury . . .	0,10 centigrms.	(gr. iss.)
Sal-ammoniac	2 grms.	(ʒss.)
Alcohol . . } of each	15 grms.	(ʒss.)
Distilled water of bitter almonds }		

Dissolve the salts in the distilled water and the alcohol, and add:

Emulsion of bitter almonds . .	500 grms.	(ʒxvi.)

Mix them carefully, and label the mixture " For *external* use."
Used, when made into lotions, in pityriasis, acne, and chronic eczema, &c.

3. *Preparations in which the action of the corrosive sublimate is modified by mixture with extractive matters.*

Antisyphilitic Pills (Dupuytren).

Take of Bichloride of mercury	0,02* centigrms.	(gr. 1/3.)
Gummy extract of opium	0,40 centigrms.	(gr. vi.)
Extract of guaiacum	0,80 centigrms.	(gr. xii.)
Excipient	q. s.	

Mix, and divide into 16 pills, each of which contains 12 millegrammes (gr. 1/5) of corrosive sublimate. (§. The French formula above (0·02) cent.) is evidently a misprint for 0·20 cent., for the former quantity would only furnish gr. 1/48 instead of gr. 1/5 in each pill). From 1 to 4 to be taken daily.

Used in constitutional syphilitic affections. The opium makes the sublimate more easily borne by the patient.

Antisyphilitic Pills.

	ADULTS.	CHILDREN.
Take of Bichloride of mercury	0,50 centigrms. (gr. viii)	0,10 centigrms. (gr. iss.)
Starch	4 grms. (ʒi.)	2 grms. (ʒss.)
Syrup of sugar	q. s.	q. s.

Mix, and divide into 50 pills. From 1 to 4 to be taken daily in the same cases as above.

Antisyphilitic Gargle.

	ADULTS.	CHILDREN.
Take of Bichloride of mercury	0,05 centigrms. (gr. 3/4.)	0,01 centigrms. (gr. 1/6.)
Barley water	200 grms. (ʒvi.)	200 grms. (ʒvi.)
White honey	60 grms. (ʒii.)	60 grms. (ʒii.)

Mix. For a gargle to be used several times a day in syphilitic ulceration of the mouth.

4. *Preparations in which the corrosive sublimate undergoes some change from combination with albuminous substances.*

Antisyphilitic Tisane.

	ADULTS.	CHILDREN.
Take of Van Swieten's solution (p. 240)	10 grms. (ʒiiss.)	2 grms. (ʒss.)
Milk	1000 grms. (℥xxxii.)	1000 grms. (℥xxxii.)

(§. * Should be 0,20 centigrms. (gr. iii.) See note, above).

R 2

Mix. To be taken by cupfuls in the course of the day. *Used* in constitutional syphilitic affections.

Antisyphilitic Gargle.

	ADULTS.	CHILDREN.
Take of Bichloride of mercury (corrosive sublimate).	0,05 centigrms. (gr. 3/4.)	0,02 centigrms. (gr. 1/3.)
Water . . .	q. s. about 10 grms. (ʒiiss.)	
Fresh milk . .	200 grms. (ʒvi.)	200 grms. (ʒvi.)

Mix. For a gargle to be used in syphilitic ulcerations of the mouth.

Pills of Corrosive Sublimate, with Gluten.

	ADULTS.	CHILDREN.
Take of Bichloride of mercury .	0,10 centigrms. (gr. iss.)	0,02 centigrms. (gr. 1/3.)
Fresh gluten . .	1,60 centigrms. (gr. xxiv.)	1 grm. (gr. xv.)
Powdered marsh-mallow .	0,60 centigrms. (gr. ix.)	0,60 centigrms. (gr. ix.)
Excipient . . .	q. s.	q. s.

Mix carefully by trituration in a marble mortar, the corrosive sublimate and the marsh-mallow, add the gluten by degrees, and then the excipient, if one is necessary, and divide into 16 pills. From 1 to 5 to be taken daily in secondary syphilis.

In this preparation, part of the sublimate remains free, but the greater part enters into combination with the gluten.

Pills of Sublimate and Bread-Crumbs.

	ADULTS.	CHILDREN.
Take of Corrosive sublimate .	0,05 centigrms. (gr. 3/4.)	0,01 centigrms.* (gr. 1/6.)
Bread-crumbs .	1,20 centigrms. (gr. xviii.)	1,20 centigrms. (gr. xviii.)
Distilled water .	0,20 centigrms. (gr. iii.)	0,20 centigrms. (gr. iii.)

Triturate the sublimate in a mortar, add the bread-crumb by degrees, then the distilled water, and divide into 12 pills, each of which contains gr. 1/16 for adults or 1/32 of a grain for children. Even in these pills the corrosive sublimate is somewhat modified,

(‡. * There is evidently some mistake here in the dose, which ought probably to be 0,025 milligrms. (gr. 3/8), instead of 0,01 centigrms.; for in the further account of the pills, the quantity in each pill is stated to be 1/32 of a grain; whereas it would be 1/72 grain if the whole quantity was only 0,01 centigrms., as stated in the text.)

but according to M. Guibourt, a portion remains in a free state. They are employed in the same cases as the preceding.

N.B. We must repeat here that mercurial pills ought never to be silvered or gilt.

5. *Preparations in which the sublimate is entirely decomposed.*

Yellow Phagedenic Water. (Yellow wash.)

Take of Bichloride of mercury   0,10 centigrms. (gr. iss.)
Lime-water . . 22 grms.   (℥vss.)

Dissolve the sublimate in a little water, and mix the solution with the lime-water. A yellow precipitate of hydrated binoxide of mercury is formed, and when the above proportions are used, the decomposition is complete.

The yellow phagedenic wash is employed in a turbid state, the bottle containing it being well shaken up each time it is used, in order to suspend the binoxide of mercury. From 1 to 3 table-spoonfuls of this mixture are put into a glassful of very warm water.

Used for *lotions* in cutaneous diseases (dartres), and in impetiginous inflammation of the face, the eyelids and the scalp; for *injections* into the nasal fossæ, the nose, and the vagina, in cases of chronic coryza, or of whites accompanied with eczema and itching of the vulva; itching of the anus, &c.

Black phagedenic water (black wash) is made from 0·05 centigrammes (gr. 3/4) of protochloride of mercury, and 32 grammes (℥i) of lime-water. It possesses the same properties as the preceding, but is less active.

PROTO-IODIDE OF MERCURY.

The proto-iodide (iodide, Ph. L.) of mercury used in medicine, has long been obtained by decomposing proto-nitrate or proto-acetate of mercury by iodide of potassium; but as thus prepared, its composition is variable, and therefore M. Berthemot has proposed to prepare it by rubbing together mercury and iodine moistened with alcohol. But even in this case, according to M. Mialhe, it always contains a variable proportion of biniodide of mercury. He therefore advises that it should be washed with boiling alcohol, in order to remove any biniodide which it may contain; an operation to which pharmaceutists ought always to subject it, in order to have it perfectly pure.*

Pills of Proto-Iodide of Mercury.

Take of Proto-iodide of mercury . 1 grm.   (gr. xv.)
    Aqueous extract of opium 0,25 centigrms. (gr. iv.)
    Extract of guaiacum   . 4 grms.   (ʒi.)
    Excipient .   .   . q. s.

Mix them with care, and divide into 100 pills. From 1 to 4 to be taken daily in the treatment of secondary and tertiary syphilis.

Pomatum of Proto-Iodide of Mercury.

Take of Proto-iodide of mercury . 2 to 4 grms. (ʒss to ʒi.)
    Lard   .   .   .   30 grms. (ʒi.)

Mix them carefully. For an ointment to be used with friction in obstinate scaly eruptions, and in syphilitic ulcerations.

Pomatum of Bi-Ioduret (Biniodide) of Mercury.

Take of Biniodide (binioduret) of mercury . 0,50 centigrms. (gr. viii.)
    Lard.   .   .   .   . 10 grms.   (ʒiiss.)

Mix for a pomatum. Used in the treatment of secondary syphilitic ulcerations.

Anthelmintic Glyster.

Take of Biniodide of mercury   .   0,01 centigrms. (gr. 1/6.)
    Iodide of potassium   .   0,10 centigrms. (gr. iss.)
    Distilled water   .   .   100 grms.   (ʒiii.)

Triturate the two salts together, and add a few drops of water. The red binoxide of mercury dissolves in the iodide of potassium, forming a colourless solution; then add the rest of the water.

Used as a glyster night and morning for several days, in children troubled with thread worms.

Suppository.

Take of Biniodide of mercury . 0,05 centigrms. (gr. 3/4.)
    Butter of cocoa   .   4 grms.   (ʒi.)

Melt the cocoa butter, and when it is nearly cold add the

(ʒ. * The same object (the separation of biniodide of mercury) may be effected more cheaply by washing the iodide with a boiling saturated solution of common salt, which dissolves and removes the biniodide, but does not affect the iodide.)

biniodide of mercury to it, rub them together and press the mass into a paper mould.

Used in the same cases as the last.

Syrup of Double Iodide of Mercury, and of Potassium,

(Iodo-hydrargyrate of Iodide of Potassium.)

Take of Biniodide of mercury	.	0,30 centigrms. (gr. ivss.)
Iodide of potassium .	.	0,60 centigrms. (gr. ix.)
Water .	.	4 grms. (ℨi.)
Simple syrup .	.	400 grms. (ℨxiii.)
Syrup of orange-flower water		96 grms. (ℨiii.)

Triturate the two salts with the water; add the solution to the syrups, and shake them together. From 1 to 4 table-spoonfuls of the syrup to be taken in the twenty-four hours. Each spoonful contains 1 centigramme (gr. 1/6) of biniodide of mercury, and 2 (gr. 1/3) of iodide of potassium.

Used in secondary and tertiary syphilis.

Mercurial Cigars.

Take of Proto nitrate of mercury	.	1 grm. (gr. xv.)
Distilled water .	.	25 grms. (ℨvi.)
Nitric acid .	.	1 grm. (gr. xv.)

Dissolve the salt in the acidulated water, and in the solution soak a piece of white blotting paper 20 centimetres by 15 (8 inches by 6). Dry it and fold it into cigarettes. Several times a day breathe gently into the bronchi 8 or 10 mouthfuls of the smoke from these cigarettes.

Used in the treatment of syphilitic inflammation of the pharynx and larynx; in common chronic laryngitis. M. Thierry advises that these cigarettes should be prepared with a solution of corrosive sublimate.

SULPHURETS OF MERCURY.

There are two sulphurets of mercury, the black or proto-sulphuret, still called Ethiop's mineral; and the red bisulphuret, cinnabar or vermillion, which is alone employed. It is used in fumigations.

Fumigations of Cinnabar.

Take of Powdered cinnabar (vermillion) . 4 to 32 grms. (ℨi to ℨi.)

Throw the cinnabar upon a plate of iron hot enough to volatilize it. The patient, placed in a chair and enveloped in a blanket, so that his head alone is free, receives the vapours, which may, moreover, be directed to any desired part of the body by means of a glass funnel. The cinnabar being partially decomposed by the oxygen of the air, the fumigation really consists of sulphurous acid, metallic mercury and bisulphuret of mercury.

Used in secondary (constitutional) syphilis and in scaly eruptions.

PREPARATIONS OF IODINE.

Solution of Iodine, for a Drink.

	ADULTS.		CHILDREN.
Take of Iodine . . .	0,20 centigrms. (gr. iii.)	{	0,05 centigrms. (gr. 3/4.)
Iodide of potassium .	0,40 centigrms. (gr. vi.)	{	0,40 centigrms. (gr. vi.)
Distilled water . .	900 grms.	(ʒxxix.)	900 grms. (ʒxxix.)
Simple syrup .	100 grms.	(ʒiii.)	100 grms. (ʒiii.)

Dissolve the iodine and iodide in a small quantity of water, and add the rest of the water and the syrup. This solution contains 1/10th of a grain of iodine in an ounce. Three or four glassfuls to be taken daily, either pure or combined with water or a tisane, in scrophulous affections.

Ioduretted Tisane.

	ADULTS.	CHILDREN.
Take of Iodide of potassium . . {	2 to 20 grms. (ʒss to ʒv.)	0,20 to 1 grm. (gr. iii to gr. xv.)
Infusion of hops, or decoction of } gentian . . . }	1000 grms. (ʒxxxii.)	1000 grms. (ʒxxxii.)
Syrup of sugar, or of gentian .	100 grms. (ʒiii.)	100 grms. (ʒiii.)

Dissolve the salt in the infusion and add the syrup. To be taken by cupfuls in the course of the day.

Used in scrophula and tertiary syphilis.

Solution for a Drink.

	ADULTS.		CHILDREN.
Take of Iodide of potassium . . .	20 grms. (ʒv.)	{	0,20 to 0,40 centigrms. (gr. iii to gr. vi.)
Distilled water . . .	500 grms. (ʒxvi.)		500 grms. (ʒxvi.)

Dissolve. One or two table-spoonfuls of this solution to be taken night and morning in half a glassful of *eau sucré* or of milk.

Used in tertiary syphilis, and for congenital syphilis and scrophula in children.

Tisane of Iodide of Starch.

Take of Starch .	.	.	10 grms. (ʒiiss.)

Dissolve it in :

Boiling water .	.	.	500 grms. (ʒxvi.)

Strain it through an open sieve, and add :

Alcoholic tincture of iodine	.	4 grms. (ʒi.)
Simple syrup .	.	.	60 grms. (ʒii.)

Mix, and shake them together when taken. This drink may be taken undiluted, or mixed with water to the extent of 30 to 100 grammes (ʒi to ʒiii) daily in the same cases as the preceding one.

Emmenagogue Potion of Iodine.

Take of Compound syrup of wormwood.	40 grms. (ʒx.)
Distilled water of balm .	.	100 grms. (ʒiii.)
Alcoholic tincture of iodine	.	30 drops.

Mix. To be taken in the course of the day, and for several days together by a table-spoonful at a time.

Used for women suffering from amenorrhœa; to be taken at the time when the menstrual period is at hand.

N.B. We may beneficially replace the infusion of balm in the mixture by an infusion of 1 grm. (gr. xv) of saffron in 100 grms. (ʒiii) of water.

Bath containing Iodine.

	ADULTS.	CHILDREN.
Take of Iodine . . .	8 to 15 grms. (ʒii to ʒss.)	1 to 4 grms. (gr. xv to ʒi.)
Iodide of potassium .	15 to 50 grms. (ʒss to ʒiss.)	4 to 10 grms. (ʒi to ʒiiss.)
Water . . .	500 grms: (ʒxvi.)	500 grms. (ʒxvi.)

Dissolve the salts in the water, and add them to a large bath.

Used in scrophulous affections.

Ioduretted Pomatum.

Take of Iodide of potassium	.	.	2 grms. (ʒss.)
Lard	.	.	.	30 grms. (ʒi.)

Dissolve the iodide in a little water, about 8 grammes (ʒii), and mix it carefully with the lard. Rub it night and morning upon the throat in goitre, in chronic enlargement of the breasts and of the joints, &c.

Ioduretted Pomatum of Iodide of Potassium.

Take of Iodide of potassium	.	.	4 grms. (ʒi.)
Iodine .	.	.	1 grm. (gr. xv.)
Water .	.	q. s. about	10 grms. (ʒiiss.)

Dissolve them, and add:

Lard . . . . 30 grms. (ʒi.)

Used in the same cases and to the same extent as the last.

Pomatum of Iodide of Lead.

Take of Iodide of lead .	.	4 to 8 grms. (ʒi to ʒii.)
Lard .	.	30 grms. (ʒi.)

Mix them carefully. Used like the preceding, and also in enlargements of the uterus.

Resolvent Bag.

Take of Powdered burnt sponges .	.	200 grms. (ʒvi.)
Iodide of potassium	.	50 grms. (ʒiss.)
Very finely powdered saw-dust	.	250 grms. (ʒviii.)

Mix by small quantities at a time, and keep the powder in a well-closed bottle. 15 or 20 grammes (ʒss to ʒv) of this powder are to be put into a kind of bag of fine linen or silk, which must be finely pricked, yet so as to retain the powder. The bag is to be applied day and night for several months to the neck of persons affected with goitre. The bag should be removed every week.

Iodine Lotions.

Take of Alcoholic tincture of iodine	.	40 grms. (ʒx.)
Alcohol at 20° (sp. gr. ·929)	.	100 grms. (ʒiii.)

Mix. To be applied twice a day as a solution, by means of a brush, to the belly, in cases of dropsical effusion from chronic peritonitis and in cases of ovarian dropsy. To the breasts in enlargement of the mammary gland. To joints affected with articular dropsy (hydro-arthrosis); and to the scrotum in congenital hydrocele in children.

Iodine Injections.

Take of Tincture of iodine	.	50 grms. (ʒiss.)
Water	.	100 grms. (ʒiii.)

Mix. To be injected into the tunica vaginalis in cases of hydrocele, or into the joints in cases of chronic hydro-arthrosis. (A glass syringe should be used whenever it is possible).

HYDRIODIC (IOHYDRIQUE) ETHER $= C^4 H^5 I$.

M. le Dr. Huette, a physician at Montargis, has just given the profession a new therapeutical agent which appears likely to us to play an important part; we mean hydriodic ether, which has long been known to chemists.

M. Huette, in a thesis sustained before the Faculty of Medicine of Paris in 1849, proposed the use of hydriodic ether in all cases in which it was desirable to saturate the system quickly with iodine; and when we wish to carry this agent directly into the lungs. It is thus that he has proposed hydriodic ether in pulmonary consumption, and in cases of tubercle in other parts of the body, but only when iodine being indicated, the lungs are in such a state that there would be no danger in using so energetic an alterative. The mode of administration which he proposes, is to put into a trial-jar with a wide mouth, a spoonful of water, mixed with 7 or 8 drops of hydriodic ether. The ether falls to the bottom, and the patient inspires the air contained in the upper part of the glass, whilst he holds the bottom of it in his hand, to favour the volatization of the ether. The whole of the ether is generally absorbed in ten minutes, and in a quarter of an hour after, iodine is found abundantly in the urine, and it may be found there for some time.

M. le Dr. Coffin, who has tried the process of M. Huette, has found benefit from it in two cases of crude tubercles, which he states that it has prevented from suppurating.

COD-LIVER AND FISH-OIL.

Syrup of Cod-Liver Oil.

Take of Bleached cod-liver oil	.	250 grms. (ʒviii.)
Powdered gum-arabic		100 grms. (ʒiii.)
Mint water.	.	100 grms (ʒiii.)
Simple syrup	.	550 grms. (ʒxviiss.)

Make a mucilage with the gum and the mint water, and add

the oil and the syrup alternately, by small quantities at a time. From 1 to 8 table-spoonfuls, or more, to be taken every day.

Used in scrophulous affections, and especially in rickets.

Mixture of Cod-Liver Oil.

	ADULTS.	CHILDREN.
Take of Black cod-liver oil. . .	90 grms. (ℨiii.)	40 grms. (ℨx.)
Yolk of eggs . . .	2	1

Mix them perfectly in a marble mortar, and add:

	ADULTS.	CHILDREN.
Syrup of orange-peel . .	50 grms. (ℨiss.)	80 grms. (ℨi.)
Distilled water of orange-flowers .	100 grms. (ℨiii.)	80 grms. (ℨiiss.)

Mix them carefully. To be taken in the course of three days, and each day's portion to be made into four doses, *i. e.* about 4 spoonfuls a day. Used in rickets.

Mixture of Fish Oil.

	ADULTS.	CHILDREN.
Take of Fish oil . . .	50 grms. (ℨiss.)	30 grms. (ℨi.)
Tartaric syrup . . .	50 grms. (ℨiss.)	30 grms. (ℨi)

Mix them accurately, and shake the mixture before taking it. To be taken in four doses during the day, in the same cases as the last.

IODURETTED OIL.

The sick often find a difficulty in taking cod-liver oil, and we have therefore given formulæ above which assist its administration. We ought to add, that this oil enclosed in gelatine capsules may be successfully employed by patients who can easily swallow masses of a certain size.

Messrs. Personne and Marchal de Calvi have proposed the employment of ioduretted oil to replace that of cod-liver oil; but we think that the energetic properties of cod-liver and fish-oil are not simply dependent upon the presence of iodine. It is probable that the volatile compounds, and the phocenate of glycerine among others, contribute to the action of these bodies. However, we think that we ought to show in this place the process employed by M. Dublanc, the head laboratorian of the central dispensary for hospitals, for preparing ioduretted oil. He takes 1000 grammes (ℨxxxii) of fresh oil of sweet almonds, which is exposed to steam so as to heat it to 80° or 100° C. (176° to 212° F.) ; he then dissolves 5 grammes (gr. lxxv) of dry iodine in this oil by careful trituration, and makes steam pass through the oil until it is completely decolorized. He then adds 5 more grammes of iodine, and renews the passage of the steam, until the oil is just decolorized ; but this time there is a trace of acidity in the liquid. He then allows it to rest, and filters the oil after having separated the water, and the filtration is continued until it is perfectly limpid.

This oil is employed like cod-liver oil, in doses of 20 to 100 grammes (℈v to ℥iii) in the twenty-four hours.

PREPARATIONS OF GOLD AND PLATINUM.

Messrs. Chrestien, Niel and Legrand, &c., have proposed the preparations of gold in syphilitic affections. Amongst the insoluble preparations, we ought to mention powdered metallic gold, and the iodide, cyanide and sulphuret of gold, which have been administered under the form of syrup, potion and pills. The following preparation appears to us to be the best : it has for its basis chloride of gold, or chloride of gold and of sodium, which are the only preparations used in the present day.

Powder or Friction with Chloride of Gold.

Take of Chloride of gold, or chloride of gold and sodium. . . . } 0,05 centigrms. (gr. 3/4.)

Lycopodium, or powdered orrice-root, exhausted by alcohol . . } 1 grm.   (gr. xv.)

Mix them accurately by trituration, and divide them into 20, the next time into 16, then into 12, and at last, by degrees, into 3 packets. The tongue and gums should be rubbed with one of these packets every day, and when under the influence of the gold they assume a purple-red colour.

We may add, that M. le Dr. Hœfer has proposed chloride of platinum under the same forms and in the same cases as the preparations of gold.

ARSENICAL PREPARATIONS.

Arsenical Pills.

Take of Arsenious acid . 0,25 centigrms. (gr. iv.)

Starch . . 5 grms.   (gr. lxxv.)

Syrup of gum . q. s.

Mix them accurately, by small quantities at a time; add the syrup, and divide the mass into 100 pills, of which from 1 to 10 may be taken daily by an adult in the treatment of obstinate neuralgias, nervous asthmas, intermittent fevers and cancerous diathesis. This medicine is to be suspended or the dose diminished when any gastric symptoms appear.

Arsenical Febrifuge Solution of Dr. Boudin.

| Take of Arsenious acid | . | . | 1 grm. (gr. xv.) |
| Distilled water | . | . | 1000 grms. (℥xxxii.) |

Boil for a quarter of an hour; add sufficient water to replace what evaporates, and fill up the quantity to 1000 grammes.

One ounce of this solution, or 8 tea-spoonfuls, contain nearly half a grain of arsenious acid. It is taken with *eau sucré*, coffee, or milk, &c.

For children the dose should not exceed *two tea-spoonfuls*, (gr. 1/8) daily; but it may be given to the extent of 10 or 15 spoonsful for adults. It is always necessary to give this dose in divided portions, and to suspend or stop altogether the use of the medicine if it shows signs of not being borne by the system, such as oppression, nausea, vomiting, &c.

This solution, to the extent of *one* tea-spoonful for children, or *four* or *five* for adults, may replace the arsenical solutions of Pearson and Fowler in the treatment of chronic diseases of the skin.

Fowler's Arsenical Solution.

Take of Arsenious acid	} of each .	5 grms. (gr. lxxv.)
Carbonate of potash		
Distilled water .	. .	500 grms. (℥xvi.)

Boil them in a matrass, allow them to cool, and add:

Compound tincture of balm (eau	}	16 grms. (℥ss.)
des carmes) . . .		
Distilled water .	. .	q. s.

To make 500 grammes (℥xvi). This solution contains the hundredth part of its weight of arsenious acid, and the fiftieth part of its weight of arsenite of potash. One drachm of the solution contains 3/5 of a grain of arsenious acid, and 1 grain and 1/5 of arsenite of potash.

In certain foreign pharmacopœias (*e. g.* Ph. Lond.) Fowler's solution is coloured red and aromatized by spirit of lavender.

Fowler's solution is used in the same doses and in the same way as the last.

Pearson's Arsenical Solution. (*Codex.*)

Take of Arseniate of soda	0,05 centigrms. (gr. 3/4.)
Distilled water	20 grms. (℥v.)

Dissolve and filter. This solution is less active than the last, (§. an illustration of the general law, that the higher the state of oxidation in metallic compounds, and the less powerful are their medicinal effects). The dose varies from a few drops to 2 grms. (℥ss.)

Used in the same cases as the last.

Arsenical Cigarettes. (Cigars of Dioscorides.)

Take of Arsenite of potash	1 grm. (gr. xv.)
Distilled water	20 grms. (℥v.)

A piece of white blotting-paper, 20 centimetres by 15 (8 inches by 6), is to be soaked with the solution by the aid of a brush; and when dry, it is to be folded after the manner of a cigarette.

Two or three times a day, 6 to 10 mouthfuls of the smoke from these cigars are to be gently inspired into the bronchi.

Used in chronic diseases of the larynx, chronic pulmonary catarrh and nervous asthma, &c.

By the combustion of the paper, the arsenious acid of the arsenite is transformed into metallic arsenic, which being introduced into the bronchi in the state of vapour, partially returns to the conditions of arsenious acid on coming in contact with the air; so that the curative effect is to be attributed to the mixture of arsenious acid and metallic arsenic.

Arsenical Glyster, Febrifuge and Anthelmintic.

	ADULTS.		CHILDREN.
Take of Arsenious acid	0,05 centigrms. (gr. 3/4)		0,01 centigrms. (gr. 1/6.)
Distilled water	100 grms.	(℥iii.)	40 grms. (℥x.)

Dissolve by the aid of heat. This glyster is administered by a glass syringe, after having first cleared the intestine by means of a common glyster.

Used in the treatment of intermittent fever, when the stomach bears arsenic with difficulty, and in cases of thread worms (ascaris vermicularis).

Escharotic Arsenical Powder of Frère Come or of Rousselot.

Take of Cinnabar . . . } of each . 15 grms. (ʒss.)
    Powdered dragon's blood . }
    Arsenious acid . . . 3 grms. (gr. xlv.)

Mix them accurately upon a porphyrizing table. To be made into a paste with water or saliva at the moment or being applied.

Arsenious acid enters into the composition of the escharotic powders of Augustin, Van Mons, Baumann, Fontanelles, Justamond, Dupuytren, &c., which are used in the topical treatment of superficial cancers.

(§. The employment of arsenious acid as an escharotic is dangerous, and has caused death. It was formerly used more frequently than it is at present, owing to this danger. If applied sufficiently strong to cause a slough with certainty, the danger is much diminished, and the risk is greater in proportion as the arsenious acid is prevented from producing this effect.

IRRITANTS.

POTASH.—SODA.

Vienna Powder. (*Lapis causticus cum calce. Potassa cum calce.* Ph. L.)

Take of Caustic potash . . . 50 grms. (ʒiss)
    Quick-lime . . . 60 grms. (ʒii.)

Reduce the two substances to powder in a heated mortar; mix them carefully and rapidly, and keep the mixture in a wide-mouthed bottle with a ground stopper. In using this caustic the powder must be moistened with a little alcohol, so as to reduce it to a soft paste, which is to be applied to the part which we wish to cauterize. The potash in this case only acts upon a circumscribed portion of skin, instead of spreading, as common caustic potash generally does; but to bound the space still more accurately, it may be surrounded by a ring of diachylon plaster.

CAUSTIC OF FILHOS.

Dr. Filhos has made the happy suggestion of preparing a caustic of potash and lime, which are to be melted together, and poured into moulds like *Pierre infernale* (lapis infernalis, nitrate of silver), which renders its employment more easy in many cases. The proportions are as follows:

Caustic potash	.	.	. 200 grms. (ʒvi.)
Powdered quick-lime	.	.	. 100 grms. (ʒiii.)

Fuse them together, and pour the mixture into leaden cylinders, which are themselves enclosed in glass tubes, to be sealed afterwards at both ends.

Alkaline Tisane.

	ADULTS.	CHILDREN.
Take of Bicarbonate of soda . .	1 grm. (gr. xv.)	0,25 centigrms. (gr. iv.)
Infusion of pellitory . .	1000 grms. (ʒxxxii.)	500 grms. (ʒxvi.)
Syrup of the 5 aperient roots (p. 167) . . .	100 grms. (ʒiii.)	50 grms. (ʒiss.)

Dissolve the salt in the infusion, and add the syrup. To be taken by a glassful at a time.

Used in certain cases of gout, and in lithic acid gravel.

Alkaline Powder.

Take of Bicarbonate of soda	.	.	15 grms. (ʒss.)
Powdered sugar .	.	.	150 grms. (ʒivss.)

Triturate, and carefully mix the 2 powders. A tea-spoonful to be taken in the milk which the child drinks during the day.

Used in the diarrhœa, which occurs at the time of weaning, or in the case of artificial milk diet which is not well borne.

Alkaline Absorbent Powder.

Take of Bicarbonate of soda	.	.	6 grms. (ʒiss.)
Calcined magnesia	.	.	4 grms. (ʒi.)
Powdered sugar .	.	.	15 grms. (ʒss.)

Rub them well together, and divide into 12 packets, three of which are to be taken daily in sugared water.

Used in dyspepsia and gastralgia, accompanied with acid eructations, and in headache, accompanied with nausea and pallor. To be followed by the use of some bitter infusion for a few days.

S

Alkaline Lotions.

Take of Subcarbonate (carbonate) of potash or soda. 100 grms. (℥iii.)
Water. .   .   .   .   . 500 grms. (℥xvi.)

Dissolve. A table-spoonful of the solution to be dissolved in 1 or 2 *litres* (2 to 4 pints) of very warm water.

Used as lotion in itching affections of the skin, and as lotions and injections in pruritus and eczema of the vulva.

Alkaline Baths.

	ADULTS.	CHILDREN.
Take of Subcarbonate of potash or soda	125 to 250 grms. (℥iv to ℥viii.)	25 to 50 grms. (℥vi to ℥iss.)

Dissolve it in a bath of water.

Used in the treatment of itch, in chronic diseases of the skin, in certain cases of acute gout, in lithic acid gravel, and in simple chronic diarrhœa.

BORAX (BORATE OF SODA).

Mixture.

Take of Borax .   •   .   . 10 grms. (℥iiss.)
Simple syrup :   •   . 10 grms. (℥iiss.)

Reduce the borax to powder; mix the syrup with it, and make a mixture, with which to rub the inside of the mouth gently several times a-day.

Used in idiopathic and symptomatic thrush, and aphthous, or mercurial state of the mouth. To be swallowed also in small quantities in acute and chronic inflammations of the mucous membrane of the pharynx.

Boracic Lotions.

Take of Borax .   .   .   . 50 grms. (℥iss.)
Water .   .   .   . 500 grms. (℥xvi.)

Dissolve. Four table-spoonsful of this solution to be mixed with 1 *litre* (℥xxxii, say 1½ pints) of warm water.

Used as lotions and injections in itching of the vulva; applied to aphthæ of the genital organs in young girls, and to parts affected with chilblains.

LIME.

Liniment of Oil and Lime, Oleo-Calcaire. (Lin. Calcis. Ph. L.)

Take of Lime-water .
Oil of sweet almonds } of each . 50 grms. (ʒiss.)

Mix, and shake them well together.

Used in the treatment of burns of the first and second degree; in impetiginous affections of the scalp and of the face; and to allay itching in diseases of the skin, and of the vulva.

Mixture to check Diarrhœa in Children.

Take of Lime-water . . . 15 grms. (ʒss.)
Distilled water of balm . . 40 grms. (ʒx.)
Syrup of quince . . . 25 grms. (ʒvi.)
Laudanum of Sydenham . . 2 drops.

Mix, and give it in the 24 hours, by table-spoonsful at a time, to children affected with subacute or chronic diarrhœa during suckling, or at the period of weaning.

Glyster to check Diarrhœa.

Take of Lime-water . . 120 to 200 grms. (ʒiiiss to ʒvi.)
Rice-water . . 300 grms. (ʒix.)
Laudanum of Sydenham . 25 drops.

Mix, and shake them well together before administering them, because the laudanum causes a precipitate of meconate of lime, and the deposition of morphia, a part of which, it is true, is dissolved in the excess of lime.

Used as a glyster in the treatment of chronic dysentery in adults.

Vapour Bath (called "The Poor Man's Vapour Bath").

Take of Quick-lime . 1 or 2 kilogrms. (1 or 2 lumps the size of the fist.)

Fold the lime in a thick cloth well soaked in water, and put the whole into a vessel four times the size of the lime, which is to be placed in the patients' bed, in a convenient situation. Moisten it from the time when the disengagement of steam diminishes. (§. This is an admirable mode of applying a vapour-bath to a patient who cannot be removed from bed; and frequent employment of it enables me to speak of its advantages in acute rheumatic fever, and cases in which a bath of any other description cannot conveniently be given. The matter is simplified by merely placing two or three lumps of lime wrapped in wet cloths, about 6 or 8 inches from different parts of the patient's body, without using a vessel for containing them at all.)

Absorbant Powder.

CHILDREN.

Take of Powdered crabs' eyes (phosphate of lime) . . . .
Sub-nitrate of bismuth (magistery of bismuth) . . . } of each 1 grm. (gr. xv.)
Powdered sugar . . . . 5 grms. (gr. lxxv.)

Porphyrize them carefully, and divide into 6 packets. 1 to be taken night and morning, during a meal.

Used for children affected with non-inflammatory, or with chronic diarrhœa.

AMMONIA.

Ammoniacal Mixture.

	ADULTS.	CHILDREN.
Take of Simple syrup . . .	40 grms. (℥x.)	40 grms. (℥x.)
Solution of ammonia . .	1 grm. (gr. xv.)	4 or 5 drops.
Water . . .	110 grms. (℥iiiss.)	100 grms. (℥iii.)

Mix, and bottle it carefully. A quarter of it to be taken every 10 minutes.

Used to dissipate intoxication; to lessen the pain in dymenorrhœa; to quicken the general circulation; to excite sweat; to bring out exanthemata to the skin, when there is no internal inflammatory action to forbid it.

Ammoniacal Potion.

Take of Spirit of Mindererus (acetate of ammonia, prepared by the ancient method) } 10 grms. (℥iiss.)
Distilled water of balm . . . 100 grms. (℥iii.)
Syrup of ether . . .
„ „ orange-flowers } of each . 20 grms. (℥v.)

Mix them carefully. To be divided into 4 doses. 1 to be taken every hour.

Used to lessen the pain in dymenorrhœa, and to abate uterine hæmorrhage.

N.B. Spirit of Mindererus has for some time been prepared from pure sub-carbonate (sesqui-carbonate) of ammonia and distilled vinegar; but formerly, the same salt was used as it was obtained by the dry distillation of deers' horns (then called volatile salt of hartshorn), by which process it was obtained, mixed with various empyreumatic products, which imparted properties to it not possessed by the pure sub-carbonate. M. Dumas has stated, that spirit of Mindererus, prepared by the ancient method, contains, amongst other foreign ingredients, cyanate of ethyle (cyanic ether), which is not found in the salt obtained by the modern method.

Ammoniacal Lotions.

Take of Sal-ammoniac (hydrochlorate of ammonia) 20 grms. (ʒv.)
Water . . . . 40 grms. ʒx.)
Vulnerary spirit.* (Alcoolat vulnéraire.} 10 grms. (ʒiiss.)
Fr. Codex.) . . . }

Dissolve the salt in the water, and add the spirit.

Used as a lotion to the hands and feet night and morning to prevent chilblains.

Ammoniacal Powder.

Take of Powdered Sal-ammoniac (Ammon. Mur.) 10 grms. (ʒiiss.)
Quick-lime, in fine powder . . 20 grms. (ʒv.)

Mix them accurately, and sprinkle with the mixture the inside of the stockings, which must be kept on during the night, to recall suppressed perspiration to the feet.

Gondret's Pomatum (Ammoniacal caustic).

Take of Suet . } of each . . . . 32 grms. (ʒi.)
Pork-fat }
Solution of ammonia at 25° (sp. gr. ·85)† . 64 grms. (ʒii.)

Melt the fat and the suet together by means of a water-bath, in a bottle with a ground stopper; add the ammonia, and shake them together in the stoppered bottle, taking care to open it from time to time to allow air to enter, so as to fill the vacuum caused by the absorption of the ammonia.

This pomatum is rubefacient in small quantities, or when applied for a short time; vesicant in larger quantities; and caustic if allowed to remain upon the skin for a length of time.

Ammonia enters into the composition of eau de Luce, balsam of Opodeldoch, and volatile liniment, all of which are rubefacient.

(§. * Obtained by the distillation of spirit from 18 different kinds of aromatic and carminative herbs. Balm, hyssop, mint, thyme, lavender and fennel, &c.)
(§. † This is rather stronger than the liquor ammoniæ fortior. Ph. L.)

CHLORINE.

Hydrochloric Collutoire.

Take of Hydrochloric acid   .   . 1 grm. (gr. xv.)
  Honey of roses .   .   . 25 grms. (ʒvi.)

Mix them accurately. To wash the mouth several times a-day, in infants affected with an aphthous mouth, or with thrush.

Chlorinated Injections.

Take of Chloride of soda (hypochlorite of soda, Labarraque's solution) .} 50 to 100 grms. (ʒiss to ʒiii.)
  Water   .   .   .   .   500 grms. (ʒxvi.)

Mix them. Used as vaginal injections in cases of infection, produced by the decomposition of a retained placenta. In glysters to destroy the fœtor of offensive stools. To relieve the pain of wounds of an unhealthy character.

Gargle to correct Offensive Breath.

Take of Decoction of yellow cinchona bark . 150 grms. (ʒv.)
  Chloride of soda (hypochlorite of soda) .   .   .} 50 grms. (ʒiss.)
  Honey of roses   .   .   50 grms. (ʒiss.)
  Spirit of cloves, triturated with a little sugar .   .   .} 4 drops.

Mix for a gargle. Used in scurvy, fœtor of the breath, and softening of the gums, &c.

CHLORIDE OF LIME.

Take of Chloride of lime (hypochlorite of lime). An indefinite quantity.

Dip a piece of tow into honey, and then roll it in the chloride of lime, and apply the mixture to the mucous surface of the mouth in children.

Used in diphtheritis of the gums, ulcerations with a pultaceous secretion, and inflamed ulcers of an unhealthy nature. The application to be repeated 3 or 4 times a-day if necessary.

NITRATE OF SILVER.

Injections into the Nasal Fossæ.

Take of Crystallized nitrate of silver   0,05 centigrms. (gr. 3/4.)
  Distilled water   .   . 200 grms.   (ʒvi.)

Dissolve. To be injected night and morning in cases of chronic coryza in young children, and in cases of ozæna.

The strength, which ought always to be very weak at first, on account of the extreme susceptibility of the pituitary membrane, may be increased in proportion as the habitual use of the remedy lessens this sensibility.

Collyrium of Nitrate of Silver (weak).

Take of Crystallized nitrate of silver . 0,05 centigrms. (gr. 3/4.)
Distilled water . . 30 grms. (℥i.)

Dissolve. 1 or 2 drops of this solution to be put between the eyelids night and morning in cases of trifling ophthalmia. Used also as an injection in gleet.

Strong Solution.

Take of Crystallized nitrate of silver . 4 grms. (ʒi.)
Distilled water . . 12 grms. (℥iii.)

Dissolve. To be applied to the pharynx and upper part of the larynx in cases of buff-coloured diphtheritis of the throat; and in chronic inflammation of the pharynx, and in changes of the tone of the voice; and to be applied to parts covered with pultaceous ulceration.

To be applied by means of a paint-brush to the everted eyelids of new-born infants in the treatment of catarrhal ophthalmia; in epidemic purulent ophthalmia, and in ophthalmia with copious mucous secretion.

To change the condition of various mucous membranes affected with chronic inflammation.

Anti-ophthalmic Pomatum.

Take of Crystallized nitrate of silver . 0,05 centigrms. (gr. 3/4.)
Lard . . . . 4 grms. (ʒi.)

Dissolve the salt in 4 or 5 drops of water, and add the lard. Mix them upon a porphyrising plate. Gently anoint the edges of the eyelids with the pomatum, in cases of chronic palpebral inflammation.

Another Pomatum.

Take of Crystallized nitrate of silver . 10 grms. (ʒiiss.)
Distilled water . . . 10 grms. (ʒiiss.)
Lard . . . . 50 grms. (℥i and ʒv.)

Dissolve the salt in the water, and mix the lard by trituration in a glass or porcelain mortar. To be smeared twice a-day over parts affected with traumatic erysipelas.

NITRATE OF SILVER (INTERNAL USE).

Pills.

Take of Crystallized nitrate of silver   0,10 centigrms. (gr. iss.)
     Fresh bread-crumbs   .   0,50 centigrms. (gr. viii.)

Dissolve the salt in 2 drops of water, and make the bread crumb absorb the solution. Divide it into 10 pills. 1 to be taken every 3 hours in cases of hæmorrhage from the stomach or intestines. From 1 to 4 pills to be taken daily in chronic diarrhœa, and in epilepsy and St. Vitus' dance.

Potion of Nitrate of Silver. (For children.)

Take of Crystallized nitrate of silver. $\left\{\begin{array}{l} 0,01 \text{ to } 0,02 \text{ centigrms. (gr. 1/6} \\ \text{to gr. 1/3.)} \end{array}\right.$
Distilled water   .   .   30 grms.   (ʒi.)
Simple syrup   .   .   20 grms.   (ʒv.)

Dissolve the salt in the water, and add the syrup. Shake them together. To be taken by a spoonful at a time in the course of the day, in cases of subacute or chronic diarrhœa, dependent upon some affection of the small intestines.

Irritant Glyster. (For children.)

Take of Crystallized nitrate of silver. $\left\{\begin{array}{l} 0,05 \text{ to } 0,10 \text{ centigrms. (gr. 3/4} \\ \text{to gr. iss.)} \end{array}\right.$
Distilled water   .   .   200 grms.   (ʒvi.)

Dissolve. For a glyster. To be given to children affected with diarrhœa and tenesmus, and a secretion of bloody mucous.

Irritant Glyster. (For adults.)

Take of Crystallized nitrate of silver.   0,25 to   1 grm.   (gr. iv to gr. xv.)
Distilled water   .   .   400 grms.   (ʒxiii.)

Dissolve. For a glyster in acute dysentery.

(§. A much stronger solution than the above (viz., gr. x in ʒi or ʒii of gruel), and a few drops of laudanum is often of service, as a glyster in chronic or subacute dysentery).

N.B. The employment of syringes, or other utensils made of metal, must be avoided with any preparation of nitrate of silver. As these preparations are decomposed by light, it will be well for the pharmaceutist to give them to the patient in coloured bottles (or bottles surrounded with paper), with the inscription, " For internal use," or " For external use."

COPPER AND ZINC.

Irritant Collyrium.

Take of Pure sulphate of zinc.	.	0,30 centigrms. (gr. ivss.)
Rose-water . .	.	100 grms. (ʒiii.)
Laudanum of Sydenham	.	4 to 8 drops.

Proceed as for the above injection. To be applied as a lotion to the eyes several times a-day, in chronic ophthalmia.

Irritant Collyrium.

Take of Sulphate of copper (or divine stone).	0,30 centigrms. (gr. ivss.)
Distilled water . .	100 grms. (ʒiii.)
Gummy extract of opium .	.	0,05 centigrms. (gr, 3/4.)

Dissolve the salt and the extract in the water. To be employed in the same cases as the last.

Anti-ophthalmic Pomatum.

Take of White oxide of zinc.	.	. 4 grms. (ʒi.)
Simple cerate	.	. 8 grms. (ʒii.)

Porphyrize. For the same cases as above. To· anoint the free edges of the eyelids.

Anti-diarrhœal Glyster.

	ADULTS.		CHILDREN.
Take of Sulphate of copper	.	0,25 centigrms. (gr. iv.)	0,05 centigrms. (gr. 3/4.)
Distilled water .	.	250 grms. (ʒviii.)	125 grms. (ʒiv.)

Dissolve. For a glyster.

Emetic Draught.

	ADULTS.		CHILDREN.
Take of Sulphate of zinc.	.	. 1 grm. (gr. xv.)	0,50 centigrms. (gr. viii.)
Distilled water .	.	. 100 grms. (ʒiii.)	40 grms. (ʒx.)
Simple syrup .	.	. 40 grms. (ʒx.)	20 grms. (ʒv.)

Dissolve the salt in the water, and add the syrup. A quarter of it to be taken every 10 minutes, until vomiting is excited. (§. I have frequently found the above quantity too small to excite vomiting in a full stomach.)

Collyrium.

Take of Sulphate of zinc .	. . 0,05 centigrms. (gr. 3/4)	
Distilled water .	. . 50 grms. (ʒiss.)	

Dissolve. A few drops to be put into the eyes night and morning, in slight catarrhal ophthalmia.

Dry Collyrium.

Take of Oxide of zinc	. . . . 1 grm. (gr. xv.)	
Powdered sugar .	. . . 15 grms. (ʒss.)	

Mix, and porphyrise them accurately. A small quantity to be blown into the eye, through a quill, in chronic ophthalmia.

Emetic Draught.

	ADULTS.	CHILDREN.
Take of Sulphate of copper .	. 1 grm. (gr. xv.)	0,50 centigrms. (gr. viii.) .
Distilled water .	. . 100 grms. (ʒiii.)	40 grms. (ʒx.)
Simple syrup .	. . 40 grms. (ʒx.)	20 grms. (ʒv.)

Dissolve the salt in the water, and add the syrup. A quarter of it to be taken every 10 minutes, until the patient has vomited 2 or 3 times.

Collyrium of Sulphate of Copper.

Take of Sulphate of copper .	. 0,05 centigrms. (gr. 3/4.)	
Distilled water .	. 30 grms. (ʒi.)	

Dissolve. Several drops to be put into the eyes night and morning in catarrhal ophthalmia.

Mixture to Remove Chorea (for Children.)

Take of Ammoniuret of copper (ammoniacal sulphate of copper) . .	0,40 centigrms. (gr. vi.)	
Water .	. . . 100 grms. (ʒiii.)	
Simple syrup .	. . 40 grms. (ʒx.)	
Laudanum of Sydenham .	. 10 drops.	

Dissolve the salt in the water, and add the syrup and laudanum.

Used in the treatment of St. Guy's (St. Vitus's) dance, (chorea). A tea-spoonful to be given to children 3 or 4 times a-day, and the dose to be gradually increased as the stomach is able to bear it, until the patient bears the whole quantity. To be continued as long as necessary.

IRRITANTS FROM THE VEGETABLE KINGDOM.

WHITE MUSTARD.

Take of White mustard seeds   .   . 1 or 2 table-spoonful.

To be taken alone, or diffused through water.

Used in constipation and imperfect digestion. (§. This was a fashionable remedy in England about forty years since for a multitude of disorders; but it went out of fashion from the bad consequences produced in some instances by the accumulation of large quantities of the seeds in the bowels, which excited inflammation).

White mustard does not contain myronic acid, but only myrosine; and it does not produce essence of mustard on contact with water.

BLACK MUSTARD.

The irritant principle of black mustard is a peculiar essence, containing sulphur and nitrogen, which does not exist ready formed in the seeds, but which takes its birth only on the contact of warm water, in consequence of the reaction of myronic acid upon myrosine, by a special kind of fermentation, to which chemists have given the name of *sinapisic*. Myrosine being coagulated by boiling water, alcohol, vinegar, acids, and most salts, it follows, that the essence fails to be formed wherever mustard comes in contact with one of these agents.

We strongly advise that simple warm water should be used either for sinapisms, or for baths of mustard.

Mustard Bath.

	ADULTS.	CHILDREN.
Take of Flour of black mustard	1000 grms. (℥xxxii.)	500 grms. (℥xvi.)
Warm water . .	2000 grms. (℥lxiv.)	1000 grms. (℥xxxii.)
,, ,, . .	q. s.	q. s.

Make a thin soup, which is to be put into a coarse linen cloth, and pressed into the bath, the water of which is to be stirred up.

Used in cases of diarrhœa resembling cholera. The patient to remain in the bath until he feels a very painful sense of burning. (§. In the case of children, until the skin is very red). To be repeated 3 or 4 times a-day, until reaction has been fairly excited in the skin.

Mustard Bandage.

Take of Flour of black mustard   .   .   .   500 grms. (℥xvi.)

Prepare the mustard as in the last case, and squeeze it out into a bucket of warm water. Soak a woollen roller in this hot mustard and water, and envelop the body of the patient by repeated folds surrounding him.

Used in the cold stage of cholera, and in cases in which an exanthematous eruption does not freely come out upon the skin.

Revulsive Sinapism.

Take of Volatile oil of mustard   .   .   .   1 part.
Alcohol at 66 per cent (25° Cartier, sp. gr. 896) .   20 parts.

Soak a piece of flannel or fine linen in the mixture, which is to be applied to the part to be reddened. The effect is produced in 2 or 3 minutes.

N.B. The bark of mezereum root, nettles, viburnum, Burgundy pitch, turpentine, and euphorbium, &c., are also employed as external rubefacients.

IRRITANTS FROM THE ANIMAL KINGDOM.

CANTHARIDES.

Cantharidin is the essential blistering principle of the cantharides; but we ought to add, that according to M. Orfila the volatile principle also possesses irritant properties.

Cantharides reduced to powder is employed in the preparation of blistering plasters. The French plaster contains one-fourth of its weight of powdered flies; the English contains one-third, and is more active.

Green epispastic pomatum contains a thirty-third of its weight of cantharides in their natural state; it is very irritating, and ought only to be used in cases in which it is difficult to excite suppuration. *Yellow* epispastic pomatum only contains the principles of the fly, which are soluble in fatty matters; and it is therefore only employed when we wish to excite a gentle irritation, in order to produce suppuration.

Tincture of cantharides has been employed in doses of 1 to 20 drops in impotence; in dysuria, caused by semi-paralysis of the bladder; and in certain chronic eczemas, which have assumed the scaly form.

Pomatum for Arresting Loss of Hair.

Take of Baume nerval* } of each	.	. 30 grms. (ʒi.)
Beef-marrow }		
Oil of sweet almonds	.	. 20 grms. (ʒv.)
Tannin . . .	.	. 2 grms. (ʒss.)
Rum . . .	.	. 10 grms. (ʒiiss.)
Tincture of cantharides .	.	. 2 grms. (ʒss.)

Melt the fatty bodies, and strain through linen; dissolve the tannin in the rum; add the solution to the mixture, and then the tincture, and stir them together until they are perfectly cold. Add aromatics at pleasure.

Extempore Blistering Plaster (Vésicatoire des campagnes).

Take of Powdered cantharides .	.	. 2 grms. (ʒss.)
Butter or lard .	.	. q. s. to give the
consistence of a thick pomatum.		

Mix them accurately, and spread the compound between two sheets of blotting paper, which are to be doubled like a letter, and then applied to the part; and kept on by a bandage.

(‡. * Beef-suet .	.	. 32 parts.
Oil of mace .	.	. 32 ,,
Oil of rosemary .	.	. 2 ,,
Oil of cloves .	.	. 1 part.
Powdered camphor .	.	. 1 ,,
Balsam of Tolu .	.	. 2 parts.
Alcohol (86 per cent) .	.	. 4 ,,

Melt, and mix together. Fr. Codex.)

EMOLLIENT OR ANTIPHLOGISTIC MEDICINES.

The class of emollients is the most numerous of the whole *materia medica*. The substances which it contains we shall content ourselves with merely naming. They are divided into seven classes, and we shall hereafter give a few formulæ for them, premising that these substances may be substituted one for another, without any inconvenience, and that their dose is, so to speak, unlimited. Lastly, we may mention, that nearly all emollients are slight laxatives.

1st CLASS. *Gummy substances.* Gum-arabic, gum Senegal, French gum, tragacanth.

2nd ,,   *Mucilaginous substances.* Linseed, quince seeds, flowers and roots of the mallow and marsh-mallow, flowers of coltsfoot (tussilago), borage, &c.

3rd ,,   *Amylaceous (starchy) substances.* Starch, sago, salep, tapioca, Iceland moss, carrageen (Irish moss), barley, rice, oats, &c.

4th ,,   *Saccharine substances and sugars.* Cane, grape, and milk-sugar; honey, dates, jujubes, figs, prunes, dog's-tooth, liquorice, &c.

5th ,,   *Albuminous substances.* Albumen, casein, gluten, &c.

6th ,,   *Gelatinous substances.* Gelatine, cartilages, isinglass, pectine, pectic acid, &c.

7th ,,   *Fatty substances.* Lard, butters, suet, olive-oil, oil of sweet almonds, poppy-oil, &c.

Emollient Tisane.

Take of Powdered gum-arabic . . 10 grms. (ʒiiss.)
Water . . . 1000 grms. (ʒxxxii.)
Dissolve the gum in the water, and add:
Syrup of gum . . . 60 grms. (ʒii.)

To be taken by glassfuls in the day; in internal inflammations, &c.

Another.

Take of Flowers of mallow or marsh-mallow .	15 to 20 grms. (℈ss to ʒv.)
Boiling water	1000 grms. (ʒxxxii.)

Infuse them, strain, and add :

Syrup of maiden hair . . .	60 grms. (ʒii.)

To be taken by glassfuls, like the last.
Used in coughs, and to soothe bronchial irritation.

Another.

Take of Rice, barley, or oats . . .	30 grms. (ʒi.)
Water	1200 grms. (ʒxxxviii.)

Boil down to 1000 grms. (ʒxxxii.) strain, and add :

Syrup of quince	60 grms. (ʒii.)

Another.

Take of Dog's-tooth	30 to 40 grms. (ʒi to ʒx.)
Water	1200 grms. (ʒxxxviii.)

Proceed as above, and sweeten at pleasure.

Emollient Gargle.

Take of Barley or rice-water . . .	250 grms. (ʒviii.)
White honey . . .	50 grms. (ʒiss.)

Mix for a gargle.
Used in inflammations of the mouth and gums.

Soothing Gargle.

Take of The four pectoral fruits . . .	40 grms. (ʒx.)
Water	500 grms. (ʒxvi.)

Boil down to 300 grms. (ʒix.) and add :

Honey	50 grms. (ʒiss.)

Mix. To be used as a gargle several times a-day, in the same cases as the last.

Another.

Take of Marsh-mallow root . .	30 grms. (ʒi.)
Water . . .	300 grms. (ʒix.)

Boil down to 150 grms. (ʒiv), and add :

Milk . . .	100 grms. (ʒiii.)
White honey . .	50 grms. (ʒiss.)

Mix for a gargle.

Jelly of Iceland Moss (free from bitterness).

Take of Iceland moss (*Lichen islandicus*) . 40 grms. (ʒx.)

Infuse it in boiling water, and throw away the water.
Wash it with cold water, until the water comes away
tasteless. Then boil the lichen in:

Water . . . . . 250 grms. (ʒviii.)

Boil it down to about 150 grms. (ʒiv), and add:

White sugar . . . . 60 grms. (ʒii.)

Cook it to the consistence of a jelly. To be taken by table-spoonsful at a time.

Used as nourishment for invalids, and to cheat the appetite of the sick (see p. 169).

Jelly of Carrageen (Irish Moss).

Take of Carrageen . . . 30 grms. (ʒi.)
Water . . . . 300 grms. (ʒix.)

Boil down to one half, and add:

Sugar . . . . 50 grms. (ʒiss.)

Melt it, and add sugar and spices. The water may be replaced by milk. To be taken like the last.

Animal Jelly.

Take of Pure gelatine, or isinglass . 25 grms. (ʒiss.)
Water . . . . 700 grms (ʒxxii.)
Sugar . . . . 500 grms. (ʒxvi.)

Dissolve the gelatine, and then the sugar, in the
water, and let it cool. We frequently add:

Citric acid . . . 2 grms. (ʒss.)

Add aromatics at pleasure.

Emollient Glyster.

	ADULTS.	CHILDREN.
Take of Linseed, or marsh-mallow root .	40 grms. (ʒx.)	20 grms. (ʒv.)
Water	500 grms. (ʒxvi.)	250 grms. (ʒviii.)

Boil down to 400 grammes (ʒxiii.) For a glyster to be used in inflammation of the bowels.

Starch Glyster.

	ADULTS.	CHILDREN.
Take of Starch . . .	15 grms. (ʒss.)	1 grm. (ʒii.)
Water	500 grms. (ʒxvi.)	200 grms. (ʒvi.)

Rub the starch with the water, boil it, and strain.

Olly Glyster.

	ADULTS.	CHILDREN.
Take of White, or poppy oil	60 grms. (ʒii.)	20 grms. (ʒv.)
Linseed tea	400 grms. (ʒxiii.)	200 grms. (ʒvi.

Mix. For a glyster.

Soothing Glyster.

	ADULTS.	CHILDREN.
Take of Decoction of bran.	500 grms. (ʒxvi.)	200 grms. (ʒvi.)
Yolks of eggs	3	2

Mix them accurately. For a glyster.

Nutritious Glyster.

	ADULTS.	CHILDREN.
Take of Starch, salep or tapioka	4 grms. (ʒi.)	2 grms. (ʒss.)
Boil it in :		
Veal broth, without salt	200 grms. (ʒvi.)	150 grms. (ʒv.)
Add :		
Yolks of eggs	3	1

Rub them together, and strain. To be administered tepid.

Used to nourish the sick when food is not easily borne by the stomach, as in gastritis and gastralgia. Glysters of milk, solution of gelatine, &c., are administered in the same cases.

Bath of Starch, or Fecula.

	ADULTS.	CHILDREN.
Take of Potato-starch, or wheat-starch	250 to 500 grms. (ʒviii to ʒxvi.)	100 to 200 grms. (ʒiii to ʒvi.)
Boiling water	q. s.	q. s.

Boil for a quarter of an hour, and add to the water of a bath.

Bath of Bran.

	ADULTS.	CHILDREN.
Take of Bran	1 to 2 kilogrms. (ʒxxxii to ʒlxiv.)	500 to 1000 grms. (ʒxvi to ʒxxxii.)

Enclose the bran in a sack, and boil it in about 10 litres (4 gallons) of water. Add the decoction to the water of a bath, and squeeze the sack into it also.

T

Gelatinous Bath.

	ADULTS.	CHILDREN.
Take of Flanders glue (gelatine) .	1000 grms. (℥xxxii.)	250 to 400 grms. (℥viii to ℥xiii.)
Hot water . . .	10 litres (4 gallons.)	4 litres (1 1/2 gallons.)

Melt the glue, and add it to a bath.

Emollient Fomentations.

Take of Marsh-mallow roots, and } of each   30 grms. (℥i.)
poppy-heads . .}

Boil them in :

    Water . . . . 1500 grms. (℥xlviii.)

Boil down to 1000 grammes (℥xxxii). For fomentations to soothe pain and inflammation.

Emollient Poultice.

Take of Barley meal . } of each . . . Equal parts.
Linseed meal }
    Decoction of mallow, or of marsh-mallow . q. s.

Rub the meal in the decoction, and cook it to a suitable consistence, frequently stirring it. The poultice to be applied between two cloths.

Starch Poultice.

Take of Potato-starch . . 120 grms. (℥iv.)
    Common water . . 1000 grms. (℥xxxii.)

Boil the water, and pour it quickly upon the starch, having first moistened it with 180 grammes. (℥vi) of cold water. Boil it for a minute, and take it from the fire.

Bread Poultice.

Take of Powdered bread-crumbs . 200 grms. (℥vi.)
    Milk . . . . 500 grms. (℥xvi.)

Mix them, and boil to a suitable consistence.

N.B. To make these poultices more soothing to inflamed parts, and more likely to hasten suppuration, from 30 to 100 grms. (℥i to ℥iii) of basilicon, or poplar ointment, or onguent de la mère,* may be added.

(§. * This is composed of olive oil, 8; pork fat, butter, mutton suet, yellow wax and litharge, of each, 4; and black pitch, 1 part. Fr. *Codex*.)

EMETICS.

EMETICS FROM THE VEGETABLE KINGDOM.

Emetic Powder.

	ADULTS.	CHILDREN.
Take of Powdered ipecacuanha root . .	2 grms. (ʒss.)	0,60 centigrms. (gr. ix.)

Divide it in 4 packets. 1 to be taken every 10 minutes, mixed with a little sugar and water (§. with plenty, *i. e.* 1 to 2 pints of warm water).

Emetic Draught.

	ADULTS.		CHILDREN.
Take of Powdered ipecacuanha	1,50 centigrms. (gr. xxiii.)		0,50 centigrms. (gr. viii.)
Water . . .	100 grms.	(ʒiii.)	40 grms. (ʒx.)
Syrup of ipecacuanha .	50 grms.	(ʒiss.)	30 grms. (ʒi.)

Mix the powder and the syrup accurately in a mortar, and add the water. Shake it up before taking it. A quarter of this draught to be given every 10 minutes.

Expectorant Tisane.

	ADULTS.	CHILDREN.
Take of Powdered senega root .	4 to 8 grms. (ʒi to ʒii.)	2 grms. (ʒss.)
Boiling water . .	750 grms. (ʒxxiv.)	250 grms. (ʒviii.)
Infuse for 2 hours, strain, and add:		
Syrup of Tolu . .	60 grms. (ʒii.)	30 grms. (ʒi.)

Mix. To be taken by small cupsful at a time, in the course of the day.

Used in catarrhal affections, when the expectoration is viscid and difficult of expulsion.

Tisane of Viola Tricolor. (Hearts'-ease—wild pansy.)

	ADULTS.	CHILDREN.
Take of Leaves or stalks of the wild pansy	40 grms. (ʒx.)	15 grms. (ʒss.)
Boil them in :		
Milk	150 grms. (ʒv.)	60 grms. (ʒii.)
Strain, and sweeten with:		
Syrup of wild pansy . .	60 grms. (ʒii.)	30 grms. (ʒi.)

To be taken night and morning for several weeks, or even months at a time, as a purifier of the blood.

Used in the treatment of cutaneous eruptions and mumps in children; and constitutional syphilis.

EMETICS FROM THE MINERAL KINGDOM.

TARTRATE OF POTASH AND ANTIMONY (TARTAR EMETIC— EMETIC).

Slightly Nauseating Drink.

	ADULTS.		CHILDREN.
Take of Barley water . .	1000 grms.	(ʒxxxii.)	500 grms. (ʒxvi.)
Tartar emetic (tartre stibié) . .	0,05 centigrms.	(gr. 3/4.)	0,02 centigrms. (gr. 1/3.)
Dissolve, and add:			
Simple syrup . .	100 grms.	(ʒiii.)	80 grms. (ʒiiss.)

To be taken by glassfuls in the course of the day.

Used in inflammatory diseases of the eyes and ears. In pain of the head, as a derivative. (§. The dose, gr. 1/9 nearly, is too small to cause much nausea; but it produces sufficient depression of the circulation to afford considerable relief in conjunctival inflammation).

Emetic Draught.

	ADULTS.		CHILDREN.
Take of Tartar emetic . .	0,10 centigrms.	(gr. iss.)	0,05 centigrms. (gr. 3/4.)
Distilled water . .	100 grms.	(ʒiii.)	40 grms. (ʒx.)
Syrup of ipecacuanha .	40 grms.	(ʒx.)	20 grms. (ʒv.)

Dissolve the salt in the water, and add the syrup. One quarter of it to be taken every 10 minutes, until vomiting is produced.

Contra-Stimulant Mixture.

	ADULTS.		CHILDREN.
Take of Tartrate of antimony (tartar emetic) .	0,30 to 1 grm.	(gr. ivss to gr. xv.)	0,15 to 0,30 cent. (gr. iiss. to gr. ivss.)
Orange-flower water .	20 grms.	(ʒv.)	10 grms. (ʒiiss.)
Linden water. .	100 grms.	(ʒiii.)	40 grms. (ʒx.)
Syrup of gum. .	30 grms.	(ʒi.)	20 grms. (ʒv.)

Dissolve the salt in the water, and add the syrup. A table-spoonful to be taken every half hour, as long as the stomach will bear it.

Used in acute pneumonia, and acute rheumatism, &c.

N.B. When it can be done, the dose may be increased.

Emetic Powder.

	ADULTS.		CHILDREN.
Take of Tartrate of antimony	. 0,10 centigrms. (gr. iss.)		0,05 centigrms. (gr. 3/4.)
Ipecacuanha .	. 1 grm.	(gr. xv.)	0,50 centigrms. (gr. viii.)

Mix accurately, and divide into 4 packets. 1 to be taken every 10 minutes, until vomiting is excited.

Tartar Emetic Ointment.

Take of Tartar emetic .	. .	4 grms. (ℨi.)
Water .	. q. s. about	10 grms. (ℨiiss.)

Rub them well together upon a porphyrizing table,

and add:

Lard	. . .	. 30 grms. (ℨi.)

Mix. To be rubbed upon the skin 3 or 4 times a-day, to produce a revulsive pustular eruption. (§. Employed in most cases when long continued counter-irritation is necessary.)

N.B. This ointment must never be applied to the face, the neck, or the upper part of the chest (in women); for the pustules leave indelible cicatrices.

Antimonial Suppository.

Take of Tartar emetic .	0,05 to 0,15 centigrms. (gr. 3/4 to gr. ii 1/3.)
Butter of cocoa .	. 5 grms. (gr. lxxv.)

Melt the cocoa-butter, and allow it to become nearly cold; add the emetic, reduced to an extremely fine powder, and mix them thoroughly. To be introduced into the anus 3 or 4 times in succession, in order to reproduce a suppressed hæmorrhoidal discharge.

SULPHATE OF ZINC AND SULPHATE OF COPPER.

(See above, p. 265, 266).

PURGATIVES AND LAXATIVES.

Laxative Tisane.

	ADULTS.	CHILDREN.
Take of Prunes	40 grms. (ʒx.)	20 grms. (ʒv.)
Water	1000 grms. (℥xxxii.)	500 grms. (℥xvi.)

Boil for ten minutes, strain, and add :

	ADULTS.	CHILDREN.
Tartaric syrup . . .	80 grms. (ʒiiss.)	40 grms. (ʒx.)

Another.

	ADULTS.	CHILDREN.
Take of Cassia pulp and tamarind pulp	15 grms. (ʒss.)	8 grms. (ʒii.)
Water	1000 grms. (℥xxxii.)	500 grms. (℥xvi.)

Boil, strain, and add :

	ADULTS.	CHILDREN.
White honey . . .	50 grms. (ʒiss.)	30 grms. (ʒi.)

Manna.

	ADULTS.	CHILDREN.
Take of Manna, in tears . . .	60 grms. (ʒii.)	40 grms. (ʒx.)

Dissolve in a cupful of hot milk. To be taken all at once.
Used as a purgative for children and old people.

Bolus of Prepared Honey.

Take of White honey . . .	200 grms. (ʒvi.)

Cook the honey until it is slightly brittle; add a sufficient
quantity of powdered marsh-mallow, and make it into boluses of
half or three quarters of an inch in diameter (1 to 2 centimetres).
These boluses are to be greased with butter, and introduced up
the seat. They form a convenient and efficacious purgative.

Laxative Mixture.

	ADULTS.	CHILDREN.
Take of Compound syrup of chicory ⎫		
Syrup of peach-blossoms . ⎬ of each 30 grms. (ʒi.)	10 grms. (ʒiiss.)	
Oil of sweet almonds . ⎭		

Mix them thoroughly. To be taken in one or two doses.

Castor Oil Mixture.

	ADULTS.	CHILDREN.
Take of Castor oil . . .	{ 15 to 30 grms. (ʒss to ʒi.)	5 to 10 grms. (ʒi to ʒiiss.)
Yolk of egg, or mucilage of gum q. s.		q. s.
Make them into an emulsion, and add		
Simple syrup } of each . .		20 grms. (ʒv.)
Mint water . }	30 grms. (ʒi.)	10 grms. (ʒiiss.)
Common water . . .	60 grms. (ʒii.)	30 grms. (ʒi.)

Mix them, and shake the mixture before taking it.

Another.

	ADULTS.	CHILDREN.
Take of Cold-drawn castor oil . .	15 grms. (ʒss.)	{ 4 to 8 grms. (ʒi to ʒii.)
Syrup of tartaric acid . .	30 grms. (ʒi.)	20 grms. (ʒv.)

Rub them in a mortar. To be taken at one dose.

Laxative Glyster.

	ADULTS.	CHILDREN.
Take of White honey or treacle . .	60 grms. (ʒii.)	40 grms. (ʒx.)
Decoction of marsh-mallow or of } linseed . . . . }	500 grms. (ʒxvi.)	200 grms. (ʒvi.)

Mix them. For a very slightly laxative glyster.

Another. (Used in the Parisian hospitals.)

	ADULTS.	CHILDREN.
Take of Honey of dogs'-mercury . .	60 grms. (ʒii.)	30 grms. (ʒi.)
Decoction of marsh-mallow .	500 grms. (ʒxvi.)	200 grms. (ʒvi.)

Mix for a glyster.

Glyster of Castor Oil

	ADULTS.	CHILDREN.
Take of Castor oil	60 grms. (ʒii.)	20 grms. (ʒv.)
Decoction of marsh-mallow .	220 grms. (ʒvii.)	200 grms. (ʒvi.)

Mix them by agitation; or better still, make the oil into an emulsion with the yolk of egg, and add the decoction by small quantities at a time.

LAXATIVES FURNISHED BY THE MINERAL KINGDOM.

Laxative Tisane.

	ADULTS.	CHILDREN.
Take of Cream of soluble tartar* (tartrate borico-potassique—*tartarus boracicus*)	60 grms. (ʒii.)	10 grms. (ʒiiss.)
Decoction of barley or dogs'-tooth	1000 grms. (ʒxxxii.)	500 grms. (ʒxvi.)

Mix, and sweeten at pleasure. To be taken by glassfuls in the course of the day.

Packets of Magnesia.

	ADULTS.	CHILDREN.
Take of Calcined magnesia	4 grms. (ʒi.)	2 grms. (ʒss.)
Bicarbonate of soda or potash (in powder)	6 grms. (ʒiss.)	4 grms. (ʒi.)
Powdered white sugar	25 grms. (ʒvi.)	10 grms. (ʒiiss.)

Mix them accurately, and divide into 12 packets. Three of them to be taken every day diffused in water.

Used in gastralgia, and dyspepsia, and headache accompanied with sickness.

After having taken this powder for four days in succession, it is desirable to take a cupful of infusion of quassia (ʒss of the quassia at a time) night and morning for eight days following.

Magnesian Medicine. (White magnesia.)

Take of Carbonate of magnesia	.	8 grms. (ʒii.)
Powdered sugar	.	50 grms. (ʒiss.)
Simple water	.	40 grms. (ʒx.)
Orange-flower water	.	20 grms. (ʒv.)

Triturate carefully and by small quantities at a time, the magnesia and the sugar, and add the water by little and little, stirring them constantly, lastly, add the orange water, and strain through a fine sieve. To be given to adults in a single dose; *to* children one table-spoonful only.

Magnesia is employed in every dose as an antidote to poisoning

(§. * This salt is made by boiling 4 parts of cream of tartar (potas. bitart.) with 1 part of crystallized boracic acid (Fr. *Codex*), which has the effect of materially increasing the solubility of the bitartrate.)

by arsenious acid. It is also employed in the form of lozenges, from 2 to 10 daily, each of which contains 0·20 centigrammes (gr. iii) of magnesia.

Royal Tisane. *(Codex.)*

Take of Senna leaves } of each .		15 grms. (ʒss.)
Sulphate of soda }		
Anise and coriander, of each		4 grms. (ʒi.)
Fresh chervil. . .		15 grms. (ʒss.)
Cold water . . .		1000 grms. (ʒxxxii.)
One citron, cut into slices.		

Macerate for 12 hours. To be taken by glassfuls in the course of the day,

Purgative Mixture for Painters. (Hospital receipt.)

Take of Diaphœnix* (electuary) . .		30 grms. (ʒi.)
Powdered jalap . .		4 grms. (ʒi.)
Senna leaves . .		8 grms. (ʒii.)
Syrup of buckthorn .		30 grms. (ʒi.)
Boiling water . .		125 grms. (ʒiv.)

Infuse the jalap and the senna in the water; add the diaphœnix; strain, and add the syrup of buckthorn. To be taken in one or two doses.

Purgative Mixture. (Purgative apozem—black draught.)

Take of Senna-leaves . .		8 grms. (ʒii.)
Powdered rhubarb .		4 grms. (ʒi.)
Tamarind-pulp . .		10 grms. (ʒiss.)

Macerate them in:

Boiling water . .		120 grms. (ʒiv.)

Strain, and add:

Sulphate of magnesia .		15 grms. (ʒss.)

Mix. To be taken at once or at twice.

Purgative Glyster.

Take of Senna-leaves . .		30 grms. (ʒi.)
Boiling water . .		300 grms. (ʒix.)

Infuse for an hour, and strain. For a glyster intended to excite uterine contractions in cases of inertia of this organ during

(§. * Diaphœnix contains: Dates, 30; sweet almonds, 14; ginger, black pepper, mace, cinnamon, carrot, fennel and rue, of each, 1; saffron, 1/20; turbith mineral, 16; scammony, 6; sugar, 30; and honey, 125 parts. Fr. *Codex.*)

delivery. As a means also of checking uterine hæmorrhage following delivery, or miscarriages such as are symptomatic of uterine cancer.

Coffee of Senna.

Take of Roasted coffee . } of each . 16 grms. (ʒss.)
   Senna fruit (follicles) }

Make an infusion of the coffee in the ordinary way, and then an infusion of the senna. Mix them, and take them with milk or sugar at pleasure.

This is an agreeable purgative for children.

Purgative Glyster for Painters.

Take of Senna-leaves .   .   .   8 grms. (ʒii.)
   Boiling water .   .   .   500 grms. (ʒxvi.)

Infuse, strain, and add:

Powdered jalap.   .   .   4 grms. (ʒi.)
Diaphœnix (see p. 281) } of each   30 grms. (ʒi.)
Syrup of buckthorn . }

Mix and stir them together. For a glyster in painters' colic.

N.B. In the country, and for poor people, the senna may be advantageously replaced by hyssop (*Gratiola officinalis—Scrophularineæ.*)

RHUBARB.

	ADULTS.	CHILDREN.
Take of Powdered rhubarb .	{ 0.30 to 0,60 centigrms.	0,10 to 0,25 cent.
	{ (gr. ivss to gr. ix.)	(gr. iss to gr. iii.)

In one powder. To be taken at the beginning of a meal by persons suffering from constipation or dyspepsia.

Rhubarb is also used under the form of a syrup, tincture, lozenges, &c.

SALINE PURGATIVES.

Lemonade of Citrate of Magnesia.

	FOR 88 GRMS.	FOR 46 GRMS.
Take of Carbonate of magnesia .	15 grms. (ʒiii, ꝺiiss.)	18 grms. (ʒiv, ꝺii.)
Citric acid . . .	23 grms. (ʒvi.)	28 grms. (ʒvii gr. x.)

Water. . . . . . 375 grms. (ʒxii.)

Make them react upon each other by gently heating them in a porcelain capsule; and when the effervescence has ceased, filter them, and add :

Syrup of lemons, of tartaric acid, or of strawberries . . . }	75 grms. (ʒiiss.)
Tincture of citron-peel . .	4 grms. (ʒi.)
Bicarbonate of soda	4 grms. (ʒi.)

Cork them carefully and quickly. To be taken by glassfuls in the day.

The lemonade may be more simply prescribed, as follows:

Lemonade of Citrate of Magnesia (not effervescing.)

Take of Officinal citrate of magnesia .	40 to 50 grms. (ʒx to ʒiss.)
Water. . . .	700 grms. (ʒxxii.)
Syrup of sugar or of gooseberries . . }	50 grms. (ʒiss.)

Mix, and filter if necessary.

We prefer this formula, because the salt can be more exactly apportioned in it. If the physician contents himself with ordering a lemonade of citrate of magnesia, the composition will vary with each druggist who prepares it; for this preparation not being officinal in the Codex, many different formulæ have been proposed. We repeat that the most simple is the best; moreover, these lemonades can easily be rendered gaseous by means of the little apparatus of Briet's* for making Seidlitz water, the employment of which is very simple.

Purgative Mixture.

	ADULTS.	CHILDREN.
Take of Sulphate of magnesia .	30 to 50 grms. (ʒi to ʒiss.)	8 to 15 grms. (ʒii to ʒss.)
Infusion of coffee .	100 grms. (ʒiii.)	100 grms. (ʒiii.)
Simple syrup . .	30 grms. (ʒi.)	30 grms. (ʒi.)

(‡. * Shown at the Great Exhibition, and now sold in most towns.)

Mix. To be taken during the day. We may repeat in this place, that coffee entirely takes away the bitterness of sulphate of magnesia.

Sulphate of magnesia (Seidlitz or Epsom salts) is the basis of Seidlitz water, and when the physician orders the water, he ought to specify whether he means the natural or the artificial, and in the latter case he should indicate the dose of the salt which he wishes to enter into each bottle. He should order :

Seidlitz water (with 8 (ʒii), 15 (ʒss), 25 (ʒvi), 30 (ʒi), 45 (ʒiss), or 60 grms. (ʒii), of magnes. sulph).

He should indicate whether he wishes it to be effervescing or not, in the absence of which the druggist will send the gaseous kind.

Purgative Apozem.

	ADULTS.	CHILDREN.
Take of Broth made with herbs	200 grms. (ʒvi.)	150 grms. (ʒv.)
Sulphate or phosphate of soda { 15 to 40 grms. (ʒss to ʒx.)		5 to 15 grms. (ʒi to ʒss.)

Mix. To be taken at once or at twice.

Purgative Tisane.

(Called Antilaiteuse—tending to suppress the secretion of milk.)

Take of Decoction of the arundo donax (canne de Provence). }	1000 grms. (ʒxxxii.)
Sulphate of potash (sal de duobus)	4 to 10 grms. (ʒi to ʒiiss.)

Mix and sweeten at pleasure. To be taken by glassfuls in the course of the day.

N.B. We have prescribed in this place the canne de Provence, which, like the periwinkle (vinca), is popularly regarded as an excellent means of suppressing the secretion of milk. It is a prejudice which is worth consulting, though these substances do not really act better than barley water in decoction of dogs'-tooth.

Tartrate of Potash and Soda. (Sel de Seignette.)

Take of Sel de Seignette	5 to 15 grms. (ʒi to ʒss.)

Dissolve in water or milk. To be taken at once in the morning fasting, to check acute diarrhœa in infants.

DRASTIC PURGATIVES.

EUPHORBIACEÆ.

Purgative Mixture.

					ADULTS.	CHILDREN.
Take of Castor oil	.	.	.	.	30 grms. (ʒi.)	10 grms. (ʒiiss.)
Croton oil	.	.	.	.	1 drop.	1/2 drop.
Syrup of lemons	.	.	.	.	30 grms. (ʒi.)	20 grms. (ʒv.)
Mint water	.	.	.	.	20 grms. (ʒv.)	10 grms. (ʒiiss.)
Pure water	.	.	.	.	40 grms. (ʒx.)	30 grms. (ʒi.)

Mix accurately. To be taken at once or at twice. Shake it up before giving it.

Croton Oil Mixture.

				ADULTS.	CHILDREN.
Take of Croton oil.	.	.	.	1 to 4 drops.	1 drop.
Mucilage of gum-arabic	.	.	5 grms. (ʒi 1/4.)	5 grms. (ʒi 1/4.)

Mix them carefully in a marble mortar, and add :

				ADULTS	CHILDREN
Simple syrup	.	.	.	40 grms. (ʒx.)	30 grms. (ʒi.)
Orange-flower water	.	.	20 grms. (ʒv.)	10 grms. (ʒiiss.)
Common water	.	.	.	60 grms. (ʒii.)	40 grms. (ʒx.)

Shake them together. To be taken at once or twice.

Croton Oil Pills.

				ADULTS.	CHILDREN.
Take of Croton oil	.	.	.	1 to 4 drops.	1 drop.
Fresh bread-crumbs	.	.	1 grm. (gr. xv.)	0,50 centigrms. (gr. viii.)

Make the bread absorb the oil, and divide into 4 pills, which are to be rolled in powdered gum. One or two to be taken in the morning, fasting.

N.B. Croton oil is employed as a revulsive, to produce a vesicular eruption upon the skin. The person who uses it ought to take care to cover the hand with a leather glove, and not to hold his face over the part which he is rubbing. (§. If this last precaution is omitted, the vapour of the croton oil sometimes produces severe inflammation of the eyes, and smarting of the skin of the face.)

Croton Oil Glyster.

				ADULTS.	CHILDREN.
Take of Croton oil	.	.	.	1 to 4 drops.	1 to 2 drops.
Yolk of egg	.	.	.	1	1

Rub them accurately together, and add :

			ADULTS.	CHILDREN.
Common water	.	.	800 grms. (ʒix.)	200 grms. (ʒvi.)

CONVOLVULACEÆ.

	ADULTS.	CHILDREN.
Take of Powdered jalap . . 4 grms.	(ʒi.)	1 grm. (gr. xv.)
Calomel . . . 0,25 centigrms. (gr. iv.)		0,05 centigrms. (gr. 3/4.)

Mix with care, and make a powder to be taken with some preserve.

Purgative Pills.

Take of Resin of jalap . . 1 grm.	(gr. xv.)
Scammony . . 0,50 centigrms.	(gr. viii.)
Extract of colocynth . 0,10 centigrms.	(gr. iss.)
Excipient . . q. s.	

Mix, and divide into 5 pills. One to be taken every two hours in the morning, fasting, until they operate.

Purgative Emulsion.

	ADULTS.	CHILDREN.
Take of Resin of jalap . . . 1 grm. (gr. xv.)		0,25 centigrms. (gr. iv.)
Yolk of egg . . . 1		1/2
Triturate them carefully, and add:		
Castor oil . . . 10 grms. (ʒiiss.)		5 grms. (ʒi 1/4.)
Water . . . 100 grms. (ʒiii.)		50 grms. (ʒiss.)
Syrup of peach-blossoms . 40 grms. (ʒx.)		25 grms. (ʒvi.)

Mix, and shake them together. To be taken at one time, in the morning, fasting.

N.B. Turbith, scammony and jalap enter into the composition of German eau-de-vie, which is a good purgative in doses of 20 to 40 grms. (ʒv to ʒx).

ALOES.

Pills.

Take of Aloes .
      Colomel
      Camboge   } of each   0,5 centigrms. (gr. viii.)
      Extract of colocynth.
      Excipient . . . q. s.

Mix, and divide into 10 pills. From 1 to 4 to be taken at bed-time, so as to obtain one or two stools the next morning. These pills may also be taken before a meal in some broth.

N.B. Aloes enter into the composition of elixir of long life, Anderton's Scotch pills, the pills of Bontius (hydragogues), and Franck's "grains of health," &c.

Gout Pills.

Take of Powdered colchicum-seeds	.	2 grms.	(ʒss.)
Calomel. . .	.	0,50 centigrms.	(gr. viii.)
Powdered digitalis . } of each	.	1 grm.	(gr. xv.)
Sulphate of quinine }			
Extract of colocynth .	.	0,50 centigrms.	(gr. viii.)
Excipient . .	.	q. s.	

Mix, and divide into 20 pills. From 1 to 4 to be taken during the day, at the commencement of an attack of gout, but we must add that this is a dangerous plan.

EXCITANTS OF THE MUSCULAR SYSTEM, OR EXCITATIVES.

NUX VOMICA.

Take of Powdered (see p. 134, 135) nux vomica	0,25 centigrms.	(gr. iv.)
Gum-arabic	2 grms.	(ʒss.)
Sugar	4 grms.	(ʒi.)

Mix, and divide into 12 packets. From 1 to 2 packets to be taken daily; one in the morning, fasting; the other on going to bed, in dyspepsia with flatulence in old people, and in very large eaters, after acute affections of the digestive organs. The same powder may be given to children affected with St. Guy's dance (chorea). In paraplegia, to the extent of 4 to 10 packets daily, or even more, until tetanic spasms are produced.

Excitant Frictions.

Take of Tincture of nux vomica .	.	30 grms.	(ʒi.)
Eau de Cologne .	.	100 grms.	(ʒiii.)

Mix. To be used with friction as an embrocation upon the affected parts, especially when the paralysis is local, as in the face (§. after inflammation of the *portio dura* of the 7th pair) or after lead poisoning.

Pills of Nux Vomica.

Take of Alcoholic extract of nux vomica	.	1 grm. (gr. xv.)
Inert excipient . .	.	q. s.

To make 20 pills; 1 to 15? to be taken daily in the same cases as the powder of nux vomica prescribed above.

Syrup of Sulphate of Strychnine.

Take of Sulphate of strychnine .	0,25 centigrm·.	(gr. iv.)
Simple syrup . .	500 grms.	(ʒxvi.)

Dissolve the sulphate of strychnine in a little water, and add the syrup. Shake them together. This syrup is employed in doses of from 3 or 4 tea-spoonfuls to even 6 or 8 table-spoonfuls in the course of the day, for children and young people affected with chorea (St. Vitus's dance), so as to produce considerable stiffness of the limbs, and a kind of tetanic twitchings. It is employed in paralysis in the same way.

RHUS TOXICODENDRON.

Pills.

Take of Extract of rhus toxicodendron 5 grms. (gr. lxxv.)
Inert excipient . . q. s.

Mix, and divide into 25 pills. From 1 to 16 to be taken daily in paraplegia without any actual organic lesion; in paralysis of the bladder and of the rectum. For children the dose should not exceed 30 to 50 centigrammes (gr. ivss to gr. viii) daily.

ARNICA.

Tisane.

Take of Flowers of arnica montana. 5 to   10 grms. (ʒi 1/4 to ʒiiss.)
Boiling water . . 1000 grms. (ʒxxxii·)

Infuse, and strain through a fine linen sieve, and sweeten at pleasure.

Emetic properties have been undeservedly attributed to arnica. This purely mechanical action was due to very delicate tufts (of crystals ?) which were suspended in the tisane when it was passed through too coarse a sieve, and it is therefore always advisable to filter the infusion carefully. It is commonly employed to cure bruises on the head, under the name of *panacea lapsorum*. It is also employed in rheumatism, gout, and especially in paralysis. We may add that it may be emetic in too large doses.

ERGOT OF RYE.

Take of Freshly powdered ergot of rye. 10 grms. (ʒiiss.)

Divide it into 10 packets. One packet to be taken every six hours, in a little sugar and water, or between two slices of bread, in uterine hæmorrhages (not puerperal); in the hæmorrhage which follows delivery, and also in inertia of the uterus during labour. Packets of 1 gramme (gr. xv) mixed with water are given to lying-in women every fifteen minutes until strong uterine contractions come on, always taking care to stop after the fourth or fifth packet, if it produces vomiting.

Mixture of Ergotine.

Take of Ergotine .	. .	2 grms. (ʒss.)
Distilled water of balm .	.	100 grms. (ʒiii.)

Dissolve, and add :

Syrup of orange-peel	. .	40 grms. (ʒx.)

Mix, and shake them together. A quarter of this mixture should be given every fifteen minutes when inertia of the uterus prevents the completion of labour, or occasions hæmorrhage after the expulsion of the child or placenta. It is used also in common uterine hæmorrhages.

In chronic congestion of the uterus, this mixture should be given in the course of the twenty-four hours.

NARCOTICS (STUPEFIANTS).

OPIUM.

Opium, one of the most heroic therapeutical agents we possess is employed under an infinity of forms, and in the most various doses. There are several extracts, and there is a syrup of opium which contains 5 centigrammes (gr. 3/4) of gummy extract of opium in every 30 grammes (ʒi) of the syrup. Opium enters into the composition of the laudanun of Sydenham and of Rousseau, into the pills of dogs'-tongue, &c. But we shall content ourselves with giving a few magistral formulæ.

Soothing Mixture.

	ADULTS.	CHILDREN.
Take of Syrup of opium . .	. 30 grms. (ʒi.)	10 grms. (ʒiiss.)
Syrup of orange-flowers .	. 20 grms. (ʒv.)	20 grms. (ʒv.)
Lettace water . .	. 100 grms. (ʒiii.)	80 grms. (ʒiiss.)

Mix. A spoonful to be taken every half hour, to allay pain and procure sleep.

Mixture for *Delirium Tremens.*

Take of Gummy extract of opium	.	2 grms. (ʒss.)
Distilled lettuce water .	.	100 grms. (℥iii.)
Syrup of gum . .	.	25 grms. (ʒvi.)
„ „ sulphuric ether*	.	15 grms. (ʒss.)

Dissolve the extract in the distilled water, and add the syrup of gum, and that of the ether. Mix, shake them together, and cork with care. This mixture may be given by a table-spoonful at a time every half hour, to patients affected with *delirium tremens,* and it must be discontinued when the agitation abates and sleep approaches. If the distress continues after the whole mixture has been taken, another must be given containing even double the dose of opium.

Antineuralgic Mixture.

Take of Gummy extract of opium .	.	4 grms. (ʒi.)
Water . .	.	q. s. to give the
extract the consistence of a syrup.		

Moisten the finger with this mixture, and wet the parts affected with neuralgia or non-inflammatory rheumatism with it, and use friction for a few minutes, taking care to keep wetting the finger and the part as fast as it dries. The rubbing being finished, cover the part, without wiping it, with a cloth moistened in the mixture, and cover it over with oiled silk.

Anti-diarrhœal Pills.

	ADULTS.	CHILDREN.
Take of Gummy extract of opium.	0,10 centigrms. (gr. iss.)	0,02 centigrms. (gr. 1/3.)
Calomel . . .	0,20 centigrms. (gr. iii.)	0,10 centigrms. (gr. iss.)
Ipecacuanha (powdered) .	0,20 centigrms. (gr. iii.)	0,10 centigrms. (gr. iss.)
Excipient . . .	q. s.	q. s.

Mix, and divide into 10 pills. One to be taken night and morning in the treatment of chronic diarrhœa.

(ʒ. * Syrup of eth. sulph.: Take ether, 1 part syrup, 16 parts (by weight). Fr. *Codex.*)

ALKALOIDS OF OPIUM.

Soothing Draught.

		ADULTS.		CHILDREN.
Take of Codeine . . .	0,10 centigrms. (gr. iss.)		{	0,01 centigrms. (gr. 1/6.)
Cherry-laurel water .	10 grms.	(ʒiiss.)		4 grms. (ʒi.)
Linden water . .	100 grms.	(ʒiii.)		80 grms. (ʒiiss.)
Simple syrup . .	30 grms.	(ʒi.)		30 grms. (ʒi.)

Dissolve the codeine in the distilled waters, and add the syrup. A table-spoonful to be taken every half hour, to soothe pain and produce sleep.

N.B. The 0,10 centigrms. of codeine may be replaced by the same weight of a salt of morphia.

MORPHIA AND ITS SALTS.

		ADULTS.		CHILDREN.
Take of Sulphate of morphia .	0,03 centigrms. (gr. ss.)		{	0,01 centigrms. (gr. 1/6.)
Magnesia (English) .	5 grms.	(gr. lxxv.)	{	0,50 centigrms. (gr. viii.)

Mix, and divide into 12 packets. One or two to be taken to check vomiting accompanied by constipation, without any mechanical obstruction.

Pills.

		ADULTS.		CHILDREN.
Take of Hydrochlorate of morphia	0,05 centigrms. (gr. 3/4.)		{	0,01 centigrms. (gr. 1/6.)
Extract of liquorice .	1 grm.	(gr. xv.)	{	0,50 centigrms. (gr. viii.)
Excipient. . .	q. s.			q. s.

Divide into 20 pills. One to be taken a quarter of an hour before every meal in diarrrhæa accompanied by lientery (white purging of undigested food), and in gastralgia and enteralgia with a tendency to diarrhæa.

Anodyne Glyster.

		ADULTS.		CHILDREN.
Take of Starch water . .	250 grms. (ʒviii.)			150 grms. (ʒiv.)
Laudanum of Sydenham .	15 drops.			1 to 2 drops.

For a glyster in diarrhæa and colic from worms.

U 2

WHITE POPPY, (*Papaver somniferum album*).

The capsules of *Papaver somniferum* (poppy heads) vary in their composition according to the species which yields them, that is to say, whether it is the white or black poppy; according as the variety taken has round heads or long ones, the latter being the most active; and according, lastly, to the period at which they have been gathered. In order to possess their full properties, poppy-heads ought to be gathered before the seeds are ripe. Those of commerce are generally collected too late, and serious consequences have resulted from substituting the green fruit for the dry capsules, which have advanced too far towards maturity.

Poppy capsules enclose seeds which are employed for preparing a sweet oil which does not possess any of the properties of the poppy, and is known in commerce by the name of *white* oil, *œillette*, or *poppy* oil. The *pericarp* (the capsule itself) is used for making the decoctions employed in lotions, fomentations, and soothing glysters, in the proportion of 10 to 20 grammes (ʒiiss to ʒv) of the heads to 1000 grammes (ʒxxxii) of water. A watery extract is also made from the capsules, the action of which is to that of opium, as about 6 to 1, (§. *i. e.* 6 parts of poppy extract equal 1 part of opium). Lastly, the extract is the basis of the syrup *diacodion*, which was formerly prepared from the decoction of the poppy-heads, but this mode of obtaining it is now abandoned (§. in the Fr. Codex, but is still retained in both the Lond. and Ed. Ph.) because of the great variation in the composition of the syrup when prepared in this way.

Soothing Glyster.

	ADULTS.	CHILDREN.
Take of Poppy capsules	16 grms. (ʒss.)	4 grms. (ʒi.)
Water .	1000 grms. (ʒxxxii.)	1000 grms. (ʒxxxii.)

Remove the seeds from the capsules, and boil for a quarter of an hour.

Used as a soothing glyster in colic and purging.

N.B. We advise physicians always to prescribe poppy heads by weight, and not by number, for their size varies much. It is better still, only to use them for external applications.

Soothing Mixture.

	ADULTS.	CHILDREN.
Take of Syrup of diacodion (or white poppy)	30 grms. (ʒi.)	4 grms. (ʒi.)
Syrup of orange-flowers .	20 grms. (ʒv.)	20 grms. (ʒv.)
Distilled lettuce water . .	100 grms. (ʒiii.)	100 grms. (ʒiii.)

Mix. A table-spoonful to be taken every half hour.

Used to soothe pain, to procure sleep, and to allay nervous colic, &c.

N.B. 30 grms. (ʒi) of syrup of diacodion contain 0,30 centigrms. (gr. ivss) of extract of poppy. This extract is employed under the form of pills, to the extent of 0,05 to 1 grm. (gr. 3/4 to gr. xv) for adults, in the 24 hours, and of 0,01 to 0,02 centigrms. (gr. 1/6 to gr. 1/3) for children.

We have already said that opium enters into the composition of compound wines of opium. Sydenham's laudanum contains opium, saffron, cinnamon, cloves and Malaga wine, and is made by maceration. (§. It therefore corresponds closely with the Vinum opii, Ph. L., which, however, does not contain saffron.) After some time the colouring matter of the saffron leaves the volatile oil with which it is united, and the laudanum becomes colourless, without however losing any of its virtues. 0·85 centigrammes (gr. xiii) of Sydenham's laudanum represent 0·10 centigrammes (gr. iss) of crude opium, or 0·05 (gr. 3/4) of extract of opium.

Rousseau's laudanum is prepared by the fermentation, for a month, of honey in contact with yeast, warm water and opium. The fermentation being completed, the liquid is distilled, and the product of the distillation is again distilled (re-coholated, *i. e.* twice distilled) and the product of the second distillation is mixed with the liquid remaining in the retort, then strained, and evaporated to a proper consistence, *i. e.* to 150 of the aerometer of Baumé (§. sp. gr. ·966). It is three times as active as Sydenham's laudanum.

Opium is a very compound product, and its constituents vary considerably. We here give the value of the different preparations which have opium or its alkaloids as their base, according to the calculations of M. Soubeiran.

1 grain of crude opium equals :						GRAINS.	1 grain of extract of opium equals : GRAINS.
Morphia	.	.	.	.	.	0,07	0,15 (gr. 1/6 nearly.)
Opium, crude	.	.	.	.	.	1	2
„ extract aqueous	.	.	.	.	0,5	1
„ „ deprived of narcotine	.	.	0,45	0,9
„ „ vinous	.	.	.	0,6	1,2
„ „ acetous	.	.	.	0,6	1,2
Tincture of opium (crude).	.	.	.	12	24
„ „ „ (extract of)	.	.	6	12
Wine of opium (simple)	.	.	.	10	20
Laudanum of Sydenham	.	.	.	8,5	17
„ „ Rousseau	.	.	.	3,6	7,2
Vinegar of opium	.	.	.	8,5	17
Acetic tincture of opium	.	.	.	10	20

In the following table, from M. Dublanc, is given the value of different extracts of poppy :

95 parts of alcoholic extract of poppy	.	.	.	contain 1 part of morphia.
333 „ „ extract of the juice of the poppy, obtained by expression	.	.	.	„ „ „
1700 „ „ extract obtained from an infusion of the dry capsules	.	.	.	„ „ „

THRIDACE, LACTUCARIUM.

Thridace, which has enjoyed a certain degree of reputation, but is now little employed, is the extract of the juice of the cultivated lettuce, which it is necessary to avoid confounding with the wild lettuce, which is much more active. *Lactucarium*, much? used in England, but little known in France, is obtained by incisions made into the same cultivated lettuce. They may, however, be used one for the other under the same forms, in the same cases, and nearly in the same doses, though lactucarium is a little the most active. Thridace is made into a syrup and pills; and into a collyrium, highly puffed by M. Rau, for relieving irritation of the conjunctiva.

Collyrium.

Take of Thridace	.	.	.	0,15 centigrms. (gr. ii 1/3.)
Distilled water	.	.	100 grms.	(ℨiii.)
Mucilage of quinine seeds.	2 grms.	(ʒss.)

Mix. A few drops of this collyrium to be put into the eyes once or twice a day, especially at night, on going to bed.

The extract of *wild* lettuce and that of *Aconitum Napellus* are employed in doses of from 0·01 to 0·05 centigrammes (gr. 1/6 to gr. 3/4).

POISONOUS SOLANACEÆ.

BELLADONNA.

Powder for Hooping-Cough.

Take of Powdered belladonna-root . 0,25 centigrms. (gr. iv.)
    „   sugar . . 5 grms.   (gr. lxxv.)

Mix them accurately, and divide into 25 packets. From 1 to 10 to be taken at once? in the morning, fasting, by children affected with hooping-cough. From 1 to 4 in the evening, in ophthalmia with great dread of light, and in obstinate constipation, and nocturnal incontinence of urine in children and young people.

Anti-epileptic and Soothing Pills.

Take of Powdered belladonna root . . 0,50 centigrms. (gr. viii.)
    Alcoholic extract of belladonna . 0,20 centigrms. (gr. iii.)
    Inert excipient .   .   . q. s.

Mix, and divide into 50 pills. One to be taken every night on going to bed for the first week; two the second week, and so on from week to week, until the patient begins to feel some disorder of vision and dryness of the throat. After this, the dose must only be increased when these symptoms become less.

They may be administered in the same way in nocturnal incontinence of urine in children and young persons, and in nervous asthma.

Stupefying (Narcotic) Mixture.

Take of Alcoholic extract of belladonna . 15 grms. (ʒss.)
    Water .   .   . q. s. to give the
    extract the consistence of syrup.

To be spread upon poultices in the proportion of 4 or 5 grms. (ʒi to ʒiʒ). Applied by means of friction to the skin covering painful parts, taking care to moisten it as it dries: spread upon the forehead and eyebrows in cases of photophobia and iritis; before operating for cataract; and also after operating for this disease.

Applied like an ointment upon the neck of the uterus in cases of rigidity, and in dysmenorrhœa. Laid upon the hypogastrum in cases of obstinate vomiting during pregnancy.

It is rubbed in small quantities upon the gums, and the inner surface of the jaws in cases of toothache and facial neuralgia, but care must be taken not to swallow it; and upon the prepuce in phymosis and paraphymosis, and also upon strangulated hernial tumours.

Belladonna Ointment.

Take of Alcoholic extract of belladonna.   . 10 grms. (ʒiiss.)
        Lard   .   .   .   . 20 grms. (ʒv.)

Moisten the extract with sufficient warm water to give it a syrupy consistence, and mix it with the lard in a mortar.

Used in the same cases as the preceding mixture, with the exception of its employment to the interior of the mouth.

Narcotic Tampon (Plug).

Take of Alcoholic extract of belladonna 0,10 centigrms. (gr. iss.)
       Extract of opium   .   0,05 centigrms. (gr. 3/4.)

Place the two extracts in the centre of a little pledget of carded cotton, and fold it up so as to enclose the extract; tie it up with a very strong thread, and leave a double thread 8 inches long attached to it.

The plug is to be introduced into the vagina by the physician or the patient herself, and placed upon the neck of the uterus, where it is to be retained from twelve to twenty-four hours. *Used* in neuralgia of the uterus. In very painful menstruation accompanied by leucorrhœa. We may add to the tampon from half a gramme to a whole one (gr. viii to gr. xv) of tannin.

Narcotic Suppository.

Take of Alcoholic extract of belladonna . 0,10 centigrms. (gr. iss.)
       Cocoa butter   .   . 5 grms.   (gr. lxxv.)

Melt the butter, and allow it to cool a little; add the extract moistened with a little water, and press it into a paper mould.

Used in cases of fissure of the anus, in painful coarctations (spasmodic contractions) of the anus, in painful hæmorrhoids, and in tenesmus of the rectum or bladder.

Narcotic Mixture.

Take of Tincture of belladonna ⎱
     „   „ opium . ⎰ of each   . 40 grms. (ʒx.)

Mix them. Used by means of friction, or poured upon the face of a poultice to the extent of one or two table-spoonfuls, to allay pain.

Narcotic Liniment.

Take of Alcoholic extract of belladonna . . . 2 grms. (ʒss.)
    Water, q. s. to dissolve the extract; about . 6 grms. (ʒiss.)
    Baume tranquille* (*Balsamum tranquillans*) . 100 grms. (ʒiii.)

Mix, and shake them together before using the liniment.

Used in the same cases as the last. A few drops are put upon cotton to relieve the pain of ear-ache.

The powdered leaves of belladonna are used in the same doses as the powdered root.

Glyster in Ileus.

Take of Dried belladonna leaves . 1 to 2 grms. (gr. xv. to ʒss.)
    Boiling water . . 250 grms. (ʒviii.)

Infuse them for an hour, and strain. To be administered as a glyster in cases of ileus from strangulated hernia, and to overcome spasmodic or inflammatory constriction of the urethra.

N.B. We have mentioned elsewhere that the different kinds of extract of belladonna possess very different properties, and it is therefore indispensable that the physician should say which kind he wishes to be used. The alcoholic extract is the most active, and the remark applies also to the extracts from the other *Solanaceæ*, and to the extracts of aconite, conium, &c.

HYOSCIAMUS (JUSQUIAME).

The leaves and seeds are employed in the same cases as those of belladonna, but the dose must be four times as large.

DATURA STRAMONIUM, (THORN-APPLE), TOBACCO.

The leaves only of tobacco are employed; and the leaves, and occasionally, but very rarely, the seeds of stramonium are used in the same form, the same doses, and the same circumstances

(ʒ. * Baume tranquille: *Fresh* leaves of belladonna, hyosciamus, solanum nigrum, tobacco, white poppy and stramonium, of each, 4 parts; *Dry* tops of absinthium, hyssop, lavender, marjorum, mentha aquatica, balsamita suaveolens, hypericun perforatum, rye, sage and thyme, of each, 1 part; *Dry flowers* of elder and rosemary, of each, 1 part: and olive oil, 97 parts.

(The fresh plants are to be bruised, mixed with the oil, and gently heated, till their water is evaporated; left for 2 hours, and then the hot oil, strongly expressed, to be poured upon the dry plants and flowers, and left for a month; then expressed, strained, and kept in well closed bottles, in a cool and dark place. Fr. *Codex.*)

as belladonna. (§. Stramonium is however used in spasmodic asthma (see below) in a manner never adopted with belladonna.)

Anti-asthmatic Cigars.

Take of Dried leaves of stramonium . . 30 grms. (ʒi.)

Moisten them with the following mixture:

   Aqueous extract of opium (thebaïca) . 2 grms. (ʒss.)
   Water . . . . 25 grms. (ʒvi.)

Dry them, and roll them in paper, to make cigarettes.

Used in attacks of nervous (spasmodic) asthma; in hysterical coughs, and in dry and obstinate coughs, symptomatic of more or less severe chronic affections of the lungs.

Others.

Take of Dry leaves of stramonium . . 30 grms. (ʒi.)
     „ „ sage . . 15 grms. (ʒss.)

Mix them, and make 20 cigars. Used in the same cases as the above. (§. Stramonium is frequently smoked to the extent of 3 or 4 pipefuls, in a common clay pipe, in the same cases as the above).

Anti-arthritic Poultice.

See "Art of Prescribing," p. 194.

This poultice should be applied for six or eight days in very painful acute or subacute inflammations of the joints.

Tobacco Glyster.

Take of Dry leaves of tobacco . 1 to 2 grms. (gr. xv to ʒss.)
   Boiling water . . 250 grms. (ʒviii.)

Infuse for an hour, and strain. To be used as a glyster in strangulated hernia. Used also in asphyxia, and especially that from drowning, though glysters of tobacco smoke have been chiefly extolled in these latter cases. Portal has proved the *danger of this kind of treatment in asphyxia.* The most simple instrument for giving these glysters in a pair of kitchen bellows, the nozzle of which is defended by a piece of leather, so as not to injure the intestine.

Narcotic Peas for Issues.

Take of Alcoholic extract of stramonium,

or:

Alcoholic extract of belladonna	. .	1 grm. (gr. xv.)
Extract of opium	. .	0,50 cent. (gr. viii.)
Macilage of gum tragacanth	} of each .	1 grm. (gr. xv.)
Finely powdered guiacum		

Mix, and make into 10 boluses, which are to be dried in a stove. They are to be used like peas for keeping open issues made by a bistoury along the vertebral column in cases of spinal tenderness (rachialgia), and between the great trochanter and the ischium in sciatica.

DULCAMARA (BITTER SWEET).

Anti-dartrous Apozem.

Take of The stems of bitter-sweet	. .	40 grms. (℥x.)
Water	. . . .	500 grms. (℥xvi.)

Divide the dulcamara into 10 packets of 4 grammes (℥i) each, and boil each in 500 grammes (℥xvi) of water down to 300 grms. (℥ix), to be taken in three doses during the day. Every other day increase the quantity from the 4 grammes, until at length it amounts to 20, 30, 40, or 60 grammes (℥v, ℥i, ℥x, or ℥ii), so that the patient may begin to feel dryness of the throat, and some disorder of vision and digestion. Continue at this dose for several weeks in succession.

Used in obstinate cutaneous diseases.

LOBELIA INFLATA.

Tisane.

	ADULTS.	CHILDREN.
Take of Lobelia inflata, (the whole plant) .	4 grms. (℥i.)	1 grm. (gr. xv.)
Infuse in :		
Water	750 grms. (℥xxiv.)	500 grms. (℥xvi.)

Strain, and sweeten at pleasure. To be taken by half a glassful at a time in the course of the day.

Used in spasmodic (nervous) asthmas, which have resisted the poisonous *Solanaceæ* (see above); in pulmonary emphysema complicated with pulmonary catarrh; and in simple chronic pulmonary catarrh, (℥. and in suffocative bronchitis).

CONIUM (HEMLOCK, CIGUE.)

Powders.

	ADULTS.	CHILDREN.
Take of Powdered conium . . .	2 grms. (ʒss.)	0,50 centigrms. (gr. viii.)
„ sugar . . .	4 grms. (ʒi.)	2 grms. (ʒss.)

Mix thoroughly, and divide into 20 packets. From 1 to 10 to be taken daily.

Used in scrophulous and cancerous diseases, &c.

Pills.

	ADULTS.	CHILDREN.
Take of Extract of hemlock with the fecula, (called Storck's. Ext. Conii. Ph. Lond.)	2 grms. (ʒss.)	0,50 centigrms. (gr. viii.)
Powdered conium . . .	2 grms. (ʒss.)	0,50 centigrms. (gr. viii.)
Excipient	q. s.	q. s.

Mix carefully, and divide into 60 pills. From 1 to 5 to be taken daily in scrophulous and cancerous affections, and in congestion of the neck of the uterus. (§. This dose (gr. ss) is much smaller than the usual one in this country, which is seldom less than gr. ii, and is increased until some effect is produced).

Resolvent Poultice.

Take of Linseed-meal poultice . q. s. about 500 grms. (ʒxvi.)

Pour over the surface of the poultice a solution made with :

Powdered conium . . .	125 grms. (ʒiv.)
Mucilage of linseed-tea . . .	q. s.

To be applied to chronic enlargement of the mammæ, ganglions, or joints, and to the abdomen in chronic inflammation of the peritoneum and of the abdominal viscera.

Narcotic medicines containing cyanogen.

Medicinal hydrocyanic acid, which has been lauded in many diseases, is a mixture of the anhydrous acid and of water, and contains 1 *volume* of anhydrous hydrocyanic acid and 6 *volumes* of distilled water; or 1 part by *weight* of anhydrous acid and 8 parts by *weight* of distilled water, (§. which makes it contain about 12 per cent. of real acid, which is six times the strength of the London acid, and must be carefully borne in mind in dispensing a French prescription in this country). From causes which it is difficult to appreciate, this acid quickly decomposes, so that we cannot reckon upon its action with certainty.* It is therefore prudent never to use this medicine either internally or externally; and it does not fulfil any purpose which is not quite as effectually attained by the distilled water of the cherry-laurel, or by the emulsion of bitter almonds, &c.

Cyanide of potassium, which is very active when pure, becomes completely inert when it is transformed into formiate, cyanate and carbonate of potash, a change which is very easily effected. We have elsewhere mentioned (p. 79) that this salt varies in composition according to the method employed in preparing it, from which it follows that it ought to be banished from internal employment as a medicine. If it is used externally, it ought to be freshly prepared.

We may repeat here, that mercurial preparations ought never to be associated with such as contain hydrocyanic acid, or are capable of producing it; for calomel becomes one of the most active poisons when it is administered in a looch prepared of bitter almonds, the hydrocyanic acid converting the protochloride into bichloride and bicyanide of mercury.

PRUSSIAN BLUE.

Anti-spasmodic Powders.

	ADULTS.	CHILDREN.
Take of Prussian blue (hydrated double cyanide of iron)	4 grms. (ʒi.)	1 grm. (gr. xv.)
Powdered sugar	10 grms. (ʒiiss.)	4 grms. (ʒi.)

Mix them accurately, and divide into 10 packets. From 1 to 10 to be taken in the twenty-four hours, in cases of epilepsy, chorea, and a chronic form of convulsions.

---

* The dilute acid of the British pharmacopœias is by no means so uncertain in its effects, or so liable to change as the French acid, which is six times as strong.

CYANIDE OF POTASSIUM.

Soothing Fomentation.

	ADULTS	CHILDREN.
Take of Cyanide of potassium	4 grms. (ʒi.)	2 grms. (ʒss.)
Distilled water	200 grms. (℥vi.)	200 grms. (℥vi.)

Dissolve the salt in the water, and keep it in a well-closed bottle in the dark. Compresses are to be soaked with this solution and applied to the skin in cases of slight neuralgia.

BITTER ALMONDS.

Looch Blanc, (White-Looch, or Loch, or Linctus.)

	ADULTS.		CHILDREN.
Take of Sweet almonds	12 grms.	(ʒiii.)	12 grms. (ʒiii.)
Bitter „	4 grms.	(ʒi.)	2 grms. (ʒss.)
White sugar	20 grms.	(ℨv.)	20 grms. (ℨv.)
Gum-tragacanth	0,40 centigrms.	(gr. vi.)	0,40 centigrms. (gr. vi.)
Orange-flower water	10 grms.	(ʒiiss.)	10 grms. (ʒiiss.)
Common water	80 grms.	(℥iiss.)	80 grms. (℥iiss.)

Pound the almonds with a little sugar, and when they are reduced to a pretty homogeneous paste, add the rest of the sugar; then pour on the water by degrees, and strain it by expression through a sieve. The gum is afterwards rubbed with a little sugar in the mortar first washed, and a mucilage is made by adding the milk of almonds by degrees, which is to be poured into a phial, and the water is to be washed with the orange-flower water, (*weighed*). This water is then added to the looch, which is to be shaken up and kept in a cool place. We may add to this looch 2, 4, or 6 grammes (ℨss, ʒi, or ʒiss) more bitter almonds than the prescribed quantity, according to the severity of the disease and the tolerance of the medicine.

Used in obstinate coughs, attacks of asthma, the dyspnœa accompanying pulmonary emphysema, and in the convulsions of children.

N.B. With very young children, we must increase the quantity of bitter almonds with great caution, and only after carefully feeling our way.

Milk of Bitter Almonds.

		ADULTS.	CHILDREN.
Take of Sweet almonds	.	4 to 6 grms. (ʒi to ʒiss.)	{ 4 to 6 grms. (ʒi to ʒiss.)
Bitter „	.	4 to 6 grms. (ʒi to ʒiss.)	{ 2 to 4 grms. (ʒss to ʒi.)
White sugar	.	60 grms. (ʒii.)	60 grms. (ʒii.)
Pure water	.	500 grms. (℥xvi)	500 grms. (℥xvi.)

Beat the almonds in a white marble mortar (after having peeled them) with the sugar, adding the water by degrees, so as to produce a homogeneous paste; then add the water by small quantities, and strain through a sieve. To this milk of almonds may be added 10 to 30 grammes (ʒiiss to ℥i) of orange-flower water. The above quantity should be taken in the course of the twenty-four hours, by a quarter of a glassful at a time.

This is the most certain and least expensive of any of the preparations which contain bitter almonds. *Used* in the same cases as the preceding looch.

Soothing Mixture.

	ADULTS.	CHILDREN.
Take of Distilled water of cherry-laurel*	10 grms. (ʒiiss.)	2 grms. (ʒss.)
„ „ lettuce .	100 grms. (℥iii.)	50 grms. (ʒiss.)
Syrup of orange-flowers	40 grms. (ʒx.)	25 grms. (ʒvi.)

Mix. To be taken by a table-spoonful at a time every hour, in the same cases as the preceding looch and emulsion.

Soothing Cerate.

Take of White wax	.	.	.	1 part.
Oil of almonds	.	.	.	4 parts.

Melt them with a gentle heat, and pour the mixture into a marble mortar, slightly heated; rub them briskly with the pestle, and add by degrees distilled water of cherry-laurel 8 parts.

To be spread upon very painful parts, and to be used with friction upon the skin in cases of superficial neuralgia.

Soothing Pomatum.

Take of Lard	.	.	.	8 grms. (ʒii)
Essential oil of cherry-laurel	.	1 grm. (gr. xv.)

Mix them. *Used* in the same cases as the above cerate.

(* ʂ. This preparation is stronger than the corresponding one in the Ph. E. and D. for in the Fr. *Codex* the weight of distilled water is to equal that of the laurel leaves employed; whilst in the British pharmacopœias a pint (20 ounces) is distilled from a pound (12 ounces) of leaves).

ANÆSTHETIC MEDICINES.

CHLOROFORM.

Potion of Chloroform.

	ADULTS.	CHILDREN.
Take of Syrup of orange-flowers.	40 grms. (ʒx.)	20 grms. (ʒv.)
Distilled water of Linden	100 grms. (ʒiii.)	40 grms. (ʒx.)
Chloroform	1 grm. (gr. xv.)	5 drops.

Mix the syrup and the chloroform by agitation, and add the distilled water. To be taken by a table or a dessert-spoonful at a time in violent colic, in neuralgias and enteralgias, and in asthma.

Chloroform Liniment.

Take of Chloroform	.	.	10 grms. (ʒiiss.)
Oil of almonds .	.	.	60 grms. (ʒii.)

Mix them accurately. Pieces of flannel are to be soaked with this liniment, and applied to the painful part in cases of nervous headache, neuralgias, rheumatic pains, hepatic, nephritic, uterine, intestinal, or saturnine colic, &c.

By adding a double quantity of oil we may use it for vaginal injections with a small syringe, which may be retained by a plug of cotton, in cases of dysmenorrhœa, uterine neuralgia, cancer of the womb, of the bladder, or of the rectum.

Anæsthetic Mastic.

Take of Powdered colophane	.	.	2 grms. (ʒss.)
Chloroform.	.	.	q. s. to dissolve the resin,

so as to make a thick solution, with which a small piece of cotton is to be impregnated, and introduced into hollow teeth, to soothe the pain. Used also in neuralgia of the teeth.

MONOCHLORIDED HYDROCHLORIC ETHER.

This ether is employed in the same cases, the same doses, and under the same forms as chloroform.

ANTI-SPASMODIC MEDICINES.

Anti-spasmodic Tisane.

	ADULTS.	CHILDREN.
Take of Flowers of the linden, or of balm . . .	20 to 30 grms. (ʒv to ʒi.)	8 to 12 grms. (ʒii to ʒiii.)
Boiling water . . .	1000 grms. (ʒxxxii.)	300 grms. (ʒix.)

Infuse, strain, and sweeten at pleasure. To be taken by cupsful in a day.

Used in nervous affections.

Anti-spasmodic Potion.

	ADULTS.	CHILDREN.
Take of Syrup of ether . .	30 grms. (ʒi.)	10 grms. (ʒiiss.)
„ „ orange-flowers .	20 grms. (ʒv.)	20 grms. (ʒv.)
Distilled water of the linden .	100 grms. (ʒiii.)	80 grms. (ʒiiss.)

Mix. To be taken during the day by a table-spoonful every hour, in nervous affections.

Another.

	ADULTS.	CHILDREN.
Take of Powdered valerian root . .	2 grms. (ʒss.)	1 grm. (gr. xv.)
Boiling water . .	100 grms. (ʒiii.)	40 grms. (ʒx.)
Infuse for half an hour, strain, and add to the liquid, when cold:		
Syrup of ether . „ „ orange-flowers } of each .	20 grms. (ʒv.)	10 grms. (ʒiiss.)

Mix. Cork it carefully, and keep it in a cool place. To be taken by table-spoonsful at a time in the course of the day.

Used in nervous affections, hysterical pains, convulsions.

Another.

See Anti-hysteric mixture, p. 184.

Antineuralgic Pills (called Meglin's Pills).

Take of Extract of valerian .
„ „ hyosciamus } of each . 2 grms. (ʒss.)
White oxide of zinc .

Mix them carefully, and make 40 pills. From 1 to 10 to be taken daily in the treatment of obstinate neuralgias.

x

ASSAFŒTIDA.

Anti-spasmodic Glyster.

	ADULTS.	CHILDREN.
Take of Powdered assafœtida . .	4 grms. (ℨi.)	1 grm. (gr. xv.)
Yolk of egg. . . .	1	1/2
Rub them in a mortar, and add:		
Distilled water of valerian . .	300 grms. (ℨix.)	150 grms. (ℨivss.)

For a glyster to be given to hysterical women, and to children affected with (§. flatulent) convulsions, or nervous symptoms.

Another.

	ADULTS.	CHILDREN.
Take of Powdered valerian root . .	10 grms. (ℨiiss.)	4 grms. (ℨi.)
Boiling water . . .	300 grms. (ℨix.)	150 grms. (ℨivss.)
Infuse, strain, and add:		
Tincture of assafœtida . .	15 grms. (ℨss.)	8 grms. (ℨii.)

Mix for a glyster in hysteria; and for children in cases of (§. flatulent) convulsions.

GUM AMMONIACUM.

Bechic (Expectorant) Potion.

	ADULTS.	CHILDREN.
Take of Powdered ammoniacum . .	4 grms. (ℨi.)	1 grm. (gr. xv.)
Mucilage of gum-arabic . .	q. s.	q. s.
Water . . .	100 grms. (ℨiii.)	40 grms. (ℨx.)
Syrup of gum . . .	40 grms. (ℨx.)	20 grms. (ℨv.)

Make the ammoniacum into an emulsion with the gum; add the water by degrees, and then the syrup.

Used in pulmonary catarrhs, accompanied with oppression, and in nervous asthma.

Expectorant Mixture.

	ADULTS.	CHILDREN.
Take of Powdered ammoniacum . .	4 grms. (ℨi.)	1 grm. (gr. xv.)
Infusion of hyssop (hyssop, ℨiiss, in water, q. s.) . . . }	100 grms. (ℨiii.)	100 grms. (ℨiii.)
Oxymel of squill . . .	30 grms. (ℨi.)	20 grms. (ℨv.)

Mix. For a potion to be taken by a table-spoonful at a time, every hour.

Used in pulmonary catarrh, in bronchitis (§. subacute or chronic) to assist expectoration, and in ascites to promote the secretion of urine.

Diuretic Pills.

Take of Powdered ammoniacum	.	.	4 grms. (ʒi.)
„ squill	.	.	2 grms. (ʒss.)
Oxymel of squill	.	.	q. s.

Mix, and make 40 pills. From 1 to 10 to be taken daily in dropsies, to increase the urinary secretion; in pulmonary catarrh, and (§. chronic) bronchitis, to assist expectoration.

Anti-hysterical Opiate.

| Take of Powdered indigo | . | . | . | 30 grms. (ʒi.) |
| White honey | . | . | . | 100 grms. (ʒiii.) |

Mix them exactly. To be taken at first by one table-spoonful every day, then two, and so on, until the whole quantity above directed is taken in the course of the day.

Used in epilepsy, nervous affections of an epileptic character, and in hysteria.

MUSK AND CASTOREUM.

Anti-spasmodic Pills.

Take of Musk	.	.	.	1 grm. (gr. xv.)
Extract of valerian	.	.	2 grms. (ʒss.)
Excipient	.	.	.	q. s.

Mix, and make into 20 pills. 1 to be taken every 2 hours, until there is a marked improvement in the symptoms.

Used in pneumonia, accompanied by delirium, especially in drunkards, and in the involuntary movements (accidents ataxiques) which are observed in fevers of a low character.

Anti-spasmodic Potion.

	ADULTS.	CHILDREN.
Take of Syrup of ether . . .	40 grms. (ʒx.)	20 grms. (ʒv.)
Distilled water of the linden .	100 grms. (ʒiii.)	60 grms. (ʒii.)
Tincture of musk } of each .	4 grms. (ʒii.)	10 drops.
„ cinnamon		

Mix. For a potion. A table-spoonful to be taken every 2 hours, in the same cases as the preceding pills.

x 2

Anti-spasmodic Glyster.

Take of Castoreum　.　.　.　.　4 grms. (ʒi.)
　　　Yolk of egg　.　.　.　.　1/2

Make them into an emulsion by trituration, and add:

　　　Water　.　.　.　.　250 grms. (ʒviii.)

For a glyster to be given to women suffering from dysmenorrhœa, or spasms of the uterus with hysterical affections.

CAMPHOR.

Pills of Camphor.

Take of Powdered camphor　.　.　1 grm.　　(gr. xv.)
　　　Gummy extract of opium　.　0,25 centigrms. (gr. iv.)
　　　Excipient　.　.　.　q. s.

Mix. To be made into 10 pills. From 1 to 4 to be taken on going to bed, to allay the pain of nocturnal erections in gonorrhœa. Used also in cystitis, and in poisoning by cantharides.

Anti-septic Powder.

Take of Red cinchona, finely powdered } of each　40 grms. (ʒx.)
　　　Powdered vegetable charcoal .}
　　　Camphor .　.　.　.　.　10 grms. (ʒiiss.)

Reduce the camphor to powder, by means of a few drops of alcohol or ether, and porphyrise the whole.

Used to sprinkle upon indolent wounds of an unhealthy character.

Camphor Liniment.

Take of Camphor　.　.　.　5 grms. (ʒi 1/4.)
　　　Olive oil　.　.　.　35 grms. (ʒix.)

Dissolve the camphor in the oil.

Used with friction in painful swellings and rheumatism.

N.B. Balsam of opodeldoch may beneficially replace the above liniment. It is made of animal soap, camphor, ammonia, and the essential oils of thyme and rosemary.

Camphorated Cigars.

To make these cigars, a little cotton is introduced into one end of quill, and the quill is then filled with powdered camphor, and to prevent it from falling out, a second plug of cotton is introduced. Care must be taken not to ram the camphor or the cotton, so as to prevent the air which is inspired from circulating freely

through it. The quill may be replaced by a tube made of glass, of turned wood, of bone or ivory, pierced with small holes.
Used in ashthma, cough, catarrh, &c.

Sedative Water.

	No. 1.	No. 2.	No. 3.
Take of Liquor ammonia (sp. gr. ·91)	60 grms. (℥ii.)	80 grms. (℥iiss.)	100 grms. (℥iii.)
Camphorated alcohol	10 grms. (ʒiiss.)	10 grms. (ʒiiss.)	10 grms. (ʒiiss.)
Common salt	60 grms. (℥ii.)	60 grms. (℥ii.)	60 grms. (℥ii.)
Common water	1000 grms. (℥xxxii.)	1000 grms. (℥xxxii.)	1000 grms. (℥xxxii.)

Dissolve the salt in the cold water; mix the camphorated alcohol and the ammonia, and shake them together every time they are used. The water, No. 3, is intended for persons whose skin is hard and callous. No. 2 is to be applied to wounds made by venomous animals; and No. 1 is employed for persons whose skin is delicate.

These waters may be aromatised at pleasure. The sedative water is employed in superficial pains; and in head-ache by means of compresses on the forehead, taking care that the water does not run into the eyes; and as a rubefacient when assisted by friction.

ETHERS.

Chemists admit three kinds of ether. (See also pp. 74, 75).

1. Those formed of a hydrocarbon, combined with an equivalent of water, *e. g.* $C^4H^4 + HO$, which may be considered as the oxide of compound radicals, named ethyle (C^4H^5); methyle (C^2H^3); cethyle ($C^{32}H^{33}$); and amyle ($C^{10}H^{11}$). Hydric ether, generally called sulphuric ether, which belongs to this class, is the only one used in medicine, and it is represented by C^4H^5O. (§. *i. e.* Oxide of the compound radicle C^4H^5, or by $C^4H^4 + HO$, *i. e.* a hydrocarbon (C^4H^4) combined with water.)

2. Those which result from the combination of the same hydrocarbons with the hydracids (*e. g.* $C^4H^4 + HCl$), which on the theory of compound radicals will be the result of the combination of these radicals with chlorine, bromine, iodine, &c.

Hydrochloric ether is the only one of this class which is occasionally employed, and in accordance with the theory it may be represented as $C^4H^5 + Cl$.

3. Lastly, ethers which are the result of the combination of an acid with one of the ethers of the first class; so that in the theory of hydrocarbons they are represented by $C^4H^4HO +$ an acid; or by $C^4H^5O +$ an acid.

To this class belong acetic ether, and nitrous (*hyponitrous*, see p. 74), commonly called *nitric ether* $C^4H^5O + NO^3$.

Ethers obtained from vinous alcohol are the only ones used, and amongst them especially sulphuric ether; so that it is this body which is commonly designated under the simple name of " ether."

SULPHURIC ETHER.

Anti-hysterical Potion.

Take of compound syrup of wormwood .	.	30 grms. (ℨi.)
Tincture of castoreum .	.	2 grms. (ℨss.)

Mix them by agitation, and add:

Orange-flower water Distilled water of valerian } of each	.	60 grms. (ℨii.)
Sulphuric ether . .	.	4 grms. (ℨi.)

Shake them together, and cork them carefully. 2 table-spoonsful to be taken every 4 hours, in hysteria.

Anti-spasmodic Potion.

	ADULTS.	CHILDREN.
Take of Simple syrup . .	30 grms. (ℨi.)	30 grms. (ℨi.)
Orange-flower water .	60 grms. (ℨii.)	30 grms. (ℨi.)
Distilled water of the linden	60 grms. (ℨii.)	40 grms. (ℨx.)
Sulphuric ether . .	2 grms. (ℨss.)	1 grm. (gr. xv.)

Mix, shake them together, and cork them with care. A table-spoonful to be taken every hour, or even every half-hour, according to the severity of the nervous affection. In spasms and flatulent convulsions.

NEURO-STHENIC TONICS.

CINCHONA.

Febrifuge Powder.

	ADULTS.	CHILDREN.
Take of Calissaya bark (pale cinchona), in fine powder	60 grms. (ʒii.)	30 grms. (ʒi.)

Divide it into 8 packets. After having vomited and purged the patient, 1 of these packets (a ʒii dose) mixed in a cup of coffee well sweetened, is to be administered as long after the vomiting as possible, and another is to be given the next morning. Then a day of rest. The following day another packet, and then 2 days rest. Another packet, and 3 days rest. Another packet, and 4 days rest; and so on, to the last packet. The treatment will thus extend over 33 days; but in nearly every instance the febrile attack does not show itself after the second day of the administration of the cinchona.

Febrifuge Glyster.

	ADULTS.	CHILDREN.
Take of Yellow cinchona, in very fine powder	8 grms. (ʒii.)	4 grms. (ʒi.)
Decoction of linseed, or of marsh-mallow	100 grms. (ʒiii.)	60 grms. (ʒii.)
Laudanum of Sydenham	10 drops.	2 drops.

Mix. For a glyster to be administered to patients who cannot, or will not swallow the cinchona.

Tonic Cold Infusion (Maceration).

Take of Gray cinchona, coarsely powdered . 5 grms. (gr. lxxv.)

Macerate for 12 hours in :

Water . . . . . 1 litre (ʒxxxii.)

Strain, and filter. To be drunk, during a meal, with wine, in cases of dysentery, at the end of chronic diseases, and after hæmorrhages.

Purgative Decoction of Cinchona.

	ADULTS.	CHILDREN.
Take of Powdered yellow cinchona .	15 grms. (ʒss.)	6 grms. (ʒiss.)
Boil it in:		
Water	1000 grms. (ʒxxxii.)	400 grms. (ʒxiii.)
Down to . . .	500 grms. (ʒxvi.)	250 grms. (ʒviii.)
Strain, whilst hot, and add:		
Sulphate of soda (Glauber's salt)	30 grms. (ʒi.)	10 grms. (ʒiiss.)

Shake it up before taking it.

This apozem is to be taken as a purgative at the commencement of intermittent fevers, before the systematic administration of powdered cinchona, or sulphate of quinine.

Powder of Cinchona and Charcoal.

Take of Powdered red cinchona	of each .	50 grms. (ʒiss.)
Porphyrized wood charcoal		

Mix. To be sprinkled upon gangrenous sores. Used as a dentifrice to strengthen the gums. In this case it is aromatised at pleasure, with essence of mint, cloves, &c.

Potion made from Extract of Cinchona.

	ADULTS.	CHILDREN.
Take of Soft extract of cinchona .	4 grms. (ʒi.)	2 grms. (ʒss.)
Mint water . .	100 grms. (ʒiii.)	80 grms. (ʒiiss.)
Dissolve the extract in the water, and add:		
Syrup of cinchona. .	50 grms. (ʒiss.)	30 grms. (ʒi.)
Tincture of cinnamon .	4 grms. (ʒi.)	2 grms. (ʒss.)

Mix. To be taken by spoonful in the course of the day. *Used* in the adynamic period (low stage) of typhus fever.

Tonic Potion.

	ADULTS.	CHILDREN.
Take of Dry extract of cinchona. .	1 grm. (gr. xv.)	0,50 centigrms. (gr viii.)
Distilled water of balm . .	100 grms. (ʒiii.)	40 grms. (ʒx.)
Syrup of orange-peel . .	40 grms. (ʒx.)	25 grms. (ʒvi.)

Dissolve the extract in the distilled water, and add the syrup. To be taken in the course of the day, in chlorosis and (ʒ. asthenic) dyspepsias, and the debility which succeeds acute illness.

Febrifuge Pills.

Take of Soft extract of cinchona. . 12 grms. (ʒiii.)
     Excipient . . . q. s.

To make 64 pills, of which 8 are to be taken at once, or better still, 4 at once, and 4 in 2 hours afterwards; pursuing the method laid down for the administration of cinchona in powder (see p. 311).

Antiseptic Pomatum.

Take of Soft extract of cinchona } of each . 10 grms. (ʒiiss.)
     ,, ,, ,, rhatany }
     Water ,, . . . 20 grms. (ʒv.)

Moisten the extract in the water, so as to make a thick solution, and add:

     Lard . . . . 50 grms. (ʒiss.)

Mix. To dress ulcers of an unhealthy character, gangrenous sores, and hospital gangrene.

Tasteless Febrifuge Powder for Children.

Take of Uncombined quinine. . 3 grms. (gr. xlv.)
     Sugar. . . 10 grms. (ʒiiss.)

Triturate them with care in a porcelain mortar, and divide into 8 packets. To be taken in a little preserve, upon the plan shown above (see p. 311).

Another Tasteless Febrifuge Powder.

                   ADULTS. | CHILDREN.

Take of Tannate of quinine . . . 6 grms. (ʒiss.) | 3 grms. (gr. xlv.)

Divide into 8 packets, which are to be taken in a little syrup or preserve, according to the method already indicated (see p. 311).

Antiseptic Gargle.

Take of Powdered yellow cinchona . . 15 grms. (ʒss.)

Boil it in:

     Water . . . . 300 grms. (ʒix.)
     Down to . . . . 200 grms. (ʒvi.)

Strain, and add:

     Syrup of cinchona . . 60 grms. (ʒii.)
     Hypochlorite of soda (chloride of soda). 20 grms. (ʒv.)
     Essence of mint . . . 6 drops.

Mix. For a gargle to be employed in ulcerations of the mouth and gums, with fœtor of the breath.

SULPHATE OF QUININE.

Febrifuge Powder.

	ADULTS.	CHILDREN.
Take of Sulphate of quinine . .	6 grms. (ʒiss.)	3 grms. (gr. xlv.)
Sugar	10 grms. (ʒiiss.)	10 grms. (ʒiiss.)

Triturate with care. Mix, and divide into 8 packets, which are to be administered in infusion of coffee, or in strong tea, exactly in the same way as the powder of cinchona (see p. 311).

The dose may be doubled or trebled, and continued every day for a longer or shorter time, in the treatment of acute articular rheumatism. In this case the powders should be given in syrup or preserve.

Febrifuge Pills.

Take of Sulphate of quinine . .	6 grms. (ʒiss.)
Extract of gentian . .	q. s.

Mix, and divide into 64 pills, of which 8 are to be taken at once, or better still, 4 at once, and 4 in 2 hours after, pursuing the plan laid down for cinchona in powder (see p. 311).

Potion of Sulphate of Quinine.

	ADULTS.	CHILDREN.
Take of Sulphate of quinine . .	1 grm. (gr. xv.)	0,30 to 0,50 centigrms. (gr. ivss to gr. viii.)
Water . . .	100 grms. (ʒiii.)	30 grms, (ʒi.)
Sulphuric acid . q. s. about	2 drops.	1/2 drop.
Syrup of orange-flowers .	40 grms. (ʒx.)	20 grms. (ʒv.)

Mix. For a potion. To be taken in the space of a few hours, in the treatment of intermittent fever. To be repeated as frequently as the powder in the ordinary method (see p. 311).

Tasteless Febrifuge Potion.

	ADULTS.	CHILDREN.
Take of Sulphate of quinine .	0,75 centigrms. (gr. xiss.)	0,25 centigrms. (gr. iv.)
Tannic acid . .	0,10 centigrms. (gr. iss.)	0,05 centigrms. (gr. 3/4.)
Sulphuric acid. .	2 drops.	1/2 drop.
Water . .	100 grms. (ʒiii.)	40 grms. (ʒx.)
Syrup of quince .	40 grms. (ʒx.)	20 grms. (ʒv.)

To be taken in 1 or 2 doses, in the treatment of intermittent fever.

Mixture of Sulphate of Quinine and Coffee.

	ADULTS.	CHILDREN.
Take of Roasted coffee . . .	10 grms. (ʒiiss.)	6 grms. (ʒiss.)
Boiling water . . .	100 grms. (ʒiii.)	60 grms. (ʒii.)
Make an infusion, strain, and add :		
Sulphate of quinine . .	1 grm. (gr. xv.)	0,25 centigrms. (gr. iv.)
Sugar	15 grms. (ʒss.)	10 grms. (ʒiiss.)

Triturate the sulphate of quinine with the sugar, and add it to
the infusion. According to the directions of M. Desvouves, the
sulphate of quinine ought neither to be acidulated nor heated in
this mixture. Shake it up before taking it. To be administered
in the ordinary way.

Febrifuge Glyster.

	ADULTS.	CHILDREN.
Take of Sulphate of quinine . .	1 grm. (gr. xv.)	0,30 centigrms. (gr. ivss.)
Water	100 grms. (ʒiii.)	60 grms. (ʒii.)
Sulphuric acid . q. s. about	2 drops.	1/2 drop.
Laudanum of Sydenham .	10 drops.	2 drops.

Mix. For a glyster. To be given in the ordinary way, and in
cases requiring quinine, when the patient cannot, or will not
swallow the febrifuge.

Pomatum of Sulphate of Quinine.

	ADULTS.	CHILDREN.
Take of Sulphate of quinine . .	5 grms. (gr. lxxv.)	2 grms. (ʒss.)
Water . . .	4 grms. (ʒi.)	4 grms. (ʒi.)
Sulphuric acid . q. s. about	6 drops.	2 drops.
Dissolve and add :		
Lard	30 grms. (ʒi.)	20 grms. (ʒv.)

Mix. For an ointment to be rubbed into the arm-pits in old
people and children, and in women who have difficulty in bearing
the preparations of quinine.—N.B. This method is most *un-*
trustworthy.

COLUMBA.

Tonic Powder.

	ADULTS.	CHILDREN.
Take of Powdered colomba . .	4 grms. (ʒi.)	1 grm. (gr. xv.)
„ aniseed . .	1 grm. (gr. xv.)	0,50 centigrms. (gr. viii.)

Mix, and divide into 20 packets. One or 2 packets to be taken daily at meal-times.

Used in chronic diarrhœa, without any severe lesion of the gastro-intestinal mucous membrane, and in dyspepsia, accompanied with acidity, and a tendency to diarrhœa.

Tonic Infusion.

	ADULTS.	CHILDREN.
Take of Columba root, coarsely powdered .	2 grms. (ʒss.)	0,50 centigrms. (gr. viii.)
Infuse it in :		
Boiling water . . .	100 grms. (ʒiii.)	40 grms. (ʒx.)
Strain and add :		
Syrup of cinchona . .	40 grms. (ʒx.)	25 grms. (ʒvi.)

Used in the same cases as the preceding powder.

SURINAM WOOD, OR QUASSIA AMARA.

	ADULTS.	CHILDREN.
Take of Quassia chips . . .	10 grms. (ʒiiss.)	2 grms. (ʒss.)

Divide it into 5 packets. Each packet to be macerated (p. 148) in a cupful of water for 12 hours, and taken night and morning for several days in succession, in the same cases as those in which columba is prescribed. Used also in headache dependant upon a bad state of the stomach, after having first administered a little magnesia or carbonate of soda for a few days.

SIMAROUBA BARK.   GENTIAN ROOT.   LESSER CENTAURY.

Used in the same cases as the preceding. Simarouba in the same doses; but gentian and centaury in rather larger ones.

LICHEN ISLANDICUS (ICELAND MOSS).

This lichen is only tonic by virtue of a bitter principle which it contains. When we wish to use it as a restorative or nutriant, we deprive it of its bitter principle by repeated infusions (see pp. 11, 272); but this must be left in, when it is to be used as a bitter tonic.

Tisane of Bitter Lichen.

	ADULTS.	CHILDREN.
Take of Fine lichen Islandicus	20 grms. (ʒv.)	8 grms. (ʒii.)
Boil it in:		
Water	1200 grms. (ʒxxxviii.)	600 grms. (ʒxix.)
down to about	1000 grms. (ʒxxxii.)	500 grms. (ʒxvi.)

Strain, and sweeten at pleasure. To be taken during the day as a restorative tonic in cases of great debility of the digestive organs, and in long and tedious convalescence.

Jelly of Bitter Lichen.

Take of Iceland moss . . . . . 60 grms.

Wash the lichen in warm water, to remove part of its bitter principle, and then boil it in:

Water . . . . 500 grms. (ʒxvi.) down

to about half. Strain and add:

Sugar . . . . . 120 grms. (ʒiv.)

Cook them together, until the liquid becomes a tremulous jelly on cooling.

OX-GALL.

Tonic Pills.

	ADULTS.	CHILDREN.
Take of Extract of ox gall	10 grms. (ʒiiss.)	1 grm. (gr. xv.)
Excipient	q. s.	q. s.

Mix, and divide into 50 pills. From 1 to 8 to be taken daily, by persons affected with constipation, and subject to flatulence and acid eructations, or to imperfect digestion after hepatic colic or jaundice.

EXCITANTS OR STIMULANTS.

UMBELLIFERÆ.

ANISEED, ANGELICA, &C.

Stimulant Infusion.

Take of the Fruit of aniseed (*Pimpinella anisum*)   2 grms. (ʒss.)
Infuse it for a quarter of an hour in :

Water   .   .   .   .   . 100 grms. (ℨiii.)

Strain, and sweeten at pleasure.

Used in intestinal flatulence, hysterical headache, hypocondriasis, and in difficulty of digestion in great eaters.

ANGELICA, CUMIN, CARRAWAY, FENNEL, DILL, AND AMMI.

Used in the same doses, and the same cases, as aniseed. As a substitute for anise, amongst the umbelliferæ may be used *Indian star-anise* or *badiane* (illicium anisatum), magnoliaceæ.

LABIATÆ.

MELISSA, MENTHA.

Stimulant Tisane.

Take of Tops of balm (melissa)   .   .   . 15 grms. (ʒss.)
                    Boiling water   .   .   . 1000 grms. (ℨxxxii.)
Infuse them, strain, and add :

Simple syrup   .   .   .   . 100 grms. (ℨiii.)

Used in the same cases as the stimulant umbelliferæ.

Stimulant Potion.

	ADULTS.	CHILDREN.
Take of Syrup of mint . .	40 grms. (ʒx.)	20 grms. (ʒv.)
Distilled water of balm .	100 grms. (ℨiii.)	40 grms. (ʒx.)
Compound tincture of balm } (Eau des Carmes)	1 grm. (gr. xv.)	15 drops.

Mix. For the same cases as the preceding. In the cold stage of fevers, in cholera, and in hysteria.

Tisane of Ground-ivy (*Glecoma*), or Hyssop.

	ADULTS.	CHILDREN.
Take of Ground-ivy, or hyssop .	15 grms. (ʒss.)	8 grms. (ʒii.)
Infuse it in :		
Boiling water . .	1000 grms. (ʒxxxii.)	400 grms. (ʒxiii).
Strain and add :		
Syrup of Tolu . .	100 grms. (ʒiii.)	100 grms. (ʒiii.)

For a tisane. To be drunk by cupsful in chronic pulmonary catarrh.

SAGE, LAVENDER.

Aromatic Wine.

Aromatic wine is an officinal preparation, obtained by the maceration of the aromatic species (see p. 202) in red wine. It is employed in lotions for pale flabby sores, with watery discharge, and for œdema of the legs, for scrophula, and chancres.

Aromatic Bath.

	ADULTS.	CHILDREN.
Take of Sage ⎫ of each .	500 grms. (ʒxvi.)	150 grms. (ʒv.)
Lavender ⎭		
Infuse them in :		
Boiling water . .	10 litres (2 gal.)	10 litres (2 gal.)
Strain and pour into a :		
Bath of . . .	250 litres (50 gal.)	100 litres (20 gal.)

For persons weakened by loss of blood, involuntary seminal discharges, and acute diseases, from which the recovery has been slow. For hysterical and hypochondriacal persons.

Aromatic Vapour-bath.

Take of Sage	200 grms. (ʒvi.)	
Lavender ⎫ of each . .	60 grms. (ʒii.)	
Juniper berries ⎭		

Pour boiling water into a wooden tub, with a cover, to warm it. Throw away this water, and then put the aromatic species into the bottom. Pour on 6 or 8 litres (a gallon, or a gallon and a half) of boiling water. The sick person is placed naked upon a chair, his body and the whole apparatus being surrounded by two or three blankets, fastened round his neck, and reaching down to the ground.

Used in the same cases as the last, and in chronic rheumatism, gout, &c.

CHAMOMILE.

Infusion of Chamomile.

Take of Chamomile . 1 grm. 50 centigrms. (gr. xxiii.)

Infuse it in :

Boiling water. 100 grms. (3iii.)

Strain, and sweeten. Used in dyspepsia, when there is flatulence and pain after a meal.

N.B. Physicians (French) are in the habit of ordering chamomile flowers by number, and not by weight; which is not an exact mode, as the flowers are not all of the same size. It is not, however, of much consequence in this case, or in any in which the substance is not very active ; but we prefer directing weights. It is only in cookery that numbers should be used. 20 heads weigh at least gr. xxiii.

Chamomile Tisane.

	ADULTS.	CHILDREN.
Take of Chamomile heads (composite flowers) . . . }	10 grms (3iiss.)	4 grms. (3i.)
Infuse them in :		
Boiling water . . .	1000 grms. (3xxxii.)	500 grms. (3xvi.)
Strain, and add :		
Simple syrup . . .	100 grms. (3iii.)	60 grms 3ii.)

To be taken by cupsful in the day, as a stomachic, carminative, and anti-spasmodic. Chamomile was the febrifuge of the ancients. In a large dose it is emetic.

Stomachic Potion.

	ADULTS.	CHILDREN.
Take of Syrup of mint . . .	40 grms. (3x.)	20 grms. (3v.)
Distilled water of chamomile .	100 grms. (3iii.)	40 grms. (3x.)
Tincture of absinthium .	2 grms. (3ss.)	20 drops.

Mix. To be taken by spoonsful in the day.

Used in flatulent, painful dyspepsia, and as a vermifuge.

Stimulant Liniment.

Take of Oil of chamomile. } of each . 30 grms. (3i.)
Baume tranquille }
Camphor . . . 10 grms. (3iiss.)

Dissolve the camphor in the oils (cold), and rub the liniment upon parts affected with flying pains, lumbago, &c.

CINNAMON.

Cordial Mixture.

	ADULTS.	CHILDREN.
Take of Red wine . . .	125 grms. (℥iv.)	60 grms. (℥ii.)
Syrup of orange-peel .	30 grms. (℥i.)	30 grms. (℥i.)
Tincture of cinnamon .	8 grms. (℥ii.)	2 grms. (℥ss.)

Mix. A spoonful to be taken every half-hour, to restore the strength exhausted by severe illness.

GINGER.

Stimulant Powders.

Take of Ginger . . . .
Aniseed, or Badiane (see p. 318) . } of each 10 grms. (℥iiss.)
Cascarilla . . .

Powder these substances coarsely, and divide them into 15 packets. Infuse 1 packet in a cupful of boiling water to make a tisane. To be taken after a meal.

Used by nervous women, whose digestion is slow and difficult, by hypochondriacs, and in convalescence retarded by dyspepsia, when febrile symptoms have disappeared.

CUBEBS.

Sedative for Gleet.

Take of Powdered cubebs . . .	100 grms. (℥iii.)
Tannin . . .	2 grms. (℥ss.)
Syrup of quince . . .	q. s. to give the
consistence of an electuary.	

Make it into boluses the size of a nut. 3 to be taken 3 times a-day.

Another.

Take of Powdered cubebs . .	100 grms. (℥iii.)
Balsam of copaiva . .	40 grms. (℥x.)
Calcined magnesia . .	15 grms. (℥ss.)
Syrup of quince . .	q. s. to give the
consistence of an electuary.	

In the same doses and cases as the above.

Y

Camphorated Cubeb-Opiate.

	ADULTS.	CHILDREN.
Take of Powdered cubebs . . .	4 grms. (ʒi.)	1 grm. (gr. xv.)
„ camphor. . .	1 grm. (gr. xv.)	0.25 centigrms. (gr. iv.)

Powder the camphor by means of a few drops of ether or alcohol; mix it with the cubebs, and divide into 4 packets.

1 to be taken 4 times a-day, in the scalding which women and young girls sometimes experience in making water.

Pills of Oleo-Resinous Extract of Cubebs. (Cubebine.)

Take of Oleo-resinous extract of cubebs		
Balsam of copaiva .	} of each .	4 grms. (ʒi.)
Powdered catechu .		
Inert excipient .	. . .	q. s.

Mix, and divide into 48 pills. From 1 to 8 to be taken daily, in gleet, and catarrh of the bladder.

Mixture for Gleet.

Take of cubebine, or oleo-resinous extract of cubebs . . .	} 1 to	2 grms. (gr. xv to ʒss.)
Mint water . . .		100 grms. (ʒiii.)
Syrup of Tolu . .		40 grms. (ʒx.)

Mix. To be taken in 4 doses during the day.

Used in acute gleet, and catarrh of the urethra and bladder.

SUDORIFICS.

Sudorific Tisane.

	ADULTS.	CHILDREN.
Take of Split sarsaparilla root 15 to	25 grms. (ʒss to ʒvi.)	8 to 12 grms. (ʒii to ʒiii.)
Infuse it in :		
Boiling water. .	1000 grms. (ʒxxxii.)	800 grms. (ʒxxvi.)
Strain, and add :		
Syrup of Cuisinier* (Syr. Sarz. Comp.)	100 grms. (ʒiii.)	60 grms. (ʒii.)

(§. * Syr. Sars. Comp. (Fr. *Codex.*) Sarsaparilla, 16; borage flowers (dry), rose petals (*Rosa centifolia*), senna and aniseed, of each, 1; sugar and white honey, of each, 16 parts. To be made into a syrup.)

Another.

	ADULTS.	CHILDREN.
Take of Sarsaparilla root Squine root . Guaiacum wood (rasped) . } of each .	8 grms. (ʒii.)	4 grms. (ʒi.)
Boil them in :		
Water . . .	1200 grms. (ʒxxxviii.)	1000 grms. (ʒxxxii.)
Down to . . .	1000 grms. (ʒxxxii.)	800 grms. (ʒxxvi.)
Strain, allow it to cool, and *macerate* it upon :		
Sassafras root (sliced) .	8 grms. (ʒii.)	4 grms. (ʒi.)
Strain it again, after 4 hours' maceration, and sweeten at pleasure.		

To be taken by glassfuls at a time, in the treatment of tertiary syphilitic affections, and in severe cutaneous diseases.

N.B. The *sudorific woods* are composed of a mixture, in equal parts, of sarsaparilla, squine, guaiacum and sassafras. The *roots* of burdock and patience, the *stems* of bitter-sweet, the *leaves* of scabious and the *flowers* of the elder are employed in the proportion of 20 or 30 grms. (ʒv to ʒi) to 1 litre (ʒxxxii) of water; the woody substances being made into a decoction, and the flowers and leaves into an infusion. Elder flowers are much used as sudorifics, and in lotions and fomentations; and violet flowers are also sudorific in doses of 8 to 12 grms. (ʒii to ʒiii) infused in 1 litre of water.

Sarsaparilla Mixture.

Take of Alcoholic extract of sarsaparilla .	15 grms. (ʒss.)	
Essence of sassafras . .	5 grms. (ʒi 1/4.)	
Dissolve them in :		
Alcohol at 21° Cartier (sp. gr. ·92).	1000 grms. (ʒxxxii.)	
Add :		
Simple syrup . . .	1000 grms. (ʒxxxii.)	

1 or 2 table-spoonsful to be taken by adults, and 2 tea-spoonsful by children, dissolved in a glass of warm water. This dose to be repeated 4 or 5 times a-day.

Used in the same cases as the preceding.

Cleansing (Depurative) Pills.

Take of Watery extract of guaiacum . Alcoholic extract of sarsaparilla } of each .	5 grms. (gr. lxxv.)	
Inert excipient	q. s.	

Mix, and divide into 50 pills. From 2 to 10 to be taken daily, in the same cases as the tisanes above.

Caraïbe's Solution.

Take of Powdered guaiacum root . 30 grms. (ʒi.)
Rum . . . . 1 litre (ʒxxxii.)

Macerate for 2 days, and filter. A small liqueur-glassful to be taken every morning for 5 days, and then 2 glassfuls.

Used in chronic gout, and in gouty concretions.

Sudorific Potion.

	ADULTS.	CHILDREN.
Take of Distilled aniseed water .	. 100 grms. (ʒiii.)	60 grms. (ʒiss.)
Tincture of cinnamon .	. 2 grms. (ʒss.)	10 drops.
Syrup of orange-peel .	. 40 grms. (ʒx.)	30 grms. (ʒi.)
Eau de Luce .	. 2 grms. (ʒss.)	10 drops.

Mix. To be taken by spoonsful in the day, in the treatment of eruptive diseases when the eruption is slow in appearing; but there is no opposing internal disorder.

N.B. Eau de Luce contains ammonia, alcohol, soap, oil of amber and balsam of Mecca (*Amyris opobalsamum*).

Mixture against Intoxication.

Take of Acetate of ammonia (spirit of Mindererus, } 10 grms. (ʒiiss.)
    see p. 260) . . . . }
Orange-flower water . . } of each . 50 grms. (ʒiss.)
Distilled water of the linden }
Syrup of orange-peel. . . . 40 grms. (ʒx.)

Mix. To be taken in 4 doses, with an interval between each of a quarter of an hour.

DIURETICS.

Swiss Apozem.

Take of Fresh cows' urine . . 700 grms. (ʒxxxii.)
Aromatize it with :

      Distilled fennel water. . 50 grms. (ʒiss.)

Warm it in a water-bath, to redissolve the deposit which forms on cooling, and take it by half-glassfuls in the course of the day. It may be sweetened with syrup of gum or of straw-berries.

Used in dropsies, and chronic diseases of the liver.

N.B. Care must be taken to renew the urine every day, especially in hot weather.

Diuretic Apozem.

Take of Aperitive species*	. .	30 grms. (ʒi.)
Boil them in :		
Water	. . . .	1000 grms. (ʒxxxii.)
Reduce it to 600 grms. (ʒxix), and add :		
Oxymel of squill	. .	100 grms. (ʒiii.)

To be taken by glassfuls, in dropsies.

Antiphlogistic Diuretic Tisane.

	ADULTS.	CHILDREN.
Take of Digitalis leaves . .	1 grm. (gr. xv.)	0,25 centigrms. (gr. iv.)
Infuse them in :		
Water	700 grms. (ʒxxii.)	400 grms. (ʒxiii.)
Add :		
Nitrate of potash . .	15 grms. (ʒss.)	4 grms. (ʒi.)
Syrup of the 5 aperient roots .	180 grms. (ʒvss.)	40 grms. (ʒx.)

To be drunk during the day, in acute articular rheumatism, and in pleurisy.

Diuretic Tisane.

	ADULTS.	CHILDREN.
Take of Pellitory leaves . .	25 grms. (ʒvi.)	10 grms. (ʒiiss.)
Infuse them in :		
Boiling water . .	1000 grms. (ʒxxxii.)	500 grms. (ʒxvi.)
Then add :		
Syrup of the 5 aperient roots .	100 grms. (ʒiii.)	60 grms. (ʒii.)

To be drunk by glassfuls in the course of the day, in dropsies.

* Roots of fennel, parsley, smallage, asparagus and butchers'-broom.

Bitter Diuretic Tisane.

	ADULTS.	CHILDREN.
Take of Squill (sliced) . . .	4 grms. (ʒi.)	1 grm. (gr. xv.)
Dry orange-peel. . .	40 grms. (ʒx.)	10 grms. (ʒiiss.)
Infuse them in :		
Boiling water . . .	700 grms. (℥xxii.)	300 grms. (℥ix.)
Strain, and add :		
Acetate of potash . .	10 grms. (ʒiiss.)	2 grms. (ʒss.)
Syrup of the 5 aperient roots .	60 grms. (℥ii.)	30 grms. (℥i.)

To be drunk by cupfuls during the day, in dropsies.

Diuretic Fomentation.

Take of Tincture of squill } of each . 60 grms. (℥ii.)
      „   digitalis }
      Water . . . . 200 grms. (℥vi.)

Mix. Soak cloths in it, which are to be applied to the thighs, and covered with oil-cloth.

Used in dropsies, when the stomach will not bear diuretics.

Diuretic Pills.

	ADULTS.	CHILDREN.
Take of Powdered root of caïnça . }		
Acetate of potash . } of each . 4 grms. (ʒi.)	1 grm. (gr. xv.)
Extract of digitalis . }		
Excipient . . . . q. s.	q. s.

Mix, and divide into 40 pills. From 1 to 10 to be taken in the 24 hours, in dropsies.

EMMENAGOGUES.

Tisane.

Take of Rue . . . . 4 grms. (ʒi.)
      Wormwood . . . 10 grms. (ʒiiss.)
Infuse them in :
      Boiling water . . . 700 grms. (℥xxii.)
Strain and add :
      Syrup of orange-peel . . 100 grms. (℥iii.)

To be drunk by glassfuls in the course of the day. In the interval between the courses.

Emmenagogue Potion.

Take of Wormwood . . 4 grms. (ʒi.)
      Saffron (the stigmata) . . 1 grm. (gr. xv.)

Infuse them in:

      Water . . . . 100 grms. (ʒiii.)

Strain and add:

      Compound syrup of wormwood . 40 grms. (ʒx.)
      Tincture of iodine . . . 30 drops.

To be taken in 4 doses for several days in succession, in cases of amenorrhœa, occurring after the courses have appeared a few times.

Emmenagogue Pills.

Take of Powdered savine .⎫
     ,,   rue .⎬ of each . 4 grms. (ʒi.)
     ,,   saffron .⎭
Syrup of wormwood . . q. s.

Mix, and divide into 20 pills. From 1 to 6 to be taken daily for several days in succession, in the same cases as the preceding potion.

POWDER OF CALOMEL AND SAVINE.

See Alteratives, p. 238.

BALSAMIC STIMULANTS.

Balsamic Pills.

Take of Turpentine (Venice or Strasburg). 5 grms. (gr. lxxv.)
      Calcined magnesia . . q. s.

Mix, and divide into 50 pills. From 1 to 10 to be taken in the 24 hours.

Used in chronic catarrh of the kidneys, of the bladder, or of the lungs; and in patients weakened by excessive suppurations.

Balsamic Syrup.

Take of Venice turpentine . . . 166 grms. (ʒv, ʒvi.)
      Simple syrup. . . . 996 grms. (ʒxxxii.)

Digest them in a water-bath for 24 hours, strain, and add:

      Rectified oil of turpentine . . 30 drops.

From 30 to 200 grammes (℥i to ℥vi) to be taken daily, in the same cases as the preceding pills.

Pills of Prepared Turpentine.

Take of Bordeaux turpentine   .   . . 25 grms. (℥vi.)

Boil it in water, until the turpentine, having lost most of its essential oil, can be rolled into pills. Then divide it into 100, which are to be kept in cold water. From 1 to 10 to be taken daily, in the above cases.

Balsamic Tisane.

	ADULTS.	CHILDREN.
Take of Savine tops . . .	40 grms. (℥x.)	15 grms. (℥ss.)
Infuse them in:		
Boiling water . . .	1000 grms. (℥xxxii.)	500 grms. (℥xvi.)
Strain, and add:		
Syrup of Tolu . . .	100 grms. (℥iii.)	50 grms. (℥iss.)

To be drunk during the day, in the same cases as the above pills.

Antineuralgic Potion.

Take of Oil of turpentine	.	.	10 grms. (℥iiss.)
Yolk of egg .	.	.	1
Water.	.	.	100 grms. (℥iii.)
Syrup of opium	.	.	10 grms. (℥iiss.)
„ „ gum.	.	.	40 grms. (℥x.)

Make an emulsion of the oil and yolk of egg, by rubbing them in a mortar; add the syrups by degrees, and then the water. To be taken in the 24 hours, for several days in succession, in the treatment of obstinate neuralgia, especially sciatica.

Antineuralgic Glyster.

Take of Venice turpentine.	.	15 grms.	(℥ss.)
Yolk of egg .	.	1	
Extract of opium .	.	0,05 centigrms.	(gr. 3/4.)
Water .	.	150 grms.	(℥v.)

Make the turpentine and egg into an emulsion, and add the water by degrees, in which the extract has first been previously dissolved. A glyster of simple water is to be first taken and returned, and then this balsamic glyster; which the patient must endeavour to retain. To be taken at first at bed-time, and after a few days twice a-day, in obstinate sciatica.

Anti-psoric Liniment.

Take of Essential oil of turpentine ⎫
     Oil of sweet almonds   . ⎬ of each   40 grms. (ʒx.)
     Lard .   .   ⎭
     Essence of citron .   .   .   4 grms. (ʒi.)

Triturate, by degrees, the lard and the oil of almonds in a mortar; and then add the essential oils, and shake them constantly. In the treatment of itch make the patient take an alkaline bath (p. 258), and on coming out of it, rub the whole body, and especially those parts which are most affected, with this liniment, for 10 or 15 minutes; and let the patient put on his clothes without drying himself. This anointing kills the acarus (scabei), and the itch is cured in a few times. The pimples remain for a short time, but are no longer contagious.

TAR.

Tar Water. (Eau de Goudron.)

Take of Tar   .   .   .   .   100 grms. (ʒiii.)
Pour a litre (ʒxxxii) of hot water upon it, and throw
  this away; then add to the remaining tar:
     Common cold water   .   . 3000 grms. (ʒc.)

Let the tar macerate for 8 days, stirring from time to time. The following day this water may be drunk, and the tar-water taken away may be replaced by fresh common water, until the liquid has lost its flavour. From 30 to 200 grammes (ʒi to ʒvi) of this tar-water to be taken daily, sweetened with syrup of Tolu, in the same cases as the tisane of savine-tops (p. 328), and the turpentine pills (p. 328) which we have indicated above.

Used for injections into the bladder, the ears, and the nose, in catarrhal discharges from these parts.

By dissolving in the cold 2 parts of white sugar in 1 part of tar-water, we obtain a syrup which may be administered internally, in the same doses and cases as tar-water.

Balsamic Bath.

Take of Bordeaux turpentine ⎫ of each   1000 grms. (ʒxxxii.)
     Tar .   .   .⎭

Mix them, and put them in the bottom of a large stoneware pot, capable of holding about 7 gallons, which is to be filled with hot water, and stirred from the bottom 2 or 3 times a-day. Put this water into the water of a large bath.

Used in the treatment of mumps in children, and in pruriginous diseases of the skin. The water may be used pure, warmed by mixture with common hot water, as an injection or lotion in pruritus of the vulva, and simple and chronic eczema and impetigo. As an injection into the bladder in chronic cataract of that organ, and into the fistulous sinuses of suppurating wounds.

Balsamic Fumigations.

Into a dish, filled with red-hot cinders, put a handful of juniper berries, and about 4 grammes (ʒi) of incense, or better still, of benzoin, to fumigate the flannels and clothes with which children are to be clad, in cases of general anasarca succeeding diarrhœa, scarlatina, or measles.

Anti-dartrous Liniment.

Take of Oil of cade (extract of *Juniperus oxycedrus*) . 15 grms. (ʒss.)

Lard „ sweet almonds } of each . . 30 grms. (ʒi.)

Essence of citron . . . . . 4 grms. (ʒi.)

Rub the lard in a mortar with the oil of almonds, and add the oil of cade by degrees, and then the essence of citron. For a liniment to anoint the parts of the body affected with mumps, with the achor of eczema, either simple or impetiginous, or with lichen *simplex* or *agrius*.

OLEO-RESIN OF COPAIVA.

(Improperly called Balsam of copaiva.)

Balsamic Pills.

Take of Oleo-resin of copaiva . . 10 grms. (ʒiiss.)

Calcined magnesia . . q. s.

Mix, and divide into 50 pills. From 1 to 15 to be taken daily, in slight gleets, and in pulmonary, renal or vesical catarrh.

N.B. Officinal solidified balsam of copaiva is made of 15 parts of oleo-resin of copaiva, and 1 part of calcined magnesia.

Balsamic Bolus.

Take of Oleo-resin of copaiva . . 15 grms. (ʒss.)

Powdered cubebs . . 20 grms. (ʒv.)

„ alum . . 5 grms. (gr. lxxv.)

Excipient . . q. s.

Mix, and divide into 50 boluses. From 4 to 10 to be taken in the 24 hours, in the treatment of acute gleet.

Balsamic Opiate.

Take of Oleo-resin of copaiva . . 30 grms. (ʒi.)
Powdered cubebs . . 100 grms. (ʒiii.)
Tartrate ferrico-potassique, (ferri } 10 grms. (ʒiiss.)
potassio-tartras) . .}

Dissolve the tartrate of potash and of iron in about 15 or 20 grammes (ʒss or ʒv) of water; add the cubebs, and then the copaiva by degrees, and then as much syrup of quince as will give the consistence of an electuary. 3 boluses the size of a nut to be taken 3 times a-day in gleet.

Copaiva Glyster.

Take of Balsam of copaiva . 5 grms. (gr. lxxv.)
Yolk of egg . . 1.
Water . . . 100 grms. (ʒiii)
Gummy extract of opium. 0,05 centigrms. (gr. 3/4.)

Make the yolk of egg into an emulsion with the copaiva in a mortar, and add the water by degrees, in which the extract of opium has been previously dissolved. To be taken twice a-day, as a glyster in gleets, when the patient cannot take copaiva by the mouth.

SULPHUROUS STIMULANTS.

SULPHUR AND SULPHUROUS PREPARATIONS.

Sulphur Ointment.

Take of Unwashed flowers of sulphur . 10 grms. (ʒiiss.)
Lard . . . 40 grms. (ʒx.)
Essence of citron . . 2 grms. (ʒss.)

Mix them accurately. To be rubbed twice a-day upon the parts affected with itch; and also in some moist forms of cutaneous disease.

Antipsoric Ointment.

Take of Unwashed flowers of sulphur . 15 grms. (ʒss.)
Common salt . . 5 grms. (gr. lxxv.)
Lard . . . 125 grms. (ʒiv.)
Essence of citron . . 4 grms. (ʒi.)

Dissolve the salt in sufficient water, and rub it in a mortar with the sulphur, then the lard and the essential oil. An alkaline bath to be taken in the evening, and the next day a quarter of this ointment to be rubbed on the affected parts every 6 hours. Each rubbing ought to last at least a quarter of an hour, and to be applied especially to the parts affected with itch vesicles. One day's treatment is sufficient (?).

Another.

Take of Sublimed sulphur	.	.	50 grms. (ʒxiii.)
Carbonate of potash	.	.	25 grms. (ʒviss.)
Lard	.	.	200 grms. (ʒvi.)
Essential oil of citron	.	.	6 grms. (ʒiss.)

Dissolve the carbonate of potash in sufficient water; and add the flowers of sulphur, and then the lard and citron. Triturate them thoroughly together.

Rub the whole body with black soap for 10 minutes, and then wash thoroughly in a bath. This being done, rub the whole body energetically with the ointment for half-an-hour, especially the parts where the itch vesicles are apparent, and then put on the clothes without renewing the ointment; and the treatment will be finished in an hour and a half. There now only remains the irritation which accompanies the itch, which goes away spontaneously, or by the use of simple baths.

Antipsoric Powder.

Take of Unwashed flowers of sulphur . 100 grms. (ʒiii.)

Sprinkle about a tea-spoonful of the sulphur every day in the bed of the person affected with itch. The bed-clothes must not be changed for 3 weeks, whilst the treatment continues.

Electuary of Sulphur.

Take of Washed flowers of sulphur	.	.	40 grms. (ʒx.)
White honey	.	.	q. s. to give the
consistence of thick electuary.			

1 drachm, or a portion the weight of a nut, according to age, to be taken 3 times a-day.

Used in chronic skin diseases, chronic rheumatism, chronic pulmonary catarrh, and scrophula.

Fumigations, or Vapour-baths of Sulphur.

Take of Common flowers of sulphur . . 30 grms. (ʒi.)

Some hot cinders are to be put into a dish, under a chair, and the flowers of sulphur are to be thrown upon them. The patient is to be seated naked, and to be surrounded by a blanket or sheet, fastened round the neck, and falling down to the ground, so as to completely envelope him, and close up all outlets for the vapour. The sulphurous acid which is produced by the combustion of the sulphur irritates the air passages violently, and causes severe coughing. It is therefore better to take these baths in a wooden frame, in which the patient can be seated with merely his head in the air, and with towels placed round the neck.

Used in itch and chronic rheumatism.

Anticatarrhal Pills.

		ADULTS.	CHILDREN.
Take of Sulphuret of calcium	.	1 grm. (gr. xv.)	0,30 centigrms. (gr. ivss.)
Alcoholic extract of aconite	.	2 grms. (ʒss.)	0,50 centigrms. (gr. viii.)
Inert excipient .	.	q. s.	q. s.

Mix, and divide into 20 pills. From 1 to 4 to be taken daily, in chronic pulmonary catarrh.

Liniment of Pihorel.

Take of Powdered sulphuret of calcium	.	20 grms. (ʒv.)
White oil (poppy oil)	.	125 grms. (ʒiv.)

Mix. This liniment to be rubbed in with the palm of the hand for 10 minutes, night and morning, in the treatment of itch.

Simple Sulphurous Bath.

		ADULTS.	CHILDREN.
Take of Solid sulphuret of potassium	.	30 grms. (ʒi.)	10 grms. (ʒiiss.)
Water . . .	.	300 grms. (ʒix.)	100 grms. (ʒiii.)

Dissolve, and add to the water of a large bath.

Used in itch, in moist cutaneous diseases, chronic rheumatism, chronic diarrhœa, and colic caused by metallic substances.

It is important that the quantity of the sulphuret should not be increased when no acid is added to the bath to decompose the salt. By adding 500 grammes (℥xvi) of common glue to this bath, we obtain the sulphuro-gelatinous bath.

Artificicial Bareges Bath.

	ADULTS.	CHILDREN.
Take of Hydrosulphate of soda (monosulphuret of sodium) crystallized	100 grms. (ʒiii.)	30 grms. (ʒi.)
Chloride of sodium . .	40 grms. (ʒx.)	10 grms. (ʒiiss.)

Dissolve in water, and add to the water of a bath.

Another.

	ADULTS.	CHILDREN.
Take of Dry sulphuret of potassium .	125 grms. (ʒiv.)	40 grms. (ʒx.)
Water	500 grms. (ʒxvi.)	100 grms. (ʒv.)

Dissolve and mix with the water of a large bath, to which the following solution is to be added:

	ADULTS.	CHILDREN.
Sulphuric or hydrochloric acid .	15 grms. (ʒss.)	5 grms. (ʒ1½.)
Water	250 grms. (ʒviii.)	25 grms. (ʒiss.)

By mixing these two liquids, sulphate of potash is produced if sulphuric acid is used, or chloride of potassium if hydrochloric acid is employed. Sulphur is deposited, and sulphuretted hydrogen is disengaged; but the quantity of acid employed is not sufficient to decompose the whole of the sulphuret.

Used in the same cases as the last.

Sulphurous Potions.

Take of Sulphuret of sodium .	.	15 grms. (ʒss.)
Distilled water .	.	150 grms. (ʒv.)

Dissolve. A tea-spoonful of this solution to be put into a litre (ʒxxxii) of very hot water for lotions. To be applied to the head in the milk-rash of infants, to the face in moist eruptions, to be inhaled up the nostrils in chronic eczema of the olfactory mucous membrane, and to be used in pruritus of the vulva.

Artificial Sulphurous or Hydrosulphurous Water.

Take of Hydrosulphate of soda .			
Carbonate of soda	} of each	0,135 millegrms.	(gr. ii.)
Chloride of sodium			
Iodide of potassium .	.	0,0001 dix-millegrms.	(gr. 1/670.)
Water free from air .	.	625 grms. (1 bottle)	(ʒxx.)

Dissolve, bottle, and cork with care. This water may be used as a substitute for the natural mineral waters of Barèges, Bagnères de Suchon, Bonnes, St. Saviour, and Cauterets. We even prefer this artificial water to the natural water sent to a distance, for it always undergoes a change, so as no longer to contain any sulphuret (hydrosulphate of soda).

Hydrosulphuric Potion.

	ADULTS.	CHILDREN.
Take of Syrup of maiden hair .	30 grms. (ʒi.)	20 grms. (ʒv.)
Distilled water of lettuce .	60 grms. (ʒii.)	30 grms. (ʒi.)
Liquid hydrosulphuric acid* .	20 drops.	5 drops.

Mix, and cork carefully. To be taken during the day by table-spoonsful at a time in chronic pulmonary catarrh, and in the early symptoms of phthysis.

SEDATIVES—CONTRA-STIMULANTS.

Antiphlogistic Powder.

Take of Powdered digitalis leaves } of each		
Nitrate of potash }	. 2 grms. (ʒss.)	
Powdered sugar .	. 10 grms. (ʒiiss.)	

Mix, and divide into 40 packets. From 1 to 4 to be taken by children, and from 4 to 10 by adults.

Used in inflammatory affections of the lungs, in acute articular rheumatism, and in diseases of the heart, and dropsies.

Tisane of Digitalis.

	ADULTS.		CHILDREN.
Take of Dry leaves of digitalis .	0,50 centigrms. (gr. viii.)	{	0.20 centigrms. (gr. iii.)
Boiling water .	. 750 grms.	(ʒxxiv.)	400 grms. (ʒxiii.)
Infuse them, strain, and add:			
Simple syrup .	. 60 grms.	(ʒii.)	40 grms. (ʒx.)

To be taken by cupsful in the course of the day, in the same cases as the preceding.

---

* This is only a solution of sulphuretted hydrogen, obtained by passing the gas through cold water under the common pressure of the air. The water then dissolves three times its volume of the gas.

Diuretic Fomentations.

Take of Digitalis leaves   .   .   100 grms. (ℨiii.)
　　　 Water   .   .   .   2000 grms. (ℨlxiv.)

Infuse, strain, and add :

　　　 Acetate of potash   .   .   60 grms. (ℨii.)

Soak flannels in it, with which the limbs and the belly are to be covered.

Used in anasarca, especially when it is caused by diseases of the heart.

Bechic (Expectorant) Pills.

Take of Extract of digitalis   .   .   1 grm.   (gr. xv.)
　　　 White oxide of antimony   .   2 grms. (ℨss.)
　　　 Inert excipient.   .   .   q. s.

Mix, and divide into 40 pills. From 1 to 6 to be taken daily by children. From 4 to 20 by adults.

Used in cases of catarrh of the pulmonary capillaries, pulmonary apoplexy, and subacute apoplexy.

Pills of Digitaline.

Take of Digitaline   .   .   0,05 centigrms. (gr. 3/4.)
　　　 Kermes mineral   .   1 grm.   (gr. xv.)
　　　 Extract of digitalis   .   1 grm.   (gr. xv.)
　　　 Inert excipient   .   q. s.

Mix, and divide into 50 pills. From 1 to 5 for children; 4 to 10 for adults.

Used in the same cases as the preceding.

Granules of Digitaline.   (Homolle and Quevenne.)

These granules are made like aniseed of Verdun. Each contains 1 milligramme (gr. $\frac{1}{60}$) of digitaline, and is equivalent in its effects to about 1 centigramme (gr. $\frac{1}{6}$) of digitalis. These granules have the triple advantage of the dose being easily fixed, of keeping for an indefinite period, and of being easily administered.

From 2 to 5 granules are to be taken in the 24 hours; seldom so many as 6 or 8. They are to be stopped on the first sign of intolerance.*

* See "Traité de Thérapeutique," de MM. Trousseau et Pidoux, vol. ii., p. 681.

ANTIMONIAL PREPARATIONS.

Expectorant Potion.

	ADULTS.	CHILDREN.
Take of White looch . .	1 (the whole quantity.)	1/2 the quantity.
White oxide of antimony .	2 grms. (ʒss.)	0,50 to 1 grm. (gr. viii to gr. xv.)

Mix, and shake them before being administered. To be taken in the course of 24 hours.

Used in febrile pulmonary catarrh.

Potion in Pneumonia.

	ADULTS.	CHILDREN.
Take of White looch . .	1 (the whole quantity.)	1/2 the quantity.
White oxide of antimony.	2 grms. (ʒss.)	1 grm. (gr. xv.)
Extract of digitalis .	0,50 centigrms. (gr. viii.)	0,15 centigrms. (gr. ii 1/3.)

Dissolve the extract in the looch; add the oxide of antimony, and stir it before it is taken. To be taken during the twenty-four hours in pneumonia.

Another.

	ADULTS.	CHILDREN.
Take of White looch. .	1 (the whole quantity.)	1/2 the quantity.
Kermes mineral .	0,25 to 1 grm. (gr. iv to gr. xv.)	0,05 to 0,20 centigrms. (gr. 3/4 to gr. iii.)
Extract of digitalis .	0,50 centigrms. (gr. viii.)	0,15 centigrms. (gr. ii 1/3.)

Dissolve the extract in the looch, add the kermes, and stir it up before administering it. To be taken in the same manner and the same cases as the last.

Bechic (Expectorant) Pills.

Take of Kermes mineral .	1 grm.	(gr. xv.)
Extract of digitalis . .	0,50 centigrms.	(gr. viii.)
Alcoholic extract of belladonna	0,10 centigrms.	(gr. iss.)
Inert excipient . .	q. s.	

Mix, and divide into 20 pills. From 1 to 10 to be taken daily.

Used in the same cases as the preceding, in nervous (spasmodic) asthma, and the pulmonary inflammations which complicate hooping-cough.

z

Antimonial Potion.

	ADULTS.	CHILDREN.
Take of Tartar emetic (émétique) .	0,20 to 1 grm. (gr. iii gr. xv.)	0,05 to 0,15 centi-grms. (gr. 3/4 gr. ii 1/3)
Lettuce water . .	100 grms. (℥iii.)	40 grms. (℥x.)
Simple syrup .	40 grms. (℥x.)	20 grms. (℥v.)

Mix. To be taken by table-spoonsful in the course of the day.

Used in acute pneumonia, and in pulmonary apoplexy. (§. It is only by virtue of the "tolerance" (see p. 94) of tartar emetic in acute pneumonia that the large doses of the above prescription can be borne without occasioning vomiting. In this country such doses generally act as emetics, whatever may be the disease present).

N.B. The preparations of opium must only be added to make the medicine tolerated by the stomach; as the opium acts in a diametrically opposite manner to sedatives of the antimonial class.

Antimonial Pills.

	ADULTS.	CHILDREN.
Take of Tartar emetic . .	1 grm. (gr. xv.)	0,10 centigrms. (gr. iss.)
Extract of digitalis .	0,40 centigrms. (gr. viss.)	0,15 centigrms. (gr. ii 1/3.)

Mix, and divide into 20 pills. From 1 to 20 to be taken in the twenty-four hours.

Used in the same cases as the preceding potion.

N.B. When tartar emetic is to be continued for several days, it ought always to be given in the form of pills. By this means, we avoid the inflammations of the mouth and throat which follow the administration of solutions of tartar emetic, and are so common, and sometimes so troublesome.

BISMUTH.

Powder.

	ADULTS.	CHILDREN.
Take of Sub-nitrate (tris-nitrate, nitrate) of bismuth . .	10 grms. (℥iiss.)	2 grms. (℈ss.)
Powdered sugar . . .	5 grms. (℥i 1/4.)	5 grms. (℥i 1/4.)

Mix, and divide into 10 packets. From 1 to 4 to be taken daily during a meal.

Used in gastralgia and enteralgia, accompanied with a tendency to diarrhœa and nervous spasms, (§. and especially with eructations of sour water into the mouth, (pyrosis).

Another.

	ADULTS.	CHILDREN.
Take of Nitrate of bismuth .	. 10 grms. (ʒiiss.)	2 grms. (ʒss.)
Powdered sugar .	. 5 grms. (gr. lxxv.)	5 grms. (gr. lxxv.)
Laudanum of Rousseau .	. 25 drops.	2 drops.

Triturate them thoroughly; mix and divide into 10 packets. One to be taken an hour before a meal in chronic diarrhœa.

Antiphlogistic Mixture.

Take of Sub-nitrate of bismuth (white cosmetic, blanc de fard) . . . . } 10 grms. (ʒiiss.)

Mucilage of quince . . . q. s. to give the consistence of a thick soup.

The suppurating and everted eyelids (in ectropion) to be covered with this mixture. To be applied also to parts affected with moist or pruriginous cutaneous diseases, and acne rosacea; to the nostrils and the ears when affected with chronic herpetic inflammations.

ANTISEPTIC ABSORBANTS.

CHARCOAL MADE FROM WHITE WOOD (e. g. WILLOW).

Charcoal Opiate.

Take of Porphyrized wood charcoal . 40 grms. (ʒx.)
Calcined magnesia . . 1 grm. (gr. xv.)
White honey . . . q. s. to give the consistence of an electuary.

One tea-spoonful to be taken every day by children, or 4 to 6 by adults, in diarrhœa and dysentery with fœtid stools; in cancerous affections of the stomach and bowels; and in gastralgia with fœtid eructations and obstinate constipation.

Antiseptic Charcoal Cerate.

Take of Porphyrized wood charcoal* . 40 grms. (ʒx.)
Extract of rhatany . . 15 grms. (ʒss.)
Cerate . . . . 100 grms. (ʒiii.)

(§. * Animal charcoal appears to me to be much more efficacious than vegetable charcoal in removing the smell from offensive and sloughing sores.)

z 2

Dissolve the extract in a sufficient quantity of water. Mix it with the charcoal, and add the cerate in small quantities by stirring them together.

Used to dress phagedenic cancerous ulcers, hospital gangrene and burns.

ANTHELMINTICS.

Anthelmintic Lozenges.

Take of Calomel lozenges of the *Codex* . . 1 to 3.

Each of these lozenges contains 0·05 centigrammes (gr. 3/4) of calomel. From 1 to 3 are given in the morning, fasting, to children who have round worms (ascaris lumbricoides). The dose is to be repeated for three days, and on the third day, an hour after the administration of the lozenges, from 10 to 15 grms. (ʒiiss to ʒss) of castor oil is to be given.

Mercurial Vermifuge Glysters.

See pages 241, 246.

Another Anthelmintic Glyster.

| Take of Calomel | . | . | 0,25 centigrms. | (gr. iv.) |
| Mucilage of linseed | . | 125 grms. | (ʒiv.) |

Suspend the calomel in the mucilage and give it as a glyster. *Used* in the treatment of thread worms (ascaris vermicularis).

Mercurial Vermifuge Suppository.

See page 246.

TIN.

Electuary of Tin.

| Take of Powdered tin | . | . | . | 4 grms. (ʒi.) |
| White honey | . | . | . | 40 grms. (ʒx.) |

Mix, and make into an electuary. Two or three tea-spoonsful of this electuary to be taken for several days in succession by children troubled with round worms (ascaris lumbricoides). One or two table-spoonsful every day for adults.

Stanno-Mercurial Electuary.

Take of Pure tin ⎱ of each . . 1 grm. (gr. xv.)
Fluid mercury ⎰

Melt the tin, and add the mercury. Powder the
amalgam when cold, and add:

White honey ⎱ of each . 40 grms. (ʒx.)
Conserve of roses ⎰

One or two table-spoonsful to be taken for several days in
succession by adults affected with tape-worms. One to three
tea-spoonsful to be taken by children.

MOUSSE DE CORSE, (CORSICAN MOSS).

Vermifuge Infusion.

Take of Corsican moss (*Fucus helminthocorton*) 4 to 16 grms. (ʒi to ʒss.)
Boiling milk . . . . 60 grms. (ʒii.)

Infuse, strain, and add:

Syrup of wormwood . . 40 grms. (ʒx.)

To be taken in one or two portions in the morning, fasting, for
three days running, in the treatment of ascarides lumbricoides.
The third day from 10 to 15 grammes (ʒiiss to ʒss) of castor oil
to be given an hour after the administration of the vermifuge
milk.

Jelly of Corsican Moss.

Take of Mousse de Corse . . . . 30 grms. (ʒi.)

Boil it for an hour in about 1000 grms. (ʒxxxii) of water,
down to 250 grms. (ʒviii.)

Strain, and add:

White sugar . . . 60 grms. (ʒii.)
Isinglass softened by water . . 4 grms. (ʒi.)
White wine. . . . . 60 grms. (ʒii.)

Cook it to the consistence of a jelly, strain and allow it to
cool.

From 1 to 2 tea-spoonsful for children, or 1 to 4 table-spoonsful
for adults; to be taken in the same cases as the foregoing milk.

SEMEN-CONTRA.

Take of Powdered semen contra (*Artemisia* ⎱ 4 to 8 grms. (ʒi to ʒii.)
contra) . . . . ⎰
White honey. . . . 16 grms. (ʒss.)

Mix for an electuary. To be taken in three doses in the morning, fasting, for two or three days running, by children troubled with round worms.

N.B. The same dose of semen contra is often administered to children under the form of biscuits, lozenges or infusion.

Lozenges of Santonine.

Take of Santonine (the crystallizable constituent of semen contra) . . . . } 1 grm. (gr. xv.)

Powdered white sugar. . . . . 50 grms. (ʒiss.)

Mucilage of gum tragacanth, made with orange-flower water. . . } q. s. to give the consistence of dough.

Divide into 50 lozenges, each of which will contain 2 centigrammes (gr. 1/3) of santonine. From 1 to 5 to be taken daily to expel ascaris lumbricoides.

POMEGRANATE ROOT, (RADIX GRANATI.)

Tænifuge Apozem.

Take of The fresh bark of the root of the wild pomegranate . . . } 60 grms. (ʒii.)

Powder it coarsely, and boil it for an hour in :

Water . . . . . 1000 grms. (ʒxxxii.)

Strain whilst hot, and add :

Compound syrup of wormwood . . 100 grms. (ʒiii.)

To be taken by glassfuls every half hour. The patient must only take weak broth at dinner the day before, and on going to bed must take a cupful of chamomile tea or infusion of germander. Three hours after taking the last dose of the decoction of pomegranate root, he must swallow at one draught 60 grms. (ʒii) of syrup of ether, and an hour afterwards, a white looch, to which have been added 3 drops of croton oil. For children, the dose must be half the above. This plan must be followed three times in nine days.

Used to expel tape worms (tæniæ).

MALE FERN, (FOUGERE MALE).

Tænifuge Bolus.

Take of Ethereal extract of the root of male fern . 4 grms. (ʒi.)

Powdered root of male fern . . . q. s. to give a consistence suitable for pills.

Divide into 8 boluses. The day beforehand the patient should submit to the regimen above described, and in the morning, fasting, he should take 2 boluses at a time every quarter of an hour. Two hours after the administration of the last two boluses, he must take at one dose 60 grammes (ℨii) of syrup of ether, and two hours later still, a white looch, with 3 drops of croton oil in it. This plan is to be repeated four days afterwards if the tapeworm is not expelled. For children, the doses should be half or one-third of the above, according to their age.

BRAYERA ANTHELMINTICA, (KOUSSO).

(Brayera anthelmintica, Rosaceæ.)

Take of Powdered flowers of kousso . . 20 grms. (ℨv.)
Infuse in :
Water . . . . . 250 grms. (ℨviii.)

Allow it to infuse for half an hour, and then drink both the infusion and the powder in two portions, leaving only a quarter of an hour between them. The day before, the patient should have submitted to the regimen above described. He should not drink after taking the kousso, and if thirsty, he must be content with sucking an orange. Six hours afterwards, if the tapeworm is not expelled, he may take a bottle of Sedlitz water. For children, the dose should be half or a third of the above. The same treatment is to be repeated every three days for three times if necessary.

SOOT.*

Vermifuge Coffee.

Take of Roasted Coffee, powdered . . 10 grms. (ℨiiss.)
Sifted soot . . . 4 to 10 grms. (ℨi to ℨiiss.)
Boiling water . . . 60 grms. (ℨii.)
Infuse for an hour, strain, and add :
Compound syrup of wormwood . 40 grms. (ℨx.)

Mix, to be taken in four doses, to destroy round worms.

(§. * The soot here prescribed is not coal soot, but that obtained from wood. Its composition varies; but it contains, in general, *acetic acid, ammonia, tar* and *creosote*, with a resinous matter called *pyretin*; all of which consist of carbon, hydrogen, oxygen or nitrogen variously combined, and are formed by the destructive distillation and volatilization of these ingredients in wood. Besides these, various

Vermifuge Glyster.

| Take of Sifted soot. | . | . | . | . | 30 grms. (ʒi.) |
| Water | . | . | . | . | 150 grms. (ʒv.) |

Boil for fifteen minutes, strain, and use as a glyster, to expel threadworms.

non-volatile substances are mechanically carried up along with them, viz., salts of iron, lime and silica, and also some carbon. Wood soot was formerly contained in the London *Pharm.*, but has been displaced, as its several constituents have been obtained in greater purity and in a less offensive form.

HELMINTHOLOGY,

HUMAN INTESTINAL (?) WORMS.

NAMES, FRENCH AND COMMON.	LATIN NAMES.	HABITATION.
DRAGONNEAU FILAIRE DE MEDINE.	Filensia Medinensis, or Dracunculus.	Cellular tissue.
TRICHOCÉPHALE DE L'HOMME. Trichocephalus.	Trichocephalus dispar.	Cœcum.
OXYURE, Oxyuris, thread-worms.	Oxyuris vermicularis. Ascaris Rudolphi.	Rectum.
SPIROPTÈRE.	Spiroptera (?)	Bladder.
STRONGLE GÉANT.	Strongylus gigas.	Kidneys.
ASCARIDE LOMBRICOÏDE, round worms.	Ascaris lumbricoïdes.	Small intestines.
OPHIOSTOME DE PONTIER	Ophiostema Pontieri.	Digestive canal.
HUMULAIRE COMPRIMÉ.	Hunnularia subcompressa.	Lymphatic vessels and bronchial glands.
DIOSTOME DU FOIE.	Diostoma hepaticum.	Liver.
POLYSTOME PINGUICOLE.	Polystoma pinguicola.	Different parts of the body.
BOTRIOCÉPHALE LARGE.	Bothriocephalus latus. Tænia lata.	Small intestines, amongst Frenchmen, Swedes and Russians.
TÆNIA CUCURBITAIN, tape worms.	Tænia solium.	Small intestines, in Germans, the English, Hollanders and the inhabitants of the East.
CYSTICERQUE DU TISSU CELLULAIRE.	Cysticercus cellulosus.	Cellular tissue.
ACEPHALOCYSTES.	Acephalocystis ovoïda. Granulata. Surculigera.	Doubtful.
ECHINOCOCQUE DE L'HOMME, Guinea worm.	Echinococcus hominis.	Liver, kidneys, &c.—Under the skin of the shoulders and ankles in persons carrying water-pots upon their shoulders in Guinea, or having to stand for some time in water.

OUTLINES OF TOXICOLOGY.

In giving a short sketch of Toxicology at the conclusion of our work, we make no pretension to saying all that is known upon this most important subject, which daily acquires new development; but we have attempted to point out concisely the symptoms and lesions caused by the principal poisons, and to give precise directions for the employment of antidotes, and for the examinations necessary to recognize the presence of a poisonous substance. For the minute details, and the complete investigation of the subject of poisons, we must refer to special works upon toxicology.

We advise a physician, when called upon for an opinion in a case of poisoning, never to give one upon preconceived notions. The symptoms and lesions ought to be his only guides in the examination which he undertakes; although the information he may receive, or the profession of the victim, may sometimes furnish him with useful hints. If everything is not as he anticipates—that is to say, if one or more symptoms or injuries are absent—it is necessary for him to remember that it seldom or never happens that all the phenomena are present which are described by authors, though some of them are so constant that, if wanting, he must see whether he has not merely got one of the many diseases which simulate poisoning.

Toxicology (from τοξικον, poison; and λογος, a discourse) is the science relating to the subject of poisons. Every substance is called a *poison* which, when taken internally, or applied in a particular manner, and in a small dose, to a *living body*, impairs or entirely destroys vitality. The expression, "living body," has been objected to, and the words, "body of man," proposed as a substitute; but although it is true that substances which are poisonous to one animal are not always so to another, the exceptions are very rare; and as a definition is only good so far as it is general, we prefer the one we have given above, which is generally adopted.

The knowledge of poisons dates from the most remote antiquity. Homer speaks of them in his poems, and it is only necessary to remember the arts of *Circe* and *Locusta* to justify the statement respecting the antiquity of poison. The father of medicine said in his speech: "I never gave poison to any one." Legislators, according to Plato's remark in his "Republic," tried to prevent the sale of poisons; and lastly, even in the time of Homer, *Moly* was engaged in looking for a universal *counter-poison*, which we are very far from having discovered even in our own days. We shall be able, however, to point out certain substances which neutralise the action of a great number of poisons; such, for example, as albumen and hydrated sulphuret of iron, in the case of metallic poisons.   •

We were for a long time contented with searching for poisons in the first parts only into which they had been carried, *i. e.*, the stomach and intestines; but in the present day, owing to the very exact instructions of M. Orfila, they have been found in various tissues, and even in secreted liquids. The Professor just named, and after him, MM. Flandin and Danger have proved that all poisons are not eliminated in the same way. Thus antimony, arsenic, and lead, are eliminated by the urine, and some others by the sweat; whilst others again, like copper, are localized in the heart.

This localization of poisons, so well established by M. Orfila, is without contradiction one of the finest discoveries in toxicology; and it is to the same author, that we owe the precise indications which enable us to distinguish poisonous substances introduced into the system, from those which the body contains in a normal condition. It is he also who has laid such just stress upon the importance in searching for poisons, of getting rid in the first instance of all animal matters; a precept entirely in opposition to all Fodéré had laid down. Experience has decided in the present day, and we can easily prove it, that it is impossible to obtain clear and distinct reactions in the presence of animal matters.

Since the spirit of classification has taken possession of all the sciences, too much importance has often been attributed to it. In toxicology a good classification ought to be. founded upon well established physiological facts; but unfortunately, these facts are wanting, and we are compelled to acknowledge that the classification of poisons proposed by Vicat, adopted by Fodéré, and modified by Orfila, is still far from being satisfactory. It contains four classes.

FIRST CLASS.

Irritant poisons, or such as inflame or corrode the parts with which they come in contact; they are also called *corrosives* or *escharotics.* This class contains:

From the mineral kingdom, phosphorus, chlorine, iodine, bromine, concentrated acids and alkalies; preparations of arsenic, antimony, mercury, copper, tin, bismuth, zinc, iron, silver, lead; alkaline sulphurets, bromides and iodides, alkaline salts, &c.; pounded glass, &c.

From the animal kingdom, cantharides, and other vesicating insects, &c.

From the vegetable kingdom, concentrated acids, and oxalic acid, drastic purgatives in large doses, the hellebores, cevadilla, most of the apocynaceæ and euphorbiaceæ, and many of the ranunculaceæ, &c.

SECOND CLASS.

Narcotic or stupefying poisons, or such as paralyse the functions of the nervous system, and embrace:

Chemical and pharmaceutical productions. Cyanogen, hydrocyanic acid, alkaline cyanides, the distilled waters of bitter almonds and cherry laurel, &c.

Vegetable products: opium, morphia, and its salts, codein, narcotine, wild lettuce, hyosciamus, dulcamara, haschich, &c.

THIRD CLASS.

Narcotico-acrid poisons, which produce at the same time narcotism, and irritation of the parts which they touch. In this class M. Orfila makes several orders which comprehend poisons that approach it the most nearly in their mode of action.

First order contains squill, œnanthe, aconite, veratria, colchicum, belladonna, stramonium, tobacco, digitalis, greater and lesser hemlock, water hemlock, rose-bay, rue, and cyanide of iodine.

Second order contains strychnine, brucia, igasurine, nux vomica, St. Ignatius' bean, upas tieuta, false angustura, worari.

Third order contains upas anthiar, camphor, Indian berry, picrotoxine.

Fourth order contains the poisonous fungi, which may be referred to the genera amanitæ and agaric.

Fifth order contains ergot of rye, odorous plants, nitrous oxide (protoxide of azote), coal-gas, and carbonic acid gas.

FOURTH CLASS.

Septic or putrefiant poisons. In this fourth class are placed the poisons which alter, liquify, or putrefy the fluids of the system, and they are called septics or putrefiants. Sulphuretted hydrogen, putrefying matters, muscles, virus, (*e. g.* small-pox), animal poisons, (*e. g.* rattle-snake), and the gases from sewers and cesspools belong to this class.

We must, however, add that some authors do not adopt the classification just given. M. Giacomi, amongst others, divided poisons into *hypo-sthenisants** and *hyper-sthenisants ;*† but some poisons, such as camphor or arsenic, may be placed in either class, according to the dose in which they are administered.

(§. * Hypo, ύπο, under; sthenos, σθενος, strength: poisons which reduce the powers of the system; *e. g.* Tartar emetic.

(§. † Hyper, ύπερ, above; sthenos, strength; poisons which increase the powers of the system (*i. e.* for a time only); such as cause inflammation; *e. g.* arsenic.

Proper mode of studying poisons.

When we wish to study any poisonous substance successfully, it is necessary to examine: 1. Its action upon the animal economy. 2. The means to be employed, in order to counteract its effects. 3. The experiments by which its presence and its nature may be proved either before or after death.

The first problem, which consists in determining the means to be employed for discovering the effects of a poison upon the animal economy, must be solved by experiments made upon living animals, and observations gathered from the effects produced upon men.

The second problem intended to establish the general means suitable for combating the effects of a poison, constitutes the treatment; which refers to the two cases: 1. in which the poison is applied externally; 2. in which it is administered internally.

In the *first case*, the part to which it has been applied ought immediately to be washed, and we must afterwards oppose its absorption by using a sucking pump (a species of cupping-glass). If the poison has been absorbed we must combat its effects by the general means which we shall point out, in speaking of the particular poisons.

In the *second* case, *i. e.*, when the poison has been administered internally, the treatment is divided into four periods.

FIRST PERIOD. *The evacuation of the poison which is still unabsorbed.*—In this stage we assist vomiting, if it is present, by giving a large quantity of some luke-warm drink, or by tickling the throat. If vomiting has not come on we excite it by administering tartar emetic in doses from 0,10 to 0,25 centigrms. (gr. iss to gr. ivss); sulphate of zinc or of copper in doses from 0,25 to 0,40 centigrms. (gr. ivss to gr. vi); or ipecacuanha to the extent of 1 to 2 grms., &c. (gr. xv to ℈ss, or more). (§. The choice of the particular emetic will sometimes depend upon the nature of the poison taken; for example, sulphate of zinc or copper, should be given in poisoning by opium in preference to tartar emetic, because the emetic action of the antimonial is so much diminished by the narcotic; but when the particular emetic to be selected is of consequence, it will be mentioned in speaking of the particular poison). If poison has been swallowed for some time, and we suppose that it has passed the pylorus, we must give a purgative glyster, or better still, one which will act both as an emetic and a purgative. Lastly, we may in some cases employ à stomach-pump to empty the stomach.

SECOND PERIOD. *Administration of the antidote, or counterpoison.*—The evacuation of the poison being as complete as possible, we must hasten to administer the antidote, which is sometimes given even in the first period, dissolved or diffused in a large quantity of water, in order to assist the vomiting, and to enable it to act chemically. Antidotes are *perfect* or *imperfect*.

A *perfect* antidote ought to possess the following properties. It must be capable of being taken in large quantities, without itself producing injury; it must act upon the poison in whatever state it may be, at a temperature equal or inferior to that of the human body; the reaction ought to be rapid, and should take place in the midst of the different liquids which the stomach may contain; and lastly, it ought to destroy all the properties of the poison. Amongst perfect antidotes we may instance *magnesia*, and *soap* and water, to neutralise the effect of *acids;* the *sulphates* of potash, soda, or magnesia, in the case of the salts of *barytes, lead,* &c.; and the *chloride* of sodium to destroy the effects of the *salts* of silver and the *proto*-salts of *mercury.*

An *imperfect* antidote is such as does not possess all the properties above-mentioned. Thus *hydrosulphuric* acid and the alkaline *sulphurets* would be excellent antidotes for *metallic* poisons, if they were not as dangerous in excess as the poison itself. So also *albumen* only partially destroys the action of the salts of *mercury* and *copper;* and *tannin* or *galls* only partially oppose the narcotic effects of morphia.

In a case of poisoning we are often ignorant of the exact nature of the poison, though the symptoms may still indicate the general class to which it belongs; and it is chiefly in these cases that a general antidote would be of such utility. If we think that it is a case of *metallic* poisoning, M. Orfila proposes *albumen* diffused in water, as it precipitates the largest number of metallic solutions, and, moreover, from its nauseous taste provokes vomiting. In the same cases, M. Mialhe employs the *hydrated protosulphuret of iron,* and M. Bouchardat the *hydrated persulphuret of iron.* If the vomited matters effervesce upon the floor, indicating the presence of an energetic *acid,* we must administer *magnesia* mixed with water, or if that is not at hand, *soap* and water. Lastly, if we suspect that the poisoning has been produced by an *organic alkali,* we must make the patient take *tannin,* or decoction of *galls.*

THIRD PERIOD. *Evacuation of the poison when absorbed.*—We are indebted to M. Orfila for some very interesting researches upon the importance of evacuating the poison after its absorption, which is accomplished by means of diuretic or sudorific drinks copiously administered.

FOURTH PERIOD. *Treatment of the illness produced by the poison.*—The means to be employed at this period will vary according to the nature of the poison. Blood-letting may now be practised, though at an earlier period it would have materially favoured the absorption of the poison; but we must abstain from it whenever we suspect that a small quantity of the poison still remains in the stomach or intestinal canal. In this fourth period we must administer soothing mucilaginous drinks, baths, lotions, and fomentations, if the poison belonged to the class of irritants. If, on the contrary, there is stupefaction, we must have recourse to stimulating drinks: tea, coffee, &c. The emetics themselves, which have been administered in the first period of treatment, will act in two ways; at first, by the expulsion of the poison, and afterwards by virtue of their action in counteracting the narcotic influence.

The third problem consists in finding out the proper means for ascertaining the nature of the poison. Three methods ought to be employed for solving this problem.

1. We must examine the poisonous effects produced upon the living system.

2. The presence, absence, or nature of these injuries.

3. The chemical reactions, which constitutes *legal* or *forensic chemistry.*

General signs of poisoning.—We ought to suspect poisoning, when a person previously in good health is seized after a meal, or after taking some liquid, with pains of a variable nature; if he complains of a sickly or noisome smell, of a disagreeable taste, or of a burning heat in his mouth, throat, or stomach; if his mouth is dry, with great thirst; if there is an unusual colour of the lips or gums; or if there is nausea, or frequent bilious, mucous, or bloody vomiting; if the vomited matters effervesce on the pavement, or make syrup of violets green, or litmus paper red; if there is hiccup, or obstinate constipation, or copious diarrhœa; if the pulse or respiration is deranged; if there are abundant cold sweats, or he has difficulty in making water; or if the face is distorted, the strength exhausted, or the intellectual faculties perverted, &c.

The means to be adopted for recognising the nature of a poison is the most important part of legal medicine; and also the one which presents the most difficulties. The symptoms and lesions may furnish some indications of the general nature of the poison; but it is to chemical researches that we are compelled to have recourse, in order to pronounce upon it in an absolute manner.

GENERAL RULES FOR THE CHEMICAL SEARCH FOR A POISON.

If we are engaged upon a solution of a poisonous substance in water, we may first discover by means of coloured tests whether it is acid, alkaline, or neutral, and we may then evaporate a drop of the liquid upon platinum foil to ascertain whether it contains an organic or inorganic substance. In the first case we shall obtain a carbonaceous matter (§. in heating the dry residue nearly to redness); and in the case of a mineral substance we may treat it with sulphuretted hydrogen, which produces (§. coloured) precipitates with the metals of the fourth, fifth, and sixth classes; but not of the first three.* The latter, when treated with hydrosulphate of ammonia (§. sulphide of ammonium), will give a precipitate in the case of metals of the third class; but not with those of the first and second. Lastly, carbonate of potash may be employed to distinguish the metals of these two classes (§. as it precipitates the second, but not the first). If sulphuretted hydrogen causes a precipitate, we

may afterwards employ yellow cyanide of potassium and iron
(§. ferrocyanide of potassium, which gives precipitates of very
characteristic colours, with several metals which are not distinguished from one another by sulphuretted hydrogen alone);
and lastly, we must use the special tests, of which we shall
speak in treating of each poison in detail.

If, however, the poisonous substance is mixed with organic
matters, we must first separate it from them, for which purpose
several methods have been adopted.

1. **Colouring matters.**—It is incorrectly stated by Fodéré, in
his article *Toxicology*, in the Dictionnaire des Sciences Médi-
cales, that it is useless to separate colouring substances, for the
mineral poisons, even when mixed with colouring matters, yield
precipitates identical with those which are produced by the tests
in a colourless solution. So far from this being the case, it is
certain that no strictly exact reaction is possible in the presence
of colouring agents, to separate which, is therefore one of the first
things to be done. For this purpose washed *animal* charcoal is
employed in *small quantities*, for it has been proved by the recent
experiments of Graham, Chevallier, and others, that the charcoal
not only retains the colouring matters, but also a considerable
proportion of metallic, as well as of other poisons. It is therefore necessary to preserve the charcoal, that it may afterwards be
tested, if merely negative results have been obtained from the
liquid under examination. In some cases chlorine or sulphurous
acid is preferable to charcoal.

2. **Solid or liquid organic matters.**—Before proceeding with
a chemical examination, the operator ought always in the first
instance to remove organic matters, for the accomplishment of
which object several processes have been recommended, the chief
of which we shall here give. If operating upon liquid substances
we may mix them with distilled water, boil, and filter them, and
then treat the liquid with absolute alcohol, or a current of
chlorine, and filter anew. Before beginning, it will be useful
to examine any sediment formed by the liquid with a good mag-
nifying glass to look for traces of any solid poison.

When operating upon solid matters, such as the liver, the
spleen, the kidneys, the lungs, the heart, or muscle, &c., vomited

substances, or blood, &c., we may destroy the organic matters by one of the following processes :

1. By nitric acid, or nitrate of potash (Orfila).

2. By sulphuric acid (Danger and Flandin), either alone, or with the addition of a little chloride of lime, in order to disengage chlorine.

3. By a stream of chlorine (Jacquelain and Millon).

4. By hydrochloric acid and chlorate of potash (Millon and Abreu).

We shall not say anything about the other plans proposed by MM. Devergie, Chevallier, Peten-Koffer, &c., which more or less resemble those just mentioned.

The organic matter being destroyed we may dissolve the residue by water, or an acid, and so obtain a product upon which we can operate with security; but before employing a test of any description whatever, it is necessary first to be assured of its purity.

Lastly, as a most sensitive method, MM. Gaultier de Claubry, Flandin, &c., have proposed the precipitation of the metals by a galvanic current; and Professor Anderson, of Edinburgh, has suggested the microscope as a general means of detecting the alkaloids.*

The presence of a poison being proved, we have still to determine in certain cases (§. copper, lead, iron), whether it is *normal* (§. *i. e.* naturally present as an essential constituent of the healthy body) or foreign; in reference to which M. Orfila has proved that the metals which are naturally present in the various organs of the body are not removed from them by being boiled in water or acidulated water, whilst the same metals, when introduced as poisons, are dissolved by it.

In order to appreciate the symptoms and lesions produced by a poisonous substance, it is necessary to make experiments upon living animals; for which purpose the rabbit, and still oftener, the dog, are chiefly selected. In these experiments, the poisons are introduced into the stomach, or are applied to the denuded skin; in the first of which cases it is indispensable to tie the œsophagus, to prevent vomiting, an operation which is performed

A A 2

in two ways: either by a simple ligature, or by a ligature after opening the canal.

It has been incorrectly asserted that tying the œsophagus is of itself sufficient to cause the death of the animal, a statement to which M. Orfila has successfully replied. He has also proved that the conclusions drawn from the action of a poison do not necessarily receive any modification from a ligature upon the œsophagus; and we might ourselves mention several instances in support of this assertion. MM. Giacomini and Devergie have therefore done wrong in opposing this practice, without which it is impossible to ascertain the action of a poison.

Of imbibition.—Practitioners may be called upon to express an opinion upon the question of imbibition. It has been proved, in the present day, that substances when in solution may rise by imbibition to parts the most remote from those to which they were originally applied. The progress of the liquid is slow; and when introduced after death, either by the stomach or the anus, it does not cause the lesions which are observed in the living body; and it is only in the neighbouring organs, and in parts immediately in contact with the digestive canal, that it is possible to prove the presence of the poisonous substance.

OF INDIVIDUAL POISONS.

FIRST CLASS.

IRRITANT POISONS.

Every substance which, when applied to the tissues, inflames, corrodes, or destroys them, deserves the name of an irritant poison, but their mode of action and their activity vary according as they are applied externally or internally, as they are solid or dissolved in some liquid, and according to the fulness or emptiness of the stomach, &c.

Symptoms produced by irritant poisons generally.—These depend upon the lesions of the digestive canal, the nervous system and the organs of the circulation. All the parts attacked by the poison are the seat of constriction and of vivid inflammation, and there is intense pain throughout the whole digestive canal, nausea, and obstinate painful *vomiting*, which, as well as the *stools*, is sometimes *bloody*. There is great disturbance of the respiration and circulation, and insatiable thirst; dysuria and strangury; cold sweats at the approach of death, loss of the intellectual faculties, and distortion of the countenance.

Lesions.—The lesions of the tissues are undoubtedly the best proofs of irritant poisoning; but these lesions, though always considerable, vary with the nature of the poison taken, its degree of dilution, and the period during which it has acted. We shall describe these lesions in speaking of the individual poisons.

General treatment.—This should be such as we have already mentioned. Whilst speaking of the treatment of poisoning in general, we insisted upon abundant and tepid mucilaginous drinks; the nervous phenomena and the vomiting must be combated by opiates in small doses; and general and local bloodletting must be practised.

PHOSPHORUS.

Phosphorus, either in powder or solution, produces death when injected into the veins; and when administered by the stomach it acts more rapidly in proportion as it is more freely divided.

Symptoms and lesions. — We must consider these in two cases: 1. When the phosphorus has been administered in small portions or in powder, the *local* irritant action is considerable : but if, 2ndly, it has been given in solution, then the irritant action is less localized, but there is excitement of the nervous system, and especially of the genital organs. In large doses, it causes violent vomiting and the most severe nervous symptoms. When applied externally, it produces deep burns.

Treatment.—Tartar emetic, from gr. i. to gr. v. Mucilaginous drinks holding magnesia in suspension, the latter being intended to neutralize the acids produced by the oxidation of the phosphorus, whilst the fluid distends the stomach and favours vomiting. Lastly, recourse must be had to antiphlogistics.

Chemical examination.—All substances containing free phosphorus are luminous in the dark, and exhale a powerful odour of garlic; and when placed upon hot bodies, they give off white fumes of phosphoric acid. But it may happen that the phosphorus has been converted into phosphorous or hypophosphoric acid; these, when boiled in water, disengage phosphuretted hydrogen, which when inflamed, burns and gives off *dense white fumes of phosphoric acid.*

IODINE.

Symptoms and lesions.—Variable, according to the dose and the state in which it has been administered. Free iodine produces vomiting, alvine dejections, and extreme pain throughout the digestive canal, but chiefly in the stomach; intense thirst, convulsions, syncope, &c.

The fatal influence which tincture of iodine exerts over dogs has been attributed to the alcohol, but this tincture is a powerful caustic, as is proved by its employment in the treatment of hydrocele, (§. and by its sometimes causing vesication, and even a slough, when applied to parts where the skin is thin). The inflammation produced in these cases is of little danger, it is true; but it is not less true that, when administered internally, it is sufficient to cause severe accidents, and even death.

Iodine and its preparations are absorbed with extreme rapidity, even in two or three minutes, and they excite the lymphatic system and the organs of generation. When applied externally, iodine produces acute inflammation (§. and intense pain for about ten minutes), but not death; and when administered internally in a solid form, animals easily vomit it.

When applied to the skin, iodine produces yellow stains which may be confounded with those caused by nitric acid or saffron; but the stains from iodine disappear of themselves in a short time (§. from one day to a week); and *immediately if the skin is washed with a moderately weak solution of liquor potassæ;* whilst those caused by nitric acid only disappear with the loss of the cuticle, and those produced by yellow vegetable tinctures, as well as by the bile, are easily washed away by water.

Treatment.—Tepid solution of starch in great abundance; starch glysters, and afterwards, antiphlogistics and sedatives, &c.

Chemical examination.—Free iodine, when heated, is driven off in beautiful violet vapours, like those obtained from indigotine; but they are distinguished by the circumstance that the latter rise but very little into the atmosphere and are immediately condensed, whilst the vapour of iodine is more permanent, (§. even this is however condensed in less than a minute after the removal of the heat). Moreover, iodine is the only known body which gives a magnificent blue colour with (§. solution of) starch, and this iodide of starch loses its colour when heated to about 70° C. (158° F.), and regains its colour when it cools. Iodine is very soluble in alcohol, ether, and sulphuret of carbon, which latter it colours purple; and these liquids remove iodine from water.

If we wish to recognize iodine when previously combined, it is necessary to set it free by means of nitric, nitrous (§. or sulphuric)· acid, of binoxide of barium (§. or by chlorine); after which we may proceed with starch as above.

When we wish to obtain iodine from the viscera, we must boil them in water and a little solution of potash, by which operation iodide of potassium and a little iodate of potash are formed, and may be recognized by means of nitric acid and starch.

IODIDE OF POTASSIUM.

This salt is rapidly absorbed and may be found for some time in the blood, the milk, the urine and the viscera. When injected into the veins to the extent of three grains it rapidly produces death. We have, however, seen patients in whom the dose of iodide of potassium had been carried to 15 or 20 grms. (℥ss to ℥v) without inconvenience, so that this salt is not as poisonous as is generally supposed. As to the effect of iodine and the iodides in causing atrophy of the glands (§. mammæ and testicles), it is not so frequent as has been stated.

Treatment.—The same as for iodine, above.

Chemical examination.—The suspected matters are to be boiled in distilled water, and the solution (§. *when perfectly cold*) is to be treated with fuming nitric acid and cold solution of starch. In addition to this, the soluble iodides, and especially the iodide of potassium, precipitate the salts of *lead* of a *yellow* colour, the *proto*-salts of *mercury* of a *greenish yellow*, and the *bi*-salts of *mercury* of a beautiful *red*, which is soluble in an excess of the reagent. As to the potash, its presence may be recognized by means of chloric acid or tartaric acid in excess (§. if the solution is moderately strong).

BROMINE.

Bromine produces the same effects as iodine upon the animal system, (§. except that when applied undiluted to the skin it causes much more severe inflammation and vesication, which is not healed for several days).

Treatment.—The same as for iodine.

Chemical examination.—Bromine is a deep red liquid when seen by reflected light, or a hyacinth red by transmitted light; its odour resembles that of chloride of iodine, and its flavour is aromatic, resembling that of saffron. It boils at 47° C. (117° F.) and its vapour (§. which rises visibly even at common temperatures) supports the combustion of inflammable bodies. It is soluble in alcohol, ether and sulphuret of carbon, which it colours purple, and these liquids remove it from water. It destroys vegetable blue colours, converting them to yellow, and it also colours solution of starch yellow. It precipitates nitrate of silver, producing a yellowish bromide, which is more soluble in ammonia than iodide of silver. If the bromine is combined, it may be set free by heating the compound with bisulphate of potash. If we are engaged in proving its presence in a viscus, it must be boiled with potash, which forms bromide of potassium, in which it may be recognized by means of nitrate of silver, or the bromine may be set free by a current or solution of chlorine being passed into the solution.

CHLORINE.

When this gas is inspired, even in small quantity, it irritates the bronchi severely, and causes violent coughing, frequently accompanied by expectoration of blood. When introduced in a small dose into the stomach, it produces severe vomiting, with inflammation of the mucous membrane, and it acts like the mineral acids.

Treatment.—Kartner proposed the inhalation of ammonia, a plan which is more injurious than beneficial, and ought to be rejected. If the chlorine has been administered dissolved in water, the patient may drink albumen dissolved in water or milk, and inflammation must afterwards be treated by soothing and emollient remedies. If the gas has been inspired, the pharyngeal or trachæal inflammation must be treated by soothing gargles, and general or local blood-letting, &c.

Chemical examination.—Chlorine is a greenish-yellow gas of a peculiar suffocating odour, and it bleaches vegetable colours. One volume of water dissolves three volumes of chlorine, and the solution tarnishes silver leaf and precipitates nitrate of silver as a white curd. This precipitate is insoluble in water, and in nitric acid, either cold or boiling, but it is soluble in ammonia, and when exposed to light it becomes dark or violet coloured. Whenever free chlorine exists in the materials under examination, its presence may be detected by its decolorizing effect upon litmus; and when such substances are distilled with water, and the vapour is made to pass over paper impregnated with starch and iodide of potassium, a beautiful blue colour is produced, which disappears with excess of chlorine.

POISONING BY ACIDS.

Acids are divided into two classes as regards their action. 1. Those highly poisonous ones which are more active in proportion as they are more diluted, and, consequently more easily absorbed, such as hydrocyanic, hydrosulphuric, arsenic, arsenious, and oxalic acids; and, 2nd. Those, on the contrary, which only act by virtue of their concentration, and which may be taken with impunity when very dilute, viz.: sulphuric, nitric, hydrochloric, acetic and tartaric acid, &c.

CONCENTRATED, OR MODERATELY CONCENTRATED ACIDS.

Symptoms of poisoning.—Acid, acrid, burning taste; intense heat in the throat and stomach, and afterwards in the abdomen; nausea, and often bloody vomiting, the vomited matters effervescing upon the pavement; hiccough; constipation; or copious diarrhœa; the pulse strong and irregular; great thirst; rigors; cold, clammy sweats; difficulty in making water, and a livid countenance.

Lesions.—Acids produce variable lesions, according to their degree of concentration. When concentrated, they corrode all the tissues and produce perforation of the stomach; or else they irritate the nerves entering into the composition of the tissues, and occasion effusion into the peritoneal cavity, and the patient dies from intense peritonitis. If the acids are diluted, the inflammation is less intense.

Treatment and antidotes. —, Water must be administered abundantly, holding in suspension *calcined* magnesia, carbonate of magnesia, or chalk (carbonate of lime). In the absence of magnesia, soap and water, solutions of bicarbonate of potash or soda, milk, or the fixed oils, (olive, &c.)

The first intention in administering liquids in abundance, is to dilute the acid, and thereby render it less corrosive; and they also distend the stomach and assist vomiting. Lastly, the antidotes just mentioned neutralize the acids, and form salts which have no chemical influence upon the system.

The subsequent inflammation must be treated by emollients, administered internally, and also applied locally to the abdomen in the forms of poultice, baths and lotions, or fomentations. The strictest attention to diet must be observed, and sometimes we must have recourse to mild narcotics. Convalescence is always tedious. The patient must be nourished by chicken· or veal broth, and by amylaceous food, and it is of the greatest importance to insist for a long period upon a *very light* diet if we wish to repair the effects of the intense gastro-enteritis. The first solid food taken must be vegetable or animal jellies; and at a later period, fish, white meats, &c.

Chemical examination.—Even the most concentrated acids are absorbed when either administered internally or applied to the skin; but the absorption takes place more easily in proportion as they are more diluted. They must be sought for in the urine, the blood, and the different organs. In this last case, these organs must be boiled for a long time in water, and we must proceed as will be mentioned in speaking of each acid in particular.

When concentrated acids are applied externally, they corrode the tissues, and death is caused by the extreme inflammation of a large extent of skin, and the consequent reaction upon the nervous system. It has been thought that as the acids destroy the parts, and are themselves decomposed, absorption would be impossible, but the experiments of Orfila have taught us that, notwithstanding these circumstances, the acids do pass into the urine.

SULPHURIC ACID.

The black or grayish stains which are remarked upon parts touched by sulphuric acid, have been put forward as proofs of this acid having been the one employed; but as all concentrated acids *char* the tissues, this character is not really of importance. If, on the contrary, we remark *blue* stains upon different parts of the body, we shall have a clear proof of its employment, by its having dissolved the blue portion of the dye (indigo), if the sufferer has been wearing clothes dyed with that substance.

Symptoms, lesions and treatment.—See Acids in general, p. 361.

Chemical examination.—Sulphuric acid is recognized in the following manner. If we operate upon the urine or the vomited matters, they must be evaporated by heat to the consistence of an extract, and the residue agitated with concentrated alcohol, or better still, with sulphuric ether, which dissolves the *free* sulphuric *acid*, but *not* neutral, or even acid *sulphates*. If we are engaged upon solid matters, they must be boiled for a long time in pure distilled water, and the liquid evaporated to the consistence of an extract, and treated as above.

The alcoholic or ethereal solution is then to be evaporated at a very gentle heat; but we ought to observe that if the liquor is coloured, it must be diluted with water, and decolorized by animal charcoal (first digested in hydrochloric acid, and then thoroughly washed, so as to remove all adhering acid before it is used for this purpose). But this operation can only be performed upon *very dilute* liquids.

The solutions being evaporated, we obtain sulphuric acid more or less concentrated, which strongly reddens litmus; causes a white precipitate in the salts of baryta, which is *insoluble in any* known reagent, unless perhaps in sulphuric acid itself. This precipitate being washed and carefully dried, and then mixed with finely powdered vegetable charcoal, and heated to redness for some time, produces sulphuret of barium, which is to be removed by water and filtered. The solution, treated by acetic or any other acid, forms a salt of barytes, and disengages sulphuretted hydrogen, which is easily recognized by its smell, and by its burning with the formation of water and the deposition of sulphur or formation of sulphurous acid. (§. A more delicate test, and one more easily applied, consists in evaporating the solution nearly to dryness and placing a drop of it upon a piece of bright silver, when a brown or black stain of sulphuret of silver will soon be perceived. Another portion is to be placed in a test-tube, and the acetic acid added, and the tube choked up with a strip of blotting-paper, moistened with a solution of diacetate of lead, which is blackened by the sulphuretted hydrogen evolved. For the burning test above-mentioned, a much larger quantity of gas is requisite than for the lead-test).

Sulphuric acid causes a white precipitate in the salts of lead, which is blackened by sulphuretted hydrogen, and is soluble in tartrate of ammonia.

As these tests are not sufficient, a few drops of the concentrated liquid suspected of being sulphuric acid must in *every case* be put into a small test-tube with a little powdered copper, mercury, or charcoal. On heating them, we obtain sulphurous acid, which is easily recognized by its smell of burning sulphur, and by its action upon a slip of paper moistened with iodic acid and solution of starch, which becomes blue as soon as the sulphurous acid comes in contact with it.

If we are engaged upon the *blue* compound (of indigo) above-mentioned, we must proceed as we have already directed, taking care in the first instance to remove the colour from the solution by means of a stream of chlorine gas.

It may happen that the greater part of the sulphuric acid has been neutralized by the antidote (magnesia, &c.) administered; but experience has proved that there always remains a small quantity of free sulphuric acid; besides which we shall still have the proof arising from the symptoms and the lesions produced;

and we may, lastly, obtain the sulphate of magnesia, potash, or soda which has been formed.

Chemists are often called upon to prove the presence of (§. free) sulphuric acid in vinegar, in which case the vinegar must be evaporated to the consistence of an extract, and treated with ether as above directed. (§. It will not, in this case, answer to adopt the much easier plan of precipitating the sulphuric acid by a salt of barytes, and treating it as directed above; for the question is not whether sulphuric acid in any form, but whether *free* sulphuric acid is present. As vinegar is made with common water, which generally contains some sulphates, sulphuric acid is almost certain to be present from this source; but if it is not *free*, there is no presumption of its having been fraudulently introduced, the suspicion of which has given rise to the examination).

It has been suggested, in order to recognize the stains produced by sulphuric acid upon clothes, that they should be subjected to dry distillation, when sulphurous acid will be set free. This is true; but the author of the suggestion has forgotten that leather and cloths of various kinds contain either sulphuric acid or alum (*sulphate* of alumina and potash). It is better to digest them for a long time in ether, and then proceed as above. We may add, that as sulphuric acid attracts moisture from the air, the spots produced by it are always damp.

NITRIC, OR AZOTIC ACID.

Symptoms.—In cases of poisoning by this acid we almost always remark a *citron-yellow* colour of the tongue, the teeth, the lips, the chin, and the fingers, &c.; and the stains only disappear with the separation of the cuticle.

Lesions of the tissues.—Nitric acid inflames, corrodes and destroys all the tissues with which it comes in contact, even when it is diluted with water, and it is capable of causing perforations. The yellow stains which we have just mentioned are sometimes formed in the stomach, where they are distinguished from marks produced by bile, by their being permanent, whilst the latter are removed when washed with water.

Treatment.—See General Treatment, p. 362.

Chemical examination. — The vomited matters, and those

contained in the digestive canal, and the intestinal tube itself, and all the organs in which we wish to search for the presence of this acid, are to be treated with cold distilled water, several times renewed. The liquors are then to be boiled in a porcelain dish to coagulate the animal matters; then filtered and neutralized by potash dissolved in alcohol. The solution is then to be evaporated nearly to dryness, and the remaining liquid introduced into a glass retort, and treated with sulphuric acid, previously boiled with sulphate of ammonia, in order to remove the nitrous compounds which it frequently contains, and afterwards diluted with half its weight of water. The retort is then to be heated, and the nitric acid collected in a receiver.

Or we may boil the different solid materials in water, with the addition of a little pure carbonate of potash, filter the solution, and evaporate it until a pellicle forms upon the surface. By this process we obtain carbonate of potash, which does not crystallize, and crystals of nitrate of potash, which fuse and scintillate upon burning coals, and which, when heated in a test-tube with some copper filings and sulphuric acid diluted with its own weight of water, give off fumes of nitrous *gas*, (§. which become red nitrous *acid* in the tube on mixing with the oxygen of the air contained in it). We may operate in the same way to recognize the presence of nitrate of potash, soda, or magnesia, when their carbonates have been employed as antidotes.

Nitric acid, when free, may be recognized by the yellow colour which it gives to organic matters, and by reddening morphia and brucia; (§. but for all these tests, except the last, it must be moderately concentrated). When mixed with a little hydrochloric acid, it dissolves gold leaf. If heated with copper, it gives off binoxide of nitrogen (nitrous *gas*), which is transformed into brownish-red vapours (nitrous *acid*) by contact with the air. The quantity of these fumes is sometimes so small that the eye cannot distinguish them; in which case they may be made to pass over paper moistened with solution of morphia or sulphate of narcotine, which becomes red, or with iodic acid and starch, which becomes blue; or better still, the gas may be made to pass into a *green* solution of protosulphate (§. green sulphate) of iron, which assumes a burnt coffee colour by the smallest bubble of binoxide of nitrogen or of hyponitrous acid, the brown colour becoming purple by a great excess of sulphuric acid.

If we are engaged in examining the stains of nitric acid upon the clothes, they must be boiled with a little potash, and treated as above directed.

HYDROCHLORIC OR CHLOROHYDRIC* ACID.

This acid, extensively used in commerce, where it bears the name of *muriatic acid* or *spirit of salt*, is one of the most energetic of mineral acids. It corrodes, destroys, and inflames the tissues.

. **Symptoms, lesions and treatment.** — See Acids generally, p. 361.

Chemical examination.—The vomited matters, and the contents of the intestinal canal, with the organs themselves, are to be submitted to distillation in a retort, after having first proved their acidity by litmus. The hydrochloric acid, mixed with water, is condensed in the receiver, and care must be taken to distil nearly to dryness, and to add water to the retort in proportion as it evaporates. The liquid contained in the cooled receiver gives off thick white fumes when a glass rod, dipped in ammonia, is brought near it ; it causes a white curdy precipitate with nitrate of silver, which is *insoluble in water or boiling nitric acid,* but is dissolved by solution of ammonia. The distilled fluid, when saturated with potash dissolved in alcohol and evaporated to dryness, yields a residue, which when distilled with sulphuric acid, gives off white fumes of hydrochloric acid, and yellowish-green fumes of chlorine if peroxide of manganese is added to the mixture previous to the application of heat. Lastly, hydrochloric acid precipitates the proto-salts of mercury white, and when mixed with a little nitric acid it dissolves gold leaf.

OXALIC ACID.

Poisoning by this acid, which is very rare in France, has become very frequent in England, which is owing to the circumstance that it is extensively used in trade, and is often mistaken for Epsom salts (sulphate of magnesia). Oxalic acid is poisonous, and *is so much more active in proportion as it has been administered in a copious amount of fluid.*

(§. * See note, p. 82.)

Symptoms.—The first symptom which manifests itself is a burning heat in the throat and œsophagus, followed by vomitings of a dark colour, and sometimes bloody, but these do not invariably occur. The nervous system is almost always affected, and the patients experience numbness, formication of the extremities, and sometimes convulsions, so that the symptoms approach those produced by strychnine, from which it is distinguished by its corrosive action and its effect upon the heart.

Lesions.—When highly concentrated oxalic acid corrodes and destroys the tissues which it touches, and it often produces perforations of the stomach and intestines. When diluted with water, it neither affects the brain nor the abdominal viscera, but the lungs exhibit red spots, and the heart loses its contractility immediately after death, when the animal dies without previous insensibility. If, on the contrary, death is preceded by a comatose state, the heart continues to beat a few moments after respiration has ceased; and in this case, the blood is black in both the arterial and venous systems, whilst in the former case the blood in the right side of the heart is black, and that in the left side red. In a word, oxalic acid exerts its influence first upon the spinal marrow, then upon the brain, and later still, upon the lungs and heart. Death is owing either to paralysis of the heart, or to asphyxia, or to both these causes united.

Treatment.—See Acids in general, p. 362; but carbonate of potash or soda must not be used unless it is unavoidable; as the oxalate of these alkalies is nearly as poisonous as oxalic acid itself.

Chemical examination.—Oxalic acid crystallizes in colourless prisms, terminated by dihedral summits, and possesses a powerfully acid taste. When heated, it is decomposed at about 115° C. (240° F.) into carbonic oxide, carbonic acid, water, and a little formic acid. When acted upon by concentrated sulphuric acid, it is converted into carbonic oxide and carbonic acid. It dissolves in water with a slight crackling; it is less soluble in cold alcohol, but it dissolves more freely in boiling alcohol.

The aqueous solution of oxalic acid precipitates all the salts of lime without distinction. The white precipitate is insoluble in excess of oxalic acid, whilst it readily dissolves in acetic, and still more freely in nitric acid. Oxalic acid, when dissolved in water, produces a white precipitate with nitrate of silver which is soluble in nitric acid; and this precipitate, when dried and heated with care (§. on platinum foil), first blackens at the edges, and then slightly detonates, giving off pure carbonic acid, and leaving metallic silver behind (§. in the form of a brownish or gray powder.

Oxalic acid is absorbed, and has been found in the urine, but not in the liver or spleen; either because it is converted into an insoluble oxalate, or rather because it remains so short a time in these organs.

If we are engaged in proving the presence of *free* oxalic acid in a liquid, we must evaporate it to dryness, and add boiling alcohol, which will dissolve the free acid, but will leave the oxalates undissolved. If, on the contrary, we are operating upon solid matters (the liver, the spleen, the lungs or stomach, &c.), we must cut them into small pieces, and boil them in pure distilled water; and the decoction must afterwards be heated with alcohol as we have just mentioned.

In cases in which we wish to prove the presence of oxalic acid, when magnesia or lime has been given as an antidote, the operation will be rather more complicated. We must first collect the precipitate, and boil it for some time with a concentrated solution of carbonate of potash, by which means carbonate of magnesia and oxalate of potash will be formed, and may be recognized by the means above indicated.

POISONING BY THE DIFFERENT VEGETABLE ACIDS.

Poisoning by the vegetable acids, such as the tartaric, citric and acetic, &c., is so rare, that we shall content ourselves with simply mentioning the characters which serve to prove the presence of these acids. In other respects, the treatment of these poisons is the same as that for acids generally.

TARTARIC ACID.

Tartaric acid is obtained from bitartrate of potash, which is itself deposited from wines in proportion as they are rich in alcohol. Tartaric acid most frequently crystallizes in regular hexahedral prisms, and it strongly reddens litmus. When heated, whilst dry, it does not begin to volatilize like oxalic acid, but it quickly decomposes, blackens, swells up, and gives off an odour of burnt sugar and acid vapours, leaving a spongy charcoal behind. It is soluble in water, and the solution precipitates the salts of lime with an organic acid, but not the sulphate, which is precipitated by oxalic acid. The precipitate of tartrate of lime is soluble in nitric acid, and in an excess of tartaric acid; and lastly, tartaric acid forms double salts, like the sel de Seignette (potassio-tartrate of soda) and tartar emetic; all which characters are sufficient to distinguish it from oxalic acid.

CITRIC ACID.

This acid crystallizes in rhomboidal prisms; it has a very acid flavour, reddens litmus, and is decomposed by heat, like tartaric acid. It does not precipitate limewater, except when boiled with it.

ACETIC ACID.

Concentrated acetic acid quickly occasions death when introduced into the stomach. It is capable of perforating the coats of the digestive canal, and it colours the mucus of the stomach and intestines—an effect which is not owing to the action of the acid upon the tissues, but is *purely the result of the chemical action exerted by acetic acid upon the blood.* Vinegar, which is a mixture of acetic acid, water and various salts, produces the same effects as acetic acid itself, but in a slighter degree.

Treatment.—See Acids generally, p. 362.

Chemical examination.—When we wish to prove the presence of free acetic acid, it is sufficient to distil the suspected matters with water; but if the acid has been combined with magnesia—for example, when this has been administered as an antidote—we must add sulphuric acid to the liquid, and distil it. The fluid obtained by distillation is then to be neutralized by pure carbonate of soda; and by evaporating the solution, acetate of soda may be obtained in crystals, which, when distilled with sulphuric acid, will yield pure acetic acid, recognized by its odour. We may now neutralize this acetic acid with pure carbonate of potash, so as to obtain an acetate, which, when distilled dry,

along with arsenious acid, will yield by the distillation Cadet's
fuming solution (alcarsine—oxide of kakodyle), the odour of
which is so characteristic (§. offensive), that it is impossible to
mistake it for anything else.

POISONING BY THE OXIDES OF THE METALS OF THE FIRST TWO CLASSES, AND THEIR SALTS.

POTASH—SODA.

These two oxides are energetic poisons. When introduced
into the veins, they cause death, by coagulating the blood; and
when taken into the stomach, they corrode and destroy all the
parts with which they come in contact. When very dilute, they
are rapidly absorbed.

Treatment.—Water, slightly acidulated with vinegar, must be
copiously administered, so as to neutralize the alkali, and assist
vomiting. Albuminous or mucilaginous liquids must be afterwards administered; and the irritation excited by the poison
must be allayed by the ordinary means.

AMMONIA.

Ammonia and its salts, especially the hydrochlorate (sal-ammoniac), are energetic poisons, and their action is exerted upon the
nervous system, but chiefly upon the stomach, which becomes the
seat of violent inflammation.

Treatment.—The same as for potash; but in the case of
ammoniacal salts, and those of potash and soda (§. except the
carbonates), it is useless to administer acidulated water; and we
must content ourselves with soothing the local inflammation and
the nervous system by antiphlogistics and opiates; and we must
always promote vomiting.

Chemical examination.—We must endeavour to isolate the
poisonous substance by means of alcohol, or by repeated crystal-
lizations, if the salt is crystallizable. If we are engaged upon
ammonia, and are operating upon putrid materials, we must

remember that ammonia is developed during putrefaction, and that this alkali may be found in the state of carbonate, or even of hydrochlorate, as has been proved by M. Chevalier. We shall content ourselves with pointing out the chemical characters of these three classes of salts:

TESTS ADDED.	SALTS OF POTASH.	SALTS OF SODA.	SALTS OF AMMONIA.
POTASH . .	No effect.	No effect.	Disengages ammoniacal gas, which is characterized by its odour, by restoring the blue colour to litmus paper reddened by an acid, and by giving off dense white fumes on contact with a glass rod dipped in hydrochloric acid.
SULPHATE OF ALUMINA, CHLORIC ACID, TARTARIC ACID, in excess.	White precipitate.	No effect.	White precipitate.
BICHLORIDE OF PLATINUM .	Granular yellow precipitate.	No effect in moderately dilute solutions.	Granulated yellow precipitate, even in dilute solutions.
ANTIMONIATE OF POTASH .	No effect.	White precipitate.	No effect.

LIME, STRONTIAN, BARYTES.

These three bodies belong to the class of alkaline earths; and their salts, especially those of barytes, irritate the parts which they touch. They are absorbed, and act upon the nervous system, especially upon the spinal marrow; and according to Brodie, upon the heart. Their presence can be proved in parts the most remote from those with which they were placed in contact.

Symptoms.—The salts of these earths, but especially those of barytes, when administered in small doses, produce nausea, frequent vomiting, vertigo and intermitting convulsions: the respiration is suspended for several moments, and the pupil is generally dilated.

Treatment.—Vomiting must be promoted, and sulphate of soda, dissolved in a large quantity of water, must be administered. Irritation must be soothed by means of antiphlogistics.

Chemical examination.—Poisoning by these substances being extremely rare, we shall content ourselves with giving the characters of the salts of lime, barytes and strontian:

TESTS ADDED.	SALTS OF BARYTES.	SALTS OF LIME.	SALTS OF STRONTIAN.
POTASH	White precipitate, soluble in excess of water.	Gelatinous white precipitate.	White precipitate, soluble in excess of water.
CARBONATED ALKALIES	White precipitate.	White precipitate.	White precipitate.
SULPHURIC ACID and SOLUBLE SULPHATES	White precipitate, insoluble in any known reagent.	White precipitate, if the solution is a concentrated one.	White precipitate, but no precipitate in a very dilute solution.
CHROMATE OF POTASH	Yellow precipitate, soluble in an excess of acid.	No effect.	No effect in a dilute solution.
HYDROFLUO-SILICIC ACID.	Crystalline white precipitate	No effect.	No effect.
PHOSPHATE OF SODA.	White precipitate, soluble in nitric acid.	White precipitate.	White precipitate.
HYDROSULPHATE OF AMMONIA	No precipitate.	No effect.	No effect.
PERCHLORIC ACID	Ditto.	Ditto.	Ditto.
FERROCYANIDE OF POTASSIUM	Ditto.	Ditto.	Ditto.
OXALIC ACID and OXALATE OF AMMONIA	Ditto.	White precipitate, insoluble in acetic acid, but soluble in nitric acid.	The salts of strontian are soluble in alcohol; and the solution, when inflamed, burns with a beautiful red or purple colour.

LIVER OF SULPHUR. (SULPHURET OF POTASSIUM.)

Liver of sulphur is a substance the composition of which varies according to a multitude of circumstances. It is most frequently a mixture of quinte-sulphuret of potassium and sulphate of potash. The following remarks will apply to quinte-sulphuret of sodium, and even, to a certain extent, to hydrosulphate of ammonia, and to the sulphurets of barium, calcium and strontium.

The offensive odour of rotten eggs, which the sulphurets give off, removes all idea of these preparations being used for purposes of homicide; but we have often seen persons poisoned by them in consequence of mistakes in their administration as medicines.

The soluble sulphurets are absorbed and carried into all parts of the system. They act like the most irritant poisons, the acids of the stomach decomposing them, and disengaging sulphuretted hydrogen, with the deposition of sulphur. When the acids are abundant in the stomach, the evolution of sulphuretted hydrogen is such, that death may take place immediately, in consequence of this gas being introduced into the blood by means of eructations (see poisoning by hydrosulphuric acid); but if the acids are in smaller quantity, death takes place more slowly. They are then absorbed, and the fatal result must be attributed to the narcotic influence which they exert upon the nervous system, after having been absorbed.

Treatment.—To excite vomiting, to administer emollient draughts, and to abate inflammation by means of antiphlogistics.

Chemical examination.—The odour given off by liver of sulphur and the soluble sulphurets suffices to discover their presence. A piece of paper, moistened with solution of acetate of lead, becomes black immediately upon being plunged into the sulphuret. The suspected materials may be heated in a retort with some acid; and the gas which is disengaged, being passed into a solution of acetate of lead, a black precipitate will be formed.

POISONING BY ARSENIC.

Arsenic is a body which has long been reckoned amongst the metals, but is now classed (§. by some chemists) in the group of metalloids, on account of the property which it possesses of forming acids with oxygen, and of combining with hydrogen. It requires very careful description, because, in all medico-legal researches upon the different arsenical compounds, it is our duty to obtain the arsenic pure; in which state it presents itself under three different forms, viz., in *mass*, in *rings*, and as mere *stains*. Under these three aspects its chemical properties are the same, though its physical characters are different.

METALLIC ARSENIC.

In Mass.

Description and chemical properties.—Metallic arsenic is solid, of a steel-gray colour, of a granular, or scaly texture, and glistening when freshly prepared; very friable, insipid, slightly odorous when rubbed, volatile; it can be sublimed, and it crystallizes in octohedra; when heated, it flies off in dark fumes, accompanied with an odour of garlic, and the vapour is converted into white arsenious acid by contact with the oxygen of the air. When acted upon by nitric acid, binoxide of nitrogen is given off, and arsenic acid is formed, if the action of the nitric acid has been sufficiently prolonged. This arsenic acid dissolves in water, and a concentrated solution of it precipitates nitrate of silver as a *brick-red* arseniate of silver. The same solution, when treated by sulphur*ous* acid, and afterwards by pure hydrosulphuric acid, assumes a yellow colour, and throws down a precipitate of *yellow sulphuret of arsenic* (§. *sesqui*sulphuret, or *ter*sulphuret of arsenic, orpiment) on the addition of a drop of hydrochloric acid. This yellow precipitate is soluble in solution of ammonia, forming a colourless solution; and when heated in a tube with *black flux* (a mixture of charcoal and carbonate of potash), it yields metallic arsenic under the form of a ring.

In Rings.

The arsenical ring possesses the same chemical properties as metallic arsenic in mass. When heated, it is volatilized, which is not the case with other metallic stains; at least not with the same facility. This ring is easily produced by heating a glass tube through which *arseniuretted* hydrogen is passing; in which case the ring is formed a *little in front of the heated point*; whilst if the gas is *antimoniated* hydrogen, the ring is formed in the part of the tube to which the heat is applied.

In Stains or Spots.

Arsenical stains present precisely the same chemical properties as arsenic in mass or in rings; and though some authors have asserted the contrary, we lay stress upon the fact. But their physical aspect is very different; and we think it necessary, therefore, to exhibit in this place the distinctive characters of all the stains which can be confounded with those of metallic arsenic.

DISTINCTIVE CHARACTER OF VARIOUS METALLIC AND OTHER STAINS.

Arsenical stains are of a *brown* colour, and very brilliant, and like a mirror, if the layer is *thin*, but of a *darker* and less glistening appearance if the deposit is *thick*, and of a canary yellow if they are mixed with organic matters or with sulphuret of arsenic. They do not disappear in the cold, but they are volatilized by the action of heat. When treated with pure and concentrated nitric acid, they instantly disappear, leaving upon the surface of the liquid some portions of the metal, which only dissolve on the application of heat. The solution, when gently and carefully heated, leaves a white residue; which, when treated with a concentrated solution of nitrate of silver, gives a *brick-red* precipitate of *arseniate* of silver; but in order that this experiment may succeed, it is necessary to allow the solution to cool, to employ only a *few* drops of very pure nitric acid, to use a *concentrated* solution of nitrate of silver, and not to raise the temperature. The arsenical stains, when dissolved in nitric acid, and evaporated to dryness, produce arsenic acid, which, if treated by a few drops of sulphur*ous* acid in the first instance, and then by hydrosulphuric acid (§. is converted into arseni*ous* acid), yields a *canary-yellow* sulphuret of arsenic, which *is soluble in ammonia*, and forms a colourless solution; and it also yields a metallic ring, if mixed with dry, black flux, and heated in a test-tube. Lastly, arsenical stains are soluble in *chloride of soda* (hypochlorite of soda); whilst antimonial stains are not soluble in this reagent.

Antimonial stains are more (§. sooty) black than arsenical ones if they are thick, and are of a tawny brown (§. not clear and glistening, like arsenic) when they are thin. They do not attract moisture from the air, or disappear in the cold. When heated, they disappear with great difficulty, and leave a residue of white oxide of antimony, which is not volatile. Nitric acid instantly dissolves them; but the solution, when evaporated, leaves a *yellowish* white residue of antimoniate of protoxide of antimony (Fremy), which does *not* produce a *brick-red* precipitate in a concentrated solution of nitrate of silver. The residue from the treatment of nitric acid, when placed in contact with hydrochloric acid, dissolves, and the solution, when treated with hydrosulphuric acid, produces an *orange*-yellow precipitate, which is *not* soluble in *ammonia.* Lastly, antimonial stains are not soluble in chloride (hypochlorite) of soda, like those of arsenic. As, however, these two kinds of stain have some resemblance to each other, we shall give a recapitulation of their distinctive characters :

TESTS.	ARSENICAL STAINS.	ANTIMONIAL STAINS.
(§. APPEARANCE AND COLOUR)	(§. Bright, glistening brown colour, where the margin becomes thin.)	(§. Dark, *sooty-black* stain, not bright brown at the margin.)
HEATED BY THE FLAME OF PURE HYDROGEN .	Disappear rapidly.	Disappear with difficulty, and leave a residue of oxide of antimony.
CHLORIDE OF SODA (HYPOCHLORITE) . .	Dissolve instantly.	Do not dissolve.
ALCOHOLIC TINCTURE OF IODINE	Dissolve after some time.	Dissolve with more difficulty, and leave a red stain.
WATERY SOLUTION OF IODINE. . . .	Solution very evident.	Solution almost entirely absent.
IODIDE OF POTASSIUM AND IODINE . .	Do not dissolve.	Dissolve immediately.

These characters suffice in the main to distinguish these two kinds of stain; and the additional proofs by nitric and hydrosulphuric acid furnish very precise distinguishing characters.

Poisoning by arsenious acid being that which is most frequently practised, we think it desirable to point out the characters of other stains, which may possibly be confounded with those produced by arsenic; but before doing so, we must say a few words upon mixed stains, *i. e.* upon those which are produced by a mixture of arsenic and antimony—in the case of a patient who, being poisoned by arsenious acid, has taken tartar emetic to produce vomiting.

Stains of antimony and arsenic.—It is evident that the appearance of these stains will vary in proportion to the amount of arsenic or antimony which they contain. If they are heated by the flame of pure hydrogen, the arsenic disappears, and the antimony remains; chloride of soda (Labarraque's solution) produces the same separation; and lastly, nitric acid, which dissolves both species of stain, produces a solution which yields, when evaporated, and boiled in distilled water, a solution of arsenious acid, and leaves a residue of antimoniate of oxide of antimony; by which, and by the characters above given, they may be distinguished from one another.

Zinc stains are produced when we employ Marsh's apparatus with *hydrochloric* (§. instead of sulphuric) acid; for the chloride of zinc which is formed being volatile, is easily carried up (§. with the hydrogen evolved). They may also be shown when sulphuric acid is used, if the action is very violent, on which account it is that we are advised to put into the leg of the apparatus in which the hydrogen is set free, pieces of asbestos or powdered china, in order to hinder the zinc from being mechanically carried up. The zinc stains have scarcely any resemblance to those of arsenic; but they may be easily distinguished by the circumstance, that when exposed to the air, they disappear even in the *cold*, and leave a residue of oxide of zinc. When treated with nitric acid, they disappear, and the solution, when evaporated, does *not* produce a *brick-red* precipitate with nitrate of silver, but forces a white precipitate with hydrosulphuric acid (sulphuret of zinc). See characters of the salts of zinc.

Iron stains.—The existence of ferruret of hydrogen, announced by M. Dupasquier, is contradicted; so that it is an exception when stains of iron form, by the use of Marsh's apparatus, either with iron alone, or with zinc containing a large proportion of iron. These stains are reddish-gray, and become red (sesquioxide of iron, rust) on exposure to the air. When heated, they do not disappear. Nitric acid dissolves them, and the solution presents the characters of the salts of iron.

Lead stains have a bluish-gray aspect, and do not disappear by heat. Nitric acid dissolves them, and forms white nitrate of lead, which is precipitated white by potash, yellow by iodide of potassium, white by sulphuric acid and the soluble sulphates, and black by sulphuretted hydrogen.

Stains arising from the earthenware itself.—The (French) Institute has properly forbidden the use of earthenware plates for receiving the arsenical stains ; because if the current of hydrogen is strong, the lead or the tin in the glaze may be reduced to the metallic state. But it is easy to distinguish these stains from those produced by arsenic, as we have just seen. (§. This objection does not apply to fine china or Berlin ware, which is not glazed with either lead or tin : it only refers to the commoner kinds of earthenware.)

Pseudo-stains.—Under this name, MM. Orfila, Danger and Flandin have brought before our notice the stains which are produced when the remains of animal matters, ammoniacal sulphites or phosphites are present in Marsh's apparatus. According to MM. Fordos and Gélis, these stains are produced by sulphur or charcoal. They are generally of a duller aspect than those from arsenic, and they either do not disappear at all, or do so with great difficulty by the action of heat or nitric acid ; and if they are at length dissolved by the acid, the solution is not precipitated by nitrate of silver or hydrosulphuric acid.

Phosphoric stains.—These are produced with great difficulty, and vary in their appearance according to their thickness, being citron-yellow, yellow, orange or red. Heat dissipates them, and nitric acid dissolves them ; and they are also readily transformed by the air alone into phosphorus and phosphoric acid ; they also attract moisture from the air. When dissolved in dilute nitric acid, they throw down a *yellow* precipitate from nitrate of silver ; and when treated with hydrosulphuric acid, they do *not* form a *yellow* sulphuret which is dissolved by ammonia with the loss of colour.

Sulphur stains are yellow, and do not dissolve in nitric acid when cold ; but by the aid of continued heat they form sulphuric acid, which is easily recognized by its own characters.

Iodine stains present a yellow aspect; and when dissolved in alcohol, they colour a cold solution of starch-blue.

Is metallic arsenic poisonous?—Notwithstanding the opinion put forward by M. Orfila in his "Traité de Toxicologie," our own experiments have induced us to return to the old opinion, and to admit that arsenic is only poisonous because it is easily converted into arsenious acid in the animal system; so that we shall refer to our future remarks upon arsenious acid for the treatment and the chemical investigations necessary for proving the presence of this body, and shall content ourselves here with mentioning the experiments upon which we found our opinion.

M. Lepetit, pharmaceutist at Caen, in the first instance, and after him M. Reveil, gave to a dog 4 grammes (ʒi) of pure, brilliant and freshly prepared arsenic. The animal, whose œsophagus was tied, died on the third day, after having exhibited the symptoms of poisoning by arsenious acid. The same dose of arsenic, mixed with 200 grammes (ʒvi) of hydrated peroxide of iron diffused in water, was given to another dog, and did not produce any severe injury, the ligature being removed from the œsophagus at the end of the fourth day. The animal passed, by stool, peroxide of iron in well formed fœcal masses, in which the presence of metallic arsenic was easily recognized. This experiment was repeated, with magnesia as an antidote, and gave the same results; and lastly, the same dog was killed by 2 grammes (ʒss) of brilliant, washed arsenic, the animal, as in the former case, having given way with all the symptoms of poisoning by arsenious acid. It is therefore indisputable that death results from the conversion of the metallic arsenic into a soluble compound; and what should this be, if it is not arsenious acid?

POISONING BY ARSENIOUS ACID.

(WHITE OXIDE OF ARSENIC).

We shall here treat simply of poisoning by arsenious acid, for the natural sulphurets (orpiment, realgar) are of little danger, owing to their insolubility; whilst the artificial yellow sulphuret (artificial orpiment) contains, according to M. Guibourt, nearly 94 per cent of arsenious acid, and therefore acts almost exactly like arsenious acid itself. As to arsenic acid and the arseniates, they are more active than arsenious acid; but they are rarely the cause of poisoning, owing to the difficulty of obtaining them; whilst arsenious acid figures in two-thirds of all the poisonings committed with criminal intentions.

This great number is explained by the facility with which it can be obtained, as it is employed by glass makers, shot manufacturers and calico printers, and it enters into the composition of Bécœur's soap, which is employed by naturalists for preserving stuffed animals. Papers stained green contain arsenite of copper (Scheele's green); and in agriculture, the grain intended for sowing is sprinkled with arsenious acid. Lastly, the poison is employed in domestic use for killing rats; and its want of colour, and almost entire absence of taste, and its energetic action, explain the preference given by poisoners to this deadly substance.

It is much to be wished that the law should regulate in the strictest manner the sale of arsenious acid. It would prevent many cases of poisoning, if dealers were obliged to colour the acid with Prussian blue, and to give it a very bitter flavour by means of aloes or colocynth.*

Signs of poisoning; physiological effects.—In whatever way arsenious acid is introduced into the animal system, it exerts the same deleterious influence, and produces the same symptoms, only they are more or less violent, and appear sooner, or more slowly, in some cases than in others. It always increases most of the secretions, diminishes the contractility of the voluntary muscles, and produces convulsions, prostration, and death. It only acts after being absorbed, and the more rapid the absorption the more intense the symptoms; but it sometimes produces no bad consequences when introduced into the stomach in the form of powder, in consequence of its being rejected in the first vomiting excited by it. In addition to the above properties, arsenious acid is a *diamorphous*† body; when freshly prepared it has a glassy appearance, and is sufficiently soluble in water; but at a later period it becomes opaque, and less soluble, from which we may imagine that the first of these two acids will act rapidly, and with the most activity; and it is also evident, that this poison will

(§. * See Appendix.)

(§. † Δις, dis, twice; μορφη, morphe, form; a body capable of forming two distinct crystalline forms.)

operate more decidedly in proportion as the solution in which it is employed is diluted.

Symptoms.—The first symptoms do not generally show themselves, until some hours after the poison has been swallowed. They are at first *nausea*, and *vomiting* of mucus, which is sometimes bloody; then anxiety, and a sense of *burning heat* in the stomach come on, and extreme *thirst* with constriction of the œsophagus; what is drunk is vomited again, and violent colic and *diarrhœa supervene*. The pulse is generally hard, and the heart's action tumultuous; the respiration difficult and panting; abundant cold, clammy sweats, followed by itching and eruptions on the skin. Violent convulsions often succeed, followed by great prostration of strength, which induces a deceitful calm. At the approach of death the heart's action abates, the skin is covered with a cold sweat, and the sufferer dies with extreme exhaustion. It may be added, that the progress of the illness is modified by the dose of the poison, and the way in which it has been administered.

Lesions produced by arsenious acid.—Very vivid redness of the mouth, œsophagus, and *stomach :* the vessels of the latter are highly injected, and there are frequently ecchymoses; the inflammation extends throughout the small intestines, and even to the rectum; but the lesions vary according as the poison has remained a longer or shorter time in any particular part. The lungs are gorged with blood, and the mucous membrane of the trachæa is reddened. The heart presents internally deep red, almost black stains, and the right cavities generally contain much blood. The nervous system is not affected; but sometimes the vessels which ramify upon the surface of the brain are gorged with blood.

It is important to be upon our guard against the presence of small rounded brilliant grains, which have been taken for arsenious acid, but which seem to be formed of fatty matters, mixed with a peculiar animal substance.

In conclusion we may add, that arsenious acid appears to localise itself in the more vascular secreting organs, in which it remains for a long time; but in the end, it is expelled either by the urine or by the other excretions. When applied externally, it is so much more easily absorbed, as the tissue upon which it is placed communicates more directly with the sanguineous system. When injected into the veins, it is more active than when introduced into the stomach, the rectum, or the vagina. When applied upon the sound and healthy skin it is absorbed with difficulty, and when placed upon the nervous tissue it does not produce any effect. The action of arsenious acid is generally *sthenic*, notwithstanding the contrary assertion of some authors who have classed it with the asthenica, or hyposthenisants.

Treatment of poisoning by arsenious acid.—If vomiting has commenced it must be promoted by tickling the throat, and administering a large quantity of gelatinous hydrated peroxide of iron, or the same oxide reduced to powder, and mixed with a large quantity of sugar and water. If vomiting has not commenced, which is rare, it must be excited by administering from 8 to 15 grains of sulphate of zinc, or ipecacuanha, and tickling the throat. We may give as much as 16 ounces of the hydrated peroxide. If the poison has been given several hours previously, and we suppose that it may have passed through the pylorus, we may administer a purgative glyster if there is constipation, and after having thus favoured the expulsion of the poison, and administered an antidote for the portion which cannot be evacuated, we must endeavour to procure the elimination of the portion which has been absorbed; for which purpose we must give *diuretics* and *sudorifics* in abundance, e. g. white wine and nitrate of potash mixed with sedlitz water. Lastly, we must combat the irritation which has been produced by emollients, sedatives, and general or local bleeding, which cannot be practised before this late period without danger.

M. Rognetta advises sthenic (stimulant or tonic) treatment, going upon the theory of arsenic being asthenic, and he therefore orders wine and brandy along with beef-tea, &c. Without saying more upon this mode of treatment, we may remark that it is injurious rather than useful.

ANTIDOTES FOR POISONING BY ARSENIOUS ACID.

We must now add a few words upon the various antidotes which have been proposed for this poison.

Hydrosulphuric acid, and alkaline sulphurets.—The solution of this acid in water is not of much use, but it may be taken without inconvenience; but the same cannot be said of the alkaline sulphurets, which precipitate arsenious acid it is true, but are at the same time very energetic irritant poisons themselves.

Charcoal.—Charcoal mixed with water has been proposed by M. Bertrand; but reason would say beforehand, that it cannot at all diminish the action of arsenious acid, and experience confirms this opinion.

Lime-water.—When mixed with milk, has been recommended by Navier. It only acts when arsenious acid is dissolved, and even then imperfectly.

Colcothar (anhydrous peroxide of iron).—Entirely without effect upon arsenious acid, and therefore useless.

Hydrated (gelatinous) sesquioxide or peroxide of iron.— This was proposed by Bunzen; and is one of the best antidotes for arsenious acid, if we take care to administer it before the poison is absorbed. It forms arsenite of iron which is insoluble, and without action upon the system. MM. Guibourt, Nonat, Deville, and Sandras, judiciously prefer the same oxide when *dry*, and reduced to powder, and mixed with water.

It is important to remember, that commercial peroxide of iron often contains arseniate of iron, which being insoluble is not poisonous, but may still give rise to serious errors in case the patient dies, and a medico-legal investigation is instituted; in which case the arsenic contained in the antidote would complicate the results. It is necessary, therefore, for the chemist to prove that there was no arsenic present in the peroxide of iron used as the antidote. It is very easy to obtain the peroxide free from arsenic, by adopting the process directed by M. Legrip, which consists in passing a current of sulphuretted hydrogen through the solution of sulphate of iron intended to furnish the

c c

peroxide, by which means the arsenic is precipitated as sulphuret and the iron is not affected.

Sulphurets of Iron.—MM. Bourchardat and Sandras advise the hydrated persulphuret of iron, and M. Mialhe prefers the protosulphuret of the same metal. Indeed, according to this last-named chemist—what is called hydrated *per*sulphuret of iron is only a mixture of *proto*sulphuret and sulphur. However this may be, these sulphurets rapidly decompose arsenious acid, and we very willingly adopt this antidote because it is of the most general character; that is to say, it acts upon nearly all the poisonous metals. Now, it may easily happen, that we are not certain about the nature of the poison, and it is evident that we should gain nothing by using peroxide of iron in poisoning by a salt of lead, and that the soluble sulphates administered in a supposed case of lead poisoning would not retard the action of arsenious acid, if that had been the poison really employed. In any case of doubt, however, the hydrated sulphuret of iron would equally decompose the salts of lead, arsenious acid, corrosive sublimate, or the salts of antimony, tin, bismuth, or silver, &c. We repeat, therefore, that we ought to give the preference to the hydrated sulphuret of iron, because it appears to act as well as the hydrated peroxide, and its action extends to a great number of poisons.

Albumen is not only a good antidote for the salts of copper and bichloride of mercury, but also for most of the metallic poisons. Albuminous water may therefore be employed with success to counteract the effects of poisoning by arsenious acid, not only because it precipitates this acid, but also because it is sickly and thereby promotes vomiting, and because its emollient action may soothe the irritation produced. Several cases of poisoning by arsenious acid have lately been successfully treated by albuminous water and diuretics.

Magnesia, which was proposed in 1796 by Mandel, a druggist at Nancy, as an antidote to arsenious acid, was forgotten, until M. Bussy clearly showed, in 1846, that it was an excellent antidote for this poison. According to him, it ought to be placed even before the hydrated peroxide of iron, because it is not only more easily obtained, but it is laxative, and thereby assists the evacuation of the poison. Magnesia has therefore, in the present day, been gained to science as an antidote, not only for acids, but also for arsenious acid, with which it forms an insoluble arsenite. It ought to be administered in large quantities, and it is best when in a gelatinous state; and druggists would do well to keep it prepared beforehand in this state.

Sugar, which was proposed by M. Duval, cannot be considered as an antidote, but only as a simple emollient; and the same thing must be said of *gum-water, milk, veal or chicken broth,* and various mucilaginous tisanes. Lastly, fatty bodies, the much be-praised theriaca, infusion of cinchona, of galls, or of other substances containing tannin, only act by virtue of their tepid water, and ought to be proscribed. As to tepid baths and demi-baths, emollients and narcotics of every description, they are only useful in soothing the irritation set up. It is also right to observe that the success of treatment depends principally upon the manner in which it is employed, and the regimen which we make the patient observe during his always tedious convalescence, during which his food ought to be scanty, and composed of feculant or other mucilaginous substances.

Chemical examination.—Arsenious acid presents itself under the form of white, vitreous, semi-transparent masses, which are opaque externally if long exposed to the air; and under that of a white powder. It is inodorous, and has a *rough*, not corrosive taste, *slightly* styptic, but not perceived until after some minutes, when it excites a secretion of saliva. When heated upon a *metallic plate*, it is volatilized, and produces white *inodorous* vapours; but if placed upon *hot cinders*, it is decomposed, and forms thick fumes of *metallic* arsenic, which have a well marked *odour of garlic*. This odour is therefore due to metallic arsenic in vapour, or to a suboxide, and not to arsenious acid. These vapours absorb oxygen as they rise in the air, and are converted into arsenious acid. This odour of garlic given off by arsenical vapours is not a sufficient proof of the presence of an arsenical compound; because garlic itself, and phosphorus, and some other substances exhale the same odour; and it is moreover easy to be deceived when trying to appreciate smells. This character ought therefore only to be considered as a hint; and the presence of arsenious acid ought to be proved beyond doubt by the following experiments:

c c 2

Liquid tests.—Sulphuretted hydrogen (hydrosulphuric acid) precipitates a yellow sulphuret (§. from an *acid*, or neutral solution of arsenious acid) which is dissolved by ammonia with *decolourization of the liquid*. *Ammonio-nitrate of silver* produces a *yellowish-white* precipitate of arsenite of silver (§. King's yellow), which becomes black on exposure to the air. *Ammoniacal sulphate of copper* produces a *green* precipitate (Scheele's green) of arsenite of copper. *Lime*-water causes a *white* precipitate. The *soluble sulphurets* precipitate arsenious acid *yellow*, like hydrosulphuric acid; but if the quantity of arsenious acid is very small, they merely produce a yellow colour and the precipitate does not fall until a few drops of hydrochloric acid are added, or the liquid is concentrated.

Reduction test.—When arsenious acid is heated in a test-tube with a little powdered *charcoal*, or the *yellow sulphuret* (obtained from the above experiments) is heated with *black flux,*[*] a ring of metallic arsenic is formed in the tube a little above the heated part. A great deal has been said about glass itself containing arsenic, and it is true that the Commission of the French Academy has proved the presence of this body in an *opaque* glass; but arsenic is not generally employed in making glass; and colourless transparent (flint-glass), or green German glass, never contains arsenic. It is as well, however, to prove beforehand that the apparatus used does not contain this substance.

Marsh's test.—The above tests were for a long time considered sufficient for proving the presence of arsenious acid; but since Marsh's discovery, recourse must always be had to the following test:

Scheele, an illustrous Swedish chemist, discovered, in 1752, that arsenic formed a compound with hydrogen, which, when burnt, left *regulus of arsenic* (metallic arsenic). Since that time,

---

(§. * A mixture of carbonate of potash and charcoal, obtained by heating nitrate of potash and bitartrate of potash to redness. The tartaric acid is decomposed, some of its carbon forming carbonic acid, with oxygen, from the nitrate of potash, and some of it remaining simply mixed with the carbonate of potash formed. As this salt is deliquescent, the black flux must always be heated to redness on a slip of platinum for a few moments before it is used. The potash (an alkali) in this test is requisite for removing the sulphur in the sulphuret of arsenic. Where arsenious acid alone (AsO^3) is present, charcoal alone is sufficient to remove the oxygen from the arsenic, and leave it in the metallic state.

arseniuretted hydrogen has been studied by Proust, Tromsdorff, Stromeyer, Gay-Lussac, Serullas, Davy, and the unfortunate Gehlen, who died from poisoning by the gas. And lastly, Marsh made known his process, which was very inconvenient as he described it, but which has been advantageously modified in several ways. We cannot point out all the modifications, more or less happy, which have been proposed; and we must confine ourselves to indicating the most simple apparatus which is now generally adopted, for which we are indebted to M. Orfila.

Into a wide-mouthed bottle capable of holding about two pints, we put about a pint of distilled water, an ounce and a half or two ounces of zinc, and about the same quantity of pure sulphuric acid. The mouth of the bottle is to be accurately closed by a good bung, which is pierced by two holes, in one of which we put a straight tube, dipping below into the fluid, and terminating in a funnel above. The second opening is occupied by a tube bent at an obtuse angle, and drawn out to a (blow-pipe) point above, whilst the lower end is cut off obliquely, forming a bevilled end. Before bending the tube, we must introduce a portion of asbestos into the lower third of the flexure.

The apparatus being thus prepared, it must be allowed to work for half an hour or more, during which time pure hydrogen is evolved, if the materials themselves have been pure; and this hydrogen, when inflamed at the pointed end, does not produce any stains upon a porcelain plate held near the flame; neither is any ring of arsenic formed, if the part of the tube containing the asbestos is heated by means of a spirit lamp. After being satisfied by long continued trial in this way of the purity of the materials introduced into the apparatus, we may pour the suspected arsenical liquid through the funnel, the animal matters having been previously destroyed by one of the methods to be pointed out hereafter. At this instant, however little arsenic may be present, the colour of the flame changes from its previous yellow to a pale blue, and we obtain, upon a porcelain plate held to it, a number of stains, of a brownish-fawn colour, more or less deep, brilliant and glistening, presenting all the characters which were described above, p. 377.

If, in addition to this, the part of the tube containing the asbestos is heated by a spirit lamp, the arseniuretted hydrogen is decomposed into arsenic, which is deposited in the form of a ring in the tube, a little above the part to which the heat is applied, and into hydrogen, which, being inflamed, deposits merely water upon the cold porcelain, if the decomposition has been complete; but arsenical stains if, on the contrary, it has not been perfect. It is a good plan to make both these experiments at the same time; that is to say, to heat the tube below the asbestos so as to obtain the ring, and to inflame the gas to obtain the arsenical stains, in case the arsenical gas has not been completely decomposed by the heat. We can recognize the presence of a millionth part of arsenious acid, and with a two-millionth part the stains begin to appear.

The asbestos is intended to accumulate a great amount of heat in one place, and also to prevent the passage of the sulphate of zinc, or of any of the liquid which may be carried up, if the production of the gas is too tumultuous, in which case it may be diminished by increasing the quantity of water in the apparatus. The bevilled end of the blow-pipe tube is intended to prevent the water which is spirted up from being retained by the capillarity of the tube, and by means of this precaution the water constantly falls back again into the bottle.

We have already pointed out some precautions which must be punctually observed, especially the one which consists in proving the purity of the materials employed, for both the zinc and the sulphuric acid may contain arsenic. It is also indispensable before inflaming the hydrogen, to allow sufficient time for all the air contained in the apparatus to be expelled, for if the hydrogen is mixed with any oxygen at the time it is set on fire, an explosion will be produced. This precaution must be more carefully attended to, in proportion as the bottle is large and the quantity of fluid contained in it is small.

It is necessary that the jet of hydrogen should not be too great; a flame from an inch to an inch and a half high is sufficient. The plate must be held in the flame, and its position should be changed every moment, as the arsenic cannot be deposited upon a hot body; and too large a flame may prevent it from being deposited at all. The materials ought to be put into the apparatus in the following order: 1. The zinc, previously acted upon by sulphuric acid and water; 2. The water; 3. The sulphuric acid. If after a trial of fifteen or twenty minutes we do not obtain any stain, we may be certain that the materials are pure. We then throw away the materials, and replace them in the above order, and after having allowed sufficient time for the expulsion of the air, we may inflame the hydrogen and add the suspected materials.

If instead of operating as above directed, we put the sulphuric acid upon the zinc, it disengages sulphu*rous* acid, which in contact with the nascent hydrogen produces water and sulphuretted hydrogen. This latter precipitates the arsenious acid in the form of yellow sulphuret, *which does not produce* stains by Marsh's apparatus. In short, in order that the stains may be produced, it is necessary that the arsenical preparation should be the *oxygenized one, or one capable of becoming oxygenized in the apparatus.* Now pure sulphuret of arsenic cannot acquire oxygen, in addition to which objection the presence of hydrosulphuric acid may cause the production of stains of sulphur.

Lassaigne's method.—Instead of inflaming the arseniuretted hydrogen as it escapes from the apparatus, so as to obtain the stains upon a porcelain plate (we have already mentioned that common earthenware is to be proscribed), M. Lassaigne proposes to make the gas pass into one of Liebig's tubes with bulbs, containing a neutral solution of nitrate of silver, in which case the silver is precipitated as a black metallic powder, and arsenious acid remains in solution. What remains of the nitrate of silver may then be precipitated by pure hydrochloric acid, and on filtering and evaporating the solution we obtain the arsenious acid, which is easily recognized by its different tests. This process is more delicate than the one above mentioned; but it is necessary to prove the presence of the arsenious acid in the solution, and not to take it for granted because the silver has been precipitated; for this may happen with pure hydrogen, and even by the mere action of light: and moreover, the black precipitate may be owing to sulphuret of silver, because the hydrogen may contain traces of sulphuretted hydrogen.

Jacquelain's method.—M. Jacquelain, after having destroyed the organic matter by means of chlorine, drives away the excess of chlorine by heat, places the liquid in an apparatus to which a tube is adapted bent at right angles, and containing in its horizontal branch asbestos calcined with sulphuric acid. This tube is surrounded towards its middle by a leaf of Dutch metal (copper leaf), and is adapted to a Liebig's tube with bulbs, containing pure chloride of gold. On heating the copper leaf, the arsenic is deposited in the interior of the tube, a little in advance of the heated part, and if any arseniuretted hydrogen escapes decomposition it reduces the chloride of gold, and forms arsenious acid, which remains dissolved in the liquid. The remainder of the gold still in the form of chloride may then be precipitated by sulphurous acid, and after filtration and evaporation we may recognize the arsenious acid by its tests. This process is more delicate than that of M. Lassaigne.

Reinsch's test.—This consists in *boiling* the suspected liquid, acidulated with about a fourth of its bulk of *pure* hydrochloric acid, in a tube containing a slip of *bright* copper. When the fluid begins to boil, the surface of the copper becomes a steel-grey, or almost black, from the deposition of metallic arsenic, according to the quantity of arsenious acid present. This test is far from possessing the delicacy which its author attributes to it. (§. The test must be carried further than this in order to be satisfactory, as tartar emetic produces a deposit of metallic antimony upon the copper, which is not easily distinguished from arsenic by its mere appearance. The coated slip of copper must therefore be *very gently* dried, and introduced into a test-tube, and heated; by which means the arsenic is sublimed (leaving the copper red, but not bright as before), and is converted by the air in the tube into arsenious acid, which can be obtained as a white glistening crystalline ring. Antimony is also separated by heat from the copper, but it *does not form any ring of glistening crystals* in a cool part of the tube. By this means I have obtained a distinct ring of crystalline arsenious acid from the $\frac{1}{1000}$th of a grain of arsenious acid dissolved in half a drachm of water. This test has the advantage of being applicable to liquids containing organic or colouring matters, neither of which interfere with the results).

Removal of organic matters.—Certain arsenious liquids which are but slightly charged with organic matters, such as clear urine, for example, may be put directly into Marsh's apparatus, taking care to pour a film of oil upon the surface of the liquid to prevent it from frothing. But if the liquid contains a certain amount of organic matter, it is *indispensable* to destroy it, for which purpose an infinite number of plans have been proposed. We shall, however, content ourselves with mentioning those which are most generally used, and pointing out which are the best.

Organic liquids.—When we are engaged in destroying animal substances mixed with the arsenious acid, such as vomited matters or the contents of the stomach, we may mix them with water and boil them. The albumen, in coagulating, carries away most of the organic matter, and the liquid may then be filtered and treated with absolute alcohol, which completes its separation. We may also successfully employ a current of chlorine, which perfectly destroys animal matters, and possesses the additional advantage of decolourizing the liquid, whilst in the process given above (boiling and alcohol) we are often obliged to have recourse to washed animal charcoal, which has the disadvantage of retaining a large portion of the poisonous substance.

Organic solids.—If, on the contrary, we have to prove the presence of arsenious acid in an organ, such as the liver, the spleen, or the kidneys, &c., we may boil these organs in distilled water, acidulated with hydrochloric acid, and afterwards proceed upon the liquid in the manner above indicated. But, in general, it is better entirely to destroy the organic matter; for which purpose the following plans have been proposed.

Orfila's method. — Mix the suspected matters with about twice their weight of pure nitrate of potash and dry the mixture in a porcelain capsule at a gentle heat, stirring it from time to time, and then throw it in small portions at a time into an earthen crucible heated to dull redness. The mixture ought to become white or gray; if it remains dark from being only charred, it shows that the amount of saltpetre was not sufficient, and a fresh quantity must therefore be added when the incineration is finished. The crucible must be allowed to cool, and distilled water is to be poured in by degrees, in order to separate all the saline matter; it is then to be poured into an evaporating dish. The liquid is to be evaporated to the consistence of a syrup, and pure concentrated sulphuric acid is to be added by degrees, until no more effervescence is produced; after which it is to be boiled until no more white fumes of nitric, or orange fumes of nitrous acid are evolved. This precaution is *indis-*

pensable, for without it these acids would not be disengaged, and explosion would be inevitable. When this operation is terminated, the saline product of the evaporation is to be taken up by distilled water and introduced into a Marsh's apparatus. If the solution is too acid, it may be neutralized by potash dissolved in alcohol.

This process has been objected to on account of its length, and the large quantity of sulphuric acid employed. It is necessary to ascertain the purity of the substances employed before using them.

Devergie's method. — After having dissolved the organic matter in potash, M. Devergie treats it with *nitrate of lime,* and takes it up again by hydrochloric acid; but when this acid is used in a Marsh's apparatus, as it is in this case, it is only zinc stains which are produced. Their characters are given at p. 379.

Flandin and Danger's method.—These chemists char the organic matters by the sixth part of their weight of sulphuric acid. The mixture is heated and stirred constantly, until it remains dry and powdery. The capsule is to be allowed to cool, and a small quantity of concentrated nitric acid is to be added, with the intention of converting the arsenious acid into arsenic acid, which is less volatile and more soluble. It is again evaporated to dryness, and the soluble matter is taken up by distilled water, filtered, and introduced into a Marsh's apparatus.

It has been objected to this process that it yields a sulphuret of carbon, and that the presence of sulphurous acid in Marsh's apparatus causes the formation of sulphuretted hydrogen, and subsequently of yellow sulphuret of arsenic, which as we have seen above (p. 391), does not give stains by means of this apparatus.

Normal arsenic.—The normal arsenic (§. *i. e.* the arsenic supposed to form part of the human body naturally) pointed out by MM. Couerbe and Orfila could not be found either by the commission of the French Institute or by M. Orfila himself. It is probable that M. Orfila, when he found the arsenic which he imagined to be normal, had been operating upon a dead body which accidentally contained this substance.

Purity of the materials.—In every medico-legal investigation it is indispensable for the chemist to ascertain the purity of his tests, and this caution especially applies to poisoning by arsenic. *Sulphuric acid.* M. Orfila has proved that commercial sulphuric acid often contains both arsenious and arsenic acid, which may be detected by neutralizing the acid with potash, and placing the sulphate formed in a Marsh's apparatus. If it contains arsenic, and we cannot obtain any other, it may be purified by distilling it from sulphuret of barium, (§. which converts the arsenic into a sulphuret, which is left behind during the distillation). *Nitric acid* does not generally contain arsenic, but we may make sure of having it free from arsenical compounds by distilling it when in contact with nitrate of silver. *Hydrochloric acid* is seldom arsenical, and when it is, it may be purified by distilling it from chloride of barium and rejecting the first portions. Its purity is recognized by saturating it with potash, introducing the chloride of potassium formed into a Marsh's apparatus, and setting this to work with hydrochloric acid. *Potash* dissolved in alcohol is scarcely ever arsenical, but we may satisfy ourselves of its purity by saturating it with pure sulphuric acid, and trying it with a Marsh's apparatus. *Nitrate of potash* (commercial) is *very rarely* arsenical. It may be tested by Marsh's apparatus with pure sulphuric acid. Lastly, it is not so common as is pretended to find *zinc* and *iron* containing arsenic; but they may also be tested by Marsh's apparatus. In addition to the above precautions, the chemist ought always to make a trial experiment, using the same reagents, and in the same quantities which he is about to employ upon the suspected materials.

Cemetery earth.—Certain earths contain arsenic, generally in the state of arsenite of lime or of sulphur, &c., both of which are insoluble. In cases of judicial disinterment of a body, the chemist ought to test the soil above and below, and on both sides of the grave, and also that of parts more or less distant from it. To do this the earth must be boiled for a length of time in distilled water, and then acted upon very concentrated sulphuric acid, and the liquors must be tested in a Marsh's apparatus.

Sulphurets of arsenic. The yellow sulphuret (orpiment) and the red (realgar), when thrown upon burning cinders, disengage alliaceous vapours, and when heated in a test-tube with black flux, they produce an arsenical ring.

Arsenic acid, as well as the arseniates, is very soluble and deliquescent. It precipitates nitrate and ammoniacal-nitrate of silver *brick-red*. It is not precipitated by sulphuretted hydrogen unless sulphurous or hydrochloric acid has been added; which latter, however, acts more slowly.

Arsenite of potash, Fowler's solution, is precipitated yellow by hydrosulphuric acid, and yellowish-white by nitrate of silver. In other respects it corresponds with arsenious acid.

We shall conclude our remarks by saying, that in poisoning by arsenious acid, as in all other cases of poisoning, it is important to lose as little as possible of the materials in applying tests; and that it is necessary, *in every case,* to endeavour to isolate the poison, and to procure either the arsenical stains or the ring.

POISONING BY THE PREPARATIONS OF ANTIMONY.

All the antimonial preparations, when taken in a large dose, occasion vomiting, alvine dejections, acute colic, and inflammation of the parts with which they come in contact; but as the copious vomiting expels the poison, it is very rare for death to result from it. It is even probable that the accidents described by Pleck as produced by metallic antimony, ought to be attributed in a great degree to the arsenic which it always contains, as has been shown by Sérullas.

Metallic antimony presents itself under three forms: in *mass,* in *rings,* and in *stains.* In the last two forms it agrees with the characters laid down in p. 378. When in mass, it is in laminæ of a bluish-white colour, brilliant, brittle, and crystallizing at its surface, somewhat in the appearance of fern leaves. When treated with concentrated nitric acid it yields solid antimonious acid, and according to M. Frémy, antimoniate of protoxide of antimony. The residue is soluble in hydrochloric acid, with which it forms a chloride which is precipitated *white* by *water,* and *orange*-yellow by hydrosulphuric acid. Oxygenized antimonial preparations, or such as can acquire oxygen in Marsh's apparatus, yield stains and rings.

We shall describe poisoning by tartar emetic only ; for all that we shall say upon it will apply to the other antimonial preparations. In short, with the exception of intensity, the lesions and symptoms are the same.

POISONING BY TARTRATE OF ANTIMONY AND POTASH.

TARTAR EMETIC, (TARTRE STIBIÉ).

Symptoms.—Metallic taste, nausea, frequent vomiting, hiccough, pain in the region of the heart, acute pain accompanied with heat in the epigastrium and stomach, abdominal colic, copious purging, syncope, small, contracted, quick pulse, and cold, or else intense heat, dizziness, loss of consciousness, convulsive motions, cramp, prostration of strength, and death. The vomiting and alvine dejections do not always occur, and in such cases the other symptoms are still more intense.

Lesions produced by tartar emetic.—These consist principally in a profound alteration of the lungs, which are of a violet colour, non-crepitant, and gorged with blood, and there are sometimes also irregular black spots. The digestive canal is deeply injected throughout its whole extent, and ecchymosis may be remarked. Sometimes, also, according to Hoffman, the stomach is gangrenous.

Treatment.—The symptoms present ought to guide us in directing our treatment. If vomiting has been abundant, and there is neither pain nor convulsive motions, mucilaginous liquids will suffice to re-establish the health. If, on the contrary, vomiting had not occurred, we must provoke it by tickling the fauces, and we must administer a strong hot decoction of galls or cinchona, and if time presses, we must administer finely powdered cinchona mixed with water. Hydrated sulphuret of iron also perfectly decomposes the tartar emetic, and forms a sulphuret of antimony which is insoluble and without action upon the system. This antidote ought to be preferred to the galls or cinchona, which act by their tannin; but the tannate of antimony formed is not completely insoluble.

When we have expelled by vomiting, or neutralized by anti-dotes the greater part of the tartar emetic, we must administer diuretic liquids in great abundance, and combat the inflammation produced by emollients and general or local blood-letting, and, lastly, we must give opium if the vomiting is excessive. (§. If, as sometimes happens, prostration is the chief symptom, wine and stimulants will be necessary.

During convalescence, we must give light food; and milk and amylaceous substances will for some time be the only diet which the patient will be able to bear.

Chemical examination.—Tartar emetic is soluble in about fourteen parts of cold water. The solution, introduced into Marsh's apparatus, gives an antimoniuretted hydrogen, from which may be obtained stains and a ring, which form even upon the very place heated, and which are further distinguished from arsenic by the characters described at p. 378. ·

The solution of tartar emetic is colourless and transparent; it has a styptic taste, and reddens litmus paper; it is precipitated white by potash, ammonia, lime-water, baryta-water, and by nitric and sulphuric acid, &c. *Hydrosulphuric acid* produces an *orange*-yellow hydrated sulphuret of antimony, which becomes redder by the action of more sulphuretted hydrogen, and is dissolved with difficulty in ammonia, the *solution remaining coloured*—see p. 388. This yellow sulphuret, when calcined with black flux, yields metallic antimony.

If the solution of the tartar emetic is very weak, the reagents which we have just mentioned do not produce any precipitate, though the sulphuretted hydrogen may produce a slight yellow turbidity, especially if a few drops of hydrochloric acid are added. This slight turbidity disappears on the addition of ammonia, and the *solution becomes colourless*, exactly as in the case of yellow sulphuret of arsenic; but if the orange-yellow precipitate of sul-phuret of antimony is treated by nitric acid, and the product diluted with boiling water, is introduced into a Marsh's appara-tus, it gives stains which are easily recognized.

If the emetic is mixed with food, it will be partially decomposed; and if we wish to recognize its presence in an organ, we may destroy the organic matters by pure nitric acid, or by nitric acid with the addition of a little chlorate of potash. The residue, diffused in water, may be introduced into Marsh's apparatus.

Animal matters decompose tartar emetic in a few days; the tartaric acid is destroyed, and the oxide of antimony is precipitated. It is *not indispensable* to prove the presence of the tartaric acid. If we obtain antimonial stains, we may conclude that the case is one of poisoning by a preparation of this metal. If we obtain a solution which is precipitated by the different reagents in the manner mentioned above, and which is not precipitated by water alone, there is very great presumption of the presence of tartar emetic; but in order to be certain of it, it must be crystallized, and the presence of tartaric acid proved, which is very difficult.

Protochloride of antimony (Butter of antimony).—It is decomposed by water, unless it is acidulated, and is converted into hydrochloric acid and oxy-chloride of antimony; it is precipitated *orange* by hydrosulphuric acid.

Kermes mineral (Hydrated oxysulphuret of antimony).— Glass of antimony, crocus metallorum, &c. All these bodies, when calcined with black flux, yield metallic antimony.

POISONING BY THE PREPARATIONS OF MERCURY.

CORROSIVE SUBLIMATE (BICHLORIDE OF MERCURY).

Symptoms.—Corrosive sublimate has an acrid, styptic, metallic taste, and produces great irritation of the throat, with a feeling of contraction; and the inflammation is so considerable, that it might suffice to cause death, without the poison having even reached the stomach. It produces intense pain in the *mouth*, the plarynx, the œsophagus, the stomach and the intestines, and causes nausea, vomiting which is often bloody, diarrhœa, and sometimes violent dysentery. These evacuations are generally more frequent than in poisoning by other metallic compounds. After these symptoms, there is an abatement, the circulation is slower, the pulse becomes small and thready, the respiration is gentle, and the skin cold; syncope then supervenes, and great general insensibility, always commencing at the pelvic extremities; and sometimes convulsions occur. The secretion of urine is generally diminished, sometimes even entirely suppressed; but patients urinate if the sublimate has been employed in a very diluted state, and if drinks have been administered. The medicinal employment of corrosive sublimate, when too long continued, produces colic, vomiting and mercurial inflammation of the mouth—or at any rate salivation. The effects are often so severe as to cause loss of the teeth, and of the palatial and maxillary bones; the face is swollen, and pain comes on in the region of the heart, dyspnœa, muscular pains, hæmoptysis, pulmonary phthysis, trembling of the limbs, marasmus and death. Other symptoms may also show themselves; and all those which we have enumerated may not always be united in the same individual; but in general, the assemblage of symptoms is what we have just mentioned.

Lesions produced by corrosive sublimate.—All the parts touched by corrosive sublimate become the seat of vivid inflammation, which exists throughout the intestinal canal, and to the most remote ramifications of the bronchi. The mucous membranes often present a blanched appearance; the stomach is sometimes the seat of ecchymoses or erosions; but the (§. small) intestines are little altered, (§. whilst there is often considerable ulceration of the cœcum and colon; the poison passing rapidly through the first, and so affecting them but slightly, but being retained in the latter, and there producing its corrosive effects). Ecchymoses have also been remarked upon the epiploon. In most cases the cavities of the heart present red or black stains. Corrosive sublimate, when applied to the sub-cutaneous cellular tissue, is absorbed, and rapidly produces death.

TREATMENT OF POISONING BY CORROSIVE SUBLIMATE.

Several antidotes have been proposed for this poison. Navier extolled the alkalies and alkaline sulphurets, which are certainly more injurious than useful. We shall mention those only which are most used.

Antidotes,

Hydrated proto and persulphuret of iron.—We do not hesitate to put the hydrated sulphurets of iron in the first place, for they instantly decompose corrosive sublimate. If, after having introduced into the mouth a weak solution of the sublimate, we place in it hydrated sulphuret of iron, *at the same instant* the harsh, styptic, metallic taste disappears, which proves the decomposition of the poison, and its conversion into an insoluble and inert sulphuret of mercury. This antidote may also be given in excess, without inconvenience; and it decomposes all the soluble mercurial compounds—even the cyanide—whereas albumen (the next antidote) has no effect upon that salt.

Albumen—Eggs.—After sulphuret of iron, we place albuminous water, made with the whites of five or six eggs, and a couple of pints of water. M. Devergie prefers the yolks of the eggs; and it is the simplest plan to administer both the yolks and whites together, mixed with water; but it is important to observe, that the precipitate which albumen forms with corrosive sublimate is soluble in an excess of albumen, which then forms a solution—less poisonous, it is true, than the corrosive sublimate, but still sufficiently so to kill animals in a short time, if they have not vomited.* Albumen is, however, a most valuable antidote, not only because of the ease with which it can be procured, but also because its sickly taste materially assists vomiting. A great excess of albumen is also requisite to redissolve completely the precipitate formed.

Gluten—Wheat-flour.—Taddei, guided by M. Orfila's experiments upon the action of albumen in poisoning by corrosive sublimate, has proposed gluten, administered in powder, or mixed with medicinal soup, and diffused in water. It is useless, at the best; for gluten is rarely kept by druggists, and in every

---

(‡. * As a practical objection to the use of eggs as an antidote for this poison, this statement is a most complete fallacy, as will be evident by attempting to redissolve the precipitate formed by dropping even a dilute solution of corrosive sublimate into undiluted white of egg. It is certainly impossible to redissolve the precipitate from a single grain in the white of one egg; and therefore a dozen or twenty eggs might be most harmlessly given for the smallest dose which is ever likely to be given or taken as a poison.)

D D

respect albumen, and still more, the hydrated sulphurets of iron, are to be preferred. (§. The substitute for gluten, placed along with it at the commencement of this paragraph (wheat-flour), is not entirely without recommendations, for it is generally at hand, and ought certainly to be freely given, mixed with water or milk, if neither eggs nor the iron preparations are at hand.)

Hydrosulphuric acid, sugar, cinchona, divided mercury, iron filings, powdered gold, and charcoal, proposed by various authors, are for the most part ineffectual, and ought to be rejected. (§. The fact is, that unless an antidote is administered within a few minutes, it generally fails of success in the case of this poison ; and therefore, whatever can be given most quickly is most valuable : and whether it be a quart of milk, or a pound of flour and water, or a dozen eggs that can be first obtained, it ought to be given forthwith, without waiting for something which may perhaps be better in the laboratory, but will in all probability be too late to be of any avail, if it has to be sent for hither and thither.)

Protochloride of tin.—This salt, proposed by M. Poumet, and to which the Institute has given its sanction, acts well when administered almost at the same time as the poison; which is impossible in most cases. Besides which, an excess of the antidote would be in itself a *most dangerous* poison, which is quite sufficient to forbid its employment.

Magnesia.—M. Bussy has proposed magnesia. The experiments made up to the present time are not sufficient to enable us to pronounce upon this substance as an antidote for corrosive sublimate.

STEPS TO BE PURSUED IN THE TREATMENT OF POISONING BY
CORROSIVE SUBLIMATE.

· On the first appearance of the symptoms we must administer the whites or yolks of eggs mixed in water, or else the hydrated sulphurets of iron. In the absence of these antidotes we may give milk, soup, or any tepid mucilaginous substance in great abundance, so as to dilute the poison, and assist vomiting. Mucilaginous drinks in great abundance ought to be preferred to the various emetics for exciting vomiting. If, notwithstanding these means, vomiting does not occur, we must not hesitate to use the stomach-pump.

After poisoning by corrosive sublimate, we frequently see most troublesome consequences, such as gastritis, enteritis, or even peritonitis. Recourse must in these cases be had to the application of leeches to the painful parts, and general blood-letting may be required; and emollients and narcotics must be administered under the form of glysters, lotions, fomentations, and local or general baths: mucilaginous fluids must be drunk, and a most careful diet observed. But if the inflammation has advanced considerably, or if it has run through all its stages, it is necessary to discard blood-letting, for gangrene is now what we have to fear, and the treatment must be that for gastro-enteritis. During convalescence, the food must be light; and milk and feculent substances can alone be allowed, though at a late period jellies and broths may be given.

Chemical examination.—Corrosive sublimate, as it is found in commerce, is under the form of regular tetrahedral prisms, or of hemispherical masses, concave on one side, and convex on the other, the lower surface of which bristles with innumerable, very crowded small crystals. The crystalline forms vary according to the process which has been employed in crystallizing it. Its taste is very powerful, styptic and metallic, and it produces a sense of constriction of the throat. When heated in a tube with a little potash, it produces metallic mercury. It is soluble in eleven times its weight of water, (§. and is also soluble in alcohol and in ether, which forms a light solution that rises to the surface in mixed liquids, and thereby removes the corrosive sublimate from organic matters with which it may be combined, and assists the subsequent steps of the examination.)

There are two forms of mercurial salts, viz., those of the protoxide and those of the binoxide. That we may the better embrace both these classes at a single glance, we have given their distinctive characters in the following table:

TESTS.	SALTS OF THE PROTOXIDE.	SALTS OF THE BINOXIDE.
POTASH or SODA . .	Black precipitate.	Orange-yellow precipitate.
AMMONIA	Ditto.	White precipitate.
HYDROSULPHURIC ACID .	Ditto.	Yellow or grayish-white precipitate, in the first instance, which varies in colour, and becomes black, with an excess of the test.
SOLUBLE SULPHURETS .	Ditto.	Ditto.
IODIDE OF POTASSIUM .	Greenish-yellow precipitate.	Bright red (§. sometimes yellow, at first) precipitate, which is soluble in an excess of the test (§. forming a perfectly colourless solution.)
CHROMATE OF POTASH .	Bright red precipitate.	Reddish-yellow precipitate.
(§. PROTOCHLORIDE OF TIN . . . .)	Black precipitate.	Precipitate white at first, but black, with an excess of the test.)
HYDROCHLORIC ACID and SOLUBLE CHLORIDES .	White precipitate.	No effect.
GOLD or COPPER WIRE (§. with a thread of zinc folded spirally round it). SMITHSON'S GALVANIC PILE	Metallic mercury.	Metallic mercury.

The above are briefly the characters of the salts of mercury; and we may add, that several of them form white precipitates on the addition of water alone—such as the sulphate and nitrate of the binoxide (persulphate and pernitrate), in which case an insoluble basic salt, and a soluble acid one, are formed. As to the specific characters of corrosive sublimate, we may add that it forms a white precipitate with sulphate or nitrate of silver (§. chloride of *silver*), which is soluble in ammonia, but is not soluble in an excess of chlorine; whilst the white precipitate which the protosalts of mercury form with hydrochloric acid and the soluble chlorides (§. chloride of *mercury*) is soluble in an excess of chlorine, and is blackened by ammonia.

Corrosive sublimate is remarkable for the facility with which it dissolves in ether, which removes it from water and all other liquids; so that if we wish to recognize the presence of the poison in any liquid, it is sufficient to shake it up with a quantity of 'ether equal to that of the liquid concerned. After shaking it for some minutes, the ethereal solution is allowed to separate by rest, and is then poured off and evaporated spontaneously; and the corrosive sublimate which remains is recognized by the characters which we have described above.

If, however, we are engaged in discovering the bichloride of mercury when mixed with food, or the contents of the digestive canal, or when combined with the tissues, it is necessary to operate in a different way, and it is important to destroy the animal matters.

All albuminous substances form compounds with corrosive sublimate, the nature of which is not well established. It is this kind of combination which has occasioned the failure of chemists who have sought for the presence of mercury in the milk of nurses under mercurial treatment; but latterly, by employing the process described below, M. Reveil has succeeded in obtaining a very small quantity of mercury from the milk of a goat, who had for several days been taking 10 centigrammes (gr. iss) of corrosive sublimate. M. Personne, chief pharmaceutist to the Hôpital du Midi, has obtained results still more conclusive, and has collected a considerable quantity of mercury from the milk of the same goat; so that it cannot be any longer doubtful that mercurial compounds do pass into and remain in the milk. The process which M. Personne employs is founded upon the principle that corrosive sublimate is dissipated by ebullition, and that it is therefore highly important not to raise the temperature of the substances containing it. This fact, previously pointed out by M. Orfila, has been placed beyond doubt by the experiments of M. Personne.

M. Lassaigne proposes to boil the mixture of animal matters and of sublimate with a solution of chloride of sodium; but according to M. Orfila, it would be difficult to apply this process to legal investigations, because the chloride of sodium does not withdraw small quantities of mercurial compounds from the masses of flesh with which they are combined.

M. Devergie dissolves the materials in concentrated hydrochloric acid, and passes a stream of chlorine gas through the solution. Orfila prefers *aqua-regia* and a current of chlorine, or better still, their carbonization by means of strong sulphuric acid in closed vessels. For this purpose he operates in a matrass, to

which is adapted a bent tube, which plunges into a jar full of
distilled water. The corrosive sublimate will be found in the
volatilized liquids and in the charcoal, which may be boiled for
twenty minutes in *aqua regia*. In operating upon blood,
M. Millon advises that the liquid should be shaken up in flasks-
full of gaseous chlorine, which is to be frequently renewed; and
we have applied this process to milk with good success. M.
Flandin employs at first sulphuric acid, and then saturates the
acid by dry hypochlorite of lime—which is a good process, but
we think that it is indispensable to operate in closed vessels.

When the solid animal matter has been destroyed, it is necessary then to operate upon the liquid, in order to prove the
presence of the sublimate. Different reagents may be employed.
Sulphuretted hydrogen which is the most delicate of all, gives a
yellowish-white, then a yellow, and ultimately, with an excess of
the gas, a black precipitate. This precipitate, collected and
heated in a test-tube with a little potash, yields metallic mercury;
but as in all cases of poisoning it is necessary to examine for
the offending substance, we advise that agitation with ether
should always be insisted upon; and liquids thus treated may be
placed in contact with several metallic plates.

Copper plate.—Copper plates, scraped perfectly clean, are
extremely sensible. M. Orfila is persuaded that by this process
he can recognize the presence of an eighty-thousandth part of
corrosive sublimate. We have ourselves shown that a plate of
yellow copper (brass?) is more sensitive than one of red copper.
Mercury when deposited upon copper, leaves a gray stain, which
becomes bright when rubbed with a cork; but if the mercurial
compound is mixed with a soluble chloride, the stain will be
white. The gray colour is owing to a mixture of metallic
mercury with a little oxide or chloride, and when this is removed
by ammonia or by hydrochloric acid, the mercury then assumes
its white colour. It is necessary to remember, that metallic
plates act with somewhat more success in proportion as the
solutions are more concentrated; and it is therefore advantageous
to boil them in a close vessel before putting the plates into them.
Lastly, it is indispensable that the metal should be perfectly
clean.

When the mercury has been deposited upon a plate of copper,

and the stains have been washed with a weak solution of ammonia,
and then in distilled water, we may test them by pressing them
between two leaves of tissue-paper.   We may cut them into
small pieces, and put them into test-tubes, drawn out so as to
taper at their extremity; and on heating them, the mercury
volatilizes, and is condensed upon the most tapering part of the
tube.   Whether we have obtained metallic mercury or not by
this means, it does not prevent our afterwards evaporating to
dryness the liquid in which the copper plate has been immersed,
charring it by sulphuric acid, and proceeding as we have mentioned above.

Smithson's (galvanic) pile.—James Smithson has proposed
to wind a strip of tin (§. or of zinc) in a spiral direction round a
plate of gold or copper; but we must take care that the tin or
zinc does not entirely cover the gold, &c.   These plates ought to
be perfectly polished.   The liquid may be acidulated with a few
drops of hydrochloric acid, and after a longer or shorter period—
sometimes only half an hour—we see the gold covered with
mercury.   The tin or zinc must then be removed, and the gold
plate dried between two leaves of tissue-paper, and it may then
be heated in a test-tube, in order to obtain metallic globules.

This pile can only be employed to exhibit the presence of a
mercurial preparation in the liquid, so far as it removes the
metallic mercury from it.   It is not sufficient proof of mercury
having been present, that the plates become white, and resume
their colour when heated, for we have seen gold or Smithson's
pile become white when plunged into a non-mercurial liquid; and
this is especially the case when the liquid is acid or contains
common salt.   There is also the tin which covered the gold plate;
and if this is heated, it regains its colour, because the tin pene-
trates into the plate; but it does not furnish metallic mercury in
globules when heated.   We may further distinguish a tin stain
from a mercurial one by putting the whitened gold plate into pure
and concentrated hydrochloric acid, which dissolves the tin, but
not mercury.

Flandin's apparatus.—The apparatus which M. Flandin has
advised for recognizing the presence of very minute quantities
of a mercurial preparation, consists in a vessel tapering at its
lower part into a tube with an opening of about the thirtieth

of an inch (1 millimetre) in diameter. The liquid to be tested is placed in this vessel, and a gold wire attached to the positive pole of a Bunsen's battery is to be placed in it (taking care that it passes down into the contracted part), and another gold wire attached to the negative pole is to be introduced into the opening at the lower end of the contracted part. The battery being excited in the ordinary way, a current is established which causes the precipitation of the mercury upon the gold wire attached to the negative pole, and however small may be the quantity of the mercurial compound, it is manifested by this process; and on heating the gold, or treating it by nitric acid, the mercury is removed. We are indebted to the kindness of M. Flandin for the opportunity of trying his apparatus, with which we obtained the most satisfactory results.

Gold plate is not so delicate as Smithson's pile or copper plate, unless it is submitted to an electric current, as we have just mentioned. It ought also, not to be used when the quantity of mercury is considerable.

Protochloride of tin precipitates mercury from its solutions, and this method may be adopted, but it is far from being so delicate as the copper plate.

In conclusion, we may add that M. Mialhe has proved conclusively that all the mercurial compounds are converted into bichloride when in contact with the alkaline chlorides of the system; from which it results that even if we do find that salt in the stomach, it does not absolutely prove that it has been introduced, as it may be the result of this reaction: and, lastly, it may happen that the corrosive sublimate may have become converted into sulphuret from contact with the sulphuretted hydrogen contained in the intestinal canal.

BICYANIDE OF MERCURY.

The bicyanide (cyanide in orig.) corresponds in its composition with the bichloride, and it is one of the most energetic poisons; but the difficulty of obtaining it is the cause of the rarity of poisoning by means of this compound of mercury.

Bicyanide of mercury crystallizes in long quadrangular prisms cut off obliquely. When heated in a tube, it yields *cyanogen, metallic mercury*, and a black product which has been called *paracyanogen.* Its solution is not affected by either potash, or iodide of potassium, which distinguishes it essentially from the other compounds of mercury; but hydrosulphuric acid and the sulphurets soon produce a sulphuret which is at first yellow, but becomes black from an excess of the test, as in the case of the bichloride. Copper plate, Smithson's pile, &c., cause the precipitation of metallic mercury; nitrate of silver forms with the bicyanide a white curdy precipitate which is insoluble in *cold* nitric acid, but is dissolved by ammonia or by *boiling* nitric acid, and in this latter case, with the disengagement of hydrocyanic acid. The cyanide of silver, when heated, gives metallic silver (§. in the form of a brownish powder) and cyanogen, which is easily recognized by burning with a *purple* flame, and being absorbed by potash.

Chemical examination.—We may operate as has been already mentioned for corrosive sublimate. If the bicyanide was mixed with urine, or any other liquid, it may be separated by means of ether.

Treatment.—It is useless to administer albumen in poisoning by this substance, for it is not precipitated by the bicyanide; but after having produced vomiting by tickling the fauces and by copious draughts, we may administer hydrated sulphuret of iron, and at a later period emollients and sedatives.

What we have already said may suffice to point out what we must do in order to combat the effects and to prove the presence of other mercurial preparations; such as the oxides, the sulphurets, nitrates, &c.

POISONING BY MERCURIAL VAPOURS.

We must, in the last place, point out the effects produced by the mercurial vapours to which gilders by the dry method, makers of barometers and thermometers, and workmen in the mercury mines are liable. Metallic mercury, when introduced into the system, acts like a poison whenever it remains long enough in the intestinal canal to be converted into bichloride. Some well established cases have been reported, proving the rapid absorption of metallic mercury, but most of the statements on this subject are inconclusive. Those reported by M. Calson deserve little confidence, and his experiments have been frequently repeated, and always with negative results : a point upon which we lay much stress.

Symptoms.—The principal are swelling and ulceration of the gums, and mercurial trembling. Antidotes are unavailing in this case ; the cause of the symptoms must be discontinued, and emollients and soothing remedies administered.

POISONING BY THE PREPARATIONS OF COPPER.

Finely divided metallic copper and its insoluble preparations are only poisonous when they become dissolved in the stomach, in which way it is that the green substance acts which is formed upon the surface of various cooking utensils, and is commonly called *verdet* or *verdigris*. This compound is in reality only hydrated bioxide of copper, or hydrocarbonate of copper, and very rarely contains oxalate, acetate, or any other salt of copper, as these are only formed when acids have been placed in contact with metallic copper. Fatty bodies, when melted and *allowed to cool* in copper vessels, greatly facilitate the oxidation of this metal.

We shall, in this place, occupy ourselves simply with poisoning by acetate of copper; and from what we shall say upon it, may be inferred what will happen with every other soluble salt of this metal.

ACETATE OF COPPER, OR VERDIGRIS.

Verdigris is a *basic** acetate of copper; *verdet* or *Venus's crystals* is a *neutral* acetate. Both of them have the binoxide†

(§. * *i. e.* having more equivalents of the base (oxide of copper) than of the acid.)
(§. † There are two oxides of copper: the first of which is red, and does not form a basis for salts; and the second, which is black, and does form a basis. Their composition is $Cu32+O4$ (red), and $Cu32+O8$ (black). English chemists generally consider the black as a *protoxide*, and the red as a *di*-oxide; in which case the latter would be represented symbolically by Cu^2+O, or $(Cu64+O8)$. and the black oxide would be written $Cu+O$, or $(Cu32+O8$, as above). By these French authors it is

-of copper for their base. We shall occupy ourselves solely with the first.

These two salts, when applied to the naked cellular tissue, or introduced into the stomach, are active poisons; they are absorbed and carried into all the organs of the body, in which it may become necessary to prove their presence. When they cause death, it is by the inflammation which they excite in the digestive canal, and also after their absorption by the influence which they exercise upon the nervous system, and probably also upon the organs of digestion and respiration.

Symptoms of poisoning by verdigris. — When introduced into the stomach, this salt produces the following symptoms. Acrid, styptic, metallic taste; dryness of the tongue, and throat, with a sensation of constriction, increased flow of the saliva, nausea, vomiting, twinges of the stomach, acute colic, frequent alvine dejections, which are sometimes bloody and black, the pulse small, irregular and frequent, syncope, burning thirst, partial suppression of urine, respiration difficult, cold sweats, cramps, convulsions, and lastly death.

We seldom find all these symptoms in the same patient. The most constant are colic and vomiting. If the poisoning has been produced by provisions cooked or allowed to remain in badly tinned copper vessels, severe headache, weakness and trembling

assumed that the red oxide is a compound of one equivalent of copper and one equivalent of oxygen; and as the equivalent of oxygen is 8, the proportions in which they combine will be Cu64+O8, as above; but in this case, the equivalent of copper is assumed to be 64, whilst English chemists generally reckon it at 32, half of 64. According to this French theory, the black oxide will be Cu64+O16, or Cu+O². English chemists consider the black oxide to be a protoxide, rather than the red, on the following grounds, which appear to be satisfactory on the point:

(1. It is a compound not liable to change, which is the general character of prot-oxides; whereas the red oxide is unstable, being converted by most acids into black oxide and metallic copper.

(2. The salts of the black oxide possess the general character of salts containing a protoxide for their base. They contain in general but one equivalent of acid, and it is a general law of chemical combination, that the number of equivalents of acid in a salt is equal to the number of equivalents of oxygen in the base.

(3. The salts of the black oxide are perfectly decomposed by a *single* equivalent of *proto*-compounds, such as potash (KO), which is inconsistent with the general laws of chemical decomposition, unless their base is also a proto-compound.

(4. The salts of the black oxide are *isomorphous* with the salts of other *prot-*oxides; which is also explicable only on the supposition that their basis is also a proto-compound; the general laws of isomorphism being, "that bodies of similar chemical constitution may crystallize together, or may be substituted for one another in various cases.")

of the limbs, cramps, abdominal pains, nausea, and vomiting with alvine 'evacuations, are experienced from eight to fifteen hours after the food has been swallowed. If the patient is promptly treated, he is generally soon restored to health; but pain in the epigastrium and colic often remain for some time.

Lesions produced by the compounds of copper. — The mucous membrane of the stomach and intestines is the seat of vivid inflammation, which sometimes forms sloughs which are quickly detached, and produce perforations through which their contents escape into the abdominal cavity.

TREATMENT OF POISONING BY VERDIGRIS.

Antidotes. — Soluble sulphurets and the alkalies ought to be proscribed for the reasons which we have already mentioned, in speaking of the treatment of poisoning by arsenious acid (p. 385) and infusion of galls, sugar and iron filings do not offer any advantages.

Albumen (white of egg) dissolved in water precipitates the salts of copper, and may be given in great abundance without any inconvenience.

Hydrated sulphurets of iron may be administered in every dose and with great advantage.

Prussiate of potash (ferro-cyanide of potassium, yellow cyanide of potassium and iron) presents all the advantages of albuminous water, and the hydrated sulphurets of iron; but when given in great excess it sometimes causes dizziness, and we therefore prefer albumen because it perfectly decomposes the salts of copper, it is easily obtained, and it promotes vomiting.

Course of treatment. — We must immediately give the whites of several eggs, with the intention of neutralizing the poison and assisting vomiting. If we cannot procure the eggs quickly, we must gorge the patient with emollient mucilaginous drinks, and tickle the fauces, and have recourse to solution of tartar emetic, unless the pain in the stomach is very severe, in which case we must abstain from it, and employ the stomach pump.

If the poison has been administered for some time, and we suppose that it has passed through the pylorus, it is useless to excite vomiting: but we must give emollient glysters, soothing drinks, and milk and water, until the effects have abated. Lastly, the irritation produced must be combatted by general and local bleeding, and by baths and emollient fomentations, and if nervous symptoms manifest themselves we must resort to antispasmodics and narcotics, to calm the spasms and convulsions.

Chemical examination.—The neutral acetate of copper and the tri-basic acetate are crystalline, are soluble in water, and possess a styptic metallic taste.

Although we have generally to deal with salts of the binoxide of copper, (the salts of the protoxide being very unstable), we think it necessary to point out the characters of both in the following table.*

TESTS.	SALTS OF THE *Dinoxide*. (In the original, "Protoxide.")	SALTS OF THE *Protoxide*. (In the original, "Binoxide.")
POTASH and SODA . .	Brownish-yellow precipitate, indissoluble in an excess of the reagent.	Bluish-white precipitate, insoluble in an excess of the reagent, and which becomes black when boiled.
AMMONIA	Precipitate soluble in excess of the reagent, forming at first a colourless solution, which becomes blue on contact with the air.	Blue or green precipitate, which is dissolved by an excess of ammonia, forming a beautiful deep-blue solution (not very delicate).
Yellow CYANIDE OF POTASSIUM and IRON .	White precipitate, which becomes brown on exposure to the air.	Marone-brown precipitate (very delicate).
Red CYANIDE OF POTASSIUM and IRON . .	—	Greenish-yellow precipitate.
HYDROSULPHATE OF AMMONIA (SULPHIDE OF AMMONIUM) . .	Brown.	Black, insoluble in an excess of the reagent.
HYDROSULPHURIC ACID .	Ditto.	Black.
IODIDE OF POTASSIUM .	Ditto.	Bluish-white.
TANNIN	Ditto.	Gray.
CHROMATE OF POTASH .	Ditto.	Red-brown.
CLEAN ZINC or IRON .	Metallic copper.	Metallic copper.

(§. * In translating the above paragraph, the terms binoxide and protoxide have been retained; but in the table I have departed from the original so far as to use the English equivalents, and have described the French binoxide as protoxide, or simply oxide, and the French protoxide as *dinoxide*. For the reasons for this change, see note to p. 410.)

When we make use of bright iron as a test, it is important that the solution should be only slightly acid. It is best to acidulate slightly with hydrochloric acid.

When we wish to recognize the presence of copper in coloured liquids, we may decolorize them by well washed animal charcoal, and then prove the existence of the copper by the tests above given. If the solution is transparent, we may pass a stream of sulphuretted hydrogen, and boil the sulphuret of copper thus obtained in pure *concentrated* nitric acid, which will form sulphate of (binoxide, Fr.) copper which is easily recognized. But if the liquid is viscid, we must first boil it, and then operate upon the filtered liquid as we have just mentioned, and treat the *coagulum* with concentrated nitric acid.

If we are engaged in discovering the presence of copper in the different organs of the body, we must calcine them with concentrated nitric acid, after which, a carbonaceous mass remains containing black oxide of copper, which is to be dissolved by nitric acid; and the pure nitrate obtained by this means contains all the characters of the salts of the black oxide (binoxide, Fr.) of copper. But in operating in this way, we run the risk of confounding the copper introduced as a poison with that which our organs naturally contain (§. *normal* copper), which is derived from various articles of food that contain it in small quantities. It is therefore necessary to boil these organs in water for about an hour, in which case the water takes up the poisonous copper, but *does not touch the normal copper*, which appears to exist in such a state of combination that water does not dissolve it.

We have already mentioned that all the salts of copper produce nearly the same symptoms and the same lesions, and possess similar chemical characters; it is therefore unnecessary to insist further upon this point, which is also forbidden by the limits which we have prescribed for ourselves.

Colic from copper.—Artificers in copper, and especially turners and polishers, are subject to metallic colic, which is easily distinguished from that produced by lead by the following difference: viz., that fever always accompanies copper colic, and the abdominal pain is increased by pressure; whilst in lead colic, as we shall see in the next chapter, the pain ceases or diminishes by pressure.

POISONING BY THE PREPARATIONS OF LEAD.

Lead is solid, bluish-white, soft, flexible, malleable and ductile; it can be scratched by the nail, and is dissolved by nitric acid with the disengagement of binoxide of nitrogen and the formation of a soluble nitrate; it is not poisonous when not dissolved by the fluids of the system. It is sometimes employed for lining kitchen utensils, and is then only dangerous when dissolved by some liquid; but when, on the contrary, it is finely divided, metallic lead is very poisonous. We know what disastrous effects are produced by saturnine emanations.

We therefore distinguish saturnine *infection*, or *chronic* poisoning, from saturnine *intoxication*, or *acute* poisoning, though both these forms of poisoning are always studied together.

Persons who use lead or its compounds, and those who handle lead preparations, or are placed in an atmosphere of their emanations, are liable to severe diseases. The principal trades in which these compounds are used are the painters, plumbers, common potters, glass-makers, printers, and especially the polishers of printing type, card-makers, assayers, chemists, colour and white-lead makers, miners, &c.

Saturnine emanations.—The symptoms produced by saturnine emanations are divided into *premonitory* or primary saturnine intoxication, and into *confirmed* effects.

Premonitory symptoms are a peculiar grayish (§. or bluish) colour upon the part of the gums nearest to the teeth. The tint of this colouration varies: it takes the name of "piping," (§. being only a narrow band of colour), and appears to be owing to sulphuret of lead. A sweetish styptic taste is perceived, and the breath is fœtid; the skin assumes a dirty yellow colour, described by the name of "lead jaundice" or "saturnine icterus," and the conjunctiva, the urine and the fœcal matters assume the same colour. Emaciation is produced, which goes by the name of "saturnine," and is chiefly remarked in the face, which becomes wrinkled.

Confirmed effects.—Saturnine emanations being absorbed, excite the nervous system of internal life (§. the ganglionic system), whilst that of the life of relation (§. the nerves of sensation and of motion) is sometimes paralyzed, sometimes exalted.

Painters' or lead colic.—When lead exerts its action upon the abdominal viscera, *colic* is developed in all its varieties, the most common symptom being pain, which is generally situated in the umbilicus, and seldom in the epigastrium or hypogastrium. It is manifested by a twisting sensation, which *diminishes when the abdomen is compressed.* There is generally constipation, seldom purging; retraction of the belly, sometimes very considerable; nausea, and sometimes vomiting of viscid, greenish matters; and eructations bitter, fetid, or sweetish, &c. We must refer to special treatises for the minute description of these symptoms.

Arthralgia.—The name of saturnine arthralgia, is given to the affection produced when lead exerts its action upon the spinal nervous system. It is characterized by pain and lesion of the functions corresponding with the affected organs, and perversion of contractility. The pain is situated in the trunk, the head, the upper and lower limbs, the loins, &c., and possesses the character of facial neuralgia or tic-doloroux. Lastly, it is accompanied by contractions, cramps, and other symptoms which it would be too long to enumerate in this place.

Saturnine, or lead palsy.—If the action of lead is exerted upon the voluntary muscles, with loss of motion of the affected parts, there is then lead palsy, which may be partial or general. Sensation may remain in the member even until it is atrophied; but if this is diminished or abolished, it is said that there is saturnine *anæsthesia*, whilst there is saturnine *arthralgia* when the sensibility is exalted.

Saturnine encephalo-pathia.—This is manifested when the lead compound exerts its influence upon the brain, in which case it produces functional disorders, such as exaltation, suspension, or perversion of the central functions. M. Tanquerel des Planches admits four forms of encephalo-pathia : 1st. delirious,: 2nd. comatose, 3rd. convulsive, and 4th. a combination of them all.*

* See "Traité des Maladies de Plomb," par Tanquerel des Planches.   Paris, 1839.

POISONING PRODUCED BY THE PREPARATIONS OF LEAD WHEN INTRODUCED INTO THE STOMACH.

The soluble saturnine compounds, or those which can be dissolved by the acids of the stomach, appear to exert their influence upon the intestines, in which they excite inflammation. They are absorbed and produce various effects, according as they have been taken in a large or a small dose. In the latter case it is not until some time after their administration that they induce any injurious consequences, such as colic, arthralgia, palsy, anæsthesia or saturnine encephalo-pathia. In a large dose, on the contrary, their action is precisely comparable to that of the most energetic irritant poisons; and death may quickly ensue even when the patient is allowed to vomit. In this case the animals (§. submitted to experiment) have given way under the inflammation of the tissues with which the poison has been in contact, and a peculiar affection of the nervous system, which is chiefly manifested when the compound of lead has been employed in solution.

Treatment of lead colic.—Several methods of cure have been proposed, which we shall describe concisely.

Chemical method.—As the chemical treatment, may be mentioned the various substances which have been proposed for combatting lead colic, which act by forming insoluble compounds with the oxide of lead; such as sulphuric and hydrosulphuric lemonade, the soluble sulphates, the hydrated sulphurets of iron, alum, &c., which have been recommended, but are considered in the present day as inefficacious.* Mercury and metallic lead, which have been suggested, ought to be rejected, as well as nux vomica, which is without any salutary influence.

Antiphlogistic method is useful when there is inflammation, but it does not offer any advantages to prevent our preferring some other method.

(§. * Mr. Benson found the free employment of dilute sulphuric acid, sweetened by treacle, of great use in preventing the occurrence of lead-poisoning in some extensive works in which it was very common previous to using this prophylactic.)

E E

Soothing method.—The administration of opium, the salts of morphia and the preparations of white poppy, constitutes this treatment. These medicines are employed under every form, but especially under that of glysters; and the treatment has good results—soothing the pain, and preventing the return of the symptoms.

Soothing and revulsive method.— This method, recommended by Dr. Ranque, consists in employing at the same time ordinary revulsives and sedatives, such as theriaca, the poisonous solanaceæ, and especially the preparations of belladonna, &c. This method renders good service.

Revulsive method.—This is generally abandoned.

Purgative method.—Purgatives, and especially the saline ones, and amongst them the sulphates of potash, soda and magnesia, are preferable to any of the methods hitherto mentioned. Their chemical effects ought perhaps to be taken into account, as well as their purgative action; but this sometimes fails; and in general, we prefer to it the method called that of " La Charité." In some cases, M. Tanquerel des Planches has proved the utility of employing croton oil in doses of from one to four drops.

The method called that of La Charite.—This treatment extends over six days :

FIRST DAY.—Purgative glyster for painters, prepared from 8 grms. (Ʒii) of senna leaves infused in 500 grms. (Ʒxvi) of water, to which is afterwards added :

Powdered jalap	.	.	.	4 grms. (Ʒi.)
Diaphœnix electuary	.	.	.	30 grms. (Ʒi.)
Syrup of buckthorn	.	.	.	30 grms. (Ʒi.)

During the day, cassia water is administered, prepared from :

Cassia pods, beaten up with the seeds . . . }	62 grms.	(Ʒii and Ʒss.)
Water	1 kilogrm.	(Ʒxxxii.)

To be boiled for a quarter of an hour, and strained. Then add :

Sulphate of magnesia .	.	32 grms.	(Ʒi and Ʒss.)
Tartar emetic .	.	0,15 cent.	(gr. ii 1/4.)

And if the disease is intense, we may add :

Syrup of buckthorn	.	30 grms.	(Ʒi.)

In the evening, the anodyne glyster for painters is given, made of :

Beet oil	.	.	.	.	. 192 grms. (℥vi.)
Red wine	.	.	.	.	. 322 grms. (℥x.)

After the glyster, the patient must take the soothing bolus, made of :

Theriaca	.	.	.	. 4 grms. (℈i.)
Opium	.	.	.	. 0,05 cent. (gr. 3/4.)

SECOND DAY.—In the morning are ordered some doses of "holy water," made of :

Tartar emetic	.	.	. 0,30 cent. (gr. ivss.)
Water	.	.	. 250 grms. (℥viii.)

When the patient has vomited, he may take the sudorific tisane, prepared of :

Rasped guaiacum wood ⎫
Sarsaparilla root . ⎬ of each . . 30 grms. (℈i.)
Squine root . ⎭

To be boiled for an hour in a litre and a half (℔iss) of water, down to a litre (℥xxxii), to which is to be added, by maceration (see p. 148):

Sassafras wood	.	.	.	. 30 grms. (℈i.)
Liquorice	.	.	.	. 16 grms. (℥ss.)

In the evening, the anodyne glyster and sedative bolus, as above.

THIRD DAY.—Sudorific laxative tisane, made of the sudorific tisane, as above; to which is added, 30 grms. (℈i.) of senna. During the day, the simple sudorific tisane. In the morning he must take the *purgative mixture for painters*, prepared from :

Diaphœnix	.	.	. 30 grms. (℈i.)
Powdered jalap	.	.	. 4 grms. (℈i.)
Senna	.	.	. 8 grms. (℈ii.)
Syrup of buckthorn	.	.	. 30 grms. (℈i.)
Boiling water	.	.	. 125 grms. (℥iv.)

In the evening, the anodyne glyster and sedative bolus.

FOURTH DAY.—The same as the third.

FIFTH DAY.—During the day, the sudorific tisane; at 4 P.M. the purgative glyster; at 6 P.M. the anodyne glyster; and at 8 P.M. the sedative bolus.

SIXTH DAY.—Purgative mixture for painters, simple sudorific tisane, anodyne glyster and sedative bolus.

If the poisonous effects still continue, and the patient has not had an evacuation, we must have recourse to the *purgative bolus for painters*, made of :

Diagrède (scammony) } of each.	.	40 grms. (ℨx.)
Resin of jalap		
Gamboge .	.	1 grm. (gr. xv.)
Confection " d'hamech" } of each	.	q.s. for 12 boluses.
Syrup of buckthorn .		

One to be taken every 2 hours.

Iodide of potassium.—According to M. Melsens, and the experiments of M. Natalis Guillot, this salt, when given in a large dose, acts favourably in lead colic, and assists the evacuation of the poison.

Saturnine arthralgia is treated by sulphurous baths alone, or united with purgatives, if the affection is complicated with colic.

Lead palsy.—Strychnine is administered with success, principally by the endermic method, in doses, gradually increased, from 0,01 cent. to 0,05 cent. (gr. 1/6 to gr. 3/4) daily. Sulphurous baths, electricity, and electro-puncture are also useful.

Saturnine encephalo-pathia. — Diluent drinks, copiously given, appear to act by themselves in a favourable manner.

TREATMENT OF POISONING BY THE SALTS OF LEAD INTRODUCED
INTO THE DIGESTIVE CANAL.

The hydrated sulphurets of iron may be employed with success, but we prefer using the sulphates of potash, soda or magnesia, as they can be administered in a large dose without inconvenience. They convert the salts of lead into an insoluble sulphate, the harmlessness of which is indisputable ; and they also assist in expelling the poison by their purgative action.

Chemical examination of the organs and fluids of the system.—In diseases produced by saturnine emanations, MM. Mérat, Barruel, Chevallier, Guibourt, &c., have been unable to prove the presence of lead in the different organs of the system ; but MM. Guibourt and Devergie have succeeded in proving the presence of a notable quantity of lead in the brain of patients

affected with saturnine encephalo-pathia. Can this have been
normal lead?

(§. Lead has been found in abundance in the muscles of the
affected arm in a case of "hand-drop.")

Though there are three well-known oxides of lead, the protoxide alone combines with acids to form neutral or basic salts.
All the salts of lead are colourless, unless they contain a coloured
acid (chromates). Nearly all are insoluble in water, and they
are attacked by acids with difficulty—the acetates and the nitrate
being the only soluble ones. The first, which are extensively
used in commerce, are the most frequent cause of lead poisoning.
The chemical characters of the salts of lead are given below:

TESTS.	PRECIPITATES.
POTASH or SODA	White, soluble in an excess of the re-agent.
AMMONIA	White, insoluble in an excess of the re-agent.
SOLUBLE CARBONATES . . .	White, insoluble in an excess of the re-agent.
YELLOW CYANIDE OF POTASSIUM and IRON	White.
RED CYANIDE OF POTASSIUM and IRON	No precipitate.
TANNIN.	Yellow salt.
HYDROSULPHURIC ACID and SOLUBLE SULPHURETS	Black, insoluble in an excess of the re-agent.
SULPHURIC ACID and SOLUBLE SUL-PHATES	White.
SOLUBLE IODIDES.	Yellow, (§. soluble in boiling water.)
NEUTRAL CHROMATE OF POTASH . .	Bright yellow.

The presence of organic matters does not prevent the salts of
lead from being precipitated by sulphuric acid, the soluble sulphates and hydrosulphuric acid.

Iron, zinc, and tin precipitate lead from its solutions, forming
the "Arbor Saturni," or "lead tree," which is produced more
easily when the liquid is acidulated with nitric acid.

If we are engaged in discovering the presence of lead in an
organ, or in a liquid containing organic matters, we must destroy
these by nitric acid, and after calcination, boil the carbonaceous
mass with the same acid which will dissolve the metal; though it
is true that by this method we obtain also the normal lead, which

is however, in very small quantity. It is therefore better to boil the organs for some time in water acidulated with acetic acid; in which case the foreign poisonous lead alone will be dissolved. It is of the first importance to be certain about the purity of the reagents, and *especially of the water.*

It sometimes happens that wine merchants treat their acid liquors (wines, beer, &c.) with litharge, which saturates the excess of acid, and gives the wines a sweet flavour. Sometimes, also, when lead shot are used for cleaning bottles, a few shot remain in the bottom, and are liable to be dissolved by the liquid kept in the bottle, which may thus produce symptoms of both lead and arsenical poisoning; for shot always contain arsenic, as may be proved by Marsh's apparatus. As to the lead, after having decolourized the liquid by means of washed animal charcoal, we may recognize its presence by the characters given above; but it is important to employ very little animal charcoal, because it always retains a portion of the salts; as may be proved by boiling it with nitric acid, and then applying the tests.

PREPARATIONS OF TIN.

Tin vessels have long been employed; and this metal is used in the present day for lining all utensils made of copper; and the experiments of Bayen, Charlard and Proust have proved that tin is not poisonous, and that the quantity of arsenic which it contains is so insignificant, that we have nothing to fear from the employment of either tin or tinned vessels. If accidents have sometimes occurred, it has been owing to the tin having contained lead.

We shall here treat simply of poisoning by the protochloride of tin (salt of tin), which is often the cause of poisoning, owing to the facility with which it can be obtained, and its extensive employment in dyeing.

Symptoms.—Salt of tin, or protochloride of tin, possesses a very decided metallic flavour, and causes nausea, vomiting, abdominal pains and copious stools; it lowers the pulse, and produces convulsive motions, and sometimes paralysis—symptoms which are almost always followed by death.

Lesions.—The lesions produced by protochloride of tin closely resemble those occasioned by corrosive sublimate. They are, acute inflammation of all the parts with which the poison has come in contact, and the gastric and intestinal mucous membrane has a deep red colour, is hardened, and frequently ulcerated; but the consideration of the symptoms and lesions alone is not sufficient to establish the nature of the poison which has been taken.

Treatment.—Milk, or, in its absence, tepid water, or, better still, mild mucilaginous decoctions, must be copiously administered. The milk acts not only as a soothing diluent, but its casein also appears to form an insoluble and inert compound with the tin. If the symptoms of inflammation of the abdominal organs are alarming, we must employ general and local bloodletting, and glysters of narcotic emollients.

Chemical examination.—Though we have only mentioned poisoning by protochloride of tin, we think it desirable to give the chemical characters of the salts of the protoxide, and also the bisalts of tin—which latter are represented by the bichloride.

TESTS.	SALTS OF THE PROTOXIDE.	BISALTS OF TIN.
POTASH	White precipitate, soluble in an excess of the test.	Gelatinous white precipitate, soluble in an excess of the test.
AMMONIA . . .	White precipitate, insoluble in an excess of the test.	White precipitate, soluble in an excess of the test.
CARBONATE OF POTASH .	White precipitate, with disengagement of carbonic acid gas.	White precipitate, with disengagement of carbonic acid.
YELLOW CYANIDE OF POTASSIUM and IRON .	White gelatinous precipitate.	White gelatinous precipitate.
RED CYANIDE OF POTASSIUM and IRON . .	White precipitate.	No precipitate.
HYDROSULPHURIC ACID .	Brown (¼. black) precipitate.	Yellow precipitate, soluble in ammonia, but without loss of colour.
SOLUBLE SULPHURETS .	White precipitate, soluble in an excess of the test.	Yellow precipitate soluble in an excess of the test.
CHLORIDE OF GOLD. .	Precipitate of purple of cassius.	No precipitate.
SHEET OF ZINC . .	Precipitate of metallic tin.	Metallic tin.

The presence of organic matters often prevents these reactions. We must proceed in our search for tin in the usual manner; *i. e.* we must destroy the organic matter by nitric acid, and must remove the carbon by *aqua regia*, with an excess of hydrochloric acid. The chloride of tin formed will then be indicated by the tests above pointed out.

PREPARATIONS OF BISMUTH.

The nitrate and sulphate of bismuth are the only soluble salts which can produce accidents. They irritate, inflame and corrode the tissues with which they come in contact; but they exert their chief influence upon the nervous system.

Symptoms, lesions and treatment.—The same as in tin.

Chemical examination.—We shall content ourselves with pointing out the characters of the salts of bismuth. They have all an acid reaction, and water decomposes them into soluble acid salts, and insoluble basic ones; but an excess of acid prevents this decomposition.

TESTS.	PRECIPITATES.
POTASH and AMMONIA. . . .	White, insoluble in an excess of the test.
SOLUBLE CARBONATES. . . .	Ditto.
YELLOW CYANIDE OF POTASSIUM and IRON	White, insoluble in hydrochloric acid.
RED CYANIDE OF POTASSIUM and IRON	Yellow, soluble in hydrochloric acid.
TANNIN	Orange-yellow.
HYDROSULPHURIC ACID and SOLUBLE SULPHURETS	Brown or black.
CHROMATE OF POTASH . . .	Yellow.
PLATE OF ZINC	Metallic bismuth.

The salts of antimony, which are also decomposed by water, exhibit many reactions similar to those of bismuth; but they are distinguished by hydrosulphuric acid, and the soluble sulphurets, which cause an orange-yellow precipitate with the salts of antimony.

POISONING BY THE PREPARATIONS OF SILVER.

Nitrate of silver, either crystallized or fused (pierre infernale —lunar caustic), is the only salt of silver which is used commercially. It rapidly destroys life by acting upon the lungs and nervous system, especially if it is injected into the veins; and when introduced into the stomach, it is absorbed, and produces acute inflammation of all the parts which it touches. When applied to the skin, or the sub-cutaneous cellular tissue, it burns them, and produces a (§. circumscribed) scar; so that it can be used as a caustic without danger (§. of its spreading beyond the desired limits).

Symptoms and lesions.—The same as those described in speaking of corrosive sublimate, only in this case perforations are frequent. We may also add, that nitrate of silver colours the skin black, or a dirty brown, and that these stains, when recent, disappear by washing them with iodide of potassium.

Treatment.—Abundant drinks, rendered slightly saline by chloride of sodium, and afterwards, emollient liquids. Bleeding, if necessary, and glysters and emollient baths, &c.

Chemical examination.—The soluble salts of silver present the following characters:

TESTS.	PRECIPITATES.
POTASH or SODA	Brown, insoluble in potash, but soluble in ammonia.
AMMONIA (very weak)	Brown, soluble in excess of ammonia.
CARBONATE OF POTASH. . . .	White, soluble in ammonia.
PHOSPHATE OF SODA	Yellow.
PYROPHOSPHATE OF SODA . . .	White.
YELLOW CYANIDE OF POTASSIUM and IRON	White.
RED CYANIDE OF POTASSIUM and IRON	Reddish-brown.
HYDROSULPHURIC ACID and the SOLUBLE SULPHURETS . . .	Black.
IODIDE OF POTASSIUM . . .	Yellowish-white, slightly soluble in ammonia.
HYDROCHLORIC ACID and the SOLUBLE CHLORIDES.	White, *clotty*, insoluble in water, or in cold or boiling nitric acid. Soluble in ammonia.
ZINC	Precipitates metallic silver.

Hydrochloric acid and the chlorides are the best tests for the salts of silver, which they precipitate, even in the midst of organic matters.

POISONING BY THE PREPARATIONS OF GOLD.

The chlorides of gold, the only soluble preparations of this metal, are violent poisons. They inflame the parts which they touch, after first staining them purple, and the symptoms and lesions resemble those produced by corrosive sublimate, but are less active.

Treatment.—We are not aware of any case of poisoning by this substance. Experiments have proved that in any such case we ought to promote vomiting, and to administer mucilaginous drinks in abundance. In short, to proceed as in the case of other irritant poisons.

Chemical Characters of the Salts of Gold.

TESTS.	PRECIPITATES.
POTASH	*None*, if the potash is in great excess.
AMMONIA and its CARBONATE . .	{ *Yellow*, fulminating gold by ammonia. By the carbonate there is also a disengagement of carbonic acid.
OXALIC ACID and SULPHATE OF PROT-OXIDE OF IRON	*Black*, metallic gold in powder.
YELLOW CYANIDE OF POTASSIUM and IRON	*Emerald-green* colour.
PROTOCHLORIDE OF TIN . . .	*Brown*, of variable shades.
HYDROSULPHURIC ACID . . .	*Black*.
HYDROSULPHATE OF AMMONIA . .	*Black*, soluble in an excess of the test.
ZINC	*Brown*, metallic gold.

The salts of gold stain the skin rose-coloured or purple, and are decomposed by most organic substances.

POISONING BY THE PREPARATIONS OF ZINC.

Metallic zinc in thin sheets is used for making sundry household or cooking utensils, which may be attacked by different acid liquids, such as wine, vinegar, (§. and milk when it has become sour), by greasy bodies, and even by water itself, which when kept in zinc vessels often holds insoluble hydrocarbonate of zinc in suspension, which being dissolved by the acids of the stomach, causes abundant vomiting. We have seen cases of poisoning produced by water which had been collected from zinc roofing.

Sulphate of zinc (white vitriol) and chloride of zinc are both well known in commerce, and have frequently caused poisoning. They are both essentially emetics, and may be safely given in large doses, if the animal is allowed to vomit; but if the œsophagus is tied, they are absorbed and carried throughout the system, and may occasion death in eighteen or twenty hours, if they have been given in a sufficient dose.

Symptoms and lesions.—Nearly the same as those produced by other irritant poisons, but amongst their symptoms vomiting is the most prominent, and in addition to their irritant action, they exercise a stupifying influence upon the brain.

Treatment.—We may administer a large quantity of soothing fluids, and milk and water, which possesses the property of decomposing the salts of zinc. Weak alkaline solutions, which have been proposed, ought to be proscribed as too irritating. Lastly, the inflammation which is excited must be soothed by ordinary antiphlogistic measures.

When the salt of zinc has acted upon the nervous system, and the vomiting has been very obstinate, we must make haste to calm these alarming symptoms, by the administration of opiates.

Chemical examination. — The suspected matters must be boiled with water acidulated with sulphuric acid, and if the liquid is coloured, it must be decolorized by animal charcoal, after which the colourless solution presents the following characters:

Characters of the salts of zinc.—Colourless salts, with a harsh styptic flavour; they have an acid reaction, and are not precipitated by any metal.

TESTS.	PRECIPITATES.
POTASH, SODA and AMMONIA . .	*White,* gelatinous, soluble in an excess of the test.
CARBONATES OF POTASH and OF SODA.	*White,* gelatinous, insoluble in an excess of the test. Soluble in potash.
CARBONATE OF AMMONIA . . .	*White,* soluble in an excess of the test.
OXALIC ACID and the SOLUBLE OXALATES.	*White,* crystalline, soluble in potash.
YELLOW CYANIDE OF POTASSIUM and IRON	*White,* insoluble in acid. It has a bluish tint, if the solution is very acid.
RED CYANIDE OF POTASSIUM and IRON	*Yellow* salt, soluble in hydrochloric acid.
HYDROSULPHURIC ACID . .	*None,* with the salts of the mineral acids; *white,* with the acetate.
SOLUBLE SULPHURETS . . .	*White,* unless the solution is acid, in which case there is no precipitate.

In short, the salts of zinc form white precipitates with every reagent except the red cyanide of potassium and iron.

POISONING BY THE PREPARATIONS OF IRON.

The salts of iron are extensively used in commerce, and are poisonous, causing acute local irritation. We were not acquainted with any case of poisoning by the salts of iron, until at the last assizes, the Court of the Lower Department of the Loire condemned a woman who had been convicted of having poisoned her daughter by means of sulphate of iron.

Symptoms, lesions and treatment are the same as those above mentioned in speaking of zinc. As to the chemical investigation, we must remember in operating by calcination that the system naturally contains iron. We must therefore content ourselves with boiling the suspected materials with acidulated water, which takes up the iron introduced as a poison, but will not touch the normal iron.

Characters of the Salts of Iron.

TESTS.	SALTS OF THE *Prot*-OXIDE. *Taste*—Astringent metallic. *Colour*—Emerald green.	SALTS OF THE *Sesqui*-OXIDE. *Colour*—Yellow or red. They redden litmus.
POTASH or SODA . .	Greenish-white precipitate, becoming green, and ultimately a dirty yellow, when exposed to the air	Reddish-brown precipitate, insoluble in an excess of the reagent.
AMMONIA . . .	Greenish-white precipitate, soluble in an excess of the test.	Ditto.
ALKALINE CARBONATES and PHOSPHATES .	White precipitate, becoming green in the air.	A brown precipitate. If a carbonate is used, carbonic acid gas is disengaged.
YELLOW CYANIDE OF POTASSIUM and IRON.	White precipitate, which becomes blue gradually in the air, and immediately under the influence of chlorine.	Precipitate of Prussian-blue.
RED CYANIDE OF POTASSIUM and IRON .	Deep-blue precipitate.	No precipitate.
HYDROSULPHURIC ACID	No precipitate.	Milky-white precipitate of sulphur, and the salt is reduced to the state of protoxide.
ALKALINE SULPHURETS	Black precipitate.	Black precipitate.
CHLORIDE OF GOLD .	Brown precipitate of metallic gold.	No effect.
SULPHOCYANIDE OF POTASSIUM . .	No effect.	Blood-red colour.
TINCTURE OF GALLS .	No precipitate.	Blue or black colour.

POISONING BY POWDERED GLASS AND ENAMEL.

These two bodies are insoluble even when reduced to powder, and are consequently without effect upon the system unless they act mechanically whilst they are retained in it. Cases of poisoning by them are rare. As treatment, we must administer an emetic and assist its action by thick mucilaginous liquids, and then have recourse to antiphlogistics if necessary.

IRRITANT POISONS FROM THE VEGETABLE KINGDOM.

A great many vegetable substances are most violent irritant poisons, which we must be contented with simply enumerating. They are: bryony, elaterium, colocynth, (*Cucurbitaceæ*); jalap resin, scammony and turbith (*Convolvulaceæ*); camboge, (*Guttiferæ*); mezereum (*Thymelaceæ*); ricinus, euphorbium and croton tiglium, (*Euphorbiaceæ*); savine, (*Coniferæ*); rhus radicans, and toxicodendron (*Terebinthaceæ*); monkshood, stavesacre, ranunculus sceleratus, bulbosus and acris, and anemone pulsatilla (*Ranunculaceæ*); and several other plants belonging to different natural orders, such as aloes, hyssop, lobelia, &c., and creosote, which is not vegetable, though of vegetable origin.

Treatment.—In cases of poisoning by irritant plants we must immediately provoke or assist vomiting, and then have recourse to antiphlogistics. Sometimes, when there is drowsiness, we administer strong coffee in large doses.

IRRITANT POISONS FROM THE ANIMAL KINGDOM.

POISONING BY CANTHARIDES.

Cantharides, *Cantharis vesicatoria, Meloe vesicatorius, Lytta vesicatoria* are insects of the order *Coleoptera*, section *Heteromera*, and of the family *Trachelides*.

When these insects are reduced to powder and introduced into the stomach, or applied to the skin or cellular tissue, they are most energetic poisons, and exert their influence principally upon the bladder and genital organs. Their deleterious property is due to *cantharidine*, to a *volatile oily principle*, and probably also to their *black* constituent, for the experiments of Orfila have proved that the *green* oil, and the *yellow* substance which are soluble in alcohol, and also powdered *cantharides itself, when exhausted by water*, do not possess any vesiccating property; whilst powdered cantharides, deprived of its volatile principle, but still containing cantharidine, acts as a caustic, though in a less degree than the common powder. Extracts of cantharides, also, which contain cantharidine, but not the volatile principle, are still very active, though they ought not to be deprived of this latter principle. Fatty bodies dissolve the poisonous principles of cantharides, and oil of sweet almonds, when digested with cantharides, furnishes an oil, which when injected into the veins, exerts its influence upon the nervous system, and especially upon the spinal column.

Symptoms of poisoning by cantharides.—Powerful offensive odour; harsh, disagreeable taste; abundant vomiting; and copious, and often bloody purging; acute colic; heat in the bladder; the *urine* sometimes *bloody;* obstinate priapism; quick, hard pulse; painful and excited respiration; intense thirst or else horror of liquids; convulsions, tetanus, delirium, &c.; in addition to which, if the powdered cantharides have been applied externally there may be sloughing of the part.

Lesions.—When introduced into the stomach in the form of powder, cantharides often produce upon the internal surface of the digestive tube fungous tubercles, swollen veins, and spots formed of extravasated blood. Inflammation of the mucous membrane of the bladder only occurs when the patient succumbs two or three days after the poison has been taken, and it never occurs in women; in addition to which, it disappears in four or five days after burial. In a man, this inflammation often produces gangrene of the penis. If the autopsy is made within twenty-four hours after death, the existence of this inflammation may furnish valuable evidence, if it can be proved that it is not owing to a cancer or ulcer of the bladder, to gangrene of the rectum after the operation for hydrocele, or to urinous infiltration consequent upon rupture of the urethra. In cases in which the powdered cantharides have been applied externally, there is infiltration of the part, and in this case the bladder and genital organs are generally inflamed, but it is not usual to find lesions of the digestive canal.

Treatment of poisoning by cantharides. — Vomiting must be excited by the administration of a large quantity of tepid mucilaginous drinks, and we must employ warm baths, and inject soothing liquids into the bladder; the gastro-intestinal inflammation is to be combatted by fomentations, emollient poultices, and general and local blood-letting. If the inflammation is very high, we may prescribe camphor internally, either alone or combined with gummy extract of opium, and the belly and the thighs may be rubbed with camphorated oil. If the poisoning is produced by the external application of the cantharides it is useless to excite vomiting, but we must use baths and administer emollient tisanes, containing spirit of nitre and camphor. The frictions of which we have just spoken may also be employed with success, and if there is acute pain in the region of the bladder or stomach, we must apply leeches, and afterwards emollient fomentations.

Medico-legal examination.—The colour of the elytra (wing scales), which are green and gold-green, and that of the antennæ, which are black, sufficiently characterises cantharides. We must therefore search for the broken wing-covers, which present themselves under the form of brilliant points, with an almost metallic lustre. Cantharides give off a peculiar nauseous odour. By treating the suspected materials with alcohol we may obtain the *cantharidine*, which forms micaceous scales, insoluble in water, but soluble in fixed and volatile oils, and fusible at 210° C. (410° F.) When strongly heated it is decomposed, and partially sublimes under the form of brilliant spangles. Hydrochloric and nitric acid dissolve it without the solution being coloured, whilst sulphuric acid colours it in dissolving it. A somewhat concentrated solution of potash or of soda dissolves it. When dissolved in a little oil and applied to the skin, it produces a blister. We may still more completely remove the *cantharidine* by the assistance of ether ; but it is not indispensable to isolate this substance in order to be satisfied of poisoning by cantharides, especially if we have succeeded in collecting the *débris* of the elytra.

POISONING BY MUSCLES.

Muscles, when eaten even in small quantities, sometimes produce severe effects, which have indeed been followed by death. The effects which they produce have been attributed to different causes ; some persons having pretended that they depend upon a morbid alteration in the animals themselves; and others, that their poisonous action is owing to substances upon which they have fed; but according to Edwards, it is impossible up to the present time, to prove the presence of any poisonous substance in muscles. It is more probable that the noxious influence is to be attributed to a peculiar disposition of the stomach (idiosyncrasy). We have certainly often found stomachs which cannot bear muscles, whilst other persons have eaten a large quantity of them without inconvenience. According to Lamouroux, muscles owe their deleterious property to a yellowish substance, which he has called scum (*crasse*), which is found in the sea. Lastly, M. Breumi thinks that it is little star-fish, which being introduced into the muscles produce the bad consequences.

Treatment.—We must immediately administer an emetic and purgative, or a substance which will act in both ways, according to the period that has elapsed since the muscles were eaten, and we must then give an ethereal draught, and vinegar and water as a tisane. If symptoms of inflammation manifest themselves in the lower part of the belly, they must be allayed by antiphlogistics.

SECOND CLASS.

NARCOTIC POISONS.

Those substances are termed *narcotics* which cause drowsiness, stupor, paralysis or apoplexy, or convulsive motions, but do not in general inflame the parts which they touch.

Symptoms.—Congestion and weight in the head, sleep, vertigo, a state resembling apoplexy, pains, slight at first, but acute afterwards, manifested by cries, furious or cheerful delirium, convulsive motions, partial paralysis, diminished sensibility, nausea and vomiting, the pulse strong, and either quick or slow, the respiration slightly accelerated, and the pupil *dilated* in some cases, and *contracted* in others.

Lesions of tissues.—When the poisoning has been of short duration we do not find any lesion, unless we have administered some irritating substance as an antidote. When applied to the denuded dermis, they produce slight irritation, analogous to what would be created by an inert or foreign body. The lungs do, however, sometimes exhibit changes, of which we shall speak further on. The cavities of the heart and the veins contain coagulated blood very soon after death; and the brain and its membranes are sometimes slightly injected. Narcotics only act after being absorbed. They produce death quickly when injected into the veins, more slowly when applied to the cellular tissue, and more slowly still when taken into the stomach.

Treatment.—We cannot give many very general directions about poisoning with narcotics; but we may say that emetics should always be given, as they answer two purposes: 1. They expel the poison; 2. They counteract, and even destroy its stupefying influence, and are therefore of great value. In the last place we must combat the drowsiness by stimulating drinks, such as coffee, tea, &c.

POISONING BY MORPHIA AND ITS SALTS.

Morphia, when introduced into the stomach, is rapidly absorbed, probably in consequence of its being converted into a soluble salt by means of the acids contained in that organ. When applied to the denuded skin, it is also very quickly absorbed by virtue of its solubility in alkaline liquids; and it is well known that lymph is constantly alkaline. In small doses it produces the following effects:

Symptoms.—Slight headache, distressing dreams, vertigo, and *contraction* of the *pupil*, in most cases; but if its action is *violent*, the pupil may remain in its *normal* state, or may even be *dilated*. Sudden startings (" commotions "), violent vomiting, pain more or less severe in the epigastric region, in general constipation, followed by violent diarrhœa, pulse usually weak and slow, respiration, generally natural, urine scanty or absent, and dry itching of the skin, which Dr. Bally regards as a most important symptom. This itching is accompanied by small, rounded, colourless, pimples. But amongst the most constant symptoms, MM. Trousseau and Bonnet place in the first rank *increased thirst*, accompanied with dryness of the mouth and throat, and vomiting, generally without bitterness of the mouth; but this bitterness, when present, must not be considered as a precursor of vomiting, as has been stated by Bally.

Although we have observed painful dreams in cases of poisoning by morphia, we ought to mention that the sleep which is produced by this substance is often calm and peaceful, but is always accompanied by *contraction* of the *pupils* when the poisoning is slight. In a large dose, morphia produces contraction, and then irregular motions *before* causing *dilatation* of the pupils. In a great number of cases there is delirium, either slight or furious, and the aspect of the face is that of congestion, not that of stupor and prostration which is remarked when the morphia has been given in small doses. When injected into the veins, morphia and its salts act more energetically; and when applied to the nervous system, they act as they do when injected into the stomach. The absorption of morphine and its salts produces some very remarkable phenomena which have been the subject of very interesting and profound investigation by MM. Dupuy, Leuret, Deguise, Desportes, Magendie, Flourens, Orfila, &c. For the full description of phenomena produced by these poisons we must refer to Special Treatises on Toxicology.

Treatment.—The same as for Opium, p. 438.

Chemical examination. —Besides morphia, opium contains codein combined with meconic or sulphuric acid; and narcotine, which is partly free, and partly combined with resinous matter. As regards intensity, these three organic alkalies produce the same phenomena, but we cannot describe each of these substances in detail in this work, but must content ourselves with pointing out the chemical characters that serve to distinguish them. We must however remark, that in order to be certain that the case is one of poisoning by morphia or its salts, it is *necessary* to prove clearly all the characters which distinguish it, and which we shall now give. We may add, that in cases of judicial disinterment, morphia may be discovered long after burial. The following are the characteristics of the three principal alkaloids of opium.

TESTS.	MORPHIA.	CODEIN.	NARCOTINE.
SOLUBILITY IN WATER.	Slight.	Soluble.	Slight.
SOLUBILITY IN ALCOHOL.	Soluble.	Soluble.	Soluble.
SOLUBILITY IN ETHER	Insoluble.	Slightly soluble.	Soluble.
SOLUBILITY IN CAUSTIC ALKALIES	Soluble.	Insoluble.	Insoluble.
FLAVOUR	Very bitter.	Bitter.	Slightly bitter.
NITRIC ACID	Produces a blood-red colour.	Does not redden it.	Red colour.
PERSALTS OF IRON	Blue colour.	No colour.	No colour.
IODIC ACID	Decomposes this acid, and sets iodine free.	No decomposition.	No decomposition.
PERCHLORIDE OF GOLD	Yellow precipitate, then blue, and lastly, violet.	Yellow precipitate.	Yellow precipitate.

We therefore see by this table that morphia is distinguished by its solubility in alcohol and caustic alkalies, and it is also soluble in fixed volatile oils; by its insolubility in ether, which dissolves narcotine; and lastly, by the *blood-red* colour produced by *nitric acid*, the *blue* by the *persalts* of *iron*, and by its decomposing iodic acid; a combination of characters which is not presented by any other known substance. (§. None of these tests are very delicate : the solution must be moderately strong for the effect to be evident).

POISONING BY OPIUM.

Opium is a very complex product, and of variable composition, of which we have already spoken in the Art of Prescribing, (p. 121). The proximate principles which it contains are however always the same, and it is merely their proportions which are variable. It is a very powerful poison, its toxical properties being principally attributable to morphia, though its other principles assist in rendering it more poisonous. It acts rapidly when injected into the veins; less so when applied to the cellular tissue; and still less so when introduced into the stomach or rectum.

The dregs of opium, deprived of morphia and narcotine by water or by alcohol, are without action upon the animal system; but if deprived of narcotine alone, by means of ether or by the process of M. Limousin-Lamothe, it possesses all its properties, and even acts with still more energy. M. Orfila has also proved the presence of a volatile principle in opium which may be obtained by distillation, and is capable of exciting vertigo, though without being very poisonous. It is impossible at present to say what part each of the proximate principles of opium plays, in cases of poisoning by this drug. MM. Desportes and Flourens have proved that opium acts principally upon the cerebral lobes.

An attempt has been made to establish an identity between the action of opium and alcoholic liquors, but M. Orfila has proved conclusively that there is a great difference between the action of these two classes of substances.*

Symptoms of poisoning by opium.—They are nearly the same as those produced by morphia, but opium appears to exert a more stimulant influence, and according to M. Bailly, painful dreams are more frequently produced by opium than by morphia, and the same is the case with the itching and eruption of which we spoke in treating of morphia.

Treatment. — Different substances have been proposed as antidotes for opium, which we will examine in order, and point out the value of each:

1. **Vinegar and vegetable acids.**—Whenever the opium has not been vomited, the vegetable acids aggravate the symptoms: but if vomiting has occurred, and the poison has been expelled, vinegar and water and the vegetable acids diminish the symptoms, and may even cause them to cease.

2. **Very strong coffee** does not decompose the opium in the stomach, nor can it be regarded as an antidote; but it has not,

---

* "Traité de Toxicologie," de M. Orfila.

like vinegar, the disadvantage of increasing the symptoms. Even if vomiting has not occurred there is no harm in using coffee, whilst there is if we employ vinegar under the same circumstances. We may also add, that very strong coffee, frequently administered, rapidly diminishes the effects of opium, and may even cause their cessation.

3. **Decoction of galls,** owing to the tannin which it contains, possesses the property of precipitating the organic alkalies of opium, and of forming but slightly soluble *tannates*, which are much less poisonous than opium itself. The employment of this decoction is therefore advantageous if we take care not to administer it in such excess as to re-dissolve the precipitate first formed.

4. **Chlorine water** does not present any real advantages and ought to be rejected.

5. **Camphor** is certainly not an antidote to opium, but when administered in small doses, it may nevertheless abate the symptoms produced by a large dose of opium.

6. **Water and mucilaginous drinks** are of no use when given in great abundance, and can only aggravate the evil by diluting the poison, and so facilitating its absorption.

7. **Ioduretted iodide of potassium,** dissolved in water, precipitates the organic alkalies of opium well enough, and forms insoluble compounds with them ; but as an excess of the antidote may produce very severe symptoms of irritation it ought to be rejected.

8. **Bleeding** does not appear to be injurious in any case, and it will be useful in strong plethoric persons, especially if some time has elapsed since the poisoning, and we have no occasion to fear that it will hasten absorption.

Steps to be pursued in the treatment.—The following is a summary of the physician's duty in treating a case of poisoning by opium. He must administer 25 or 30 centigrammes (gr. iv or gr. ivss) of tartar emetic *dissolved* in a *very small quantity* of of water, and 75 centigrammes or 1 gramme (gr. xiss to gr. xv) of sulphate of zinc; or 10 to 25 centigrammes (gr. iss to gr. iv) of sulphate of copper. (This last salt, in a large dose, is capable of exciting acute inflammation of the digestive tube, and

of causing death). After having given the emetics, he must
administer decoction of galls or strong coffee after the vomiting
has been copious; and if the subject is plethoric, he may then
take blood from the arm. He may afterwards give coffee, or
acetic, or tartaric, or citric lemonade as a drink; and from time
to time he must make rough friction upon the arms and legs,
(§. and must compel the patient, even if necessary by flogging,
to keep in motion for some hours after the poison has been taken).
Lastly, he may give a camphorated glyster, or a purgative one,
if he supposes that the poison has passed through the pylorus.

Chemical examination.—We cannot here give the chemical
and physical characters of the different preparations of opium,
for such a description would only be fit for a complete treatise on
toxicology. But we may remark that poisoning by Sydenham's
laudanum* is the most common; and that its extreme bitterness,
yellow colour, and vinous, slightly poisonous and aromatic odour
are sufficient for recognizing it.

It is difficult to isolate crystallized morphia and meconic acid
when we operate upon small quantities; and it is not sufficient
to prove merely its bitterness, and the colour produced by the
tests for morphia, in order to affirm positively that the suspected
liquid contains opium. It is necessary to isolate the morphia
and meconic acid, in order to pronounce with certainty; but if
to the reactions indicating their presence, we can add the *symptoms* of poisoning by opium the presumption becomes very
strong.

Process.—If we are operating upon liquid matters we must
evaporate them to the consistence of a thick syrup by a very gentle
heat; but if, on the contrary, we are engaged upon solid organs,
we must boil them in water slightly acidulated with acetic acid,
and after this evaporate the solution to the consistence of a thick
syrup. This is then to be treated twice with boiling concentrated alcohol; and the solution obtained by it is to be filtered
when cold, and again evaporated to the consistence of syrup.
We must now re-dissolve in distilled water, and filter a second
time. The filtered liquid is then to be treated with basic acetate

(§. * Sydenham's laudanum corresponds closely with the London vinum opii,
whence the *vinous* and *aromatic* odour spoken of, which are not present in common
laudanum.)

of lead (§. liq. plumb. diacet.), which forms a precipitate of meconate of lead, which must be separated by filtration and carefully preserved. A current of hydrosulphuric acid is then to be passed through the solution, to precipitate the excess of lead, and after again filtering it the liquid is to be evaporated in a water-bath, after being decolorized by animal charcoal if necessary. Lastly, the evaporation is to be completed under an air-pump receiver, by which means we obtain a shapeless mass of crystals, which present all the characters above assigned to morphia. As to the precipitate of meconate of lead, it is to be boiled with water acidulated with sulphuric acid, which will form an insoluble sulphate of lead, which may be separated by filtration. The liquid, when evaporated, furnishes either crystals or an amorphous powder of *meconic acid*, the solution of which precipitates the salts of the peroxide of iron (§. Tinct. ferri. sesquichlor.) of a deep blood-red.

NARCOTICS OF THE NATURAL ORDER OF SOLANACEÆ.

Hyosciamus, and the plants of the genus *Solanum*, especially bitter-sweet (*Solanum dulcamara*) and common nightshade, (*S. nigrum*) approach opium in their effects. Although *hyosciamia* has been extracted from hyosciamus, and *solanine* from the different solanums, it is very difficult to prove their presence in the animal system unless we operate upon large quantities. The treatment will be the same as that for opium : but as poisoning by these substances is extremely rare, we shall refer to special treatises on toxicology for the particulars.

Some authors have placed saffron amongst narcotics. If the substance is injurious, it is in a very feeble degree. The wild lettuce and the yew also produce symptoms analogous to those caused by opium.

POISONING BY HYDROCYANIC (PRUSSIC) ACID.

The hydrocyanic acid of Gay-Lussac is, with *nicotine* and *cicutine*, the most active of known poisons. The diluted (medicinal) acid acts in the same way, but about ten times the dose is necessary. It acts more quickly and with greater intensity when it has been dissolved in ether or alcohol. When exposed to the air, and even when carefully excluded from it, it (§. the strong acid) rapidly loses its properties, and is converted into an imperfecty understood black matter.

It acts upon animals of all classes, but principally upon those whose nervous system is the most developed; and it is absorbed whether it is introduced by the stomach or through the denuded skin; but it does not act when placed upon the nerves, the *dura mater*, or any of the white organs. The intensity of its action varies according to a great number of circumstances.

Symptoms.—The symptoms produced by hydrocyanic acid are so important, that we shall describe them with care. They may be divided into three periods.

FIRST PERIOD is very short: Weight of the head, dizziness, unsteady gait, difficult respiration, and increased pulsation of the heart.

SECOND PERIOD. — Convulsion, the head drawn backwards, tetanic spasms, general insensibility, and during this period there is frequently involuntary emission of urine or fœces.

THIRD PERIOD.—Continued insensibility, profound coma, great muscular relaxation, complete loss of motion, difficult respiration. This period, which is of some length, terminates in death; but it is sometimes interrupted by a fresh attack of tetanic spasms of short duration; and lastly, in certain cases, epigastric pain is observed.

Lesions of tissues.—When hydrocyanic acid kills quickly, it does not inflame the parts with which it has been in contact, and if the contrary takes place, the acid has not been pure; the muscular contractility is annihilated; the vascular system is gorged with thick, black, oily-looking blood; the veins of the brain may be slightly injected; but there are *never* clots of blood, or cerebral hæmorrhage, which essentially distinguishes poisoning by prussic acid from apoplexy, properly so called. (§. Though it may not be called true inflammation, still the mucous membrane of the stomach is often *deeply injected* in cases of poisoning by ordinary prussic acid, in which death has been as rapid as usual with this poison.)

TREATMENT OF POISONING BY HYDROCYANIC ACID.

Several antidotes have been proposed; viz., ammonia, strong coffee, oil of turpentine, bleeding, dashing cold water upon the head, the inhalation of chlorine, and latterly, the hydrated carbonate ferroso-ferrique (hydrated protoxide and peroxide of iron).

Ammonia.—The inhalation of ammonia from a moderately strong solution may prevent death from prussic acid, by stimulating the nervous system; but it is necessary that this antidote should be employed early. It is necessary also to abstain from using solution of ammonia of the ordinary strength, as it excites acute inflammation.

Strong coffee is of no use, and ought to be abandoned.

Oil of turpentine produces no good effect, either when inhaled, or when taken into the stomach.

Blood-letting has been extolled by Hume, but the experiments of Orfila prove that it has no sensible effect. It may, however, diminish cerebral congestion.

Affusion of cold water.—These affusions are practised along the spine, and chiefly along the cervical vertibræ; they act beneficially and may produce a speedy recovery.

Chlorine.—Inspirations through water, slightly impregnated with chlorine or with the condensed chloro-vinegar of M. Mialhe, prevent the action of hydrocyanic acid, probably by decomposing it, and separating its hydrogen. The condensed chloro-vinegar just mentioned is prepared by spreading a thin layer of dry chloride of lime upon a towel, folding this into the form of a cravat, and moistening it with vinegar, which disengages the chlorine by degrees, and allows it to be inspired through the mouth and nostrils.

Hydrated carbonate of protoxide and peroxide of iron (Hydrated carbonate of ferroso-ferrique).—This product is obtained from a mixture of equal parts of sulphate of protoxide and sulphate of peroxide of iron, decomposed by means of carbonate of soda, which causes a brown precipitate, with a mixture of hydrated carbonate of the protoxide and carbonate (?) of the peroxide of iron. This is the mixture recommended by Messrs. Smith (of Edinburgh), but it does not act so favourably as chlorine or affusions of water; and as it is rapidly converted by the air into peroxide of iron, it must be prepared in the moment of need, by which we then lose very precious time.

Steps to be pursued in the treatment.—If the poison has been administered by the stomach, we must make haste to administer an emetic (§. and to irritate the fauces by a feather), or give a purgative glyster, if we are summoned at a later period. We must then make the patient inhale chlorinated water or solution of ammonia (1 part of ammonia to 12 parts of water*); but the chlorine answers the best. We must insist upon these inspirations, and must dash cold water down the back, and put a bladder of ice upon the head. At a later period the symptoms of cerebral congestion must be combatted by general bleeding, or by leeches placed behind the ears.

Chemical examination.—When hydrocyanic acid is *pure and anhydrous*, it exists under the form of a liquid at common temperatures, which is colourless, of a powerful odour, resembling that of bitter almonds, of a sharp, hot flavour, which excites coughing; it slightly reddens litmus paper, and boils at 25° C. (77° F.); it rapidly decomposes, inflames on the approach of a burning body, and is soluble in water, constituting the medicinal acid, which presents the same physical characters as the concentrated acid, only in a less degree; but when it is poured upon paper, it does not congeal, as the anhydrous acid does, nor is it inflammable. If, however, it is distilled, the condensed products may be inflammable.

(§. * Liquor ammonia fortior contains about 1 part of ammonia in 3; and it can therefore be reduced to the above strength by mixing 1 part of liquor ammonia with 8 parts of water.)

Pure or diluted hydrocyanic acid produces a white precipitate with nitrate of silver; and the cyanide of silver which is formed is white, clotty, and insoluble in water or in *cold* nitric acid, though it *dissolves* in *boiling nitric acid*, and also in *ammonia*. When the precipitate is washed and carefully dried, and then heated in a test-tube, it is decomposed into metallic silver (§. which remains in the tube as a brown powder), and into cyanogen, which burns, when inflamed, with a purple colour, and is absorbable by potash; but if the cyanide of silver has been badly dried, it does not produce cyanogen. Instead of decomposing the cyanide of silver by heat, M. O. Henry proposes to boil it with chloride of sodium and a very small quantity of distilled water, by which means chloride of silver and cyanide of sodium are formed; but we must take care not to use an excess of chloride of sodium, and to boil it a sufficient length of time. We must then allow the liquid to cool, and must filter it, and afterwards add to the liquid a small quantity of freshly prepared *green* hydrated oxide of iron (protoxide, mixed with a little sesquioxide); heat it slightly, and again filter. By this means we form yellow cyanide of potassium* and iron, which being treated with sulphate of sesquioxide of iron (§. or with tinct. ferri-sesquichlor,), produces a beautiful blue precipitate of double cyanide of iron (*Prussian blue*).

M. Lassaigne prefers decomposing the cyanide of silver by means of potassium in a very small tube; cyanide of potassium is formed which produces a beautiful precipitate of Prussian blue, when treated with mixed sulphate of protoxide and peroxide of iron (sulphate ferroso-ferrique).

The salts of iron are not precipitated by hydrocyanic acid; but if we add a little potash to a mixture of sulphate of protoxide and sulphate of peroxide of iron, hydrocyanic acid then produces the precipitate of Prussian blue. If, however, the potash has been added in excess (which is generally the case), the precipitate will be greenish or reddish, instead of blue, because it will be mixed with a little red sesquioxide of iron; (§. but on the addition of a few drops of hydrochloric acid, this sesquioxide is

---

(§. * This is evidently a mistake, and should be cyanide of *sodium* and iron, no potassium having been present throughout the process. If chloride of potassium was substituted for the chloride of sodium directed to be employed, then the text would be correct.)

dissolved, and then the characteristic deep blue is evident.) This reaction of hydrocyanic acid upon the salts of iron is not, however, of great value as a test; nor does it by any means equal that of the same acid upon nitrate of silver. (§. This test is, however, both delicate and of great value in the opinion of English toxicologists. If the acid is in a nearly colourless solution, as when it has been distilled from the contents of the stomach, it scarcely ever fails to give conclusive evidence of its presence.)

Hydrocyanic acid alone does not precipitate sulphate of copper; but on the addition of liquor potassæ we obtain a precipitate, the tint of which varies from *apple*-green to *yellowish*-green, according as the solution is concentrated or weak, and according also to the amount of potash which is added.

(§. Liebig has proposed a test of great delicacy and value. A few drops of recently prepared hydrosulphate of ammonia (sulphide of ammonium) are to be placed upon the concave surface of a glass dish, watch glass, or porcelain dish, and they may be spread upon the surface by means of a cork or camels'-hair pencil. This dish must be inverted over the vessel containing the suspected materials, and by the aid of a *very gentle* heat, the hydrocyanic acid is volatilized, and is received upon the moistened surface of the dish After continuing the process for a few minutes, the dish may be removed, and the hydrosulphate of ammonia (which has become converted into sulpho-cyanide of ammonium if prussic acid has been present), must be evaporated to dryness by a *gentle* heat. If a rod, dipped in a solution of persalt of iron, is drawn over the glass, blood-red streaks of sulpho-cyanide of iron are formed; or if the quantity is considerable, a blood-red solution is obtained by placing one or two drops of the iron salt upon the glass.)

If we are engaged in proving the presence of hydrocyanic acid mixed with organic substances, such as vomited or other matters, we must subject the materials to distillation, adding distilled water from time to time. (§. We may try Liebig's test either before distilling the suspected matters, or with a portion of the product of the distillation). And we must treat another portion with nitrate of silver, when the cyanide of silver obtained may be recognized by the characters given above. (§. With another portion we may try the Prussian-blue test.) If we wish to ascertain the quantity of hydrocyanic acid contained in a liquid, instead of distilling it, it is better to treat it with nitrate of silver, after having satisfied ourselves that the liquid does not contain chlorides or hydrochloric acid; and the cyanide of silver formed must be washed, dried and weighed with care. A fifth of the weight of this cyanide represents exactly the quantity of anhydrous hydrocyanic acid contained in the liquid submitted to analysis.

Before subjecting the materials to analysis, it is important to smell them to ascertain whether they do not exhale the odour of hydrocyanic acid, which character, when *decidedly present*, is of the highest importance.

We may add, in conclusion, that proving the presence of hydrocyanic acid in the vomited matters, in the digestive tube, or in the liver of a person supposed to have been poisoned by this acid, is not an absolute proof that poisoning has really taken place; for this acid is sometimes developed both in healthy and sick persons; and it is not quite certain that it may not form during the decomposition of azotized matters. Lastly the hydrocyanic acid may have been added after death.

POISONING BY CYANIDE OF POTASSIUM.

Cyanide of potassium has for some time been extensively employed in plating with gold and silver. The salt is seldom pure; but when well prepared, it is highly poisonous. It rapidly changes on contact with the air, and still more so with water; indeed, M. Pelouze has proved that under these circumstances it disengages ammonia, and forms formiate of potash; it also gives rise of carbonate of potash.

Pure cyanide of potassium acts like hydrocyanic acid; whilst the substance commercially sold for manufacturing purposes under the name of cyanide of potassium is nearly inert.

Chemical examination.—Cyanide of potassium is a white salt, inodorous at first, but soon acquiring the smell of bitter almonds, owing to its being decomposed by contact with the air. It precipitates the persalts of iron, *blue*, the salts of binoxide of copper,* *apple-green*, and nitrate of silver, *white ;* and the cyanide of silver formed presents all the characters mentioned above (p. 445).

(§. * See note, p. 413.)

The distilled water of cherry-laurel *(cerasus, lauro-cerasus—Rosaceæ)*, and that of bitter almonds, contain a volatile essence which is poisonous, and also contain a small quantity of hydrocyanic acid. Their poisonous effects will be the same as those mentioned in speaking of prussic acid; and we ought to pursue the same course of treatment in a case of poisoning, either by the essence, or the distilled water of these two substances.

We have already mentioned, and we lay stress upon this point, that all the substances which contain hydrocyanic acid, or which are capable of forming it, being placed in contact with mercurial preparations, and especially with calomel, transform them into bichloride and bicyanide of mercury, both of which are highly poisonous. Such a combination ought therefore to be carefully avoided.

THIRD CLASS.

NARCOTICO-ACRID POISONS.

This class ought to contain only substances which produce inflammation of the parts they touch, and at the same time narcotism; but it is made to embrace a great number of poisons which do not inflame the tissues, and which, moreover, do not occasion narcotism. We therefore coincide with the opinion of Professor Orfila, who forms several groups under this class, which we shall but briefly name; for it will be impossible to give a complete description of every poisonous substance, within the limits which we have laid down for ourselves.

FIRST SECTION.

This contains squill, œnanthe, aconite, veratria, colchicum, belladonna, stramonium, tobacco, digitalis, various species of hemlock, oleander, rue and cyanide of iodine.

Symptoms produced by these poisons. — The poisonous

action of these substances is manifested by convulsions of the muscles of the face and extremities, by delirium and sharp cries, and by dilatation of the pupil, which is, however, sometimes contracted, or in a natural condition. The pulse is very variable; there are abdominal pains, nausea, obstinate vomiting, and alvine dejections; and sometimes we observe a kind of intoxication, prostration, insensibility, and general trembling.

Lesions.—The poisons of this section inflame the parts which they touch, and serious changes are observed, chiefly in the lungs, the blood and the nervous system, upon which they more especially act after having been absorbed; to which action, rather than to any local irritant effect, death ought to be attributed.

Treatment.—We must administer tartar emetic in doses of from one grain and a half to two grains and a half, when the poison has not been taken long; and we may also give from fifteen grains to half a drachm of ipecacuanha, and assist the action of the emetics by tickling the fauces. These evacuants act in two ways: first, by expelling the poison which has been swallowed, and afterwards by counteracting its narcotic effect. If, on the contrary, some time has elapsed since the poison was taken, we must administer purgative glysters, or give an emeto-cathartic, composed of two grains and a half of tartar emetic, and an ounce or an ounce and a half of sulphate of soda. If at this period symptoms of cerebral congestion show themselves, we must practise a single bleeding, which may be repeated according to the strength of the patient, and the good effects produced. We must afterwards give vinegar and water; but this drink would be injurious before the evacuation of the poison, because it does not assist the vomiting, and it favours the absorption of the poison. At a later period still we can only calm the irritation which has been excited by means of mucilaginous drinks, and the application of leeches to the abdomen.

Although it is very seldom that poisoning is produced by the external application of these substances, we must add that, if such should be the case, the treatment must be the same, even to the administration of evacuants. We ought also to oppose absorption by the application of cupping glasses and by ligatures.

We shall conclude this article by making a few remarks upon

G G

some of the substances contained in this class, which are the most frequent cause of poisoning.

BELLADONNA *(Atropa belladonna—Solanaceæ)*.

This plant owes its properties to atropia, an alkaloid which is found in all parts of the plant. It possesses a transparent crystalline form, and is little soluble in water, but it is soluble in alcohol and ether. When heated in closed vessels, atropia is volatilized, and it burns in contact with the air, leaving no residue. With acids it forms crystallizable salts, which are precipitated *citron-yellow* by chloride of gold, *dove-coloured* by chloride of platinum, and *white* by solution of galls. Their solution, even when when very dilute, causes persistent dilatation of the pupil.

Belladonna, and, in a higher degree still its extract (obtained by evaporating the juice of the fresh plant at a very gentle heat), possesses very poisonous properties. Their local action is almost nothing; but if they are absorbed, they act upon the nervous system, and cause phenomena which are not however sufficient to characterize poisoning by them.

It is chiefly the fruit of belladonna which has been the cause of poisoning, from being mistaken for black cherries and black grapes. These different kinds of fruit are distinguished by the following characters :

Belladonna fruit.—*Bi-*locular berry, accompanied by a persistent calyx, and containing *kidney-shaped* seeds.

Cherries.—Drupes, having a deciduous calyx, and containing a single stone, produced by the hardening of the endocarp.

Black grapes.—Berries with a deciduous calyx, containing *pyriform* seeds, marked by a longitudinal furrow; the fruit is also *uni-*locular, owing to the destruction of the dissepiments.

Dr. Runge has proposed, in order to recognize poisoning by belladonna, that the blood of the animal supposed to be poisoned should be placed upon the eye of a rabbit, the pupil of which becomes dilated, if the poison was present. This test does not appear to us to be of much value.

(§. The characteristic effects of belladonna as a poison are, that it produces remarkable *dilatation* of the pupil, *dryness* and constriction of the *throat*, with difficulty in swallowing, and *gay delirium*, without convulsions.)

Treatment.—See p. 449.

TOBACCO, AND VARIOUS KINDS OF HEMLOCK.

We should not have spoken of poisoning by tobacco, or at any rate by nicotine, if a celebrated case had not lately occurred, which called the attention of toxicologists to this very poisonous substance, which has been studied with remarkable care by MM. Orfila and Stass.

Nicotine, the organic alkali of the different species of tobacco, and *conicine*, or *cicutine*, which exists in the hemlocks, are undoubtedly the two most energetic poisons in the vegetable kingdom; and we greatly regret that we cannot enter into the full details of poisoning by them. We must content ourselves with giving their distinctive characters, which we borrow from the splendid work presented by M. Orfila to the Academy of Medicine of Paris. In this work the learned Professor has proved: 1. That we can characterise pure nicotine as easily as if it were a poison from the mineral kingdom; 2. that we can discover this alkali in the alimentary canal, and prove that it exists there, even when the canal contains only a few drops of it; and 3. that it is easy to prove its presence in the liver and in the other organs after it has been absorbed.

Nicotine and conicine are both volatile organic alkalies, which probably exist in the state of acetate, tannate or gallate in the plants yielding them, from which, as well as from various matters with which they may be mixed, they can be separated by repeated careful distillation in contact with potash, which in order to be successful, ought to be made in a current of hydrogen, owing to the facility with which these alkalies change when in contact with air.

The following are the distinctive characters of these two alkalies:

TESTS.	NICOTINE.	CONICINE.
STATE	Liquid.	Liquid.
COLOUR	Colourless, when pure—becomes brown in the air.	Yellow.
ODOUR	Pungent, disagreeable—resembling tobacco.	Resembling that of the urine of mice.
ACTION UPON REDDENED LITMUS	Restores the blue colour.	Restores the blue colour.
ACTION OF WATER . .	Very soluble in water.	It floats, and does not easily dissolve in water.
ACTION OF HEAT .	Volatilizes at 250° C. (482° F.), diffusing a very irritating odour of tobacco.	Volatile; diffuses an odour of celery, mixed with that of the urine of mice.
ALCOHOL and ETHER .	Very soluble. These liquids remove it from water.	Very soluble.
SULPHURIC ACID, CONCENTRATED and COLD .	Produces a port-wine colour.	No change.
NITRIC ACID . . .	Orange-yellow colour, by the aid of a gentle heat.	Topaz colour, unchanged by heat.
NEUTRAL ACETATE OF LEAD	White precipitate.	No precipitate.
TANNIN	Ditto.	White precipitate.
CHLORIDE OF PLATINUM .	Yellow precipitate.	Yellow precipitate.

One of the most curious characters of nicotine is that which it presents in contact with the acetate of binoxide (§. protoxide, Eng.) of copper, with which it forms a *blue* precipitate soluble in an excess (§. of the nicotine), producing a *blue* solution, like that with ammonia; a character which may cause this last base to be confounded with nicotine; but nicotine is precipitated *yellow* by iodised water, whilst ammonia removes the colour from this test without rendering it opaque.

Treatment of poisoning by tobacco, the hemlocks, nicotine and conicine, see p. 449.

We cannot conclude this reference to the history of the hemlocks, without giving the distinctive characters of the *Cicuta virosa* (water hemlock) and *Cicuta maculata* (spotted hemlock) of the *Æthusa cynapium* (fools' parsley) and the *Petroselinum sativum* (true parsley).

CHARACTERS.	CICUTA VIROSA.	CICUTA MACULATA.
Roots	Whitish, perpendicular, fleshy, hollow in the centre, and full of a milky juice.	Long, spreading, horizontal.
Stem	Entirely green.	Marked with purple spots, like Conium maculata.
Leaves	Elongated, lancolate, straight, acute, deeply serrated with irregular teeth.	Oval, acute leaflets, regularly toothed.
Leaflets of the partial involucre	As long, and frequently longer, than the umbels.	Shorter than the umbels.

CHARACTERS.	ÆTHUSA CYNAPIUM.	PETROSELINUM SATIVUM.
Odour	That of mice.	Aromatic.
Stem	Erect, branched, cylindrical, slightly striated, glaucous, reddish internally, having the leaves three times divided, the leaflets being straight, acute, cut, and of a dark-green colour.	Furrowed, green; the leaves large, and divided into three lobes, nearly cuneiform, and tcothed.
Flowers	White, and disposed in terminal umbels, composed of about a score of rays, those of the circumference being the longest; no general involucre, but the *partial* ones composed of three, four or five *linear* leaflets, *bent downwards*, and hanging all upon *one side*.	Yellowish-green, with a general involucre, of six or eight leaflets.
Fruit	Globular, compressed, of a dark-green colour, with five rounded projections on each leaf.	Elongated, ovoid, slightly marked with scarcely visible longitudinal lines.

Lastly, we may add that accidents have been occasioned by mixing the fruits of hemlock with those of aniseed; which latter are green and globular, slightly elongated, and carrying the remains of the peduncle at their base, whilst those of hemlock, on the contrary, are white, slightly bent into a crescent shape, and have no persistent peduncle.

SECOND SECTION OF NARCOTICO-ACRIDS.

This section comprehends strychnine, igasurine, brucine, nux vomica, St. Ignatius' bean, false Angustura bark, and upas tieuté.

Symptoms produced by these substances.—The predominant phenomenon in poisoning by these substances is the special influence exerted upon the nervous system, which is manifested by a general contraction of all the muscles of the body, with rigidity of the spinal column. A profound calm soon succeeds, which is followed by a new tetanic seizure longer than the first, during which the respiration is quickened. These symptoms then cease, the breathing becomes easy, and there is stupor followed by another general contraction. In dogs, the front legs are stiff and drawn together, being directed backwards, and the vertebral column is rigid, the head being drawn back upon the neck; and the animal falls upon its lower jaw, and soon after upon its side. When the spasm is complete, the thorax is immovable and respiration ceases, and the lips and gums assume a violet colour. This state of asphyxia continues for one or two minutes, and unless it is extreme the organs of sense and the brain continue to perform their functions. After some time the tetanus ceases and the breathing returns. These attacks are renewed with increasing violence for four or five times, and death follows the fifth. One phenomenon which deserves to be mentioned, and which is only to be found in poisoning by these substances, is, that touching any part of the body, or even threatening to do so, instantly produces the tetanic spasm.

Lesions.—The same changes are observed as in persons asphyxiated, but in a great number of cases there is no lesion in the alimentary canal.

STRYCHNINE.

This organic alkali is one of the most virulent poisons with which we are acquainted, and the symptoms and lesions produced by it are such as we have just described.

Treatment.—The treatment which we are about to mention for strychnine applies to poisoning by brucine, nux vomica, St. Ignatius' bean, false Angustura bark, camphor and Indian berries, or to *picrotoxine*, the proximate principle obtained from them.

Persons wounded by the *Upas* employ chloride of sodium as an antidote; but MM. Magendie and Delille have proved that this salt does not produce any effect, whether it is applied externally or is introduced into the stomach. Now as upas produces the same symptoms as strychnine and the other poisons of this section, it follows that poisoning by it ought to be treated in the same manner; that is to say, that we ought speedily to administer an emetic to excite vomiting, which should be promoted by tickling the fauces. It is also of primary importance to counteract the asphyxia, which is the principal cause of death, by performing tracheotomy,* and blowing air into the lungs. If the poison has been applied to the limbs by arrows impregnated with the poison, or by any other means, we ought immediately to cauterize the part, and apply a ligature tightly above the wound. If the poison has been swallowed for some time, we should give a purgative glyster, and administer draughts containing sulphuric ether or oil of turpentine, which in most cases produce a salutary effect. Lastly, injections of chlorine and decoction of tannin are of value, principally in cases of poisoning by strychnine, brucine, or nux vomica. We may add, that in every case artificial respiration, practised with diligence and with care, is the most efficacious remedy in poisoning of this nature.

Chemical examination for strychnine and brucine.—These two organic alkalies only act when they have been absorbed. They are both easily recognized even when mixed with coloured organic liquids, but it is sometimes difficult to prove the whole of their characters. If we are engaged in proving their presence

---

(*. Artificial respiration may in many cases be efficiently practised without resorting to this measure. If powerful pressure is made upon the sides of the chest and *upon the abdomen* at the same time, the cavity of the thorax is diminished, and the air contained in the lungs is expelled. As soon as the compression is withdrawn, the elasticity of the ribs causes them to resume their old expanded positions; the chest is again enlarged, a partial vacuum is formed, and air rushes into the lungs, to be again expelled by pressure upon the ribs and abdomen as before. By this means artificial respiration may be kept up for a great length of time, without the use of bellows, or any other apparatus.)

when mixed with organic matters, it is necessary to boil the materials either with concentrated alcohol or with water acidulated with acetic acid. In the first case, we may thus isolate the principle by itself; and in the second, its combination with the acetic acid may be decomposed by ammonia, which precipitates the strychnine and brucine; which two alkaloids are distinguished by the following characters:

TESTS.	STRYCHNINE.	BRUCINE.
TASTE	Extremely bitter.	Bitter.
CRYSTALLIZATION . .	Octohedral, or four-sided prisms, terminated by four-sided pyramids.	Right prisms, with a rhomboidal base.
CONCENTRATED NITRIC ACID	*Yellow* colour.	*Blood-red* colour, which passes into violet by protochloride of tin.
NITRATE	Easily crystallized.	Not crystallizable..
ALCOHOL	Insoluble in diluted alcohol.	Soluble in diluted alcohol.
SULPHURIC ACID and BINOXIDE OF LEAD, or BICHROMATE OF POTASH	Very beautiful violet colour.	No effect.

We ought to add, that commercial strychnine is very often impure, containing brucine, which causes it to be reddened by nitric acid. It would seem also from the recent experiments of M. Desnoix, which we regret not being able to introduce in this work, that the red colour produced by treating strychnine with nitric acid, is owing to a very energetic base, which he has isolated and named *Igazurine*; an alkaloid which is specially distinguished from the preceding by its ready solubility in water. It is indeed more easily reddened by nitric acid than even brucine itself.

NUX VOMICA.

Nux vomica, St. Ignatius' bean and false Angustura bark owe their influence to the strychnine and brucine which they contain, so that poisoning by these substances is precisely similar to that produced by strychnine. The alcoholic extract of nux vomica is the most active of all the pharmaceutical preparations of this seed.

If we are engaged in discovering the presence of nux vomica

mixed with animal substances, it is necessary to boil them several times in water; the filtered liquid is then to be precipitated by thick milk of lime, which forms an insoluble igasurate of lime, which is precipitated along with the strychnine, the brucine and the excess of lime. The deposit, after being carefully dried, is to be exhausted by boiling alcohol, which dissolves the two organic alkalies, and leaves them as a residue when evaporated. We must then proceed to their separation and purification by the ordinary means, and prove them by their tests.

False Angustura bark, attributed at first to the *Brucia antidysenterica*, is a bark known commercially, in which MM. Pelletier and Caventou have discovered *brucine*. It is now known that it is produced by the *Strychnos nux vomica*. It has sometimes been confounded with true Angustura bark produced by the *Cusparia febrifuga*, of the family *Rutaceæ*. The chemical tests which have been pointed out by M. Guibourt* for distinguishing these two barks are given below, and are as follows:

CHARACTERS.	FALSE ANGUSTURA.	TRUE ANGUSTURA.
BARKS	Thick, rugous, rolled upon itself. Edges cut perpendicularly.	Flat, or rolled up, little wrinkled, edges bevilled.
COLOUR	Brown, or greenish yellow, presenting protuberances or excrescences, produced by the great development of the corky layer, which has a still more yellow colour.	Grayish-yellow.
TASTE	Very bitter.	Bitter.
Nitric acid . . .	*Red* colour when dropped upon the bark.	*Yellow* colour.

THIRD SECTION.

This section contains upas anthiar, camphor and Indian berry (coque du Levant).

The members of this section are of little importance, and are

---

* "Histoire naturelle des drogues simples," 4th ed., tome iii., p. 512.

seldom the cause of poisoning. They irritate the parts which they touch, producing vomiting and convulsions. Poisoning by their means is to be treated like poisoning by opium.

FOURTH SECTION.

POISONOUS FUNGI (MUSHROOMS.)

We exceedingly regret not being able in this place to give all the distinctive characters of the different species of poisonous and edible fungi (mushrooms); but we can only advise physicians to consult the excellent work of M. Roques. The genus *Boletus* contains few poisonous species; it is to the genera *Agaricus* and *Amanita* that the poisonous fungi chiefly belong.

The genus *Amanita (Agaric-bourse)* contains mushrooms proceeding from a bag or volva, being furnished on its lower surface with leaves or lamellæ, which radiate below; its head which is supported by a pedicle more or less swollen at its base, being marked on its under surface by radiating laminæ. This group contains the false orange-agaric (la fausse orange), a variety of the *Amanita auriantaca* of Persoon, *Agaricus muscarius* of Linneus, *Agaricus pseudo-aurianticus* of Bulliard. This fungus is very poisonous, and is often confounded with the true orange-agaric *(Amanita aurantiaca)*, which is an excellent article of food. Their distinctive characters are given below.

CHARACTERS.	TRUE ORANGE-AGARIC.	FALSE ORANGE-AGARIC.
VOLVA . . .	Entirely covers the mushroom when young, giving it the appearance of an egg.	Imperfectly covers the mushroom.
HEAD . . .	Without white warty prominences.	Spotted with white warts.
COLOUR . . .	Orange *yellow.*	Scarlet-*red*, or bright orange-*red*.
LOWER LAMINÆ . .	Slight yellow.	White.

Most of the other amanites are poisonous. We shall content ourselves with pointing out the characters of the two species which most frequently give rise to fatal mistakes.

The genus *Agaric* contains mushrooms unprovided with an envelope (bourse) or volva. The head consists of radiating laminæ, generally simple, and alternately long and short. This genus which contains several poisonous, and also some edible species, is divided into four groups: 1. The group of *Lactuaires* or *Lactésiens*, Persoon; 2. Group of agarics with a naked pedicle, which is lateral or excentric; 3. Agarics with a full pedicle and a fleshy head, the laminæ not being adherent to the pedicle, and not becoming black as they grow old; 4. Group of agarics provided with a collar.

Symptoms of poisoning by mushrooms (fungi).—We have mentioned that the symptoms produced by poisonous fungi are of two kinds—the one evidenced upon the heart and nervous system, the other upon the alimentary canal. It is very difficult to establish a classification of fungi according to their symptoms, because they vary from a multitude of circumstances—amongst which, we think it is very important to note the age, more or less advanced, of the mushroom, and the manner in which it has been seasoned. We are, however, far from agreeing in the opinion of some persons, who think that all mushrooms are poisonous when they have been badly prepared, whilst others assure us that the seasoning and alcoholic liquors with which they are accompanied as articles of diet, take away the poisonous properties even of those which are reckoned the most injurious.

In most cases it is not until some hours after the mushrooms have been eaten that their effects manifest themselves; the patient then feels pain in the stomach, severe colic, extreme thirst, great heat, especially in the abdominal region, small, hard, wiry and frequent pulse, and impeded respiration. Then follow cramps, convulsions and faintings, without loss of the intellectual faculties. The disease continues from two to six days, and terminates in death, if the patient is not quickly relieved by treatment. In some cases, the symptoms of a gastro-intestinal affection are the most prominent, and there is also occasionally muttering delirium and drowsiness. Lastly, in some cases the nervous symptoms just mentioned are not preceded by those indicative of any gastro-intestinal affection.

Cases have been mentioned in which mushrooms have acted like septic poisons, the skin becoming pale, cold, and covered with sweat, the pulsations at the heart and wrist being scarcely perceptible, and death occurring without suffering. In a few cases there have been convulsive motions ushered in by locked-jaw.

Lesions.—These vary much, according to the kind and quantity of the mushrooms eaten. We most frequently observe a swollen belly, an injected conjunctiva, contraction of the pupils, and inflammation or irritation of the stomach and bowels, which often present gangrenous spots. The skin is mottled with violet stains, and the lips exhibit the same colour; the lungs are inflamed, and gorged with black blood. This engorgement is found in all the veins of the abdominal viscera, in the liver, the spleen and the mesentery. Gangrenous spots have also been found upon the membranes of the brain, upon the pleura, the lungs, the diaphragm, the bladder, the mesentery, the uterus, &c. The substance of the brain has been found marked with red points.

Medico-legal researches.—Chemistry is of no use in the examination of poisonous fungi, the botanical characters of which ought to be noted when possible. Chemical analysis has proved the existence of a great number of principles in mushrooms, but none of them present characteristic features. M. Pouchet, professor of natural history in Rouen, has stated that fungi, boiled for about a quarter of an hour in water, lost all their poisonous properties, whilst the decoction caused violent death in dogs to whom it was given.

TREATMEMT OF POISONING BY FUNGI.

Many substances have been proposed to counteract this kind of poisoning; we shall enumerate them, and assign their true value to each.

Vinegar.—The active principles of fungi are very soluble in vinegar, from which it follows that the liquid must facilitate absorption, which in fact does take place. It is, however, of use *after* the poison has been expelled by vomiting or purging.

Chloride of sodium.—Common salt possesses all the advantages and disadvantages of vinegar.

Sulphuric ether.—The internal employment of ether, and of Hofmann's anodyne liquor (Spt. Æth. Sulph. Co.) after evacuants, is of great use.

Tartar emetic, or other emetics, as well as emeto-cathartics, are of great value, and ought to be considered as the basis of all treatment.

Ammonia.—The volatile alkali has been proposed, but the frequently repeated experiments of Paulet prove that it is injurious rather than beneficial. As to other substances which people are in the habit of giving, such as theriacum, oil, butter, milk, &c., &c., they do not produce any good effect.

From all which it follows, that in poisoning by poisonous fungi, the physician ought with speed to excite evacuations, either by the aid of emetics, of emeto-cathartics, or of purgative draughts or glysters; the latter generally act the best, because it nearly always happens that the symptoms of poisoning do not manifest themselves until the poisonous substance has passed through the pylorus. After the evacuation has been as complete as possible, we may administer vinegar and water as a drink, and a strong ethereal mixture, by a table-spoonful for a dose, from time to time.

In this kind of poisoning, it sometimes happens that tartar emetic by itself will not produce vomiting; and we must therefore associate it with ipecacuanha, as in the following powder:

Powdered tartrate of antimony   .   15 to 30 centigrms. (gr. ii 1/4 to gr. ivss.)
    „   ipecacuanha root   .   2 grms. (ʒss.)

when the intestinal inflammation is considerable, or there is fever with intense thirst and dryness of the tongue and throat, it is necessary to be careful in giving irritant purgatives. In this case we must have recourse to bleeding and other antiphlogistic means. Lastly, M. Chansarel asserts that he has obtained good results from the use of 2 grammes (ʒss) of tannin in a litre (℥xxxii) of water, or of a *decoction* of 15 grammes (ℨss) of galls, or of 30 grammes (ℨi) of powdered cinchona in a litre of water.

We shall content ourselves with barely mentioning poisoning by a kind of fungus, which it is impossible to confound with those which are taken as food, viz., ergot of rye (*sclerotium clavus*, Decandolle, or *sphaccælia segetum*, Léveillé. Poisoning can only be produced when this substance has been administered in too large a dose as a medicine, and the treatment will be the same as that already mentioned for poisoning by fungi generally.

In the class of narcotico-acrids are still some substances of trifling importance which we shall merely enumerate, viz., spirituous liquors, intoxication, *lolium temulentum*, and odorous plants. Amongst gases we may mention *protoxide of nitrogen* (laughing gas) *phosphuretted hydrogen, arseniuretted hydrogen*, the character of which we gave when treating of poisoning by arsenious acid, *bicarbonated hydrogen, coal-gas, carbonic acid* and *carbonic oxide*. We shall say, a few words only upon poisoning by the last two gases, and shall treat in a more extended manner of poisoning by the vapour of charcoal.

--- --- ---

POISONING BY CARBONIC ACID.

Nysten attributed the poisonous effects of carbonic acid gas to its not containing any free oxygen, but the experiments of Collard de Martigny have sufficiently proved that this gas is itself deleterious. According to M. Leblanc, dogs suffer severely when the air contains 10 per cent of carbonic acid, and the inconvenience is even well marked when it contains only 5 per cent. When injected into the veins in small quantity it is not deleterious, for it only mixes with the blood, and escapes by the lungs when the liquid traverses these organs.

Treatment.—See Charcoal Vapour, p. 467.

Medico-legal examination.—Carbonic acid gas is colourless and transparent, its flavour is tartish, and its odour pungent; it extinguishes burning bodies, reddens litmus paper, and causes a white precipitate in lime water, which precipitate is soluble in an excess of carbonic acid.

The air contains about four parts of carbonic acid in ten thousand. This gas is produced by the combustion of all organic substances; it is disengaged by the calcination of earthy carbonates, and especially when carbonate of lime is heated, which circumstance has procured for it the name of chalk acid. It is produced also by the putrefaction of organic matters, and during the fermentation of all substances containing sugar, when this fermentation is effected under the influence of an active ferment, (§. and by the respiration of all animals). Lastly, carbonic acid exists in some mineral waters and in volcanic eruptions.

The presence of carbonic acid in large quantity is easily proved in any place if a candle will not burn in it, an experiment which wine makers and brewers ought always to make when they wish to go into the vats or cisterns which contain the fermenting liquors. If we wish to measure the carbonic acid, we must make the gaseous mixture pass through baryta-water, when insoluble carbonate of barytes will be formed, which must be collected, dried and weighed; after which, it is easy to calculate the quantity of carbonic acid gas.

POISONING BY CARBONIC OXIDE GAS.

Nysten placed carbonic oxide amongst those gases which are not injurious of themselves, though he recognized that it exerted a peculiar influence upon the nervous system; but in the present day it is established that it is one of the most deleterious gases. The experiments of M. Tourdes have proved that air mixed with a *thirtieth* of carbonic oxide killed a rabbit in thirty-seven minutes; with a *fifteenth* an animal of the same kind perished in about twenty-three minutes; and with an *eighth* death took place in seven minutes. M. Leblanc has recently proved by repeated and careful experiments that *a hundredth* part of carbonic oxide mixed with the air, killed a bird at the end of two minutes. If when death is approaching we remove the animal from the poisonous mixture, it may return to life; but the symptoms of paralysis will disappear with difficulty.*

Treatment.—See charcoal vapour, p. 467.

* "Annales de chimie et de physique," 3rd series, vol. v., p. 19.)

Medico-legal researches.—Carbonic oxide is a gas colourless, inodorous, insipid, transparent, elastic and inflammable on the approach of a burning body; it burns with a *blue* flame, and produces carbonic acid. If it is pure, it is not absorbed by potash, nor does it precipitate lime-water. It may easily be confounded with proto-carburetted hydrogen, but in burning the latter produces carbonic acid and water, whilst carbonic oxide produces carbonic acid alone. Carbonic oxide gas is produced when large quantities of charcoal are burnt at once, as in deep furnaces.

Of unrenewed air.—Unrenewed air is not only an irrespirable gas, but it is also a poisonous one, by virtue of the large quantity of carbonic acid which it contains. Two causes may lead to the increase in the quantity of the gas; first the combustion of organic matters, and second the respiration of a great number of people assembled in a space in which the air is not renewed. Beside the deficiency of oxygen and the predominance of nitrogen and carbonic acid it is necessary to point out the presence of the *animalized* aqueous vapour which is exhaled from the skin and lungs.

The experiments of M. Leblanc have taught us that the quantity of carbonic acid is sometimes very great in unrenewed air. In the great amphitheatre of the Sorbonne when a thousand people have remained in it for an hour and a half, the proportion of carbonic acid was raised to 1 per cent, although two doors were kept constantly open. This is therefore a great source of vitiation of the air, even without taking into account the animalized vapours, which certainly materially assist in rendering the air unwholesome.

The analysis of unrenewed air is made by the ordinary methods which we shall briefly point out in speaking of asphyxia by charcoal vapour.

POISONING BY ILLUMINATING (COAL) GAS.

Illuminating gas possesses a very complicated composition; it nearly always contains the same gases, but their proportion varies with the process employed for obtaining it. Oil gas, the óne which is most frequently used (in France), contains: *bicarburetted hydrogen, tetrahydruret of carbon, carbonic oxide, hydrogen, sulphuret of carbon,* a small quantity of *pyrogenous oil, hydrosulphuric acid gas,* and *carbonic acid,* either *free* or combined with *ammonia.*

It is true that illuminating gas is generally purified by making it pass through milk of lime or solid lime; and by this means it is almost completely deprived of carbonic acid, hydrosulphuric acid, and hydrosulphate and carbonate of ammonia; but we must, in a general way, agree with M. Tourdes in saying that the odorous properties of the gas are really a very valuable safeguard to the public, and it is doubtful whether a perfectly inodorous gas might not present true dangers, from its escape not being always prevented.

Coal gas may cause death even when it is present in a smaller proportion than an eleventh. Its injurious properties are to be attributable to *bicarburetted hydrogen,* other *carburets of hydrogen,* and especially to carbonic oxide. Its action is principally exerted upon the nervous system and the respiratory apparatus.

Treatment of poisoning by coal gas.—The first thing to be done in this, as in all other cases of asphyxia, is to remove the patient from the asphyxiating cause, to which we must add slightly stimulating draughs of tea or linden. If the respiratory organs act freely, but there are signs of visceral congestion, we may have recourse to blood-letting, as well as to energetic revulsives to the skin and the alimentary canal. As to the state of asphyxia, we must treat that as if it arose from any other cause, as we shall mention in speaking of asphyxia from the vapour of charcoal.

POISONING BY THE VAPOUR OF CHARCOAL.

The vapour of charcoal, or more properly speaking, the gases formed by the combustion of charcoal, (for this body cannot be converted into vapour,) is a mixture the ingredients of which vary in quantity and quality, according to the combustible matters which have given rise to them.

H H

These gases do not merely produce simple asphyxia, that is to say, cessation of respiration, but they cause true poisoning, for most of the gases are deleterious, and we may place carbonic oxide in the first rank.

Symptoms of poisoning by the vapour of charcoal. — It is very difficult to exhibit the general symptoms observed in this form of poisoning, but in most cases the patient feels a great weight in the head, with buzzing and ringing in the ears, great debility in the senses, and an irresistible propensity to sleep. The breathing is slow and difficult, and at last ceases altogether.

The heart beats at first with violence, then its pulsations become weaker, and again they increase in strength; the blood becomes so coagulable that at the end of a few moments it forms a thick firm clot. Some patients utter complaints and groans, which prove that they are in great suffering, whilst others, on the contrary, fall into a kind of ecstacy which continues until the complete loss of the intellectual faculties. Sometimes general discolouration of the skin is observed, and at other times the face presents a violet-red tint, with great placidity of the limbs. According to Dr. Marye this red colouration is limited to the ears and face. Lastly, a tetanic rigidity has been observed, which disappears some time after death, to reappear again in a few hours; nausea and vomiting are not so frequent as has been affirmed; during the tetanic seizure the urine and fæces are sometimes expelled involuntarily.

Lesions of tissues.—We shall follow Dr. Marye in recounting the signs on the body of a person dead from asphyxia, during the three or four hours which succeed death.

The skin is nearly always pale throughout, but the thighs are sometimes marbled. It has been said that the dead body quickly loses its heat, especially if exposed to the air, and the tetanic rigidity is very great. We have observed rose-coloured spots about the neck and cheeks; the mouth is closed; the eyelids dropped; the ball of the eye glassy; the pupils *seldom dilated;* the face is pale, and also the hands and the feet: the fingers and nails are never violet coloured; nothing is observed as having been expelled by the mouth or anus.

The colour of the blood varies as the poisoning has been more or less rapid. As for engorgement of the veins of the pulmonary cells, their particular colour is not characteristic of this poisoning, for Dr. Marye has proved that the same characters are to be found in the bodies of persons who have died from other causes.

Treatment of poisoning by the vapour of charcoal.—The patient should be laid naked upon his back, in a free current of air, with the head and chest raised, and tepid, or even cold water if the surrounding temperature is not too low, should be dashed with force upon the whole body, but especially upon the chest and face; the whole body, especially the trunk, should be briskly rubbed with flannels impregnated with some aromatic liquid, and then the parts which have been wetted must be rubbed with warm towels, and again the frictions must be renewed. We must persevere with these means until respiration is thoroughly re-established, and we must, moreover, irritate the soles of the feet, the palms of the hands and the spine by dry frictions. We may also irritate the pituitary membrane by ammonia, or by means of a burning sulphur match, and the nasal fossæ may be stimulated by the feather of a quill. It will be useful to inflate the lungs gently with air,* and to administer stimulating glysters or vinegar and water, common salt, or sulphate of magnesia. If the symptoms of asphyxia continue, but the animal heat remains, we may let blood from the foot, or better still, from the jugular vein, and this last plan is better than giving tartar emetic, which is injurious rather than beneficial. We may, however, always give this medicine after the patient has regained his consciousness, if he experiences nausea and a weight at the stomach. Glysters and fumigations of tobacco ought to be banished; and we must also avoid giving liquids before respiration is perfectly re-established, because deglutition being performed with difficulty, part of the liquid may enter the trachæa, and cause a true asphyxia.

When, on the contrary, the patient is perfectly restored to life, and has been placed in a warm bed with the windows kept open, we may give him a few spoonsful of some generous wine or a cordial draught. We may add, that all measures of relief ought to be applied with the utmost promptitude, and they should be continued for some time even after the patient appears

(†. * See p. 455.)

dead, and should only be stopped when cadaveric rigidity comes on : but we must take care not to confound this with convulsive rigidity. We have seen patients restored to life after twelve hours of treatment.

Medico-legal researches.—The gas produced by the combustion of charcoal consists of oxygen, nitrogen, carbonic acid, carbonic oxide and carburetted hydrogen, which gaseous mixture may be collected by emptying in the room a bottleful of mercury, or in default of this, of very dry sand.

The gaseous mixture collected in the bottle may be forced by means of mercury or oil to pass through an apparatus composed in the following manner and carefully closed. 1. A Liebig's tube with bulbs, containing strong sulphuric acid, and a U tube containing pumice-stone impregnated with sulphuric acid in order to absorb the water. 2. A second apparatus, adjusted to the first, and composed, like it of a tube with bulbs containing a concentrated solution of caustic potash, and of a U tube containing fragments of pure potash; these two tubes retain the carbonic acid. 3. A horizontal glass tube surrounded with copper leaf, and containing black oxide of copper raised to a high temperature; through which will pass the nitrogen, oxygen, carbonic oxide and carburetted hydrogen. These last two, taking oxygen from the black oxide, will be converted into carbonic acid and water, which are to be retained by an apparatus disposed as above, (1. 2.), containing potash to absorb the carbonic acid, and sulphuric acid to retain the water, the weight of both of which being ascertained, it will be easy to calculate the proportion of carbonic oxide and carburetted hydrogen which were contained in the gaseous mixture. The apparatus is terminated by a second horizontal tube, also surrounded by copper leaf and heated, and containing metallic copper, which is intended to retain both the oxygen which existed in the gaseous mixture, and the azotized compounds that may have been formed by the passage of the nitrogen over the black oxide of copper. After this tube comes a bent one, which opens under a graduated bell glass full of mercury, in which the nitrogen may be measured. As to the oxygen, its quantity is determined by the difference.[*] The apparatus which we have just described may

se several steps may perhaps be rendered clearer by an example. Suppose be modified in different ways; and the three gases which it is chiefly important to measure are the carbonic acid, carbonic oxide and carburetted hydrogen.

Several medico-legal questions have arisen in connection with asphyxia from the vapour of charcoal, but we cannot discuss them here, and must refer to the excellent treatise on toxicology by M. Orfila.

100 cubic inches of the gaseous mixture to be taken, and passed through the 1st and 2nd parts of the apparatus, which have first been carefully weighed; suppose that the 1st part (that containing sulphuric acid) gains 1 grain in weight—that is due to 1 grain of water which was in the form of vapour at the temperature of the experiment —say, 60° F. But 100 cubic inches of vapour at 60° F. are known to weigh 19·38 grains; therefore this 1 grain will equal 5·16 cubic inches of watery vapour.

(Suppose that the 2nd part of the apparatus gains 12 grains in weight, that will be owing to carbonic acid; but 100 cubic inches of CO^2 are known to weigh 47·262 grains; therefore this 12 grains will equal 25·39 cubic inches of carbonic acid.

(The remainder of the mixed gases is now passed over the oxide of copper, by which the carbonic oxide CO is converted into carbonic acid CO^2, and the carburetted hydrogen, H^2C, is converted into water, HO, and carbonic acid, CO^2.

(Suppose that the sulphuric acid apparatus now gains ·9 of a grain in weight, it will be owing to water; but water consists of 1 part by weight of hydrogen, and 8 parts by weight of oxygen; therefore this ·9 of a grain will contain ·1 of a grain of hydrogen. But this hydrogen was in the form of carburetted hydrogen, H^2C, and in this gas there are 2 parts by weight of hydrogen to 6 parts of carbon; therefore this ·1 gr. of hydrogen would be combined with ·3 gr. of carbon, and form ·4 of a grain of carburetted hydrogen. Its carbon is converted into carbonic acid; and as 6 grains of carbon are known to form 22 grains of carbonic acid, the ·3 of a grain will form 1·1 gr. of CO^2, to which we must return shortly. 100 cubic inches of H^2C are known to weigh 17·417 grains; therefore the ·4 of a grain of H^2C will equal 2·29 cubic inches of carburetted hydrogen, which was in the mixture.

(Suppose, now, that the potash part of the apparatus gains 7 grains in weight, it will be from carbonic acid; but 1·1 gr. of this is owing to the carbon of the carburetted hydrogen, and therefore only the remaining 5·9 grs. will be owing to the carbonic oxide. But as 22 grains (the equiv.) of carbonic acid are formed from 14 grains (the equiv.) of carbonic oxide, the above 5·9 grs. will represent 3·527 grs. of carbonic oxide. Now 100 cubic inches of this gas are known to weigh 30·207 grs.; therefore this 3·527 grs. will equal 11·67 cubic inches of carbonic oxide.

(We have now only the nitrogen and oxygen to account for; but the latter is removed by the copper, and the nitrogen is collected in the graduated jar. Suppose there are found to be, say, 49·50 cubic inches of gas, this will be nitrogen, and the oxygen alone remains undiscovered.

(We have found, however:

5·16 cubic inches of	watery vapour,
25·39 „ „	carbonic acid,
2·29 „ „	carburetted hydrogen,
11·67 „ „	carbonic oxide,
49·50 „ „	nitrogen,

Which together make 94·01 „ „ gases for which we have accounted.

(But 100 cubic inches were taken; and the oxygen absorbed by the copper is the only gas not accounted for; and 100 minus 94·01 = 5·99 cubic inches of oxygen.)

FOURTH CLASS.

SEPTIC OR PUTREFACTIVE POISONS.

This name is applied to poisons which produce general prostration, decomposition of the fluids of the body, and syncope, but
do not affect the intellectual faculties.

SULPHURETTED HYDROGEN, OR HYDROSULPHURIC ACID.

Hydrosulphuric or sulphhydric* acid is a colourless gas with a
fetid odour, resembling that of rotten eggs; it reddens litmus,
and is inflammable, burning with a blue flame, and producing
water and sulphurous acid if the combustion is complete; but
allowing of the deposition of sulphur if it is not complete. It is
decomposed by chlorine, iodine, and bromine, which separate its
hydrogen, and cause the sulphur to be deposited. It is soluble
in water, and precipitates the salts of *lead black*, those of *antimony orange* yellow, those of *arsenic yellow*, and those of *zinc
white*, under the influence of acetate of soda.

Hydrosulphuric acid is one of the most energetic poisons,
especially when it is respired; it is less poisonous when introduced into the stomach or the veinous system; it is absorbed
without decomposition, and causes great prostration with a
change in the texture of organs, and especially of the nervous
system. If it is injected in very small quantities only into the
veins, it does not produce fatal symptoms.

Treatment.—(See p. 472).

GAS FROM CESSPOOLS.

The gas from cesspools, generally known (in France) under
the name of *plomb* (sink gas) varies much in its composition. It
always contains much azote, little oxygen, free carbonic acid or

carbonate of ammonia, and hydrosulphate of ammonia. We see, therefore, that the physical properties of this gaseous mixture will vary according as one or other of its constituents predominates, from which it follows that the symptoms and lesions will also vary according to the composition of the gaseous mixture.

If the disease is slight the patient experiences uneasiness, nausea, convulsive motions of all parts of the body, but principally of the muscles of chest and jaws; the breathing is irregular, the skin cold, and the pulse slow, feeble and thready.

If the patient is more severely affected there are syncope, a violet colour of the face and limbs, the mouth is frothy and bloody, the eyes are dull and closed, and the pupils dilated, the pulse is frequent and small, and the heart's action tumultuous, the breathing is convulsive and difficult, and the limbs are in a state of great relaxation. Sometimes indeed in the most severe cases we observe violent contractions of short duration, and the sufferer utters cries denoting acute pain.

MEPHITIC GAS FROM SEWERS.

Like the gas from cesspools that from sewers varies in its composition. The gases which it contains are nearly always the same, but the proportions vary from a great number of circumstances. The gas from sewers generally contains more azote and less oxygen than the air, and also more carbonic acid, and hydrosulphuric acid, the proportion of which is sometimes as high as 3 per cent.

Symptoms.—Nightmen are subject to a species of ophthalmia called *mitte*, whether caused by the action of the gas, or by the direct contact of dirt. This disease which is slight in many cases, manifests itself by inflammation of the conjunctiva, which soon extends to the cornea, and is often followed by cerebral affections. Emollients nearly always increase the mischief, whilst astringent collyria soon cause the inflammation to disappear.

The diseases to which nightmen are liable are lumbago, headache, general feeling of illness, and nausea, symptoms which give way by the employment of diluted acid drinks, and of tartar emetic. There is sometimes violent colic, which yields to purgatives. Lastly angina *tonsillaris*, erysipelas, and jaundice, have been sometimes observed.

M. Labarraque has employed the hypochlorite of soda (chloride of soda) with success in assisting the cleansing or repair of sewers. Free currents of air ought also to be established either by lighting a good fire at one end of the sewer, or by means of a ventilator; but we must observe, that if the mephitic gas contains a large quantity of hydrosulphuric acid gas, the air of the sewer when influenced may produce a violent detonation, on which account it is more prudent to employ the chloride of soda and a ventilator.

The gas from cesspools in which hydrosulphate of ammonia predominates is what principally causes the phenomena just mentioned, and the lesions are the same as those described in speaking of hydrosulphuric acid; that is to say, the alterations are chiefly manifested in the nervous system.

If, on the contrary, carbonic acid or carbonate of ammonia predominates in the gaseous mixture there is difficulty of breathing, which becomes noisy, and there is great prostration of strength, without any notable lesion of the nervous system. Death is to be attributed in this case rather to the want of respirable air than to poisoning.

As a lesion the arterial system is found full of very black blood.

Treatment of poisoning by gas from cesspools.—The first thing is to expose the patient to a free current of air, to use smart and rough friction over the body, and to dash it with cold vinegar and water; we ought also to make him inspire the condensed chloro-vinegar, which was described in speaking of poisoning by hydrocyanic acid (see p. 443). These inhalations must be managed with care, for fear of irritating the lungs.

If we imagine that the patient has swallowed any of the water contained in the cesspool, we must excite vomiting either by tickling the fauces, or by administering a mixture of half a drachm of powdered ipecacuanha, and 1½ to 3 grains of tartar emetic. If these means are not sufficient we must practice bloodletting, which must be repeated if necessary, and the nervous disorder, the spasms and convulsions must be calmed by antispasmodics and cold baths. If notwithstanding all these means the state of syncope continues, we must apply sinapisms to the feet, and blisters to the calves of the legs.

If the patient has been asphyxiated by hydrosulphuric acid gas, or by hydrosulphate of ammonia, we must act as has been directed in speaking of poisoning by the vapour of charcoal, joining to that mode of treatment inhalations of chlorine made by means of the condensed chloro-vinegar (see p. 443).

PUTRIFIED ANIMAL MATTERS.

Putrified animal matters, black puddings, and especially the " foie grass" (enlarged goose liver) produce consequences analogous to those caused by septic poisons, and the same accidents sometimes occur, even when the food which has been taken does not exhibit any signs of change. In all cases we must hasten to make the patient vomit, and then combat the symptoms by the means indicated in the particular case.

VENOMOUS ANIMALS.

Certain venomous animals possess a reservoir of poison, even a slight wound with which produces severe symptoms, sometimes followed by death; whilst other animals, under certain circumstances contract diseases in which the different fluids of the system are so altered as by their contact with living animals to produce very dangerous affections, such as pustules, ulcers of the hands, gangrene, hydrophobia, &c. We must refer to works on external pathology for the study of these affections.

As to animals with a poison reservoir, we shall merely say a few words upon the adder and the viper. We shall point out their distinctive characters, and mention the various modes of treatment which have been proposed to counteract the effects produced by the bite of these reptiles.

Distinctive Characters of the Viper and the Adder.

CHARACTERS.	VIPER. *Vipera Berus—Coluber Berus.*	WATER ADDER. *Coluber Natrix.*
CLASS	Reptiles.	Reptiles.
ORDER	Ophidians.	Ophidians.
SECTION . . .	With poison fangs.	Without poison fangs.
LENGTH . . .	About 65 centimetres (25 ¼ inches).	7 to 14 decimetres (27¼ to 55 inches.)
HEAD	Depressed, flattened, larger than the neck, which is contracted, and of a triangular form.	Oblong, oval, depressed, with a black ring upon the back part of the head.
COLOUR . . .	Variable, whiteish, gray, blackish, yellowish, reddish tint interrupted by spots, which have a certain degree of regularity upon the top of the head; behind the eyes are always found two black linear marks in the form of a V.	Ashy, black spots upon the back, becoming larger along the sides.
TAIL	Terminating abruptly.	Terminating insensibly.
FANGS	Two moveable ones.	None.

We can easily distinguish the wound made by a viper from that made by an adder, for the first has a V form, and presents towards its middle two larger wounds formed by the poison fangs.

The bite of the adder is not venomous. This reptile feeds upon insects, fishes, shell-fish, birds, and small quadrupeds, but never upon fruit. The poison of the viper is on the contrary mortal, even when the wound is made by the fangs of a dead viper; but it is a curious thing that the poison of the viper, like worari, does not produce any bad consequences when introduced into the healthy stomach, whilst it causes death if this organ presents the smallest erosion; moreover, the poison of the viper is innoxious to the viper itself, to slow-worms, to leeches, and to snails. The cat sometimes resists it, and sheep more frequently still, whilst man experiences terrible effects, which generally terminate in death, unless means are employed to counteract them.

The symptoms which are first observed are, an acute pain in the wounded part which is considerably swollen, and becomes hot, shining, and red, and afterwards violet, cold, and nearly insensible. The inflammation and pain extend to the great nervous trunks and the lymphatic vessels; the eyes become red and glaring, and weep copiously. Then follow fainting, nausea, gastralgia, dyspnæa, cardialgia, bilious vomiting, cold sweat, tympanitis, acute colic, lumbar pains, great relaxation of the sphincter of the anus, a kind of paralysis of the neck of the bladder, and involuntary evacuations of urine and fæces; the pulse is small, wiry, intermittent and jerking; the skin becomes yellow, and the blood black, and a sanious liquid oozes from the wounded part; at a later period if relief is not obtained, the parts of the body affected with œdema are covered with bloody blabs (phlytenæ), and they soon become gangrenous.

It is to the celebrated Fontana that we are indebted for what we know about the poison of the viper, which is in the form of a thick liquid, neutral to test papers, without any decided flavour; it becomes yellow on concreting, like mucous or albumen; and it may be kept for a long time without alteration in the cavity of the fang, whether separated or not from the bone which supports it.

We shall not speak in this work of the poisonous serpents which do not exist in Europe, neither shall we dwell upon venomous insects, which only cause death when the wounds from them are excessively numerous, such as bees, hornets, &c., and we shall conclude our history of the viper by pointing out the means to be employed for counteracting its bite.

Preservatives.—Many specifics have been mentioned, either for combatting the bites of poisonous serpents, or for preventing them from biting at all. Unhappily most of these remedies are powerless.

MM. Humboldt and Bonpland were the first to point out in their "Plantes Equinoxiales" the guaco (*Milhania guaco*), which grows in the kingdom of Grenada. This plant has been confounded with the Ayapana of Brazil, *Eupatorium ayapana*. The properties of the guaco are incontestible; for the authority of Humboldt's name does not allow of doubt. When the negroes rub their hands and bodies with this plant the most dangerous serpents will not bite them, and it is sufficient to make the wound bleed and introduce a little of the juice of the guaco to prevent bad consequences when they have been bitten.

Arsenious acid, arsenite of potash, ammonia and *eau de luce* have been regarded as excellent specifics against the bite of venomous serpents. We shall now give the treatment which ought to be pursued.

TREATMENT OF THE BITE OF VENOMOUS ANIMALS.

External treatment.—We must apply a ligature lightly immediately above the wounded part, which ligature ought only to remain a few minutes, and should be made of flat ribbon. We may bleed the wound before removing the compression, or better still, may remove it and apply cupping glasses, or we may suck the wound with the mouth, if we are certain that the lips and the cavity of the mouth do not present any excoriation, and we must wash it with tepid water.

If the disease is severe, the pain acute, and the swelling considerable, we must avoid making incisions, which only increase the mischief; but we may cauterise it with red-hot iron, or by means of protochloride of antimony (butter of antimony) which are considered as the best caustics in the case. In default of them we may however employ nitrate of silver, caustic potash, the caustics of Vienna or of Filhos, sulphuric acid, boiling oil, moxas, caustic ammonia, or the pomatum of Gondret, &c., but nothing must be allowed to delay the application of cupping glasses. At a later period we may apply to the wound lint soaked in a mixture of one part of strong liquor ammoniæ and two parts of olive oil; and later still, olive oil only slightly ammoniated, by way of friction as a lotion. When the wound no longer presents any danger it may be dressed like a simple sore.

Internal treatment.—We must endeavour to assist transpiration and to obtain sleep, and at the same time that we are applying external treatment, we must administer linden water rendered slightly ammoniacal, and place the patient in a hot bed, and carefully cover him, making him take from time to time a tablespoonful of some cordial composed of four ounces of Bordeaux wine, an ounce of syrup and a drachm of tincture of cinnamon; or else a few mouthfuls of Sherry or Madeira. If bilious vomiting or jaundice show themselves, we must give an emetic of ipecacuanha (gr. xv) and tartar emetic (gr. 3/4). If gangrene is progressing, we must add to the above cordial two drachms of soft extract of cinchona. If, on the contrary, the symptoms cease or abate in violence, we must continue the same treatment, taking great care during convalescence about the diet, which should be very light for a few days.

If the disease is slight, we may content ourselves with bleeding the part, cauterising it with ammonia and administering infusion of linden, camomile, or other bitters, to each cupful of which we have added six or eight drops of liquid ammonia.

APPENDIX.

AN. 14, VIC. REG., CAP. XIII.

AN ACT TO REGULATE THE SALE OF ARSENIC.

June 5, 1851.

WHEREAS the unrestricted Sale of Arsenic facilitates the Commission of Crime: Be it enacted by the Queen's most Excellent Majesty, by and with the Advice and Consent of the Lords Spiritual and Temporal, and Commons, in this present Parliament assembled, and by the Authority of the same, as follows:

I. Every Person who shall sell any Arsenic shall forthwith, and before the Delivery of such Arsenic to the Purchaser, enter or cause to be entered in a fair and regular Manner, in a Book or Books to be kept by such Person for that Purpose, in the Form set forth in the Schedule to this Act, or to the like Effect, a Statement of such Sale, with the Quantity of Arsenic so sold, and the Purpose for which such Arsenic is required or stated to be required, and the Day of the Month and Year of the Sale, and the Name, Place of Abode, and Condition or Occupation of the Purchaser, into all which Circumstances the Person selling such Arsenic is hereby required and authorized to inquire of the Purchaser before the Delivery to such Purchaser of the Arsenic sold, and such Entries shall in every Case be signed by the Person making the same, and shall also be signed by the Purchaser, unless such Purchaser profess to be unable to write (in which Case the Person making the Entries hereby required shall add to the Particulars to be entered in relation to such Sale the Words "cannot write"), and, where a Witness is hereby required to the Sale, shall also be signed by such Witness, together with his Place of Abode.

II. No Person shall sell Arsenic to any Person who is unknown to the Person selling such Arsenic, unless the Sale be made in the Presence of a Witness who is known to the Person selling the Arsenic, and to whom the Purchaser is known, and who signs his Name, together with his Place of Abode, to such Entries, before the Delivery of the Arsenic to the Purchaser, and no Person shall sell Arsenic to any Person other than a Person of full age.

III. No Person shall sell any Arsenic unless the same be before the Sale thereof mixed with Soot or Indigo in the Proportion of One Ounce of Soot or Half an Ounce of Indigo at the least to One Pound of the Arsenic, and so in proportion for any greater or less Quantity: Provided always, that where such Arsenic is stated by the Purchaser to be required, not for Use in Agriculture, but for some other Purpose for which such Admixture would, according to the Represention of the Purchaser, render it unfit, such Arsenic may be sold without such Admixture in a Quantity of not less than Ten Pounds at any One Time.

IV. If any Person shall sell any Arsenic, save as authorized by this Act, or on any Sale of Arsenic shall deliver the same without having made and signed the Entries hereby required on such Sale, or without having obtained such Signature or Signatures to such Entries as required by this Act, or if any Person purchasing any Arsenic shall give false information to the Person selling the same in relation to the Particulars which such last-mentioned Person is hereby authorized to inquire into of such Purchaser, or if any Person shall sign his name as aforesaid as a Witness to a sale of Arsenic to a Person unknown to the Person so signing as Witness, every Person so offending shall for every such Offence, upon a summary Conviction for the same before Two Justices of the Peace in *England* or *Ireland*, or before two Justices of the Peace or the Sheriff in *Scotland*, be liable to a Penalty not exceeding Twenty Pounds.

V. Provided, That this Act shall not extend to the Sale of Arsenic when the same forms Part of the Ingredients of any Medicine required to be made up or compounded according to the Prescription of a legally qualified Medical Practitioner, or a Member of the Medical Profession, or to the Sale of Arsenic by Wholsale to Retail Dealers, upon Orders in Writing in the ordinary Course of Wholsesale Dealing.

VI. In the Construction of this Act the Word "Arsenic" shall include Arsenious Acid and the Arsenites, Arsenic Acid and the Arseniates, and all other colourless poisonous Preparations of Arsenic.

THE SCHEDULE.

DAY OF SALE.	NAME AND SURNAME OF PURCHASER.	PURCHASER'S PLACE OF ABODE.		CONDITION OR OCCUPATION.	QUANTITY OF ARSENIC SOLD.	PURPOSE FOR WHICH REQUIRED.
1 September, 1851.	John Thomas.	Hendon.	Elm Farm.	Farm Labourer.	5 lbs.	To steep Wheat.

(Purchaser's Signature.)   Witness,   (Seller's Signature.)

JOHN THOMAS.   JAMES STONE,   GEORGE WOOD.

Grove Farm, Hendon.

Or, if Purchaser cannot write, Seller to put here the Words, "cannot write."

INDEX.

A.

Absorption of medicines (rate of), 88.
Accumulation of action, 89.
—— doses, 89.
—— medicines, 89.
Acetate of ammonia, 64, 260.
—— copper, neutral, 68.
—— lead, neutral, 68.
———— tribasic, 68.
—— potash, 62.
Acétolats, 6, 162.
Acétolés, 6, 158.
Ache, 34.
Acids generally, poisoning by, 361.
———— poisoning, lesions, symptoms
and treatment of, 361.
———— nomenclature of, note upon,
82.
—— acetic, 74.
———— poisoning by, 370.
———— tests for, 370.
—— arsenious, 72.
———— poisoning by, 381.
———— tests for, 387.
—— azotic (see Acid, nitric), 60.
—— boracic, 62.
—— carbonic, 62.
———— poisoning by, 462.
———— tests for, 463.
—— chlorhydric, 60.
———— (note upon), 82.
———— poisoning by, 367.
———— tests for, 367.
—— citric, 369.
—— cyanhydric (see Acid, hydrocyanic),
62.
—— hydrochloric, 60.
———— poisoning by, 367.

Acid, hydrochloric, tests for, 367.
—— hydrocyanic, 62.
—— hydrocyanic, poisoning by, 442.
———— tests for, 444.
—— hydrosulphuric, 60.
———— poisoning by, 470.
—— juices, 142.
—— lactic, 74.
—— muriatic (see Acid, hydrochloric),
60.
—— nitric, 60.
———— poisoning by, 365.
———— tests for, 365.
—— oxalic, 74.
———— poisoning by, 367.
———— tests for, 368.
—— phosphoric, 62.
—— prussic (see Acid, hydrocyanic) 62,
442.
—— sulphuric, 62.
———— poisoning by, 363.
———— tests for, 363.
—— sulphurous, 62.
—— sulphydric (see Acid, hydrosulphuric), 60.
—— tartaric, 74.
———— poisoning by, 369.
Aconitum napelus, 50.
Acorus, 12.
Acotyledons, 10.
Adder, characters of, 474.
—— poisoning by, 474.
Adjuvant of a prescription, 209.
Æthusa cynapium, 36, 453.
Affusions, 127.
Agaric, 10.
Ages, considerations relative to, 90.
Albumen, vegetable, 140.
Albuminous substances, 270.

I I

Alcohol, 74.
—— nitric, 179.
—— sulphuric, 62.
Alcoolata, 6, 162.
—— vulnéraire, 261.
Alcoolés, 6, 156.
Aldehyde, 74.
Ales, medicated, 158.
Algæ } products from, 10.
Algues }
Alkali, volatile, 64.
Alkanet, 28.
Alkekenge, 28.
Almonds, 40.
—— bitter, 41, 303.
—————— (essence of—formation of), 41.
—— milk of, 155, 303.
Aloes, 16, 286.
Alteratives, 236.
Althæa officinalis, 46.
Alum, 66, 228.
Amadou, 10.
Ambergris, 52.
Amidon, 15, 146.
Ammomées, natural family of, 16, 17.
Ammonia, preparations of, 260.
—— chlorhydrate of, 64.
—— hydrochlorate of, 64.
—— poisoning by, 371.
—— tests for, 371.
Ammoniacum, 36, 306.
Ampélidées, natural family of, 44.
Amygdalin, 41, 110.
Amygdalus, 40.
Amylaceous roots, 150.
—— (non) roots, 151.
—— substances, 270.
Anæsthetics, 304.
Analeptics, 15, 218.
Analysis of mixed gases, mode of, 468.
Anamirta cocculus, 50.
Anatripsalogic method, 98.
Anchusa, 28.
Angustura bark (false), 30, 456.
—— (true), 44.
—————— distinctions between, 457.
Animal kingdom, medicines from, 52 to 57.
—— parasitic, 345.
—— venomous, 473.
—————— poisoning by, 473.
Aniseed, 36.
Annelides (products of), 54.
Anthelmintics, 340.
Anthemis, 32.
Anti-emetic draught of Rivière, 110.

Antimony, and its compounds, 72.
—— butter of, 205.
—— poisoning by, 396.
—— tests for, 398.
Antiphlogistics, 270.
Antiseptics, 339.
Antispasmodics, 305.
Aperient roots, 17.
Apium petroselinum, 36.
Apocynées } natural family of, 30.
Apocynaceæ }
Apozems, 152.
—— antidartrous, 299.
—— antiscorbutic, 153.
—— diuretic, 325.
—————— (Swiss), 324.
—— purgative, 284.
—— tænifuge, 342.
—— vermifuge, 342.
Appendix, 478.
Archil, 10.
Arctium lappa, 32.
Aristolochiées } natural family of, 22.
Aristolochiaceæ }
Arnica, 32, 288.
Aroidées } natural family of, 12, 13.
Aroideæ }
Arrow-root, 16.
Arsenic, 60.
—— Act of Parliament for regulating the sale of, 478.
—— poisoning by, 375.
—— preparations of, 72, 253.
—— rings of, 376.
—— stains of, 377.
—— sulphurets of, poisoning by, 395.
—— tests for, 376.
Artemisia, 32.
Art of prescribing, 77.
Arum family, 12, 13.
Asarabacca, 22.
Asparaginées } natural family of, 16, 17.
Asparagineæ }
Asparagus, 16.
Asplenium adianthum nigrum, 13.
Assafœtida, 36, 306.
Astragalus, 42.
Astringents, mineral, 227.
—— vegetable, 230.
Atropa, 26, 450.
Atropia, 450.
Aurantiacées } natural family of, 44.
Aurantiaceæ }
Avena, 12.

B.

Badiane, 318.
Bag, resolvent, of iodine, 250.
Balm, 24.
Balsams, 144, 187.
—— of copaiva, 42.
—— of Fiovarenti, 196.
—— of Peru, 43.
—— of Tolu, 42.
Balsamum sulpharis, 160.
—— tranquillans, 297.
Balsomodendron myrrha, 42.
Bandage, mustard, 268.
Barley, 14.
Barytes, hydrochlorate of, 64.
—— poisoning by, 372.
—— tests for, 374.
Baryum, chloride of, 64.
Basis of a prescription, 208.
Baths generally, 200.
—— alkaline, 258.
—— aromatic, 202, 319.
—— balsamic, 329.
—— Barèges (artificial), 334.
—— bran, 273.
—— of corrosive sublimate, simple, 241.
———— compound, 242.
—— of fœcula, or starch, 273.
—— ferruginous, 226.
—— gelatinous, 202, 274.
—— ioduretted, 249.
—— of lime, 259.
—— mercurial, 202.
—— of mustard, 267.
—— poor man's (vapour), 259.
—— sulphurous, 203, 332, 333.
—— vapour, aromatic, 319.
Baume de condom, 160.
—— nerval, 269.
—— de soufre, 160.
—— tranquille, 297.
—— de vinceguère, 160.
Bay (sweet), 22.
Beaver, 52.
Beer, medicated, 158.
Bees, 56.
Beet, 24.
Belladonna, 26, 295.
—— poisoning by, 450.
Benoîte, 40.
Benzoin, 30.
Bernard's experiments, 110.
Berthollet's law, 114.
Bicarbonate of soda, 64.
Bichloride of mercury, 70.

Bichloride of mercury, poisoning by, 399.
—— preparations of, 240.
—— tests for, 403.
Bile, extract of, 53.
Biniodide of mercury, 70.
Binoxide of mercury, 70.
Birds, 52.
Birthworts, 22.
Biscuits (ferruginous), 222.
Bismuth, 68, 338.
—— poisoning by, 424.
—— tests for, 425.
Bistort, 24.
Bisulphuret of mercury, 70.
Bitartrate of potash, 62.
Bitter-sweet, 26.
Black draught, 281.
—— flux, 388.
—— maiden hair, 13.
—— (phagedenic) wash, 68.
Blanc de fard, 339.
Blistering plasters, 190.
Boluses, 175.
—— balsamic, 330.
—— of cooked honey, 278.
—— of Nancy, 66, 223.
—— tænifuge, 342.
Boraginées } natural family of, 28.
Boragineæ }
Borage, 28.
Borate of soda (borax), 258.
Boswellia serrata, 42.
Boudin's solution of arsenic, 254.
Bouillons, 153.
Boules de Nancy, 66, 223.
Box-tree, 22.
Brayera anthelmintica, 40, 343.
Bromine, 61.
—— poisoning by, 360.
Broths, 153.
Brucia, brucine, 454, 455.
—— tests for, 455.
Brutolés, 158.
Bryonia, 38.
Buckthorn, 42.
Buck-wheat tribe, 25.
Burdock, 32.
Butcher's broom, 17.

C.

Cachou, 42.
Cainca, 34.

Camboge, 44.
Cameliées, 44.
Camphor, 22, 308.
Canary seed, 192.
Cannabinaceæ, 20.
Cannabis indica, 20.
Canne de Provence, 12.
Cantharides, 56, 268.
—— poisoning by, 431.
—— tests for, 433.
Caoutchouc, 20.
Carbonic oxide, poisoning by, 463.
Capacy, 31.
Capillaire du Canada, 12, 13.
—— de Montpellier, 12,13.
Caprifoliaceæ, 34.
Capsules, 175.
Caraïhe's solution, 324.
Carbonate of soda, 64.
—— (sub) of iron, 66.
—— of lead (cerussa), 68.
Cardamome, 16.
Carex, 12.
Carminatives (umbelliferæ), 318.
Carragheen, 10, 272.
Caryophyllées ⎱ 46.
Caryophyllaceæ ⎰
Cascarilla, 22.
Cassia fistula, 40.
—— pulp, 40.
—— senna, 40.
Castoreum, 52, 307.
Castor oil, 22.
Cataplasms (see Poultices), 192.
Catechu, 42, 232.
Catheretics, 204.
Cats'-foot, 32.
Caustics, generally, 204.
—— ammoniacal, 261.
—— arsenical (of Frère Côme, or Rous-selot), 205.
—— of Cauquoin, 205.
—— of Filhos, 63, 205, 256.
—— of Gondret, 261.
—— lunar, 72.
—— sulpho-safranique of Rust and Velpeau, 205.
—— of Vienna, 62, 205, 256.
Celandine, 48.
Celery, 34.
Centuary (lesser), 28, 316.
Cerasus lauro-cerasus, 40.
Cerates, 185.
—— of charcoal (antiseptic), 339.
—— of Galien, 186.
—— simple, 185.

Chamomile, 32, 320.
Champignons (mushrooms), 10.
—— poisoning by, 458.
Charcoal, 339.
Charcoal, vapour, poisoning by, 465.
Chelidonium majus, 48.
Chenopodiaceæ, 24.
Cherry laurel, 40.
—— mixture of, 303.
—— pomatum of, 303.
Chicory, 32.
Chiendent, 12.
Chiococca, 34.
Chloride of barium, 64.
—— lime (hypochlorite of), 262.
—— silver, 72.
—— sodium and gold, 72.
Chlorine, 60, 262.
—— poisoning by, 360.
Chloroform, 74.
—— preparations of, 304.
Chloro-vinegar (Mialhe's), 443.
Chologogue purgatives, 84.
Chromule, 140.
Churrus, 21.
Cicuta maculata, 453.
—— virosa, 453.
Cicutine, 451.
Cigarettes, anti-asthmatic, 298.
—— arsenical, 255.
—— camphorated, 308.
—— of Dioscorides, 255.
—— mercurial, 247.
Cigue, 36.
Cinchona barks, 34, 311.
—— rules for administering, 311.
Cinnabar, 70, 247.
Cinnamon, 22, 321.
Citrine ointment, 72.
Citron, 44.
Civet cat, 52.
Clove pink, 46.
Cloves, 38.
Club mosses, 12, 13.
Coal gas, poisoning by, 464.
Cocculus indicus, 50.
—— palmatus, 50.
Coccus cacti, 56.
Cochineal, 56.
Cochlearea armoracia, 46.
Cocoa, 46.
Codein, 50, 291.
Cod-liver oil, 54, 251.
Coffee, 34.
—— of senna, 282.
—— vermifuge, 343.

Cbing, 38.
Colchicaceæ, 14, 15.
Colchicum, 14.
Colcothar, 66.
Cold seeds (four), 39.
Collutoires, 197.
—— astringent, of alum, 229.
—— boracic 197.
——— (dry), 198.
—— of catechu, 233.
—— hydrochloric, 262.
—— odontalgic, 198.
Collyriums, 194.
—— dry, 195, 239, 266.
—— irritant, of sulphate of copper, 265, 266.
——— zinc, 265, 266.
—— narcotic, 195.
—— of nitrate of silver, 196, 263.
—— simple, 196.
—— soft, 195.
Colocyath, 38.
Colombo root, 50, 315.
Combinations of medicines, rules for, 105.
Comfrey, 28.
Compositæ, 30, 32.
Confections, 168.
Coniciue, 451.
—— tests for, 452.
Coniferæ, 18.
Conium, 36, 300.
Conserves, 168.
Considerations relative to ages, 90.
——— climates, 92.
——— diet, &c., 91.
——— diseases, 96.
——— medicines, 78.
——— national difference, 92.
——— patients, 90.
——— professions, 91.
——— sexes, 90.
——— temperaments, 90.
Contrayerva, 20.
Convolvulaceæ, 26.
—— purgatives from, 286.
Copaiva, 42, 330.
Copper, and its compounds, 66, 265.
—— note upon the oxides of, 410.
—— poisoning by, 410.
—— tests for, 413.
Copperas, blue, 68.
—— green, 66.
Coque du Levant, 50.
—— poisoning by, 457.
Coquelot, 48.
Coral, red and white, 10, 56.

Coralline de Corse, 10.
Coriaria myrtifolia, 41.
Corrective or corrigant in a prescription, 208.
Corrosive sublimate, 70.
—— preparations of, 240.
—— poisoning by, 399.
—— tests for, 403.
Corsican moss, 10, 341.
Cotton, 46.
Couperose, bleue, 68.
—— vert, 66.
Cousso, 40.
Crabs, 54.
—— eyes, 54, 55.
Craw-fish-eye lichen, 10.
Cream of tartar, 62.
—— soluble, 62.
Creosote, 234.
Cresson de fontaine, 46.
Crocus metallorum, 72.
Croton oil, 22.
Cruciferæ, 46, 48.
Crustacea, 54.
Cubebs, 18.
Cucumis colocynthis, 38.
Cucurbitaceæ, 38.
Cupuliferæ, 18.
Currants, 38.
Cusparia, 44.
Cuttle-fish, 54.
Cyanide (double) of iron (prussian blue), 301.
—— of mercury, 408.
——— poisoning by, 408.
—— of potassium, 302.
——— poisoning by, 447.
Cyanogen, (medicines containing), 306.
Cydonia, 38.
Cynips gallæ, 56.
Cynodon dactylon, 13.
Cynoglossum, 28.
Cyperaceæ, 12, 13.

D.

Daphnées, 22.
Dates, 14.
Datura stramonium, 26.
Decantation, 130.
Decoction, 148.
—— of cinchona (purgative), 312.
—— of rhatany for injections, 233.
—— white of Sydenham, 153.

Decompositions, chemical, (Berthollet's law of), 114,
Delphinium staphisagria, 50.
Dextrine, 147.
Diacodium, 49.
Diamorphism, 382.
Dianthus caryophyllus, 46.
Diaphenix, 281.
Diastase, 15, 147.
—— animal, 82.
Dicotyledons, 18 to 51.
Digestion, (preparation of medicines by), 148.
Digitalis, 26.
Digitaline, 27.
—— preparations of, 336.
Dipterix odorata, 41.
Distillation, 160.
Distilled waters, 161.
Diuretics, 324.
Dog's-tooth, 12.
—— grass, 13.
Dorstenia contrayerva, 20.
Doses of medicine, 102.
Douches, 203.
—— with sulphuret of sodium, 203.
Dover's powder, 108.
Dragon's blood, 14, 232.
Drimys winterii, 45.
Drying of medicines, 126.
Dulcamara, 26, 299.

E.

Eau celeste, 68.
—— de clous ou ferrée, 222.
—— de goudron, 329.
—— de javelle, 64.
—— phagédenique jaune, 68.
———— noir, 68.
—— de Rabel, 62.
Ecussons, 189.
Egyptian ointment, 69.
Eispnote method, 98.
Elæo-cerolés, 185.
—— sacchara, 170.
Elæoptène, 145.
Elaterium, 38.
Elder, 34.
—— rob, 35.
Elecampane, 32.
Electuaries, 168, 171.
—— astringent, 171.

Electuaries, with mercury and tin, 341.
—— with myrrh, 171.
—— with sulphur, 332.
—— with tin, 340.
Eleolées, 159.
Elimination of medicines, 87.
Elm, 20.
Embrocations generally, 99, 128.
Emetics, 275.
Emetic, (tartar), 276.
———— poisoning by, 397.
———— tests for, 398.
—— draught of ipecacuanha, 275.
———— sulphate of copper, 266.
———————— zinc, 265.
———————— tartar emetic, 276.
Emmenagogues, 326.
Emollients, 270.
Emulsin, 110.
Emulsions, 154.
—— of castor-oil, 155.
—— copaiva, 155.
—— jalap resin, 286.
—— simple, or milk of almonds, 155.
Encens, 42.
Endermic method, 100.
Enepidermic method, 98.
Epsom salts, 64.
Ergot of rye, (de seiglè), 10, 288.
Ergotine, 11, 289.
Errors, chemical and pharmaceutical, to be avoided, in the administration of a medicine, 112.
Erysimum officinale, 48.
Escharotics, 204.
—— powder of arsenic, Frère Côme, Rousselot, 256.
Esprits (see Spirits), 162.
Essence of bitter almonds, 41.
—— mustard, 49.
—— soap, 202.
Etain (see Tin), 422.
Ethérolats, 6, 162.
Ethérolés, 6, 159.
Ethers, 74, 309.
—— note upon classes of, 74, 75.
—— acetic, 74.
—— chlorhydric, 74.
Ether, hydrochloric, 74.
—— hydriodic, 251.
—— iodhydric, 251.
—— mono-chloré, 304.
—— nitrous, 74.
—— sulphuric, 310.
Ethiops, martial, 66.
—— mineral, 247.

Euphorbiaceæ, 20, 22.
—— purgatives from, 285.
Euphorbium, 20.
Evaporation, 131.
Everlasting (mountain), 32.
Excipient of a prescription, 208.
Excitants (general), or stimulants, 318.
—— of the muscular system, 287.
—— balsamic, 327, 330.
—— emmenagogue, 326.
—— sulphurous, 331.
Extractive vegetable, 140.
Extracts generally, 163.
—— of conium (Storck's), 300.
—— lead, 68.
—— male fern, 342.
—— nux vomica (alcoholic), 287.
Extrait de Saturne, 68.

F.

Fatty preparations, 185.
—— substances, 270.
Feculæ, 146.
Fenugreek, 42.
Fermentation, various kinds of, 141, 267.
Fern, male, 4, 11, 342.
Ferns, products of, 10, 11, 12.
Fer, réduit, 218.
Ferruginous pills, 218, 219.
—— preparations, 218.
—— poisoning by, 429.
Ferrugo, 66.
Fève de St. Ignace, 28.
Figs, 20.
Figwort tribe, 26.
Filhos' caustic, 256.
Filtration, 130.
Fishes, products from, 54.
Fleas, 56.
Fleur-de-lis, 16.
Flowers of sulphur, 60.
Flux, black, 388.
Foie de soufre, 62.
Fomentations generally, rules for, 128.
—— antineuralgic, 130.
—— diuretic, 326, 336.
—— emollient, 274.
—— soapy, 129.
—— soothing, 302.
Fools-parsley, 36.
Formules (prescriptions), 207.

Formules, rules to be observed in writing, 210.
—— model of, 215.
Fougères, 10, 11, 12.
Fowler's solution of arsenic, 12, 254.
Foxglove, 26.
Frictions with chloride of gold, 253.
—— nux vomica, 287.
Frogs, 54.
Fruits, pectoral, (four), 15.
Fumariaceæ, 48.
Fumaria officinalis, 48.
Fumigations, 132.
—— aromatic, 133.
—— balsamic, 330.
—— of cinnabar, 247.
—— nitric acid, 133.
—— soothing, 123.
—— sulphurous, 332.
Fungi, 10, 11.
—— poisoning by, 458.

G.

Gadus morrhua, 54.
Galangale, 16.
Galbanum, 37.
Galingale, 12.
Galipea cusparia, 44.
Galls, 18, 56, 231.
Garance, 34.
Gargles, 196.
—— acidulated, 197.
—— antiseptic (of cinchona), 313.
—— antisyphilitic, 241, 243, 244.
—— astringent of alum, 234.
—— subacetate of lead, 227.
—— of corrosive sublimate, 241.
—— emollient, 271.
—— for fetid breath, 262.
—— of the four pectoral fruits, 271.
—— hydrochloric, 197.
—— rhatany (extract of), 234.
Gas (coal), poisoning by, 464.
—— from cesspools and sewers, 470, 471.
Gayac, 44.
Gelées, 169.
Gelatine, 270, 272.
Gelatinous substances, 270.
Genevrier, 18.
Gentian, 28.
Gentianaceæ, 28.
Geracy, 31.

German tinder, 10.
Geum, 40.
Ginger, 321.
Girofle, 38.
Glass, poisoning by, 430.
Glauber's salt, 84.
Glucose, 147.
Glycyrrhiza, 40.
Glysters, 198.
—— anodyne, 291, 292.
—— anthelmintic, 235, 241, 246, 255, 340, 344.
—— antidysenteric, 228, 265.
—— antineuralgic, 328.
—— antispasmodic, 199, 308.
—— astringent, 228, 231, 238, 259.
—— —— of tannin, 230.
—— of copaiva, 331.
—— croton-oil, 285.
—— emollient, 272.
—— febrifuge, 311, 315.
—— for fissures of the anus, 199.
—— irritant, for children, 284.
—— laxative, 279.
—— mercurial (vermifuge), 340.
—— nutritious, 273.
—— oily, 273.
—— purgative, 281, 282.
—— of starch, 199, 272.
—— of tobacco, 298.
Gnaphalium, 32.
Gold, and its compounds, 72, 253.
—— poisoning by, 426.
—— tests for, 427.
Gomme gutte, 44.
Gossypium herbaceum, 46.
Goulard's extract of lead, 68.
Gourd tribe, 38.
Graisses médicamenteuses, 186.
Gramineæ, 12.
Granateæ, 38.
Granatum, 342.
Granules, 175.
—— of digitaline, 336.
Grape tribe, 45.
Grasses, 12.
Gratiola, 26.
Grenadier, 38.
Groseille, 38.
Grossulariaceæ, 38.
Guiacum, 44.
Guimauve, 46.
Gum adragante, 42.
—— ammoniacum, 36.
—— arabic, 42.
Gummy substances, 270.

Guttiferæ, 44.

H.

Habituation to medicines, 94.
Hartshorn, 52.
Hart's tongue, 13.
Hashish, 21.
Hedge mustard, 48.
Hellebore, black and white, 14, 15, 50.
Helminthology, table of, 345.
Hemlock, 36.
—— water, 36.
Hemp, Indian, 20.
Hempworts, 21.
Henbane, 26.
Hoffman's solution, 79, 178.
Homberg's sedative salt, 62.
Honeys, 56, 167.
Hops, 20.
Horse-radish, 46.
Hound's tongue, 28.
Huile de cade, 18.
Huiles essentielles, 145.
Hydrogen (bicarburretted), poisoning by, 464, 465.
—— (sulphuretted), 470.
Hydrolats, 6, 161.
Hydroléts, 149.
Hydromel, 168.
Hyosciamus, 26, 297.
Hyper-sthenisants, 349.
Hypochlorite of lime, 262.
—— soda, 262.
Hypo-sthenisants, 349.
Hyssop, 24.
—— hedge, 26.

I.

Iatraleptic method, 98.
Ice, artificial, 60.
Iceland moss, 10.
Idiosyncracy, 90, 97.
Igazurine, 456.
Ignatius' (St.), bean, 28.
Illicium anisatum, 318.
Incompatible substances, table of, 118.
Indian berry (see Coque du Levant), 50.
—— rubber, 20.
Indigo, 42.
Infusions, 148.

Infusion of chamomile, 320.
—— cinchona, 311.
—— columba, 316.
—— stimulant, 318.
—— vermifuge, 341.
Ingestion, method by, 100.
Inhalation, 134.
Injections, 198.
—— astringent, 228, 231, 232.
—— of chlorine, 262.
—— of galls, 232.
—— iodine and iron, 224.
—— iodo-ferrée, 224.
—— ioduretted for hydrocele, 250.
—— irritating, 198.
—— of pine-water (distilled), 198.
—— silver (nitrate of), for the nasal fossæ, 262.
—— soothing, 198.
Insects, pharmaceutical products from, 56.
Intermedium of a prescription, 208.
Inula, 32.
Iodide of iron, 66.
—— lead, 250.
—— mercury, 70.
—————— and potassium, 247.
—— potassium, 62.
—————— poisoning by, 359.
Iodine, poisoning by, 358.
—— preparations of, 60, 248.
Iodo-hydrargyrate of iodide of potassium, 247.
Ipecacuanha, 34.
Irideæ, 16, 17.
Irish moss, 10.
Iron, and its compounds, 66, 218.
—— poisoning by, 429.
—— tests for, 430.
Irritant medicines, 256, 267.
—— poisons, 356.
Ivory, 52.

J.

Jalap, 28.
Jasminaceæ, 30.
Jellies, 169, 272.
—— of bitter lichen, 317.
—— Corsican moss, 341.
Juglandaceæ, 20.
Juices, 140.
—— acid, 142.
—— aqueous, 140.

Juice, extractive, 140.
—— inspissated, 163.
—— milky, 145.
—— oily, 143.
—— preservation of, 142.
—— resinous, 144, 145.
—— saccharine, 141.
Jujubes, 42.
Juleps generally, 175.
—— soothing, 176.
Juniper, 18.
Juniperus oxycedrus, 330.
Jusquiame, 26.

K.

Kermes, mineral, 73.
Kino, 43, 232.
Koumarouma odorata, 41.
Kousso, 40, 342.
Krameria triandria, 46.

L.

Labiatæ, 24, 26.
—— preparations from, 318.
Lactate of iron, 66.
Lactucarium, 31, 145, 294.
Lapis infernalis, 205.
Laudanum, Rousseau's, 293.
—— Sydenham's, 293.
Lauraceæ, 22.
Laurier cerise, 40.
—— rose, 30.
Lavements, 198.
Lavender, 24.
Law's method of administering mercury, 71.
Laxatives, 280.
Lead, and its compounds, 60, 227.
—— poisoning by, 415.
—————— treatment of, 417.
—— tests for, 420.
Leeches, 54.
Leguminosæ, 40, 42.
Lemonades generally, 152.
—— of citrate of magnesia, 283.
—————— gaseous, 283.
—— citric, 152.
—— sulphuric, 152.
Lettuce, 30, 31.
Levigation, 135.
Lice, 56.

Lichens, 10, 11.
—— Icelandicus, 10, 316.
—— pixidé, 11.
Liebig's test for prussic acid, 446.
Liliaceæ, 16, 17.
Lily (water), 50.
Lime, preparations of, 259.
—— phosphate of, 64.
—— poisoning by, 372.
Linaceæ, 46.
Linctuses, 176.
—— white pectoral, 176, 302.
Lindenblooms, 45.
—— tree, 44.
Liniments generally, 99.
—— antidartrous, 330.
—— antipsoric, 329.
—— of camphor, 308.
—— chloroform, 304.
—— narcotic, for piles, 200.
—— of oil and lime (oleo-calcaire), 259.
—— of Pihorel, 333.
—— stimulating, 320.
—— volatile, 200.
—— of white precipitate, 239.
Linseed, 46.
Linum usitatissimum, 46.
Liparolés, 186.
Liquorice, 40.
Litharge, 68.
Liver of sulphur, 62.
Lixiviation, 149.
Lobelia inflata, 299.
Lochs, 176, 302.
Logoniaceæ, 28, 30.
Loks, 176.
Looches generally, 176.
—— of antimony, (white oxide of), 177.
—— blanc or white, 176, 302.
—— (demi), 176.
—— kermetized, 177.
—— laxative, for children, 177.
Lotion, alkaline, 258.
—— ammoniacal, 261.
—— antidartrous, 236.
—— antiherpetic (mercurial), 130.
—— astringent, 227.
—— boracic, 258.
—— cosmetic of corrosive sublimate, 242.
—— ferruginous, 225.
—— of iodine, 250.
—— sulphurous, 334.
—— with vegeto-mineral water, 130.
Lozenges, 170.
—— anthelmintic, 340.

Lozenges of santonine, 342.
Lunar caustic, 72.
Lungs of the oak, 11.
Lycopodiaceæ, 12, 13.
Lycopodium, 12, 13.

M.

Mace, 25.
Macerations generally, 148.
—— of cinchona, 311.
—— of quassia, 316.
Madder, 34.
Magistral formulæ, 112.
—— prescriptions, 207.
Magnesia, and its compounds, 64, 280.
Maiden hair, Canadian, 12, 13.
—— Venus', 12, 13.
Mallow, 46.
Malva sylvestris, 46.
Malvaceæ, 46.
Mammalia, medicines furnished by the, 52.
Manna, 30, 278.
Marjoram, 24.
Marsh's test for arsenic, 388.
Massicot, 68.
Mastic, anæsthetic, 304.
—— odontalgic, of Foulon, 229.
Meadow saffron, 14.
Measures, French, tables of, 4, 217.
Medicines, definition of, 206.
—— absorption of, 81.
—— accumulation of, 89.
—— action, 89.
—— doses, 89.
—— action, mode of, 86.
—— administration of, rules for, 86.
—— application of, methods of, 98.
—— augmenting the action of, 105.
—— changes in, 81.
—— Classification of, by natural families, 9 to 57.
—— combination of, rules for, 105.
—— commercial kinds of, 78.
—— diminishing the action of, 108.
—— doses of, table of, 102.
—— elimination of, 87.
—— forms particular given to, 112, 127.
—— habituation to, 94.
—— influence of climate, &c., upon the action of, 96.
—— disease, upon the action of, 96.

Medicines, intervals for the administration of, 102.
—— mutations of, 81.
—— narcotic, containing cyanogen, 300.
—— periods for the administration of, 104, 105.
—— tolerance of, 94.
—— to obtain the effects two or more at the same time, 109.
—— to obtain new and peculiar effects, 109.
Melanthaceæ,14, 15.
Melilot, 40.
Melissa, 24.
Mellites, 167.
Menispermeaceæ, 50.
Mercurialis annua, 20.
Mercury, and its compounds, 68, 70, 79, 239.
—— bichloride of, 240.
———— poisoning by, 399.
———— preparations of, 239.
—— bicyanide of, 408.
———— proto-iodide of, 245.
———— sulphurets of, 247.
———— tests for, 403.
—— vapours of, poisoning by, 409.
Metals, classes of, 82.
Mezereum, 22.
Milk, asses' 52.
Milk-wort tribe, 47.
Mineral crystal, 62.
—— kingdom, medicines from, 60 to 74.
Mint, 24.
Mixtures, 177.
—— against intoxication, 324.
—— of alum, for croup, 229.
—— of ammonia, 260.
—— of ammoniacum, 181.
—— anthelmintic, 182, 185.
—— antihysterical, 184.
—— antineuralgic, of lead, 227.
———— opium, 290.
—— antiphlogistic, 276, 339.
—— antispasmodic, 180.
—— of borax, 258.
—— of camphor, 182, 183.
—— of castor oil, 181, 279.
—— for chilblains, 178.
—— for chorea, 266.
—— of cod-liver oil, 252.
—— of copaiva, 181.
—— cordial, 321.
—— of croton oil, 182, 285.
—— for delirium tremens, 290.
—— for diarrhæa, 259.

Mixture, diuretic, 179.
—— emetic, 184.
—— of ergot (obstetric), 178.
—— expectorant, 306.
—— ferruginous, 222, 223, 224.
—— of fish oil, 252.
—— for gleet, 322.
—— kermetized, 184.
—— laxative, 278.
—— narcotic, 289, et subs.
—— purgative, 189, 263.
———— for painters, 281.
—— of quinine and coffee, 315.
—— sudorific of sarsaparilla, 323.
—— tonic, 178.
—— vermifuge, 182, 185.
Mollusca, 54.
Momordica, 38.
Monkshood, 50.
Monocotyledons, 12, 13.
Monœsia, 234.
Morées, 20.
Morelle, 26.
Morphia, and its salts, 50, 291.
—— poisoning by, 435.
—— tests for, 436.
Morus nigra, 20.
Moss, Corsican, 10.
—— Iceland, 10.
Mousse de Corse, 10, 341.
Moxas, 205.
—— Percy's, 205.
Mucilages generally, 154.
Mucilaginous substances, 270.
Mugwort, 32.
Mulberry, 20.
Mullein, 26.
Muscles, 54.
—— poisoning by, 433.
Mushrooms (family of), 10.
—— poisoning by, 458.
Musk, 52, 307.
Mustard, 48, 267.
—— essence of, 49.
Mutations of medicines, 81.
Myristaceæ, 24.
Myrolées (solutions by essential oils), 6, 160.
Myronic acid, 49.
Myrosine, 49.
Myroxylon toluiferum, 42.
Myrrh, 42.
Myrtaceæ, 38.

N.

Narcotico-acrids, poisoning by, 448.
Narcotics, 289.
—— poisoning by, 434.
Narcotine, 50.
Nenuphar, 50.
Nerprun, 42.
Neuro-sthenic tonics, 311.
Nicotine, 27, 451.
—— tests for, 452.
Nightshade, common, 26.
—— deadly, 26.
—— woody, 26.
Nitrate of bismuth (sub) *blanc de fard*
—*cosmetic, or pearl white,* 68.
—— of mercury, 70.
—— of potash, 62.
———— (fused), 62.
—— of silver, 72.
Nitric alcohol, 179.
Nomenclature (pharmaceutical), 5.
Noyer, 17.
Nut-galls, 18.
Nutmegs, 24.
Nux vomica, 28.
—— poisoning by, 456.
—— preparations of, 287.
Nymphæa, 50.
Nympheaceæ, 50.

O.

Oak, 18.
—— bark, 231.
Oats, 12.
Œillet rouge, 46.
Œnéolés, 157.
Œnolés, 6.
Officinal formulæ, 206.
Oils generally, 143.
—— of Cade, 330.
—— castor, 22.
—— classification of, 143.
—— cod liver, 251.
—— composition of, 145, 144.
—— croton, 22.
—— essential, 145.
—— fish, 251.
—— ioduretted, 252.
—— medicated, 159.
—— olive, 30.
—— of paper, 236.
—— poppy (test for), 159.

Oil, of vitriol, 62.
—— volatile, 145.
Ointments, 187.
—— antipsoric, 331, 332.
—— of belladonna, 296.
—— of Cyrillus, 241.
—— plasters, 188.
—— of sulphur, 331.
—— tartar emetic, 277.
Oleander, 30.
Olibanum, 42.
Olives, 30.
Onguent de la mère, 274.
Opiates, 171.
—— antiblenorrhagic, 321, 331.
—— antihysterical, 307.
—— balsamic, 331.
—— of charcoal, 339.
—— of cubebs and camphor, 322.
Opium, 48.
—— its alkaloids, 291.
—— poisoning by, 437.
—— preparations of, 289.
———— table of, 294.
—— tests for, 440.
Opoponax, 37.
Orange, 44.
Orchidées, 18, 19.
Orchidaceæ, 18, 19.
Ordonnance, 207.
Orge, 14.
Orpiment, 72.
Orseille, 10.
Ox-gall, 317.
Oxygen, 60.
Oxysulphuret of antimony, 72.
Oysters, 54.

P.

Palmaceæ, 14, 15.
Palma Christi, 22.
Palms, 14.
Papaveraceæ, 48, 50.
Papaver rheas, 48.
—— somniferum album, 48.
Parelle d'Auvergne, 10.
Parietaria, 20.
Parsley, 36.
Pastes, 169.
Pastilles, 170.
Pâtes, 169.
Patience, 24.
Paullinia, 234.

Peach, 38.
Pearson's solution, 72, 255.
Peas (narcotic) for issues, 299.
Pectoral fruits (four), 14.
Pellitory, 32.
—— of the wall, 30.
Peony, 50.
Pepper, 18.
Pepsin, 82.
Percolation, 157.
Percy's moxas, 205.
Periwinkle tribe, 31.
Phalaris canariensis, 192.
Pharmacy, short sketch of, 125.
Phellandrum aquaticum, 36.
Phocenic acid, 52.
Phosphate of lime, 64.
—— of soda, 284.
Phosphorus, 60.
—— poisoning by, 357.
Pierre infernale, 72.
Pills generally, 172.
—— of aloes, 286.
—— alum, 228.
—— anti-arthritic (gout), 287.
———— catarrhal, 333.
———— chlorotic, 219.
———— diarrhœal, 290.
———— epileptic, 295.
———— gastralgic, 174.
———— neuralgic, 173, 305.
———— spasmodic, 307.
———— syphilitic, 236, 243.
—— antimonial, 338.
—— arsenical (febrifuge), 253.
—— astringent, 227, 228, 232, 233.
———— tonic, 225.
—— balsamic, 327, 330.
—— bechic (expectorant), 336, 337.
—— Belloste's, 68.
—— Bland's, 67, 220.
———— modified, 220.
—— of calomel, 239.
—— of camphor, 308.
—— for chronic catarrh of the bladder
or bronchi, 174.
—— of conium (extract of), 300.
—— of copaiva, 174.
—— corrosive sublimate, 244.
—— croton oil, 285.
—— cubebine, 322.
—— depurative, 323.
—— of digitaline, 336.
—— diuretic, 307, 326.
—— emmenagogue, 327.
—— expectorant, 336, 337.

Pills, febrifuge, 313.
—— ferruginous, 218, 219, 225.
—— gout, 287.
—— hemlock (extract of), 300.
—— of iron, citrate and lactate, 226.
—— jalap, 286.
—— Meglin's (anti-neuralgic), 305.
—— of mercury (protiodide), 246.
—— morphia (hydrochlorate of), 291.
—— nux vomica (alcoholic extract of),
287.
—— ox-gall (tonic), 317.
—— purgative, 286.
—— of quinine (sulphate of), 174, 314.
—— Sedillot's, 68.
—— silver (nitrate of), 264.
—— of tannin, 230.
—— turpentine (prepared), 328.
—— Vallet's, 67, 220.
—— of white precipitate, 238.
Piperaceæ, 18.
Pitch, Burgundy, 18.
Pivoine, 50.
Plasters, 188.
—— blistering, 190.
—— diapaline, 188.
—— of gum diachylon, 188.
—— softening, 237,
—— Vigo's, 68.
Platinum, preparations of, 253.
Poisoning by acids generally, 361.
———— acetic, 370.
———— arsenic } 381.
———— arsenious
———— carbonic, 462.
———— citric, 370.
———— hydrochloric, 367.
———— hydrocyanic, 442.
———— hydrosulphuric, 470.
———— nitric, 365.
———— oxalic, 367.
———— prussic, 442.
———— sulphuric, 363.
———— tartaric, 369.
———— vegetable, 369.
—— ammonia, 371.
—— angustura bark (false), 454.
—— antimony, 396.
———— tartrate of, 397.
—— arsenic, 375.
———— sulphurets of, 395.
—— barytes, 372.
—— belladonna, 450.
—— bismuth, 424.
—— bromine, 360.
—— cantharides, 431.

Poisoning by carbonic acid, 462.
——— oxide, 463.
—— cesspool gases, 470.
—— charcoal fumes, 465.
—— chlorine, 360.
—— coal-gas, 464.
—— copper, 410.
—— corrosive sublimate, 399.
—— enamel, 430.
—— fungi, 468.
—— glass, 430.
—— gold, 426.
—— hemlock (water, &c.), 451.
—— hyosciamus, 441.
—— iodine, 358.
—— iodide of potassium, 359.
—— iron, 429.
—— lead, 415.
—— lime, 372.
—— mercury bichloride, 399.
——— bicyanide, 408.
——— vapours, 409.
—— morphia and its salts, 435.
—— muscles, 433.
—— mushrooms, 458.
—— narcotics, 434.
—— narcotico-acrids, 448.
—— nux vomica, 456.
—— opium, 457.
—— phosphorus, 357.
—— potash, 371.
—— potassium, cyanide of, 447.
——— sulphuret of, 373.
—— putrifying animal matters, 473.
—— putrefiants, 470.
—— septics, 470.
—— sewer gases, 471.
—— silver, 425.
—— soda, 371.
—— solanaceæ, 441.
—— strontian, 372.
—— strychnine, 454.
—— sulphuretted hydrogen, 470.
—— tartar emetic, 397.
—— tin, 422.
—— tobacco, 451.
—— vegetable irritants, 431.
—— venomous animals, 473.
—— viper, 475.
—— zinc, 427.
—— general rules for the detection of, 353.
—— general signs of, 352.
Poisons, classification of, 348.
—— irritant, 348, 356.
——— lesions, symptoms and treatment of, 357.

Poisons from the vegetable kingdom, 431.
—— narcotic, 348, 434.
——— lesions, symptoms and treatment of, 434.
—— narcotico-acric, 349, 448.
—— septic, or putrefactive, 349.
Polygala Senega, 46.
Polygalaceæ, 46.
Polygonaceæ, 24.
Polypi, 56.
Pomatums generally, 186.
—— antimonial, 187.
—— anti-ophthalmic, 263.
——— of red oxide of mercury, 237.
—— anti-psoric, 236.
——— septic, 313.
—— for arresting loss of hair, 269.
—— astringent (of sulphate of iron), 226.
—— of binoxide of mercury, 245.
—— citrine, 72.
—— of creosote (desiccative), 235.
—— Cyrillus's, 241.
——— modified, 241.
—— epispastic, green, 268.
——— yellow, 269.
—— Gondret's, 261.
—— of iodide of lead, 186, 250.
——— mercury, 245.
——— potassium, 187, 249.
——— (ioduretted), 187, 250.
—— quinine (sulphate of), 315.
—— resolvent (mercurial), 237.
—— for ulcers (phagedenic), 296.
—— of zinc, oxide, 265.
Pomegranate, 38.
Poplar, 20.
Poppy red, 48.
—— white, 48, 292.
——— compounds of, 62, 64, 256.
Porphyrization, 134.
Potash, acetate of, 62.
—— bitartrate of, 62.
—— borico-tartrate of, 62.
—— caustic, 62.
—— chloride of, 64.
—— hydriodate of, 62.
—— hypochlorite of, 64.
—— nitrate of, 62.
—— poisoning by, 371.
—— prussiate of, 62.
—— sulphate of, 62.
—— tests for, 372.
Potassium, cyanide of, 62, 447.
——— poisoning by, 447.

Potassium, iodide of, 62.
———— poisoning by, 359.
—— sulphuret of, 62.
———— poisoning by, 375.
Potato, 26.
Potions generally, 175, 178.
—— ammoniacal, 260.
—— anthelmintic (of soot), 235, 343.
—— anti-blenorrhagic, 322.
———— diarrhœal (of nitrate of silver), 264.
———— hysteric, 310.
———— monial, 337, 338.
———— neuralgic, 328.
———— spasmodic, 305, 310.
———————— with musk, 307.
—— astringent of alum, 228, 233, 234.
—— bechic (expectorant), 306.
—— of chamomile, 320.
—— of cinchona, extract of, 312.
—— emmenagogue, 327.
———— of iodine, 249.
—— expectorant, 306, 337.
—— febrifuge, 179.
———— tasteless, 314.
—— ferruginous, 223.
—— hydrosulphuric, 335.
—— for pneumonia, 337.
—— of quinine (sulphate of), 314.
—— stimulant, 318.
—— sudorific, 324.
—— sulphurous, 334.
—— tonic, 312.
Poultices (see also Cataplasms), 197.
—— anodyne, 194.
—— anti-arthritic, 194.
—— bread, 274.
—— emollient, 274.
—— resolvent of conium, 300.
—— starch, 274.
—— suppurative, 194.
—— vinegar, 194.
Powders generally, 134.
—— absorbent, 260.
———— and alkaline, 257.
—— ammoniacal, 261.
—— anti-diarrhœal, 338, 339.
———— neuralgic, 221.
———— phlogistic, 335.
———— psoric, 332.
———— septic, 308.
———— spasmodic, 301, 338.
—— astringent, of tannin, 230.
—— of bismuth, 338.
—— of calomel, for internal or external use, 238.

Powder, caustic (Vienna), 256.
—— of charcoal and cinchona, 312.
—— dentifrice, 138, 222.
———— for cleaning teeth blackened by iron, 138.
—— emetic, 275, 277.
—— escharotic, of arsenic, 256.
———— Frère Côme, 256.
———— Rousselot, 15, 256.
—— febrifuge, of yellow cinchona, 311.
———— tasteless, for children, 313.
———— of quinine, 314.
—— ferruginous, 220.
———— for children, 221.
—— of ginger (stimulating), 321.
—— of gold (chloride of), 253.
—— hemlock, 300.
—— for hooping cough, 295.
—— impalpable, mode of preparing, 136.
—— of magnesia, 280.
—— mercury, binoxide of, 237.
—— morphia, sulphate of, 291.
—— nux vomica, 287.
—— stomachic, 221.
—— of tannin, 230.
—— tonic, 221, 315.
—— Vienna, 256.
—— of white precipitate, 237, 238.
Preface, Authors', v.
——— Translator's, vii.
Prescription, model of a, 215.
—— rules for writing a, 210.
Primæ viæ, 81.
Prussian blue, 66, 301.
Pulmonaire de Chêne, 11.
Pulps generally, 138.
Pulverization, 134.
Punica granatum, 38.
Purgatives, 278.
—— drastic, 285.
—— saline, 283.
Putrefying poisons, 470.
Pyrothonide, 236.

Q.

Quassia amara, 44, 316.
Quercus infectoria, 18.
—— robur, 18.
Quince, 38.
Quinine, sulphate of, 314.

R.

Raifort sauvage, 46.
Ranunculaceæ, 50.
Rapontic, 24.
Rasori's theory of "tolerance," 95.
Realgar, 72.
Reconstituants (analeptics), 218.
Radoul, 41.
Red precipitate, 70.
Reglisse, 40.
Reinsch's test for arsenic, 392.
Reptiles, products furnished by, 54.
Resins, kinds of, 144, 145.
—— preparations of, 185.
Resolvent farnia, 43.
Respiration, artificial, 455.
Retinoles mous, 187.
—— solides, 188.
Rhamnaceæ, 42.
Rhamnus catharticus, 42.
Rhatany, 46.
Rhubarb, 24.
Rhus toxicodendron, 288.
Ricinus, 22.
Rivière's anti-emetic draught, 110.
Robs, 164.
Rocella tinctoria, 10.
Rochelle salt, 64.
Roots, aperient, greater, 167.
———— lesser, 167.
—— containing starch, 150.
—— not containing starch, 151.
Rosaceæ, 38, 40.
Rose, 40.
Rouille, 66.
Rousselot's escharotic powder, 15.
Rubiaceæ, 34.
Rue, 44.
Rutaceæ, 44.

S.

Sabadilla, 14.
Saccharine substances, 270.
Saccharolés, 165.
—— mous, 168.
—— solides, 170.
Saccharures, 170.
Saffron, 16.
Safran de Mars, 66.
Sagapenum, 37.
Sage, 26.

Sago, 14.
Sal-ammoniac, 64.
—— de duobus, 62.
—— prunelle, 62.
Salep, 18.
Salicaceæ, 20.
Salicine, 21.
Salt of Saturn, 68.
Sambucus, 34.
Sang-Dragon, 14, 232.
Saponaria officinalis, 46.
Sarasin, 24.
Sarsaparilla, 16.
—— German, 12.
Sassafras, 22.
Savine, 18.
Scammony, 28.
Scilla, 16.
Scolopendrum officinale, 13.
Scrophularineæ, 26.
Second ways (secundæ viæ), 81, 92.
Sedatives, 335.
Sedges, 12, 13.
Seidlitz salts, 64.
Seignette salts, 64.
Sel de duobus, 62.
—— prunelle, 62.
Semen contra, 32, 341.
Senega, 46.
Senna, 40.
Septic, or putrefying poisons, 470.
Serpentary, 22.
Sexes, considerations relative to, 90.
Shields, 189.
Silver, and its compounds, 72, 262.
—— poisoning by, 425.
—— tests for, 426.
Simarouba, 45, 316.
Sinapis, 48.
Sinapisms, 192, 268.
Sisymbrium nasturcium, 46.
Smilax squina, 17.
Smithy water, 67.
Snails, 54.
Soaps, 72.
Soapwort, 46.
Soda, and its salts, 64, 256.
—— poisoning by, 371.
—— tests for, 372.
Solanaceæ, 26, 28, 295.
—— poisoning by, 441.
—— nutrient, 27.
Soluble tartar, 280.
Solution, medicines prepared by, 147.
—— by alcohol, 156.
—— arsenical, of Boudin, 254.

Solution, arsenical, Fowler, 254.
——— Pearson, 255.
——— astringent, for erysipelas (Velpeau's), 256.
———Caraïbe's, 324.
—— of corrosive sublimate, 240.
—— by essential oils, 160.
—— by ether, 159.
—— ferruginous, 223.
—— of iodine, 248.
—— Van Swieten's, 240.
——— modified, 241.
Soot (preparations of), 234, 343.
Spanish flies, 56.
Sparadraps, 189.
Species, aperitive, 325.
—— aromatic, 202.
—— carminative, 37.
Spermaceti, 52.
Spirit of Mindererus, 64, 260.
Spirits, 162.
—— acetic, 162.
—— ethereal, 162.
Sponge, 56.
Spurge tribe, 21.
Squill, 16.
Squine, 17
Star-anise, 318.
Starch, 146.
—— roots containing, 150.
——— not containing, 151.
Starchy substances, 270.
Stavesacre, 50.
Stearates, 188.
Stearoptine, 145.
Stimulants generally, 318.
—— balsamic, 327.
—— sulphurous, 331.
Storax tribe, 30.
Stramonium, 26, 297.
Strawberry tribe, 38.
Strontian, poisoning by, 372.
—— tests for, 374.
Strychnine, 29, 454.
—— doses of, 29.
—— poisoning by, 454.
—— tests for, 455.
Strychnos nux vomica, 28.
—— poisoning by, 454.
Sublimate (corrosive), 70.
Substances soluble in acids, 82.
——— alkalies, 82.
——— alkaline chlorides, 82.
Succedanea, 87.
Sucs, 140.
Sudorifics, 322.

Sudorific woods (four), 23.
Sugars, 141.
—— cane, 12, 141.
—— grape, 141.
—— milk, 141.
—— mushroom, 141, 142.
Sulphur, flowers of, 60.
—— liver of, poisoning by, 375.
—— magistry of, 60.
—— precipitated, 60.
—— vegetable, 12.
Sulphuretted hydrogen, poisoning by, 470.
Suppositories, 191.
—— anthelmintic, of binoxide of mercury, 246.
—— antimonial, 277.
—— purgative, 191.
—— to recal hæmorrhoids, 191.
—— of tannin, 231.
Sureau, 34.
Surinam wood, 316.
Symphytum, 28.
Synantheraceæ, 30, 32.
Synaptase, 41.
Syrups generally, 165.
—— balsamic, 327.
—— of cod-liver oil, 251.
—— cuisinier (Syr. Sals. Co.), 322.
—— of ether, 74, 75, 290.
—— ferruginous, 224.
—— of iodide of iron, 224.
——— mercury and potassium, 247.
—— iodo-ferré (Mialhe), 224.
—— of iron and rhatany, 222.
—— of Karabé, 80.
—— preservation of, 167.
—— Ricard's, 222.
—— of strychnine (sulphate of), 287.

T.

Table of helminthology, 345.
—— incompatible substances, 118.
—— measures, 4, 217.
—— opiate preparations, 294.
—— weights, 1.
Tablettes, 170.
Tampons, astringent, for uterine hæmorrhage, 231.
Tannin, 18, 230.
Tapioca, 20.
Tar, 329.
—— water, 329.

Tartar emetic, 72.
Tartarus boracicus, 280.
Tartrate borico-potassique, 62, 280.
Tea, 44.
Temperaments (considerations relative to), 90.
Terebinthaceæ, 42.
Ternströmiaceæ, 44, 45.
Terra foliata tartari, 62.
Theobroma cacao, 46.
Theriaca, 171, 206.
Thorn apple, 297.
Thrydace, 31, 294.
Thyme, 24.
Thymelaceæ, 22.
Tillia Europœa, 44.
Tilliaceæ, 44.
Tilleul, 44.
Tin, 68, 340.
—— poisoning by, 422.
—— tests for, 423, 424.
Tinctures, alcoholic, 156, 157.
—— ethereal, 159.
Tisanes, 149.
—— alkaline, 151, 257.
—— antilaiteuse, 284.
—— antispasmodic, 305.
—— antisyphilitic, 243.
—— astringent, 230, 232.
—— of balm, 318.
—— balsamic, 328.
—— of chamomile, 320.
—— of digitalis, 335.
—— diuretic, 325.
—— emmenagogue, 325, 326.
—— emollient, 270, 271.
—— expectorant, 275.
—— of Feltz, 153.
—— ground ivy, or hyssop, 319.
—— iodide of starch, 249.
—— ioduretted, 248.
—— laxative, 278, 280,
—— of lichen, Islandicus (bitter), 317.
—— royal, 281.
—— stimulant, 318.
—— sudorific, 151.
—— of wild parsley, 275.
Tobacco, 26, 297.
—— poisoning by, 451.
—— tests for, 451, 452.
Tolerance of medicines, 94.
Tonics, 218.
—— neuro-sthenic, 311.
Tonka bean, 41.
Toxicology, Outlines of, 346.
Tragacanth, 42.

Treatment of poisoning generally, 350.
Trochisques, 204.
—— escharotic, 204.
Turbith, 28.
—— nitrate, 71.
Turpentines, 144.
—— Bordeaux, Strasburg, Venice, 18.

U.

Ulmaceæ, 20.
Umbelliferæ, 34, 36, 318.

V.

Valerianaceæ, 32.
Van Swieten's solution, 71.
Vanilla, 18.
Vapour of charcoal (poisoning by), 465.
Vaporization, 131.
Vegetable drugs, collection of, 125.
—— grease, 144.
—— sulphur, 12.
Vegeto-mineral water, 69.
Velpeau's caustic sulfo-safranique, 63.
Venomous animals, poisoning by, 473.
Venus, crystals of, 68.
Veratrine, 15.
Verbascum, 26.
Verdet, 68.
Verdigris, 68.
Vermilion, 70, 247.
Veronica, 26.
Vesicatories, 190.
Vienna caustic powder, 256.
Vigne, 44.
Vigo's plaster, 68.
Vine, 44.
Vinegars, medicated, 158.
Violaceæ, 46.
Violet, 46.
Viper, distinctive characters of the, 54, 474.
—— poisoning by, 475.
Virgin's milk, 31.
Vitriol, blue, 68.
—— green, 66.
—— oil of, 62.
—— white, 66.
Vulnerary spirit, 261.

W.

Walnut, 20.
Wash, black (phagedenic), 68, 245.
—— yellow (phagedenic), 68, 245.
Water-cress, 46.
—— dropwort, 36.
—— ferruginous, de Boules, 223.
—— nail, or rusty, or smithy, 222.
Water-lily, 50.
Waters, alkaline, 60.
—— distilled, 161.
—— ferruginous, 60.
—— gaseous, 60.
—— muriates (containing), 60.
—— purgative (saline), 60.
—— sedative, 309.
—— sulphurous, 60, 334.
—— white, 69.
Wax, 56.
Weights, tables of, 1 to 4.
White cosmetic, 68, 339.
—— precipitate, 70.

Willow, 20.
Wines, aromatic, 319.
—— medicated, 157.
Winter's bark, 45.
Wood-louse, 54.
Woods, sudorific, 323.
Worms, table of, 345.
Wormwood, 32.

Y.

Yellow phagedenic wash, 68, 245.

Z.

Zinc, and its compounds, 66, 265.
—— butter of, 205.
—— poisoning by, 427.
—— tests for, 428.
Zingiberaceæ, 16, 17.
Ziziphus vulgaris, 42.

THE END.

LONDON:
Printed by Schulze and Co., 13, Poland Street.

ERRATA.

Page 62, line 49, *for* "tartrate," *read* "borico-tartrate."

  „ 62, „ 50, *for* "soluble tartar," *read* "soluble cream of tartar."

  „ 72, „ 25, *after* "kermes," *omit* the apostrophe.

  „ 246, „ 20, *after* "syphilitic," *add* "and phagedenic."

  „ 334, „ 22, *for* "potions," *read* "lotions."

STANDARD SCIENTIFIC WORKS,

PUBLISHED BY

HIPPOLYTE BAILLIERE,

219, REGENT STREET, LONDON;

AND

290, BROADWAY, NEW YORK, U.S.

J. B. BAILLIERE, LIBRAIRE, RUE HAUTEFEUILLE, PARIS.

BAILLY BAILLIERE, LIBRAIRE, CALLE DEL PRINCIPE, MADRID.

MR. BAILLIERE *having lately opened a house at* 290, BROADWAY, NEW YORK, *for the sale of Scientific Works, begs respectfully to state that he shall now be enabled to supply any American Books on Science and General Literature, immediately after Publication, at the rate of Five Shillings the Dollar on the New York Prices.*

H. B. continues to receive a weekly parcel from France, containing the newest Works on Science and General Literature, which he supplies at the rate of One Shilling per Franc on the advertised Price in Paris. He begs to acquaint his friends and the Patrons of German Scientific Works, that he is able to furnish German Works and Periodicals every Month, at the rate of Three Shillings and Sixpence the Rix-Dollar.

Chemistry, Physics, Mineralogy, Geology, Astronomy, Rural Economy, &c.

	£ s d
Blakey (R.) History of Logical Science from the Earliest Times to the Present Day, by Robert Blakey, Professor of Logic and Metaphysics, Queen's College, Belfast, Author of the History of the Philosophy of Mind, in 1 vol. demy 8vo. . . .	0 12 0
Boussingault. Rural Economy; in its Relations with Chemistry, Physics and Meteorology. By J. B. Boussingault, Member of the Institute of France. 2nd Edition, with Notes, carefully revised and corrected, 1 vol. 8vo. cloth boards. London, 1845 . .	0 18 0

£ s d

Brewster (Sir David). The Natural History of Creation, in 1 vol. royal 8vo. Illustrated with Engravings and Woodcuts. *In preparation.*

Campbell. A Practical Text-Book of Inorganic Chemistry including the Preparations of Substances, and their Qualitative and Quantitative Analyses, with Organic Analyses. By Dugald Campbell, Demonstrator of Practical Chemistry to the University College. 12mo. London, 1849 . . . . . 0 5 6

Chapman. A Brief Description of the Characters of Minerals; forming a familiar Introduction to the Science of Mineralogy. By Edward J. Chapman. 1 vol. 12mo. with 3 plates. London, 1844 . 0 4 0

———— Practical Mineralogy; or, a Compendium of the distinguishing Characters of Minerals; by which the Name of any Species or Variety in the Mineral Kingdom may be speedily ascertained. By Edward J. Chapman. 8vo. Illustrated with 13 engravings, showing 270 specimens. London, 1843 . . . . . 0 7 0

Chemical Society (Quarterly Journal of the). 4 vols. 8vo. London, 1848—52 . . . . . 2 12 0

———————— Published Quarterly. Each Part . . . 0 3 0

Cook. Historical Notes on the Discovery and Progressive Improvements of the Steam Engine; with References and Descriptions to accompany the Plates of the American condensing Steam Engine for River Boats. 18mo. and a large fol. coloured plate on a roller and canvas. New York, 1849 . . . . . 0 18 0

Dumas and Boussingault. The Chemical and Physiological Balance of Organic Nature: an Essay. By J. Dumas and J. B. Boussingault, Members of the Institute of France. 1 vol. 12mo. London, 1844 . . . . . . 0 4 0

Fau. The Anatomy of the External Forms of Man (for Artists). Edited by R. Knox, M.D., with Additions. 8vo. and 28 4to. plates. 1842. Plain 1 4 0

———————— Coloured 2 2 0

———————— The Text separately with the four additional Plates, for Persons possessing the French edition. Plain . . 0 12 0

———————— Coloured . . 0 14 0

Fourier. The Passions of the Human Soul. Translated from the French by the Reverend John R. Morrell, with Critical Annotations, a Biography of Fourier, and a General Introduction, by Hugh Doherty. 2 vols. 8vo. London, 1851 . . . 1 1 0

Frazer (W.) Elements of Materia Medica, Containing the Chemistry and Natural History of Drugs; their Effects, Doses, and Adulterations, with the Preparations of the British Pharmacopœas, 8vo. London, 1851 . . . . . 0 12 0

Gordon (L.) A Synopsis of Lectures on Civil Engineering and Mechanics. 4to. London, 1849 . . . . 0 7 6

Gordon and Liddell. Exposition of a Plan for the Metropolitan Water Supply, showing that the Thames at Maple-Durham is the most eligible source from which a supply of pure soft water can be brought for the inhabitants of London and its suburbs. 8vo. London, 1849 . . . . . 0 1 0

£ s d

Graham. Elements of Chemistry; including the Application of the Science in the Arts. By T. Graham, F.R.S. L. & E., Professor of Chemistry at University College, London. 2nd Edition, entirely revised and greatly enlarged, copiously illustrated with Woodcuts. Vol 1, 1850 . . . . . . 1 1 0
———————— Part IV. separately, to complete the Volume . 0 3 0

Humboldt. Kosmos: a General Survey of the Physical Phenomena of the Universe. By Baron A. Humboldt. The original English Edition. 2 vols. post 8vo. London, 1848 . . 0 15 0

Kæmtz. A Complete Course of Meteorology. By L. F. Kæmtz, Professor of Physics at the University of Halle. With Notes by Ch. Martins, and an Appendix by L. Lalanne. Translated, with Additions, by C. V. Walker. 1 vol. post 8vo. pp. 624, with 15 Plates, cloth boards. 1845 . . . . 0 12 6

Knapp. Chemical Technology, or Chemistry applied to the Arts and Manufactures. By F. Knapp, Professor at the University of Giessen. Edited, with numerous Additions, by Dr. E. RONALDS, Professor of Chemistry at Queen's College, Galway; and Dr. THOMAS RICHARDSON, of Newcastle-on-Tyne. Illustrated with 600 large Woodcuts and 7 Coloured Plates. 3 vols. 8vo. London, 1848—1851 . . . . . . 3 4 0
———————— Vol. III. Containing Sugar, Tea, Flour, &c. With 7 Coloured Plates 1 2

Knipe. Geological Map of the British Isles. Coloured. In a case. London, 1848 . . . . . . 4 4 0

Leon (John A.) The Art of Manufacturing and Refining Sugar, including the Manufacture and Revivification of Animal Charcoal. With 14 Plates, illustrative of the Machinery and Building. Large folio. London, 1850 . . . . . 3 3 0

Liebig. Chemistry and Physics, in relation to Physiology and Pathology. By Baron Justus Liebig, Professor of Chemistry at the University of Giessen. 2nd Edition. 8vo. London, 1847 . 0 3

Memoirs of the Literary and Philosophical Society of Manchester. (Second Series.) Vol. 9. 8vo. with Woodcuts and Plates. London, 1851 . . . 0 7 6

Mitchell (J.) Manual of Practical Assaying, intended for the use of Metallurgists, Captains of Mines and Assayers in General. With a copious Table, for the purpose of ascertaining in Assays of Gold and Silver the precise amount, in Ounces, Pennyweights, and Grains, of noble Metal contained in one ton of Ore from a given quantity. 1 vol. post 8vo. London, 1846 . . 0 10
———————— Treatise on the Adulterations of Food, and the Chemical Means employed to detect them. Containing Water, Flour, Bread, Milk, Cream, Beer, Cider, Wines, Spirituous Liquors, Coffee, Tea, Chocolate, Sugar, Honey, Lozenges, Cheese, Vinegar, Pickles, Anchovy Sauce and Paste, Catsup, Olive (Salad) Oil, Pepper, Mustard. 12mo. London, 1848 . . . . 0 6

Muller. Principles of Physics and Meteorology. By J. Muller, M.D. Illustrated with 530 Woodcuts, and 2 coloured Plates. 8vo. London, 1847 . . . . . . 0 18 0

£ s d

Nichol. Astronomy Historically and Scientifically developed, showing the Rise of the Science from its Growth, and the Character of the illustrious Men who have contributed to it. By J. P. Nichol, Professor of Astronomy in the University of Glasgow. 2 vols. 8vo. Illustrated by Plates and Woodcuts. *In preparation.*
—— The Architecture of the Heavens. Ninth Edition, entirely revised and greatly enlarged. Illustrated with 23 Steel Engravings and numerous Woodcuts. 8vo. London, 1851 . . . 0 16 0

Quekett (J.) Lectures on Histology, delivered at the Royal College of Surgeons of England. Illustrated by 159 Woodcuts. 8vo. London, 1852 . . . . . 0 10 6
—— Practical Treatise on the Use of the Microscope. Illustrated with 12 Steel Plates and Wood Engravings. 2nd Edition. London, 1852 . . . . . . 1 2 0
—— Practical Treatise on Minute Injection, and the Application of the Microscope to Diseased Structure. 8vo. Illustrated with Engraved Plates and Woodcuts. *In the press.*

Reid. Rudiments of Chemistry, with Illustrations of the Chemistry of daily Life, by D. B. Reid, M.D., Lecturer on Chemistry, formerly one of Her Majesty's Commissioners for the Health of Towns in England. 4th Edition, with 130 Woodcuts. 12mo. 1850 . 0 2 6

Regnault. An Elementary Treatise on Crystallography, Illustrated with 108 Wood Engravings, printed on black ground. 8vo. London, 1848 . . . . . . 0 3 0

Reichenbach (Baron Charles). Physico-Physiological Researches on the Dynamics of Magnetism, Electricity, Heat, Light, Crystallization and Chemism, in their Relations to Vital Force. The complete Work from the German Second Edition, with Additions, a Preface and Critical Notes, by JOHN ASHBURNER, M.D. 8vo. With Woodcuts and One Plate. London, 1850 . . 0 15 0

Richardson. Geology for Beginners; comprising a Familiar Exposition of the Elements of Geology and its Associate Sciences, Mineralogy, Fossil Conchology, Fossil Botany, and Paleontology. By G. F. Richardson, F.G.S. 2nd Edition, post 8vo. With 251 Woodcuts. 1843 . . . . . 0 5 0

Richardson and Ronalds. Metallurgy; and the Chemistry of the Metals. In 3 vols. 8vo. Illustrated with numerous Wood Engravings. *In the press.*

Stars and the Earth. The Stars and the Earth; or, Thoughts upon Space, Time, and Eternity. 4th Edition, Eighth thousand, 2 Parts in 1, 18mo. London, 1850 . . . 0 2 0

Stockhardt. The Principles of Chemistry, illustrated by Simple Experiments. Translated from the German Edition. With 218 Woodcuts. 12mo. Cambridge, 1850 . . . 0 7 6

Thomson. Chemistry of Organic Bodies—Vegetables. By Thomas Thomson, M.D., F.R.S. L. & E., Regius Professor of Chemistry in the University of Glasgow. Corresponding Member of the Royal Academy of Paris. 1 large vol. 8vo. pp. 1092, boards. London, 1838 1 4 0
—— Heat and Electricity. 2nd Edition, 1 vol. 8vo. Illustrated with Woodcuts. London, 1839 . . . . 0 15 0

		£ s d
Thomson. Chemistry of Animal Bodies. 8vo. Edinburgh, 1843	.	0 10 0

Thomson (R. D.) British Annual and Epitome of the Progress of Science. By R. D. Thomson, Assistant Professor in the University of Glasgow. 3 vols. 1837, 38, 39. 18mo. cloth boards, lettered, each 0 3 6

Weisbach (J.) Principles of the Mechanics of Machinery and Engineering. 2 vols. 8vo. Illustrated with 200 Wood Engravings. London, 1848 . . . . . . 1 19 0

Anatomy, Medecine, Surgery, and Natural History.

£ s d

Ashburner. On Dentition and some Coincident Disorders. 18mo. London, 1834 . . . . . . 0 4 0

Canton (A.) The Teeth and their Preservation, in Infancy and Manhood to Old Age. 12mo. with Woodcuts . . . 0 4 0

Courtenay. Pathology and Rational Treatment of Stricture and Urethra in all its Varieties and Complications, with Observations on the Use and Abuse of Urethral Instruments. The whole illustrated by numerous Cases. By F. B. Courtenay, M.R.C.S., &c. 4th Edition, 8vo. London, 1848 . . . . 0 5 0

——— A Few Words on Perineal Section, as recommended by Professor Syme, for the Cure of Stricture of the Urethra. 8vo. London, 1850 . . . . . . 0 1 0

——— Practical Observations on the Chronic Enlargement of the Prostrate Gland in Old People: with Mode of Treatment. By Francis B. Courtenay. 8vo. with numerous Cases and Plates, boards. London, 1839 . . . . 0 7 6

——— A Treatise on the Cure of Stricture of the Urethra; with Practical Observations on the Treatment of Spermatorrhœa by Cauterization. 8vo. 1851 . . . . 0 3 6

Cruveilhier and Bonamy. Atlas of the Descriptive Anatomy of the Human Body. By J. Cruveilhier, Professor of Anatomy to the Faculty of Medicine, Paris. With Explanations by C. Bonamy. Containing 82 Plates of Osteology, Syndemology and Myology. 4to. London, 1844. Plain 3 0 0

——— Coloured 5 15 0

Fau. The Anatomy of the External Forms of Man (for Artists). Edited by R. Knox, M.D., with Additions. 8vo. Text, and 28 4to. Plates. London, 1849. Plain . . . 1 4 0

——— Coloured . . . 2 2 0

Gerber and Gulliver. Elements of the General and Microscopical Anatomy of Man and the Mammalia; chiefly after Original Researches. By Professor Gerber. To which is added an Appendix, comprising Researches on the Anatomy of the Blood, Chyle, Lymph, Thymous Fluid, Tubercle, and Additions, by C. Gulliver, F.R.S. In 1 vol. 8vo. Text, and an Atlas of 34 Plates, engraved by L. Aldous. 2 vols. 8vo. Cloth boards, 1842 . . . 1 4 0

£ s d

Grant. General View of the Distribution of Extinct Animals. By Robert E. Grant, M.D., F.R.S. L. & E., Professor of Comparative Anatomy at the University College, London. In the "British Annual," 1839. 18mo. London, 1839 . . . . 0 3 6

———— On the Principles of Classification, as applied to the Primary Divisions of the Animal Kingdom. In the "British Annual," 1838. 18mo. Illustrated with 28 Woodcuts. London, 1838 0 3 6

———— Outlines of Comparative Anatomy. 8vo. Illustrated with 148 Woodcuts, boards. London, 1833—41 . . . 1 8 0

———— Part VII. with Title-page 0 1 6

Hall (Marshall). On the Diseases and Derangements of the Nervous System, in their Primary Forms, and in their modifications by Age, Sex, Constitution, Hereditary Predisposition, Excesses, General Disorder and Organic Disease. By Marshall Hall, M.D., F.R.S. L. & E. 8vo. with 8 engraved Plates. London, 1841 . 0 15 0

The following is an Appendix to the above Work.

———— On the Mutual Relations between Anatomy, Physiology, Pathology, Therapeutics and the Practice of Medicine; being the Gulstonian Lectures for 1842. 8vo. with 2 Coloured Plates and 1 Plain. London, 1842 . . . . . 0 5 0

———— New Memoir on the Nervous System, true Spinal Marrow, and its Anatomy, Physiology, Pathology, and Therapeutics. 4to. with 5 engraved Plates. London, 1843 . . . 1 0 0

Henriques. Ethiological, Pathological and Therapeutical Reflections on the Asiatic Cholera, as observed in Europe, Asia Minor, and Egypt. 8vo. London, 1848 . . . . . 0 1 6

Honigberger. Thirty-Five Years in the East. Adventures, Discoveries, Experiments, and Historical Sketches, relating to the Punjab and Cashmere, in connection with Medicine, Botany, Pharmacy, &c., together with an original Materia Medica, and a Medical Vocabulary in four European and five Eastern Languages. By J. M. Honigberger, late Physician to the Court of Lahore. Royal 8vo. with numerous Engravings. London, 1852 . 1 11 6

Hufeland. Manual of the Practice of Medicine; the Result of Fifty Years' Experience By W. C. Hufeland, Physician to the late King of Prussia, Professor in the University of Berlin. Translated from the Sixth German Edition by C. Bruchhausen and R. Nelson. 8vo. bound. London, 1844 . . . . . 0 15 0

Jones (W.) An Essay on some of the most important Diseases of Women, with a Description of a Novel Invention for their Treatment and Relief. Second Edition. 8vo. London, 1850 . 0 1 0

———— Practical Observations on the Diseases of Women, showing the necessity of Physical Examination, and the Use and Application of the Speculum. Illustrated by Cases, Woodcuts, and Coloured Plates. 8vo. London, 1850 . . . . 0 7 0

Lebaudy. The Anatomy of the Regions interested in the Surgical Operations performed upon the Human Body; with Occasional Views of the Pathological Condition, which render the interference of the Surgeon necessary. In a Series of 24 plates, the Size of Life. By J. Lebaudy. Folio. London, 1845 . . . 1 4 0

Hippolyte Bailliere's Publications.

£ s d

Lee. The Anatomy of the Nerves of the Uterus. By Robert Lee,
M.D., F.R.S. Folio, with 2 engraved Plates. London, 1841 . 0 8 0

Maddock. Practical Observations on the Efficacy of Medicated
Inhalations in the Treatment of Pulmonary Consumption. By Dr.
Maddock. 3rd Edition. 8vo. with a coloured Plate. London, 1846 0 5 6

Martin. A General Introduction to the Natural History of Mammiferous Animals: with a particular View of the Physical History
of Man, and the more closely allied Genera of the Order " Qua-
drumana," or Monkeys. Illustrated with 296 Anatomical, Osteo-
logical, and other Engravings on Wood, and 12 full-plate Repre-
sentations of Animals, drawn by W. Harvey. 1 vol. 8vo. London, 1841 0 16 0

Moreau (Professor). Icones Obstetricæ; a Series of 60 Plates
and Text, Illustrative of the Art and Science of Midwifery in all
its Branches. By Moreau, Professor of Midwifery to the Faculty
of Medicine, Paris. Edited, with Practical Remarks, by J. S.
Streeter, M.R.C.S. Folio. Cloth boards. London, 1841. Price Plain 3 3 0
—————— Coloured 6 6 0

Owen. Odontography; or, a Treatise on the Comparative Anatomy
of the Teeth, their Physiological Relations, Mode of Development,
and Microscopical Structure in the Vertebrate Animals. By Richard
Owen, F.R.S., Corresponding Member of the Royal Academy of
Sciences, Paris and Berlin; Hunterian Professor to the Royal College
of Surgeons, London. This splendid Work is now completed. 2 vols.
royal 8vo. containing 168 plates, half-bound russia. London, 1840—45 6 6 0
—————— A few copies of the Plates have been printed on India paper,
2 vols.,4to. 10 10 0

Phillips. Scrofula: its Nature, Prevalence, Causes, and the Principles of Treatment. By Benjamin Phillips, F.R.S., Surgeon and
Lecturer on Surgery to the Westminster Hospital. 8vo. with an
engraved Plate. London, 1846 . . . . 0 12 0
—————— A Treatise on the Urethra; its Diseases, especially Stricture,
and their Cure. 8vo. boards. London, 1832 . . 0 8 0

Prescriber's (The) Complete Handbook. *See* TROUSSEAU.

Prichard. The Natural History of Man; comprising Inquiries into
the Modifying Influence of Physical and Moral Agencies on the
different Tribes of the Human Family. By James Cowles Prichard,
M.D., F.R.S , M.R.I.A. Corresponding Member of the National
Institute, of the Royal Academy of Medicine, and of the Statistical
Society of France; Member of the American Philosophical Society,
&c. &c. 3rd Edition, enlarged, with 50 coloured and 5 plain Illustrations, engraved on Steel, and 97 Engravings on Wood, royal 8vo.
elegantly bound in cloth. London, 1848 . . . 1 16 0
—————— Appendix to the First and Second Editions of the Natural
History of Man, large 8vo. with 6 coloured Plates. London, 1845
and 1848. Each 0 3 6
—————— Six Ethnographical Maps, as a Supplement to the Natural
History of Man, and to the Researches into the Physical History
of Mankind, folio, coloured, and 1 sheet of letter-press, in cloth
boards. 2nd Edition. London, 1850 . . . . 1 4 0

£ s d

Prichard. Illustrations to the Researches into the Physical History of Mankind. Atlas of 44 coloured and 5 plain Plates, engraved on Steel, large 8vo. Boards. London, 1841 . . . . 0 18 0
——— On the Different Forms of Insanity, in Relation to Jurisprudence. (Dedicated to the Lord Chancellor of England.) 12mo. London, 1842 . . . . 0 5 0

Rayer. A Theoretical and Practical Treatise on the Diseases of the Skin. By P. Rayer, M.D., Physician to the Hôpital de la Charité. Translated by R. Willis, M.D. 2nd Edition, remodelled and much enlarged, in 1 thick vol. 8vo. of 1300 pages, with Atlas, royal 4to. of 26 Plates, finely engraved, and coloured with the greatest care, exhibiting 400 varieties of Cutaneous Affections. London, 1835 . 4 8 0
————————— The Text separately, 8vo. in boards . . 1 8 0
————————— The Atlas 4to. separately, in boards . . 3 10 0

Ricord. Illustrations of Syphilitic Disease. Translated from the French by Betton. 4to. 50 Coloured Plates. Philadelphia, 1851 5 5 0

Ryan. The Philosophy of Marriage, in its Social, Moral, and Physical Relations; with an Account of the Diseases of the Genito-Urinary Organs, with the Physiology of Generation in the Vegetable and Animal Kingdoms. By M. Ryan, M.D. 4th Edition, greatly improved, 1 vol. 12mo. London, 1843 . . . . 0 6 0

Shuckard. Essay on the Indigenous Fossorial Hymenoptera; comprising a Description of the British Species of Burrowing Sand Wasps contained in all the Metropolitan Collections; with their habits, as far as they have been observed. 8vo. with 4 Plates. London, 1837. *Plate I. is wanting* . . . 0 10 0
——— Elements of British Entomology. Part 1. 1839. 8vo. . 0 8 0

Streeter (J. S.) *See* Morrau.

Trousseau and Reveil. The Prescribers Complete Handbook, comprising the Principles of the Art of Prescribing, a Materia Medica containing all the Principal Medicines employed, classified according to their Natural Families, with their Properties, Preparations and Uses, and a Concise Sketch of Toxicology. By M. Trousseau, Professor of the Faculty of Medicine, Paris, and M. Reveil. Edited, with Notes, by J. Birkbeck Nevins, M.D. London, 1852. 12mo. 0 6 6

True and False Spermatorrhœa. 8vo. 1852 . 0 5 0

Vogel and Day. The Pathological Anatomy of the Human Body. By Julius Vogel, M.D. Translated from the German, with Additions, by George E. Day, M.D., Professor to the University of St. Andrews. Illustrated with upwards of 100 plain and coloured Engravings, 8vo. cloth. London, 1847 . . . 0 18 0

Waterhouse. A Natural History of the Mammalia. By G. R. Waterhouse, Esq., of the British Museum. Vol. I, containing the Order Marsupiata, or Pouched Animals, with 22 Illustrations, engraved on Steel, and 18 Engravings on Wood, royal 8vo. elegantly bound in cloth, coloured Plates 1 14 6
————————— Plain 1 9 0

£ s d

Waterhouse. A Natural History of the Mammalia. By G. R. Waterhouse, Esq., of the British Museum. Vol. II. containing the Order Rodentia; or, Gnawing Mammalia: with 22 Illustrations, engraved on Steel, and Engravings on Wood, royal 8vo. elegantly bound in cloth, coloured Plates. London, 1848 . 1 14 6

———————— Plain 1 9 0

The Natural History of Mammalia is intended to embrace an account of the structure and habits of all the known species of Quadrupeds, or Mammals; to which will be added, observations upon their geographical distribution and classification. Since the fossil and recent species illustrate each other, it is also intended to include notices of the leading characters of the extinct species.

The Genera, and many of the species, are illustrated by Engravings on Steel, and by Woodcuts. The modifications observable in the structure of the skulls, teeth, feet, and other parts, are almost entirely illustrated by Steel Engravings.

Williams. Elements of Medicine: Morbid Poisons. By Robert Williams, M.D., Physician to St. Thomas's Hospital. 2 vols. 8vo. London, 1836—41 . . . . . 1 8 6

———————— Vol. II. separately. 1841 . . . 0 18 0

Willis. Illustrations of Cutaneous Disease: a Series of Delineations of the Affections of the Skin, in their more interesting and frequent forms; with a Practical Summary of their Symptoms, Diagnosis and Treatment, including appropriate Formulæ. By Robert Willis, M.D., Member of the Royal College of Physicians. The Drawings are after Nature, and Lithographed by Arch. Henning. These Illustrations are comprised in 94 Plates, folio. The Drawings are Originals, carefully coloured. Bound in cloth, lettered. London, 1843 . . . . . . 6 0 0

———————— On the Treatment of Stone in the Bladder by Medical and Mechanical Means. London, 1842 . . . . 0 5 0

Botany.

£ s d

Babington. Primitiæ Floræ Sarnicæ; or, an Outline of the Flora of the Channel Islands of Jersey, Guernsey, Alderney, and Sark. 12mo. London, 1839 . . . . . 0 4 0

Fielding and Gardner. Sertum Plantarum; or, Drawings and Descriptions of Rare and undescribed Plants from the Author's Herbarium. By H. B. Fielding; assisted by G. Gardner, Superintendent of the Royal Botanic Gardens, Ceylon. 8vo. London, 1844 1 1 0

Hooker. Icones Plantarum. By Sir W. J. Hooker, Director of the Royal Botanic Gardens, Kew. New Series, Vols. I.—IV, containing 100 Plates each with Explanations. 8vo. cloth. London, 1842— 1844. Each vol. 1 8 0

———————— Vol. IV. Part 2. London, 1848 . . . 0 14 0

£ s d

Hooker. The London Journal of Botany. Vols. I—VI, with 24
Plates each, boards. 1842—47 .   .   .   . 6 0 0
Now reduced to 20 Shillings each Vol.

———— Notes on the Botany of the Antarctic Voyage, conducted by
CAPTAIN JAMES CLARK ROSS, R.N., F.R.S., in H.M.S. *Erebus and
Terror;* with Observations on the Tussac Grass of the Falkland
Islands 8vo. with 2 coloured Plates. London, 1843 .   . 0 4 0

———— Niger Flora; or, an Enumeration of the Plants of Western
Tropical Africa, Collected by the late Dr. Th. Vogel, Botanist to
the Voyage of the Expedition sent by Her Britannic Majesty to the
River Niger in 1841, under the Command of Capt. H. D. Trotter,
R.N., including Spicilegia Gorgonea, by P. B. Webb, and Flora
Nigritiana, by Dr. J. D. Hooker and George Bentham. With 2
Views, a Map, and 50 Plates. 8vo. London, 1849 .   . 1 1 0

Mather (W.) Outlines of Botany. Part I, with 7 Plates, 12mo.
cloth boards. London, 1848 .   .   .   . 0 2 6

Miers (J.) Illustrations of South American Plants, Vol. I. 4to.
With 34 Plates. London, 1847—50 .   .   . 1 15 0

Schleiden. The Plant; a Biography, in a Series of Popular Lectures on Botany. Edited and Translated by A. Henfrey, F.L.S.
8vo. with 5 coloured Plates, and 13 Woodcuts. London, 1848 . 0 15 0

Wight. Illustrations of Indian Botany; or, Figures Illustrative of
each of the Natural Orders of Indian Plants, described in the
Author's Prodromus Floræ Peninsulæ Indiæ Orientalis; but not
confined to them. By Dr. R. Wight, F.L.S., Surgeon to the
Madras Establishment. Vol. I, published in 13 Parts, containing
95 coloured Plates. Madras, 1838—40 .   .   . 4 17 6

———————— Vol. II. 3 Parts, containing 200 coloured Plates.
Madras, 1841—50 .   .   .   .   . 4 12 0
Odd Parts may be obtained to complete Sets.

———— Icones Plantarum Indiæ Orientalis; or, Figures of Indian
Plants. By Dr. Robert Wight, F.L.S., Surgeon to the Madras
Establishment. Vol. I, 4to. consisting of 16 Parts, containing
together 318 Plates. Madras, 1838—40 .   .   . 4 0 0

———————— Vol. II, consisting of 4 Parts, containing together 418
Plates. Madras, 1840—42 .   .   .   . 5 5 0

———————— Vol. III, Parts 1 to 4, with 426 Plates. Madras,
1842—47 .   .   .   .   .   . 6 0 0

———————— Vol. IV, Parts 1 to 4, with 458 Plates. Madras,
1848—50 .   .   .   .   .   . 6 0 0

———————— Vol. V, Part 1, with 140 Plates. Madras, 1851 . 2 0 0
Odd Parts may be obtained to complete Sets.

———— Contributions to the Botany of India. By Dr. Robert Wight,
F.L.S., Surgeon to the Madras Establishment. 8vo. London, 1834 0 7 6

———— Spicilegium Neilgherrense; or, a Selection of Neilgherry
Plants, Drawn and Coloured from Nature, with Brief Descriptions
of each; some General Occasional Notices of their Economical
Properties and Uses. By Dr. Robert Wight, F.L.S., Surgeon to
the Madras Establishment. 3 Parts, 4to. with 150 coloured Plates.
Madras, 1846—48 .   .   .   .   . 4 10 0

£ s d

Wight. Prodromus Floræ Peninsulæ Indiæ Orientalis; containing abridged Descriptions of the Plants found in the Peninsula of British India, arranged according to the Natural System. By Drs. Robert Wight, F.L.S., and Walker Arnott. Vol. I, 8vo. London, 1834   .   .   .   .   0 16 0

Wilson. Practice of the Water Cure, with authenticated Evidence of its Efficacy and Safety. Part 1, containing 70 authenticated Cases, the Opinions of English Medical Practitioners, a Sketch of the History and Progress of the Water Cure, and an Account of the Processes used in the Treatment. 8vo. London, 1844   .   0 1 6
——— The Water Cure, Stomach Complaints and Drugs, Diseases, their Causes, Consequences and Cure by Water, Air, Exercise and Diet. 8vo. Third edition, 1843   .   .   .   .   0 4 6

Bernstein (L.) Selections from the best German Authors in Prose and Poetry; also some Commercial Letters, 12mo. London, 1842 . 0 6 0

Boniface. Modern English and French Conversation; containing Elementary Phrases and new Easy Dialogues, in French and English, on the most familiar Subjects: for the Use of the Traveller and Student. By M. Boniface. Sixteenth edition, 18mo. London, 1845   .   .   .   .   0 3 0

Ollendorff. A new Method of Learning to Read, Write and Speak the German Language in Six Months. By H. G. Ollendorff. Translated from the Fifth French Edition. By G. J. Bertinchamp, A.B. Fourth edition, revised and considerably improved. 12mo. bound, 1851   .   .   .   .   0 9 0
——— A Key to the Exercises. 12mo. bound, 1851   .   .   0 4 6

219, Regent Street, London, and 290, Broadway, New York.

Just Published. 8vo. Cloth. Price 22s.

VOL. X. OF THE

LIBRARY OF ILLUSTRATED

STANDARD SCIENTIFIC WORKS.

𝔄lready 𝔓ublished.

I.

Professor Muller's Principles of Physics and Meteorology.
WITH 530 WOODCUTS AND TWO COLOURED ENGRAVINGS. 8VO. 18s.

II. AND V.

Professor Weisbach's Mechanics of Machinery and Engineering.
2 VOLS. WITH 900 WOODCUTS. £1 19s.

III. IV. AND X.

Professor Knapp's Technology; or,
Chemistry Applied to the Arts and Manufactures.
EDITED BY DR. RONALDS, AND DR. T. RICHARDSON.
3 VOLS. SPLENDIDLY ILLUSTRATED, PRICE £3 4s.

VI.

Quekett's (John) Practical Treatise on the Use of the Microscope.
SECOND EDITION, WITH 12 STEEL AND NUMEROUS WOOD ENGRAVINGS. 8VO. £1 2s.

VII.

Professor Fau's Anatomy of the External Forms of Man.
𝔉or 𝔄rtists.
EDITED BY R. KNOX, M.D.
8VO. AND AN ATLAS OF 28 PLATES 4TO. PLAIN £1 4s. COLOURED £2 2s.

VIII.

Professor Graham's Elements of Chemistry, with
Its Application in the Arts.
SECOND EDITION, WITH NUMEROUS WOODCUTS. VOL. I. £1 1s.

IX.

Professor Nichol's Architecture of the Heavens.
NINTH EDITION, WITH 23 STEEL PLATES AND MANY WOODCUTS. LONDON, 1851. 16s.

𝔍n the 𝔓ress.

A Complete Treatise on Metallurgy, and the Chemistry of the Metals.
BY DRS. RONALDS AND RICHARDSON.
With Illustrations.

LONDON: PRINTED BY SCHULZE AND CO., 13, POLAND STREET

LaVergne, TN USA
15 August 2010
193365LV00003B/62/P